Africa Unchained

Africa Unchained

The Blueprint for Africa's Future

George B. N. Ayittey

First published in hardcover in 2005 by
PALGRAVE MACMILLAN™
First PALGRAVE MACMILLAN™ paperback edition: September 2006
175 Fifth Avenue, New York, N.Y. 10010 and
Houndmills, Basingstoke, Hampshire, England RG21 6XS.
Companies and representatives throughout the world.

PALGRAVE MACMILLAN is the global academic imprint of the Palgrave
Macmillan division of St. Martin's Press, LLC and of Palgrave Macmillan
Ltd. Macmillan® is a registered trademark in the United States, United
Kingdom and other countries. Palgrave is a registered trademark in the
European Union and other countries.

ISBN-13: 978-1-4039-7386-3 paperback
ISBN-10: 1-4039-7386-5 paperback

Ayittey, George B. N., 1945–
    Africa unchained : the blueprint for Africa's future / George B. N.
Ayittey.
        p.   cm.
    Includes bibliographical references and index.
    ISBN 1-4039-6359-2 (cloth)
    ISBN 1-4039-7386-5 (paperback)
    1. Africa—Economic policy.   2. Africa—Economic conditions—1960–
3. Poverty—Africa.   4. Africa—Politics and government—1960–   I.
Title.

HC800.A985   2004
338.96—dc22

                                                      2003066355

A catalogue record of the book is available from the British Library.

Design by Letra Libre.

10   9   8   7   6   5   4   3   2

Printed in the United States of America.

Contents

CHAPTER 1

CHAPTER 2

CHAPTER 3

CHAPTER 4

DEDICATIONS

ALGERIA:

Abdelbaki Djabali, a correspondent of the daily *El Watan,* who escaped "death by road accident" on December 7, 2000, when his car was rammed off the road by a careening truck. His crime? Unrelenting exposés on corruption.

Lounes Matoub, a Berber singer, gunned down on June 26, 1998, at a roadblock on the road to his village in Beni Douala, for his outspoken criticisms of the government and Islamic groups. The Armed Islamic Group claimed responsibility.

BURKINA FASO:

Norbert Zongo, a popular journalist, playwright, and human rights activist, whose investigations into official corruption earned him both a widespread audience and numerous death threats. He was gunned down in an ambush on December 13, 1998.

CHAD:

Souleymane Guengueng, who after being unjustly imprisoned and tortured for two years in the late 1980s by the brutal Hissène Habré's regime, fought back courageously. He founded the Association of Victims of Political Oppression, and spent the next decade gathering testimony from fellow survivors and their families—over 700 people in all. The evidence provided critical material for Chadian and international human rights organizations to pursue a case against Habré, who fled to Senegal with $11 million in loot after being overthrown in December 1990. In January 1999, an indictment was brought against Habré in Senegal's Supreme Court. Although the case was thrown out in March 2001, Guengueng should be honored for bringing about Africa's first "Pinochet case."

EGYPT:

Salaheddin Mohsen, whom the authorities made a "martyr of free speech" (*Index On Censorship*, March 2001; p.132). He was sentenced to three years in prison with hard labor on January 27, 2001 for the crime of writing a book, *Shivering of the Lights*, which the authorities claimed "defamed Islam."

Saad Eddin Ibrahim, an internationally acclaimed sociologist and founder of the Ibn Khaldun Center for Development Studies. He is a courageous and strong advocate of independent judiciary review of voting to counter electoral fraud in Egypt. He has spoken against religious intolerance and the rising tensions between Egypt's Muslim majority and Christian minority. In a crass attempt to hunt and silence the sociologist, Ibrahim was put on trial and government prosecutors accused him of harming Egypt's image with exaggerated reports, of accepting foreign donations without government permission, of using donated money for personal enrichment, and of bribing newscasters to report favorably on the center's work. But as it turned out, "the government had infiltrated the center and planted evidence, framing Ibrahim" (*The New York Times*, April 22, 2001; p.5). On May 21, 2001, he was sentenced to jail for seven years. "This is politically motivated and the sentence is politically dictated," Ibrahim told the Associated Press on a mobile phone as the police escorted him from the courtroom. "It is a struggle and it will go on. I do not regret anything I stood for" (*The New York Times*, May 22, 2001; p.A7).

ETHIOPIA:

Israel Sboka, publisher and editor-in-chief of the weekly *Seife Nebelhal*, and Samson Seyoum, former editor-in-chief of *Ethiop*, both of whom, under persecution, fled the country in December 2000. Professor Asrat Woldeyes and Ato Tesfaye, gunned down by Tigrayan Peoples' Liberation Front assassins.

Ato Assefa Maru, an unrelenting advocate of freedom of association and individual rights, shot in cold blood by security forces in May 1997.

Alebatchew Goji, beaten and tortured to death while in police custody in July 1994.

Mustafa Idris, who mysteriously disappeared in 1994.

GHANA:

Tommy Thompson, the intrepid publisher of the newspaper, *Free Press.*

LIBERIA:

J. Milton Teahjay, who mysteriously vanished in 2001.

Opposition leader Togba-Nah Tipoteh and human rights activist James Verdier, whose lives have been under threat (*Africa Insider*, April 15, 2001; p.5).

MOROCCO:

Mehdi Ben Barka, a Moroccan exile who vanished in Paris in 1965. Ahmed Boukhari, a retired member of the secret police unit known as CAB–1 (created in 1960 to intimidate, torture, and kill members of the opposition), claimed that "Ben Barka was killed on the orders of those at the top of the Moroccan secret services, with the approval of cabinet ministers" (*The Economist* February 16, 2002; p.44).

MOZAMBIQUE:

Carlos Cardoso, an investigative journalist, who was murdered in November 2000 for uncovering a bank scandal in which about $14 million was looted from Mozambique's largest bank, BCM, on the eve of its privatization. The official in charge of banking supervision, Antonio Siba Siba, was also murdered while investigating the banking scandals.

Salamao Moyana, editor of the independent weekly, *Savana,* and its senior reporter, David Kashweka, who were placed on a death list on December 14, 2000. Anonymous callers had threatened them with death because they "talk too much" and "stick their noses into things" (*Index on Censorship,* March/April, 2001; p.109).

NIGERIA:

Kamsulum Kazeem, a security man at the newspaper *City People,* who was shot dead when armed persons attacked the offices of Media Techniques Limited, publishers of the paper, in the early hours of January 10, 2001.

Tunde Oladepo, a senior editor of *The Guardian,* who was gunned down in his Ogun state home in front of his wife and children on February 27, 1998.

Tunde Salau, a prominent student activist who was hacked to death on February 13, 2002, at Lagos University just after he had appeared for an examination. Salau, president of the Lagos state university students' union, was attacked with machetes by unknown assailants. He died of severe wounds. Salau had recently led a student protest against the murder of justice minister Bola Ige by unknown gunmen in the southwestern town of Ibadan.

RWANDA:

Hon. Burakiri Evarist, a progressive politician from Commune Rutare and a member of Parliament for the Liberal Party, who was murdered in cold blood by one of the soldiers in President Paul Kagame's military intelligence squad and buried in a mass grave at commune headquarters.

Former Rwanda Patriotic Front (RPF) Minister Seth Sendashonga, who resigned and fled to Nairobi, where he was assassinated because he had evidence concerning deliberate killings. Hon. Col. Lizinde Mugabushaka, who also resigned his RPF Parliamentary seat and fled to Nairobi via Kinshasa, where he was similarly assassinated to destroy evidence.

SUDAN:

Yousif Kuwa Mekki, who for 16 years led a guerrilla division of the Sudan People's Liberation Army in the Nuba mountains of central Sudan and was the figurehead of the Nuba people's struggle for survival against the repression meted out by the Islamic government in Khartoum. His life was dedicated to raising the Nubas' awareness of and pride in their own culture. Before joining the ranks of the Sudanese People's Liberation Army (SPLA) he was a teacher and cultural activist, and served as an elected politician in the regional assembly. He grew up in a milieu in which to be Nuba was to be regarded almost as a slave. As a Muslim from the geographical north, but dedicated to a tolerant, multicultural Sudan, he was the embodiment of the "New Sudan" philosophy of the SPLA leader Colonel John Garang. As a governor, Kuwa always sought consensus and democracy, insisting that sound civil administration, functioning courts, and religious tolerance were the foundation of liberation. Mekki, teacher, soldier, and politician, died on March 31, 2001 in Norwich (*The Independent,* [UK] April 4, 2001).

TUNISIA:

Sihem Bensedrine, Mohammed Bechri, and Omar Mestiri, members of the Committee for Rights in Tunisia, who have been threatened, harassed, and assaulted in their campaign to improve human rights in Tunisia.

UGANDA:

Jimmy Higenyi, who was shot dead on January 12, 2000, by armed police who also injured ten others during a rally organized by the opposition against global terrorism and dictatorship. "'By ordering police to use live ammunition to disperse a peacefully demonstrating crowd, President Museveni has demonstrated he does not support our international struggle against global terrorism and dictatorship,' said Dr. James Rwanyare, chairman of the Uganda People's Congress (UPC). Dr. Rwanyare was later arrested with one of his female aides and taken to an unknown destination" (*New African,* February 2002; p.15).

ZAMBIA:

Ronald Penza, former finance minister, who was named in 1994 by *Euromoney,* a World Bank and IMF publication, as the world's second-best finance minister and was gunned down at his home on November 6, 1998. Police claimed he was killed by "armed robbers" but his family accused the government of complicity and cover-up.

ZIMBABWE:

Shepherd Ndungu, a schoolteacher, beaten to death by Zimbabwe African National Union–Patriotic Front (ZANU-PF) thugs for leafing through the pages of the *Daily News,* a newspaper critical of the government. The thugs accused him of supporting the opposition, Movement for Democratic Change (MDC), marched him to his house and ransacked it. Finding no evidence linking him to the MDC, "they dragged him to a crossroads market where, before startled shoppers, they hammered him with iron bars and lashed him with chains until he died" (*The Economist,* February 23, 2002; p.28).

ACKNOWLEDGMENTS

In my travails, various people, both Americans and Africans, and foundations, institutes, and agencies have provided me with support and encouragement. I owe each one of them a huge debt of gratitude. David B. Kennedy, president of the Earhart Foundation in Ann Arbor, Michigan, provided me with funding to support field trips to Africa and research. The Lynne and Harry Bradley Foundation of Milwaukee, Wisconsin, also provided funding for the editing of this book. I am also grateful to Richard Gilder of the Gilder Foundation in New York and the Matt Essieh Family Foundation.

During my tenure at American University, I have been fortunate to receive critical reviews and encouragement from Professors Robert Lerman, Alan Isaac, Walter Parks, Robert Feinberg, and Jon Wisman, and excellent secretarial support from Sheila Budnyj, Sharon Childs-Patrick, and many others in the economics department.

The Board of Directors of The Free Africa Foundation, its staff, scholars, and associates must also be mentioned. Emmanuel Odamten, John Orleans-Lindsay, Ambassador Imru Zelleke, Felix Amankona-Diawuoh, Koshin Mohamed, Fred Oladeinde of the Foundation for Democracy and Development of Africa, as well as Roger Ream of Fund for American Studies, Ed Feulner of the Heritage Foundation, Ian Vasquez of the Cato Institute, and Ed Crane, president of Cato Institute, Phil Harvey of DKT International and Mary Kaplan of the J.M. Kaplan Fund have been extremely supportive.

There are many others (Americans, Canadians, South Africans, and others) to whom I still owe a debt of gratitude: Lynne Criner, Learned Dees of the National Endowment for Democracy, Tony Ellison, Robert Fox, John Fund (*The Wall Street Journal*), Georgie Ann Geyer (nationally syndicated columnist), Cliff Gosney, Sandy and Margaret Matheson, Audna Nicholson, Ralph Phillips, Gregory Simpkins, and others.

Last but not least have been the numerous Ghanaians and other Africans who have shown unflappable support for my work and writings. Worthy of mention are Dr. Emmanuel Ablo, Jerry Simpson, Mohamed Idris, Karanta

Kalley, Dr. Charles Mensa, Ablorh Odjijah, Rev. G. B. K. Owusu, William and Adwoa Steel, and many, many others. Rev. Seth Tetteh and Alfred Vanderpuije must also be mentioned for their vision to craft a "Brave New World."

A special gratitude is owed to Emmanuel Odamten, an administrative assistant at The Free Africa Foundation, for his diligence, steadfast support, and research assistance, and Alberta Amoaning-Yankson, who painstakingly made the stylistic and punctuation changes requested by the copyeditor.

In the final analysis, however, the views expressed in this book are my own and any errors or misstatements are my sole responsibility.

George B. N. Ayittey, Ph.D.
Washington, D.C.—November, 2004

PROLOGUE

In the battle of ideas and the campaign to push Africa in a new direction, certain experiences become memorable. They may come as innocent, everyday, run-of-the-mill events but have profound import.

One memorable experience occurred in July, 2003, when I was writing this book. I had been invited to Ghana by Dr. Charles Mensa, executive director of the Institute of Economic Affairs, to participate in a three-day workshop at Elmina. My task was to give a series of lectures on globalization and rent-seeking activities to a group of young African graduates. There were about 30 of them from Nigeria, Ivory Coast, Senegal, Sierra Leone, and, of course, Ghana.

These young African graduates were quite energetic and intellectually agile. What made my day at the workshop was a young Sierra Leonian called Mustapha—about 24 years old. He had told his friends that he was going to take part in a workshop in Ghana. Thereupon they asked him who were going to be the speakers. When he mentioned Professor Ayittey, his friends became "ecstatic" (his own words) and demanded "proof" that I would indeed be speaking. They insisted that Mustapha record every word I said.

Upon arriving in Ghana, Mustapha went to town and purchased a small tape recorder but lost it just before he got to the workshop. Thinking that he would be in "big trouble" (his words) if he returned to Sierra Leone without the tape, he rushed back to town and scrounged for hours before finding another tape recorder to purchase. By the time he got back, my lectures were over. Poor guy. To save his neck, he got me to repeat "I am Professor George Ayittey" over and over on the tape recorder. I also gave him copies of my lectures.

I may have saved his neck but he left a deep impression on me. Mustapha comes from a new generation of young African graduates and professionals, who look at African issues and problems from a totally unique perspective. They may be classified as the *cheetah generation*—Africa's new hope. They do not relate to the old colonialist paradigm, the slave trade, nor Africa's postcolonial nationalist leaders such as Kwame Nkrumah, Jomo Kenyatta, Kenneth Kaunda, or Julius Nyerere. The cheetahs know that many of their current leaders are hopelessly corrupt, and that their governments are ridiculously rotten and commit flagitious human rights violations. They brook no nonsense about corruption, inefficiency, ineptitude, incompetence, or buffoonery. They understand and stress transparency, accountability, human rights, and good governance. They do not have the stomach for colonial-era politics. In fact, they were not even born in that era. As such, they do not make excuses for or seek to explain away government failures in terms of colonialism and the slave trade. Unencumbered by the old shibboleths over colonialism, imperialism, and other external adversities, they can analyze issues with remarkable clarity and objectivity.

Their outlook and perspectives are totally different from many African leaders, intellectuals, or elites, whose mental faculties are so foggy and their reasoning or logic so befuddled that they cannot distinguish between right and wrong. They see a Western imperialist plot in every African adversity and would rally to the defense of such African leaders as Robert Mugabe of Zimbabwe, who fought against colonial rule. Having liberated their countries, such leaders have been transformed into semi-gods and can do no wrong. This is the *hippo generation*—intellectually astigmatized and stuck in their colonialist pedagogical patch. They can see with eagle-eyed clarity the injustices perpetrated by whites against blacks, but they are hopelessly blind to the more heinous injustices perpetrated—right under their very noses—by the Mugabes, the Ghaddafis, the Eyademas, the Obiangs, and others against their own people. The hippos only see oppression and exploitation when perpetrated by Westerners or white people. The cheetahs are not so intellectually astigmatized. Perhaps a mention of a few *cheetahs* besides Mustapha would be appropriate.

The Ghana Cyberspace Group (GCG), led by Yaw Owusu, is a pack of cheetahs, who mobilized young Ghanaian professionals in the diaspora to effect political change in Ghana in 2000. Subsequently, after the defeat of the tyrannical Rawlings regime in Ghana, they transformed themselves into an "investment club" (Ghana Investment Club, GIC) to mobilize funds for investment in Ghana. They were not waiting for the World Bank to do it for them. Nor are they globetrotting, begging for foreign aid.

Paul Sunwabe, a Liberian, styles himself as "Ayittey's number 1 fan." He and Chantelle Abdul, a Nigerian, mobilized a group of young African students at George Washington University in Washington, D.C., holding a series of conferences and seminars to push a different perspective on Africa. They have vowed to work tirelessly to expose the crimes committed by African despots and to block the grant of political asylum to any such despot.

James Shikwati, the executive director of the Inter Regional Economic Network (IREN), is a Kenyan cheetah. I have been much impressed by the activities of IREN, and participated in a conference James organized in November 2003. Most of the attendees were young—under 30 years old—and represented all walks of Kenyan life. There were journalists (from the *East Standard,* and the *Daily Nation,* among other papers) and also reporters for the Kenya Broadcasting Corporation (KBC). I told them at the conference that our generation has failed Africa miserably and has left a horrendous trail of chaos, instability, destruction, and vapid corruption across Africa. And, instead of taking full responsibility for this sordid record, our generation is constantly inventing new excuses to defend our failures. For this reason, only Africa's young professionals can take Africa in a new direction. Their minds are not polluted with all this anticolonial rhetoric and garbage. As such, they are capable of clear thinking, can see things with acute clarity, and can understand that the leadership must be held accountable for the mess in Africa.

This new breed of young African professionals I met in Kenya impressed me greatly. They are not into the blame game. Blaming colonialists and imperialists does not cut it with them. These young Africans do not just sit there, expecting Western colonialists to come and fix Africa's problems. Nor do they call upon the government to come and do everything for them. Three cases impressed me greatly. The first was a presentation by Students in Free Enterprise (SIFE)—a group of young university students that are involved in community-based entrepreneurship projects in the Marurui and Kibera slums in Nairobi. They teach petty traders, hawkers, small artisans, market women, and those in the informal and traditional sectors about simple accounting techniques, how to secure microfinance, how to secure a job, and how to improve the productivity of their businesses, among other things, so as to make these self-employed artisans self-sufficient. Among their projects are Jitegemee Project (*"Jitegemee"* is a Swahili word meaning "self reliability") and Msingi Was Biashara (basic money-making). They also teach people in the informal sector how to find skills that the community could use to profitably earn a living. For example, making beads, household decorations, and leather items; identifying markets; marketing goods; and plowing profits back into the business.

The second was a young Kenyan man, Jackson Kyengo, the director of Distance African Tours. Frustrated after years of working in government as a civil service employee, he quit his job and started his own safari touring company. His mini-buses, which were clean and efficiently run, provided transportation for the conference.

The third was Akinyi June Arunga, a female cheetah who blazed a trail across Africa—from Cairo to Cape Town—and produced the BBC documentary *The Devil's Footpath.* Displaying tremendous courage and determination, she traveled through Egypt, Sudan, Congo, Angola, Namibia, and South Africa, coming face to face with deprivation, the unspeakable horrors of war in the Congo, collapsed infrastructure, and devastated economies. She captured the misery endured by the average African and a remarkable spirit of resilience that allowed Africans to remain undaunted in their daily struggles.

I will relate one last story, which illustrates the difficulties this new generation faces. Strive Masiyiwa is another cheetah; he has been hounded and persecuted in Zimbabwe for refusing to submit to President Mugabe's corrupt rule. In 1993, Masiyiwa challenged Mugabe, demanding his right to start a cell-phone business. For almost five years, the president tried to prevent him from setting up his company, fearing the establishment of any telecommunications network outside official control. But Masiyiwa was not deterred and fought back through the courts, arguing that the behavior of the state telephone monopoly violated the constitutional right to free speech.

In 1995, the Supreme Court ruled in favor of Masiyiwa, and he started setting up base stations around Harare, with the help of Swedish telecommunications giant Telefon AB L.M. Ericsson. It was then that Mugabe entered the fray. "Mugabe issued a presidential decree, making it illegal for any private business to build a cellular network. Offenders faced two years in jail" (*The Wall Street Journal*, April 24, 2000; p.A24). Ericsson abandoned the project at one point and Masiyiwa had to hide in the trunk of his car to avoid arrest. But the Supreme Court struck down the decree as unconstitutional and Mugabe backed down.

In June 1998, Econet Wireless Ltd. hit the microwaves, which were by this time also being used by two other cellular operators: one owned by the government and the other owned by a group of ruling-party loyalists, including Mugabe's nephew, Leo Mugabe. Within weeks of coming online, Econet captured 45 percent of the market, a number that by February 2000 had grown to 60 percent, with more than 100,000 subscribers. Econet's market capitalization on the Zimbabwe stock exchange rose 2,000 percent, making it the country's second-largest company. International investors snapped up shares of Econet. But Mugabe's government grew suspicious of growing foreign interest in the company.

The turning point came at a February 15, 2000 referendum, when opposition activists used Masiyiwa's telecommunication network. Zimbabwe's economy was in tatters, wracked by mismanagement and shortages of fuel and commodities. To divert attention from his economic woes and unpopular involvement in Congo's war, Mugabe asked for draconian emergency powers to seize white farmland in a referendum. The opposition retaliated, transmitting a simple digital text around Zimbabwe from cell phone to cell phone, hundreds of thousands of times. All it said was: "No fuel. No forex.

Vote NO.'" Masiyiwa's offense was that it was his company that carried the messages.

According to newspaper reports and government insiders, a furious Mugabe brought the subject up in several cabinet meetings, cursing Masiyiwa and accusing him of being behind the message campaign. Masiyiwa pointed out that he had conducted an investigation, ordering overnight billing and system-diagnostics records, and discovered that the messages originated from subscribers themselves, mostly youngsters, who are the biggest users of the free short-message service. But Mugabe was not convinced. That Econet was the only cell-phone company with no ties to the government only heightened his suspicions.

"Making me responsible for the messages sent on my network is like holding me responsible for the contents of private conversations," said Masiyiwa. "I was told that the president was so angry that he actually said I should be eliminated" (*The Wall Street Journal,* April 24, 2000; p.A24).

Though the government denied the president made such a remark, shortly after the referendum, which the opposition won, the Zimbabwe Africa National Union-Patriotic Front (ZANU-PF)—dominated parliament passed a bill granting the government sweeping powers to intercept and monitor all telecommunications and internet traffic, as well as the authority to force telecommunications companies to suspend certain services. Many observers and diplomats said the bill was aimed at Econet. Fearing for his life, Masiyiwa fled to South Africa, where a pride of cheetahs is growing strong.

Zulu musician Bonginkosi Thuthukani Dlamini, who calls himself Zola, has become a celebrity in South Africa. Ten years after the dismantling of apartheid, Zola's musical career has rocketed, making him a household name in South Africa. As *Washington Post* correspondent Lynne Duke described:

> His music is *kwaito,* the hard-pumping South African style that is the soundtrack of the harsh lives and pastel dreams of a black township generation that came to adulthood after apartheid's fall. In the black township slang called *isicamtho,* kwaito (pronounced KWAY-toe) means "cool, wicked talk," though some say it takes its name from an old township gang, the AmaKwaitos. It's akin to rap, but its rhythms and languages are distinctly African, along with the music they call Zulu hip-hop, which is filling the airwaves here. (*The Washington Post,* April 14, 2004; p.C1)

Zola grew up in an impoverished place down in Soweto, one of the nation's largest black townships, which is still mired in squalor and poverty. Though the post-apartheid government has brought some telephone service and electricity to the township, other basic services are lacking. He grew up among the humble, the powerless, and the frustrated. Now, he says he is of those young-generation people who need to be heard. Most of South Africa's black heroes hail from the old South Africa—from the struggle against white minority rule in the 1970s and 1980s. But Zola did not come from that era. Born a year after the 1976 police massacres of the bloody Soweto uprising, he appreciates and respects what the black heroes struggled for. But as he sees it, the younger generation is striving to reach far beyond the struggle of their parents.

> "We're still connected with that apartheid umbilical cord thing. We don't look at the old generation—our moms and dads—as ignorant but as a deprived nation. They [apartheid's leaders] did not give them [the old generation] education or gave them wrong education. And we have to go back to them and explain the things we learn of the world. We live in a global village, from which they were excluded and we need to tell them that this is how life is now." (*The Washington Post,* April 14, 2004; p.C1)

Zola is not yet ready to cut the umbilical cord completely but his music conveys a certain kind of message: Life is what you make of it yourself, and people, millions of people, are listening.

This is the basic thrust of *Africa Unchained:* unleashing the entrepreneurial talents and creative energies of the real African people—the peasants, affectionately called the Atingas in Ghana because of their loyalty, dependability, and trustworthiness. The Atingas do not sit in some government office, dressed in "zoot and tai," pushing pen and pencil on paper. They are found in the informal and traditional sectors, weaving mats and making *garri.* The old paradigm, whereby the West took center stage in every African problem, is now obsolete. Kaput. But many African leaders, scholars, and intellectuals in the West still cling to it. My most vociferous critics come from this group, the *hippo generation.* Some have accused me of "bashing Africa," of "washing Africa's dirty linen in public," and called me such names as "Uncle Tom," "a sell-out," and "a traitor." If only they would make a distinction between African *leaders* and the African *people.* The leaders are the problem, not the people. When I challenged them to name just 10 good postcolonial African leaders—out of 198—since 1960, they could not come up with 10 names! When one accused me of being an "imperialist lackey" because I do not criticize the West, I wrote this response and posted it on many African Internet discussion forums, including Mwananchi (mwananchi@yahoo.com) and Naijanet (naijanet@e-groups.com) on August 13, 2003:

As an African, I know from historical experience that the West has committed atrocities and exploited my people. The West does not give a hoot about us (Africans) and the West is not alone. The Arabs don't give a damn about Africans; neither do the French, the British, the Russians, Japanese, or Koreans. Certainly, the Chinese don't come to Africa because they love black people. Every foreigner or entity who visits Africa comes to pursue *their* interests, not ours (Africans).

As an African, I also have a *leader* who is supposed to pursue our interest. But he pursues only his own selfish interests and does not give a damn about me. He has oppressed me, brutalized me, beaten me, and stolen my money to accumulate a huge personal fortune in Swiss banks. After only four and a half years in power, the late General Sani Abacha ("The Butcher of Abuja") amassed a personal fortune worth more than $5 billion. General Ibrahim Babangida did better, accumulating more than $7 billion. He walks freely, thumbing his nose at the people. More than $400 billion in oil revenue has flowed into Nigerian government coffers since 1970. Nobody knows where that oil money is. Explain to me why Nigeria, an oil-producing country, has gasoline shortages and must import refined fuel.

I also have a *politician* who is supposed to represent me. After I voted for him, his first act was to grant himself and fellow legislators hefty salary increases and allowances to furnish their offices and purchase cars. Remember Senator Chuba Okadigbo?

"As Senate President, he controlled 24 official vehicles but ordered 8 more at a cost of $290,000. He was also found to have spent $225,000 on garden furniture for his government house, $340,000 on furniture for the house itself ($120,000 over the authorized budget); bought without authority a massive electricity generator whose price he had inflated to $135,000; and accepted a secret payment of $208,000 from public funds, whose purpose included the purchase of Christmas gifts" (*New African,* Sept 2000; p.9).

I also know that as an African, we have very fine intellectuals and professionals but many of them act like intellectual prostitutes, selling off their conscience and integrity to serve the dictates of barbarous military regimes. In fact, according to Colonel Yohanna A. Madaki, when General Gowon drew up plans to return Nigeria to civil rule in 1970, "academicians began to present well researched papers pointing to the fact that military rule was the better preferred since the civilians had not learned any lessons sufficient enough to be entrusted with the governance of the country" (*Post Express,* Nov 12, 1998; p.5).

Nigeria's Senator Arthur Nzeribe once declared that General Babangida was good enough to rule Nigeria. When pressed, he confessed: "I was promised prime ministerial appointment. There is no living politician as hungry for power as I was who would not be seduced in the manner I was to invest in the ABN, with the possibility and promise of being Executive Prime Minister to a military president" (*The Guardian,* Nov 13, 1998; p.3).

Now, let me ask a practical, not academic question: If I have a very sharp cutlass (machete) whom should I go after?

George B. N. Ayittey,
Washington, D.C.

Now, some hippos want to borrow "Ayittey's cutlass." The cheetahs already have theirs.

Chapter 1

Why Africa Is Poor

Instead of being exploited for the benefit of the people, Africa's mineral resources have been so mismanaged and plundered that they are now the source of our misery.

> —United Nations Secretary-General, Kofi Annan
> at the Organization of African Unity (OAU) Summit
> in Lome (*Daily Graphic*, July 12, 2000; p.5).

Ghana was the first sub-Saharan nation to win its independence from a colonial power in 1957. Yet the average per capita income of my people is lower now than in the 1960s, four decades after independence. Some of the blame for this we Ghanaians must accept. My country must acknowledge that corruption has been a canker on our public and economic life and must be contained.

One hundred years ago, our trading was limited to the supply of raw materials, mainly gold, timber and cocoa. One hundred years later, our trading consists of raw materials, mainly gold, timber and cocoa.

I must admit that Ghana's path towards self-reliance has not been smooth. I am painfully aware that our past can be characterized by one step forward and two steps backward.

> —President John A Kufuor of Ghana
> (*The Financial Gazette*, May 3, 2002; p.5).

INTRODUCTION: THE AFRICAN PARADOX

In February 2002, British Prime Minister Tony Blair warned that the West could face new terrorist threats unless measures were taken to relieve African poverty (*BBC World Service*, Feb 6, 2002). Comparing the continent's plight to that of Afghanistan ten years ago, when it was allowed "to deteriorate into a failed state living on drugs and terrorism," Tony Blair said: "In the end the impact was felt on the streets of America" (*The Times of London,* Feb 6, 2002).

Economic conditions in Africa have deteriorated alarmingly, which should not have been the case given the continent's immense development potential and untapped mineral wealth. As an old continent, it is the source of strategic minerals, such as tantalite, vanadium, palladium, uranium, and chromium. It has the bulk of the world's gold, cobalt, diamonds, and manganese. Compared to the Asian continent, Africa is not overpopulated. Therefore, it "has enormous un-exploited potential in resource-based sectors and in processing and manufacturing. It also has hidden growth reserves in its people—including the potential of its women, who now provide more than half of the region's labor force" (World Bank, 2000a; p.12).

Africa could well be the next and final frontier for roaring market-based capitalism. Yet, paradoxically, a continent with such abundance and potential is inexorably mired in steaming squalor, misery, deprivation, and chaos. The Congo basin is extremely rich in minerals, but its people are yet to derive any substantial benefit from that wealth. Instead, they have slipped with indecent haste back to near stone-age existence. Provision of basic social services—such as education, health care, sanitation, clean water, and roads—is nonexistent. In the eastern part of the Democratic Republic of the Congo (DRC), particularly in Goma, there is no government. Freelance banditry and pillage are the daily fare. No one is in control of anything—rebel groups do not even control their own people.

When Ghana gained its independence on March 6, 1957, it stood at the same level of development as South Korea. Both countries had income per capita of $200. At independence, there was much hope for Ghana. The country's economic potential was enormous: It had rich endowments of minerals (gold, diamonds, bauxite, manganese), cash crops (cocoa, coffee, kola nuts), and timber. In addition, Ghana had a well-educated population, with a relatively larger professional and educated class than many other African countries. But 40 years later, South Korea's income per capita is ten times that of Ghana: $4,400 versus $420.

Nigeria also stood at the same stage of development with South Korea in 1960, but 40 years later, Africa's most populous nation found itself mired in convulsive violence and grinding poverty with nearly the same per capita income as in 1960—as if the economy went into hibernation. Between the inception of civilian rule in May 1999 and 2003, after decades of villainous military rule, more than 10,000 people had died in ethnic and religious clashes. The army continued to massacre hundreds of civilians with impunity. Even the respected justice minister Bola Ige was assassinated in December 2001. His killers have not been found. On February 2, 2002, fighting between members of the Yoruba and Hausa ethnic groups claimed the lives of more than 100 people in Lagos. "By all accounts, the fighting began in Idi Araba on Saturday afternoon after a Yoruba youth defecated in front of a house owned by Hausas" (*The New York Times*, Feb 8, 2002; p.A3). "Every occurrence of violence erodes the legitimacy of the state and its leaders, leaving democracy to stand alone and exposed to those who want to subvert it further or destroy it altogether," said a hopelessly weak and frustrated President Olusegun Obasanjo (*The New York Times*, Feb 8, 2002; p.A3).

Independence and freedom did not bring the prosperity promised by the nationalist leaders. Poverty levels instead increased sharply in the postcolonial period. By the early 1990s, the dreams of many Africans had turned sour: They were economically worse off than they were at independence (World Bank, 1989; p.4).

Bleak Prospects

Africa's postcolonial economic performance remains dismal and prospects for the new millennium are, to put it bluntly, bleak. Sub-Saharan Africa, consisting of 48 countries, is the least-developed region of the Third World despite its immense wealth in mineral and natural resources.

Since 1990, the United Nations Development Program (UNDP) has ranked 162 countries in terms of their progress on human development, using the Human Development Index (HDI). It determines the overall achievements in a country based on life expectancy, educational attainment (adult literacy and combined primary, secondary, and tertiary enrollment), and adjusted income per capita in purchasing power parity (PPP) U.S. dollars (UNDP, 2001; p.14). Each year, African countries compete for the lowest distinctions. In 2001, for example, the 28 countries at the bottom of the ranking were all from Sub-Saharan Africa (UNDP, 2001; p.142). Furthermore, compared to other regions in the Third World, Sub-Saharan Africa lags far behind in terms of economic performance. Not only have already low incomes fallen but per capita GDP growth over the period 1975 to 1999 averaged –1 percent. In 1999, Madagascar and Mali had per capita incomes of $799 and $753—down from $1,258 and $898 25 years ago. In 16 other Sub-Saharan African countries, per capita incomes were also lower in 1999 than in 1975 (UNDP, 2001; p.12).[1] The following table shows the comparative performance of Sub-Saharan Africa in stark terms.

Gross domestic product relates to domestic economic activity and excludes income produced outside the country. Measures for income per

Table 1.1　Comparative Economic Performance 1975–1999

Region	GDP Per Capita, 1999	Annual Growth of GDP Per Capita, 1975–1999	Annual Growth of GDP Per Capita, 1990–1999
East Asia and Pacific	$3,950	6.0	5.9
Latin America and Caribbean	$6,880	0.6	1.7
South Asia	$2,280	2.3	3.4
Sub-Saharan Africa	$1,640	-1.0	-0.4

Source: UNDP, *Human Development Report*, 2001; p. 181.

capita, which take into account external transactions such as trade and income transfers, have not performed well either. For Sub-Saharan Africa, gross national product (GNP) per capita has dropped steadily from $624 in 1980 to $513 in 1998. A similar trend was registered for all of Africa: a drop from $749 in 1980 to $688 in 1998 (World Bank, 2000a; p.35).[2]

Prognosis for the new millennium is widely acknowledged to be disheartening:

Sub-Saharan Africa enters the new century with many of the world's poorest countries. Average income per capita is lower than at the end of the 1960s. Incomes, assets, and access to essential services are unequally distributed. And the region contains a growing share of the world's absolute poor, who have little power to influence the allocation of resources.

Moreover, many of the development problems have become largely confined to Africa. They include lagging primary school enrolments, high child mortality, and endemic diseases—including malaria and HIV/AIDS—that impose costs on Africa at least twice those in any other developing region. One African in five lives in countries severely disrupted by conflict. Making matters worse, Africa's place in the global economy has been eroded, with declining export shares in traditional primary products, little diversification into new lines of business, and massive capital flight and loss of skills to other regions. Now the region stands in danger of being excluded from the information revolution (World Bank, 2000a; p.1).

The United Nations Conference on Trade and Development's (UNCTAD) Report, *Least Developed Countries, 2002,* noted that both the extent and depth of poverty have increased dramatically in Sub-Saharan Africa: "The proportion of people in 29 African countries living below $2 per day increased from 82 percent in the late 1960s to 87.5 percent in the late

1990s. For those in extreme poverty—under $1 per day—the increase was from 55.8 per cent to 64.9 percent. The number of African[s] living in extreme poverty rose dramatically from 89.6 million to 233.5 million over the same period" (*Africa Recovery,* Sept. 2002; p.9). The report noted that not only is poverty widening in Africa, but it is also becoming more severe.

On July 8, 2003, the UN issued a stern warning about worsening economic and social conditions in black Africa, just as U.S. President George W. Bush began a five-day tour of the continent. In its Human Development Report (2003), the UNDP warned that:

> Unless things improve it will take sub-Saharan Africa until 2129 to achieve universal primary education, until 2147 to halve extreme poverty and until 2165 to cut child mortality by two thirds. For hunger no date can be set because the region's situation continues to worsen. (*Financial Times,* July 9, 2003; p.1)

The report noted that while most of the world's economies expanded in the 1990s, people in 54 developing countries had become poorer; the majority of these countries were in Africa.

The number of poor in Africa, defined as those making less than a dollar a day, has increased sharply in both relative and absolute terms. The absolute number of poor in Africa has grown five times more than the figure for Latin America, and twice that for South Asia. For example, in 1995 the population of Africa was estimated to be 580 million.[3] Of these,

- 291 million people had average incomes of below one dollar a day in 1998;
- 124 million of those up to age 39 years were at risk of dying before 40;
- 43 million children were stunted as a result of malnutrition in 1995;
- 205 million were estimated to be without access to health services in 1990–1995;
- 249 million were without safe drinking water in 1990–95;
- More than 2 million infants die annually before their first birthday. (World Bank, 2001; p.xiii)

The Challenge

Turning things around requires development or economic growth, and the key to growth is investment—both foreign and domestic. Investment then is the way out of Africa's economic miasma and grinding poverty. Africa needs investment in agriculture, manufacturing, education, health care, telecommunications, and infrastructure. But the continent has remained unattractive to investors. In fact, UNCTAD concluded that "Africa has lost attractiveness as market for Foreign Direct Investment (FDI) as compared to other developing regions during the last two decades" (*The African Observer,* Nov 30-Dec 13, 1998; p.21).

This is ironic because rates of return on investment in Africa are among the highest in the world. "Since 1990, the rate of return in Africa has averaged 29 percent; since 1991, it has been higher than in any other region, including developed countries as a group, and in many years by a factor of two or more" (UNCTAD, 1999; p.12). Net income or profit from British direct investment in Sub-Saharan Africa (not including Nigeria) increased by 60 percent between 1989 and 1995 (Bennell, 1997a, p.132). Furthermore, in 1995, Japanese affiliates in Africa were more profitable (after taxes) than in the early 1990s, and were even more profitable than Japanese affiliates in any other region except for Latin America and the Caribbean and West Asia (UNCTAD, 1999; p.12). Earlier studies by UNCTAD also confirmed the high rate of return of foreign affiliates of transnational corporations in Africa (UNCTAD, 1995). But foreign investors have stayed away from Africa: "Too often, Africa has been associated only with pictures of civil unrest, starvation, deadly diseases and economic disorder, and this has given many investors a negative picture of Africa as a whole" (UNCTAD, 1999; p.12).

For much of the time since 1970, foreign direct investment (FDI) into Africa has increased only modestly, from an annual average of almost $1.9 billion in 1983–1987 to $3.1 billion in 1988 to 1992 and $6.0 billion in 1993 to 1997. While inflows to developing countries as a group almost quadrupled, from less than $20 billion in 1981 to 1985 to an average of $75 billion in the years 1991 to 1995, inflows into Africa only grew two-fold during that period. As a result, Africa's share in total inflows to developing countries dropped significantly: from more than 11 percent in 1976–1980 to 9 percent in 1981 to 1985, 5 percent in 1991 to 1995 and to 4 percent in 1996 to 1997 (UNCTAD, 1999; p.13). Net private direct investment in Sub-Saharan Africa dwindled to $3.9 billion in 2002 —a paltry sum and worse than in six of the seven previous years. Even rich Africans do not invest in Africa: an estimated 40 percent of the continent's privately held wealth is stashed offshore (*The Economist,* Jan 17, 2004; Survey, pp.4 and 11).

Paucity of Economic Success Stories

Largely due to pressure from African Americans (or black Americans), Western economic analysts have over the decades tried in vain to focus on Africa's economic success stories in order to accentuate the positive or avoid painting too negative a portrait of Africa for reasons of political correctness. Multilateral lending institutions, such as the World Bank and the International Monetary Fund, also engage in this sport, but for reasons other than political correctness. By touting a country as an "African economic success story," it is their hope that other African countries may emulate that country's policies. Unfortunately, political correctness can lead one astray, and success stories often fall on deaf ears and blind eyes.

Of course Africa's situation is not altogether hopeless. To be sure, there are economic success stories in Africa, but they are distressingly few. In 2001, this tiny coterie included Benin, Botswana, Madagascar, Mali, Mauritius, Mozambique, and Uganda, because they were registering impressive growth rates according to international aid agencies. This suggests that the vast majority of the 54 African countries are economic basket-cases. The real danger in focusing on the tiny number of success stories is that it ignores the much, much larger sordid picture. Furthermore, the economic success stories are themselves small country examples and are unlikely to serve as regional powerhouses to pull their neighbors or the rest of the continent out of its economic doldrums. Having Nigeria, Sudan, Congo (DRC), Ethiopia, or Angola as success stories would be more meaningful and strategic than Lesotho and Equatorial Guinea. Most unsatisfactorily, the list of economic success stories keeps changing. The Gambia, Nigeria, Ghana, Tanzania and Zimbabwe have vanished from the success list the World Bank trumpeted in 1994.

It is also true that a number of African countries have initiated economic reforms aimed at increasing the role of the private sector and moving to a market economy. State-owned enterprises have been privatized and various state controls have been removed. In addition, steps have been taken to restore and maintain macroeconomic stability through the devaluation of overvalued national currencies and the reduction of inflation rates and budget deficits.

Furthermore, African countries have also improved their regulatory frameworks for FDI, making them far more open, permitting profit repatriation, and providing tax and other incentives to attract investment. For example, 26 of the 32 least-developed countries in Africa covered in a 1997 survey had a liberal or relatively liberal regime for the repatriation of dividends and capital (UNCTAD, 1997b). Reforms have also been made in other areas that are important for the FDI climate, such as trade liberalization, the strengthening of the rule of law, and improvements in legal and other institutions, as well as in telecommunications and transport infrastructure (World Economic Forum, 1998, p.20).

Yet, all these reforms in the policy framework for FDI have not been enough to spur economic growth, overcome the negative image of Africa, and attract foreign investors. Instead of addressing those issues that create the negative image—such as ending insane civil wars—many African governments have established investment promotion agencies and engaged in PR campaigns to change this image, in the hope that the PR campaigns would attract investors. In the Southern African Development Community (SADC), for example, all 14 member states have established such agencies, 7 of which were set up only in the 1990s (Mwinga et al., 1997). Much of this effort, however, is likely to prove futile.

First, the investment promotion agencies cannot be effective when SADC members do not follow the rules of their own organization and have failed consistently to erase the negative image that afflicts their own region. Foreign investment does not occur in a vacuum but in a stable environment where the rule of law prevails. For example, President Festus Mogae of Botswana has persistently complained that the Zimbabwean crisis is hurting the region's economy, and southern African government agencies seeking to attract foreign investment have dithered over ending the violent political crisis in Zimbabwe that could destabilize the entire region. Foreign investors fled South Africa when two white Zimbabwean farmers were murdered on April 18, 2000. According to *The Wall Street Journal* (May 4, 2000), the South African bond market witnessed an outflow of R1.8 billion ($263 million) (p.A16). And the Kenyan shilling experienced a six-month low against the dollar as traders feared a Zimbabwe contagion (*The Washington Times,* May 6, 2000; p.A5). It was clear that the economic interests and needs of an entire region were being held hostage by Zimbabwe's leadership, which refused to respond appropriately to the breakdown of law.

Finally, on January 14, 2002, leaders of the fourteen-member SADC gathered in Blantyre, Malawi to discuss the political crisis in Zimbabwe that was spiraling out of control. Opposition supporters in Zimbabwe were being brutalized and killed by government-backed thugs. And Zimbabwe's parliament was considering passing a draconian bill that would severely restrict press freedoms. So how could SADC leaders call Zimbabwe President Mugabe to order when most of them do not respect these freedoms in their own countries? Perhaps, these southern African leaders would change their ways. But as is often the case, "change" comes too late. Such were the cases of Julius Nyerere and Kenneth Kaunda.

Julius Nyerere

As the investment climate in southern Africa continues to deteriorate and, with that, the prospects of an economic rejuvenation, the leaders, believing that investment occurs in space, establish one investment promotion agency after another with the task of attracting foreign investors to Africa. The late Julius Nyerere, former president of Tanzania, eventually recognized the folly of this exercise. In a speech at his alma mater (the University of Edinburgh) on October 9, 1997, he was direct:

> In my view, three factors militate against economic and social growth in Africa. The first of these is corruption. This is a widespread cancer in Africa. The second factor which makes business reluctant to invest in Africa is political instability. But even if African countries were to become paragons of good governance and political stability, despite the corruptive and disruptive nature of poverty itself, foreign investors would not be coming rushing to Africa. Most African countries still lack the necessary physical infrastructure and the education and training in skills needed for rapid economic and social development. This, in my view, is the third and the most important factor militating against significant flows of foreign direct investment to Africa. (*PanAfrican News*, September 1998)

It was an astonishing statement to come from Nyerere, an avowed African socialist who was deeply suspicious of private capital. The irony—or more appropriately, the tragedy—is that he never honored or paid heed to the very points he made in his speech when he was the president of Tanzania from 1962 to 1984. His domestic record and legacy were riddled with massive economic failures and policy blunders that left Tanzanians worse off than they were at independence in 1962. With current income per capita of $210, Tanzania is among the seven poorest nations in the world.

Commenting on Africa's independence struggle in that remarkable speech, he also said that: "In practice, colonialism, with its implications of racial superiority, was replaced by a combination of neocolonialism and government by local elites who too often had learned to despise their own African traditions and the mass of the people who worked on the land" (*PanAfrican News*, September 1998). This was yet another remarkable statement by Julius Nyerere.

The supreme irony of it all is that Julius Nyerere, who denounced Britain's colonial project, eventually sought medical help from Britain. He died at St. Thomas Hospital in London from leukemia on October 14, 1999, at the age of 77. The socialist medical system he established in Tanzania was in shambles and could not save him.

Kenneth Kaunda

Kenneth Kaunda is another of the "old guard," whose reeducation came rather late. He led Zambia to independence from Britain in 1964 and ruled

Zambia for 27 years. Like Nyerere in Tanzania, Kaunda banished any opposition to his rule, and established a one-party state which failed miserably.
It "built an unmanageable, socialist-style economy on subsidies and foreign
debt that resulted in food shortages and food riots" (*New York Times,* January 31, 2002; p.A4). In 1991, following the collapse of the Soviet Union, the
democratic winds of change swept across Africa, claiming Kenneth Kaunda
as a prized victim.

A decade later, he was a changed man: "Why should anyone in public life
impose himself on the people? The decisions must be made by the people.
In my case, it was a call for change. The tide was for change in the country.
I respected it. Look at me now. You are watching a relaxed old man. I'm very
happy with what I'm doing" (*The New York Times,* Jan 31, 2002; p.A4).

Perhaps, something good after all can be said about African leaders—
when they are out of power and senile! But can Africa afford to wait that
long for current sit-tight leaders to grow "wise"—once out of office—before
talking about sound economic policies that help the people? And at 80 years
of age, how much more old must Robert Mugabe grow to acquire "wisdom"?

ATINGA: THE AFRICAN PEASANT

An assessment of the performance of Africa's postcolonial leaders on the development front always generates intense controversy, given the personal sacrifices they endured and the arduous struggle they waged against
colonialism. Having won independence for their respective countries, most
should have retired and passed the baton to a new set of leaders to wage the
war against poverty and underdevelopment. The skills and expertise required
to wage a successful liberation struggle are not the same as those needed for
successful economic development. The liberation struggle entailed battling
an "enemy"—a Western colonial power—with such tactics as civil disobedience, ambush, and frontal attacks. In the struggle against underdevelopment
and poverty, the "enemy" was not an external power and the tactics could
not be clearly defined. As a result, liberation theology and anticolonial
rhetoric seeped into the development arena, creating a confusing paradigm
with the West and modernization/industrialization occupying center place.

After winning independence for their respective countries, African leaders were in a hurry to develop Africa. The negative imputations about
African racial inferiority needed to be erased quickly, and they wanted to
prove to the Western world that Africa too was capable of success. This psy-
chological disposition, while understandable, plunged many African countries into a development quagmire.

First, it perilously corrupted the purpose of economic development. Twin
confusing and potentially incompatible objectives of development emerged:

To "prove something" to the world and to seek material improvement in the standard of living of the average person. Perhaps, to prove that it is "developing" and not wallowing in economic backwaters,

> Nigeria, one of the world's poorest countries, is to launch its own space program in the form of an agency that will develop rocket and satellite technology.
>
> Transport Minister Ojo Madueke said the Government had allocated three billion naira ($6.7 million) for the program and that the agency would receive 2.5 billion naira a year in the next three years with the aim of becoming self-financing. (*New Zealand Herald,* June 7, 2001)

Such conscious and deliberate effort to prove that one is not "backward" may well end up proving the opposite. In September 2003, Nigeria launched its first satellite, built by a British firm for $13 million, which the Nigerian government claimed will "enhance the quality of life of people" and alleviate poverty. How exactly? "The government says the satellite will help Nigeria 'leap-frog' from its present state (awful roads, telephones that rarely work), into the space age. But Sam Chukwujekwu, an engineering professor, thinks the money would be better spent on education: 'You can't leap-frog from a mud foundation,' he says" (*The Economist,* Sept 13, 2003; p.43).

Second, a development paradigm infused with a liberation theology unnecessarily places the West at the center and profoundly politicizes and insufferably injects alien ideologies into the debate. The object of economic development is to raise the living standard of the average African, which is measured by income per capita.[4] He is not an elite but a peasant—an illiterate, poor, and rural person, whose primary occupation is agriculture or such primary activities as fishing and lumber, as well as such secondary activities as baking, sewing, trading, and repair business. We shall call this average African peasant "Atinga." He has two wives, with eight children, and they all live under some traditional authority, such as a chief, in a village. He has much more respect and reverence for the chief than the central government seated hundreds of miles away in the capital city. The chief is closer to him, listens to him, and cares about his needs.

Atinga is well versed in and proud of his tribal customs, religion, and philosophical beliefs, in which he has carefully instructed his children. He believes that there are supernatural forces and spirits who observe and control his daily activities. These supernatural forces are assumed to have emotional intelligence and prohibitions against certain types of human behavior. Compliance with these rules is rewarded in the form of longevity, freedom from sickness, and individual prosperity. Violations may elicit such punishment on an individual basis as sudden death, affliction by a terrible disease, or financial ruin, and collectively with poor harvests and barren women in the tribe. The ancestral spirits, for example, supervise and maintain the social norms that have been handed down by oral tradition from time immemorial. Atinga assumes these ancestors have continuing concern for the safety, welfare, and progress of living members of his kin group. Therefore, his moral code is dictated by abiding by the wishes and injunctions of these ancestors. It is necessary to communicate with these gods and spirits, to placate them in order not to incur their displeasure or wrath, and to make atonement in cases of wrongdoing to prevent vengeful acts or misfortune, such as a bad harvest.

Atinga has two plots of land, five acres each. He inherited one plot from his father and acquired the other from the village chief, who is the custodian of unoccupied land. Individuals or "strangers" may approach the chief for a plot of land to farm on term basis only.[5] Cultivation of food crops is generally a female avocation, following the traditional division of labor along sexual lines. The wives and the daughters cultivate cassava and vegetables on one plot. Harvest produce is carried on the head to the homestead. Surpluses beyond the family needs are taken by the wives to the village market for sale, explaining why village market activity is dominated by women.

By the traditional sexual division of labor, the cultivation of such cash crops as cocoa, coffee and tea; hunting, fishing, building the homestead, and defending the village are reserved for men. Thus, Atinga grows coffee on the other plot of land. The farming technique used in both food and cash crop cultivation is slash-and-burn, and the technology is primitive, restricted to such implements as the cutlass and the hoe.

The Atinga family goes about its economic activities using centuries-old traditions and customs. If the family makes a little more money than it needs, the savings are placed under a mat, in a pot, or some *susu* (revolving credit) scheme. And if he or any member of his family is sick, they rely on traditional medicine. For his transportation needs, he relies on the *mutatis, tro-tro,* or mammy wagons. Two of his front teeth are missing and the rest are discolored by *goro* (kola nuts).

These Atingas produce Africa's real wealth—they farm the food and cash crops (cocoa, tea, coffee, sisal, etc.) and mine Africa's gold, diamonds, uranium, and other minerals—the wealth that the elite plunder. But in the postcolonial period, they did not feature in the grandiose schemes African governments and the elite drew up to "develop" Africa, for two reasons.

Neglect of the Atingas

The elite were more preoccupied with industrialization than with agriculture—roundly castigated as an inferior form of occupation. Peasant farmers, the Atingas, received little or no help from their respective governments. Instead, heinous brutalities, brutal repression, and vapid exploitation were meted out to them. Oftentimes, they have been uprooted and their economic livelihoods disrupted by never-ending cycles of civil war. According to Rachel Swarns, an American reporter,

> Today, one of every five Africans lives in a country severely disrupted by conflict. . . . The World Food Program struggles to feed nearly a million people. And every day, about 500 children die from malnutrition, disease and exploding land mines. Leprosy and polio—illnesses virtually eradicated in the West—are rampant. Rebels and bandits roam freely through vast swaths of the country, making roads impassable. And since the national airline refuses to fly to most stretches of the interior, most Angolans are stranded in remote towns that seem like islands in dangerous waters. (*The New York Times,* Dec 24, 2000; p.S2)

Congo's war has claimed more than 3.5 million lives and the looting of diamonds, gold, and timber has left the 53 million Congolese among the poorest people in the world. The World Bank estimates that 80 percent of the population lives on less than 50 cents a day. Congo has almost no paved roads. According to *The Economist* (Aug 9, 2003):

> In Matonge, one of Kinshasa's densest neighborhoods, there have been no public services for years, despite constant "tax collection" by police and the government. The streets are paved with a thick layer of rubbish. Politicians driving their sparkling Mercedes cars through the market have to dodge meter-deep potholes. (p.40)

Only death will separate African politicians and elites from their Mercedes. In East Africa, they are called the *wabenzi*—men of Mercedes Benz—in Swahili. "They are all selfish," says Christina Furuha, a mother of six in Goma, of Congo's political leaders. "They do not care about the people" (*The Washington Post,* Aug 30, 2002; p.A12). A recent estimate by an American aid agency, the International Rescue Committee, "put the death toll as between 3.1 million and 4.7 million people, most of whom perished from the starvation and disease that result when civilians are in almost perpetual flight from armed men" (*Economist,* May 17, 2003; p.40).

African leaders who rail against racism and demand better treatment of blacks from whites often display contemptuous disregard for the welfare of their own citizens. Despite a looming famine situation, the president of Zimbabwe bought a new presidential fleet, consisting of a state-of-the-art limousine for himself, a second limousine for one of the vice-presidents, two

Mercedes Benz sedans and 19 presidential escort trucks with total value of $250 million. The presidential fleet was to be delivered by air from Bonn, Germany, at a cost of $4.4 million. According to *The Standard* (Nov 18, 2001):

> The purchase of the VIP fleet brings to $469 million the amount government has spent in 2001 alone on luxury cars for use by the president and his wife, the vice presidents, ministers and their deputies, the speaker of parliament and senior judges. In addition, government had set aside $219 million for a fleet for ministers, their deputies, judges and the speaker of parliament. The supply of the other 38 Mercedes Benz sedans was put on hold by the High Court after Harare businessman, Stanley Botsh, alleged tender fraud in the vehicle deal by Zimoco and top government officials.

The Atingas of Angola, Sierra Leone, and vast stretches of the Niger Delta in Nigeria are hurt by these excesses. "The war, the war, the war," said Jose Machel, a barber. "With our Angolan government, it is always the war that prevents them from doing anything for the people. But they live well" (*The Washington Post*, November 20, 2001; p.A16). As the incidence of poverty soared in Africa, many Atingas resorted to desperate measures to survive. Said Josiah Makawa, a warehouse worker in Harare, Zimbabwe:

> My family has not eaten meat in months. Sometimes we eat only raw vegetables for supper because we have no money to buy [fuel] for cooking. This government has had 20 years to do something about the land problem and they did nothing. Now that's all they want to talk about. No one is listening. (*The Washington Post*, November 23, 2000; p.A45)

In June 2000, two friends, Frederick Frimpong, 50, a well digger, and Owusu, 42, a mason, appeared before a circuit tribunal at Kumasi for offering two young men for sale at 40 million *cedis* ($6,000) each. According to the police chief inspector, Lucy Taylor, "they were selling the boys because they were fed up with poverty" (*Ghanaian Times*, June 29, 2000; p.1). Said Charles Onyango-Obbo, editor of the Kampala daily, *The Monitor*, "I know many people who are having to sell everything because they have lost their jobs. Farmers barely an hour from Kampala are selling off their daughters in return for sacks of corn: three for a pretty girl, two for a less attractive one. Ugandans are so numbed, they read these stories and laugh. And it is going to get worse" (*The Washington Times*, December 25, 1997; p.A11). This was not what independence from colonial rule was supposed to lead to.

The Atingas have no political voice or say in the decisions affecting them; nor have they been given any on account of their illiteracy. Neither do they have representation in the "one-party state" systems that were foisted upon

Africa after independence. Politically, Africa is the most "un-free" continent, having more despots per capita than any other region. Fewer than 16 of the 54 African countries are democratic, and the vast majority of Africans labor under brutally repressive and corrupt regimes.

Famine, civil wars, devastated agriculture, collapsed infrastructure, and political repression have sapped the vitality of Africa and sentenced the Atingas to near stone-age existence. As if these challenges were not enough, a new threat, HIV, now threatens the very survival of a beleaguered continent.

The HIV/AIDS pandemic has killed at least 20 million of the more than 60 million people it has infected thus far, leaving 14 million orphans worldwide. On the continent of Africa, nearly 30 million people have HIV virus—including three million children under the age of 15. Nearly 20 million HIV-infected men, women, and children, representing almost 70 percent of the total number of HIV/AIDS cases in all of Africa and the Caribbean, are concentrated in just 14 countries: Botswana, Ivory Coast, Ethiopia, Guyana, Haiti, Kenya, Mozambique, Namibia, Nigeria, Rwanda, South Africa, Tanzania, Uganda, and Zambia. In some countries in Africa, more than one-third of the adult population carries the infection. Africa has already lost some 12 million people from AIDS—more than the total number of deaths from all of the wars in Africa combined—and 11,000 new cases are diagnosed every day. But the leadership has done little to stem the rising pandemic.

At a Cairo forum in May 2001, Urban Jousson, the regional director for East and Southern Africa at United Nations Children's Fund, suggested that current African leaders be made to answer for their failure to adequately address the HIV/AIDS pandemic. He expressed fears that most of the "millions of dollars now being promised to fight AIDS in Africa would go into the pockets of leaders and members of national AIDS committees if adequate control measures were not immediately taken."[6]

If the Atingas voice any whiff of criticism of the elite-run government, soldiers with bazookas swoop down to raze their villages. In October 2001, soldiers apparently avenging the killing of 19 comrades massacred more than 200 ethnic Tiv villagers in central Benue state. Survivors gave gruesome accounts of how the soldiers, pretending to be on a peace mission, assembled men in Zaki-Biam and shot them down before embarking on a systematic destruction and looting of the town of 50,000. "Soldiers ravaged the market. Some looted, stealing motocycles, furniture and even yam, residents said" (*New York Times,* October 30, 2001; p.A3). "We want out of the Federal Republic of Nigeria," said Joseph Gaji, 34, an agricultural specialist. "Why should we be part of a federal government that cannot build anything for us, only destroy?" (*New York Times,* October 30, 2001; p.A3).

Consensus is growing among economists that governance, economic management, institutions, and economic freedom have more to do with successful economic development than natural endowments alone (Olson, 1996). Burnside and Dollar (1997) found that better-managed countries had higher levels of economic growth. In fact, there have been suggestions that "poor countries have been held back not by a financing gap (lack of capital) but by an 'institutional gap' and a 'policy gap'" (Dollar and Pritchett, 1998; p.33).

The Atingas have never had economic freedom, which is built with property rights and choice. According to the Heritage Foundation of Washington, D.C., and the Fraser Institute of Vancouver, Canada, "Individuals are economically free if property that they have legally acquired is protected from invasions or intrusions by others, and if they are free to use, exchange or give away their property so long as their actions do not violate other people's similar rights" (*Economist,* Jan 13, 1996; p.21).

The concept may sound abstract and esoteric but is relevant in everyday activities. Perhaps, like democracy, it is easier recognize its absence than to define it. Economic freedom does not exist when a government arbitrarily can confiscate private property (residential or commercial); conscript individuals for military service or forced labor; dictate prices at which commodities may be sold and purchased; restrict access into certain occupations, economic sectors, and markets; prohibit the production and consumption of certain commodities and services; and even impose on its citizens the use of a currency rendered worthless by reckless monetary policies.

The Heritage Foundation and *The Wall Street Journal* annually compile an Index of Economic Freedom. According to their 2001 index:

> Sub-Saharan Africa remains the most economically unfree—and by far the poorest—area in the world. Of the 42 sub-Saharan African countries graded, none received a free rating. Only five (12 percent regionally) received a rating of mostly free—a decline from last year's seven—while 29 were rated mostly unfree and two were rated repressed. (Angola, Burundi, Democratic Republic of Congo, Sierra Leone, Somalia and Sudan were excluded from the study because of the unreliability of available data caused by political instability, outright civil war, or lack of central government).
>
> The index demonstrates that sub-Saharan Africa's poverty is not the result of insufficient levels of foreign aid; on a per capita basis, many sub-Saharan African countries are among those receiving the world's highest levels of economic assistance. Rather, the main cause of poverty in sub-Saharan Africa is the lack of economic freedom embodied in policies that these countries have imposed on themselves, as well as the rampant corruption systemic in many of these countries. (p.4)

There were some improvements in 2004. According to the Heritage Foundation and *The Wall Street Journal* Index of Economic Freedom (2004), 9 African countries came to be classified as "mostly free" (Botswana, Uganda, South Africa, Cape Verde Islands, Morocco, Mauritania, Tunisia, Namibia, and Mauritius). Zimbabwe was the worst African performer, ranking 153 out of 155 countries. However, no African country received a free rating.

Economic research supports the hypothesis that economic freedom is highly correlated with economic growth. Adkins, Moomaw, and Savvides (2002) found that "increases in economic freedom are associated with improved economic performance in that increases in economic freedom move countries closer to the production frontier" (p.105–6). Other research studies—Gwartney, Lawson, and Holcombe (1999) and Easton and Walker (1997)—reached similar conclusions.

Unfortunately, for much of the postcolonial period, the economic freedom of the Atingas has been stripped by a plethora of government regulations, price controls, and *diktats*. What type of crops they could produce, who to sell them to and for how much were all dictated by so-called "revolutionary" African regimes. Under Sekou Toure of Guinea's program of "Marxism in African Clothes,"

> Unauthorized trading became a crime. Police roadblocks were set up around the country to control internal trade. The state set up a monopoly on foreign trade and smuggling became punishable by death. Currency trafficking was punishable by 15 to 20 years in prison. Many farms were collectivized.
>
> Food prices were fixed at low levels. Private farmers were forced to deliver annual harvest quotas to "Local Revolutionary Powers." State Companies monopolized industrial production. (*The New York Times*, Dec 28, 1987; p.28)

Various devices, such as development levies, price controls, and marketing boards, were used to milk them of their produce. Huge amounts of resources were skimmed off cocoa, coffee, and tea export earnings—ostensibly for development for the entire country to benefit all. But much of the resources extracted from the Atingas were used by the ruling elite to develop only the urban areas where the elites lived. The rest was looted by the ruling elite to amass huge personal fortunes abroad.

Indeed, in Ivory Coast, the late President Felix Houphouet-Boigny admitted in his 1988 new year's address to the nation that the country's farmers had over the years parted with four-fifths of the value of what they produced to enable the government to finance economic development. Much of this money went to the State Marketing Board. Nevertheless, the development that took place was concentrated in Abidjan and other urban areas and thus bypassed the rural peasants. Large sums were also channeled into the creation and maintenance of unwieldy and unprofitable parastatal corporations. The president's proteges used the rest of the Atingas' money for self-enrichment. *West Africa* reported, "The number of financial scandals involving top political figures which have come to light in the past decade give some indication of the extent to which self-enrichment is tolerated" (May 1–7, 1989; p.677).

Houphouet-Boigny himself was reputed to hold a vast personal fortune. In 1983 he declared, "I do have assets abroad. But they are not assets belonging to Cote d'Ivoire. What sensible man does not keep his assets in Switzerland, the whole world's bank? I would be crazy to sacrifice my children's future in this crazy country without thinking of their future" (*La Croix* [Paris], March 13, 1990). According to *Africa Report,* one anonymous tract estimated the president's fortune to be CFA 3,353 billion ($1=CFA 285 in April 1990) (May-June 1990; p.14). In the *Guardian Weekly* (London) Paul Webster claimed that Houphouet-Boigny "was siphoning off French aid funds to amass a personal fortune as high as 6 billion [francs]" (June 17, 1990; p.9).

While amassing a fortune abroad, Houphouet-Boigny was reducing the official price paid to the Atingas who grow cocoa and coffee by 50 percent for the 1989 to 1990 growing season. In the early 1980s he also froze the nominal incomes of most Ivorians while inflation raised the cost of living. By 1990 prices had gone up some 50 percent without any compensating adjustment in wages.

It is the Atingas who ultimately bear the brunt of their leaders' greed and neglect. On January 27, 2002, a small fire from a gas station near a central market in Lagos spread to the weapons depot at the Ikeja military base, touching off massive explosions that propelled shrapnel and shockwaves for miles through the crowded slums and working-class neighborhoods that surround the base. The huge blasts sent thousands of residents fleeing in panic. Many, including children, jumped into a nearby canal without realizing how deep it was and drowned. The death toll from the blasts and the drowning exceeded 2,000, according to private newspapers.

Residents had many reasons to be angry. The provision of basic social services, law, and order was nonexistent. The crime rate had soared. "Some police officers had been convicted of robbery or aiding bandits over the last year" (*The New York Times,* Feb 3, 2002; p.WK6). And when the explosions occurred in January 2002, there were no fire and rescue operations because the city had no trucks. Angry residents wanted to know how and why bombs, shells, and rockets were stockpiled in a heavily populated area. They demanded that President Olusegun Obasanjo cancel a scheduled trip to the

United States to attend the World Economic Forum in New York. He visited the devastation site to express his grief to the victims' families. When the distressed crowd of mothers of missing children urged him to take a closer look, he reacted in anger: "Shut up! I don't really need to be here. After all, the governor of the state is here" (*The Washington Post*, Feb 10, 2002; p.A20). He later apologized, saying "he was unaware at the time that lives had been lost." "How could Obasanjo have not known that people had died?" asked Jonah Nnachi, a 22-year-old trader. "If he was a person who cared for people, he would not have said those things" (*New York Times*, February 10, 2002; p.A5).

There are hundreds of examples. With more than 300,000 Liberian refugees across West Africa under his care, the United Nations high commissioner for refugees, Ruud Lubbers, flew to Monrovia to see their president, Charles Taylor. Taylor was not interested; the chief of his cabinet, Blamoh Nelson, was dispatched to deliver a retinue of excuses for denying aid to refugees—there was no money, no medicines, and enemies in neighboring countries arming rebels and plunging Liberia into war. Mr. Lubbers was visibly angered by Taylor's ambivalence. "'I am here to say to you the situation is getting from bad to worse," he said, his fingers tapping the table in a conference room in the presidency. 'You're killing your own people'" (*New York Times*, May 15, 2003; p.A3). President Taylor did not give a hoot.

The elites have turned almost every elementary concept of development upside down. The purpose of "government" is not to serve but to fleece the people. Development, to the elites, means developing their pockets, and foreign investment means investing the booty in a foreign country! Thus, to the Atingas, development means robbery, brutality, impoverishment, a starvation diet, and a gun to the head. They have been betrayed. This is not the freedom and development the Atingas hoped for after independence.

Africa's Salvation and Future

Just as it is important to distinguish between African *leaders* and the African people, so too is it important to distinguish between three Africas, which are constantly clashing. The first is traditional or indigenous Africa, which historically has been castigated as backward and primitive. Yet it works—albeit at a low level of efficiency. Otherwise, it would not have been able to sustain its people throughout the centuries. Today it is struggling to survive. The second Africa is the modern one, which is lost. The third is the informal sector, a transitional sector between traditional and modern. Most of Africa's problems emanate from its modern sector. They spill over onto the traditional, causing disruptions, dislocations, and claiming innocent victims. Most Westerners generally have difficulty dealing with and reconciling these two Africas—a view expressed by Nick Thompson, an American writer who traveled through Africa in 1998:

> When I left the United States, I had two contrasting images of Africa in my head. First, the stereotypical images of anarchy, starving children and poverty that seem to dominate every American's impressions of the continent. Beyond these desperate images, I also expected to find a continent that I had roman-ticized: an isolated land of music, magic, strong traditional culture and beau-tiful people that have survived with dignity through terrible hardship; a land captured in a flaming black-and-orange painting of elegant silky figures cross-ing a river in a canoe, a painting that a Ghanaian artist had once traded me in a New York subway. (*The Washington Post,* 8 Nov 1998, p.E1)

Most Western teachers and analysts erroneously assume that the two Africas operate by the same principles and logic. Traditional or rural Africa is the home of the real people of Africa—the Atingas, the peasant majority, who produce the real wealth of Africa: agricultural produce, cash crops, tim-ber, minerals, sculpture, and other artifacts. They lack formal education, but with their raw native intelligence and skills, some of them have been able to produce great works of art. The sculptures of Yoruba, Ibo bronzes, the beads of the Masai, Fang masks, Zulu headrests, and Sotho snuff containers "are masterpieces by any standard" and their artists "did so much, via Picasso, Derain, Braque and Matisse and Gris and others, to change the face of 20th-century European art" (*Economist,* Oct 7, 1995; p.97). "Rockefellers and Rothschilds were early connoiseurs of Shona sculpture. Prince Charles has become a collector" (*Newsweek,* September 14, 1987; p.80).

Nick Thompson found the "real Africa" at Ndiabene Toure:

> It is a small village in rural Senegal that has been around for 900 years: A beautiful, isolated village that may be poor by Western standards but where poverty doesn't matter. The village is divided into large family compounds, three or four men each with three or four wives and each wife with three or four children. Everyone eats from communal bowls without utensils. The day consists of planting what can be planted, harvesting what can be harvested and cooking what can be cooked. Every day, someone will go to the nearest city to sell whatever is left over and to buy whatever else is needed. The day ends when the sun goes down because there's no electricity, and, it being the desert, there's nothing to burn for light but sand and dry air. (*The Washington Post,* Nov 8, 1998; p.E1)

African natives have always been free enterprisers, going about their daily economic activities on their own volition. They do not queue before their rulers' palaces or huts for permission to engage in trade, fishing, or agriculture. They produce surpluses that are sold in free village markets, where prices are determined by bargaining, not dictates from the tribal government. Their traditional societies are generally peaceful and stable. They live not only in harmony with others but also with their natural environment, including wildlife. They run their societies with their own unique political and economic institutions.[7]

A careful study of their "primitive" societies reveals an astonishing degree of functionality: participatory forms of democracy, rule of customary law, and accountability. Their system of government was so open that some allowed participation by foreign merchants. No modern country, even the United States, can boast of such an open government. Africa's traditional rulers were no despots, despite their characterization as such by European colonialists in order to justify various pacification campaigns.

The ruler was surrounded by various councils, bodies, and institutions to prevent abuses of power and corruption. Furthermore, the ruler was held accountable for his actions at all times and could be removed at any time if he was corrupt or failed to govern according to the will of the people. "Under most traditional African constitutions, bad or ineffective rulers were more readily removed from office than most modern constitutions allow. Divine kingship does not absolve a ruler from removal if he fails to live up to his responsibilities or constitutional duties. Important decisions were made only after necessary discussions and consultations had been made. Akan kings had no right to make peace or war, make laws, or be directly involved in important negotiations such as treaties without the consent of their elders and/or elected representatives" (Boamah-Wiafe, 1993; p.169).

Modern Africa, by contrast, is the abode of the elites, the vampire parasitic elite minority group. This sector is a meretricious fandango of imported or borrowed institutions that are little understood by the elites themselves. The end product is a mass of confusion and an internally contradictory system that bears no affinity to either the indigenous system or the colonial state. It is a ludicrous monstrosity that was created by the ruling elites themselves after independence by copying and grafting here and there from a foreign system they hardly comprehended. Over time it evolved into the present-day bizarre politico-economic system that admits of no rule of law, no accountability, no democracy of any form, and even no sanity. There is utter institutional chaos and misgovernance. Here common sense has been murdered and arrogant lunacy rampages with impunity. At the helm of the affairs of the state is a "hardened coconut" who has debauched all key institutions of government—the military, the judiciary, civil service, banking, and the government itself. "Government" has ceased to exist in many

African countries, replaced by a vampire or a gangster state, which evolves into a coconut republic and eventually implodes.

From the 1970s and up to the twenty-first century, considerable effort and resources were invested in cajoling the ruling vampire elites to reform the African mafia state. They were bribed with foreign aid to reform their abominable political systems. The World Bank and the IMF popped in with structural adjustment loans to help reform decrepit state-controlled economies. Buzz terms, such as "reliance on the private sector," "market economies," "accountability," "transparency," and "governance" all punctuated the air. But much of this drive fizzled with billions of dollars wasted. The democratization process stalled and economic liberalization went kaput. The ruling vampire elites were just not interested in reform. Instead, they performed the "Babangida boogie"—one step forward, three steps back, a flip, and a sidekick to land on a fat Swiss bank account. Reform became a vulgar charade.

A strange version was the "Abacha cha-cha-cha." General Sani Abacha, head of state of Nigeria, created various committees and commissions supposedly to shepherd the country toward democratic rule. But many of them, including the National Mobilization and Persuasion Committee headed by Dr. Godwin Dabo, the Transition Implementation Committee (TIC), the National Reconciliation Committee (NARECOM), and the Committee on Devolution of Powers between Federal, State, and Local Governments, were actually working to help Abacha succeed himself as "civilian president" (*The Vanguard,* July 16, 1998). And all the five political parties Abacha legalized promptly adopted him as their presidential candidate, taking lunacy to new heights of imbecility. Why not just declare the country to be a one-party state, where one buffoon is the sole candidate and always wins 99.9 percent of the vote?

But Abacha was not alone. In the nightclubs of Kinshasa, Congo, couples were dancing "the *dombolo,* a step created to mock the President, Laurent Kabila's ponderous style" (*New York Times,* May 21, 1998; p.A1). He was still pondering—never mind what!—when he was shot dead by his own security detail in January 2000.

It should be clear that the modern sector is beyond redemption and non-reformable by the ruling vampire elites. They are simply not interested in reform—period. In fact, it would be economically and politically suicidal for them to do so. In Egypt, the National Democratic Party (NDP), the lumbering colossus that holds all but a few seats in Egypt's rubber-stamp parliament, announced in October 2003 that it had embraced a platform of sweeping economic, political, and social reform. Were Egyptians impressed? According to *The Economist* (October 4, 2003):

By and large, no. They have heard such promises before. Few Egyptians are convinced that the ruling elite is capable of real reform. The dominant suspicion is that the game is not change, but a bid to smooth the transfer of power to another generation within the same entrenched establishment (p.45).

In Kenya, "the Mount Kenya mafia, as the Kikuyu cabal became known within weeks of Mr. Mwai Kibaki's inauguration, appears to have renounced reform in favor of shoring up its ailing patron's power" (*The Economist*, October 11, 2003; p.52). In September 2003, Odhiambo Mbai, a leading political scientist and key man in efforts to redraft Kenya's lumpen constitution and introduce fundamental reforms, such as paring the president's almost limitless powers and independent judiciary, was assassinated in his home. "Three men were charged with the murder but not the senior government figure they accuse of hiring them. Three top people from the *East African Standard* newspaper were also arrested after publishing one of the suspects' confessions—minus the alleged paymaster's name. Mbai's fellow delegates to Kenya's constitutional review team have since accused the ruling politicians of bribery and intimidation" (*The Economist*, October 11, 2003; p.50). On July 8, 2004, angry Kenyans clashed with police in a violent street protest in Kisumu to express their fury at the government's failure to enact a new constitution. One person was killed and at least half a dozen others were injured (*The New York Times*, July 8, 2004; p.A6).

The refusal of the ruling elite to implement real reform will continue to produce never-ending crises on the continent. In fact, for much of the past 40 years or so, the bulk of the energies of gangster African governments has been absorbed in damage control and crisis management—managing scandals and budget, debt, foreign exchange, AIDS, agricultural and environmental crises—affording them little time to devote to real African development. When one is shuttling back and forth between creditors in ragged clothes, begging for alms, one has little time to craft a new vision for Africa.

At some point, even perpetual Afro-optimists would be rudely awakened to the law of diminishing returns: That pumping more and more aid into Africa's leaky bowl to induce gangster regimes to implement reforms will yield less and less in results. The African rogue state should be left to the fate it deserves—implosion and state collapse. This may sound cruel but it is a cold, hard, African reality. As the saying goes: "The wise learn from the mistakes of others, while fools repeat them. Idiots, on the other hand, repeat their own stupid mistakes."

What this discussion suggests is that the future of Africa does not lie, for the moment, in the crisis-laden modern sector. Nor does it ride on the backs of dysfunctional elites who are incapable of learning from their own stupid mistakes. Rather, it rides on the backs of the Atingas and their cutlasses and "primitive" implements. The real challenge of economic development is how to use or improve upon their existing institutions and technology to lift them out of poverty. It entails approaching them with humility, appreciating the contributions they can make, studying their traditional system, asking them what sort of assistance they need, and devising new initiatives and simple technologies that fit into their cultural and socioeconomic environment. It requires going to the villages and living with the Atingas. In short, it requires a completely new mentality and willingness to give the Atingas a better deal in the current economic and political dispensation.

Unfortunately, few have been able to meet this challenge in Africa, despite a swarm of foreign aid workers and development experts working in partnership with various African governments. African governments and elites have held the Atingas in contempt. Few have been willing to live in the villages. And if they have ever visited the villages, they have arrogantly marched off to "educate" and "teach" the Atingas about "modern and scientific" farming techniques and feed them empty revolutionary slogans. This old development approach, characterized by "elite dysfunctionalism," gets Africa nowhere. That elite model is geared toward wiping out the Atinga and the traditional system because they are "backward," and imitating symbols of modernity either to "prove something" or to "impress" foreigners. It treats Atingas as eyesores and does not fit them into modernization schemes.

From the outside, few of the multitudes of development experts and foreign aid workers were in a position to help the Atingas. For one thing, they have to work through corrupt elite-run governments to reach the Atingas, with frustrating results. The cultural gap was another problem. Few understood the Atingas cultural practices, beliefs, and the complexities of the traditional system. Thus, one often encounters a situation where foreign aid workers, in noble humanitarian endeavors, are trying to help people they don't understand. Innocent but tragic miscalculations often occur.

From this analysis, it is easy to understand why Africa's postcolonial record has been such a disaster. The object of development is to raise the living standards of the average African (the Atinga). African elites constitute the major problem in this task. Seduced by sophisticated modern gadgetry and pre-occupied with aping foreign paraphernalia, the elites seldom consider the Atingas "partners in development." Worse, African governments run by the elites repress, brutalize, and plunder the wealth of the Atingas. How then does development occur in such an atmosphere?

To take Africa to the next level, a completely new approach or paradigm is required. The new paradigm turns the old one completely upside-down. It shatters myths, places Atinga full-square at the center, and starts from the bottom up, rather than the old "top-down" approach. Furthermore, it seeks to liberate Atinga from the chains of tyranny, mismanagement, misgovernance, ignorance, disease, and abject poverty. Instead of elites marching off to the villages to "teach" Atinga, perhaps it is rather Atinga who can teach the dysfunctional elites a thing or two about agriculture and governance. After all, the Atingas have been farming for centuries. Elitism is just a new phenomenon, emerging after independence. And the elite better be humble enough to learn from the Atingas because their supposedly "backward and primitive" systems have survived for centuries while the so-called modern and scientific systems introduced by the elites barely survived forty years after independence and have been collapsing all over the continent. Moreover, there is a treasure trove of useful knowledge embedded in the Atingas' traditional system that the elite can discover, extract, and use. This is especially true of traditional medicine. In fact, this realization has already dawned upon some African scholars.

At a May 2000 conference on medicinal plants and traditional medicine for the new millennium, conferees issued "The Nairobi Declaration":

Formally Recognizing Traditional Medicine

We, the participants of the Nairobi Conference on Medicinal Plants, Traditional Medicines and Local Communities in Africa: Challenges and Opportunities of the New Millennium do hereby confirm our commitment to the collective goal of Health for All through the primary health care approach and the principles of conservation and sustainable development outlined in the Convention of Biological Diversity.

Whereas:

In sub-Saharan Africa in 1999, there were 6,027 deaths a day due to the HIV/AIDS epidemic, 2,345 deaths a day due to malaria, and 8,181 deaths a day due to diarrhea; and traditional medicines are often the only affordable and accessible forms of healthcare for the majority of the African rural population; and local health traditions—many of which are oral in nature and therefore largely undocumented—are being lost;

And

Traditional health systems have not been replaced by the "Western" system because traditional healing is deeply embedded in wider belief systems and remains an integral part of the lives of most African people;

We draw attention to the fact that:

African governments have not acknowledged or built upon this traditional knowledge resource-base, thereby making the goal of Health for All more difficult to achieve unless these resources are mobilized and used more effectively; the unsustainable, unregulated and indiscriminant harvesting of medicinal plant species is being compounded by the very low level of understanding of the biology and ecology of the species concerned; it is unlikely that social, technical or economic changes in developing countries over the next decade will reduce significantly the dependency of rural peoples on medicinal plant species resources; though there are few reliable data on global trade of medicinal plants, the loss of species would be a catastrophic blow to productivity, balance of payments, national debt, and GDP.

We call on the Presidents of all African countries to declare the period 2000 to 2010 the decade of African Traditional Medicine and commit their governments through the appropriate ministries to:

- Formally recognize the value of Traditional Health Systems alongside modern health systems in national primary healthcare as an available intervention option in the fight against HIV/AIDS and other communicable diseases;
- Identify compelling scientific methods to evaluate and standardize traditional herbal remedies in order to promote their safe, effective and affordable use;
- Develop comprehensive strategies/policies for the conservation, management and sustainability of supply of medicinal plant species;
- Identify legal strategies that protect the Intellectual Property Rights (IPR) of knowledge holders; formally recognize the value and contribution of ethno-veterinary knowledge in livestock healthcare;
- Establish an annual recognition week that acknowledges the important role that women play in home healthcare through their knowledge and use of medicinal plant species;
- Work with the World Trade Organization (WTO) to identify a process that effectively regulates the international trade of African medicinal plant species and protects individual countries' resources and rights;
- Establish a partnership of countries to protect and enhance this aspect of African cultural heritage.

Nairobi, Kenya
May 19, 2000 [8]

Perhaps another declaration is required, formally recognizing the critical role the Atingas can play in Africa's economic future and giving them a better deal. This is what this book is about: throwing away the chains of economic hardship and suffering that postcolonial African governments have shackled their people with.

PLAN OF THE BOOK

The thrust of this book is blunt and two-fold: First, African problems must be solved by Africans. The prevailing, deep-seated tendency—largely orchestrated by African despots to conceal their own failures—blames Africa's problems on external factors—colonial legacies, the lingering effects of the slave trade, Western neocolonialism, imperialism, and the World Bank, among others. This externalist orthodoxy, which held sway for more than forty years after independence, portrays Africa as a "victim" and suggests that the solutions to Africa's problems must come from external sources. This orthodoxy has lost its relevance and validity. It is kaput.

Second, Africa must be developed by Africans, using their own "African model," not one copied from the United States, Russia, Asia, or Jupiter. What works in Asia or Argentina may not work in Africa. This blueprint for Africa's future lies in Africa. It rests on the backs of its Atingas but their backs are broken and their lives traumatized by decades of brutal repression, naked exploitation, and rampant corruption. They live in fear and insecurity, most often in refugee camps. They are angry, which is the subject of chapter 2.

Chapter 3 examines the postcolonial elite development model. The principal grievance of African nationalist leaders in the 1950s against the colonial authorities was that there had been no development. Colonial objectives were not to develop Africa but to undertake only such forms of development that were compatible with the interests of European metropolitan powers. Since the colonizing nations were mostly industrialized, the colonies were envisaged to function as nonindustrial appendages to the metropolitan economy as consumers of European manufactured goods and providers of mineral, agricultural, and sylvan commodities. As a result, the development of the colonial economies was perniciously "skewed": overspecialized in one or two main cash crops (mono-export culture), making African economies highly vulnerable to gyrations in commodity prices on the world market.

Specialization in cash crops, it was argued, also destroyed Africa's ability to feed its people and supply their other needs internally. Most domestic industries collapsed from competition from cheaper—and probably better—imported manufactures. Because of collusion among foreign firms and discrimination from colonial banks, the modern sector was completely in foreign hands. Thus, most of the surplus profit generated by the economy flowed overseas and was not invested in the colony. Local industrialization was flatly discouraged.

The prime motivating force behind colonialism was exploitation, not social development. Infrastructural facilities provided by the colonialists were pitiful. Only a few roads, schools, and hospitals were built. As Nkrumah (1973) scolded:

> Under colonial rule, foreign monopoly interest had tied up our whole economy to suit themselves. We had not a single industry. Our economy depended on one cash crop, cocoa. Although our output of cocoa is the largest in the

world, there was not a single cocoa-processing factory. There was no direct rail link between [the cities] Accra and Takoradi. There were few hospitals, schools and clinics. Most of the villages lacked a piped water supply. In fact the nakedness of the land when my government began in 1951 has to have been experienced to be believed (p.395).

Kwame Nkrumah of Ghana, Julius Nyerere of Tanzania, and other African leaders vowed to demolish that miserably distorted colonial economic structure Africa had inherited and erect in its place alternatives that would serve the needs and interests of Africa, not those of Europe. To accomplish this, Africa could not rely on markets, which in any case were introduced by the colonialists and as such constituted decaying relics of the old colonial order. Nor could Africa rely on its peasants for an agricultural revolution because, according to Nkrumah, these peasants were "too slow to adapt or change their practices to modern, mechanized scientific methods" (Uphoff, 1970; p.602).

African development, according to African nationalist leaders, required a carefully planned and massive transformation of African economies. Such an investment could only be undertaken by the state. Furthermore, transformation of African societies required state control of the economy. This set the stage for massive state interventionism in the 1950s and 1960s. In Francophone Africa, industries were nationalized, tariff barriers erected, and the state assumed near-total control of the national economy (*Africa Analysis,* October 2000, p.4). Rather interestingly, the World Bank, USAID, the U.S. State Department and even development experts from Harvard University supported these arguments and accordingly channeled much aid resources to African governments (Bandow, 1986).

To initiate development, it was widely held that the African state needed wide-ranging powers to marshal the resources from the rural area and channel them into national development. Extensive powers were conferred upon African heads of state by rubber-stamp parliaments. Other heads of state simply arrogated unto themselves these powers. If a piece of land was needed for highway construction, it was simply appropriated by the state, and if an enterprise was needed, it was established by the government without any consultation with the people it was intended to benefit. In this way, *all* African governments, regardless of their ideological predilections, came to assume immense powers. Most of these powers were ultimately vested in the hands of the head of state. As President Felix Houphouet-Boigny of Ivory Coast put it succinctly: "Here in Ivory Coast, there is no Number 1, 2, or 3. I am Number 1 and I don't share my decisions" (*West Africa,* August 8, 1988; p.1428).

The drift toward state interventionism and development planning, however, was accentuated by the socialist ideology. After independence, many African elites and intellectuals argued for an ideology to guide the government on the road to development. The choice almost everywhere was socialism. The dalliance and fascination with socialism emerged during the struggle for political independence and freedom from colonial rule in the 1950s. Many African nationalists harbored a deep distrust and distaste for capitalism. In fact, capitalism and colonialism were adjudged to be identical: since the latter was evil and exploitative, so too was the former. Socialism, then, was advocated as the only road to Africa's prosperity.

To undertake the massive industrialization drive, the socialist state demanded and appropriated wide-ranging powers. Huge resources were also needed by the state for investment. Tax mechanisms had to be devised to transfer these resources to the state. But things did not go well right from the beginning.

Planned socialist transformation meant the institution of a plethora of legislative instruments and controls. All unoccupied land was appropriated by the government. Roadblocks and passbook systems were employed to control the movement of Africans. Marketing boards and export regulations were tightened to fleece the cash crop producers. Price controls were imposed on peasant farmers and traders to render food cheap for the urban elites.

Under Nkrumah, socialism as a domestic policy in his Seven-Year Development Plan was to be pursued toward "a complete ownership of the economy by the state." A bewildering array of legislative controls and regulations were imposed on imports, capital transfers, industry, minimum wages, the rights and powers of trade unions, prices, rents, and interest rates. Some of the controls were introduced by the colonialists, but they were retained and expanded by Nkrumah. Private businesses were taken over by the Nkrumah government and nationalized. Numerous state enterprises were acquired. Even in avowedly capitalist countries like Ivory Coast and Kenya, the result became the same: government ownership of most enterprises and a distrust of private-sector initiative and foreign investment.

However, the fundamental mistake made by the nationalist leaders was that they spurned their own indigenous African heritage and never went back to their own African roots to build on Africa's indigenous institutions. Most of the models and systems they introduced or imposed on Africa were alien. In particular, the one-party state system and socialism as an economic ideology can never be justified upon the basis of African tradition. Chapter 4 looks at this perfidious cultural betrayal.

To develop Africa required huge resources. Chapter 5 is an examination of how African governments attempted to secure such resources by borrowing abroad or simply printing money. This kind of development finance created its own problems.

Chapter 6 is an examination of the first-generation problems that emerged when impatience to develop bred intolerance of criticism of government policies and general dissent. Regimes that had won independence and freedom for their respective citizens began to drift toward autocracy. Further, the industrialization drive began to sputter. State enterprises had been acquired haphazardly, with little feasibility study and planning. They could not deliver the goods, and if they did, their products were shoddy and more expensive than the imports they were supposed to replace. And the huge resources needed for investment could not materialize since domestic sources of taxation were limited. Recourse was taken to foreign borrowing.

In Tanzania, for example, many Western aid donors, particularly in Scandinavia, gave enthusiastic backing to Nyerere's *Ujaama* socialist experiment, pouring an estimated $10 billion into Tanzania over 20 years. A National Maize Project under this program was funded by USAID from 1979 to 1985. Aid also came from Cuba, China, and the former Soviet Union. China built the 1,200 mile Tan-Zam railway at a cost of $166 million, free of interest and two years ahead of schedule.

With the passage of time, state controls began to wreak havoc on African economies. As any economist would affirm, price controls, regardless of where they are imposed, create artificial shortages. If the free market price of a bag of maize is $5.00 and the government fixes its price at $1.00, the immediate effect is to artificially cheapen the commodity and increase its demand. But it has the opposite effect on supply. By forcing suppliers to accept a price *lower* than what they were receiving before, it discourages production and reduces supplies. The combination of increased demand and reduced supplies produce the shortage.

The problems began to feed on themselves to create new ones. Chapter 7 examines the second-generation problems, induced by the first. State controls, for example, created commodity scarcities and destroyed the productive base of agriculture, which, in turn, produced a food crisis and a foreign exchange crisis. Unable to produce food and export cash crops, African countries could not earn the foreign exchange they needed to import essential capital goods for development, thereby precipitating a foreign exchange and ultimately a debt crisis.

Chapter 8 examines the grand initiatives unveiled by African leaders in the past to develop Africa. These initiatives were pompously announced at various African summits, amid clicking champagne glasses. After the summits, nothing much was heard of them. Another initiative being touted by African leaders is the New Economic Partnership for Africa's Development

(NEPAD). If the past is to be any guide, this plan is going nowhere fast as it is flawed right from the outset.

Chapter 9 examines in greater detail Africa's own indigenous economic institutions. Markets were not invented by Europeans and transplanted into Africa. There were free village markets in Africa before the Europeans stepped foot on the continent. This is not a veiled attempt to rewrite history but a statement of fact. Timbucktu, Salaga, Kano, and Mombasa were all great market towns of yesteryear. It is rather bizarre and an act of unpardonable cultural sabotage for African governments to pursue strident anti-market policies. For example, rural market activity in Africa has always been dominated by women, and these women traders have always been free enterprisers. And free trade routes criss-crossed the continent even centuries before the arrival of the Europeans. Free village markets, free enterprise, and free trade have always been part and parcel of Africa's indigenous economic heritage. These constitute the "roots" upon which the future of Africa must be built.

Chapter 10 focuses the development debate where it belongs: as improving the economic lot of the people. In Africa, the real people are the peasant majority. By and large, African governments and elite did not craft such an "Atinga model," choosing instead a model that may be characterized as "development-by-imitation." In the Atinga model, development must start at the grassroots level. This involves studying the peasants' ways of life, their economic activities, and native institutions, with a view to *improving* upon them to make them more productive or efficient. For example, native African fishermen still use dugout canoes, which limits the size of their catches. Real development would entail improving upon their simple setup so that *more* fish can be landed. The emphasis should be on the quantity gathered since a starving person cares less about *how* the fish on his plate was caught.

Unfortunately, the traditional ways of doing things were denigrated. Agriculture, the primary occupation of the peasant majority, was shunned as an "inferior" trade. Industry, or industrialization, became the rage since the rich countries were industrialized. Wholesale importation of foreign technology and systems was undertaken. The peasants were never brought into these grand schemes to industrialize Africa. By the early 1980s, the continent was littered with the carcasses of these failed imported systems. Now there is the need to go back to the grassroots level and start doing first things first.

This chapter also looks at the role the African state can play in forging a sensible development strategy. Obviously, massive state intervention—as in the early phases of the postcolonial era—would not work. Nor would the hands-off *laissez-faire* approach. A proactive state that believes in individual ingenuity and recognizes its own limitations is needed.

As African economies become increasingly integrated into the global economy, developments elsewhere in the world may impact African economies. While globalization may present many challenges to African economies, it also presents Africa with immense opportunities. The final chapter looks at moving Africa forward in the new century and the global economy. It specifically focuses on the role of African elites. For much of the postcolonial period, Africa's elites have played a negative developmental role. This final chapter seeks to outline the positive role they can play.

CHAPTER 2

The Wrath of the People

If you had told me a year ago that I would be in the streets rioting, I would have said you were insane. But then again, if you told me I would be praying to God to deliver us from [President] Robert Mugabe a year ago, I would have said the same thing. I am not a violent man; I am not an especially religious man. But whatever it takes for Zimbabwe to finally be rid of this man, I am willing to do.

—Josiah Makawa, a 24-year-old warehouse worker in Harare, quoted in *The Washington Post,* Nov 23, 2000; p.A45

Enough is enough. I have never participated in a demonstration before. I'm sick over this. It's a masquerade, a fraud. General Guie has to leave power. If he doesn't, it's war.

—Juliette Adjoua Koffi of Abidjan, Ivory Coast, quoted in *The New York Times,* Oct 25, 2000; pA5

Each and everything they [the African National Congress] promised us is not materializing. This country is going to the dogs.

—Raphael Mohlala, 22, Johannesburg, quoted in *The Washington Times,* April 15, 2004; p.A15

ANGRY PEASANTS FIGHTING BACK

True freedom never came to much of Africa after independence. In many African countries, independence was in name only; all that occurred was a change in the color of the master—from white colonialists to black neocolonialists—and the oppression and exploitation of the African people continued relentlessly.

Far from being utilized to lift its people—the Atingas—out of poverty, Africa's great mineral wealth and resources have instead been a curse. Nigeria, Angola, Gabon, Equatorial Guinea, and Congo-Brazzaville produce substantial quantities of oil. Both Nigeria and Angola earn over $100 million a day from crude oil exports. Yet, they are ranked among the 30 poorest countries in the world. According to BBC News (March 10, 2004):

> Nigeria has earned around $400 billion from oil since 1970 [but much of it has been squandered]. Nigerians own some of the finest properties in the world's best cities, and swell some of the world's biggest bank accounts. An ongoing criminal investigation in the US shows that even in Equatorial Guinea, where oil was only discovered in 1991, the president has $700m in a US bank account.

Oil revenues benefit mostly members of a tiny ruling elite and the companies that have worked with them. The oil bonanza reaped by Angola, Cameroon, Equatorial Guinea, Gabon, Nigeria, and other countries has been squandered and frittered away in conspicuous consumption.

The Angolan government earns around $3.5 billion from oil sales a year, but what happens to the revenue is a closely guarded secret: "The bulk of the money bypasses the budget, disappearing straight into the hands of the presidency. Angolans, who have long suspected something of the kind, call the nexus of the presidency, the Central Bank and Sonangol, the state oil company, the Bermuda Triangle: the place where money vanishes without a trace" (*The Economist*, Jan 15, 2000; p.48). Much of the money was used to finance a war that devastated the country and to finance the lifestyles of the super-rich "oligarchy" with whom the president surrounded himself. "When the cash runs out, the powers-that-be take out short-term, high-interest loans, guaranteed against future oil production. Thus, the entire profits from Angola's oil production for the next three years are said to have already been spent" (*The Economist*, Jan 15, 2000; p.48).

In February 2002, *African Business* reported that "a study into Angola's revenue accounts that compares state and oil company financial data has found that billions of dollars are missing. Numbers that do not tally occur mainly in the vast oil-backed loans used by the state to buy arms and prop up the war battered economy, economists and analysts engaged in the study have found" (p.6).

Cabinda, which accounts for about 60 percent of Angola's estimated one million barrels daily of oil production, derives little benefit from it. In a straw poll organized by the Campaign for a Democratic Angola in February 2004, people were asked whether oil had benefited ordinary Cabindans. Out of 2,200 responses, only three people ticked the "yes" box. "We die here every single day because of the oil. We've already told the [ruling] MPLA [party], 'If what you want is oil, you can just build a pipeline from here to Luanda and pump all the oil you want. Just leave us alone,'" said Cabindan journalist Raul Danda (*IRIN News,* March 22, 2004).

Father Jorge Congo, an influential Catholic priest and spiritual leader of the 300,000-strong community, agreed: "We've never benefited from it, so oil does not make any difference in the struggle. What's happened is that Cabindans have become victims of the oil—that's for sure" (*IRIN News,* March 22, 2004).

A group of angry Cabindans want their independence from the vampire elites in Luanda. Although the Cabinda Enclave Liberation Front (FLEC) is much weaker than it used to be and can only muster intermittent attacks, they have been increasing their attacks on government soldiers. The conflict smolders, despite the government offensive in the province in October 2002.

In October 2000, a consortium led by Exxon Mobil Corp. and including Chevron/Texaco Corp. and Petronas of Malaysia began the construction of a $3.7 billion underground oil pipeline that stretched 650 miles from oil fields in landlocked Chad through neighboring Cameroon and out into the Atlantic Ocean. When the first oil tankers, with 950,000 barrels of crude, left Cameroon in October 2003 for refineries abroad, local aid organizations held a silent protest and declared it a national day of mourning.

Under an agreement signed between the World Bank, the oil consortium, and the government, most of the Cameroonian government's share of oil income, expected to average $100 million a year, would be kept in a London escrow account. The government passed a law stipulating that 80 percent of the income would be used to finance education, health programs, infrastructure, water management, and rural development. Ten percent will go to a fund to benefit future generations, and 5 percent for development in the Doba oil-field area. A nine-member Revenue Management College made up of Chadians from civil society, parliament, the supreme court and government must approve disbursement of the funds. But the government spent $4 million of a $25 million signing bonus from the oil companies to buy weapons. Naturally. And President Idriss Deby tried to amend the constitution so that he could run for a third term and appointed his brother-in-law as governor of the central bank, a position that puts him on the Revenue Management College that manages the oil revenue. "You see, there are really crucial problems," said Theresa Mekombe, a citizen representative on the Revenue Management College. "So far, the oil has done nothing to help us. Do you see any hospitals or schools being built yet?" (*The Washington Post,* March 13, 2004; p.A16).

The Congo basin is extremely rich in minerals but its people are yet to derive any substantial benefit from that wealth. Feeling cheated and betrayed, the Atingas—the real people of Africa—are now angry and rebelling, which partly explains why Africa is in such turmoil today. They are fighting back against vampire governments that suck their economic blood out of them.

On January 26, 2003, for the first time ever in Senegal's history, tens of thousands of farmers from across the country marched on the capital to vent their grievances and anger. They converged on the largest stadium in Dakar to demand policies that would increase their incomes, reduce rural poverty, and lift them from the status of "second-class citizens." In so doing, they shattered the common elite misconception of peasant farmers as silent and passive. "Farmers, more than ever before, are mobilizing to better their conditions of life," declared Mr. Mamadou Sall, president of the largest national farmers' group, the *Conseil National de Concertation et de Coopération des Ruraux* (CNCR) (*Africa Recovery*, May 2003; p.14). The organization presented government officials with a "Farmers' Manifesto." It noted that agricultural productivity remains very low and that most rural people live below the national poverty line. "Agriculture has been in crisis since the end of the 1970s, and this has led poverty and food insecurity to become generalized throughout the rural areas," the manifesto stated (*Africa Recovery*, May 2003; p.14).

Although agriculture provides livelihoods for around 60 percent of the Senegalese population and accounts for 18 percent of GDP, it has perfidiously been neglected. It receives only 10 percent of all public investments. For many decades—including the French colonial era—the groundnut sector took the lion's share of public financing for agriculture. In fact, since independence in 1960, almost all the government's training, subsidies, and agricultural extension services have been devoted to peanut production for export. Neglected, most villages lack running water or electricity. In many rural areas the soil has eroded or become acidic and a succession of droughts in the late 1970s and early 1980s brought environmental degradation and rural impoverishment.

In Ivory Coast, once touted by the World Bank as an African "success story," resentment had been bubbling under the surface for nearly ten years—well before the country imploded into civil war in August 2002. Back in 1992, angry citizens took to the streets to protest hopeless life in perpetual poverty. Anger had been seething in the countryside, where 80 percent of the country's 12 million population lives. They produce over 80 percent of the country's wealth—cocoa, coffee, cotton, bananas, and pineapples. Years of neglect by the government and lack of development finally prompted them to take action. As *West Africa* (Dec 7–13 1992) reported:

They are not only disappointed, they are also very, very angry because, as producers of the nation's wealth, they have been denied their due share of that wealth. They held a meeting at Anyama, on the outskirts of Abidjan, after which they issued an ultimatum to the government to address their demands, which included better prices for their produce. A deadline of 15 October was set.

Realizing that things were getting out of hand, President Felix Houphouet-Boigny himself hosted the leaders [of the farmers] at his private residence in Yamassoukrou. The angry farmers demanded that they should be involved in selling direct to the consumers, to ensure that they know how much the country is earning from abroad. The government agreed. (p. 2098)

The Atingas are fed up with crooked politicians who make vain promises to seek election but, once elected, break their promises and become more preoccupied with the frenzied plunder of the state treasury:

Alarmed at what they see as the total neglect of the Volta Region, the majority of participants at the second regional parliamentary forum held at Ho in December 1998, used the occasion to verbally chastise their MPs for making vain promises to obtain their votes and abandoning them to their fate. The forum was organized in a bid to bring Parliament closer to the people and to strengthen the relationship between Parliament and civil society. Out of the seven speakers, only four were able to do so.

The Chairman for the forum, Mr. Theodore Adzoe, had to call proceedings to a halt at exactly 2 P.M. in view of the noticeable anger of the people.

Participants booed and hooted at MPs who attempted to offer excuses. The outgoing Volta regional Minister, Lt. Col. Charles Kofi Agbenaza (rtd) could not offer any explanation to tell them why the people of the region should continue to pay TV licence even though they enjoy poor reception. He was, therefore, hooted at and asked to proceed on his transfer to Upper West. Dr. Alex Ababio, MP for South Dayi, was put on the carpet when he tried to explain the work of the Volta Caucus in Parliament.

"Sit down, you people are cheats, crooks and punks. After giving us promises you only go to Parliament to amass wealth," they said. (*Ghanaian Chronicle,* Dec 4–6, 1998; p.12).

Kenyans too have every reason to be angry. "Kroll, a British firm, hired to recover money stolen under the old regime [of Daniel arap Moi], says it has traced some of the $3 billion stashed abroad by Moi's cronies" (*The Economist,* July 10, 2004; p.42). Some African villagers are openly defying tax officers: "The Loulouni district chief was thrown out of the village when he tried to collect taxes on 2 February 1995. The chief returned on February 9 with a battalion of police and paramilitary gendarmes. Enraged villagers met them with clubs and hunting rifles. Two peasants and eight policemen were wounded in the ensuing clash" (*African News Weekly*, March 3, 1995; p.5).

Africa has a police force, which is supposed to protect the Atingas. But more often than not, they are on the take or in cahoots with the ruling elite *bazongas* (raiders of the public treasury). For two weeks in May 2003 in Bunia, a town in Ituri in northeastern Congo, residents cowered under an unrelenting shower of mortars and grenades as tribal militias pillaged, murdered, and maimed their victims outside the United Nation's barracks. The town's 700 United Nations peacekeepers were helpless in halting the mayhem. The Congolese government sent 600 policemen to Ituri to protect the people and restore peace and order. But the policemen sold their guns to the Lendu militias and then took refuge themselves in the UN barracks (*The Economist*, May 17, 2003; p.40).

Fed up with corrupt and incompetent police, an enraged mob completely burned down the Barikese police station in the Atwima district of Ashanti, Ghana, on November 13, 1999, after sending the policemen and their families fleeing into the bush for dear life. According to *Ghanaian Times* (Nov 16, 1999),

> The mob action followed the death of a cargo truck driver, Iddrisu Mahama, through a gun shot allegedly fired by Sergeant S.Y. Boadu of the station, during a scuffle over the policeman's rifle. Sergeant Boadu is reported to be in custody in Kumasi, on the orders of the Ashanti Regional Police Commander, Mr Yaw Adu Gyimah. The paper says the body of the driver has been deposited at the Komfo Anokye Teaching Hospital mortuary for autopsy. (p.1)

Similar conditions have been simmering at Obuasi, a gold-mining town in Ghana for a long time:

> Fears are mounting over the growing tension between the illegal miners and gold-mining companies in Ghana as unemployed youths become more desperate to grab a piece of the wealth they see being extracted from around their villages. At least 1,000 illegal miners, known as *galamsey*, a local word that means "gather them and sell," armed themselves with blow guns, clubs, knives and machetes in June and attacked Ashanti Goldfields security men who tried to run them off a particularly rich site. The miners also stole about 50,000 chickens from the company's poultry farm, ransacked the building and injured three policemen. (*The Washington Post*, July 16, 1996; p.A10)

The clashes between local communities and mining companies in Ghana have become frequent, prompting this editorial from *Ghanaian Chronicle* (Dec 11–13, 1998):

Hardly any day passes in Ghana now without one hearing of disturbances and violent clashes between some indigenous communities and mining companies. Some of the spots that have witnessed such clashes include Kwabeng in the Eastern Region, Tarkwa in the Nzima East district of the Western Region, the Obuasi area of the Ashanti Region, and the Dunkwa and Ayamfuri areas of the Central Region, among others. In fact, the chiefs of one of the towns in the Western Region donned their mourning costume and went on a protest march against the activities of mining companies in their locality. And in the Obuasi area, the inhabitants of a certain community went on the rampage, destroying plant, machinery, equipment and even a poultry farm belonging to a local mining company. (p.5)

The rebellion is spreading to many African countries where the Atingas, fed up with exploitation, have vowed not to sit down and take it anymore. At a market in Freetown, Sierra Leone, "hundreds of civilian youths tried to lynch six soldiers who had seized bags of corn from a trader without paying. They reportedly set upon 17 the soldiers with sticks and stones before a military patrol intervened" (*The Washington Post,* Jan 5, 1998; p.A13).

Nigeria's oil wealth is produced in the Niger delta, which has been the scene of one such rebellion. Nigeria's state oil company, working with partners that include Shell, Chevron, Mobil, Amoco, and Texaco, produces 2 million barrels of oil—worth $30 million to $40 million—each day. But for years, most of that river of cash has flowed to military governments that have broken promises to spend fixed percentages of it to bring electricity, clean water, village clinics, and schools to the oil belt. The regime of General Sani Abacha, for example, promised to return 13 percent of Nigeria's oil proceeds to develop the oil communities but the funds were siphoned off by corrupt officials. "If we would honestly put even 3 percent of the oil revenues into these communities, it would make a big difference," said Frank Efeduma, a Shell oil spokesman in Warri, Nigeria (*The Washington Post,* Nov 9, 1998; p.A18). In the 1990s, the Ogonis, Nembe, Ijaws, and other ethnic groups have escalated protest to violence, often seizing oil facilities and oil company workers.

The entire delta area with 6 million people, consisting of 20 tribes, has been devastated. As *The Washington Post* (Nov 9, 1998) put it: "The curse of natural wealth has fallen heavily around the Niger River delta, Africa's most lucrative oil field. Nearly 40 years of oil production, directed mostly by military governments, has left the delta peoples poorer, sicker, less nourished and less educated than the rest of the country. Oil spills have damaged fishing grounds and farmland" (p.A18). For instance, in Nembe, home to several thousand people on the edge of Nigeria's largest oil field, there is no electricity, clean water, roads, or other basic amenities. Gas is burned there, causing environmental pollution. Nor does the area have a major oil refinery. In a

policy that defies economic sense, oil is piped from the delta area hundreds
of miles to the north, where it is refined to provide employment and industrial activity to the Hausa-Fulani, who have monopolized political power
since Nigeria's independence in 1960.

Hardest hit in the Niger delta are the Ogoni, who number 500,000 and
sit on top of billions of dollars of oil reserves. But "we get no benefit from
it, absolutely none," complained Chief Edward Kobani, a senior elder of the
Ogoni. Their homeland is an environmental mess. Gas—a byproduct of the
oil industry for which there is no use—is burned 24 hours a day, producing
acid rain and toxic pollution. Air and water quality has suffered, and crops
have been damaged. The health toll is enormous: There are high levels of
skin rashes, allergies, abscesses and infections. Ken Saro-Wiwa started the
Movement for the Survival of the Ogoni People (MOSOP), demanded $10
billion for environmental damage and royalties from the federal government
and Royal Dutch/Shell, and threatened to secede the area from Nigeria. The
group wrote an Ogoni national anthem, designed a national flag, and
printed a national currency. Frightened of another Biafra, the military government attacked Ogoni villages. In May 1995 Saro-Wiwa was arrested; he
and eight others were hanged on November 10, 1995 despite a chorus of international pleas for clemency. But the Ogoni have not given up their fight.

On October 4, 1998, militant Ijaws seized oil facilities throughout their
land. At the Batan station, they ordered the pumping station's crew to shut
it down and leave. "We are like mad dogs," said Augustine Egbane, an Ijaw
leader (*The Washington Post,* Nov 11, 1998; p.A28). The oil field at Batan
was producing 26,000 barrels—worth $380,000—a day but little money
went back to the village. In the 35 years that Shell has operated the Batan
field, oil spills have spoiled the village's traditional livelihood of fishing. Further, villagers must paddle for three hours to find clean water. The village has
no clinic and no real school, only an unequipped classroom that villagers
built themselves. In 1993, a government development agency strung electrical lines in the village but never connected them to the outside (*The Washington Post,* 11 November 1998; p.A28).

The delta youths demand not just equity from the state but also in the
redistribution of income from their oil. A first attempt at secession was led
by Isaac Adaka Boro, who called for a Niger Delta Republic in 1965. The
rebellion was short-lived and faded into history, but the anger in the delta
was reignited with Saro-Wiwa's MOSOP. The Abacha military regime, as
well as Western oil companies, felt threatened. Despite Saro-Wiwa's hanging
and the militarization of the entire Ogoniland, the groups were not deterred.

On December 11, 1998, 5,000 Ijaws signed a declaration in Kaiama—
Adaka Boro's birthplace—and asserted ownership of all resources in their

swamps and creeks, and served notice to oil companies operating in the area. In addition, they formed the Niger Delta Volunteer Force, modelled after Boro's army, and vowed to go to war.

Since the Kaiama declaration, the Abdusallam Abubakr military regime, which succeeded Abacha's, promised to raise the revenue to resource-producing states from 3 percent to 13 percent and give N15.3 million ($184,000) in development funding. The promises, however, have not been fulfilled. According to *The Washington Post* (November 9, 1998), "The deep poverty of the delta—alongside the luxurious homes and lives of the military rulers, their political allies and the U.S. and European oil firms who are their partners—has left people desperate, frustrated and bitter. Bitter enough that, in recent years, youths have formed militias, stolen guns, seized oil facilities and made war on their ethnic rivals" (p.A18). Groups in the 9 oil-producing states of Nigeria's 36-state federation have for years demanded that they should receive more money than the rest of the country from the oil sales, since Nigeria earns around 90 percent of its $10 billion foreign currency earnings from oil and gas sales. The impoverished oil-producing areas charge that they only see a tiny percentage of that money ever spent in their regions.

On October 7, 1998, angry youths opposed to Nigeria's government took control of 9 Shell oil pumping stations, blocking the daily flow of about 250,000 barrels of petroleum. The facilities were seized in several areas by groups of demonstrators charging that "government election preparations are unfair," according to Shell Nigeria Managing Director Ron Van Den Berg. Two of the company's helicopters and an oil rig were seized by the angry mobs. According to *The Washington Post:*

> Registration for the 1999 presidential vote began with youth groups in the oil-rich Niger River delta region using the occasion to protest what they say is their exclusion from the political process. Communities in Nigeria's southern states say their interests are not represented in federal politics, which is dominated by northerners. Although rich in oil, the Niger River delta states are among the poorest and most neglected in Nigeria. (Oct 9, 1998; p.A38)

Elsewhere in Africa, anger is boiling over. Secession, formerly a taboo, is now being openly discussed and sought. In January 1998, the Bubi people on Equatorial Guinea's main island of Bioko launched separatist attacks in their bid for self-determination. Five were killed. On August 28, 1998, hundreds of angry Nigerian pensioners, who had not received their pensions since 1993, stormed the offices of Kogi State to protest. "When an official tried to calm down the pensioners, they beat him senseless and stripped him naked" (*The Daily Times,* Lagos, August 29, 1998; p.3).

On August 2, 1999, a small band of rebels unsuccessfully tried to seize the town of Katima Mulilo in Namibia. They were routed and 14 people died in the melee. The rebels had hoped their action would draw attention to their cause: independence for the Caprivi strip, a sliver of land sticking out of the north eastern corner of Namibia. Caprivi is home to about 100,000 Lozi-speakers, who resent being ruled by the country's Ovambo majority. The Ovambo dominate the South West Africa People's Organization (SWAPO), the ruling party, and hold the choicest jobs.

Another hot spot has been the island of Anjouan, in the Indian Ocean archipelago of the Comoros. Anjouan broke away from the Comoran Islamic Federation in August 1997. In December 1998, clashes between rival militias left 60 people killed (*The Washington Times,* Dec 13, 1998; p.A10).

On October 1, 2001, English-speaking activists, operating under the banner of the Southern Cameroon National Council (SCNC), organized demonstrations with the goal of breaking away from Cameroon and forming their own English-speaking country. According to *New African* (Nov 2001),

> The main grouse is that they have not been fairly treated by the union leaders, now under the command of President Paul Biya, who has been in power since 1982.
>
> They say "the promise of unity has been betrayed by Biya" and that their part of the country has been totally neglected and starved of development.
>
> "The road infrastructure, the academic institutions, there has been an effort to erase every practice that was of Anglophone tradition," says Dr. Christopher Fomunyoh, an English-speaking Cameroonian who now works with the National Democratic Institute for International Affairs in Washington DC.
>
> In an interview with AllAfrica.com in mid-October, Fomunyoh said: "Take the military: Cameroon has 25 generals. Only two of them are Anglophone. Public administration, the same thing. In key departments of government, an Anglophone has never been foreign minister, minister of defense or minister of finance. People see this, and feel that they are being marginalized and that they will never be able to feel like they belong. A lot of people are for decentralization. Northerners, Southerners, English speakers, French speakers. It's the government that doesn't want to do that. Biya has been there forever and is looking to stay in power as long as possible." (p.14)

MORE ANGRY VOICES

An increasing number of Africans—including even children—are voicing their outrage at the contumacious failure of African leaders to bring development to the continent. At the United Nations Children's Summit held in

May 2002 in New York, youngsters from Africa ripped into their leaders for failing to improve their education and health. "You get loans that will be paid in 20 to 30 years . . . and we have nothing to pay them with, because when you get the money, you embezzle it, you eat it," said 12-year-old Joseph Tamale from Uganda (*BBC News* website, May 10, 2002).

An irate Horace Awi, a member of the Concerned Professionals Group and a drilling engineering manager with a multinational oil company in Lagos, Nigeria, wrote on a naijanet discussion forum on November 16, 2001:

> The more you read about Africa, the more it becomes evident that African leaders are a strange lot. These guys are worse than space aliens. And some-body wants me to believe our problem is the white man. Rubbish. I posit that colonial rule was better. Obasanjo, the Nigerian leader regards himself as the best black leader in the world today. Maybe Mandela is white. This is why Obasanjo gallivants all over the globe. Let's concede that perhaps he is. Then Africa is really in trouble. If the best rules like they are doing in Nigeria today, frittering away our poor income on nonsensical projects, you begin to won-der what hope the African has? (Quoted with permission).

On April 14, 1999, soldiers swooped down on La Cite Indigene, a sec-tion of Kinshasa, Congo, where most of the city's six million people live. President Laurent Kabila was coming to visit the area. The soldiers manned checkpoints and replaced billboards that the people had taken down. *"C'est l'homme qu'il fallait!"* proclaimed one such billboard, showing President Lau-rent Kabila's beaming face. Residents had been mocking the message: "It's the man we needed!!" "With time, we hope there will be a change in lead-ership, because the current ones are the same as the ones in the past," said Mbiya Kalondji, a petty trader at the market in Masina (*The New York Times,* May 24, 1999; p.A3).

The next day, sirens wailed and amid helter-skelter commotion, President Kabila's long motorcade rolled into Masina. The residents were ready and wait-ing. They had purchased whistles to blow a symbolic *"fin de match"* (end of game) for the president. As the motorcade sped through the city, "youths hurled rocks and women bared their bellies to call attention to food shortages" (*The New York Times,* May 24, 1999; p.A3). Kabila never paid attention. On Janu-ary 19, 2000, President Kabila was assassinated by one of his own bodyguards.

In 2001, an angry Zambian tribal chief—Chief Bright Nalubamba of the Ila people of Namwala—withdrew cooperation with the Chiluba's then-rul-ing Movement for Multi-Party Democracy (MMD) government until all leaders who had committed crimes were brought to book. Commenting on exposure of serious scandals and financial mismanagement by some MMD ministers, Chief Nalubamba urged villagers to exercise their citizen's right to arrest MMD leaders when the leaders visited their villages to campaign. "How can we allow these MMD crooks to come to our villages to ask for more years to complete their destruction of our mother Zambia?" chief Nalubamba asked. "How can I lend my support to state-propelled hooliganism, vandalism, corruption and scandals?" Chief Nalubamba asked Zambians to effect citizen's arrest, and to manhandle and cage all MMD "big corrupt thieves" into places designed for crooks and dangerous national lawbreakers because the police had failed to arrest them. "All of them must be placed under wanted list by the people as the police have failed the nation lamentably," he said (*The Post*, Lusaka, May 29, 2001).

In August 2001, the Sierra Leonian government tried urging people to stop jeering and throwing stones at former military ruler Captain Valentine Strasser, who became Africa's youngest head of state when he seized power at the age of 25 in 1992 and was overthrown in a bloodless coup in 1996. "A government statement said Captain Strasser had been embarrassed by people throwing stones at him and booing him when he ventured out on the streets of the capital, Freetown" (*The Daily Graphic,* Aug 18, 2001; p.5).

Prominent and eminent Africans are speaking out, too. On a JOY FM radio interview in Accra in July 2000, Kofi Annan, the U.N. secretary-general, lamented that sometimes he is "ashamed to be an African" because of the never ending crises in Africa. At the Organization for African Unity Summit in Lome, Togo, on July 10, 2000, he blasted African leaders for the mess on the continent. Ghana's state-owned newspaper, *The Daily Graphic* (July 12, 2000) reported:

> At the recent OAU Summit in Lome on July 10, United Nations Secretary General Kofi Annan told African leaders that they are to blame for most of the continent's problems. "Instead of being exploited for the benefit of the people, Africa's mineral resources have been so mismanaged and plundered that they are now the source of our misery." (p.5)

Former South African president Nelson Mandela weighed in, urging Africans to take up arms and overthrow corrupt leaders who have accumulated vast personal fortunes while children have gone hungry. He urged "the public to pick up rifles to defeat the tyrants" (*The Washington Post,* May 7, 2000; p.A22). And no less a person than Nobel laureate Archbishop Desmond Tutu added his voice. In an interview with the *Saturday Star* newspaper in Johannesburg, he said: "Robert Mugabe of Zimbabwe seems to have gone bonkers in a big way. It is very dangerous when you subvert the rule of law in your own country, when you don't even respect the judgments of your judges then you are on the slippery slope of perdition. It is a great sadness what has happened to President Mugabe. He was one of Africa's best leaders, a bright spark, a debonair and well-read person" (*Saturday Star,* Jan 12, 2002).

ECONOMIC RETROGRESSION

An uncomfortable and ugly truth about Africa is the fact that present African governments are, in many countries, far more invidious and worse than the hated, authoritarian colonial state that Africans overwhelmingly rejected in the 1960s. Under colonialism, Africa's resources and wealth were plundered for the development of metropolitan European countries. Today the tiny, parasitic ruling elites use their governing authority to exploit and extract resources from the productive members of the society. These resources are then spent lavishly by the elites on themselves.

In Liberia, President Taylor "zooms around Monrovia in a ten-vehicle convoy, bristling with goons in dark glasses who gun down the odd driver who gets in their way" (*The Economist,* Jan 8, 2000; p.44). The only radio station that reaches the whole country is owned by President Taylor. He has made the army and police irrelevant and keeps control of the country through the secretive anti-terrorist unit, which is run by his son. Most politicians have fled the country; the few that stayed were either beaten up or have "disappeared." Much of the economy is controlled by President Taylor and his cronies. The Lebanese businessmen who financed his war against the late Samuel Doe have been rewarded with exclusive monopolies to import rice and fuel. "The President grants licenses to exploit forests and diamond mines without consulting parliament. As a foreign observer put it caustically: Liberia, he said, was a 'demented circus of crooks trying to outdo other crooks'" (*The Economist,* Jan 8, 2000; p.44).

What incentives do the Atingas have to produce more when they are robbed of their surpluses through devious taxes and levies? The Atingas may be illiterate and "backward" but they are no fools. As we have seen, they will rebel against brutal repression, naked exploitation, and meretricious venality. Back in 1982, Yaw Amoafo, an irate ordinary Ghanaian, expressed exactly this:

> Despite noises being made about the exploitation of the people, it is the STATE, as the Chief Vanguard, and her so-called Public Servants, Civil Servants which actually exploit others in the country. The money used in buying the cars for Government officials, the cement for building estates and other Government bungalows which workers obtain loans to buy, the rice workers eat in their staff canteens, the soap, the toothpaste, textiles cloth

which workers buy under the present distribution system all come from the
farmers' cocoa and coffee money.

This STATE-MONOPOLY CAPITALISM has been going on since the
days of the colonial masters and even our own Governments after independence have continued the system.

The farmers realizing this naked exploitation decided unconsciously that
they would no longer increase cocoa and coffee production, they would not
increase food production and any other items which the State depends on for
foreign exchange. In effect, there will be no surplus for the State to exploit.
(*The Daily Graphic*, Feb 17, 1982; p.3)

People become alienated, as the Nigerian scholar Claude Ake noted eloquently:

> Most African regimes have been so alienated and so violently repressive that
> their citizens see the state as enemies to be evaded, cheated and defeated if
> possible, but never as partners in development. The leaders have been so en-
> grossed in coping with the hostilities, which their misrule and repression has
> unleashed that they are unable to take much interest in anything else includ-
> ing the pursuit of development. These conditions were not conducive to de-
> velopment and none has occurred. What has occurred is regression, as we all
> know only too well (1991b; p.14).

The rebellion by angry Atingas has dire economic consequences. They
refuse to produce cash or food crops to avoid exploitation by a vampire
state. The economy contracts and the contraction is accelerated by large-
scale flight out of the formal economy. Desperate people turn increasingly
to clandestine economic transactions in the parallel or informal economy
to keep their incomes and assets out of the reach of the state bandits. These
survival mechanisms involve hoarding, exchange of goods above the official price, smuggling, and illegal currency deals. With time, larger and
larger segments of the economy slip out of the control of the mafia state,
which soon finds that its control does not extend beyond a few miles of
the capital—as was the case with General Samuel Doe of Liberia in 1990
and Charles Taylor in 2003.

The refusal by the Atingas to produce surpluses for a vampire state to exploit adversely impacts agricultural production and exports. Indeed, food
production per capita has declined steadily over the decades after independence in the 1960s and continued well into the 1990s. For example, with
1989–91 as the base year, food production per capita index for Africa was
105 in 1980 but 92 for 1997 (World Bank, 2000b; p.225). Countries such
as Kenya, Malawi, Sierra Leone, and Zimbabwe that were self-sufficient in
food production now face sharp escalation in food import bills.

In September 2001, the International Food Policy Research Institute, a Washington think tank, released an alarming report (2020 Global Food Outlook) warning of rising hunger on the continent. "The study concludes that without massive investment in irrigation, roads to take the harvest to market and crop research, Africa might have 49 million malnourished children by 2020, a rise of 50 percent" (*The Washington Post,* Sept 4, 2001; p.A12).

The report noted that African governments would need to invest $133 billion over the next 20 years to avert the predicted sharp rise in malnutrition. Asked if African governments would pay any attention to the report, Mark W. Rosegrant, the primary author, said: "To date, only a handful—including Uganda, Botswana, Ghana and Mozambique—share their citizens' preoccupation with feeding themselves" (*The Washington Post,* Sept 4, 2001; p.A12). Inability to feed itself means Africa must resort to food imports. These rose an astonishing 65 percent between 1988 and 1997 from $8.89 billion to $14.69 billion (World Bank, 2000b; p.107). By 2000, food imports had reached $18.7 billion, slightly more than donor assistance of $18.6 billion to Africa in 2000 (*Africa Recovery,* Jan 2004; p.16).

The rebellion of the Atingas against mafia African states can also be seen in Africa's declining share of world trade. As the World Bank (2000b) noted: "Africa's share of world trade has plummeted since the 1950s from more than 3 percent: it now accounts for less than 2 percent of world trade or 1.2 percent if South Africa is excluded. Three decades ago, African countries were specialized in primary production and highly trade dependent. But Africa missed out on industrial expansion and now risks being excluded from the global information revolution" (p.8). Worse, "strongly trade oriented in the 1960s, Africa was the only region to then experience a decline in real dollar exports per capita. The erosion of Africa's world trade share in current prices between 1970 and 1993 represents a staggering annual income loss of $68 billion—or 2.1 percent of regional GDP" (World Bank, 2000b; p.20).

Of course, there are other factors that account for Africa's declining share of world trade, such as trade barriers in the industrialized countries, worsening terms of trade, failure to diversify exports, and domestic policies that discouraged private investment. However, the trade barrier argument holds little water when the actual physical volume of many primary commodities from Africa has been declining and the increased supplies on the world market came from other regions, namely Southeast Asia. For example, the physical volumes of such African exports as forest products, copper, iron, phosphates, groundnuts, oil palm, sisal, and meat have dropped dramatically from 1980 to 1997 (World Bank, 2000a; p.90-104).

While some African countries have suffered terms of trade losses, Africa's oil exporters made massive terms of trade gains. "But as with most oil exporters, the gains have not been used to place countries on a path of sustainable growth" (World Bank, 2000b; p.21). Nor have the gains been used to alleviate poverty.

The rebellion by Africa's Atingas has been vastly costly. Had they been given a better deal, they would have produced enough food and thereby saved the nearly $18 billion Africa annually wastes on food imports. They would also have produced enough exports to prevent the loss of Africa's share of world trade, which cost a staggering $68 billion annually. Adding these two up yields an astonishing $83 billion annually. But there is more.

The withdrawal of the Atingas from the formal sector to escape the tentacles of the vampire state has implications for tax revenue. As they withdraw, they take with them potential tax revenue. A shrinking economy also contracts the tax base. Increasingly, the vampire state finds itself unable to generate the tax revenue needed to finance its soaring expenditures. Budget deficits grow ever larger. The country resorts to foreign aid and printing money. Recourse to foreign aid, which is merely a "soft loan," increases the country's foreign debt and money creation fuels inflation, with deleterious economic consequences. The country is trapped in a vicious cycle of debt, stagnation, and dependency on foreign aid.

In 2000, donor assistance to Africa amounted to $18.6 billion (*Africa Recovery,* Jan 2004; p.16). This aid would not have been needed if the Atingas had not rebelled and had produced enough to feed Africa—thereby saving $18 billion—and produced enough to export, thereby saving Africa $68 billion.

AFRICA'S SALVATION AND FUTURE

The causes of Africa's crises or poverty have little to do with artificial colonial borders, American imperialism, racism, or the alleged inferiority of the African people. "If colonialism was what held Africa back, you would expect the continent to have boomed when the settlers left. It didn't" (Guest, 2004; p.9). And the incessant whining about the legacies of colonialism and blaming them for Africa's woes "gives little clue as to how these woes could be ended" (Guest, 2004; p.11).

Africa's woes have more to do with bad leadership and the enabling role played by the Western governments and institutions. The centralization of both economic and political power turns the state into a pot of gold that all sorts of groups compete to capture. Once captured, power is then used to amass huge personal fortunes, to enrich one's cronies and tribesmen, to crush one's rivals, and to perpetuate one's rule in office. All others are excluded (*the politics of exclusion*). The absence of mechanisms for peaceful transfer of power leads to a struggle over political power, which often degenerates into civil strife or war. Chaos and carnage ensue. Infrastructure is destroyed. Food production and delivery are disrupted. Thousands are dislocated and flee, becoming internal refugees and placing severe strains on social systems of the resident population. Food supplies run out. Starvation looms.

The Western media bombards the international community with horrific pictures of rail-thin famine victims. Unable to bear the horror, the conscience of the international community is stirred to mount eleventh-hour humanitarian rescue missions. Foreign relief workers parachute into the disaster zone, dispensing high protein biscuits, blankets, and portable toilets at hastily erected refugee camps. Refugees are rehabilitated, repatriated, and even airlifted. At the least sign of complication or trouble, the mission bogs down and is abandoned (see, for example Somalia in 1995). That is, until another vampire African state implodes and the same macabre ritual is repeated year after year. It seems nothing—absolutely nothing—has been learned by all sides from the melt-downs of Somalia, Liberia, or Rwanda.

At the next crisis, African leaders mount their high horses and appeal incessantly to the international community to save the continent, globe trotting with a bowl in their hands, begging, begging for aid. They cannot see that Africa's begging bowl is punched with holes. What comes in as foreign aid and investment ultimately leaks away. Total foreign aid and investment into Africa from all sources amounts to $18 billion annually. But capital flight out of Africa exceeds $20 billion annually. Destructive wars cost more than $10 billion annually in weapon purchases, damage to infrastructure, and social carnage. According to a UN estimate, in 1991 alone, more than $200 billion in capital was siphoned out of Africa by the ruling gangsters and briefcase bandits (*The New York Times,* Feb 4, 1996; p.4). Note that this amount was more than half of Africa's foreign debt of $320 billion. Furthermore, capital flight out of Africa, on an annual basis, exceeds what comes into Africa as foreign aid. The World Bank estimates that more than $250 billion flowed into Nigeria's coffers alone between 1970 and 2000, but much of that leaked away. Nigerian President Olusegun Obasanjo stunned representatives of African civic groups meeting in Addis Ababa, Ethiopia, in June 2002, with the statement that corrupt African leaders have stolen at least $140 billion from their people in the decades since independence (*The London Independent,* June 14, 2002). And according to the *London Observer,* Zimbabwe's economic collapse had caused more than $37 billion worth of damage to South Africa and other neighboring countries (*The Observer,* Sept 30, 2001). It defies common sense to pour more water into a leaky bucket. We shall expand at length on the issue of leakages in chapter 8.

ABYSMAL FAILURE OF WESTERN POLICIES TOWARD AFRICA

We shall have more to say about Western aid programs for Africa in chapter 5, but suffice it to say here that Western aid policies toward Africa have failed miserably over the decades to reverse the continent's economic decline. While other factors such as design flaws and bureaucratic red tape played a significant role, the policies themselves were structured on false premises. The first is the persistent belief by Western governments, agencies, and individuals—despite massive evidence to the contrary—that there exists in Africa a "government" that cares about its people, represents their interests, and is responsive to their needs. This is a delusion on a grand scale. In many African countries, the institution of government has been corrupted and transformed into a criminal enterprise. The ruling elites do not enter government to serve but to fleece the people. In fact, politics is the gateway to fabulous wealth in Africa. Ministers do not resign; neither do presidents. They stay and stay and stay in power (10, 20 and even 30 years or more. Mobutu of Zaire was in power for 32 years; Eyadema has been in power for 34 years. In fact, since 1960, there have been 198 African heads of state; less than 20 resigned or stepped down from power.

What exists in many African countries is a vampire or pirate state (a government hijacked by a phalanx of gangsters, thugs, and crooks who use the instruments of the state to enrich themselves, their cronies, and tribesmen. All others are excluded. The richest persons in Africa are heads of state and ministers. And quite often, the chief bandit himself is the head of state. Their primary instinct is to loot the national treasury, perpetuate themselves in power, and brutally suppress all dissent and opposition. And the worst part is, they do not invest their booty in their own African countries but choose to stash it in Swiss and foreign bank accounts.

The second flaw inherent in Western policies toward Africa is the baffling inability to make a distinction between African *people* and African *leaders*. It is always important to make this distinction because leaders and people are not synonymous. The leaders have been the problem, not the people. And leadership failure is not tantamount to failure of Africans as people. The vast majority of African leaders do not represent nor are chosen by the Atingas (the people). Unfortunately, there are many Western organizations and governments that seek to establish "solidarity" or a "relationship of deep friendship" with the African people. But somehow, these Western organizations and governments rather naively believe that that they can best help the African people by working with or forming partnership with African leaders.

Failure to make this distinction led to the demise of President Clinton's policies toward Africa. To his credit, President Clinton paid more attention to Africa than previous U.S. administrations. He placed Africa on the front burner and adopted a proactive engagement with Africa—largely to placate the African American constituency. High profile White House conferences with African ministers, trade missions to Africa, and tours by senior government officials were regular fares. First Lady Hillary Clinton and Chelsea visited Africa in February 1997, and in March 1998, President Clinton himself visited Africa for the first time as president.

He pledged to support African nations undergoing transformations toward peace, democracy, human rights, and free markets through expanded economic opportunities and stronger cooperation. A series of new initiatives were launched, including Africa Growth and Opportunity Act (AGOA), to expand U.S.-Africa trade and investment. Another was the African Crisis Response Initiative (ACRI), consisting of African troops to be deployed to intervene in serious crisis situations to avert a Rwanda-like conflagration. All well-intentioned, perhaps, but accomplishing little as the continent's woes worsened.

During his March 1998 trip, President Clinton painted a rosy portrait of Africa, making "giant steps toward democracy and economic prosperity." He hailed Presidents Laurent Kabila of Congo, Yoweri Museveni of Uganda, Paul Kagame of Rwanda, Meles Zenawi of Ethiopia, and Isaias Afwerki of Eritrea as the "new leaders of Africa" and spoke fondly of the "new African renaissance sweeping the continent." Steeped in political correctness and gushing with guilt over the iniquities of Western colonialism, President Clinton appeased tyrants of Africa's coconut republics with euphonious verbiage. In Uganda, he apologized for America's involvement in the transatlantic slave trade but said nothing about slavery next door in Sudan. In fact for eight years, President Clinton was silent about the enslavement of blacks by Arabs in Mauritania and Sudan, until December 6, 2000, when he did denounce "the atrocities of Sudan," including "the scourge of slavery," on Human Rights Day. Before then, however, his Sudan policy had been crippled by a massive intelligence debacle: The August 1998 cruise missile attack on the El Shifa pharmaceutical plant in Khartoum, ostensibly in retaliation for the terrorist bombing of the U.S. embassies in Kenya and Tanzania. As it turned out, the plant was not owned by Osama bin Laden, as alleged by the Clinton administration but by Salah Idris, a reputable Saudi businessman who sued the U.S. for $30 million. The United States quietly unfroze $24 million of Idris's assets. This fiasco handed a public relations bonanza to Sudan, a country widely loathed in sub-Saharan Africa for sponsoring state terrorism and Arab slavery.

But barely two months after President Clinton's return to the United States, Ethiopia and Eritrea were at war. They pounded each other, apologized for innocent civilian casualties, took a break to bury the dead, rearmed, and then hammered each other again. The "new African renaissance" touted by the Clinton administration thus evaporated and the rest

of the "new leaders"—so enthusiastically embraced by President Clinton—
were at each others throat in the Congo conflict. As if the embarrassment
of seeing its friends at war was not enough, the administration's other
African "partners in development" turned out to be crocodile reformers and
crackpot democrats.

Further, the "giant steps" touted by President Clinton turned out to be
ungainly baby steps. Africa's growth rate in the 1990s came nowhere near the
7 percent needed to reduce poverty rates. It averaged a paltry 4.3 percent,
which, given a 3 percent population growth rate, meant stagnant per capita
income. Accordingly, the list of African economic success stories touted by
the Clinton Administration in 1994 (Gambia, Burkina Faso, Ghana, Nigeria, Tanzania, and Zimbabwe) shrunk to two (Ghana and Burkina Faso), although four new countries were added in 1998 (Guinea, Lesotho, Eritrea,
and Uganda). However, the coup in Guinea, the senseless Ethiopian-Er-
itrean war, and the eruption of civil wars in western and northern Uganda
have knocked off most of the new "success stories."

Nor was Africa's democratization process successful under Clinton's
watch. Although Senegal and Ghana had made successful democratic tran-
sitions in 2001, the number of African democracies has remained at 16—
out of 54 African countries—since 2003. The democratization process in
Africa has been stalled by political chicanery and strong-arm tactics. Incumbent autocrats appoint their own electoral commissioners, empanel a fawn-
ing coterie of sycophants to write the constitution, massively pad the voter's
register, and hold what Africans call "coconut elections" to return themselves
to power.

And more African countries imploded since President Clinton took office in 1992: Somalia (1993); Rwanda (1994); Burundi (1996); Zaire
(1996); Congo-Brazzaville (1997); Sierra Leone (1997); Congo (1998);
Ethiopia/Eritrea (1998); Guinea (1999); and Ivory Coast (2000).

Clinton's Africa policy came under fire even in the black American community he sought to please. In April 2000, a black American congress-
woman, Rep. Cynthia McKinney (D-GA), berated: "I am sorry to say this
administration has no Africa policy—or what it has has tremendously failed"
(*The Washington Times,* April 14, 2000; p.A17). And in a January interview
with the *East African* newspaper, she described Clinton's Africa policy as
"such an abysmal failure." "How can someone so friendly end up with such
an outrageous, atrocious, horrible policy that assists perpetrators of crimes
against humanity, inflicting damages on innocent African people?" she
asked. Similar sentiments were expressed by Randall Robinson, executive director of TransAfrica, which spearheaded the campaign against apartheid in
South Africa. He dismissed Clinton's policies in Africa as a "disaster."

The most spectacular policy failure was the African Crisis Response Initiative (ACRI), announced on September 28, 1996, by the Clinton administration. It was supposed to deal with crisis situations before they escalated into Rwanda-like conflagrations. By organizing and training an African peacekeeping team, ACRI hoped to improve the capacity of African nations to respond to humanitarian crises in a timely fashion. The Clinton administration, with congressional approval, allocated $35 million for ACRI's startup costs. But few African leaders participated in the program. Most needed their troops to crush their people's aspirations for freedom at home. The program's inglorious demise came in 2000. It trained 740 of Ivory Coast's soldiers at a cost of $1.7 million, but in October of the same year, the last date the State Department posted an update on its ACRI web site, that country imploded. "Clinton promised a lot of things but we never got one of them," said Abdul Musa Baba, a workshop manager, in Ushafa—20 miles from Abuja—where President Clinton got an avenue named after him and ecstatic crowds hailed him as Africa's savior (*The Guardian,* July 1, 2003).

But Clinton was not alone in failing to deliver. Over the past decades, other Western governments, international aid organizations, and multilateral financial institutions have crafted various initiatives to tackle Africa's woes. Though well-intentioned, most of these initiatives came to ignominious grief.

Against this backdrop, the new U.S. president, George W. Bush, announced on March 14, 2002, in Monterrey (Mexico) that the United States would increase its foreign aid programs by 50 percent to $15 billion a year under a program called the "Millennium Challenge Account" (MCA). MCA would complement existing aid programs by providing additional aid to governments in developing countries that "rule justly, encourage economic freedom, and invest in people" (MCA website:).[1]

I was at a White House event in the Eisenhower Executive Office building on July 13, 2004, when President Bush signed into law a bill extending AGOA well into the future in the presence of African diplomatic corps and key Congressional lawmakers. A Nigerian officer, attached to the Nigerian Embassy and seated next to me, quipped: "The United States has done its part, let's hope African leaders would do their part." "Would they?" I queried. He scanned the faces of the African ambassadors at the ceremony and gently shook his head.

To be effective, the Bush administration's Millennium Challenge Account and aid programs must avoid three fundamental pitfalls of Clinton's Africa policy. First, President Clinton relied almost exclusively on black Americans for counsel in the formulation of U.S. Africa policy. While

African American legislators may mean well, they lack an operational understanding of Africa's current woes. For example, the appointment of Rev.
Jesse Jackson as special envoy to Africa was a major blunder. When he was
sent in June 1994 to help defuse Nigeria's political crisis, pro-democracy
forces refused to meet with him due to his support of the former military
dictator, General Ibrahim Babangida. Some even threatened to stone Rev.
Jackson if he stepped foot in Nigeria. And Sierra Leonians have not forgiven Rev. Jesse Jackson for brokering the 1999 Lome Accords which
awarded a ministerial position to Foday Sankoh, the barbarous warlord
whose band of savages (the Revolutionary United Front) chopped off the
limbs of people, including women and children, who stood in their way.
Sierra Leonians were outraged when Rev. Jackson compared Fodah Sankoh
to Nelson Mandela.

Second, the Clinton administration's Africa policy was "leader-centered." It sought to develop warm, cozy relationships—euphemistically
called "partnerships"—with the "new leaders" of Africa. The Clinton administration invested in the rhetoric of African leaders pretending to be
Abraham Lincoln and, seeking to transform their African society. By styling
themselves as Lincoln wannabes, Western governments set themselves up to
be suckered by hucksters and charlatans. These African leaders parrot
"democracy" not because they believe in it but because they know that is
what unlocks the floodgates of Western aid. As Grace Bibala wrote in the
East African, "William Jefferson Clinton's desperate and possibly naïve
search for a partnership with a 'new breed' of African leaders was doomed
to failure" (Jan 18, 2001).

Third, the "African renaissance" that Clinton spoke fondly of quickly fizzled because of his administration's failure to distinguish between outcomes
and the processes or institutions required to achieve those outcomes. While
a democratic Africa, based on the free market system, is desirable, it is the
outcome of often long and arduous processes. A market economy, for example, cannot be established without secure property rights, the free flow of
information, the rule of law, and mechanisms for contract enforcement.
Since these processes or foundations are missing in most African countries,
the free markets the Clinton administration hoped to establish there proved
elusive.

A new U.S. policy toward Africa must be fundamentally altered by de-
politicizing and deracializing it. The problems Africa faces today have little
to do with the slave trade, colonialism, or racism, and more to do with bad
leadership and bad governance, originating from the establishment of defective economic and political systems. Native-born African dissidents and exiles living in the United States understand Africa better and need to be

consulted by the United States administration in formulating its Africa policy.

Second, a new approach must be adopted that places less emphasis on the rhetoric of African leaders and more emphasis on institution building. Leaders come and go but institutions endure. Six institutions are critical: An independent central bank, an independent judiciary, an independent and free media, an independent electoral commission, a neutral and professional armed security forces, and a professional and efficient civil service. These institutions are vital for the establishment of the environment Africans need to craft solutions to their own problems. These institutions will help end the vicious brutalities meted out to the Atingas and the rapacious plunder of their wealth. And these institutions are established by civil society, not leaders. The Clinton administration was misguided in its belief that it could micromanage African affairs from Washington. The United States can help but it cannot supplant the initiative and efforts Africans themselves must make to solve their own problems. Nor can the United States be of much help if African leaders and governments are unwilling to establish the institutions needed for Africa to progress. But will the Bush administration learn? In an editorial, *The Washington Post* (April 12, 2004) noted:

> The largest obstacle to President Bush's democracy initiative in the greater Middle East may be Hosni Mubarak, the president of Egypt. Mr. Mubarak, 75, is an unrepentant autocrat who has ruled his country under emergency law for 23 years; his repressive policies, including unrelenting persecution of Islamic political movements, have helped fuel al Qaeda, whose top leadership has included a number of Egyptians. In recent months, Mr. Mubarak has waged a vigorous campaign to block, dilute or co-opt the administration's plan to promote political liberalization in the region this year. He has denounced it as an outside imposition; claimed it can't happen before an Israeli-Palestinian settlement; argued that the only beneficiaries of democracy will be Islamic extremists; and insisted that in any case Egypt is already democratic and becoming more so all the time.
>
> Since it signed a peace accord with Israel in 1979, the United States has showered the regime with some $50 billion in aid while asking for little outside a cooperative foreign policy. Mr. Mubarak's quasi-socialist economic system meanwhile has kept millions of Egyptians mired in desperate poverty, and his suppression of alternatives to his nationalist ideology has strengthened Islamic extremism." (p.A18)

What Africa needs is tough love and straight talk since most of its leaders don't use their heads. Even more tragic is the fact that the Westerners who set out to help Africa don't use theirs either. Says *The Economist* (Jan 17, 2004):

"For every dollar that foolish northerners lent Africa between 1970 and 1996, 80 cents flowed out as capital flight in the same year, typically into Swiss bank accounts or to buy mansions on the Cote d'Azur" (Survey; p.12).

Oftentimes, for fear of being labeled "racist," "foolish northerners" shy away from criticizing African leaders, which does not really help Africa since there is only so much the international community can do to help Africa. If African leaders are not willing to step up to the plate and tackle Africa's woes, there is little the outside world can do to turn Africa around. UN Secretary-General Kofi Annan said exactly that to African heads of state who had gathered in Maputo, Mozambique for the African Union's annual summit: "The U.N and the rest of the international community can appoint envoys, urge negotiations and spend billions of dollars on peacekeeping missions, but none of this will solve conflicts, if the political will and capacity do not exist here, in Africa" (*Associated Press* July 10, 2003; web posted: www.ap.com).

CHAPTER 3

The Postcolonial Elite Development Model

Africans want change because there is so much suffering here. But Africans are above all else devoted to their ancestors, and they do not want to betray that by becoming something that they are not.

> —Patekile Holomisa, an *inkhosi* (chief) and head of the
> Congress of Traditional Leaders in South Africa,
> in *The Washington Post,* Dec 18, 2000; p.A1.

The prevailing African State, in all African countries, is an implant from the European countries whose colony each African country was. The present postcolonial State in Africa did not grow organically out of the body of Africa: it is an implant on the African body, hence the grotesque features of some, or many, of the elements of the contemporary African State, and of contemporary Political Parties in Africa, which are also implants on the African body: the African body is rejecting many of these elements of the Western State.

> —Herbert W. Vilakazi, Commissioner of the Independent Electoral
> Commission at the KZN Election Indaba, Durban,
> 17 Sept 2002 (web posted: www.ifp.org.za)

INTRODUCTION

In the 1960s, when many African countries gained their independence from Western colonial rule, the euphoric cry "free at last" rang across the continent. New national flags were unfurled to the chimes of new national anthems. Africa was to develop in its own image, but into what? The challenge was daunting.

African nationalist leaders waged the arduous struggle against colonialism, endured economic hardships, and made personal sacrifices to win independence for their respective countries. Kwame Nkrumah of Ghana, Julius Nyerere of Tanzania, and Kenneth Kaunda of Zambia, for example, gained international stature for their fight against colonial injustices and their freedom crusades. They shared some common characteristics. First, they sought recognition and respect for their newly fledged African nations and won their deserved seats in the hall of nations. Second, they were in a hurry to develop Africa. Development formed part of the logic of the liberation struggle because the colonialists undertook little social and economic development. The impatience to "catch up" with the rich countries—or narrow the gap between the rich and the poor—afflicted almost all African nationalist elites. Nkrumah expressed it best when he said, "We must achieve in a decade what it took others a century" (Nkrumah, 1973; p.401). The need to "catch up" was understandable, but the impatience led to haste, which made waste.

Having settled on the objective, a model or mechanism was needed. At that time, three development paths were available:

1. A free-market capitalist approach in which the private sector serves as the "engine of growth"
2. A state-directed and controlled (*dirigiste*) path in which the state plays a hegemonic role in the economy
3. A modernized indigenous African approach

The first option (capitalism) was rejected because of its association with Western colonialism. The third option was not considered because of a pervasive belief among African nationalists and elites that Africa's own indigenous institutions were "too backward," "too primitive" for the rapid development and transformation of Africa. Almost everywhere in Africa, the native institutions were castigated as "inferior." Ashamed of the label of "backwardness," the elites embarked upon a program of development that placed obtrusive emphasis on industry. No longer should Africa be relegated to the "inferior" status of "drawers of water and hewers of wood." Industrialization was synonymous with development. Consequently, agriculture and other primary activities—engaged in by the Atingas—were shunned as too "backward."

The natives were urged to abandon their backward ways and adopt "modern methods." For example, Kenya's minister of national guidance and political affairs, Mr. James Njiru, banned the magazine *True Love* in February 1989, for publishing a cover photograph of naked girls, clad in tribal dress, dancing before King Mswati of Swaziland:

He argued that Kenyans should abandon backward cultures for modern ones that are acceptable to foreigners, but this seems to deny that Africans should be proud of their African culture. There is nothing intrinsically virtuous or respectable in Western modes of dress and behavior. (*New African*, March 1989; p.28)

It was widely assumed, not only by African elites but outside experts as well, that the adoption of foreign values was necessary for successful economic development. Development became synonymous with "change." Nkrumah, again, best expressed this attitude. Though agriculture was the main economic activity of indigenous Africa, he felt he could not rely on peasant farmers for a rapid agricultural revolution because they were "too slow to adapt or change their practices to modern, mechanized methods" (Uphoff, 1970; p.602).

Accordingly, virtually all postcolonial African states opted for the second (*dirigiste*) approach for ideological, nationalistic, and situational reasons. The state was to spearhead economic development. It was believed that only the state can raise capital quickly, marshal resources, and accelerate development. Various edicts and devices were enacted to transfer massive resources to the state for investment. With few exceptions, agriculture—the primary occupation of the Atingas—was neglected in favor of industry.

IDEOLOGIES FOR AFRICA'S POSTCOLONIAL DEVELOPMENT

To develop Africa, the nationalist leaders uniformly rejected those ideologies underpinning the colonial structures. Consequently, they needed an alternative, and four distinct official ideologies emerged. The first was socialism, practiced by Kwame Nkrumah of Ghana, Ahmed Sekou Toure of Guinea, Modibo Keita of Mali, Gamal Abdel Nasser of Egypt, Julius Nyerere of Tanzania, and Kenneth Kaunda of Zambia. They expounded the creation of an egalitarian, just, and self-sufficient polity. The mechanism for the attainment of these goals was the *state*, which would furnish the pivot of critical identities, organize the economy, and supervise the second, societal phase of decolonization (Chazan, et al., 1992; p.155). They extolled political centralization and mobilization as the vehicles for real transformation.

The second ideology was political pragmatism, espoused by such leaders as Felix Houphouet-Boigny of Ivory Coast, Abubakar Tafawa Balewa of Nigeria, Hastings Banda of Malawi, and Daniel arap Moi of Kenya. Declaring themselves to be non-ideological, they stressed economic growth and prosperity. In their countries, the state was charged with the task of fostering entrepreneurship, attracting foreign investment, and creating a climate conducive to material advancement. But as Chazan, et al. (1992) explain, "The pragmatic worldviews were no less statist than the more populist-socialist theories; they were however advanced for different reasons and with other goals in mind—related, also to the preservation of elite privilege. Centralization, therefore, was delineated not in a social or political but in an administrative sense; it nevertheless was as deeply ensconced in the political attitudes of pragmatists as in those of self-proclaimed socialists" (p.156).

The third ideology, military nationalism, was supplied by the first batch of military leaders who burst onto the political scene in the late 1960s and early 1970s: Idi Amin of Uganda, Jean-Bedel Bokassa of Central African Republic, Mobutu Sese Seko of Zaire, and Gnassingbe Eyadema of Togo. Mobutu, for example, wrote that, "We in Zaire spent a lot of time building a strong central state which could resist Soviet aggression quickly and effectively. This enabled us to decisively make the uniform decisions that were necessary to fulfill our national defense obligations and our commitments to the United States" (*The Washington Times,* June 14, 1995; p.A23).

These military strongmen exhibited a dictatorial bent. They had not been central to the independence struggles and felt the need to develop alternative ideologies to supplant those of the leaders they overthrew. They glorified African military tradition and shunned foreign ideals. They revived certain traditional practices. In the economic arena, they exercised full control over national resources, not only to deflect pressures from external creditors but also to account for statist monopolies. But their ideologies were scarcely impressive:

> They are by and large bereft of intellectual content, they are replete with contradictions, they address key issues haphazardly. These orientations, at best, may be viewed as feeble attempts to legitimate their purveyors; in most instances, they have provided the cover for the exercise of brute force. Manifestations of this sort of military nationalism resurface periodically, as insecure leaders with dwindling support bases find refuge in cultural symbols in a desperate effort to gain some loyalty and legitimacy. (Chazan, et al., 1992; p.158)

The fourth ideology was Afro-Marxism, which was the official policy of Angola, Mozambique, Congo, and Ethiopia. It attributed the malaise of African economies to the lingering effects of imperialism and the continuing machinations of neocolonialism, both within and outside Africa. It envisaged the creation of a totally new social order, in which private ownership of the means of production would be abolished and the state would become the supreme patron of economic destiny.

Socialism

Socialism, however, was by far the most predominant ideology adopted by African nationalist leaders. The hegemonic role in economic development envisaged for the state was driven by this ideology since many African nationalist leaders were suspicious of capitalism. The courtship and fascination with socialism emerged during the struggle for political independence and freedom from colonial rule in the 1950s. Many African nationalists harbored a deep distrust and distaste for capitalism, which was falsely identified by most African nationalist leaders as an extension of colonialism and imperialism. Therefore, freedom from colonial rule was synonymous with freedom from capitalism. This spawned the belief among African leaders that the most appropriate strategy by which they could undertake national development was socialism. Furthermore, having just emerged from the colonial era, all African leaders were naturally poised to jealously protect the hard-won sovereignty and to strenuously guard against another episode of "colonial" and foreign exploitation. This was only possible if the state maintained a large enough presence in the economy, ostensibly to control the activities of foreign companies.

The strength of these convictions was reflected in the almost universal adoption of "African socialism." But as Bandow (1986) argued:

> "African socialism," for instance, was more a Western than an indigenous concept. Burkina Faso's External Relations Minister, Leandre Bassole, captured the essence of the issue during the UN's recent special session: "Africa's development has almost always been the brainchild of persons who have had and still have a very questionable understanding of our profound being." (p.18)

Nonetheless, a wave of socialism swept across the continent as almost all the new African leaders succumbed to the contagious ideology. The proliferation of socialist ideologies that emerged in Africa ranged from the "*Ujamaa*" (familyhood or socialism in Swahili) of Julius Nyerere of Tanzania; to the vague amalgam of Marxism, Christian socialism, humanitarianism, and "Negritude" of Leopold Senghor of Senegal; to the humanism of Kenneth Kaunda of Zambia; to the scientific socialism of Marien N'Gouabi of Congo (Brazzaville); to the Arab-Islamic socialism of Muammar Ghaddafi of Libya; to the "Nkrumaism" (consciencism) of Kwame Nkrumah of Ghana; to the "Mobutuism" of Mobutu Sese Seko of Zaire. Only a few African countries, such as Ivory Coast, Nigeria, and Kenya, were pragmatic enough to eschew doctrinaire socialism.

Socialism in Africa was to be a distinctive ideology based on the continent's unique social and cultural traditions. Though the ideology was copied

from the East, many African leaders frowned upon becoming a satellite of
the Soviet Union or China in the early 1960s. They chose "nonalignment"
in the arena of international politics although in practice they participated
in anti-West bash fests in Havana and Harare.

The major differences among the African nationalist leaders, however,
could be found in two areas: how to proceed with development and the nature of state intervention. While Houphouet-Boigny and Jomo Kenyatta of
Kenya were willing to proceed slowly, Nkrumah and Toure of Guinea were
in a hurry. The other differences were of the degree of state ownership, intervention, and the role of foreign private capital in economic development.
The few African leaders—such as Hastings Banda of Malawi, Felix
Houphouet-Boigny, and Jomo Kenyatta, who opted for the "capitalist"
road—allowed a role for private capital, while the overwhelming majority of
socialist African leaders placed severe restrictions on it. For example, in Ivory
Coast, Kenya, Liberia, Malawi, Senegal, and Zaire, foreign companies were
welcome. In the socialist countries, they were generally not. Rather, existing
foreign companies were nationalized.

There were further divisions even within the socialist camp. Though socialist African leaders adopted socialism in order to remedy the exploitative,
capitalistic tendencies of colonial structures, there were individual differences on the need for the ideology. Nkrumah of Ghana, widely regarded as
the "father of African socialism," was convinced that "only a socialist form
of society can assure Ghana of a rapid rate of economic progress without destroying that social justice, that freedom and equality, which are a central
feature of our traditional life" (Seven-Year Development Plan. Accra: Government of Ghana, 1963; p.1).

Nkrumah declared socialism to be his ideology and his political party in-
distinguishable from the state: "Convention People's Party is the state and the
state is the party. The Party has always proclaimed socialism as the objective
of our social, industrial and economic programs. Socialism however will remain a slogan until industrialization is achieved" (Nkrumah, 1973; p.190).
He went on to reiterate, "Let me make it clear that our socialist objectives demand that the public and co-operative sector of the productive economy
should expand at the maximum possible rate, especially in those strategic
areas of production upon which the economy of the country depends."

Furthermore, he surmised that "socialist transformation would eradicate
completely the colonial structure of our economy" (Nkrumah 1973; p.189).
Additionally, Nkrumah believed "Capitalism is too complicated for a newly independent state; hence, the need for a socialist society" (Nkrumah, 1957; p.9).

Nkrumah was at times incoherent and unclear about the choice of the socialist ideology. Nor were the goals of socialism clearly defined. At one point,

he believed socialism would assure "a rapid rate of economic progress." At another, he believed the socialist transformation would demolish the colonial structure of Ghana's economy. He stated,

> Ghana inherited a colonial economy and similar disabilities in most other directions. We cannot rest content until we have demolished this miserable structure and raised in its place an edifice of economic stability, thus creating for ourselves a veritable paradise of abundance and satisfaction. Despite the ideological bankruptcy and moral collapse of a civilization in despair, we must go forward with our preparations for planned economic growth to supplant the poverty, ignorance, disease, illiteracy and degradation left in their wake by discredited colonialism and decaying imperialism. (Nkrumah 1973, p.195)

Nkrumah was constantly haunted by the specter of imperialism and neo-colonialism, which "is only the old colonialism with a facade of African stooges." He believed that only socialism could effectively check the evil machinations of neocolonialism and felt obliged to enlighten his fellow African heads of state. His socialist homilies spilled over from Ghana's borders to the rest of Africa. The socialist state he envisioned for Ghana was to be,

> in the vanguard of the African revolutionary struggle to achieve continental liberation and unity. Ghana, under my government, was a haven for the oppressed from all parts of Africa. Freedom fighters trained there. [One of these freedom fighters was Robert Mugabe, current premier of Zimbabwe]. Ghana was revered all over the African continent, as a country which all who fought oppression and exploitation could depend upon. Our political and economic achievements were closely studied and admired. (Nkrumah, 1957; p.7)

When all is pieced together, socialism was to serve for Nkrumah no less than six objectives:

1. To generate rapid economic growth,
2. To create a "veritable paradise of abundance and satisfaction,"
3. To check the "evil machinations of imperialism and neocolonialism,"
4. To foster "economic independence" in adverse colonial heritage,
5. To serve "in the vanguard of the revolutionary struggle,"
6. To liberate the oppressed continent of Africa.

Nyerere of Tanzania, on the other hand, based his socialist ideology on African cultural traditions. He was first exposed to socialism, as were many African socialists, in the West—during his schooling in Scotland. He castigated capitalism or the money economy, which in his view, "encourages individual acquisitiveness and economic competition" (Nyerere, 1966; p.23).

The money economy was, in his view, foreign to Africa and it "can be catastrophic as regards the African family social unit." As an alternative to "the
relentless pursuit of individual advancement," Nyerere insisted that Tanzania be transformed into a nation of small-scale communalists ("*Ujamaa*")
(Nyerere, 1966; p.54).

Earlier, in 1962, Nyerere wrote:

> The foundation and the objective of African socialism is the extended family.
> The true African Socialist does not look on one class of men as his brethren
> and another as his natural enemies. He regards all men as his brethren—as
> members of his ever extending family. That is why the first article of Tanzania
> African National Union's (TANU's) creed is: "*Binadamu wore ni ndugu zangu,
> na Afrika ni moja.*" ["I believe in Human Brotherhood and the Unity of
> Africa"]. "ujamaa," then, or "Familyhood" describes our Socialism. It is op-
> posed to Capitalism, which seeks to build a happy society on the basis of the
> exploitation of man by man; and it is equally opposed to doctrinaire social-
> ism which seeks to build its happy society on a philosophy of inevitable con-
> flict between man and man. (qtd. in Bell, 1987; p.117)

Nyerere, according to Bell (1987):

> claimed that the traditional African economy and social organization were based
> on socialist principles of communal ownership of the means of production in
> which kinship and family groups participated in economic activity and were
> jointly responsible for welfare and security. The socialist system of co-operative
> production appeared to be more compatible with African culture than the in-
> dividualism of capitalism and on the basis of these cultural roots Nyerere sought
> to emphasize the distinctive characteristics of African socialism. (p.117)

The planned socialist transformation of Africa was understood to mean
the institution of a plethora of legislative instruments and controls. All unoccupied land was appropriated by the government. Roadblocks and passbook systems were employed to control the movement of Africans.
Marketing boards and export regulations were tightened to fleece the cash
crop producers. Price controls were imposed on peasant farmers and traders
to render food cheap for the urban elites. A bewildering array of legislative
controls and regulations were imposed on imports, capital transfers, industry, minimum wages, the rights and powers of trade unions, prices, rents,
and interest rates. Some of the controls were introduced by the colonialists
but were retained and expanded on by Nkrumah. Private businesses were
taken over by the Nkrumah government and nationalized. Numerous state
enterprises were acquired. Even in avowedly capitalist countries like Ivory

Coast, Malawi, Nigeria, and Kenya, the result became the same: government ownership of most enterprises and a distrust of private-sector initiative and foreign investment. The problem was, no aspect of this economic ideology was in consonance with Africa's own indigenous economic heritage.

Statism

> If the twentieth century taught us anything, it is that large-scale centralized government does not work. It does not work at the national level, and it is less likely to work at the global level.
>
> —Kofi Annan, U.N Secretary-General
> *(The New York Times,* Sept 13, 2000; p.A12).

Statism may be defined as the employment of the instrumentalities of the state to promote and direct economic development to achieve various objectives. After independence, a large economic role was envisaged for the state in economic development. The drift toward statism was influenced by many factors:

a. Ideological—to repudiate capitalism and adopt socialism as the basis for national development;
b. Economic nationalism—to achieve economic sovereignty and to promote indigenous ownership or "indigenization";
c. Situational—to remove domestic obstacles to rapid social development;
d. Colonialism-related—to protect the country against foreign exploitation, and to right colonial wrongs or economic injustices; and
e. Faddish—to follow the prevailing economic orthodoxy in the Third World.

No one single factor can be isolated as the main driving force behind statism, however. All played a role, although the colonial factor seems to have been prevalent.

During colonial rule, there was little social development, or encouragement of indigenous businesses and entrepreneurs. Thus in Uganda, for example, the Uganda Development Corporation created in 1963 a subsidiary known as African Business Promotions Ltd., whose objective was to "establish and promote our own people in the trade and commerce field generally so that Ugandans may play a reasonable part and hold a reasonable share of the country's commerce" (Thomas, 1969; p.266). Similarly, in Kenya, due to the lack of sufficient indigenous private entrepreneurs after independence, government created parastatals "to fill the existing entrepreneurship gap" (Eckert 1987; p.446). Thus, public enterprises "served as a means to promote the establishment of private African enterprises" (Eckert 1987; p.446).

In 1955 in Kenya, among registered companies, there were about 246 new companies owned by Europeans with a nominal capital of £8.9 million (£ = $1.83), 99 companies belonging to Asians with a nominal capital of £3.6 million, and only one company belonging to an African with a nominal capital of £250. Government therefore set up some parastatals in order to implement the program of indigenization: the Industrial and Commercial Development Corporation (ICDC), the Development Finance Corporation of Kenya (DFCK), the Industrial Development Bank (IDB), the Kenya Industrial Estate Program (KIE), and the Rural Industrial Development Centers (RIDC). Although the objective of the Industrial Development Corporation at its inception in 1954 was to promote the industrial and economic development of Kenya, by 1967 it had been extended to include the indigenization of the Kenyan economy.

The activist role of the state, as an engine of economic development, was also girded by prevailing orthodoxy and circumstances in the 1950s and 1960s. First, it was widely believed that the enormous and urgent problems of development could not be solved by private enterprise alone and that governments must abandon their traditional caretaker and regulatory functions and move into an era of active participation in the productive sector. This encouraged governments to establish state enterprises to go into actual production, ministries of agriculture into actual agricultural production, and ministries of mines into actual mineral exploitation. For example, Nigeria's Second National Development Plan (1970–74, p.6) declared that "the Government will seek to acquire, by law of necessity, equity participation in a number of strategic industries that will be specified from time to time. In order to ensure that the economic destiny of Nigeria is determined by Nigerians themselves, the Government will seek to widen and intensify its positive participation in industrial development."

Second, it was believed that poverty was a pathological condition that needed to be eradicated. Though various causes were isolated, the ultimate culprit was held to be an inadequate rate of capital accumulation. Not enough was being invested to raise income. Inadequate investment, in turn, was due to low savings, which was produced by low levels of income. Thus, the poor were caught in a "low-level equilibrium trap" or a vicious circle of poverty. Private enterprise and markets could not be relied upon to break the circle. Markets in the developing countries were either nonexistent or underdeveloped and as such could not provide reliable guidance for development. The only way out of the poverty trap was somehow to raise the national and per capita incomes to the point at which savings and capital accumulation would be possible on a sufficient scale. A "big push" was all that was needed to do the trick and the economy would take off into self-sustaining growth. These ideas were associated with such names as Gunnar Myrdal, W. W. Rostow, S. Kuznets, Harvey Leibenstein, and H. W. Singer.

This was the grand strategy of the 1950s and early 1960s. The question was how to engineer that "big push." Before this could be answered, it was universally agreed that colonialism must end, since the colonial state lacked the legitimacy and therefore the self-confidence to undertake fundamental social engineering. The onus, therefore, must be on the first successor states just beginning to emerge in Africa, with Ghana moving toward independence and the rest of the continent not so far behind. As Fieldhouse (1986) aptly described it: "On these states and their character the economists—like the 18th century philosophes, with whom they had much in common, before them—placed great faith. Their rulers were assumed to be both enlightened and efficient, and so fit to be the main instruments of change and development" (p.88). It is important to keep in mind the assumption that the rulers were "enlightened and efficient."

Accordingly, the rulers and their economic advisors placed great emphasis on economic management and planning as the alternative to the market on account of the widespread belief that market prices were distorted and did not reflect true social values. Development under state planning could overcome such market deficiencies, imperfections, or distortions. This period (1950s and 1960s) was characterized by a proliferation of development plans and an expanding role of the state in economic development.

In many African countries, socialism provided an additional if not the principal driving force behind the drift toward statism. Regardless of the individual justification for its adoption, socialism, where adopted in Africa, was understood to mean increasing participation of the state in virtually every sector of the economy. In the case of Ghana before independence, the economy could be stratified into three layers: At the top were the Europeans and Levantines owning the large commercial enterprises; in the middle were the Asians and Middle Easterners engaged in wholesale and retail trading with a virtual monopoly of general transport services including motor spare parts; at the bottom were the Africans engaged in cash crop agriculture, farming, petty trading, and rudimentary services (Ankomah 1970; p.123). Originally, the establishment of state enterprises was intended primarily to promote economic growth. Government legislation (the Ghanaian Enterprises Decree of 1968) was directed at increasing the participation of Ghanaians in the modern sector of the economy. However, this was overtaken by a more radical ideological objective.

Kwame Nkrumah, Ghana's first president, was quite emphatic about the meaning of socialism: State participation as a domestic policy was to be pursued toward "the complete ownership of the economy by the State" (Seven-Year Development Plan). Nkrumah's socialist transformation of Ghana was to be rapid. As such, there was to be a rapid expansion of the state sector and "various state corporations and enterprises were to be established as a means of securing our economic independence and assisting in the national control of the economy" (Nkrumah, 1957; p.398–99). State participation was also expected to achieve another objective: rapid industrialization.

The technique of planning was adjudged superior to the nineteenth-century doctrine of *laissez-faire*. A Seven-Year Development Plan 1963/64–1969/70 was drawn up. Furthermore, it was stated that, "government interference in all matters affecting economic growth in the less developed countries (LDCs) is today a universally accepted principle" (Nkrumah, 1963; p.109). Accordingly, a horrendous array of instruments was employed to assure state participation and regulation of the economy. Numerous state enterprises were acquired haphazardly, with little foreplanning or regard to costs.

A battery of legislative controls were instituted—on imports, capital transfers, on industry, on minimum wages, on the rights and powers of trade unions, prices, rents, and interest rates. The state under this scheme emerged as a major entrepreneurial and socioeconomic force.

The state was also to serve as the primary source of capital formation (or investment). The rationale was stated by Krobo Edusei, one of Nkrumah's ministers, quite cogently:

a. Private enterprise, with its profit motive, feels willing to enter fields with high and quick returns only;
b. Private enterprise does not want to plough back their profits but prefers to reduce our hard-won foreign currency by transferring a proportion of their profits abroad;
c. Savings for investment could be most quickly and effectively generated only on a communal basis through creating surpluses in annual government budgets. (qtd. in Killick, 1978; p.215)

Tanzania's Julius Nyerere stated clearly that it was the role of the state to intervene actively in the economy (Fieldhouse, 1986; p.174). In Kenya, Jomo Kenyatta's Kenya African National Union (KANU) adopted socialism as its policy objective (Sessional Paper No. 10—"African Socialism and its Application to Planning in Kenya," Republic of Kenya, 1965). The role of the state was expanded accordingly:

> As a proportion of GDP, the state's share increased from 11 to 20 percent from 1960 to 1979, while private consumption decreased from 72 to 65 percent. Between 1964 and 1977 public employment rose from 32 to 42 percent of total wage employment. The state also took controlling position in agriculture. In form, at least, Kenya therefore adopted much the same state-centered approach to development as most other African countries. (Fieldhouse, 1986, p.165)

Kenya established such state monopolies as the Maize and Produce Board, the Kenya Tea Development Authority, the Kenya Meat Commission, and other state bodies with near-monopoly control over the distribution of food crops. Its government also drew up national plans and adopted an import-licensing system, the hallmarks of a state-controlled economy (Fieldhouse, 1986; p.165).

In comparing KANU's Sessional Paper No. 10 with Tanzania's Arusha Declaration, Bell (1986) found that "Both documents display a commitment to equality and social justice, and to reducing international and internal inequalities" (p.118). For example, the Kenyan document stressed at the outset that "In African socialism every member of society is important and equal. The State has an obligation to ensure equal opportunities to all its citizens, eliminate exploitation and discrimination, and provide needed social services such as education, medical care and social security" (Republic of Kenya, 1965; p.4).

Similarly, the Tanzania African National Union Constitution acknowledged as the first socialist principle "that all human beings are equal" and pledged that the government would give "equal opportunity to all men and women," and would eradicate "all types of exploitation" so as to "prevent the accumulation of wealth which is inconsistent with the existence of a classless society" (Republic of Tanzania, 1967, p.1). Tanzania's Second Five-Year Plan for Economic and Social Development laid emphasis on the fact that "considerable benefit will accrue in the long run from the expansion of public ownership because (a) it will be possible to create a genuine Tanzanian industrial know-how faster than under conditions of unrestricted private enterprise; (b) it will be possible to pursue a more effective industrial strategy than is possible under private enterprise; (c) the profits made in industry will be re-invested in United Republic of Tanzania." Thus, the government as the representative of the people regarded ownership of the means of production by Tanzanians as an "antidote to capitalist exploitation" (Second Five-Year Development Plan 1964–69; p.iix).

Although Nigeria is often touted as "capitalistic" and "open," its basic economic strategy and policies were decidedly statist and typical of post-colonial Africa. As Fieldhouse (1986) described:

> Lagos, exactly like Accra, aimed to concentrate the largest possible share of the national product in its own hands, to expand the public sector and to develop import-substituting industry by means of tariffs, import licensing and other stimuli. At the same time, agricultural prices were to be kept down by marketing boards to benefit both industry and the urban consumer and to provide government income. (p.151)

In 1954 the Talakawa Party declared that: "Only a free and independent Nigeria can establish a socialist system of production; and that only such an establishment of socialism can enable our people to plan the use of our material and productive resources in such a way as to guarantee to every Nigerian citizen real security, the right to work and leisure, a rising standard of living, liberty, and equal opportunity for a full and happy life" (Olaniyan 1985, p.177).

The state apparatus was also to be used to protect Nigerians from foreign exploitation. The First Development Plan (1962–68) called for economic independence and stated that indigenous businessmen should control an increasing portion of the Nigerian economy. The 1963 Immigration Act and the government's 1964 statement on industrial policy, when taken together, were designed to encourage personnel and local-content indigenization (Biersteker, 1987; p.71). Three years later an Expatriate Allocation Board was created in part because of a large influx of Lebanese and Indian merchants engaged in both wholesale and retail sales of textile goods in the Lagos trading area.

In April 1971 the state acquired 40 percent of the largest commercial banks, and the Nigerian National Oil Company (NNOC) was established, with the government keeping a majority participation. Four years later the government acquired 55 percent of the petroleum industry and 40 percent of National Insurance Company of Nigeria (NICON). The following year the acquisition was extended to other insurance companies when the government took 49 percent of their shares.

Nigeria's Second Development Plan (1970–74) was unequivocal, declaring that:

> The interests of foreign private investors in the Nigerian economy cannot be expected to coincide at all times and in every respect with national aspirations. A truly independent nation cannot allow its objectives and priorities to be distorted or frustrated by the manipulation of powerful foreign investors.

It is vital therefore for Government to acquire and control on behalf of the Nigerian society the greater proportion of the productive assets of the country. To this end, the Government will seek to acquire, by law if necessary, equity participation in a number of strategic industries that will be specified from time to time. (The Second National Development Plan, 1970–74: Program of Post-War Reconstruction and Development, 1970; p.289)

This was followed by the third and fourth development plans (1975 and 1980), reflecting the Nigerian government's abiding faith in the potency of state planning and interventionism, even though Nigeria maintained an open economy and a "capitalist" posture.

Zambia under Kaunda fit the classic mold of the command economy: "Through companies it controlled, the state ran virtually everything, from the cultivation of maize to the baking of bread to the mining of copper. Payrolls were heavily padded, with employees receiving housing, cars and free airfare on the national airline. Even food was subsidized" (*The Washington Post*, Sept 12, 1995; p.A12).

State interventionism was also the order of the day in Francophone Africa, drawing much impetus from French socialists and the French colonial system. In Francophone Africa, statism evolved from the peculiar nature of the French colonial experience. The authoritarian colonial state was an extractive tool utilized by the French to make rules and control, regulate, and organize the local economy to extract maximum profit. It was not meant to empower the people to make them masters of their destinies or principal actors in their own development. The French never envisioned independence for their colonies. French colonial policies stressed assimilation, under which the colony was to become an integral part of the mother country rather than a separate but protected state, as under British colonial policy of "indirect rule." Thus, the French colonial state actively intervened and interfered with the native systems to enforce assimilation with French culture. The French had no intention of using the traditional rulers as intermediaries as the British did. The French allied themselves with African rulers in order to neutralize them until they could be eliminated or deposed at convenience. Those who remained were put in the position of serving as agents of the colonial state rather than rulers in their own right. For example, when the French conquered Dahomey in 1894, General Dodds dismembered the kingdom. Only the central province, the area around the capital of Abomey, remained; the rest of the provinces were placed under direct French rule or made into new kingdoms. Where there were no central authorities, as in stateless African societies such as the Fulani and Somali, the French created new chiefs. Thus, French colonial policies of assimilation and tutelage posed the greatest threat of obliterating indigenous African culture, though in many places the culture survived.

To be sustainable, the colonial system partly relied on a small and selected proportion of the indigenous population. At first, it relied on pliant local chiefs or colonial appointees and acculturated elites, who were shaped by the French educational system. In exchange for their cooperation, the French colonial state would reward them with grants, scholarships to study in France, among other things.

In this scheme of things, the struggle for independence was perceived differently by these actors. The French wanted continuity; the local elites wanted to replace French officials. A new relationship could be crafted: Continuity of colonial rule with a black face (Saumon, 2000). The local elite stood to reap enormous gains by replacing French officials and using the colonial state for their own benefit. The social, political, and economic order prevailing in Francophone Africa was not questioned by the local elite, and the status quo was to be maintained in the name of nation building. Thus, the indigenous people were not involved in this new arrangement; they were excluded from the creation of the independent state (Saumon, 2000).

The primacy of the state was necessary for the affirmation of the new independent nation, and this setup rendered statism inevitable since any vision of development by any nationalist leader—regardless of his ideology—could not be achieved except through the apparatus of the state. To a large extent, this was also true of many Francophone African countries.

Patrick Manning (1988) noted that:

> In Guinea, a state-dominated socialist economy was set up beginning with independence in 1958, in Congo-Brazzaville, a similar decision was taken in 1967, and in Benin, a socialist state was proclaimed in 1975. At the same time, the economy of Ivory Coast, which may be labeled one of state capitalism (since it draws private investment funds, but invests them under state control) is in some ways very similar. (p.129)

Though the purported objectives of statism were always "national development" and "the sovereign interests of the independent nation," in practice, the beneficiaries always turned out to be an elite minority, not the majority of the population—the peasants or the Atingas. Remarkably, this type of governance—economic apartheid—was the norm across postcolonial Africa. The use of the term "apartheid," which evokes ugly racial connotations, may appear strange but is deliberate. In pre-1994 South Africa, statism was officially known as apartheid—the use of the instruments of the state to promote the economic welfare of whites. Caldwell (1989) asserted:

In fact, apartheid has been nothing but a series of anti-capitalist laws designed to strengthen central government and prevent South Africa from developing, free market-style, into a rich, multi-racial country: 1911 Native Labor Regulation Act and 1932 Native Service Contract Act (preventing black miners and farm workers from leaving their jobs without employer consent), 1951 Native Building Workers Act (excluding blacks from skilled building work in white urban areas), 1952 Native Services Levy Act (imposing a monthly tax on urban black workers to discourage their hiring), Job Reservation Determination No. 3 of 1958 (reserving 15 metals-industry jobs for whites) among hundreds of others. Then there have been land restrictions, influx control, District Labor Control Boards, and all the rest. (p.50)

Although Botswana has been a shining black African economic star, statism has also been discernible and specifically benefits the cattle-owning and agricultural elite, who were instrumental in establishing the dominant political party. According to Libby (1987):

From 1962 to 1973, the government's approach to agricultural development was to concentrate its extension services upon roughly 10 percent of the farmers who had the necessary cattle to plough and who were receptive to modern farming techniques (these included the more educated and successful farmers). Once registered in the scheme, farmers received considerable support and advice from government extension agents.

The government also supported public marketing institutions that were primarily designed to serve the large successful farmers. For example, the Botswana Meat Commission (BMC), a parastatal corporation with a monopoly over the export of Botswana's cattle and beef, caters primarily to large cattle owners.

In 1974, the government established the Botswana Agricultural Marketing Board (BAMB) with several buying depots throughout the country. Although BAMB has been successful in providing a market for the small farmer, it does nothing to assist the roughly 50 percent of all rural households who produce no surplus at all. (pp.113–15)

Evidently, the application of the labels "capitalism" and "socialism" to African countries is not particularly useful and probably more apt to create confusion. The relevant ideology has always been statism since virtually all postcolonial African governments have been statist. Its precise characteristics have varied according to the social, economic, and political peculiarities within each particular country and also over time, in response to changing internal and external pressures. However, it needs to be emphasized that statism did not suddenly emerge from the blue. Its roots were laid in colonial administration policies. Perhaps a few examples would be instructive.

The Portuguese in Guinea-Bissau actively intervened in the economy, discouraging internal trade in order to persuade peasants to concentrate more on the production of cash crops for export trade. In Mozambique, the colonial administration during the *Estado Novo* era was paternalistic, encouraging both large company plantations and the African population to become heavily dependent upon the state for their prosperity and economic security (Libby, 1987; p.219).

In the 1930s, government in the French and Belgian colonies was a formidable power and essentially autocratic. Over the years, it took on greater powers and the most widely known aspect of this growth of government was the postwar development plans drawn up by the French and Belgians. They involved huge expenditures on public works: ports, airports, roads, public buildings, dams. The French program, for example, was known as FIDES, a name chosen because the acronym means "faith." The Belgian campaign for public investment in its colonies was formally adopted in the 1952 Ten-Year Plan. As Manning (1988) put it:

> Government, in the late colonial years, not only carried out great expenditures in public works and increased its spending in social services, but opened up a great deal of new public enterprise. This government intervention in areas which might have been left to the private sector was a heritage of the early colonial years, when French colonial government took over railroads. Now colonial governments built new ports, founded development corporations to expand agriculture, and established marketing boards to direct commerce in export crops. (p.126)

Along with the growth of public works projects, the central state apparatus grew as well. And in response to growing nationalist criticisms, the colonial administrations began more active interventions in African economies to meet their demands. Marketing boards, for example, were all set up during the colonial era with the declared purpose to protect small African peasant producers from the vagaries of the world market. Marketing boards fixed prices well below world market levels, and the difference was to be used for the purposes of rural development.

During World War II, many European countries introduced price controls to elicit sacrifices for the war effort. As Killick (1978) observed about Ghana:

> Attempts to control prices, rents and interest were all initiated in the colonial period and there were other major pieces of interventionism, notably the wartime creation of a statutory marketing board with a legal monopoly over the exportation of cocoa. Szereszewski has shown the key role of the colonial gov-

ernment in an earlier period of the Gold Coast's development and another writer observed that "Nkrumah did not need a socialist ideology in order to follow a well-beaten track." (p.48)

In Zambia and Zimbabwe, measures introduced by the colonial administration were, like most of Africa, retained by the incoming black government. In Zimbabwe, the controls on imports, exports, foreign exchange transactions, as well as the state security system introduced by Ian Smith, were all retained by the Robert Mugabe government.

Bauer (1984) noted that:

> Without the policies of the closing years of colonial rule the incoming governments would not have inherited the effective and comprehensive state controls established in the 1950s, especially the state export monopolies and the large reserves accumulated by them. They would not have inherited the methods, potentialities and wherewithal for establishing quasi-totalitarian policies, nor the same inducement for attempting to do so. Without these controls, and especially the state export monopolies, the prizes of political power would have been far less and there might have been less scope for large-scale organized oppression and brutality. (p.94)

This colonial precedent argument is somewhat disingenuous as it seeks to place the blame elsewhere. There was no need for African nationalist leaders to repeat colonial mistakes. Of more importance however was the substantial intellectual, moral, and financial support African statists received from scores of Western scholars and aid agencies. Bandow (1986) pointed out that:

> The London School of Economics, which promoted the socialist development model, was perhaps the most important educational institution for English-speaking colonial subjects. British socialist Beatrice Webb explained in her autobiography that she and her husband felt "assured that with the School as the teaching body, the Fabian Society as a propagandist organization, the (London County Council) as object lesson in electoral success, our books as the only elaborate original work in economic fact and theory, no young man or woman who is anxious to study or to work in public affairs can fail to come under our influence." As a result, leaders throughout the underdeveloped world adopted this particular British economic philosophy as their own. (p.20)

Bandow (1986) continued that, as culpable as the menagerie of Western economic advisers who developed the statist philosophies adopted by developing nations were, the governments of the industrialized nations did worse:

They have paid the Third World leaders to adopt the *dirigiste* model. The activities of international agencies, such as the World Bank, the IMF, and UN Development Program, as well as programs initiated by the US Agency for International Development (AID) and philanthropic foundations, have all helped Third World officials put into effect the collectivist nostrums advanced by Lenin, Myrdal and others. . . .

Even such an institution as the World Bank has not been exempt from the same influences. For example, in 1983 Stanley Please, then a senior adviser to the World Bank's Senior Operations Vice President, reflected that when he joined the institution two decades before "as a committed socialist. . . . I was surprised and shocked by the emphasis which the Bank at the time gave to the public sector in general and to the government in particular. Here was an institution which had the reputation of being ultra free enterprise and market-oriented, yet had more confidence in the rationality, morality and competence of governments than I ever had." (p.23)

The World Bank's support for statism was reflected in its lending policies. Most of its loans focused on infrastructure projects devised by governments. For example, throughout the 1980s, the bank committed about 80 percent of its funds to government enterprises, or parastatals. The IMF, on the other hand, provided less direct support for statism. Its focus was on balance of payment disequilibria. Furthermore, its loans were subject to conditions such as devaluation, trimming budget deficits, and general macroeconomic management. But IMF emphasis and insistence on conditionalities and macromanagement rather perversely, or perhaps inadvertently, supplied further impetus to the notion of state management and control. For example, IMF prescriptions on reducing budget deficits and insistence on sound macroeconomic management always implied austere measures to be taken by the state, reinforcing the notion of an activist state.

Many Western governments and international aid agencies also supported—perhaps inadvertently—this orthodoxy of state interventionism. Foreign direct investment was deemed incapable of breaking the vicious circle of poverty. This type of investment, it was argued, tended to be "selective" and concentrated in "enclaves" that are insulated from the rest of the host economy. In economic jargon, it lacked forward and backward linkages. Thus, foreign investment, it was concluded, did not contribute significantly to the process of capital accumulation or the creation of local skills and know-how. To remedy these, foreign aid would be a better alternative. It needs to be remembered that such thinking coincided with the time when war-torn Europe was recovering splendidly with the Marshall Aid Plan. Why not use a similar plan to help postcolonial Africa break out of the poverty trap?

Accordingly, as Whitaker (1988) noted:

From the early 1960s, the World Bank and its soft loan window, the International Development Association, supplied the lion's share [of development assistance], at least 25 percent on average. Over the years, US aid fluctuated widely, doubling during both the Kennedy and Carter presidencies, and falling back in the mid-1980s as the United States itself became a major world debtor.

   Like the World Bank, the United States saw the development process in those days the way most Africans did: governments would expand and diversify the economy by creating industries and services, moving into areas where Europeans and sometimes Asians held a near monopoly. . . .

   So the United States and the World Bank actively supported national planning to provide the basis for both government activity and their own projects. Ghana proved an apt student of this new science, pioneering the multi-year comprehensive development plans, and Nigeria's independence gift (of $225 million) was based on a blueprint for its first five years. The plans grew increasingly sophisticated as economists invented new techniques, including input-output analysis, growth simulation models, and dynamic programming. Development programs, national planning boards, and industrial development corporations sprang up everywhere. (p.66)

The United Nations agencies also are not blameless in their support for statism. For example, all United Nations Development Program (UNDP) funds go to governments and the agency consciously avoids projects that do not involve close public sector involvement. Bandow (1986) would also include the UN General Assembly, UN Conference on Trade and Development (UNCTAD), as well as USAID and nongovernmental organizations. For example, "throughout the postwar period, the Ford Foundation, the Harvard Institute for International Development, and the MIT Center for International Studies have all supported the local and central planning bureaucracies of India and Pakistan. Though American economists generally advised the adoption of modest market incentives—such as higher prices for farmers—all three groups endorsed the transcendent goal of state planning" (p.25).

   In the final analysis, however, the ultimate responsibility for the adoption of statism rested with African leaders. Providing convenient alibis for misguided economic policies only serves to compound Africa's economic woes.

STRATEGIES FOR DEVELOPMENT

Most African leaders equated development with industrialization. The logic was elegantly simple: the developed countries were industrialized and therefore development meant industrialization. However, Nkrumah, for example, was skeptical about basing Ghana's industrialization on an indigenous entrepreneurial class, which, at any rate, hardly existed in sufficient numbers in the 1950s. Various attempts had been made to promote and expand Ghanaian entrepreneurs in the late 1950s, but Nkrumah became quickly disillusioned in these efforts and with the capability of nascent Ghanaian entrepreneurs to industrialize Ghana at the speed he desired. In a broadcast on October 9, 1960, he revealed his government policy on private enterprise:

> I have stated that the economic structure is divided into four different sectors. . . . the state-owned sector; . . . the joint state-private enterprise sector; . . . the co-operative sector and . . . the purely private sector. I have also stated that the Government intends to place far greater emphasis on the development of Ghanaian co-operatives rather than encourage Ghanaians to start private business enterprises.
>   In the past, the Government has given considerable assistance to Ghanaian private enterprise but the result has been negligible and disappointing. So disappointing in fact that, the Government feels that its assistance must be channeled in a more productive manner. (qtd. in Killick, 1978; p.120)

Nkrumah went further than merely channeling resources to the state. When in May 1961, W. A. Wiafe, a leading businessman in Parliament, criticized Nkrumah's government policies for the confusion they had created in the commercial life of the country to the detriment of African businessmen, he was promptly imprisoned without trial under the Preventive Detention Act of 1961 (Garlick, 1971; p.121). Also, C. C. K. Baah, another businessman and government back-bencher, had to flee the country when he criticized the government's attitude toward private enterprise.

More dramatic, however, was the testimony of Mr. Ayeh-Kumi before the Ollennu Commission (1967), which was set up after Nkrumah was overthrown in 1966 to investigate allegations of corruption in the grant of import licenses. Ayeh-Kumi tendered in evidence a document memorandum prepared by Mr. Amoako-Atta (former minister of finance) and Mr. Djin (former minister of trade) outlining Nkrumah's policy directions regarding big European business and Ghanaian traders. He testified that:

> It has been the system to gradually stifle the big businessmen and the small Ghanaian businessmen in this country to be replaced by State Corporations, and there has been a move towards this in putting all sorts of inconveniences in the way of merchants and traders in the country. The steps to be taken against them were income tax, various types of taxation, (import) license restrictions; African businessmen must not be given licenses and if they per-

sisted they should be given such licenses as would make them incapable of doing business. (Ollennu Report, 1967; p.10, para.59)

Overtly and surreptitiously, there was a massive transfer of investable resources to the state for investment in those economic fields with "low and slow" returns. The rapid growth of the state's share in capital formation was reflected in the fact that by 1965 it had jumped to 65 percent from 25 percent in 1958 (Economic Survey of Ghana, 1969; p.24).

New factories, roads, schools, and bridges were built at an incredible speed. The beneficiary of the government's investment thrust was the industrial sector, to the almost total neglect of the peasant or rural sector. There was a sharp rise in the number of manufacturing concerns owned wholly or partly by the state. The state's share in gross manufacturing rose from 11 percent in 1962 to a little over 25 percent in 1967.

Nkrumah was explicit about his emphasis on industry:

Industry rather that agriculture is the means by which rapid improvement in Africa's living standards is possible. There are, however, imperial specialists and apologists who urge the LDCs to concentrate on agriculture and leave industrialization for some later time when their population shall be well fed. The world's economic development, however, shows that it is only with advanced industrialization that it has been possible to raise the nutritional level of the people by raising their levels of income. (Nkrumah, 1957; p.7)

The strategy on industrialization was based upon import-substitution (I-S) and state ownership. High tariff walls were erected to protect I-S industries that were expected to conserve foreign exchange by replacing goods previously imported. Securing a domestic market for I-S industries and assuring a ready supply of imported inputs was one of the objectives of the import-licensing program.

When Nkrumah belatedly recognized the immense contribution that agriculture could make to the country's economic development, he took his socialist program to that sector as well. This resulted in increased state participation and massive investments in the agricultural sector, which was to be mechanized and diversified. Nkrumah also saw mechanization and socialization as the quickest means of achieving the agricultural revolution. Just as he felt he could not rely upon Ghanaian entrepreneurs for rapid industrialization, he also believed he could not rely upon the peasant farmers for rapid agricultural transformation because they were "too slow to adapt or change their practices to modern mechanized scientific methods" (Uphoff, 1970; p.602).

To realize the potential contribution of these farmers toward the agricultural revolution, they were to be taught and encouraged to adopt modern farming techniques through extension services and demonstration (state) farms. This came across clearly in Nkrumah's public speeches:

> Mr. Speaker, the back-bone of Ghana's agriculture has always been its farmers who, particularly in recent years, have made a fine contribution to the economy and expressed their patriotism in a number of unselfish ways. The developments the Government is proposing in the areas of State and Co-operative farming will bring them a share of local facilities they have so long been denied. More than this, they will have the opportunity to share in the up-to-date techniques of farming that must be employed if greater yields and diversity of crops are to be attained.
>
> I want our farmers to understand that the State Farms and Co-operative enterprises are not being encouraged as alternatives to peasant farming. The interest of peasant farmers will not be made subservient to those of the State Farms and Co-operatives. We need the efforts of our individual farmers more than ever if we are to achieve, at an increased pace, the agricultural targets we have set ourselves. We look to our individual peasant farmers for the enlargement of investment in our agriculture. (Speech to the National Assembly on March 11, 1964, reprinted in Nkrumah, 1973; p.195)

Mechanization was to be the guiding principle of the agricultural revolution for reasons other than increased productivity. To Nkrumah, industrialization and development were synonymous with the adoption of advanced machinery. To demonstrate and encourage the use of modern farming techniques, he set up and designated the following bodies with those responsibilities: the United Ghana Farmers' Council was charged with organizing co-operatives and the provision of extension services. State Farms Corporation, Workers Brigade, and Ghana Young Farmers' League were established. The State Farms were to be models of collective production of food; the Workers Brigade was to run settlement farms, and the Young Farmers were expected to be mechanized farmers. Finally, a Food Marketing Board was created to fix maximum prices for all foodstuffs and to improve the efficiency of the distributive system. Through these institutions, Nkrumah hoped to create "a complete revolution in agriculture on our continent [and] a total break with primitive methods and organizations and with the colonial past" (Nkrumah, 1963; p.27).

After being established in 1963, the State Farms expanded their operations rapidly and by 1964 they were cultivating about 51,226 acres and by 1965 were managing a total of 105 farms (Wheetham and Currie, 1967; p.174). Their labor force was over 30,000 at the end of 1965, while the Workers Brigade and Ghana Young Farmers' League had between them over 15,000 persons on payroll. The United Ghana Farmers' Co-operative Council, which was the sole cocoa-buying agency, engaged over 30,000 workers on farms and in cocoa buying (Ahmad, 1970; p.117).

The peasants, the chiefs, and the indigenous sector generally did not fit into the grandiose schemes Nkrumah drew up to industrialize Ghana. His Seven-Year Development Plan (1963–69), for example, devoted only two paragraphs to the whole of the agriculture sector, and the 1965 foreign exchange budget allocated a paltry $2 million to agriculture, compared to $114 million and $312 million for manufacturing and imports, respectively.

Nkrumah was overthrown in a military coup in 1966. But his statist experiment did not end then. Successive Ghanaian governments retained, and in some cases expanded, the state interventionist behemoth Nkrumah had erected. Foreign mining companies were subsequently nationalized. More state enterprises were set up and a denser maze of controls were placed on prices, rents, interest, foreign exchange exports, and imports. By 1970, nearly 6,000 prices, relating to more than 700 product groups, were controlled in Ghana (World Bank, 1989; p.114). Tragically, this statist development strategy was replicated in many other African countries, although the scale and intensity were somewhat different.

In 1967, Tanzania's ruling party's Arusha Declaration established a socialist state where the workers and peasants controlled and owned the means of production. The Arusha Declaration sought to encourage self-reliance primarily through an expansion of agricultural production for domestic consumption. Banks, insurance companies, and foreign trading companies were nationalized. A "villagization" program was adopted to encourage the communal production, marketing, and distribution of farm crops. Between 1967 and 1973, the number of rural villagers officially designated as residing in *ujamaa* (familyhood) villages increased from one-half million to two million (an estimated 15 percent of the rural population). In the next several years after 1973, a major drive to bring rural Tanzanians into villages resulted in the creation of villages throughout the entire country. Ethiopia adopted a similar program—forced resettlements on government farms.

In Mozambique, the Mozambican Liberation Front (FRELIMO) sought to establish a socialist state replete with collectivized agriculture, crop-growing schemes, village political committees, and health programs. The party took over about 1,000 "fortified villages" that the Portuguese regime had initially created to cut off villager contact with FRELIMO. These were converted into communal villages, with about one million inhabitants. Other communal villages were set up in the aftermath of the Limpopo and Zambezi Valley floods in 1977 and 1978, and still more were created in response to the resurgence of the National Resistance Movement (MNR) guerilla war in Manica and Sofala.

According to Libby (1987):

> The centerpiece of Frelimo's rural social program for Mozambique was the collectivization of agriculture into communal villages and cooperative farms. Agricultural cooperatives were intended to provide an integrated production base for the communal villages. Hence, villagization was designed to increase food and cash crop production and to make available common facilities for farming as well as provide social services such as education and health comparable with *ujamaa* villages in Tanzania. (p.216)

Strange as it might sound, the statist system established in Tanzania, Ghana, Mozambique, and elsewhere in Africa was no different from that which operated under apartheid South Africa. In fact, one of the cruelest jokes perpetrated on a gullible world was the misconception that the South African economy under apartheid was a "capitalist and free market." For example,

> D. F. Malan, who would lead the National Party to victory in 1948, told the Volkskongress in 1934: "If war should come, it will mean, in my opinion, the end of the capitalist system. But whether this happens with or without war, by revolution or evolution, the capitalist system which is based on self-interest and the right of the strongest is in any case doomed." (Caldwell, 1989; p.50)

Under apartheid, the South African economy was characterized by severe state interventionism: Where blacks could live and work, and what type of jobs they could take, were all determined by the state. The fictional link of apartheid to capitalism remained well into the 1990s, even though the National Party government operated a horrendous array of programs to maintain a heavy presence in the economy. "For small-scale black, family, and cooperative companies, there's the Small Business Development Corporation. To encourage village industry, there are homeland subsidies, the Development Bank, and the Decentralization Board. To finance larger industry, there's the Industrial Development Corporation. Export subsidies are given to industrialists. And control boards guide agricultural production and distribution. This is all done by the National Party government in the hopes of promoting a mixed economy that serves national interests" (Caldwell, 1989; p.51).

According to Andrew Kenny, a liberal South African engineer and freelance journalist, "Grand apartheid was a piece of socialist engineering which shoved people—mostly blacks—around like earth in front of a bull dozer, much in the same way as the schemes of Stalin in the USSR, Pol Pot in Cambodia and Nyerere in Tanzania's *ujamaa*. The main idea was to push the blacks, who accounted for more than 70 percent of the South African population, into 'homelands' or 'Bantustans,' which made up 13 percent of the land area" (*The Spectator,* July 5, 2003; p.24). Kenny went on to claim that, "The apartheid regime and the ANC (African National Congress) resemble each other in thought. Both are obsessed by racial ideology and state control. The ANC government has allowed more free enterprise than apartheid ever did but without ever relinquishing a tight commanding grip. South Africa today is not so much capitalist as corporatist or fascist, along the lines of what Mussolini wanted for Italy, with the masters of big business, the trade unions and the government doing coercive deals among themselves to control the whole economy" (*The Spectator,* July 5, 2003; p.25).

THE INITIAL MISTAKES

At independence, African nationalist leaders faced the formidable task of developing their countries with little to work with. Under colonialism, there had been spartan social development. The colonialists built a few thousand miles of road and dreadfully inadequate schools. At independence in 1961, Tanzania had less than a hundred university graduates. Said Julius Nyerere, former head of state, in a speech at the University of Edinburgh on October 9, 1997:

> Tanzania or Tanganyika then had approximately 200 miles of tarmac road, and its "industrial sector" consisted of 6 factories—including one which employed 50 persons. And despite the Education and Health services provided by some Christian Missionaries and later begun by colonial governments, at independence less than 50 percent of Tanzanians children went to school— and then for only four years or less; 85 percent of its adults were illiterate in any language. The country had only 2 African Engineers, 12 Doctors, and perhaps 30 Arts graduates, I was one of them. (*PanAfrican News,* Sept 1998)

Guinea-Bissau was even less lucky. According to Lamb (1985): "What the Portuguese left as a legacy of three hundred years of colonial rule was pitifully little: 14 university graduates, an illiteracy rate of 97 percent and only 265 miles of paved roads in an area twice the size of New Jersey. There was only one modern plant in Guinea-Bissau in 1974—it produced beer for the Portuguese troops—and as a final gesture before leaving, the Portuguese destroyed the national archives." (p.5)

Industrial development had not been encouraged, as the colonies were not conceived of to compete with the industries of Europe. The object of infrastructure, where it was erected, was to serve the needs of the resident expatriate community and to help evacuate minerals and cash crops from the interior. The large rural sector and the interior of Africa were largely left untouched. Recall Nkrumah's complaint at Ghana's independence in 1957 that: "We had not one single industry. Our economy depended on one cash crop, cocoa. There were few hospitals, schools and clinics. Most of the villages lacked a piped water supply" (Nkrumah, 1957; p.395).

To initiate development, African nationalist leaders had to work with a small cadre of inexperienced bureaucrats. Few of the leaders had any experience running the ship of state. Most had spent time in jail for agitating for freedom, or in the bush, fighting for independence for their respective countries. Under those circumstances, mistakes were bound to be made. But some of the mistakes were too elementary to be excusable and could have been avoided with a little more introspection and study. Specifically, many of the avoidable mistakes related to the nature of the leadership itself—in particular, attitude, motivation, and character flaws.

LEADERSHIP FLAWS

Inferiority Complex

Most of the African nationalist leaders suffered from an inferiority complex that compelled them to "prove something"—either that they were not "racially inferior" or that Africa was just as "capable" as the West. This predisposition influenced their development policies and led them to undertake grandiose development projects, not out of considerations of economy and efficiency but to show off or "prove a point." Understandable as this desire might have been, given the humiliation Africans endured during the slave trade and the degradation of African civilization during the colonial period, it led the leaders to imitate foreign metropolitan symbols and paraphernalia, to place obtrusive emphasis on high-tech gadgetry when simple technology would have sufficed. For example, mechanization of agriculture in the 1960s was bull-headedly pursued at a time when Africa was not ready and labor was in abundant supply. Driven more by emotional impulses than by reason or rationality, African nationalist leaders blindly copied truckloads of foreign cultural paraphernalia and systems that were garishly out of place.

The all-consuming mentality was: If American farmers use tractors, so, too, must African farmers. If New York has skyscrapers, so, too, must Africa. If London has double-decker buses, so, too, must Lagos. If Rome has a basilica, so, too, must Yamassoukro in Ivory Coast. China has state farms, so, too, must Africa. The United States has two political parties, so, too, must Nigeria. Accordingly, the military regime of President Ibrahim Babangida created two political parties: the Social Democratic Party and the National Republican Convention.[1] To add more insult, the military regime also wrote their party manifestoes. The list of this type of unimaginative aping ("so-too-must-we" syndrome) in Africa is endless. Name any foreign system and there is a collapsed replica somewhere in Africa.

Back in 1963, Nkrumah demanded a bylaw from the Accra-Tema city council requiring all advertisements in Accra to be illuminated by neon lighting so that the main streets of the city would resemble Picadilly Circus. The city council approved the bylaw despite the insistence of the Ghana Chamber of Commerce that the lights were impractical in a country where most businesses had few employees and limited capital (Werlin, 1973; p.261).

When Sir Arthur Lewis disagreeably pointed out to an African prime minister that the minister was proposing to spend 50 percent of his entire development budget on his capital city, which had only 5 percent of the population, the prime minister was surprised. "But why not?" he asked. "Surely when you think of England you think of London, when you think of Russia you think of Moscow and when you think of France you think of Paris" (Lewis 1962, p.75). The most bizarre instance of this "so-too-must-we" syndrome occurred in 1977 when President Bokassa spent 20 percent of the GNP of the Central African Republic ($20 million) to crown himself "emperor" to prove that, like France, black Africa can produce emperors. And since the United States has a space program, "Nigeria, one of the world's poorest countries, is to launch its own space program in the form of an agency that will develop rocket and satellite technology" (*New Zealand Herald*, June 7, 2001).

There was hardly any pretense at understanding why London has double-decker buses or why American farmers use tractors. It is a shame that African elites and leaders lack original ideas and cannot use their imagination to craft authentically African solutions to African problems. If all they can do is to imitate, then they might as well bring back the foreigners to come and rule Africa. At the very least, if African leaders and elites were bereft of original ideas, they could copy or improve Africa's own indigenous systems. Before long, most of these foreign imitation projects began collapsing because they had no roots in the indigenous culture. Huge sums of foreign aid were wasted in the process. Africa's enormous $350 billion foreign debt in 2002 was testimony to the carcasses of numerous "black elephants" littering the continent. Poor African peasants (the Atingas) must now pay off a huge foreign debt incurred through elite stupidity.

Functional Illiteracy

Blind copying is the product of functional illiteracy. The functional illiterate is "educated" and possesses a degree, diploma, or some military title, but does not understand its import or the meaning of things. He is imbued with symbolism and characterized by rote behavior. He mimics his teacher and regurgitates material taught in class as gospel truth. He is incapable of independent thought or rational reasoning and lacks initiative. He cannot on his own assess the inherent merit or consistency of an idea. If the teacher approves of an idea, he accepts it without question.

In the classroom, the functional illiterate was taught that LAND + TRACTORS = BOUNTIFUL AGRICULTURAL HARVEST. Upon graduation, he finds that the "food equation" in traditional Africa is: PEASANT FARMER + LAND + SHIFTING CULTIVATION + MANURE + INCENTIVES = LIMITED AGRICULTURAL OUTPUT. Where are the tractors? The functional illiterate is stuck. "Tractors there must be! Even if they must be imported from Jupiter!" Else, there could be no agricultural revolution.

Accordingly, tons of sophisticated agricultural machinery were imported into Africa, costing huge amounts of scarce foreign exchange or credit. In the 1970s Tanzania was using combine harvesters to grow wheat. Much of this agricultural machinery operated for a few months, broke down, and was then abandoned in the fields to rust.

Fishing is another example. To Africa's functionally illiterate elite, the modern way of fishing is by using laser-guided trawlers, aided by global positioning systems, and the catch is preserved through refrigeration. Never mind that Africa's native fishermen have been fishing in dugout canoes and preserving fish by smoking and salting it—techniques which require no foreign exchange expenditure. But to the elites, the traditional methods are not good enough—as if a starving person cares if the fish on his plate was caught by a modern trawler or a primitive dugout canoe. Only African elites would insist that fish caught by a modern trawler tastes better!

Africa's educational system is probably at fault: It produces graduates who spend more time arguing about the causes of Africa's problems than about how to fix them. Nigeria, by its sheer size, has more graduates than any other African country. Bragged Chieke Evans Ihejirika of Temple University in Philadelphia: "One thing nobody can say that Nigeria lacks is a class of some of the best scholars the world has ever known" (*African News Weekly,* March 3, 1995; p.17). And how have they tackled their country's problems with all that intellectual prowess? In a blistering commentary, Reverend S.J. Esu, a Nigerian pastor, wrote:

> Most educated Nigerians, who are good copycats of foreign behavioral patterns, will like to flaunt their Euro-American amoral (and in fact immoral) tendencies in our face. Not even the decadence of those societies, despite their wealth and technologies, will make our elites have a rethink about those systems.

The quality of our elitism is so appallingly apelike that they are quite unable to distinguish a substance from a label. Whatever is out there is simply repeated here—root, stalk and leaf. It is a shame today that we are being taught by Europe to breast-feed our babies. Today, almost every Nigerian woman wears a bleached skin and the curly hair strand of another race group.

It is time that we have a rethink. And we ask our elites to ship in or ship out. (*Vanguard*, Lagos, Aug 5, 1999)

Religion of Development

The notion of "development" was widely misconstrued by the nationalist leaders. It was misinterpreted to mean the adoption of "modernity" or modern and scientific ways of doing things—by implication, a rejection of existing ways as "old and backward." The logic was simple and observed. The developed countries were industrialized and used modern scientific techniques. Therefore, development meant industrialization and modernity. The tendency to equate industrialization and modernism to development was a manifestation of a pathological condition known as "religion of development." This religion, which shaped or directed much of the elite's postcolonial development effort, was characterized by the following:

- An excessive preoccupation with sophisticated gadgetry, signs of modernism, an inclination to exalt anything foreign or Western as sanctified and a tendency to castigate the traditional as "backward."
- A tendency to emphasize industry or industrialization over agriculture.
- A misinterpretation of the so-called characteristics of underdevelopment as causes of economic "backwardness" and for development to mean their absence.
- A tendency to seek solutions to problems from outside rather than from inside Africa.
- Attempts to model African cities after London, Paris, New York, or Moscow.

This religion of development propelled African nationalist leaders and elites to opt for obtusely expensive and inappropriate capital-intensive techniques of production when simple, less costly techniques were available. It also contributed to the neglect and consequent decline of African agriculture. Peasant agriculture was too "backward" and was simply excluded from the grandiose plans drawn up by the elites to industrialize Africa. Nor was any role envisaged for Africa's peasant majority—the Atingas. Derided as "uneducated," "slow to change," and "bound by tradition," they and their

"primitive implements" were shunned. In fact, many of their other traditional practices in the rural sector—such as traditional medicine—were os-
tracized as well. In many countries the natives were debarred from many
economic fields.

Perhaps the most serious malady was economic illiteracy. How wealth is
created was not well understood by the nationalist leaders. Confusion prevailed over the meaning of "socialism" and "capitalism." The confusion was
compounded by the alleged association of capitalism with colonialism.
Colonialism was detested with a vengeance by the nationalist leaders and
African elites. It was rightly denounced as evil, exploitative, and oppressive.
However, because "capitalism" was identified with "colonialism," it was rea-
soned that capitalism, as an ideology, must also be evil and exploitative—a
common syllogistic error, or error by association. Kwame Nkrumah, the first
president of Ghana, for example, described Western capitalism as "a world
system of financial enslavement and colonial oppression and exploitation of
a vast majority of the population of the earth by a handful of the so-called
civilized nations" (Nkrumah, 1962; p.13). Soviet propaganda and literature
also tied capitalism with colonialism. Marxist-Leninist ideology also supported the idea that any return on private capital amounted to exploitation.
Therefore, many African nationalist leaders adopted socialism—the antithesis of capitalism—as their ideology. Lost in the ideological shuffle was the
more important question: How is wealth created?

Wealth, almost everywhere, is created by individuals in the private sector.
The government does not create wealth; it only redistributes it. Furthermore, government does not solve all problems. Quite the contrary, government often creates problems. It would be interesting to challenge African
elites to name one single problem their respective governments have been
able to resolve in the postcolonial period. If they cannot, then we must ask
why they call upon the government to solve more and more problems.
Clearly, any model of development that seeks to create wealth through heavy
reliance on the state is doomed to failure in Africa.

Perversion of the Notion of Development

Since "development" was almost everywhere in Africa misinterpreted to
mean "change," it gravitated toward mimicry—the approach was akin to
what educators call the "refrigerator fallacy." All teachers have refrigerators,
and therefore if one acquired a refrigerator, one would become a teacher!
The developed countries were industrialized, and therefore if one acquired
enough industries (and perhaps a nuclear bomb)—presto—one would become a developed country. Clearly, this perverted way of looking at things

shifted the emphasis away from the rigorous process of training needed to become a teacher to the rather facile task of acquiring a "symbol" of the occupation. Similarly, the emphasis was shifted from understanding the *modus operandi* of development to a preoccupation with its symbols. If an African head of state showed off a brand new shiny piece of imported tractor, it would "prove" that agriculture had been "mechanized"—a symptom of the same "inferiority complex" syndrome noted earlier. Precisely what that tractor was supposed to do to improve agricultural productivity or whether a mechanical support infrastructure existed or not, was of little importance. The mere presence of the tractor was of overriding importance. Such antics and obsession with symbolism betrayed a woeful lack of understanding of the development process.

Economic development does not mean the wholesale and blind acquisition of the symbols and signs of modernity. Nor does it mean everything about indigenous Africa must be rejected in favor of alien systems. In fact, the true challenge for development practitioners is *how to use the existing so-called "primitive, backward, and archaic" institutions to generate economic prosperity.* These institutions can never be alienated from Africa's peasants. They are part of their culture. One cannot expect these peasants to suddenly renounce their age-old traditions and ways of doing things. Nor is such abjuration absolutely necessary, as demonstrated by the stupendous success of the Japanese. The Japanese did not have to become "Americanized" or "Sovietized" in order to develop.

Development simply means improving upon the existing ways of doing things to make the processes more efficient and productive than before. "Productivity" means producing more from the same or even fewer resources; or alternatively, producing the same amount by using fewer inputs. In the African context, development means using the *same indigenous system* (or the existing system) to produce more output. The principal beneficiaries of economic prosperity ought to be the peasants, not the tiny parasitic elite minority, which constitutes less than 10 percent in any African country. But one can only improve the efficiency and performance of an automobile if and only if one understands how it operates.

As stated in chapter 1, this challenge was, in most cases, not met by Africa's leaders and elites, which explains why Africa is still mired in poverty. First, African governments and elites held the Atingas in contempt and denigrated their traditional systems. The elites were more obsessed with "modern and scientific" technologies than "primitive" ones. Second, they repressed, brutalized, and exploited the Atingas, never considering them to be "development partners." Third, foreign aid workers, experts, and agencies were not of much help as they did not understand the traditional system of

the Atingas. Since few appreciated or understood how the indigenous system operated, its performance and productivity could not be improved. Fig-
uratively speaking, when the peasants' agricultural machinery needed
ordinary firewood to continue operation, African elites, with much help
from Western donors, multilateral banks, and experts, were pouring in
rocket-jet fuel! The "modern" fuel was of course not only useless but destructive as well. It is debatable whether the elites willfully set out to destroy
the indigenous machinery or acted on the basis of innocent ignorance or
sheer stupidity. Whatever the case, the result was stalled machinery. This
issue is crucial, and perhaps an elaboration would be instructive.

Again, I take the native fishing industry as an example. Africans have
been fishing in dugout canoes for centuries. The object of development here
is to land more fish. *How* that fish is caught is immaterial to a destitute and
starving African country. True development in this case would mean improving the indigenous system so that more fish could be landed—in this
case, widening the boats to permit bigger catches of fish to be landed. But
the elites interpreted "improvement" differently. In their development paradigm, "improvement" meant jettisoning the traditional (existing technology), importing or copying a brand new technology (high-tech fishing
trawlers), which they did not understand, to produce *more* (land more fish).

The wooden dugout canoes were considered to be too "primitive." "Modern and scientific" methods were supposed to be better. Accordingly, Ghana's
elites completely ignored the native fishing industry and set up a State Fishing
Corporation, equipped with "state of the art" trawlers, so to speak. And when
government drew up plans to build modern boats, it chose pleasure aluminum
boats. Worse, "The State Boatyard at Mumford in the Apampam District
launched only 6 vessels with a workforce of 40 employees after operating for
9 years" (*Daily Graphic,* Accra, August 14, 1981; p.8). And the State Fishing
Corporation fishing vessels? They were impounded in foreign ports for non-
payment of mooring charges and the corporation itself eventually collapsed.

Meanwhile, the primitive dugout canoes continued to faithfully plug
away, delivering the fish, sometimes bumper catches, with little assistance
from the Ghanaian government. In 1981, for example, when Ghanaians
were starving, large catches of fish landed by dugout canoes were rotting on
the beaches. Native fishermen along the coastal areas of the central and western regions were reported "to be refusing to go to sea because there were no
prospective buyers following the bumper catches in those areas" (*Ghanaian
Times,* July 13, 1981; p.3). The government of Ghana provided no assistance
to the native fishermen because "the cold storage facilities of the State Fishing Corporation had broken down and there was no foreign exchange to import spares" (*Daily Graphic,* August 4, 1981; p.5).

This waste also occurred in 1971, 1972, 1975, 1979, 1980, and 2003—all because the "educated" officials had never heard of the traditional forms of fish preservation: smoking and salting—practical solutions. They only know of refrigeration (cold storage facilities). This author was in Accra on August 1, 2003, when frustrated native fishermen, unable to sell their catch of herring, threw the fish back into the sea.

African elites took this peculiar development approach and its concomitant neglect and deprecation of indigenous systems to many other fields as well. *The Washington Post* columnist Jim Hoagland reported an experience that occurred to him in the early 1970s during a tour of a gleaming new hospital built near Monrovia with U.S. aid. A young Liberian doctor told him: "We will never be able to staff this hospital and keep it supplied. We could have spent the same money on a dozen rural health clinics that we could sustain. But then there would not have been a big and well-publicized dedication ceremony attended by your congressmen and high-level aid administrators, and by our ministers." (*The Washington Post*, July 9, 2003; p.A27)

Indeed, in 2003, that "modern" hospital in Liberia stood as a bombed-out shell, a victim of mismanagement, inept administration, and a casualty of war—a decayed monument to American munificence. In this same way, the success of almost every production activity organized by the elites became totally dependent on imported inputs—the very inputs Africa did not have or possess the foreign exchange to pay for. Agriculture, for example, now required chemical fertilizers, tractors, and combine harvesters since "mechanization" was all the rage. Without these inputs, the elites were stuck.

Common sense requires using the resources or inputs Africa has more of: labor and wood. Scientific and capital-intensive techniques are productive and efficient, but in a different environment, where the relative costs of inputs are different and where the infrastructure exists to maintain the machinery. In Africa, the more appropriate technology is *labor-intensive*. It is not only *cheaper* but creates employment as well. But then again in modern Africa, common sense is the scarcest commodity in officialdom.

SUMMARY

Africa's postcolonial development effort may be described as one giant false start. The nationalist leaders, with few exceptions, adopted the *wrong* political systems (sultanism or one-party states); the *wrong* economic system (statism); the *wrong* ideology (socialism); and took the *wrong* path (industrialization via import-substitution). Equally grievous, perhaps, was the low caliber of leadership. Functionally illiterate and given to schizophrenic posturing and sloganeering, the leadership lacked basic understanding of the development process. Preoccupied more by the need to "prove something," they copied blindly. As a result, the development that took place in postcolonial Africa can be described as "development-by-imitation." Such development can scarcely be described as "organic" but rather as an "enclave economy," where nearly all the inputs are imported to manufacture a previously imported commodity. The "enclave" economy has little or no "roots" or "linkages" with the local economy, except for the labor that is extracted.

Development does not mean blind imitation of the attributes or symbols of modernity. Nor does development mean total rejection of Africa's cultural and traditional systems. Development deals with people; in Africa, these people are the peasant majority—the Atingas. The real challenge of development is to take what is there—at the local level, anchored in the traditional system—and *improve* upon it, so as to make it *more efficient, more productive, more hospitable, and more elegant.* Such development is alternatively called "organic development," "participatory development," "grassroots development," or "bottom-up development." Africa remains poor because most of African nationalist leaders and copy-cat elites never met the real challenge of development. As such, the poverty of Africa is not due so much to the "backwardness" of the peasant majority as it is to the intellectual backwardness of the leadership and the elites.

CHAPTER 4

The Cultural Betrayal

The ANC [government of South Africa] wants to transplant customs from other countries here, and that will destroy the Zulu nation and all that we value. We are poor, but do you see any beggars in the streets like you do in the cities? The *inkhosi* (traditional chief) makes sure that we are all provided for. The municipality will make beggars of us. When I have a problem, I can go see the *inkhosi* any time, day or night. I don't need an appointment. They can have their civilization, brother.

—Benjamin Makhanaya
in *The Washington Post,* Dec 18, 2000; p.A1.

This is a vibrant, diverse country. Hardly anyone wants to see it homogenized into a pseudo-Gulf state. We are not Arabs.

—Nima El-Bagir, a Sudanese journalist
in *The Economist,* June 28, 2003; p.48.

"Your "modern" politics [in Africa] is dictated by personal greed, power and suppression of thought. Our forefathers believed in participatory democracy. They saw politics as a way to liberate and build nations . . . The "modern" school [in Africa] taught us to read and write but not where we came from or where we are going to. The schools again teach us how to acquire money but not how wealth is created. We want to bring people's awareness back to their roots . . .
The chief represents the people. Without the people there is no chief. They have one goal. The people make the rules and the laws and both the chief and the people adhere to the same rules . . . We as a people have deserted our traditions in favor of [foreign ones]. We need to go back in time and learn every aspect of our traditions that served our forefathers well.

—Asantefuohene Nana Osei-Bonsu
in *African Monthly,* July, 1995; p.10.

THE IMPOSITION OF ALIEN SYSTEMS ON AFRICA

As noted in the previous chapter, African nationalist leaders believed they could not rely on Africa's "backward" indigenous institutions for the rapid development they envisaged after independence. As such, they searched for some foreign systems to adopt for Africa. But then, they possessed only a perfunctory understanding of these foreign systems. One could not expect African nationalists to be completely conversant with the intricacies and the internal mechanics of the British, French, Russian, or Chinese political systems. Each of these systems had evolved through time and reflected the unique cultural and political experiences of their peoples. In every political constitution there is a cultural imprint. The political events experienced by Africans are decisively different from those of Americans and other people. Obviously, it would be absurd to implant an American or Soviet constitution in an African country and expect it to work.

African nationalist leaders and elites were in a fix; their choices were limited. The adoption of Western systems was generally out of the question, as they symbolized a submission to Western notions of "superiority" and validated decades of colonial exploitation and oppression. Since capitalism was synonymous with colonialism, it too was evil and exploitative.[1] The inevitable choice was socialism, the antithesis of capitalism, as noted in the previous chapter. As the guiding ideology, only socialism could check the evil machinations of neocolonialism, imperialism, and capitalist exploitation, African nationalist leaders argued. Moreover, socialism could be accorded some authenticity by such African concepts as "family pot," "strong sense of community or tribalism," and "sharing." These arguments provided the rationale for the near-universal adoption of one-party socialist state systems under life-presidents in Africa. One convenient argument was that "there was only one African chief and he ruled for life." But these nonsensical arguments for one-party socialist dictatorships could in no way be validated by African tradition. Indigenous African systems were grossly distorted by various African dictators to suit their political purposes. True, African chiefs are chosen to rule for life, but they can be removed.

The One-Party State System

Indigenous African governments were gerontocracies (government by elders). But the elders were not infallible. Nor was respect for the elders a form of servility. Young adult members of the community could participate in the decision-making process by either attending the council meetings or the village assembly. They could express their opinions openly and freely. The chief or councilors did not jail dissidents or those with different viewpoints. Nor did the chief loot the tribal treasury and deposit the booty in Swiss and foreign banks. This native system of government was misunderstood by many foreign observers who were more preoccupied with its "primitive" external manifestations. "Primitive" *tontons* summoned the village assembly, not by a public announcement over the radio or a published notice in a newspaper. There were no administrative clerks to record the proceedings meticulously. The venue was under a tree or at an open market square, not in an enclosed roofed structure.

Granted, the facilities were "primitive." But there was a tradition of reaching a *consensus,* which is the more important observation. There was a *forum* (village assembly) and *freedom of expression* to reach this consensus. There was a *place* (village market square) to meet and the *means* (talking drums) to call such a meeting, however "primitive." And never mind the fact that no administrative clerk recorded the proceedings in writing. The institution was there, before the colonialists set foot on the continent.

More crucial was the existence of the institution, not the outward manifestations or its form. Although elections were not held in precolonial Africa, the African king or chief was chosen; he did not choose himself. Moreover, he could be removed at any time. As Oguah (1984) argued, "If a democratic government is defined, not as one elected by the people but as one which does the will of the people, then the Fanti system of government is democratic."

The Kenya Government concurred. In a Sessional Paper (No.10 of 1963/65), it asserted:

> In African society a person was born politically free and equal and his voice and counsel were heard and respected regardless of the economic wealth he possessed. Even where traditional leaders appeared to have greater wealth and hold disproportionate political influence over their tribal or clan community, there were traditional checks and balances including sanctions against any possible abuse of power. In fact, traditional leaders were regarded as trustees whose influence was circumscribed both in customary law and religion. In the traditional African society, an individual needed only to be a mature member of it to participate fully and equally in political affairs (paragraph 9).

At the Pan-African Congress in Mwanza, Tanzania, in 1958, the delegates shrilly wailed over the fact that: "*The democratic nature of the indigenous institutions of the peoples of West Africa* has been crushed by obnoxious and oppressive laws and regulations, and replaced by autocratic systems of colonial government which are inimical to the wishes of the people of West Africa" (quoted in Langley, 1979; p.740). It demanded that: "The principle of the Four Freedoms (*Freedom of speech, press, association and assembly*) and the Atlantic Charter *be put into practice at once . . . Democracy must prevail throughout Africa from Senegal to Zanzibar and from Cape to Cairo*" (quoted in Langley, 1979; p.741). The Congress stoically resolved to "*work for the establishment and perpetuation of true parliamentary democracy in every territory within the African continent.*" It vowed an "*uncompromising safeguarding of liberty of every citizen* irrespective of his race, colour, religion or national origin." It declared publicly that it was "dedicated to *the precepts and practices of democracy.*" It made it plain that "*The safeguards and protection of citizen's rights and human liberties will be buttressed by:*

a. Uncompromising *adherence to the Rule of Law*
b. Maintenance of the *absolute independence of the Judiciary*
c. *The exercise of the right to vote or stand for any office* and
d. The *constant observance of the declaration of the Universal Human Rights and the United Charter.*

Further, the Congress called "*upon the Government of East and Central Africa to remove all legal restrictions against the freedom of the press and particularly condemns the unjust prosecution and convictions which have taken place in some of these Territories against the African press in particular*" (quoted in Langley, 1979; p.742).

Treacherously, the Pan-Africanists failed to establish these lofty principles and ideals (democracy, the vote, freedom of the press, of assembly, etc.) after independence. In 2004, only 16 out of the 54 African countries had multiparty democracy. The Banjul Charter of Human and People's Rights in 1965 was for show. Freedom of the press, of speech, and of political association was rarely upheld by the nationalist leaders. Nor did they build upon the "democratic nature of the indigenous institutions of the peoples of Africa."

Suddenly after independence, the same African nationalist leaders and elites who railed Western misconception about Africa were singing a different tune. Democracy was now a "colonial invention" and therefore alien to Africa. For example, according to Kwame Nkrumah of Ghana, an insidious dogma propagated by the imperialists was that "Western democracy and parliamentary system are the only valid ways of governing; that they constitute the only worth-while model for the training of an indigenous elite by the colonial power" (Nkrumah, 1968; p.8). Democracy an "imperialist dogma?"

Then the Kenyan government, after independence, suddenly decided that, in African society, a person was no longer born free and equal and his voice and counsel were not to be heard unless he belonged to KANU—the sole legal party. Participation in the political decision-making process, regardless of wealth and political affiliation, was not African after all. Claiming that democracy was alien, many other modern African leaders justified the imposition of autocratic rule on Africa. They declared themselves "presidents-for-life," and their countries to be "one-party states." Military dictators pointed to the warrior tradition in tribal societies to provide a justification for their rule, while other African dictators claimed that the people of Africa did not care who ruled them. Most of these claims, of course, betrayed a rather shameful ignorance of indigenous African heritage.

Professor Eme Awa, the former chairman of Nigeria's National Electoral Commission (1987), vigorously challenged these claims:

> I do not agree that the idea of democracy is alien in Africa because we had democracy of the total type—the type we had in the city-states where everybody came out in the market square and expressed their views, either by raising their hands or something like that. (*West Africa*, Feb. 22, 1988; p.310)

In a similar blistering rebuttal, Ellen Johnson-Sirleaf, the Finance Minister of Liberia in 1985–86, retorted:

> They tell us that democracy is a luxury in Africa; that a multi-party political system is inappropriate to our traditions; that the electoral process is foreign to our heritage and that participatory politics is potentially exploitative of our masses. Such rubbish is repeated in one form or fashion by even some of our renowned continental leaders. But we know and can see clearly through their attempts to halt the development of political institutions merely to perpetuate themselves in power. This social African legacy has led to succession only through the barrel of a gun—a legacy which now threatens us with two political forces—the military and the civilian, the latter with no means to ensure full political choice or expression. Add to this a growing disguised military as a political force in the form of civilianized soldier[s] and we will realize how much behind Africans are falling in this important aspect of *national development*. (*Index On Censorship*, May 1987; p.14).

After independence, African nationalist leaders did not only deny their people political participation but also muzzled them as well. In Africa's so-called "backward and primitive" system, the people could express their views and wishes *freely* without fear of arrest or detention by their chiefs. But after independence and for much of the postcolonial period, this freedom of expression insidiously vanished in much of Africa. Recall that in 2003, only 8 out of 54 African countries had freedom of the press and of expression: Benin, Botswana, Cape Verde Islands, Ghana, Mali, Mauritius, Sao Tome & Principe

and South Africa. Seventeen are partly free and the rest labor under brutal intellectual repression.[2]

Socialism: An Alien Economic Ideology

While it is true that Africans are imbued with a greater sense of community
awareness than most Western cultures, the concept of the individual was not
completely absent. According to a Fanti proverb: "Life is as *you* (the individual) make it." And in the general African phrase: "I am because we are,"
in which the "we" connotes community, the "I" (the individual or person-
hood) was not entirely absent. An analogous situation is supplied by the
phrase: "Man is a social animal." The meaning here is that the human being
desires the company of others and abhors living alone. Accordingly, each
person yearns for some "togetherness" or "a community." But it cannot be
inferred from this disposition that "man is a socialist."

Being a "social animal" (sociable or socialistic) is totally different from
being a socialist. Another distinction should be made: socialism as public
policy and socialism as an economic ideology. Public policy and responsible
government mandate that the state should care about the poor, the handi-
capped, the unemployed, the sick, and the elderly. In that sense, even the
U.S. government is very socialist. However, that should not be confused
with socialism as an ideology, which is rooted in political, economic, and intellectual *control by the state.* The ideology of socialism, as understood and
practiced, entails government ownership of the means of production; government control and direction of economic activity; the operation of state
enterprises to the exclusion of privately owned businesses; price-fixing by the
state and a myriad of state regulations and controls; one-party states and
government ownership of the press. In other words, there is an absence of
private ownership, free markets, political and *intellectual freedom.*

Indigenous African economic systems are *not* characterized by these ab-
sences and therefore cannot be classified as "socialism." Economic, political,
and intellectual repression as well as state *controls,* were *never* part of indigenous African tradition. Nor could traditional African rulers establish a "socialist" (state-controlled) economy if they had wanted to since the logistics
were well beyond their reach. The control mechanisms and measures needed
to control the economy were not yet developed.

Many of Africa's nationalist leaders either misread their own indigenous
African economic systems or were ignorant of them. Nyerere (1962), for example, was right in pointing to the communalism of African peasants. It is
true the people of Africa pooled their resources together (family pot or fund,
working bees, extended family systems, etc.) and helped one another ("com-

munal labor"). But that feature of traditional African society cannot be interpreted as readiness for socialism. One can be socialistic or communalistic without necessarily being a socialist or communist. Many rural folks in America are socialistic in the sense that they care about their neighbors, offer voluntary labor to help neighbors rebuild homes devastated by tornadoes, and watch over neighbors' property (neighborhood crime watch). But they are hardly socialists or communists. Neither are the Amish of Pennsylvania.

Being communalistic or socialistic did not necessarily mean the African peasant was communist or socialist and therefore willing to share his wealth equally with all members of the extended family. Julius Nyerere, ex-president of Tanzania, for example, mistook the peasant's emphasis on kinship and community as readiness for socialism—*ujamaa* (Nyerere, 1962). But even then, the sense of community did not extend beyond one's kinship group. It was this fundamental inability on the part of African nationalist leaders to distinguish between "communalism" and "socialism" that caused many of them to adopt an ideology which they erroneously thought could be justified by African tradition. This resulted in some sort of comedy of errors after independence when they attempted to copy an alien system they did not understand to graft onto an indigenous system they did not understand either. One could well imagine the consequences.

Among Western writers and analysts, there has also been pervasive mythology about indigenous African heritage. One of the most strikingly misleading statement has been the claim of "communal ownership of the means of production." There was/is no such thing as "communal ownership" of cattle or land. Forests, rivers, lakes, and the ocean were for common usage. However, a community could set aside some grazing land for such use. In general, however, land was privately owned—controlled by lineages. In traditional Africa, the person who first settles on unoccupied land becomes the owner. He may pass this land on to his descendants and they can pass it to their descendants. Thus, the land becomes "lineage-owned" or controlled, belonging to the first ancestor, the original settler. Kings and chiefs may hold royal land or "stool land" in trust but it does not belong to them or the state.

The myth of communal ownership of land may have arisen innocently out of confusion or misinterpretation. When a European colonialist asked an African who a plot of land belonged to, the African would have replied: "It belongs to us. We own the land." To the African, the "we" meant his extended family or lineage, but the European might have assigned a much wider interpretation to the "we" to mean the entire village community or the tribe. Hence, "communal ownership of land."

Furthermore, in indigenous Africa, all the means of production were privately owned. The economic factors of production—labor, capital, and the entrepreneur—were owned by the peasants, not their chiefs or the state.[3] Huts, spears, and agricultural implements were all private property. The profit motive was present in most market transactions. Free enterprise and free trade were the rule in indigenous Africa. The natives went about their economic activities on their own initiative and free will. They did not line up at the entrance of the chief's hut to apply for permits before engaging in trade or production. What and how much they produced were their own decisions to make. The African woman who produced *kenkey,* *garri,* or *semolina* herself decided to produce those items. No one forced her to do so. Nor did anyone order the fishermen, artisans, craftsmen, or even hunters what to produce.[4] In modern parlance, those who go about their economic activities on their own free will are called "free enterprisers." By this definition, the *kente* weavers of Ghana, the Yoruba sculptors, the gold and silver blacksmiths, as well as the various indigenous craftsmen, traders, and farmers were free enterprisers. The Masai, Somali, Fulani and other pastoralists who herded cattle over long distances in search of water and pasture to fatten them also were free enterprisers. So were the African traders who traveled great distances to buy and sell commodities— an economic risk-taking venture. They all go about their economic activities on their own initiative, not at the behest of their traditional rulers—the chiefs. For centuries, they have been selling their produce and wares in open, free, village markets. African chiefs do not harass them, impose ridiculous price controls on them, or even fix wages and jail violators; Africans bargain over prices. Nor do these chiefs monopolize the tribal economy, or operate "tribal government enterprises," the equivalent of state enterprises.

Indigenous African markets have always been hospitable to foreigners. Nigerian traders are welcome, and can indeed be found, in virtually every West African market. The local chiefs do not expel them. Arab and Hausa long-distance traders have for centuries traded freely in African markets. So too did the Europeans, until they rolled out their guns and abused African hospitality. Free trade and private enterprise were the rules in indigenous Africa.

There were classes in indigenous African society: the royal family, commoners, strangers, and slaves. But these distinctions carried no economic significance. Anyone, even slaves, could own property and rise to high social status. The Jaja of Bonny in Nigeria, for example, rose from being a slave to being king.

There were inequities in the distribution of income in traditional African societies. There were rich merchants, traders, and poor peasants. Inequalities of wealth were very much a feature of indigenous Africa. For example,

"Among the Igbo (of Nigeria) inequality was recognized in age, status, wealth, religion, birth and descent. Royalty was in name and not in fact, as the Igbo recognized achievement rather than hereditary-bestowed greatness" (Olaniyan, 1985; p.24).

African beliefs in inequalities of wealth were expressed in many proverbs. According to the Masai (Kenya) proverb, " *Merisio ilkibunyeta le tunyanak*" ("the fingers of people are not all the same length"). The Fantis of southern Ghana, known for their proverbs, had this one: "All mushrooms grow in the same place but some are eaten and others are not." The Fanti also had the proverbs, "the wealthy man is senior" and "a good name cannot be eaten but it is money that counts."

Most people tend to conceive of wealth as money, oversized bank accounts, fancy mansions and so on. But in traditional African society, there was wealth of a different type. The Masai in Kenya and the Zulus of South Africa counted their wealth in cattle. Among the Gikuyu, "cows give the owner a prestige in the community. The owner of a large number of cattle was sentimentally satisfied by praise names conferred upon him by the community in their songs and dances" (Kenyatta, 1938; p.62). "All the Tsimihety of Madagascar aspire to keep large numbers of cattle" (Wilson, 1967; p.253). The Somali for wealth is *hoolo*, which means primarily wealth in livestock. Camels were the most prized possession. To the Sonjo of Kenya, goats and beehives constituted wealth. Certainly, since not all Africans had the same heads of cattle or goats; there was unequal distribution of wealth in the form of cattle.

Africans accumulate wealth just as westerners do. The pursuit of wealth was a cultural occupation! Prestige, status, honor, and influence were all attached to wealth in indigenous systems. The wealthy were important people with influence in governmental affairs. Hammer notes "Sidamo men (of Ethiopia) aspire to positions of wealth" (1970; p.339). In Kuba society of Zaire, "wealth is a powerful means of acquiring prestige, and prestige is the basic value of society. Wealth is displayed in order to give prestige; it has to be shown in rich clothing, furniture and hospitality" (Vansina, 1962; p.326). Among the Igbo, "the attainment of wealth meant the attainment of prestige and influence, through respect, clientage, assumption of titles, and achievement of political influence" (Carlston, 1968; p.191). Among the Hausa, "customary exchange of gifts marks wealth and its pursuit as legitimate at the same time that it demonstrates status and affirms prestige. The generosity of wealthy men evokes admiration for wealth and emulation in its pursuit. It also leads the Hausa to set high value on the freedom to pursue wealth limits set by Islam on the one hand and by customary norms on the other" (Smith, 1962).

There was no indigenous Africa law that forbade individuals from accumulating wealth or acquiring valuable possessions. And there was no law that mandated that wealth, individually acquired, must be shared equally with all kinsmen. There were, however, two important caveats that were operative in many ethnic societies. The first was that the pursuit of wealth should be within certain boundaries defined by religion, Islam, for example, and social norms. It would be wrong, for instance, for an individual to pursue prosperity at the expense or injury of his kinsmen. In other words, a tribesmen should not exploit a fellow tribesman for his own advancement. Such exploitation in most indigenous African systems was a taboo.

Centralized government control and direction of economic activity were the exceptions, rather than the rule, in traditional Africa. In fact, state intervention in the economy was not the general policy, except in the kingdoms of Dahomey and Asante. Even in commerce, African states lacked state controls and ownership. In Gold Coast, for example, gold-mining was open to all subjects of the states of Adanse, Assin, Denkyira, and Mampong. Some chiefs taxed mining operations at the rate of one-fifth of the annual output. In some states, all gold mined on certain days was ceded to the throne. But the mines were in general not owned and operated by the chiefs. Rather, chiefs granted mining concessions.

Precolonial Africa was characterized by great freedom of movement of people and of trade. A dense web of trade routes criss-crossed the continent, along which the natives moved freely and engaged in trade. Africans have long had an ingrained cultural propensity to trade. Throughout their history, they have been known to travel great distances to purchase goods from strangers at cheaper prices to sell at higher prices to make a profit. Much of this activity was free from state controls and regulations. State intervention in trade, commerce, and markets by Africa's traditional rulers was also the exception rather than the rule. There was no native African law which forbade Africans from entering into businesses if they wished. By nature and tradition, Africans have always been free enterprisers. Markets were the nerve-centers of traditional African societies.

Worse, true socialism was never practiced by African nationalist leaders. The socialist state, with its coercive powers, became an instrument of oppression and exploitation. Those who expressed views different from the party line saw lives abruptly disrupted and themselves hauled into jail. Under African "socialism," the same socialist party hacks and functionaries were now the bourgeoisie riding about in Mercedes Benzes. Thus the "socialism" practiced in Africa was a peculiar brand of "Swiss-bank" socialism that allowed the head of state and a phalanx of kleptocrats to rape and plunder their state treasuries to deposit funds in Swiss and foreign banks. Under "Mobutuism," the president of Zaire presided over a heinous kleptocracy with a personal fortune that exceeded $8 billion in Swiss bank accounts—a fortune that incidentally was greater than Zaire's entire foreign debt of $6 billion.

While preaching socialism, Nkrumah himself was stashing millions of dollars abroad. Nye (1967) put his fortune at $30 million, and the Ghana Government Commission of Enquiry placed it at £12,322,009 (The Apaloo Report, 1967). Nobody came closer to the African definition of socialism than Krobo Edusei, an ex-Minister in the Nkrumah government, when he said: "Socialism doesn't mean if you have made a lot of money you can't keep it" (Fitch and Oppenheimer, 1966; p.23). This was the same minister who attempted to import a $3 million gold bed into Ghana in 1964. Back in 1962, a member of Ghana's National Assembly, B. E. Kusi, excoriated these so-called "socialists":

> Many children go about in the streets because they cannot get accomodation in secondary schools, while those Ministers who are in charge of the money send their children to international schools and to University. Most of them ride in Mercedes Benz (220s) and yet call themselves socialists. This is very bad. If we want to build a socialist country, then we must let the President know that we are serious about the use of public funds and that we do not pay mere lip service to socialism (LeVine, 1975; p.12).

Asked what he understood by socialism, one of Robert Mugabe's ministers replied: "In Zimbabwe, socialism means what's mine is mine but what's yours we share!" (Dostert, 1987; p.43). Edgar Tekere, an outspoken critic of Mugabe's government, lambasted poignantly:

> We all came from Mozambique with nothing; not even a teaspoon. But today, in less than two years, you hear that so-and-so owns so many farms, a chain of hotels and his father owns a fleet of buses. Where did all that money come from in such a short period? Isn't it from the very public funds they are entrusted to administer? (*New African*, March 1989; p.21)

When African socialist elites chanted "food for the masses" they meant "food for the elites." More equitable distribution of income, of course, also meant more for the elites. Using their governing authority, the elites extracted wealth from the productive peasants and spent it in prestigious projects, status symbols, and luxurious living (Mercedes Benzes, BMWs, grand public buildings, and airports) in imitation of the higher standard of the richer metropolitan countries in the West. In 1980, Ghana police were riding about in BMWs, insisting that they needed a fleet of faster cars to catch robbers. The peasants were not amused. In East Africa, they coined an apt Swahili term for them: the *wabenzi*—men of Mercedes Benz.

In Ghana, an avowed Marxist revolutionary, Fte./Lte. Jerry Rawlings, cruised about in a sprightly Jaguar. Rawlings drew much inspiration from Col. Muammar Ghaddafi of Libya's "Green Book," which laid out Ghaddafi's official ideology—an idealized blend of socialism and Islamic fundamentals. According to the Green Book, "wage workers are a type of slave" and the "final solution to economic ills is the abolition of profit" (qtd. in *The Washington Post,* Jan 3, 2004; p.A14). Recall that "profit" was never an alien word in Africa. Under Ghaddafi, private enterprise was essentially banned. Said Libya's prime minister, Shokri Ghanem, "The policies of full socialism led to imprudent management and corruption" (*The Washington Post,* Jan 3, 2004; p.A14). Julius Nyerere was perhaps the only true practicing socialist, but his Chama Chamapinduzi (CCM) party was hopelessly riddled with corruption.

Much of the indigenous economic system still exists today, where African governments have not destroyed it through benighted implantation of alien ideologies and systems. Women traders still can be found at most markets in Africa. They still trade their wares for profit. And in virtually all traditional African markets today, bargaining over prices is still the norm—an ancient tradition. Traditional African chiefs do not fix prices. And it is this indigenous economy system, characterized by free village markets, free trade, and free enterprise that Africa must turn to for its economic rejuvenation.

To conclude, in postcolonial Africa, socialism was the wrong ideology at the wrong place and the wrong time, practiced by the wrong leaders for the wrong people.

Religious Imperialism

In the postcolonial period, the clash between Christianity and Islam has been pushed beyond the absurd into lunacy because neither Islam nor Christianity is indigenous to Africa. Islam was originally introduced to Africa by Arab traders, conquerors, and slave raiders, and Christianity by European traders, conquerors, and slave raiders. Strictly from the black African historical perspective, the Arabs were no different from the Europeans. Both groups were invaders, colonizers, and slavers, who used their religions—Christianity and Islam—to convert, oppress, exploit, and enslave blacks. Jomo Kenyatta, the first president of Kenya, once said that: "When the Christian missionaries came to Africa, we had the land and they had the Bible. They taught us how to close our eyes and pray. When we opened them, they had the land and we had the Bible" (cited by Lamb, 1985; p.58).

While the Europeans organized the West African slave trade, the Arabs managed the East African and trans-Saharan counterparts. Over 20 million black slaves were shipped from East Africa to Arabia. Enslaving and slave trading in East Africa were peculiarly savage in a traffic notable for its barbarity. Villages were razed, the unfit villagers massacred. The enslaved were yoked together, several hundred in a caravan, on their long journey to the coast. It is estimated that only one in five of those captured in the interior reached Zanzibar. Some historians believe the slave trade was more catastrophic in East Africa than in West Africa. Diseases such as smallpox and cholera, introduced by marauding Arab caravans penetrating the interior in search of slaves, decimated entire local populations and were far more devastating than the actual export of slaves to Indian Ocean markets.

For the trans-Saharan slave trade, an estimated 9 million captives were shipped to slave markets in Fez, Marrakesh (Morocco); Constantine (Algeria); Tunis (Tunisia), Fezzan, Tripoli (Libya); and Cairo (Egypt). The official Libyan and Arab line on slavery is that: "The Arab countries are a natural extension to the African continent. The African Arabs, or those who carried the indulgent message of Islam, were the first to effectively oppose slavery as inhumane and unnatural. The claim that Arabs were involved in the trade at all is a mischievous invention of the West, made in order to divide the Arabs from their brothers and sisters who live in the African continent" (*New Africa*, Nov 1984; p.12). Black Africans know better. If the Europeans had not colonized Africa, the Arabs would have. And the Arabs never forgave the West for beating them to the punch.

During the black struggle for civil rights in the United States and independence in Africa in the 1950s and 1960s, Afro-Arab differences and ill-feelings were buried. Black leaders, seduced by the fallacious premise that "the enemy of my enemy must be my friend," made common cause with the Arabs. In the United States, many blacks dropped their "European" or "slave" names and adopted Islamic ones. In Africa, black leaders entered into alliances and sought support from Arab states for the liberation struggle against Western colonialism. Grand Afro-Arab solidarity accords were pompously announced. Drooling, grandiloquent speeches announced meretricious Afro-Arab summits. Little came out of them, and since independence, black Africans have gradually realized that the Arabs regard them as "expendable." The Arabs are just as ready as the French to use them as pawns to achieve their chimerical geopolitical schemes and global religious imperialism/domination.

The first crack in the Afro-Arab solidarity facade came with the 1973 oil embargo, which sent many African economies careening into the doldrums and debt. Arab oil-producing states raked in billions of dollars in profits. Black African leaders looked expectantly to the Arab world for economic assistance but little came, as was also the case with subsequent oil price shocks in the early 1980s.

In 1979, a terrorist bombing of the Norfolk Hotel in Nairobi further rattled Afro-Arab amity. The bombing was in retaliation against Kenya for permitting Israeli commandos to use its airspace in a dramatic rescue of Israeli hostages in Entebbe, Uganda. Not a single Arab country condemned the bombing in Nairobi. The implicit message was particularly arrogant and maddening: that black Africa had no right to pursue an independent foreign policy and must kowtow slavishly to the Arab world.

Prior to the bombing, anti-Arab feelings had long been simmering among black Africans. Crass attempts to impose Arabic names and Islamic law have stuck in Africans' craws. According to the Amazigh (Berber) Cultural Association in America, a Moroccan law, enacted in November 1996 and referred to as Dahir No. 1.96.97, "imposes Arabic names on an entire citizenry more than half of which is not Arabic." The Berbers in Algeria, too, are up in arms. Fed up with years of discrimination and persecution at the hands of the Arab majority, Berbers, who make up 20 percent of Algeria's 32 million people, seek more autonomy in the eastern region of Kabylie. They were the original inhabitants of North Africa when invading Arabs introduced Islam in the seventh century. Old tensions erupted into violence after a Berber schoolboy died in police custody in April 2001. There were street clashes in Kabylie between the police and Berber militants, and more than 100 protesters were killed. "The Berbers also want the government's police force, which they accuse of being partisan, to withdraw from Kabylie, and they want their language, Tamazight, to be recognized as an official language" (*The New York Times,* June 30, 2003; p.A4).

The continued enslavement of black Africans in this day and age by Arabs in Sudan and Mauritania has been a constant source of outrage. Though slavery of blacks was officially abolished in Mauritania and Sudan in 1980 and 1987 respectively, heinous practices and mistreatment of blacks continue. In 1988, for example, a group of black political prisoners in Mauritania, including Tene Youssouf Gueye, Lt. Abdoul Ghoudouss Ba, Ibrahim Sarr, Amadou Moctar Sow, and Ly Mamadou Bocar were beaten and tortured to death in prison. Their deaths brought this angry reaction from Kwaku O. Sarpong:

> Abuse of black people by Arabs, especially Syrians and Lebanese, has been ignored for too long. The painful fact is that this abuse occurs under our noses in African towns and cities where they have come to enjoy our hospitality. It

is high time Arabs were made officially aware of this and reminded of the black solidarity they have enjoyed for years in their conflict with Israel.

In the late 1970s, it was an open secret in New York that Arab diplomats never invited their black counterparts to their receptions. (*West Africa,* March 7, 1988; p.27)

The Mauritanian government of Maaouya Ould Sid Ahmed Taya claimed to have outlawed slavery at least five times since the early 1980s:

> The government continues to insist that there is no more slavery in Mauritania. But treatment of *harantines* is still a highly controversial issue.
>
> As if to demonstrate its expressed commitment to right past wrongs, the Taya government this week named Sghair Ould M'Barek, a 49-year-old lawyer from a family of *haratines*, as its new prime minister.
>
> There was no official explanation, but some saw the selection as a bid to secure *haratine* loyalties with elections scheduled for November 2003. The new prime minister is known for his Arab nationalist sympathies. (*The Washington Times,* July 10, 2003; p.A15)

Taya seized power as a colonel in a military coup in 1984. Since 1991, he has run a "crocodile" multiparty democratic system where his ruling Democratic and Social Republican Party retains complete control. In 1992 and 1997, he shed his military uniform, donned civilian clothes, and ran and won fraudulent elections that were boycotted by the five-party Opposition Front. The 1997 election gave Mr. Taya's party 54 of 56 seats in the Senate and 64 of 81 seats in the National Assembly.

In Sudan, Arab militias, formed and armed by the Islamic government of Lt. Gen. Omar Bashir, traffic in slaves: People, mostly women and children from the southern Dinka tribe, are seized in raids and either kept by the militias or sold north. On March 22, 1995, the black Catholic bishop of south Sudan, Macram Max Gassis, testified before a U.S. Congressional Committee that black people are bought and sold in Sudan, "some for as little as $15 and some in slave markets (at Shendi)" (*The Washington Times,* April 27, 1995; p.A18).

It is reputed that even Lt.-Gen Omar Bashir himself has Dinka and Nuer slaves (*New African,* July 1990; p.9). "The allegations against me are all lies," he claimed, though he "acknowledges that he has four 'students' living in his house. One of them, a young black boy from the Nuweir tribe, escaped this year (1995)" (*The Washington Times,* April 27, 1995; p.A18). On March 8, 1995, the UN Human Rights Commission summoned the courage to issue the fiercest censure resolution it has ever adopted. It condemned Sudan "for abuses including torture, summary executions and slavery" (*The Washington*

Times, March 11, 1995; p.A8). Finally bowing to international pressure, the government of Bashir began to tackle the problem of slavery. "In April, 2000, 65 women and children were released from remote farms in western Sudan and flown to the army base of Aweil in Bahr al-Ghazal province. They were to return to their villages on foot" (*The Washington Times,* June 1, 2000; p.A12).

The Bashir regime was unrelenting in its brutal treatment of blacks and non-Muslims. In February 1992 the government drove 400,000 squatters—mostly black refugees fleeing the war in the south—out of Khartoum at gunpoint and into the desert, where temperatures can reach 120 to 135 degrees. At least a dozen squatters who resisted eviction were shot. "The scale of the callousness is hard to imagine. That the government wasted no time bulldozing the homes is matched in ruthlessness only by the official decision to send the displaced to campsites where water, food, sanitation, health facilities and adequate shelter are wholly insufficient or don't exist at all," wrote *The Washington Post* in an editorial (March 14, 1992; p.A12).

Bashir's brutal treatment of non-Muslims was also evident in his use of food as a weapon. During the famine in 1990, the Muslim north deliberately blocked supplies to the south, where previous famines have hit hardest: According to the U.S. State Department, "Trains and barges have been held up, surplus food stocks exported overseas and the Sudanese Air Force has even bombed relief sites" (*The Washington Post,* Oct 6, 1990; p.A22). In addition, in 1990 the Bashir regime exported 300,000 tons of sorghum, a staple food, to Libya and Iraq for the purchase of arms to use against rebels in the south. Nevertheless, in September 1990 Bashir attended the United Nations Summit for Children in New York and won applause when he claimed that his government's priority was children. As he spoke, his war planes were bombing civilian targets in southern Sudan and killing hungry black children. According to Robert Hadley, information officer for the UN Operation Lifeline Sudan, Khartoum has relentlessly bombed civilian population centers in the south, usually with old Soviet-made cargo planes flying at 12,000 feet or higher over rebel-held areas and dropping 500-pound bombs. Congressman Frank R. Wolf (R-VA), who visited the village of Kajo Kaji near the Ugandan border, which had been the target of recent bombings, said he saw 10 bomb craters in the village and old people and women suffering from shrapnel wounds (*The Washington Post,* Feb 12, 1993; p.A33).

Back in June 1989, the military regime of Lt. Gen. Bashir of Sudan, who overthrew Sadiq al-Mahdi's elected civilian government, vowed to re-impose the *sharia.* Under this law theft is punishable by amputation of the right hand or, if there are more than three people or weapons involved, cross amputation: right hand, left foot. Defamation and alcohol consumption are punishable by flogging, as is adultery or, if both of the partners are married, by stoning to death. Apostasy, defined as the renunciation of Islam, is punishable by public execution with the body left on public display.

"My junta will destroy anyone who stands in the way and amputate [the limbs of] those who betray the nation," said Bashir. Indeed, a prosperous merchant was hanged, despite diplomatic protests, for illegal possession of a small amount of foreign currency, and others were executed for foreign currency offenses. Amnesty International reported widespread torture and killings of civilians (www.ai.com).

Hassan al-Turabi, the chief fiery Islamist ideologue, was the mastermind behind these diabolical schemes. In 1999, after falling out with President Bashir, he was ousted and jailed. Subsequently placed under house arrest, his wife, Weza al-Mahdi, became conciliatory: "Islam is a free religion. People should be free to choose" (*Economist,* June 28, 2003; p.50). Must one to two million Sudanese die needlessly before the authorities recognize that they have the right to choose their religion? Maybe more African officials need to be placed under house arrest for them to come to their senses. But this is hoping against hope.

Just when a peace accord was signed to end Sudan's deadly 20-year conflict in the south in November 2003, another humanitarian crisis flared up in the Darfur region in the western part of Sudan. Government-sponsored Arab militia, known as *janjaweed,* launched a massive, indiscriminate pogrom against blacks in the region. By July 7, 2004, "the violence ha[d] killed up to 30,000 people, displaced 1.2 million and forced more than 120,000 into refugee camps in neighboring Chad. The United Nations has accused Sudan's government of encouraging the attacks by Arab militias against black Muslims in what officials call a campaign of ethnic cleansing" (*The New York Times,* July 8, 2004; p.A4). UN Secretary General Kofi Annan said "villagers he had talked to in the camps told of attacks from government planes, helicopter gunships and 'horrendous cleanup attacks' by *janjaweed* militia involving 'killing, plundering, burning, and widespread rape'" (*The New York Times,* July 8, 2004; p.A4).

This kind of leadership is an outrageous disgrace to Africa. More disgraceful was the silence of the African Union and black American leadership, especially the U.S. Congressional Black Caucus. This is yet another example of the "intellectual astigmatism" that afflicts black African leadership, which was discussed in the previous chapter: The remarkable ability to see with eagle-eyed clarity the injustices perpetrated against blacks by whites but hopelessly blind to the same atrocities committed by black African governments against their own black citizens.

Aloysius Juryit of Nigeria was bitter: "Events in the Sudan and Mauritania (to mention only a few) have shown that the worst racists are Arabs, especially when it comes to dealing with blacks" (*New African,* March 1990; p.6).

In August 1998, Islamic terrorists bombed U.S. embassies in Kenya and Tanzania, claiming more than 240 African lives. Not a single Arab country condemned these attacks. Then, on August 26, 1998, terrorists blew up the Planet World restaurant in Cape Town, South Africa, killing one person and injuring 27. A group calling itself "Moslems Against Global Oppression" claimed responsibility and said that the bombing was in retaliation for the U.S. strikes in Sudan and Afghanistan. Africa, ravaged by grinding poverty, famine, AIDS, and a never-ending cycle of war, faced a new threat—religious imperialism.

In November 2002, Islamic terrorists struck again with an attack on the Paradise Hotel in Mombasa, killing at least 30 people. It hit Kenya's tourism industry hard. Industry officials estimated that, 10 months later, 15,000 tourism jobs had been lost in the coastal region, a disaster for perhaps 150,000 or more people dependent on those wages. "The attacks scared off tourists for months, hitting a sector still recovering from the 1998 US embassy bombing in Nairobi that killed more than 200 people, mostly Kenyans. Hotel occupancy, normally about 40 to 45 percent at this time of the year, has slumped to an average of about 20 to 30 per cent in the shoreline tourist hotels, hotel officials say" (*East African Standard,* Aug 26–Sept 1, 2003).

If the Islamic terrorists thought they could count on black Africans for sympathy while using them as cannon fodder for their cause, they terribly miscalculated. They only succeeded in shattering the crucible of Afro-Arab solidarity and purchasing an excess supply of black African wrath in the bargain. The twin bombings in East Africa blew the lid off anti-Arab rage. Said an irate Nigerian medical doctor, Segun Tonyin Dawodu: "Why on an African soil? Damn the stupid imbeciles. The OAU and other African Organizations should condemn this unprovoked atrocities against black people. All Arabs . . . should immediately be rebuked without mincing words and there should be a blanket ban on issuance of visa for entry into any African country by these bigots" (naijanet@esosoft.com, August 8, 1998).

Particularly vexing was the callous rape of African hospitality by Arabs and Islamic terrorists. In the twin-bombing of the U.S. embassies, one of the suspects—a Palestinian (Mohammed Saddiq Odeh)—moved to Mombasa in 1994 to set up a fishing business. He married a Kenyan woman, Nassim, but readily abandoned her, despite her pregnancy, and fled to Pakistan after the dastardly deed. Some payback for African support of the Palestinian cause.

Discrediting Islam

Many would agree that Islam is a fine religion but its cause is being increasingly hijacked and debauched by zealots. After the September 11, 2001 tragedy, Muslim fanatics, carrying posters of Osama bin Laden, held demonstrations in Kano, Nigeria, to protest U.S.-led bombings in Afghanistan. Nigeria is almost evenly split between northern Muslims (50 percent of the population) and southerners who practice Christianity (40 percent), with some traditional African religions. Religious and ethnic clashes have been a staple of Nigerian life and to avert religious conflict, Nigeria wisely adopted a secular constitution on May 4, 1999. Chapter I, part II, section 10 states: "The Government of the Federation or of a State shall not adopt any religion as State Religion." The adoption of the *sharia* by any state is clearly unconstitutional, except in domestic matters. But several northern states, in defiance of the Constitution, went ahead and adopted the *sharia* as their state religion anyway. Zamfara first adopted the *sharia* on October 26, 2002, barely five months after President Obasanjo assumed office. It rapidly spread to 12 of Nigeria's 36 states.

The adoption of the sharia has accentuated religious strife and communal violence which has claimed more than 10,000 lives since President Olusegun Obasanjo took office in May 1999. Christians, Muslims, and others have been hacked to death with knives and swords, in conflicts precipitated by the new laws. Churches and mosques have been destroyed in Kano. Commenting on the rise of Muslim *sharia* law in parts of Nigeria, Professor Chinua Achebe lamented: "I am now not optimistic of the benefits that will come to Nigeria because of democracy. We have dug ourselves into *sharia;* into a situation where we have become a laughing stock of the world, because we are discussing things like stoning women to death in the 21st century" (*BBC World News Service,* Nov 22, 2002). Dismayed by what he termed "the tragedy of Nigeria," Achebe reflected on the divisions apparent in modern Nigeria: "Religious differences have not just been introduced. Muslims and others have always been there, but somehow they didn't wipe each other out. What is happening today is that some people are using these differences to promote their ambition and this is an abuse of politics. That's why the selfishness of the elite stands out so clearly" (BBC World News Service, Nov 22, 2002).

Hizbah (religious enforcers) vigilantes mete out harsh, on-the-spot, extralegal punishments for such "un-Islamic" activities as violating dress codes and questioning Islamic teachings. Women caught riding alone in taxis are subject to physical abuse by the Hizbah. In May 2001, an Islamic court in Katsina state ordered the removal of the left eye of Ahmed Tijjani, who was found guilty of partially blinding a friend during an argument. Two months later in Birnin-Kebbi, a *sharia* court ordered 15-year-old Abubakar Aliyu's hand amputated for stealing the equivalent of $300. In October 2001, 35-year old Safiya Hussaini was condemned to death by stoning for allegedly committing adultery. International outcry helped save her but on March 23, 2002, a second woman, 30-year-old Amina Lawal, was sentenced to death by stoning by a regional court in Katsina state for having a child outside marriage. Rioting by Muslim youth and clashes with Christians, which claimed more than 200 lives, led to the cancellation of the World's Beauty Pageant in November.

Governors of northern Nigerian states fanned the embers of religious fanaticism with irresponsible and incendiary pronouncements. The Zamfara state governor, Ahmed Sani, claimed on October 3, 2001, that some northern state governors had contributed the staggering amount of 100 million *naira* ($1 million) to buy arms for the purpose of fighting for their faith because there were no longer army generals of northern extraction who were also Muslims that would protect the north. In May 2001, the deputy governor of Kano State, Alhaji Mar Ganduje, led a horde of *sharia* enforcers on a raid on top-class hotels and recreational centers where alcoholic drinks were allegedly being sold in contravention of the *sharia* code. They descended on Kano Club, Daula Hotel, Central Hotel, Magwan Water Restaurant, Hotel Tropicana, among others, smashing windows and bottles and wreaking wanton destruction. The Hotel, also in Kano, was doused with gasoline and set ablaze. And the Justice Niki Tobi Judicial Commission, investigating the causes of the September 2001 ethnoreligious riot that engulfed Jos and Bukuru, was told that the arms and ammunition said to have been used by Muslims during the riot were supplied by Bauchi state governor Alhaji Adamu Muazu and the most recent former Plateau state commissioner of police, Alhaji Mohammed Abubakar.

The rise in religious fundamentalism across Nigerian society can be understood as a response to soaring unemployment, increasing poverty, social decay, destitution, and rising levels of violent crime. But religious bigotry and intolerance could plunge Nigeria into another civil war, which could destabilize the entire West Africa region. Ivory Coast was ripped apart by civil war between the Muslim northerners and Christian southerners in 2001. More important, Muslim militants are misguided in their belief that strict adherence to the Islamic code will cure Nigeria's ills.

The problems they lament are often created by corrupt and incompetent governments with misaligned priorities. In a region where clean water is scarce, Kano state in September 2000 approved 86.5 million naira (about $860,000) for the construction and renovation of *sharia* courts, and the importation of amputation machines for the enforcement of the *sharia*. In November 2001, more than 700 people died in northern Nigeria in a outbreak of cholera, which is often the result of poor sanitation or contaminated water. The most affected area was the state of Kano, but the neighboring states of Katsina and Jigawa were also affected. Records in the infectious diseases hospital in Kano clearly show that at least 250 people have died as a result of the cholera outbreak (*BBC* World Service, Nov 13, 2001). After weeks of denying the seriousness of the outbreak, the Kano State government conceded it was facing a crisis: "The epidemic has been worse than we expected," said state Health Commissioner Mansur Kabir (*The Washington Times,* Nov 29, 2001; p.A17).

The Kano state government was caught off guard because it had been more preoccupied with the brutal enforcement of the *sharia,* in violation of section 10 of Nigeria's own 1999 federal constitution. The ensuing religious strife and clashes claimed more than 2,000 Nigerian lives between 1999 and 2001.

In some states, the *sharia* was blatantly exploited for political gain and capriciously enforced. Political campaigns mixed candidate posters with praises for *sharia* law, from which the rich and powerful are exempt. In August 2001, when Mohammed Sani, a tailor in Zamfara state, asked why government officials were allowed to keep their satellite dishes and VCRs when the two cinemas in town were closed, *sharia* police promptly arrested and jailed him for four months. "Islam does not permit someone to criticize the government," explained Abdul Kadir Jelani, the paramount Islamic leader and an adviser to the governor.

On October 12, 2001, a group of angry Muslims, carrying posters of Osama bin Laden and anti-American banners, embarked on a peaceful march in Kano to protest U.S.-led bombings in Afghanistan. The group attacked a small group of Christians (*The Washington Post,* Oct 15, 2001; p.A9). Clashes spread across the city. Crowds began to loot and burn buildings. By the time the violence was quelled, as many as 200 lay dead. Never mind that neither Islam nor Christianity is indigenous to Africa. Said President Olusegun Obasanjo in Paris:

> What is happening in northern Nigeria is that some people do not understand, and they need to be made to understand, that pursuit of those who have committed terrorism is different from fighting Islam. Some people mix the two, and anyone who supports terrorism in Nigeria or any other place in the world must need to see a psychiatrist. (*The Washington Times,* Nov 1, 2001; p.A18)

Why should Africans kill themselves over foreign religions? Maybe it is Nigeria's political leaders who need to see witch doctors. They sat on their hands while the violence was spilling out of control. In a terse statement titled, "Stop the Madness," the Catholic secretariat berated Nigeria's political leaders: "While the nation burns and the people die in their thousands, our leaders at all levels have generally displayed a shocking sense of insensitivity. They are busy bickering over political fortunes and investing in re-election" (*New African,* Dec 2001; p.22).

The threat of Islamic fundamentalism is spreading across West Africa. Many fundamentalist Muslim movements from Mali, Nigeria, Niger, Chad, and Senegal do share the goal of returning to strict Islamic law or *sharia* and eradicating the secular state. "Our problems are not ideological or religious, they are economic," said Aminata Traore, a Malian sociologist. "People want schools, they want medical attention for their children, but who is listening to them? Islamists, who provide them with water and fertilizer, believe the solutions are found in religion. And many see violence as the only resort—and why not, if there is no solution on Earth for them?" (*The Washington Post,* Sept 30, 2001; p.A24). But if each aggrieved party has to resort to violence to seek redress, how much of Africa would be left?

Rather sadly, fanatical Muslim zealots pick on the vulnerable, the powerless, and the poor—mostly women. A married Muslim woman who commits adultery can be sentenced to death by stoning but married men who commit the same offense go scot-free. A person's hand can be amputated for stealing, but not the hands of those who steal public money. Nigeria ought to have been the giant of Africa but kamikaze bandits—mostly Muslim (Babangida, Buhari, Abacha, Abubakr, etc.)—plundered the country clean. Worse, General Sani Abacha was alleged to have died in 1998 from a Viagra-induced sex orgy with Pakistani prostitutes. In Sokoto, grey-haired men are often married to under-age girls. In Kano male prostitutes are common, and in Kaduna, both male and female prostitution exist. Hadiza Mamane, the madam of Sokoto bar, complained bitterly: "When they install *sharia* in Nigeria, the rich know how to get around it. They do all sorts of things in hotels or in their big houses, at the same time that poor people like us are chased away. Hypocrites, they're all hypocrites" (*The New York Times,* Feb 2, 2001; p.A3).

Even the Muslims themselves became disillusioned about the *sharia.* Said Professor Abubakar Saddiq, of the Center for Democratic Development in Zaria:

> People have noticed that some of the governors who have adopted *sharia* have no real interest in social justice. Rather, they want to harness religion to win or hold on to power, with all its perks. Not long after the first thieves had their hands cut off, people started to grumble that the big-time crooks in high places were going unpunished. (*The Economist,* June 28, 2003; p.50)

Indeed, in the West African region, the division between Muslims and Christians has dangerously been widened and exploited by power-hungry politicians—especially in Nigeria and Ivory Coast. What is more, the religious problems spill over to neighboring countries, risking the further destabilization of an already fragile region.

The imposition of alien ideologies, religions, and systems by African leaders is tearing the continent apart. Islamic imperialism is a no-win proposition in Africa, as it will inevitably provoke a backlash, with destructive consequences. If Muslims are allowed to establish an Islamic state, should the same privilege be extended to Christians? If not, why not?

When Zamfara state imposed the *sharia,* the House of Assembly of the southern state of Cross River threatened to declare itself a "Christian state" if Obasanjo failed to respond. It also passed a resolution enjoining the federal government to forbid the use of oil resources of the Delta states to implement the *sharia.* In fact, Nigeria's northern Islamic states are already paying a hefty price: gas (petrol) shortages. "Gas stations stand empty or with mile-long queues: in the north, on a recent 300-mile drive along the highway from the northern border down to the capital, Abuja, there was not a drop of fuel in any station. Instead, countless young men, sometimes boys as young as 10, sold fuel in jerrycans—at triple or four times the official rate of 19 cents a liter" (*The New York Times,* Feb 2, 2001; p.A3).

It would be grotesquely unfair, however, to portray Muslims as "villains" in Africa since they, too, have suffered persecution and discrimination. Because Zambia is 70 percent Christian, former President Frederick Chiluba contemplated declaring Zambia a "Christian" nation; Christian churches opposed the move, saying it would be divisive. In Ivory Coast, former President Henri Konan Bedie launched a xenophobic campaign of *"Ivoirité"* (Ivorian-ness), ostensibly to check against the influx of foreigners but in reality to target mainly Muslims from the north. In Chad, French-educated Christian southerners who governed the country in the 1960s discriminated against northern Arabs and Muslims. The Muslims rebelled and civil war ensued. In Ethiopia, Muslims have long been persecuted, under both Emperor Haile Selassie and Comrade Mengistu Haile Mariam. In Uganda, rebels of the Lord's Resistance Army (LRA) want Uganda to be ruled by the Bible's Ten Commandments. The LRA, led by Joseph Kony, operates in the north from bases in southern Sudan. The LRA kill, torture, maim, rape, and abduct large numbers of civilians, virtually enslaving numerous children. More than 6,000 children were abducted during 1998, although many of those abducted later escaped or were released.

And it must be said that Muslims did play a positive and protective role in Rwanda during the 1994 genocide; as a result, large numbers of Rwandans have converted to Islam. Of the 8.2 million people in Rwanda—Africa's most Catholic nation—Muslims now make up 14 percent, twice as many as before the killings began (*The Washington Post,* Sept 23, 2002; p.A10).

Many Rwandans converted to Islam because of the role that some Catholic and Protestant leaders played in the genocide. During the genocide, many Christian clerics allowed Tutsis to seek refuge in churches and then surrendered them to Hutu death squads. In some cases, Hutu priests and ministers even incited their congregations to kill Tutsis. Among those facing genocide charges at the U.N.-created International Criminal Tribunal for Rwanda were clergymen and even nuns. Said Jean Pierre Sagahutu, a Tutsi who converted to Islam from Catholicism after his family members were slaughtered: "I know people in America think Muslims are terrorists, but for Rwandans they were our freedom fighters during the genocide. I wanted to hide in a church, but that was the worst place to go. Instead, a Muslim family took me. They saved my life" (*The Washington Post,* Sept 23, 2002; p.A10).

THE DESTRUCTION OF AFRICA'S HERITAGE

The Indigenous Versus Western Institutions

Incredible as it may sound to many, the colonialists did not really introduce any new institutions into Africa. What they introduced were merely more efficient forms of already existing institutions—both good and bad. It was probably for this reason that colonialism lasted for nearly a century. Had it introduced institutions that were diametrically antithetical to the existing ones, the demise of colonialism would have come sooner.

The introduction of different forms of the same institutions did not mean the colonialists "invented" those institutions—an extremely important distinction. There were weapons in indigenous Africa: spears, bows and arrows. The Europeans introduced guns, which were more efficient in their killing, although the "primitive" weapons did occasionally triumph in the Ashanti and Zulu wars in the nineteenth century. But it is incorrect to assert that the colonialists "invented" weapons and the institution of war. Similarly, in precolonial Africa, the natives gathered under a tree or at the village market square and debated an issue until they reached a consensus. When the colonialists came, they erected a building and called it "parliament," which means a "place to talk." It did not mean the colonialists "invented" the institution of public debate and free speech.

Another example was the institution of money. Generally, money serves as a means of exchange and facilitates production and trade. Without money, an economy would grind to a snail's pace. Lenin recognized this when he said, "The best way to wreck the capitalist system is by debauching its currency."[5] Africans were using various commodity monies (cowrie shells, gold dust, salt, iron bars, etc). It was the colonialists who introduced coins and paper currency, the more efficient forms of money. They did not invent the institution of money.

Africa had bows and arrows; the colonialists brought guns. Africa had periodic rural village markets; the Europeans introduced the urban supermarket. Africa was moving goods and people by foot (human porterage), caravans, horses, and canoes. The colonialists brought more efficient forms of transportation: steamers, roads, automobiles, and railways. The colonialists did not invent these institutions; they only introduced different forms of these institutions.

Failure on the part of many African leaders to make this distinction led to an indiscriminate and quixotic assault on many institutions perceived to be "colonial" or "Western." Markets, for example, are ancient institutions in Africa. As Skinner (1964) remarked: "Markets were ubiquitous in West Africa. There were a few regions where aboriginal markets were absent—in parts of Liberia, southwestern Ivory Coast, and in certain portions of the plateau regions of Nigeria. Nevertheless, even here people engaged in trade, and benefited from the markets of contiguous areas. The markets served as local exchange points or nodes, and trade was the vascular system unifying all of West Africa, moving products to and from local markets, larger market centers, and still larger centers" (p.215).

There were two types of markets and trade: the small village market and the large markets that served as long-distance interregional trade centers. Rural markets often were sighted at bush clearings or at the intersection of caravan routes. As Polly Hill (1986) asserted: "Rural periodic markets are such ancient institutions in many parts of West Africa and the literature on African markets is vast" (p.54).

Many of the precolonial rural markets of West Africa provided for the needs of local producers, consumers, and traders and also served as foci for long-distance traders. Some rural markets operated daily, depending on the volume of trade. In Nigeria, "Every village and town had markets which were attended in the morning or evening and in some cases, throughout the day. These markets were held either daily or periodically. The daily markets were local exchange points where producers, traders and consumers met to sell and buy. The periodic markets were organized on a cyclical basis of every three, four, five and sixteen days to feed the daily markets. Every community had a market cycle which enabled traders and buyers to attend different markets on different days" (Falola, 1985; p.105).

The local markets had two important characteristics. The first was their cyclical periodicity (Skinner 1964, p.215). Market days would be rotated among a cluster of villages. For example, Yoruba, Dahomey, and Guro markets operated on five-day cycles. Igbo rural markets were on a 4-day or multiple of the 4-day cycle, while Mossi markets ran on a 3-day or 21-day cycle.

The second characteristic of rural markets was the segregation of vendors or merchants according to the products they sold. Tomato sellers, for example, were all seated in one section of the market. The object was to promote competition. As Falola (1985) observed, segregation "made it convenient for buyers to locate the regular section of each commodity, to choose from a wide variety of goods, and to buy at a fair price since the traders had to compete with one another at the same time" (p.106).

Suddenly after independence, the market was denounced as a "western institution" by functionally illiterate African leaders, and trading, which Africans have engaged in for centuries, was banned. Recall that under Sekou Toure of Guinea's program of "Marxism in African Clothes," "unauthorized trading became a crime. Police roadblocks were set up around the country to control internal trade" (*The New York Times,* Dec 28, 1987; p.28). Even the supposedly "backward" chiefs of Africa seldom banned any market trading activity. But the most outrageous perfidy occurred in Ghana between 1981 and 1983.

Denouncing markets as dens of profiteers, the military regime of Ft./Lte. Jerry Rawlings (Provisional National Defense Council) of Ghana imposed stringent price controls on commodities and established Price Control Tribunals to enforce them and hand down stiff penalties. Market women who violated the price controls had their wares confiscated, their heads shaved, and were stripped naked, flogged, and thrown into jail. Markets were burned and destroyed by Air Force personnel when traders refused to sell at government-controlled prices. Economic lunacy was on the rampage. Having jailed the traders and destroyed their markets, the government of Ghana discovered to its chagrin that there was no food to feed the people it had jailed. "Thirty prisoners died in Sunyani prison for lack of food; 39 inmates died at another" (*West Africa,* July 15, 1983, p.1634). More will be said on this price-control exercise in the next chapter, but the benighted assault on perceived "Western institutions" by African leaders not only impaired their own progress but also arrested the natural evolution of the indigenous institutions as well. Specifically, the rural village market could not develop into an urban market since that particular market was perceived to be "Western" and was being destroyed. By allowing the "Western" roads and bridges to deteriorate, the movement of goods and people was impeded. Further, the decay of the colonial schools and universities meant that the indigenous institutions could not evolve into formal educational structures.

The onslaught against the "colonial" institutions, more generally, showed a woeful lack of understanding of the purpose of those institutions. The purpose of "parliament," for example, was to provide a forum to debate national issues. Such a forum existed in indigenous Africa under a tree. To expunge all reminders of the hated episode of colonialism was understandable. But it did not require, for example, a destruction of the "parliament" building. A mere change of name to, say, "Indaba" would have sufficed (just as several African countries adopted African names after independence: Gold Coast to Ghana, Rhodesia to Zimbabwe), and the "parliament" building, whatever it was called afterward, would have continued to serve its purpose.[6] But in blowing up the colonial parliament without providing an alternative forum, many African leaders denied their people public discourse of national issues and participation in the decision-making process—an African tradition.

The Plight of the African Chief

Traditional African rulers (chiefs and kings) were perhaps the most persecuted group after independence. During colonial rule, African kings and chiefs who did not submit to the colonial administrators were replaced or exiled. The onslaught against chiefs continued after independence, and they were betrayed along with the rest of the African population. Additional humiliation was inflicted upon the traditional rulers when they were stripped of much of their traditional authority and their powers severely curtailed.

Recall that traditionally the chiefs had always been custodians of land in precolonial Africa. But after independence, they lost this authority when the administration became much more centralized: The government took over unoccupied land and customary law lost virtually all standing. In several Francophone African countries—such as Guinea, Cameroon, and Zaire—land law was changed. Other states simply nationalized all land. The government of Sekou Toure in Guinea justified the nationalization of land by citing the need to transfer control from the colonialists and mining companies to the people as a whole.

In British Africa, the policy of "indirect rule" enabled the chiefs to have a substantial role in government. Toward this end, the British established a House of Chiefs in almost all of its African colonies. In the early stages of colonialism, this house was mainly responsible for the collection of graduated head tax. Subsequently, its functions were expanded to include local government, and it was charged with additional functions such as road maintenance and construction. However, the general centralization of administration that occurred in almost all of Africa after independence left little scope for effective participation of the traditional rulers in government.

The nationalists and elites were determined to reduce the powers of the chiefs and exclude them from government.

In most ex-British colonies, the chiefs did not resist the encroachment on their traditional powers. In Ghana, for example, Nkrumah reorganized local government and subordinated the chiefs to elected councilors. The House of Chiefs was subsequently abolished, with muted complaints from the chiefs. In Uganda, however, the *Kabaka* (local chief) put up a fierce resistance, which was largely responsible for the rise of Idi Amin and Milton Obote and the subsequent degeneration into political instability and carnage. Mozambique's traditional leaders, known as *regulos,* fought bitterly against the governing party's efforts to get rid of them. And in Zimbabwe, President Robert Mugabe was forced to court the public approval of chiefs from the country's two main tribes—the Shona and the Ndebele—after independence in 1980.

In the case of Ghana, Arhin (1985) charged that:

> From 1951 to the present day, the Governments of Ghana have taken away the authority of traditional rulers by passing laws (or acts) and decrees. In 1951, the Legislative Assembly passed the Local Government Ordinance which substituted Local Councils for the Native Authorities or the Council of traditional rulers. The Ordinance intended that elected persons rather than traditional rulers should act as the guardians of the welfare of the community. In 1954, another Ordinance of the Government deprived the traditional rulers of their representation in the Local Councils. In 1958 (a year after Ghana became independent), the Local Courts Act abolished the courts of traditional rulers and took away the authority that the Colonial Government had given them to settle disputes among the people, as they had done in the days before colonial rule itself. Also in 1958, the Legislative Assembly passed the "House of Chiefs' Act," which confirmed that traditional councils and the Houses of Chiefs could resolve disputes among traditional rulers. (p.110)

There were subsequent laws in 1962, 1969, 1971 and various amendments. But,

> The manner in which the Governments of Ghana have applied some of these laws has greatly weakened the position of traditional rulers and made it clear even to those who had no idea of the new laws that the traditional rulers can act only if the central Government wishes them to do so. The Governments have had certain rulers removed from their stools by notifying the public in the Gazette that they no longer "recognize" those rulers. The most famous examples are the removal of the rulers of Akyem Abuakwa and Wenchi by the Government of Kwame Nkrumah, and the rulers of Akyem Kotoku, Wenchi and Yendi by the National Redemption Council under the Chairmanship of the late General I.K. Acheampong. (Arhin, 1985; p.113)

Nigeria was supposed to be the exception, since its federal constitution provided for some devolution of authority toward local authorities and traditional rulers. Furthermore, in the struggle for independence, there was little friction between the traditional rulers and the elites. In fact, the position of the National Council of Nigeria and Cameroon in its 1954 manifesto was quite explicit: "Our Emirs and Obas, Obongs and Etubons and Amayonabos, are sovereigns in their own rights. This is the verdict of our history. Accordingly, our National Rulers must fit into the position of Constitutional monarchs." But it did not turn out that way.

Beginning under Nigeria's first president, Abubakar Balewa, the northern region government abolished the chiefs' status of sole native authority. In 1963, the Emir of Kano was capriciously removed by the federal government. After the Nigerian military coup of 1966, the traditional rulers had hoped their fortunes would improve but it was never to be. As *West Africa* put it:

> They lost their Native Authority police forces under one military head of state; under another they lost more of their role and responsibilities through the Local Government reforms of 1976; they lost their critical authority over land use under a third; and they lost their own forum, the House of Chiefs, under the incoming civilian administration of the Second Republic in 1979. Under the next military government, they were forced for good measure, as it were, to witness the humiliation of two of their senior most colleagues, the Emir of Kano and the Ooni of Ife, whose passports were withdrawn in 1984 for displeasing the military government; in military idiom, the rulers were further humbled by being ordered not to leave their domain without the prior permission of their Local Government chairmen, the new and sole channel of communication between the traditional rulers and Government. Twenty-five years after the brusque removal of the Emir of Kano, the traditional rulers watched the dismissal of the Emir of Muri, once again as the outcome of a clash with government, along with central intervention over the appointment of the Sultan of Sokoto himself. (20–26 March, 1989; p.431)

The insidious assault against the traditional rulers was partly driven by the mistaken belief among the nationalist leaders that the indigenous institutions, along with chieftaincy, were "too anachronistic" to permit the rapid transformation of Africa. Chiefs were regarded as "too conservative" and as stumbling blocks. They were identified with "the old system," which after independence was to be demolished and replaced with "the new," "the modern," and industry. The chiefs, tied up with the land and peasantry, did not fit into the grandiose schemes drawn up to modernize and industrialize Africa.

Another reason was the widespread but unjustified claim that Africa's traditional rulers were "collaborators" of the colonial system, setting the stage for a diminution of their powers and desecration of their authority. According to Dr. S. K. B. Asante,

> In the eyes of Kobina Sekyi, those chiefs who co-operated with the colonial government by supporting the Provincial Council and the "interventionist" system of indirect rule, were committing triple betrayal. First, they were betraying their old allies, the educated elite, who had now only a minor place as "attendants" in the Provincial Council system, and who were left out of the machinery of the colonial administration. Second, by accepting new government legislation which sought to strengthen the authority and the legal position of the native authorities, the chiefs were betraying the democratic principles of the traditional political system. Third, the chiefs were betraying themselves; for in accepting the support of the colonial government they were becoming increasingly dependent upon the British, losing their autonomy and freedom of action and becoming the tools of the colonial administration, mere subordinates in the official hierarchy. (*West Africa,* Jan 10, 1982; p.83)

However, the real motivation for the charges of betrayal against the chiefs could be found in the power struggle between them and the nationalist leaders. The intelligentsia was quite naturally miffed at the perceived reluctance of the chiefs to grant them what they regarded as their proper share of influence in the colonial administration. After independence, power-hungry elites launched a calculated campaign to exclude the chiefs from power-sharing arrangements and governance. Moreover, the same charges of triple betrayal could also be leveled against the elites themselves, who, after independence, assumed and concentrated power in their own hands, refusing to share it. Further, the elites themselves betrayed the democratic principles of the traditional political system and became puppets or tools of foreign ideologies.

The general portrayal of the chiefs as "collaborators" of colonial government was disingenuous. In fact, many African chiefs put up a gallant struggle against colonialism. But their weak military positions, poor organization, and the sporadic nature of the resistance enabled the colonial forces to crush them easily and brutally. Moreover, during the struggle for independence, many chiefs gave leaders of the struggle much logistical help. But incredibly, after independence, African nationalist leaders and elites chose to ignore these acts of bravery and cultural patriotism, branding the chiefs as "collaborators." Said *African News Weekly* (July 7, 1995):

> When Mozambican President Joaquim Chissano's Frelimo Party won independence from Portugal in 1975, the chiefs were accused of having been puppets of

the Portuguese and stripped of their power. During the liberation war between 1964 and 1974, chiefs in the province of Niassa gave vital support to Frelimo and their rejection after independence left them particularly disgruntled. (p.3)

But even where such collaboration had been the case, it developed because most chiefs took decisions considered appropriate under prevailing circumstances to ensure the survival of their people. Faced with certain death and the routing of their tribes under the heels of the mighty colonial war machine, "cooperation" was perhaps the most expedient method to preserve their realms.

The African chief's foremost responsibility was the survival of their people. An African chief generally did not make policy or take decisions by himself. He only executed the will of the people. He could not "sell off" his people and expect to remain chief. If a chief "collaborated," it was the collective decision of the people to seek cooperation or an alliance with the colonialists, as this offered the best means of survival. Indeed, many African ethnic groups sought alliances with Europeans as protection against belligerent neighboring groups. The Fanti of Ghana, for example, entered into such an alliance with the Dutch in the sixteenth century. Within this context, the depiction of chiefs as "collaborators" by the elites was not only unfair but dishonest as well.

Those "chiefs" who openly collaborated with the colonial government were, in many cases, colonial appointees ("canton chiefs" in French West Africa and "ward chiefs" in British colonial Africa). Generally, because these "canton chiefs" derived their authority from the colonial government and felt they had the colonial army behind them, many became corrupt and autocratic. The reaction of their people is worth recalling. The African people refused to recognize some of these "chiefs" and destooled them (removed them from office). The Ga of Ghana, for example, had no chief with political authority. But the Dutch—like other Europeans—had it in their head that every community must have a head. Accordingly, they created the position of *mantse*, or political head, for the Ga people. But the Ga promptly destooled their *mantse* and created the post of *mankralo* (caretaker).[7]

In some African societies, the people took extraordinary steps to protect their real chiefs. In Mali, for example, French colonialists discovered to their chagrin a ruse by the natives. Throughout the Malian countryside, villages set up fictitious chiefs and councilors to meet with the French colonial administrators when they came visiting to give orders. The French gleefully extracted treaties from these chiefs, who were only too glad to oblige. Only, the natives knew that treaties with fake chiefs were not valid.

It may also be recalled that the Asante organized *asafo* companies (vigilante groups), prior to the outbreak of the First World War, to destool chiefs suspected of collaborating with the colonialists. Some of these quislings were shunned or killed by their people. In the Gold Coast, the British colonialists came to the stunning realization that the provincial councils on which the chiefs served were of little use. As A. F. E. Fieldgate, the acting secretary for native affairs, summed it up in 1937: "In my opinion, little importance can be attached to the activities of these (Provincial) councils. For the most part the chiefs do not carry their people with them" (cited in *West Africa,* Jan. 10, 1982; p.83).

If anything, a strong case of collaboration or even cowardice can be leveled at African elites themselves. The struggle for independence was protracted, and those elites who lacked the courage to fight colonialism had several options. They could Westernize themselves for defensive purposes. Indeed, many did, aping the trappings of Western culture in the hope that if they acted as Westerners, the colonialists would not destroy them. Other elites exercised the option of joining the colonial administration, an even more blatant case of collaboration.[8]

The final option open to the elites was exit. They could migrate or exile themselves, and many did so, choosing to live in Europe for some time. The traditional rulers had no such option. It was they who had to remain, whether they liked it or not, and face the colonialists as well as their people, day in day out. They were in the eye of the struggle, constantly determining how best to deal with the situation. The elites in Europe never had to face this danger. In Angola, chiefs who failed to secure the required number of slaves demanded by the Portuguese were themselves enslaved in the 1570s. Over a hundred chiefs and notables were sold into slavery in a single year (1573) and another hundred murdered by the Portuguese. It was blatant dishonesty for Westernized elites and those who abandoned the struggle, even temporarily, to accuse the traditional rulers of collaboration.

There are reasons for this vigorous defense of the chiefs. First, the humiliation of chiefs and desecration of traditional authority were acts of cultural treachery. From time immemorial, the chiefs had been the custodians and defenders of African culture, traditions, and institutions. An attack against them was synonymous with an assault on indigenous African culture, the very culture the elites vowed to defend with such slogans as "Negritude" and "African personality." And far from being "illiterate" laggards dead set in their old ways, the chiefs have shown themselves capable of transforming themselves. Many of today's African traditional rulers are not "illiterate and backward." In fact many of them are highly educated and have held enviable careers in the civil service.

Second, an African economy cannot be developed without the people (the peasants) and their natural leaders (the chiefs). The chiefs are closer to the people, and understand their needs as well as local conditions far better than the bureaucrats sitting in air-conditioned offices in the capital cities. "I don't know whether I can trust some politician who I have never met and who I hear others say is corrupt. But the chief I know I can trust. It is not like he makes any decisions that his people are opposed to. Everything he does, he first consults with his [headmen]. He speaks for us, yes, but he says what we want said," quipped Mqtutuzi Ngwaza (*The Washington Post,* Dec 18, 2000; p.A1).

In Ghana, Osagyefo Amoatia Ofori Panin, the king of the Akyem Abuakwa state, complained bitterly about ten years of constitutional rule (1993–2003) that paid only lip service to the institution of chieftaincy and traditional councils. Although Article 270 of Ghana's Constitution insulates and protects the chieftaincy from the predations of manipulative governments, it does not assign any participatory role to the institution in the administration and development of the country. Panin wrote:

> While the majority of our towns and villages are governed on a day-to-day basis by stools and skins (traditional councils), hardly any attempt is made to involve chiefs in national development planning agenda. There is no opportunity to comment on parliamentary bills or local government by-laws or social policy initiatives. Thus programs set out in such agenda end up as unworkable or ill-designed. In fact, the institution has remained the most enduring of all our national institutions since pre-colonial era. Thus, it is important to determine why in spite of its longevity, acceptance and effectiveness, stools and skins (traditional councils) are largely excluded from the scheme of local government. None of the constitutional provisions on local government and decentralization include measures enabling the participation of stools and skins (traditional councils). Traditional authorities have no right to participate in the work of District Assemblies and may only be represented if they are included among the President's appointees. (*Governance Newsletter,* Sept 2003, a publication of the Institute of Economic Affairs, Ghana)

Furthermore, one cannot reach the African people without the use of chiefs as intermediaries. Even the British colonialists recognized this when crafting their colonial policy of "indirect rule." Far from being useless appendages of the "old system," these chiefs are in fact Africa's most important human resource, vital for development purposes:

> In Ghana, Gomoa Nyiresi citizens recently met with the chief of their town, Nana Kwesi Esuon II, to begin planning for a 45 million cedi electric power

project in their town. At the meeting it was agreed that 150 poles would be erected for the project, which is designed to bring electric power to the entire community. Elders in the town were to contribute 40,000 cedis each, while the remaining amount would be attained through fund-raising measures. (*Africa News Weekly,* March 5, 1993; p.10)

The authority of South Africa's chiefs was undermined by the white government, which paid them and replaced them at will. They still receive salaries from the central government, but many in the African National Congress (ANC) government view them as anachronisms. King Goodwill Zwelithini, king of the Zulus, argues that this is foolish, because in rural areas it is hard to promote development without the chiefs. Some chiefs undoubtedly wish to make life better for their people, to whom they are closer than the bureaucrats in Pretoria, the capital. The average rural South African has no idea how to file a complaint with the local government, but she knows where the chief lives. Working with tribal chiefs can make it easier to establish schools, water supplies, and sewerage systems.

Tragically, the misguided marginalization of chiefs that occurred in post-colonial Africa is being repeated in post-apartheid South Africa. "Since the 1994 election (that saw the end of apartheid), traditional leaders—many installed and sustained by apartheid authorities because they did what they were told—have hovered at the margins of the new order, grumbling at their lack of official status, power and pay. The chiefs, in part because they were dependent on the money that the apartheid machinery doled out, do not have a long history of supporting the liberation movement and are often looked at with suspicion by the African National Congress. "Since the 1994 elections, the chiefs have been given a national council, which has advisory powers and is supposed to promote the role of traditional leadership within a democratic constitution. But what their future role will be in local community government and in distributing farming and water rights on tribal lands remains the question" (*The New York Times,* April 27, 1999; p.A3).[9]

More than a third of South Africa's 44 million people live under the jurisdiction of one or another of the nation's 800 tribal chiefs, or *amakhosi* as they are referred to in the Zulu language. "Traditional leaders here have endured colonialism, war and nearly 50 years of oppressive white minority rule, only to face extinction at the hands of the black-majority government that vanquished apartheid six years ago and installed democracy" (*The Washington Post,* Dec 18, 2000; p.A1).

The ruling African National Congress made little effort to disguise its contempt for traditional authorities, even though former president Nelson Mandela hailed from a royal tribal family. It allowed its dislike of its political rival, the Inkatha Freedom Party (IFP)—a predominantly Zulu party led by Chief Buthelezi—to color its decisions regarding the role of traditional leaders in the new South Africa. As elsewhere in postcolonial Africa, the ANC government laid claim to thousands of acres of land that tribal authorities have held in a community trust for decades. As custodians of that land, the chiefs customarily decide how the land is to be used and by whom, and members of the tribe pay no taxes on it. In local elections held across South Africa in December 20002, the ANC, in a bizarre instance of functional illiteracy, sought to abolish the traditional system by extending municipal government to remote rural areas that had, in some instances, been ruled by *amakhosi* for more than 400 years. "The new system sought to replace each local chief, or *inkhosi,* and his headmen, or *indunas,* with a mayor and city council, similar to the structure of municipal governments in the West" (*The Washington Post,* Dec 18, 2000; p.A1). But the *amakhosi* fought back. Militant chiefs organized a boycott and shutdown of one voter registration site. Their protests drew thousands of supporters.

Said one irate tribal chief of Quadi, Mzunjani Ngcobo: "How can a politician decide what is right for my people better than myself or my son, who has been preparing his entire life for the moment when he must lead? I am not running for re-election. This is not my career. It is my duty. I have served my people for 48 years and will continue to serve them until I die" (*The Washington Post,* Dec 18, 2000; p.A1). Officials of the governing ANC insist with pompous effrontery that a municipal government, with its ability to collect taxes, draw upon skilled technical staff members, and coordinate development efforts with other government officials, would be better suited to enforce laws; to build roads, schools, and sewer systems; and to attract investors to South Africa's impoverished countryside. "Some people see you as the gatekeepers to the past, opposed to all things modern," Yunus Carrim, the government's director of municipal elections, told a gathering of traditional leaders in December 2000 (*The Washington Post,* Dec 18, 2000; p.A1). "The challenge is whether traditional leaders are ready to transform their leadership to the realities of today." No, the problem is whether Africa's ruling elite are ready to reform their backward mentality.

The functionally illiterate misconstrues "development" to mean "change," and change must be total: the obliteration of the traditional and its replacement by the "new." "Africans want change because there is so much suffering here," said Patekile Holomisa, an *inkhosi* and head of the Congress of Traditional Leaders in South Africa. "But Africans are above all else devoted to their ancestors, and they do not want to betray that by becoming something that they are not" (*The Washington Post,* Dec 18, 2000; p.A1).

Negotiations between the ANC and traditional leaders collapsed after the *amakhosi* rejected as insufficient the government's proposal to provide them with a single seat on each municipal council. The chiefs have proposed a two-tiered system of governance in which elected officials address regional matters and they, the *amakhosi,* handle local matters, keeping their communities intact. ANC government officials balked but an African "curse" awaits them.

Across Africa, there has been chronic tension between African tradition, which places ancestral land in the hands of local tribes, and the modern African state, which reserves land in the hands of the government.

Ronald Mwangangi, a primate researcher, and his colleagues went to the village of Baomo, Kenya, to scan the lush riverside treetops for a rare colobus monkey. Villagers were irate, suspecting that they wanted local land to expand the nearby Tana River Primate Reserve. The land issue had simmered since 1976, when the reserve was first sketched on maps and the people who had been farming it were told not to expand their plots. They refused, claiming that it was their ancestral land. But as pressure grew on the unique ecosystem, a favored habitat of the rare red colobus and mangabey monkeys, the Kenya Wildlife Service, with financial support from the World Bank, offered the residents free land elsewhere. But many in the village didn't budge. When the researchers arrived at the village, about 50 women "mooned" them.

As Karl Vick, an American correspondent reported:

> The women approached the visitors in formation, the eldest at the rear, where they would remain, fully dressed. The younger ones cavorted in front, chanting, clapping and, at the climactic moment, turning their backs and hoisting their skirts toward their visitors—a half-dozen men of science struggling to maintain the detachment befitting their profession.
>
> "That was to curse us," said Ronald Mwangangi, recalling the scene at this remote oasis two months ago. "They said we were going back to the womb," Mwangangi said. "You can be educated, but that sort of traditional practice has got a lot of influence on you—deep."
>
> But that open conflict [over land] pales beside the conflict inside the stunned men who watched 50 mothers show them their bare backsides. Like almost everyone raised in this part of Africa, they understood that the sight was intended to hasten their deaths. By flashing their private parts, local residents said, the mothers had not only insulted their targets but reminded them where they had come from. (*The Washington Post,* Feb 26, 2001; p.A14)

In another remote Kenyan town, a dozen researchers took to their heels and fled after the women showed up after dark. "Naked women scare scientists," read the headline in the *Daily Nation.* "When you see African women stripping, that is a very serious matter," said Islam Juma, a teacher (*The*

Washington Post, Feb 26, 2001; p.A14). "They are collaborating with the environment." Indeed, the women had concluded their protest by picking up a handful of sandy gray soil and flinging it at the researchers.

In recent years, stark naked stripping by women has increasingly been employed to knock some cultural sense into dim-witted elites. In 1983 when a group of women marched in downtown Nairobi to protest police torture, the police pounced on them, beating them up to disperse the demonstration. Thereupon, the women stripped and bared their essentials. "'They resorted to something they knew traditionally would act on the men,' said Wangari Maathai, one of those who tore off her clothes and saw young policemen turn their faces away" (*The Washington Post,* Feb 26, 2001; p.A14). They stripped to show their nakedness to their sons since in Africa it is a curse to see one's mother naked. On the land dispute in Boama, Maathai said: "See, the government operates like a Westerner, following laws which are really Western laws." "And the local people at that time were acting very local" (*The Washington Post,* Feb 26, 2001; p.A14). Indeed.

At the conference on "Democracy, Sustainable Development and Poverty: Are They Compatible?," the eminent African scholar, Prof. Ali Mazrui (2001), asked in a keynote address,

> Who killed African democracy? The cultural half caste who came in from Western schools and did not adequately respect African ancestors. Institutions were inaugurated without reference to cultural compatibilities, and new processes were introduced without respect for continuities. Ancestral standards of property and legitimacy were ignored. When writing up a new constitution for Africa these elites would ask themselves "How does the House of Representatives in the United States structure its agenda? How do the Swiss cantons handle their referendum? I wonder how the Canadian federation would handle such an issue?" On the other hand, these African elites almost never ask how did the Bunyoro, the Wolof, the Igbo or the Kikutu govern themselves before colonization? (p.7)

In a vile and perfidious act of cultural betrayal, the functionally and culturally illiterate elites sought to mould Africans in the image of others. Foreign cultural practices and systems were foisted on the African cultural body politic. Disaster was inevitable as these foreign systems did not fit into Africa's sociocultural milieu. The turmoil, chaos, and destruction that have ravaged postcolonial Africa can be seen as the rejection of these transplanted foreign organs. The continent is littered with the carcasses of failed foreign systems, imposed on the African traditional body.

CHAPTER 5

Development Finance

Foreign aid has done more harm to Africa than we care to admit. It has led to a situation where Africa has failed to set its own pace and direction of development free of external interference. Today, Africa's development plans are drawn thousands of miles away in the corridors of the IMF and World Bank. What is sad is that the IMF and World Bank "experts" who draw these development plans are people completely out of touch with the local African reality.

—Dr. Joshat Karanja, a former Kenya member of parliament,
in *New African,* June 1992, p.20.

I've never seen a country develop itself through aid or credit. Countries that have developed—in Europe, America, Japan, Asian countries like Taiwan, Korea and Singapore—have all believed in free markets. There is no mystery there. Africa took the wrong road after independence.

—President Abdoulaye Wade of Senegal, in *The New York Times,*
April 10, 2002; p.A3.

THE RESOURCE GAP

To spearhead development, the state needed power and resources. When additional powers were needed, the state simply arrogated them or secured them through a rubber-stamp parliament. Resources could be secured in a variety of ways:

- Use of foreign exchange reserves
- Taxation

- Inflationary finance
- Domestic borrowing
- Foreign borrowing
- Windfall from a mineral export (diamonds, gold or oil)

Foreign Exchange Reserves

At independence, few African countries had foreign exchange reserves to finance development. Ghana, for example, had about $400 million in reserves but these were quickly depleted to finance Nkrumah's industrialization drive. Resources could also be extracted through special "development levies," export and import taxes. Inflationary finance simply meant printing money to finance development projects—for example, increasing agricultural production—in the hope that resultant increase in production would "absorb" the excess liquidity that had been created. Domestic borrowing involved creating special savings accounts from which the government could borrow—for example, postal office savings accounts, government savings bonds, farmers' savings bonds and workers savings accounts, as well as borrowing from the banking system through the sale of government securities. Resources could also be borrowed from foreign sources: from private banks, foreign governments in the form of "foreign aid," and multilateral institutions such as the World Bank and the IMF. And under fortuitous circumstances, an African country may obtain resources for investment from an export windfall. For example, high oil prices pumped billions of dollars into the coffers of the governments of Equatorial Guinea, Nigeria, Angola and Gabon. High copper prices in the 1970s swelled the coffers of Zaire and Zambia, while Botswana enjoyed a diamonds bonanza in the early 1980s. Although African governments availed themselves of all these modalities, the most common approach was to extract resources from the peasantry, print money, and borrow from foreign (Western) governments.

Milking the Peasants

Under statism and development planning, African governments envisioned huge surpluses in the rural sector to be tapped for development. Large resources could be transferred to the state by extracting wealth from peasant producers. The milking devices used included the following: poll taxes, low producer prices, export marketing boards, hidden export taxes, price controls, development levies, and forcing peasant farmers to sell annual quotas to government organs. The assumption was that such resources, ceded to the state, would be used by development planners for the benefit of all.

The prices peasants received for their produce were dictated by many African governments, not as determined by market forces in accordance with African traditions. Under an oppressive system of state controls, Africa's peasants came to pay the world's most confiscatory taxes.[1] They faced stiff penalties and outright confiscation of their produce if they sold above the government-controlled prices.

When the Kenyan National Cereal and Produce Board was established in 1979, it was mandated as the sole purchaser, handler, and storer of all grains nationwide. In addition, it set the producer and consumer prices. One ostensible reason was to milk the agricultural sector and transfer resources to the state. For example, according to *West Africa* (Feb 15, 1989):

> On the average, between 1964/65 and 1984/85, the peasants of Gambia were robbed of 60 percent of the international price of their groundnuts! For 20 years, the Jawara Government "officially" took, free of charge, 3 out of every 5 bags, leaving the peasant with a gross of 2. With deductions for subsistence credit fertilizer, seeds, etc., the peasant would end up with a net one bag out of five . . . With these facts, it is simply wrong to say that the poverty of the peasant derives from the defects of nature—drought, over-population, laziness, and so on (p.250).

In 1981, the Government of Tanzania paid peasant maize farmers only 20 percent of the free market price for their produce. In Sierra Leone, taxation levels in the agricultural sector averaged between 30 and 60 percent of gross income (*West Africa,* Feb 15, 1982; p.446). In 1984 cocoa farmers in Ghana were receiving less than 10 percent of the world market price for their crop. In Ethiopia, Guinea, Tanzania, and many other African countries, peasant farmers were forced to sell their produce or quotas only to state produce-buying agencies.

Recall that in Malawi, former Life-President Hastings Banda "was able to extract economic surplus from peasant producers and transfer it to the state sector through two commercial banks, his holding company—Press Holdings—and the parastatal Agricultural Development and Marketing Corporation (ADMARC)" (Libby, 1987; p.191). He then used the resources to reward his political supporters by transforming the latter into commercial agricultural estate owners whose prosperity and economic security depended on their personal loyalty to the president.

Prices of agricultural produce were also fixed to render food cheap for the urban elites—the basis of political support for African governments. For example, when the Zambian government instituted a maize-meal coupon program in the 1970s that subsidized the cost of maize meal for urban and semi-urban families, the program excluded rural citizens—even though they were recognized as being the poorest segment of the population—because it was rationalized that they could grow their own maize. When traders refused to sell their produce at government-dictated prices, authorities raided markets in May 1988. They arrested hundreds of people, took their money, and tore down market stalls, seizing sugar, detergents, salt, maize meal, soft drinks, candles, flour, and clothing. Back in 1984 in Ghana, Kwame Forson, the Agona Swedru District Secretary, "called on some unidentified soldiers who make brief stopovers at Swedru to check prices, and instead threaten and rob innocent traders, to desist from such acts" (*West Africa*, July 23, 1984; p.1511).

In this way, the peasantry was systematically robbed of considerable resources. For example, in a January 1989 New Year's address, President Houphouet-Boigny of Ivory Coast admitted that peasant cash crop producers "have over the years parted with four-fifths of the value of what they produced to enable the government to finance development" (*West Africa*, May 1–7, 1989; p.677). But development for whom? Much of this money went to the State Marketing Board and the bulk of the development that took place was concentrated in Abidjan and other urban areas, bypassing the rural peasants. For example, over 80 percent of the "development" of the Ivory Coast was concentrated in Abidjan for the benefit of the urban elites, not the rural peasants. Large sums of the peasant's money were also channeled into the creation and maintenance of unwieldy and unprofitable parastatal corporations. The president's protégés used the rest of the money for self-enrichment.

The standard of living enjoyed by the elites far outstripped that of the peasants. Contrast the plush and subsidized amenities of the ruling class in the urban areas with the dingy and wretched lives of the rural peasants. In Mauritania, for example, while the elites, the Arabs, had access to subsidized tap water supplies, the peasants, often black, paid seven to forty times more for their water from sellers with donkey carts. In 1982, while the leadership in Zaire was making $5,000 to $9,000 a month, a peasant was lucky to make $50 a month (*Africa Now*, March, 1982; p.17). In 1985, Cameroon, with a per capita income of less than $1,000 a year, was the world's ninth-largest importer of champagne. The elites were living high.

Gradually over the postcolonial period, the African state evolved into a predatory monster that used a convoluted system of regulations and controls to pillage and rob the productive class—the peasantry. Those who complained about the rape were brutalized, jailed, or killed. By the early 1970s, the outline of a mafia state—a neopatrimonial state—were clearly visible.

"Only socialism will save Africa!!" African leaders and nationalists chanted. But the socialism practiced in Africa was a peculiar type—"Swiss bank socialism"—which allowed the head of state and a platoon of bandits (armed government looters) to rape and plunder African treasuries for deposit in Switzerland. As African economies deteriorated, Africa's tyrants and elite cohorts furiously developed pot-bellies and chins at a rate commensurate with the economic decline. While Africa's peasants were being exhorted to tighten their belts, vampire elites were loosening theirs with fat bank balances overseas. In Angola, the socialist system operated as a kind of reverse Robin Hood, funneling the richest benefits to the least needy:

> Angolans who own cars can fill their tanks for less than a dollar, and international telephone calls cost only pennies. One local boasts of getting a round-trip ticket to Paris on Air France for the equivalent of two cases of beer. Luanda does not even pick up its own garbage; the job is contracted out to a foreign company using Filipino workers lured to Angola with fat paychecks, special housing and First World garbage trucks.
>
> Of course, the chief beneficiaries of all this are the city's westernized elite and their foreign business bedfellows. Many of life's necessities, on the other hand are not available at subsidized prices. For the poorest residents, survival is impossible without resort to *candonga*, or illegal trading. (*Insight*, Oct 1, 1990; p.13)

But the Atingas, despite their lack of formal education, proved that they were no pushovers and rebelled against naked state exploitation by withholding their produce, switching to other crops, producing enough to feed themselves, and simply by smuggling their produce to places where it fetched higher prices.

In fact, at one time in 1981, Ghana's cocoa farmers threatened to invade the Cocoa Marketing Board (CMB) head office in Accra with machetes, hoes, and axes because "Since the establishment of the Cocoa Marketing Board (CMB) in 1947 nothing has been done for the welfare of the farmers in this country. While farmers are suffering, the Board gives huge sums of money to their officials to put up houses which are later rented to the Board at fantastic rates" (*The Punch*, August 28 - Sept 3, 1981; p.1). Other cocoa farmers were threatening to destroy cocoa trees because "farmers in the country had been cheated for far too long and they would not sit idle for a few individuals to take them for a ride" (*Daily Graphic*, March 4, 1981; p.8). Ghana earns the bulk of its foreign exchange from cocoa and the farmers did not make vain or empty threats. At the time of independence in 1957, cocoa farmers were selling about 400,000 tons of their produce to the CMB for export. For the 1981/82 crop year the amount sold to the CMB was only 220,000 (*West Africa*, Oct 18, 1982; p.2731).

Peasant farmers do not have guns, political power, or connections, but they can also rebel passively against the exploitative socioeconomic system and oppressive price controls by curtailing production. In Ghana, for example, production of local staples like maize, rice, cassava, and yam in 1982 was half the level in 1974. Ghana therefore had to import maize from Mozambique. "'Ghana spends at least 72 million *cedis* ($2 million) annually on the importation of maize,' the Ashanti Regional Secretary, Mr. Kwame Kessie said" (*West Africa,* Aug 23, 1982; p.2188). Indeed, Ghana's total imports of food stood at 200 million *cedis* annually (*West Africa,* Feb 7, 1983; p.370).

The results elsewhere in Africa were falling agricultural and export production. As I noted in chapter 1, with 1989–91 as the base year, food production per capita index for Africa was 105 in 1980 but 92 for 1997 (World Bank, 2000a; p.225). Countries such as Kenya, Malawi, Sierra Leone, and Zimbabwe that were self-sufficient in food production now face sharp escalation in food import bills. Declines in export production were noted way back in the 1980s. For example, in 1988, diamond dealers and miners in Sierra Leone told Mr. A. R. Turray, the governor of the Central Bank, that, "The government's gold and diamond marketing board (GGDO) was being sidestepped because it does not offer attractive enough prices. Mr. Turray admitted that smuggling could be minimized if the GGDO paid better prices" (*West Africa,* Jan 23–29, 1989; p.125). GGDO did not, and consequently between April and December 1988, its purchases were nil. In Tanzania, the amount of maize and rice sold through official channels in 1984 was less than one-third the level in 1979.

In 1983, the government of Ghana complained that cocoa smuggling was depriving the nation of at least $100 million in foreign exchange annually. Diamond smuggling cost Angola and Sierra Leone at least $200 million and $60 million, respectively, yearly. In Sierra Leone, in just one year, "the diamond output of 731,000 carats in 1975 was reduced to 481,000 in 1976 (34 percent decline) mainly by the activities of smugglers" (*West Africa,* July 18, 1977; p.1501). Uganda coffee was regularly smuggled to Kenya. Guinea-Bissau diamonds and coffee ended up in Ivory Coast. Nigeria's consumer goods and petrol were regularly smuggled to Cameroon.

Denouncing smuggling as an economic felony, African governments responded by closing their borders and issuing threats: "Convicted cocoa smugglers in Ghana will be shot by firing squad in future, the Chairman of a Public Tribunal, Mr. Agyekum, has said in Accra" (*West Africa,* Dec 6, 1982; p.3179). In February 1989, Nigeria's justice minister, Prince Bola Ajibola, declared that, "Henceforth, anyone caught smuggling or in possession of smuggled items will be sentenced to life in prison" (*Insight,* Feb 6, 1989; p.38). For almost a decade, 1975–84, Tanzania closed its border with Kenya to prevent smuggling, but to no avail. Economic lunacy was running amok.

In the 1980s, Zimbabwe was a net food exporter, but by 1992, it was importing food. It is true the 1991–92 drought devastated agricultural production in southern Africa. But in the case of many countries in southern Africa, the drought merely exacerbated an already precarious food supply situation. In Zimbabwe, the culprit was low government-dictated prices. As John Robertson, the chief economist of the First Merchant Bank in Harare, observed: "The Government [of Robert Mugabe] could have avoided half the total food import with better policies. In the last several years, the Government decided to pay a low price to farmers who grew corn, the staple crop. This meant that the farmers switched to other crops" (*The New York Times*, July 10, 1992; p.A11).

Inflationary Finance

Virtually all African governments have run persistently high budget deficits since independence due to the operation of two factors: a small tax base and soaring, out-of-control government expenditures. An African economy consists of three main sectors: a very large traditional sector, where the majority of the population live and operate; a small formal sector, where formal employment, salaries, pensions, taxes, and paperwork are done; and the informal sector, a transitional sector between the traditional and the modern. Quite often, the government is the largest employer, as the private sector is tiny or nonexistent. Thus, income taxes are paid by civil servants, workers in state enterprises, and private companies. The bulk of government revenue is derived from excise taxes on commodities (for example, gasoline taxes), import duties, and export levies.

An African government that seeks to raise revenue has few options. Excise taxes and import duties have built-in inflationary effects. That is, increasing the excise tax on gasoline or import duties on corn, for example, would ultimately raise their prices to the consumer and could provoke a strong consumer reaction. For example, civil servants and trade unions may demand higher salaries, which in turn will cause government expenditures to increase as the government is the main employer. The problem with African government finances, however, is not so much the narrowness of the tax base but rather expenditures that have spun wildly out of control in the postcolonial period.

Traditionally, budget expenditures are broken down into two categories. The first is "Recurrent Expenditures," which cover administration, civil servant salaries, provision of social services (education, health care), law enforcement, and the like. The second is "Capital Expenditures," which cover purchases of new equipment and machinery, such as new computers, new aircraft, new tanks for the military, and the construction of new schools. Capital expenditures also include an important item, "Development Budget"—essentially expenditures on new development projects, such as the construction of new roads, new factories, and the like to spur the country's rate of development.

In the 1950s, during colonial rule, the capital expenditure item was very small as the colonial administrators did not undertake much social development. Therefore, revenue collected was sufficient to balance colonial budgets and leave a small surplus. After independence, ever-burgeoning capital expenditures—to compensate for neglect of development under colonial rule—were added, throwing budgets out of balance and producing ever-growing budget deficits. In the 1970s, 1980s, and 1990s, the deficits grew larger and larger on account of the following factors:

• Increasing expenditures on the military and security forces to shore up unpopular and illegitimate regimes
• The patronage system—perks, gifts, and emoluments to maintain the existing support base, "jobs for the boys" in the civil service and state corporations, and hand-outs to buy new political support
• Corruption—inflation of government contracts, embezzlement of public funds, malpractices in the administration of import and price controls, cost overruns in the face of commodity shortages
• Losses accumulated by state enterprises to be covered by government subventions.

For ten years, there was no audit of public accounts in either The Gambia or Ghana. An audit in 1994 revealed an embezzlement of 535,940 *dalasis* at the Ministry of Agriculture and misuse of 60 million *dalasis* by the Gambian Farmers' Cooperative Union. In Ghana, the 1993 Auditor-General's report detailed a catalog of corrupt practices, administrative ineptitude, and the squandering of over $200 million in public funds. The former minister of finance, Dr. Kwesi Botchwey, himself admitted to chaotic public expenditure management, with the treasury and spending agencies operating at cross purposes (*Ghana Drum,* Jan 1995; p.14). A September 27, 1994 audit in Nigeria revealed that a total of $12.4 billion—more than a third of the country's foreign debt—was squandered by its military bandits between 1988 and 1994. "The Speaker of the Lagos State House of Assembly, Dr. Olorunnimbe Mamora, revealed that the Lagos government account since 1994 has not been audited" (*P.M. News,* July 26, 1999). In Sierra Leone, President Momoh declared to parliament on June 2, 1989, that austerity and self-sacrifice must prevail—but not for his government. Large, uncontrollable expenditure items had rendered the budget meaningless. Momoh "explained that the government had continued to fund its activities by printing money, spending in excess of tax revenue, and borrowing from the Central Bank, while the nation's meager resources were used for imports that were irrelevant to the needs of the economy" (*West Africa,* June 12–18, 1989; p.958).

In 1995 in Zimbabwe, barely a month after Mugabe's government stipulated a 10 percent annual salary increase ceiling, top government officials awarded themselves increases exceeding 50 percent. In 1999, President Mugabe further rewarded them by tripling and quadrupling their salaries, calling for "his cabinet ministers to receive more than $21,000 a year while members of parliament received increases of nearly 300 percent, to $12,800" (*The Washington Post,* Dec 2, 1999; p.A37). In Tanzania, senior government officials and major politicians exempted themselves from taxes. In 1993 there were over 2,000 such exemptions, costing the treasury $113 million.

Parts of the deficits were financed by simply printing money (money creation), and the rest was financed through a combination of taxes on the peasantry and borrowing from both domestic and foreign sources. Generally, printing money to finance a deficit can be undertaken without serious long-term adverse economic consequences—but under rather tight conditions. That is, if money is created to finance an economic activity that results in increased production, then the extra goods produced would absorb the excess liquidity that had been created. If no increase in production occurred, then the increased money supply would simply produce inflation—a phenomenon where too much money is chasing too few goods. The problem with inflationary finance in Africa was that, while the money supply was increasing, production—especially food production—was *declining,* as Table 5.1 shows.

Table 5.1 shows that food production per capita has consistently been declining from its base year of 1989–91 (inadequate production), while the money supply has been increasing in double digits.[2] The result has been inflation. Consider the GDP deflator entry of 120.8 for 1998. This means that what cost $1.00 in the local currency in 1995 cost almost $1.21 in 1998. That is, a 20.8 percent increase in prices *over a 3-year period,* giving an average annual inflation rate of about 7 percent.

In Africa, a general rule of thumb regarding annual percent increase in the money supply is that it should not exceed 5 percent. That is the minimum rate of growth of domestic output required to absorb such an increase in the money supply in order to have inflation-neutral effects. Any rate above 5 percent would be economically irresponsible. But for the entire decade of the 1990s, gross domestic output in Africa did not even grow at the rate of the population increase (3 percent). Clearly, even a modest growth of 5 percent in the money supply can be inflationary, other things being equal.

Table 5.1

	1990	1991	1992	1993	1994	1995	1996	1997	1998
Per Capita Food Production Index (Average 1989–91 = 100)									
Sub-Saharan Africa	100	99	96	96	95	97	95	94	—
All Africa	100	99	97	97	94	97	97	92	—
Money Supply Growth (Annual Percentages)									
Sub-Saharan Africa	10	14	12	12	34	15	14	15	8
All Africa	14	13	12	12	25	11	13	15	9
GDP Deflator (Local Currency Series) Index 1995 = 100									
Sub-Saharan Africa	62.1	64.4	71.0	71.0	90.1	100.0	109.1	118.2	120.8
All Africa	62.1	64.9	71.4	71.4	90.5	100.0	108.9	116.8	120.3

Source: African Economic and Financial Data, UNDP/World Bank. Washington, D.C.: World Bank, 2000.

Overprinting of money to finance deficits occurred mostly in Anglophone and Lusophone African countries. In Francophone African countries, special budgetary arrangements were made with France and the operation of the sister franc *Communaute Financiere Africain* (CFA). This was created for the former French colonies in 1948 with its valued pegged at 50 CFA to 1 French franc (FF). France also set up a Department of Cooperation to provide French colonies with financial aid, tariff concessions, and support for their currencies. The department had an African aid budget five times greater than that of Britain. In 1988, for example, France spent $2,591 million in aid to Africa; Britain spent $516 million. More than half of French foreign aid went to Africa, making France the continent's foremost patron. In 1993, for example, France's budget for overseas aid was $7.9 billion (*The Economist*, Aug 12, 1995; p.35). And bailing out Francophone African governments by financing budget deficits was becoming expensive, costing the French treasury $2 to $3 billion annually.

The common currency (CFA) and its link to the FF stabilized prices in Francophone Africa but at a tremendous geopolitical cost. By linking the CFA to the French *franc* and by insisting that Francophone African countries keep 30 to 35 percent of their deposits with the Bank of France, French banking connections were able to exercise "a far more effective system of control than any form of colonization" (Biddlecombe, 1994, 30). Furthermore, the linkage of the monetary system accelerated flight of capital out of Francophone Africa: "Over $500 million worth of local CFA currency was being illegally shipped out every year, about one-third of all the notes in circulation" (Biddlecombe, 1994; p.34). On January 11, 1994, the CFA was devalued from 50 CFA to 100 CFA for a French *franc*, touching off a wave of demonstrations, labor disputes, prices increases, and clashes across West Africa. The devaluation was deemed necessary in order for France to comply with entry requirements in the European Union (EU).

Thus, while much of Francophone Africa, with the exception of Guinea, Zaire, and Maghreb nations, enjoyed relative monetary stability, the rest of Africa was characterized by currency over-issue. Coupled with declining domestic production, the results were inflation and valueless currencies—the *cedi, naira, zaire, kwacha* and other African currencies. In Ghana, for example, the black market rate for the *cedi* stood at C40 to the U.S. dollar in 1981 (the official rate was C2.75 to the dollar). Even after a successful economic recovery program and greater availability of goods, the black market rate for the *cedi* in 1996 was 1,780 to the dollar (the official rate was closed after the adoption of weekly foreign exchange auctioning system in 1987). By 2004, the rate had reached 9,500 *cedis* to the dollar.

The basic cause of currency overissue, excess liquidity and the resultant inflation, and worthless currencies has been the fact that central banks in Africa are not independent. An independent central bank is one of the key institutions required to help establish an enabling environment for investment. The absence of an independent central bank means that monetary policies are subordinated to the fiscal whims of the central government. Reckless fiscal spending is accommodated by a servile central bank. In some cases, central governments literally hold a gun to the heads of governors of central banks and order them to release money for budgetary purposes—sometimes without even a semblance of an explanation. The worst offenders were military regimes. During the regimes of the late General Sani Abacha of Nigeria and Flt./Lte. Jerry Rawlings of Ghana, trucks were driven to the basements of central banks in the middle of the night and loaded with bundles of new cash. Such heists were often used to finance election campaigns. To win the 1992 presidential election, Fte./Lte. Rawlings granted civil servants a hefty 80 percent increase in salaries, which he financed largely by printing money.

In Nigeria, military rulers brought the banking system to the verge of collapse. Having frittered away the oil bonanza on extravagant investment projects, a new capital at Abuja with a price tag of $25 billion, and the highly ambitious Third Development Plan (based upon the false projections of oil output and revenue), the fall in oil prices in 1981 left Nigerian governments desperate for new sources of funds. To maintain income and the consumption binge, Nigerian governments borrowed heavily. The country's foreign debts quadrupled from $9 billion in 1980 to $36 billion in 1990. When external sources of credit started drying up, Nigeria's military governments raided the banking system to finance its profligacy, injecting substantial liquidity into the economy.[3] In 1974, for example, the Central Bank of Nigeria (CBN) loans to the government constituted less than 1 percent of the bank's asset portfolio. By 1986, they had reached 63 percent. Excess liquidity in the banking system has been a constant problem, and according to Ralph Osayameh, president of the Chartered Institute of Bankers of Nigeria, "The cause of that is government expenditure" (*West Africa,* Feb 1–7, 1993; p.153).

Control of government expenditure was nonexistent. Chaos reigned. Established budgetary procedures were flagrantly skirted by top government officials. For example, soon after Gen. Babangida signed a Structural Adjustment Program (SAP) agreement with the IMF in 1986 to rein in extrabudgetary spending and escalating defense expenditures, he formed his own private army (called the National Guards) and showered officers of the armed forces with gifts of cars worth half a billion *naira.* He exempted the military from belt-tightening. In July 1992, his military regime took a delivery of 12 Czechoslovakian jet trainers (Aero L–39 Albatros) in a secret deal believed to be part of a larger order made in 1991 and worth more than $90 million. Earlier in 1992, Nigeria had purchased 80 British Vickers Mark 3 tanks, worth more than $225 million.

In 1986, Gen. Babangida established a "dedication account" with 20,000 barrels of oil per day to fund the Liquefied Natural Gas (LNG) project. Earnings from the allocation were paid into a special account with the Midland Bank of London. In 1988, other special accounts were created to fund specific development projects: Stablization, "Signature Bonus," and Nigerian National Petroleum Corporation (NNPC) accounts. Receipts for the various accounts between 1988 and June 30, 1994, totaled $12.441 billion. But the receipts were never reflected in the federal budget.

> The dedication and special accounts were parallel budgets for the presidency and the decision of what projects to be financed was made by Babangida alone, depending upon the pressures brought to bear on him by sponsors of specific items. (*Newswatch,* Jan 16, 1995; p.11)

The former governor of the CBN, Alhaji Abdulkadir Ahmed, was the only one who, as governor, had the authority to effect payment on the authority of the president. According to *Newswatch* (Jan 16, 1995):

> If money from the dedicated account was needed for any undertaking, a note was sent by Ahmed to the CBN's director of foreign operations stating that he should release so many million dollars for such project. It would then be stated that the note should stand as a directive and a receipt for such money. In all cases, the accounts were debited accordingly. The Bank did not request, demand or was it given any documentary evidence of the services or projects paid for because these were deemed classified.
>
> In the case of payment of contractors, only certificates of performance were lodged with the bank and at no time were the original contract documents made available to CBN. It was therefore not possible to check requests for payment against the total value of the contract so as to guard against double payment or inaccurate claims. In a number of cases, there were variations between amounts approved for payments and the actual amount disbursed. (p.12)

Money from these accounts was hardly applied to the purpose for which it was originally intended. For example, out of the NNPC dedication account, according to *Newswatch* (Jan 16, 1995), Ahmadu Bello University received $17.90 million for the purchase of television and video equipment;

$27.25 million went to medical equipment for Aso Rock Clinic; $3.85 million to the army for the purchase of ceremonial uniforms; $323.35 million to the Ministry of Defense; $59.72 million for security; and $25.49 million to defense attaches in Nigerian embassies abroad—all of which bore no relation whatsoever to liquefied natural gas.[4]

From the dedicated account, $5.304 billion were spent, between 1988 and 1994, on grandiose investment projects with little economic viability. The Ajaokuta Steel Plant, which was commissioned in 1979, received $1.473 billion. By 1995, it had cost more than $3 billion but was not yet fully operational.

Improved revenue collection would have helped narrow deficits, but weak administrative capacity and susceptibility to graft and venality limited its prospects. Fraud pervaded customs and other revenue collection agencies. For example, in 1992, the Ministry of Petroleum could not account for some $1.5 billion in crude oil sales between 1980 and 1986. NNPC was even worse. "Last October, Emmanuel Abisoye, a retired major-general, who headed a panel that looked into the activities of the corporation, discovered that N71.39 billion ($3.2 billion) earned in oil revenue and lodged in several accounts of the NNPC between 1991 and 1993 had been misappropriated. In his report to government, Abisoye observed: 'NNPC does not respect its own budget. NNPC does not respect its own plans. NNPC does not respect constituted authorities'" (*Newswatch*, Jan 16, 1995; p.13).

Nigerian governments vowed to launch investigations, but the probes, the "war on corruption," and the vaunted rhetoric of "accountability" by Nigeria's military rulers were dismissed by the people as crude oil jokes. "For all the promises of probity, the military elite has been as corrupt as any regime that preceded it, taking kickbacks on contracts and diverting government funds" (*Financial Times*, May 22, 1992; p.6).

By 1995, Nigeria's banking system was on the verge of collapse. Most banks were unable to meet their obligations to customers. Depositors often were not allowed to withdraw amounts in excess of 1,000 *naira* ($110), irrespective of their credit balances. In June 1995 hundreds of irate depositors took action. At the Onitsha branch of the Mercantile Bank at Owerri Road, they held the staff hostage and demanded to withdraw their money from the bank. "The bank manager maintained that there was not enough cash on hand to satisfy this great number of customers. In response, the depositors blocked all entrances to the bank and would not permit staff members to leave" (*African News Weekly*, June 2, 1995; p.12). Depositors were infuriated by a notice on the door to the Ikolaje/Idi-Iroko Community Bank stating that "we have been forced to close shop as a result of external auditors certification. A team of auditors had examined the bank's records and found them wanting (*African News Weekly*, June 9, 1995; p.15).

Elsewhere in Africa, civilian goat-heads also engage in the same reckless practice of overspending and printing money to finance their excesses. In Kenya's 1992 election campaign, "Moi's cronies established a network of 'political banks' that siphoned money out of the Central Bank and pumped it into the ruling party's campaign. This brazen abuse of the monetary system to finance the campaign almost doubled the money supply in six months, creating 100 percent inflation" (*The Atlantic Monthly*, Feb 1996; p.33). In many cases, a simple directive was issued to the central bank without explanation and money was promptly released. Consider: "In a series of letters between April and July 1993 from the Finance Permanent Secretary, Dr. Wilfred Koinange, directed the Central Bank Governor, Mr. Eric Kotut to transfer a total of Ksh 5.8 bn ($102.5 million) to Kenya Commercial Bank (KCB). The letters indicated neither the purpose or reason for the transfers" (*African Business*, Oct 1996; p.33).

More galling, some African heads of state *knew* of the disastrous consequences of reckless inflationary finance. In fact, all Ghanaian heads of state did recognize the problem. For example, the late General I. K. Acheampong of Ghana recognized that "In the battle against inflation, one main weapon must be the control of government expenditure itself. Recourse to the Central Bank to support the Budget and the consequent very high level of monetary expansion in recent years must be halted" (*West Africa*, Aug 15, 1977; p.1658). The governor of the Bank of Ghana himself also noted that "budget deficits have been the major source of inflation in the past 3 years, 1974–77" (*West Africa*, Dec 19, 1977; p.2583). And the 1978/79 government budget statement itself admitted, "Analysis of the changes in the money supply shows that as the size of the budget deficit continued to expand so did government borrowing from the Bank of Ghana. Furthermore, over the past 5 years, more than 70 percent of every budget deficit has been financed by the Bank of Ghana, resulting in the injection of substantial amounts of new money into the economy" (p.2).[5] The budget statement continued:

Between 1971 and 1977, the money supply rose from an average of C280.6 million to C1,761.1 million—an increase of C1,480.5 million or over 500 per cent. Crudely expressed on an annual basis, the average rate of increase over this period was more than 80 per cent. This situation may by compared with increases of less than 7.5 per cent per annum in the period of 1969 to 1971, less than 2 per cent in 1965 to 1969, and about 20 per cent per annum in the First Republic 1960 to 1965. Clearly, the rates of increase in money supply over the 1971 to 1977 period and therefore of overall liquidity have been excessive. This was especially so between 1974 and 1977 when the money supply rose from C581.1 million to C1,761.1 million. (Sept 12, 1978; p.3)

From the PNDC Revised Budget Statement, 1981–82:

Public corporations have been so grossly mismanaged that most of them have come to depend on government for outright subventions, subsidies and guarantees of loans from the banking system. Instances of the most blatant incompetence can be cited in the conduct of affairs at the Black Star Line, State Farms, Food Products Corporation and numerous other public boards and corporations where financial administration and controls have been loose or even do not exist; indeed some of these institutions have not had any accounts published for as many as 4 years or even more. Even the central government accounts are in arrears by three years. Under these circumstances, expenditures are undertaken in the most irresponsible manner and without any sense of financial discipline.

In order to finance all these financial demands on the government, the previous Limann Administration resorted to the printing of more money. As a result, even though the 1981–82 Budget estimated a deficit of 4,500 million *cedis*, that deficit had reached about 3,000 million *cedis* by December 1981. With the already existing shortages in the supply of all types of goods, including essential items such as drugs and food, the funding of any such large deficit simply by printing more money would have created further escalation of price inflation, which, already at the existing rate of about 116 percent, constituted further indirect taxation of the working classes.

The Limann Government's woeful failure to curb expenditure and narrow the deficit on recurrent account was matched squarely by its cynical and incompetent handling of cocoa evacuation. (p.ii)

Yet the pattern continued, and no one in the Ghanaian government made any serious efforts to rein in government expenditures that were careening out of control. In fact, the PNDC's own finance minister, Dr. Kwesi Botchwey, "attacked some members of his own government for mismanagement, 'by heart' spending, lack of satisfactory accountability, transparency and corrupt procurement practices" (*Ghana Drum,* Jan 1995; p.14). And the ruling PNDC's own party paper, *Ghana Palaver,* published in its June 16–19, 1995 issue an article entitled, "The High Money Supply," by Charles Abban. Abban writes:

In 1988 money supply (total money and quasi money in circulation) was 181.1 billion *cedis* and in 1993, it stood at 661.6 billion *cedis*. [That is, the money supply in 1993 was three-and-half times what it was in 1988. The rate of increase over the 5-year period was an astonishing 265 percent, or, on an annual basis, 53 per cent per annum.] The causes of this trend [increase in the money supply] have been budget deficits. (p.3)

Ghana government budgetary management in the postcolonial period has been characterized by reckless spending and the production of record budget deficits, financed in the main by printing money. Excess liquidity (money) in the economy, other things being equal, sparks inflation, which has deleterious effects on the economy, as I shall discuss in chapter 7. Inflation discourages savings, depreciates the value of the local currency (the *cedi*), increases the cost of living, and raises government spending. These effects may generate their own negative social consequences. For example, increase in the cost of living may stir labor unrest if civil servants, teachers, university professors, and workers embark on strike action to demand higher wages. Since the government is the largest employer in Africa, acceding to these increased wage demands would increase the government's wage bill or expenditures. Besides wages, inflation would also push up the cost of goods and services acquired by the government. Now, inflation-induced increase in government spending may increase the budget deficit and lead to another bout of money creation and inflation. Thus, a veritable vicious circle emerges where budget deficits and inflation feed on each other. When a government cannot maintain any fiscal discipline by living within its means—like most African governments—one effective way of breaking that vicious circle is to erect a wall to stop raids by the central government on the central bank, which prints money. The establishment of an *independent central bank,* which I called for in chapter 2, would provide such a check against fiscal excesses. But there have been no such checks on the money supply, leading an irate Ismail Yamson, chairman of Unilever of Ghana, to declare that:

> There is no reason why Ghana should not achieve the consistently high growth rates of certain parts of Asia. All the favorable conditions that we see in such fast growing economies are to be found here and even more. Yet we are not growing. The reasons are not far-fetched. They can be found in the deteriorating macroeconomic environment and the poor performance of the manufacturing sector as well as weaknesses in the management and control of government expenditure.
>
> Budget deficits in 1992 and 1993 pushed the inflation rate to around 25 percent, halved the value of the *cedi,* and forced the Bank of Ghana to raise interest rates to over 40 percent to check the expansion of money supply. Just what any country needs to scare away investors and destroy industry. (*Africa Report,* March/April, 1995; p.36)

By 1997, the *cedi* was worthless and Ghanaians were increasingly resorting to the use of dollars. On September 25, 1997, the Institute of Statistical, Social and Economic Research (ISSER) of the University of Ghana issued a report, "The State of the Ghanaian Economy." It noted that the major problem facing Ghana's economy was the high rate of inflation and the increasing "dollarization." ISSER said the excessive increases in money supply because of financing of fiscal deficits by the central bank and high food prices were primarily responsible for the inflationary pressures in the economy. "Therefore, if recent statements by the Governor of the Bank of Ghana that the Bank would no longer finance government deficits and take effective measures to stop the 'dollarization of the economy' and if austere measures are put into effect then positive results will be seen in the crusade to stabilize the economy," said Kwadwo Asenso-Okyere from ISSER (*The Ghanaian Times*, Sept 27, 1997; p.3). To be able to carry these intentions through, the independence of the central bank had to be assured, ISSER cautioned. But no heed was paid to this advice. The government continued to resort to extensive domestic borrowing from the central bank, thereby injecting more money into the economy (*The Ghanaian Chronicle*, June 30–July 2, 2000; p.6).

Foreign Borrowing

Finally, an African government may borrow resources from abroad for investment. It may borrow from foreign private commercial banks or from foreign governments, often Western. Foreign private bankers and investors have not found Africa an attractive place to extend credit to or invest in and have been retreating; the void has increasingly been filled by Western governments and multilateral agencies in the form of foreign aid.

There are three types of foreign aid: humanitarian relief aid, given to victims of natural disasters such as earthquakes, cyclones, and floods; military aid; and economic development assistance. Much confusion surrounds the third, also known as official development assistance (ODA). Contrary to popular misconceptions, ODA is not "free." It is essentially a "soft loan," or loan granted on extremely generous or "concessionary" terms.

For example, an African government that needs $50 million to build a dam may borrow the said amount from a foreign private bank at 10 percent rate of interest for 10 years—a prototype of a typical foreign commercial loan. However, a Western government aid agency, say USAID, may provide the funds at 2 percent interest for 20 years, with a five-year grace period. This ODA differs from a normal foreign commercial loan in three respects: It has a lower rate of interest, a longer term to maturity, and a "grace period." Still, it is a "soft loan" that must be paid back; it is *not* free.

Africa's experience with official development assistance dates back to the colonial era. One of the charges African nationalists leveled against the colonial powers was that colonialism failed to promote credible social and economic development for Africans. And the critics were right. Colonial administrations were frugal and fiscally conservative. The colonies were expected to pay their own way instead of draining the finances of the mother country. Further, the development of Africa required large capital outlays that the home administrations were not prepared to undertake. Where investment was necessary—to lay down some minimal infrastructure for the exploitation of minerals and raw materials—the mother countries expected such expenditures to be financed by the colonies themselves. If the colonies borrowed any funds, they were supposed to service their own debts.

In the British colonies, the only "aid" offered consisted of grants under the 1929 Colonial Development Act to meet the cost of repaying loans approved for capital projects. The French colonies obtained comparable assistance under *Fonds d'investissement pour le Developpement Economique et Social*. No such arrangements existed for the Belgian colonies.

After World War II, grudging contributions to colonial development were made by the British and the French in token appreciation of African soldiers who aided in the war effort: "In 1959, for example, British East Africa (Kenya, Uganda and Tanganyika) received £5 million in official grants; by 1962 that had risen to £23 millions. Nigeria received an official donation of £5 millions in 1960. These, of course, were in addition to commercial loans raised on the London money market. But these were quite modest. Nigeria, for example, raised only £6.8 millions in new loans between 1946 and 1955, Tanganyika £6.69 millions. Kenya was a heavy borrower in these years, it borrowed £18.7 millions; and in addition, the East African High Commission borrowed £31.5 millions, whose burden was spread between the three countries" (Fieldhouse, 1986; p.244).

FOREIGN AID AFTER INDEPENDENCE

After independence, African nationalists settled down to the task of developing Africa—in its own image. A large role was envisaged for an activist and centralized state, gathering resources from traditional economic activities and investing them in modernization. Much of these resources were to be secured domestically through increased savings, sacrifice, and belt-tightening. The remainder was to be sought through foreign aid requests.

Initially, foreign aid was expected to fill the gap between domestic savings and investment. The rationale was the banal "vicious circle of poverty": Savings or investible resources were low because of poverty and incomes were low because of low investment, which in turn was due to low savings. Foreign aid therefore could supplement domestic savings, enable a higher rate of investment to be attained, and propel the economy out of its "low-level equilibrium trap." Foreign aid was thus seen as an essential prerequisite to economic advancement.

Even if domestic savings were adequate, a more mundane rationale was used to justify foreign aid requests. African countries lacked capital-producing sectors and needed to import tractors, equipment, and machinery, as well as intermediate goods such as fuel, lubricants, and spare parts essential for development. But foreign exchange was required to import these critical goods, and since most African currencies are not freely convertible, ample domestic savings in *cedis or kwachas* cannot be used to purchase tractors unless they were first converted into foreign exchange through exports. Such foreign exchange receipts could then be used to import machinery and equipment. Thus, an African country's effective savings is the difference between its foreign income (export earnings) and imports of consumer goods. The country can obtain more foreign exchange to finance imports of capital goods if it earns more abroad or curtails its import of such luxury items as caviar, pickled French sausages, or Mercedes Benzes, for example.

The development frenzy received further impetus when the United Nations declared the 1960s as the "development decade." Advocates of foreign aid determined that an African country's capacity to earn more foreign exchange through exports was limited by the following constraints: an inelastic foreign demand for African exports, an unjust international economy system, protectionist policies of industrialized nations, and monopolistic as well as oligopolistic practices of multinational corporations. Therefore, even if imported consumer goods were reduced to the barest minimum—assuming African elites would consent to an abstemious diet—the foreign exchange earnings saved would still be insufficient to finance huge capital imports. Given those assumptions, foreign aid was expected to play a vital role in accelerating development by financing critical imports (Chenery and Strout, 1966; pp.679–733).

Such theoretical arguments for greater foreign development assistance were buttressed with emotional invective. Colonialism raped and plundered Africa, argued the newly independent African states. Therefore, it was the responsibility—in fact, the moral duty—of the West to repair the damage, return the booty, and rectify the injustices perpetrated against black Africans. It is difficult to determine whether the West was persuaded more by academic arguments or succumbed to its own collective guilt over the iniquities of colonialism and slavery.

It is important to remember that reservations against this dominant paradigm by one brave economist, Peter Bauer, were ignored. He warned that, politically, centralized power could lead to corruption, authoritarianism, to-talitarianism, and human misery. He cautioned that under this scheme of things, government essentials such as maintenance of law and order, effective management of monetary and fiscal systems, and even agricultural extension work, would be neglected by a regime concerned with micromanagement of the economy (Bauer, 1972; pp.90–91).

Nevertheless, the West responded to African appeals with generous contributions of aid. As Whitaker (1988) noted:

> Even in 1965, almost 20 percent of Western countries' development assistance went to Africa. In the 1980s, Africans, who are about 12 percent of the developing world's population, were receiving about 22 percent of the total, and the share per person was higher than anywhere else in the Third World— amounting to about $20, versus $7 for Latin America and $5 for Asia. (p.60)

Earlier, the World Bank (1984) had reached similar conclusions:

> External capital flows to sub-Saharan Africa have been quite high. Between 1970 and 1982, official development assistance (ODA) per capita increased in real terms by 5 percent a year, much faster than for other developing countries. In 1982, ODA per capita was $19 for all sub-Saharan African countries and $46 per capita for low-income semiarid countries—compared, for example, with $4.80 per capita for South Asia. Aid finances 10 percent of gross domestic investment in Africa as a whole, but up to 80 percent for low-income semiarid countries and over 15 percent for other low-income semiarid countries. For some countries, ODA finances not only all investment, but also some consumption. During the 1980–82 period, however, ODA levels stagnated, even though sub-Saharan Africa's share in the total increased from 21 percent in 1980 to 24 percent in 1982. (p.13)

Changing Foreign Aid Patterns

Official development assistance to Africa may be delineated into four phases. Phase one covers the period from independence in the 1960s to the beginning of the 1970s, during which bilateral aid was the main source of development finance in Africa. Private foreign investment was not significant, largely as a result of the socialist rhetoric and policies of African nationalist leaders. There was some recourse to private credit markets in the West, but this was insignificant, and, where utilized, tended to be of very high cost, as was the case with supplier's credit. "Foreign direct investment was limited mainly to minerals and oil extraction, and in some cases to the production of wage goods such as beverages and textiles" (UNCTAD, 1998a; p.116). Although the former colonial powers (Britain, France, and Belgium) provided the bulk of bilateral assistance, other countries such as Canada, Norway, Sweden, the Soviet Union (mostly military aid), and the United States assumed an increasingly prominent role in aid disbursements to Africa.

However, as early as the 1960s, a growing concern over the effectiveness of foreign aid had begun to surface. USAID officials had realized that project support made little sense unless recipient governments improved the incentive framework for economic activity. As a result, the Peterson Commission was established by the Nixon administration to evaluate and reform U.S. foreign aid programs. It recommended that the primary function of USAID be shifted back to project lending and technical assistance, while the IMF and World Bank would provide overall policy frameworks for developing countries.

Thus, phase two began in the early 1970s when multilateral institutions, such as the IMF, the World Bank, the European Development Bank, the OPEC Special Fund, the International Fund for Agricultural Development, the UNDP, the Arab Bank for Economic Development in Africa, the African Development Bank, and the Commonwealth Development Corporation, became increasingly important sources of development assistance. For example, in 1970, aid from multilateral sources accounted for only 13 percent of the total; by 1987, that had grown to 34 percent. The following table illustrates the phenomenal growth of multilateral aid in the 1970s and 1980s.

By contrast, private commercial lending, including net foreign investment in Africa, declined sharply between 1980 and 1990, although it picked

Table 5.2   Gross Disbursements of External Loans to Sub-Saharan Africa
($ Millions)

Disbursements	1970	1980	1987	1990	1994	1996
Bilateral (concessional)	432	2,552	4,868	4,915	4,808	4,156
Multilateral	151	1,697	2,345	2,327	1,451	939
Private	593	6,330	3,346	2,533	4,636	4,426
Total	1,176	10,579	10,559	9,775	10,895	9,521

Sources: World Bank, *Financing Adjustment in Sub-Saharan Africa, 1986–199.* Washington, D.C.: World Bank, 1988; World Bank, *African Development Indicators, 1998–99.* Washington, D.C.: World Bank, 2000; UNCTAD, *Trade and Development Report, 1998.* New York: United Nations Publication, 2000.

up in 1994. Between 1990 and 1995 the net yearly flow of foreign direct investment into developing countries quadrupled to over $90 billion, but Africa's share of this fell to only 2.4 percent. According to the World Bank, in 1995 a record $231 billion in foreign investment flowed into the Third World. Singapore by itself attracted $5.8 billion, while Africa's share was a paltry 1 percent, or $2 billion—less than the sum invested in Chile alone (*The Economist,* Nov 9, 1996; p.95). "Even that meager proportion has been disputed by some analysts who believe the true figure to be less than $1 billion," said *The African Observer* (April 11–24, 1996; p.20). Although it increased dramatically to $4.7 billion in both 1996 and 1997, it dropped to $3 billion, leading United Nation's Conference on Trade and Development (UNCTAD) to conclude that "Africa has lost attractiveness as market for Foreign Direct Investment as compared to other developing regions during the last two decades" (*The African Observer,* Nov 30-Dec 13, 1998; p.21).

This view is corroborated by the Organization for Economic Cooperation and Development (OECD), which noted that, though private capital flows to developing countries over the period 1990–97 exceeded $600 billion, the flow to all of Sub-Saharan Africa barely amounted to $10 billion. Even then, of that total, fully $9 billion accrued to one country, South Africa—meaning that the other 49 countries and 560 million people of Sub-Sahara attracted essentially no net new private capital during the greatest international investment boom ever witnessed (Eberstadt, 2000; p.B4). Thus, Sub-Saharan Africa has steadily grown ever more reliant on foreign aid, with the multilateral development banks (MDBs) and bilateral donors simply filling the void vacated by private commercial lenders.

Much of the loans extended by the MDBs during the second phase were project specific: They had to be used to fund infrastructural development (roads, dams, telecommunications, and schools)—public goods that were vital for an African country's development. A hydroelectric dam, such as the Akosombo Dam in Ghana financed by the World Bank, generated not only electricity but also provided large "externalities": a low-cost power grid for an industrial base, and a man-made lake that could provide income-earning opportunities from tourism and fishing. Road construction and telecommunications also fall in this category, since they facilitate movement of goods and commerce. Similarly, a steady supply of a well-educated labor force aids industrial expansion. Multilateral Development Bank loans were also used to finance agricultural and industrial projects, which were largely owned by the state.

Phase three began in the early 1980s when it became apparent that most African economies were in crisis. Although the crises were triggered by the oil price shocks of 1979 and the Third World debt crisis of 1982, there was a general recognition that decades of misguided government policies had contributed immensely to Africa's economic morass. In fact, in May 1986, African leaders themselves collectively admitted on their own accord, in a rare moment of courage and forthrightness, before the United Nations Special Session on Africa, that their own capricious and predatory management had contributed greatly to the continent's deepening economic crisis. In particular, they pointed to their own "past policy mistakes," especially the neglect of agriculture. The 1985 Organization for African Unity Report, which served as the core of the African sermon at the United Nations, urged African nations "to take measures to strengthen incentive schemes, review public investment policies, and improve economic management, including greater discipline and efficiency in the use of resources" (*West Africa,* April 21, 1986; p.816). Most notably, the report pledged that "the positive role of the private sector is to be encouraged." Even a year before that, the African Development Bank and the Economic Commission for Africa had produced reports that had been adopted at the OAU meeting in July 1985. These reports stressed a change of direction of economic policy "toward more market freedom, more emphasis on producer incentives, as well as reform of the public sector to ensure greater profitability" (*West Africa,* 21 April 1986; p.817).

Subsequently, African leaders agreed to the World Bank's structural adjustment programs (SAPs) in return for loans to ease balance of payment, debt servicing, and budgetary difficulties. In June 1987, African leaders reaffirmed their determination to pursue the SAPs at a conference organized by the Economic Commission on Africa at Abuja, Nigeria. Under a structural adjustment program, an African country would undertake to devalue its currency to bring its overvalued exchange rate in line with its true value. Supposedly a more realistic exchange rate would reduce imports and encourage exports, thereby alleviating the balance-of-trade deficit. The second major thrust of SAPs was to trim down the statist behemoth by reining in soaring government expenditures, removing the plethora of state controls on prices, rents, interest, and the exchange rate, while eliminating subsidies, selling off unprofitable state-owned enterprises, and generally "rationalizing" the public sector to make it more efficient. By 1989, 37 African nations had formally signed up for over $25 billion in Western donor support.

Phase four began after the collapse of communism in the eastern-bloc countries in 1989, when Western donor governments and the MDBs finally recognized the importance of a democratic order and added various "conditionalities" to the receipt of their aid: respect for human rights, establishment of multiparty democracy, etc. For example, on May 13, 1992, "the World Bank and Western donor nations suspended most aid to Malawi citing its poor human rights record, a history of repression under its nonagenarian "life-president" Hastings Banda. The decision came after protest by workers turned into a violent melee in Blantyre. Shops linked to Banda and the ruling party were looted and government troops fired point-blank at the protesters, killing at least 38" (*The Washington Post,* May 14, 1992; p.A16).

The total amount of funds transferred to African governments during the four phases has been quite substantial. According to OECD, "the net disbursement of official development assistance (ODA), adjusted for inflation between 1960 and 1997 amounted to roughly $400 billion. In absolute magnitude, this would be equivalent to almost six Marshall Aid Plans" (Eberstadt 2000; p.B4). Since ODA is merely a "soft loan," this accumulated foreign aid forms the bulk of Africa's $350 billion foreign debt. Of this, 40 percent is owed to or guaranteed by Western governments and 36 percent is owed to multilateral financial institutions, such as the World Bank and the IMF (Nafziger, 1993; p.29). Private commercial loans, as a share of Africa's total debt, dropped from a high of 36 percent in the 1980s to about 20 percent in the 1990s, reflecting a declining private commercial lending interest in Africa. Much of the private unsecured commercial debt is accounted for by Nigeria, Ivory Coast, Congo, Gabon, and Zimbabwe, with Nigeria alone responsible for an estimated 50 percent of Sub-Saharan Africa's total commercial debt.

Between 1980 and 1990, Africa's debt grew faster than any other region in the Third World. By 1990, 27 African countries were classified as heavily indebted, meaning that 3 of 4 key ratios were above critical levels: debt to GDP was above the critical level of 30–50 percent; debt to income of all goods and services was above the critical level of 165–275 percent; accrued debt service to exports was about the 18–30 percent level; and accrued interest to exports above the critical 12–20 percent level (Nafziger, 1993; p.30). In the period 1978–83, Africa's debt ratio (outstanding debt over export earnings) doubled to over 200 percent. For some individual countries, the debt ratios at the end of 1985 skyrocketed. Sudan's debt ratio reached 1,232 percent; Mozambique's 1,518 percent; and Guinea-Bissau's 1,042 percent (IMF, 1986).

THE FAILURE OF FOREIGN AID PROGRAMS IN AFRICA

That foreign aid has failed to accelerate economic development in the Third World generally is no longer in dispute. An empirical study of foreign aid by Boone (1995) shows that "there was no significant correlation between aid and growth" but that "government consumption rises by approximately three quarters of total aid receipts" (p.4). So, according to Boone, aid in its usual government-to-government form does little to promote a long-term economic growth but does induce growth in government bureaucracy. As far as the poor are concerned, regardless of regime type, "aid flows primarily benefit a wealthy political elite" (Boone 1995; p.5). One indicator of this is infant mortality rates, which are sensitive to even tiny changes in nutrition for the poor. However, there is "no significant impact of aid" on these indicators (Boone 1995; pp.4–5). According to Doug Bandow of the Cato Institute, a Washington-based libertarian organization, "The United Nations [in 1999] declared that 70 countries—aid recipients all—are now poorer than they were in 1980. An incredible 43 were worse off than in 1970. Chaos, slaughter, poverty and ruin stalked Third World states, irrespective of how much foreign assistance they received" (*The Washington Post,* Nov 25, 1999; p.A31). Except for Haiti, all of the 13 foreign aid failures he cited— Somalia, Sierra Leone, Liberia, Angola, Chad, Burundi, Rwanda, Uganda, Zaire, Mozambique, Ethiopia, and Sudan—were in Sub-Saharan Africa. The African countries that received the most aid—Somalia, Liberia, and Zaire—have slid into virtual anarchy.

Similarly, food aid has induced an import food dependency in Ghana, according to Young and Kunz (2000). Despite Ghana's relatively small size, it is the sixth largest recipient of food aid. Ghana uses PL 480,[6] given on easy credit terms to the government to sell for development money, which is then used to fund development projects, or to use for a specific sale for agricultural improvement/food security. A country can save on foreign exchange and raise capital by getting these types of aid. Yet, as a USAID report itself concludes, the general direction of the country's growth has not been positive. Cocoa, a major export, now suffers in spite of the aid that was supposed to help Ghana develop.

Further, humanitarian aid may have created an import dependency as the two major aid components of "wheat and rice tend to end up on the plates of the better-off" (Young and Kunz, 2000). Internally, "natural resource depletion, declining agricultural productivity, low private savings, low investment rates, and a high population growth rate" spell an unstable future for Ghana, especially concerning agriculture and famine. To sum up USAID's presence in Ghana, "only a small percent of the population in need were served" by development initiatives (Young and Kunz, 2000). As far as consumption inequality is concerned, the lowest 10 percent in Ghana consume 3.4 percent of total consumption, whereas the top 10 percent consume 27 percent of total consumption (World Bank 1997; pp.222–23).

Nor has adjustment lending been successful in Africa. According to UNCTAD (1998b), "Despite many years of policy reform, barely any country in the region has successfully completed its adjustment program with a return to sustained growth. Indeed, the path from adjustment to improved performance is, at best, a rough one and, at worst, disappointing dead-end. Of the 15 countries identified as 'core adjusters' by the World Bank in 1993, only three (Lesotho, Nigeria and Uganda) are now classified by the IMF as 'strong performers'" (p.xii).

Reasons for Failure: From the Donors' Side

Perhaps what contributed most to the grievous failure of Western aid to Africa was a donor culture of doublespeak and inconsistencies in policy actions that achieved a confusing and overlapping array of objectives. As noted, foreign aid comes in three forms: economic development assistance, military aid, and humanitarian relief assistance for humanitarian crisis situations. Despite being cloaked in "development" garb, economic development assistance to Africa has over the decades been used as an instrument by the donors to achieve a variety of noneconomic (geopolitical and political) objectives, such as the containment of Communist expansionism in Africa, democratization, and promotion of human rights, among others. But some of these are also the stated policy objectives of U.S. foreign military aid, which seeks to promote stability, democracy, and human rights among U.S. allies. The two key elements of that program have been foreign military financing, which provided allies with grants, military equipment, and related technical services; and international military education and training, which provided extensive training of foreign military officers and police forces in a wide variety of operations. Such U.S. military aid went to brutal military regimes in Liberia (under the late Samuel Doe), Ghana (under Jerry Rawlings), Somalia (under the late Siad Barre), and Zaire (under Mobutu).

First, the West poured much foreign aid into Africa to support cold war allies (the late Mobutu Sese Seko of Zaire; the late General Samuel Doe of Liberia; the late General Siad Barre of Somalia), and to woo various Marxist leaders from the Soviet bloc (Flt./Lte. Jerry Rawlings of Ghana; Joaquim Chissano of Mozambique; Jose Eduardo dos Santos of Angola). After the cold war, Western foreign policy objectives were overhauled. Greater emphasis was placed on promotion of democracy, respect for human rights, better governance, transparency, and accountability, among other goals. However, nothing much changed. Western policies remained leader-centered—devoted to the rhetoric of a "charismatic leader"—as was exemplified by President Clinton's March 1998 trip to Africa during which he hailed the presidents of Ethiopia, Eritrea, Uganda, Congo, and Rwanda as the "new leaders of Africa."

Second, foreign aid allocations were often cocooned in bureaucratic red tape and shrouded in secrecy. The programs lacked transparency and the people being helped were seldom consulted. Third, much Western aid to Africa was tied and riddled with cronyism, thereby eclipsing its effectiveness. About 95 percent of procurement by USAID went to a few firms that only did business with USAID. "They were inside-the-Beltway firms that employed former AID staffers," said Larry Bryne, the assistant administrator for management (*The Washington Times,* August 19, 1996; p.A8). Known as "a cadre of Beltway Bandits, these Washington-based firms, or firms with Washington offices, were experienced in winning US AID contracts and cornering a large portion of US AID contracts to Central and Eastern Europe and the former Soviet Union" as well (Wedel, 1998; p.27). Similarly, "an estimated 80 percent of French aid comes back in salaries, orders and profits," according to Biddecombe (1994; p.33).

A large part of the donor funds goes to feed a hungry Western NGO bureaucracy. Aggressive lobbying campaigns often are launched to provide justification for the continuation of food relief aid. Ken Hackett, director of Catholic Relief Services, pitching the idea of food aid, told the U.S. Congress: "Each food aid dollar has at least a double impact. First, the funds are spent primarily in the United States on U.S. commodities, processing, bagging, fortification, and transportation. This enhances economic activity and increases the tax receipts to the U.S. government. Second, the food is provided to people and countries, which cannot afford to import adequate amounts of food on a commercial basis. Finally, when PVOs are involved, we leverage funds and services and gain broad public participation" (Maren, 1997; p.201).

According to Claude de Ville de Goyet, director of the World Health Organization's emergency preparedness and disaster relief coordination program in the Americas, such "crisis junkies" do more harm than good:

> Instead of supporting local emergency and medical services, they inundate them with un-requested, inappropriate and burdensome donations of clothes, medical equipment and packaged food. Many misguided individuals seem motivated as much by the chance to raise their own profiles at home as by a genuine opportunity to do some good. You see hundreds of small agencies turning up at the scenes of disasters. Some of them pop up because there is money or because there is media coverage, which is emotionally appealing. People tend to consider that, just because it is an European or American from a developed country, they can do better than a national would do in a disaster, I am sorry, but that is wrong. (*The Washington Times,* Sept 4, 2000; p.A11)

De Goyet lamented that the helicopters sent to Mozambique in March 2000 were not only too late to rescue the majority of the victims of massive flooding but that the money spent on them could have better paid for thousands of villagers to rebuild their shattered lives. "Dispatching Western medical teams was worse than useless, as they absorbed large chunks of the aid budget but arrived long after the critical 24 hours when acute medical care was needed. They then departed too quickly to help local doctors deal with the long-term consequences of the disaster, he said" (*The Washington Times,* Sept 4, 2000; p.A11).

Fourth, Western governments and development agencies failed to exercise prudence in granting aid and loans to African governments. Much Western aid to Africa was used to finance grandiose projects of little economic value and to underwrite economically ruinous policies. There are many horrifying blunders. In Somalia, Italy sponsored 114 projects between 1981 and 1990, costing more than $1 billion. According to Wolfgang Achtner, an Italian journalist, "with few exceptions (such as vaccination programs carried out by NGOs [nongovernmental organizations]), the Italian ventures were absurd and wasteful" (*The Washington Post,* Jan 24, 1993; p.C3). One example was the $250 million spent on the Garoe-Bosaso road, which stretches 450 kilometers across barren desert but is crossed only by nomads on foot.

Fifth and finally, Western donor governments and organizations allowed themselves to be duped by shrewd and corrupt African despots. Structural adjustment programs, or "adjustment lending," failed because of design flaws, sequencing, pedagogical inanities, and a weak commitment to reform. African dictators accepted reform—both economic and political—only reluctantly. And even when they accepted it, they performed the acrobatics around it, getting it to suit their whims.

Foreign loans and aid programs in Africa were badly monitored and often stolen by corrupt bureaucrats. "We failed to keep a real hands-on posture with aid," said Edward P. Brynn, former U.S. Ambassador to Ghana. "We allowed a small, clever class that inherited power from the colonial masters to take us to the cleaners. It will take a whole lot of time and money to turn Africa around" (Harden, 2000; p.1).

More maddening, the donor agencies *knew* or should have known all along the motivations and activities of corrupt African leaders and that billions of aid dollars were being spirited into Swiss banks by greedy African kleptocrats. "Every franc we give impoverished Africa, comes back to France or is smuggled into Switzerland and even Japan," wrote the Paris daily *Le Monde* in March 1990. Patricia Adams of Probe International, a Toronto-based environmental group, charged that, "in most cases, Western governments knew that substantial portions of their loans—up to 30 percent, says the World Bank—went directly into the pockets of corrupt officials, for their personal use" (*Financial Post,* May 10, 1999). The World Bank itself estimates that "nearly 40 percent of Africa's aggregate wealth has fled to foreign bank accounts" (*The Washington Post*, Nov 25, 1999; p.A31). Yet, the bank considers these same bandit African governments as "partners in development." As Gourevitch (1998) noted in regards to the late Rwandan president, General Juvenal Habyarimana, "Development was his favorite political word and it also happened to be a favorite word of the European and American aid donors whom he milked with great skill" (p.69).

World Bank loans and foreign aid to Africa have bailed out tyrannical regimes. After its economy was shattered by crass "revolutionary" policies in 1983, the Marxist Provisional National Defense Council regime in Ghana found its days numbered. The Soviets and Cubans could no longer provide assistance. It made overtures to the West, which responded with alacrity, eager to win one more "convert." The regime signed a structural adjustment agreement with the World Bank in 1983. Slight improvements in the economy were hysterically hailed and Ghana was declared a "success story," a "role model for Africa." Twelve years later and after the infusion of more than $4 billion in World Bank loans and credit, the World Bank itself admitted in its own 1996 Country Assessment Report that declaring Ghana a "success story" was a mistake and not in the country's own best interest.

The same thing happened in Mozambique and Angola, whose economies had been devastated by years of senseless civil wars. The Marxist regimes in both countries, under siege from freedom fighters, were about to collapse. They did what any clever Marxist would do to survive: blamed apartheid South Africa for funding insurgency activity in their country, eschewed doctrinaire Marxism, expunged all references to this ideology from government documents, and signed a structural adjustment agreement with the World Bank. Eager to woo these countries from the Soviet orbit, Western financial and technical assistance poured into Mozambique in the late 1980s, at the rate of $800 million a year. Britain even provided military assistance and personnel to help Zimbabwean forces crush the insurgents in Mozambique and to rebuild and reopen the Beira Corridor, which allowed goods to flow from the interior to the port city of Beira. Suddenly these resistance forces or freedom fighters, who for years put up a courageous struggle against brutal Marxism, were now characterized as "bandits" and forsaken by the West. The same fate befell the resistance forces in Angola. In July 1989, when Angola was faced with imminent economic collapse, President dos Santos took up membership in the IMF. A year later his government formally abandoned Marxist-Leninism and announced that it would introduce a market economy. The new Clinton administration cheered and the State Department made diplomatic exchanges with Angola. Dos Santos was invited to the United States, just as Jerry Rawlings had been officially invited. The rehabilitation and bailout of Marxist tin gods was complete.

In this way, World Bank–sponsored SAPs provided failing regimes the door to redemption in the West and, more important, to their own survival. Had the World Bank insisted on signing SAP agreements with only democratic countries and those at peace, the course of history in Ghana, Mozambique, and Angola would have been different and their people would have breathed easier. The very act of signing an existing SAP agreement was an admission of failure. Johnson (1993) noted that:

> Western experts who had backed the rapid transfer of power argued that Africa, in particular, was going through a difficult transition, and that patience—plus assistance of all kinds—was imperative. That view is now discredited. During the 1980's it came to be recognized that government-to-government aid usually served only to keep in power unsuccessful, unpopular and often vicious regimes. (p.7)

Uganda, dependent on foreign aid for 55 percent of its budget, was hailed as a "success story" by the World Bank and the IMF, despite growing concerns about its undemocratic political system, defense spending, inane intervention in the Congo conflict, and rampant corruption. Yet, on December 11, 1999, Uganda's aid donors announced the country's biggest-ever dollop of aid: $2.2 billion, with no visible strings attached. Of this amount, $830 million was to be given quickly as budget support and the rest was to come in chunks over three years. "Cynics might say that Uganda can hold the world to ransom because the World Bank, the IMF and the other foreign donors cannot afford to let their star pupil go under" (*The Economist*, Feb 12, 2000; p.61).

Reasons for Failure: From the Recipients' Side

It is easy for African leaders to put the blame somewhere else; for example, on Western aid donors or on an allegedly hostile international economic environment. But as the World Bank (1984) observed, "genuine donor mistakes and misfortunes alone cannot explain the excessive number of 'white elephants'" (p.24). Certainly, the recipients—African governments—are also responsible for the failure of aid programs.

It must be stated that there is nothing wrong with borrowing money. The cardinal principle of borrowing requires that the loan be used productively to generate a net income over and above that required for debt repayment or amortization. Unfortunately, this has not been the case in many African countries. External loans were not used productively. Some were used to finance reckless spending, to establish grandiose loss-making state enterprises and other "black elephants," or to purchase weapons to slaughter the African people; the rest was simply squandered.

Consumption Loans

There are three ways in which foreign aid or loans are "consumed." The first is borrowing from abroad to finance a budget deficit on the current account. Such a loan simply finances recurrent expenditures: for example, paying civil servants' salaries. The use of the loan generates no foreign exchange or return to pay back the loan. If the loan is used to finance a deficit on the capital account, such as a new office building or telephone system, it must produce or save enough foreign exchange to service the loan. But in general, this is difficult to achieve.

A second type of consumption loan is borrowing abroad to finance imports of consumer goods (corned beef, sardines, Mercedes Benzes, TV sets, etc.). In this case, the loan is simply consumed and there will be nothing to show for it: no foreign exchange saved or earned. Ghana, Nigeria, and Cameroon borrowed much abroad to buy consumer goods. In the early 1980s, for example, more than half of Tanzania's imports was financed by loans from foreign governments.

The third type of consumption loan is that taken to purchase arms and ammunition—the most useless and pernicious use of foreign aid. No income is generated to repay the loan. Ethiopia, Angola, Mozambique, Libya, Chad, Somalia, and Uganda all took foreign loans to buy weapons to wage various campaigns. If conflicts can be settled through dialogue and negotiation at very little cost, then what is the sense for a poor nation to borrow heavy amounts and wage military conflicts? What Africa spends on arms, much of which are bought with foreign loans, in the teeth of its famine crisis, defies logic. In Africa's most idiotic war, between Ethiopia and Eritrea (1998–2000), both countries were spending $1 million a day on weapons while their people were being ravaged by AIDS and famine:

> According to figures from the Institute for International Strategic Studies in London, Ethiopia, a country of 60 million, spent $480 million on arms in 1999; Eritrea, a nation of 3 million, spent $306 million. They spent slightly smaller amounts in 1998.
>
> This year [2000], Ethiopia's defense budget is set to rise to $533 million. Yet before the first outbreak of war in 1998, Ethiopia's defense budget was a little more than $100 million, the Institute said.
>
> In the last four years, Ethiopia received $924.9 million from the World Bank, more than two-thirds of it in 1998 after a first round of fighting, according to the World Bank. Eritrea, a much smaller country, received less. The

World Bank never threatened to stop the money, bank officials said, although Ethiopia lost is program with the IMF because of excessive military spending. (*The New York Times,* May 22, 2000; p.A9)

Unproductive Investments: Prestigious "Black Elephants"

Though foreign aid was used to finance specific development projects, they tended to be grandiose projects and state enterprises, dictated more by considerations of prestige than by concerns for economic efficiency. The late Mobutu Sese Seko of Zaire once declared, "I know my people. They like grandeur. They want us to have respect abroad in the eyes of other countries" (*The Wall Street Journal,* Oct 15, 1986; p.6). Accordingly, half of Zaire's foreign debt of $6 billion went to build two big dams and the Inga-Shaba power line, as well as a $1 billion double-decked suspension bridge over the Congo River. The upper level is for a railroad that does not exist.

By 1983, Ghana had more than 240 state enterprises (SEs), but their performance has been nothing short of the scandalous. These enterprises, set up with foreign loans, were supposed to earn or save Ghana the foreign exchange needed to service or pay back the loan. Instead, they racked up losses upon losses, and used up more foreign exchange to compound the debt crisis. The state enterprises could not fill the shortfall in production. Inevitably, the results were greater inefficiency, excess capacity, and economic retrogression. Similar results were obtained in other African countries such as Nigeria, Tanzania, and Zaire, as we saw in chapter 3.

Corruption, Fraud, and Shady Deals

Considerable evidence exists to suggest that many foreign loans were contracted under rather dubious and corrupt circumstances. Nigeria, for example, does not know the true amount of its foreign debt—it could be as much as $35 billion or not. Back in 1990, Chief Olu Falae, secretary to the federal military government, announced after a debt verification exercise that "over 30 billion *naira* (or $4.5 billion) of Nigeria's external debt was discovered to be 'fraudulent and spurious'" (*West Africa,* Sept 25 - Oct 1, 1990; p.1614). And while the country sank deep into debt, Nigeria's former military rulers amassed huge personal fortunes—General Ibrahim Babangida had an estimated fortune of $8 billion and even General Sani Abacha amassed $5 billion after only 4 years in office.

Ghana's foreign debt stood at $5 billion in 1995. To finance its industrialization drive, Nkrumah had borrowed heavily from abroad under supplier's credit. In a supplier's credit arrangement, a fast-talking equipment peddler would sell Ghana an equipment over a period of time, generally four to six years. The peddler then would obtain credit from private banks and have it guaranteed by his own country's governmental export credit insurance organization. After this arrangement, any future dealings would be between Ghana and the export credit organization; not with the peddler. He was paid and gone.

Indeed, under supplier's credit arrangements, Ghana bought in many cases obsolete equipment at inflated prices and contracted a huge foreign debt between 1961 and 1966. For example, the expensive three Illyushin jets Ghana bought from the Soviets, at a time when Ghana Airways was having difficulty filling its planes, turned out to be old jets that had been repainted. The British firm Parkinson-Howard sold Ghana a huge dry dock that lay idle for nine years after it was commissioned in 1969. The German "equipment-monger" Stahlunion built a sheet-glass plant with a capacity that was nearly three times the size of the local market. The plant was never brought into operation and later had to be converted at an extra cost of 2.5 million *cedis* to bottle-making. When that was completed, the government imported large quantities of bottles from Czechoslovakia and China to make it difficult for the factory to sell its bottles. A parliamentary report suspected that the plant, which supplied Ghana's Vegetable Oil Mills, "was of pre-war manufacture and had been lying idle for more than 30 years before being shipped to Ghana" (Public Accounts Committee, 1965; p.9).

A Ghana government investigation (Apaloo Commission, 1967) reported that Parkinson-Howard, which built the Accra-Tema Motorway, the Tema Harbor extension, and the dry docks and steelworks, paid a total of $680,000 in bribes between 1958 and 1963 in three installments to certain ministers. In most cases, the bribes were 5 to 10 percent of the value of the contract.

In the 1990s, there were persistent allegations of corruption and fraud in the use of aid to Ghana: "The British environmental group, Friends of the Earth, says millions of dollars in overseas aid—going to Ghana's timber sector—have been diverted by local and foreign logging firms which got development aid from the British Overseas Development Administration and the World Bank" (*The African Letter,* March 16–31, 1992; p.1). Even refugee aid was not spared. Mattresses, rations, and other relief supplies to Liberian refugees encamped at Budunburam in Ghana were regularly pilfered by the authorities. When a Liberian refugee by the name of Oscar complained, "the Ghanaian soldiers beat him" (*Index on Censorship,* April 1996).

There have been cases upon cases of embezzlement of donor funds involving ministers and high government officials. Some examples:

- Five officials at the Payroll Processing Division of the Controller and Accountant-General Department have been implicated in the 492.5 million *cedis* ($70,000) fraud at the Sekyere West District Assembly. The money represented payment to 59 suspected "ghosts" (*Daily Graphic*, July 31, 2001; p.1).
- In 1999, public servants were found to have embezzled over 100 million *cedis* out of some 1.4 billion *cedis* sent by the UNDP as a poverty reduction fund (*The Ghanaian Chronicle*, July 3–4, 2000; p.8).
- Mr Osei-Tutu Prempeh, the former Auditor-General of Ghana, annually released auditing figures which exposed large scale corruption and financial impropriety in many government and state institutions. In July 2001, he himself was arrested for his fraudulent withdrawal of various sums of money amounting to $526,000. The monies were taken or filched $15,000 at a time from the United Nations Imprest Dollar Account kept with the Bank of Ghana (*The Daily Guide*, Aug 8, 2001; p.1).
- Mr. Charles Adjei, the former Managing Director of Ghana Water Company Ltd. (GWCL), a state-owned company, "unilaterally used his position to award a water meter contract worth 5.4 billion *cedis* ($771,000) instead of the 1.5 billion *cedis* approved by the company's board of directors" (*The Daily Guide*, Aug 23, 2002; p.1).
- In 1995, Dr. Robert Dodoo authorized the Ministry of Finance to pay 70 million *cedis* to Messrs Electrovator Engineering Ltd for the installation of two lifts (elevators) in the Civil Service Annex Building. When the building was completed in 1999, the elevators had not been installed and Mr. W. Parti, the managing director, had fled the country for London (*The Daily Graphic*, Aug 21, 2002; p.3).
- "The former Minister of Trade and Industry, Mr. Dan Abodakpi, is to face charges of conspiracy, fraud, and allegedly causing $400,000 financial loss to the state. The amount was paid to Dr. Frederick Owusu-Boadu of Leebda Corporation of the U.S. for preparing a feasibility study into the establishment of a Science & Technology Park in Ghana. But contrary to the claim that Dr. Owusu-Boadu conducted feasibility studies for which payment of $400,000 was authorized by Mr. Abodakpi, documents available to the Special Investigation Team indicate that the purported study was indeed a proposal from Dr. Owusu-Boadu for the implementation of the project. It could not be called a feasibility study for which a huge sum needed to be paid because it lacked such key indicators as market analysis, financial projections and analysis to determine the viability of the project" (*Daily Graphic*, July 14, 2001; p.3).

The effectiveness of World Bank programs, themselves seriously flawed to begin with, were severely impaired in the pervasive culture of corruption and brazen looting by high government officials. One such example was "The Community-based Poverty Reduction Program of 1999."

A loan of $5 million was granted in 1999 for this program, whose purpose was to test the mechanism for the delivery of poverty reduction interventions to marginalized groups through community nutrition for street children, and to build capacity for monitoring and evaluating poverty reduction programs. Under this project were two sub-specific ones,

a. The Core Welfare Indicators Questionnaire, and
b. The Ghana Living Standard Survey (GLLS).

However, the main task, the distribution of funds to farmers in the Eastern Region, never materialized due to the misappropriation of funds. Many of the farmers were left in limbo and put into a state of despondency. Out of the $5 million for the project, $68,000 was misappropriated and the government interdicted [the following] officials responsible for the co-ordination and implementation of the projects. Authorities suspected the officials misappropriated $26,000 or 130 million *cedis* intended for distribution to the small community farmers in the Afram Plains: Col. D. I. K. Sarfo, I. G. Tetteh, P. P. Adade, C. K. Gyamfi, D. Attrama, E. K. Addai, and B. Acheampong (*Serious Fraud Office [SFO] Report, 1999*). The 1999 SFO Report also indicated that the chief executive of the project, Lt. Col. Lord Sarfo, was found to have taken part in the embezzlement. In addition, "The DCE, the district coordinating director, the District planning Officer and the Social Welfare Officer, together with the NGO called Ghana Development Youth Chambers, were involved in various deals amounting to C136, 299,000"(SFO Report, 1999; p.27, para.4A).

On the sub-specific programs, the Ghana Statistical Service headed by Dr. Oti Boateng, the government statistician, had the responsibility for the Core Welfare Indicators Questionnaire. The government statistician was alleged to have misappropriated $11,000 or 58 million *cedis* intended for conducting the survey (SFO Report, 1999; p.28). The law enforcement authorities interdicted Dr. Oti Boateng. Another sum, 155.4 million *cedis* provided by the World Bank to the Ghana Statistical Service for a "Living Standards Survey," was misappropriated by Dr. Atadika through the inflation of car rentals and seminar fees. In another example,

A total amount of 650 million *cedis* (about $278,000) allocated to the Tema Municipal Assembly toward the implementation of its Poverty Alleviation Program for the last two years cannot be traced. According to reliable sources, there is no record of the total amount released by the Ministry of Local Government and Rural Development in two batches of 400 million *cedis* for 1997 and 250 million *cedis* in 1998 respectively having been expended on any project or projects to alleviate poverty in the Assembly's area of jurisdiction. Political observers questioned the Assembly's integrity under the leadership of Nii Armah Ashietey. "He calls himself a mafia and says only God can remove him from the Assembly," an observer remarked, adding that he is a law unto himself so far as matters of the municipality are concerned. (*Free Press,* Jan 13–19, 1999; p.1)

According to Goosie Tanoh, leader of the newly formed Ghana National Reform Party, "It is an open secret that so many grants from Japan, Canada, USA and Britain had been given to party functionaries who have misapplied it" (*Ghanaian Chronicle,* Aug 14, 2000; p.3).

On December 11, 2001, Mr. Victor Selormey, the former minister of finance, was convicted of embezzling $1.2 million of a World Bank loan granted for the computerization of Ghana's court system. He was also convicted of five other counts of defrauding by false pretence, conspiracy, and causing financial loss to the state. He was sentenced to a total of eight years imprisonment and ordered to pay a total 20 million *cedis* for the two counts of conspiracy and two counts of willfully causing financial loss to the state. His accomplice, Dr Fredrick Owusu Boadu, President of the Leebda Corporation Limited in Texas, failed to appear before the Fast Track Court in Accra to give evidence. In August 2001, Dr. Frederick Boadu was reported to have fled the United States. "The court further ordered Selormey and Dr. Frederick Owusu-Boadu, a Ghanaian consultant in the United States of America (USA), to refund $1,297,500 to the state or it will compel the prosecution to initiate civil action to recover the money" (*Daily Graphic,* Dec 1, 2001; p.1).

Ghanaians were outraged at what they perceived to be a light sentence. The office of *The Evening News* was inundated with calls from irate Ghanaians. Mr. George Sowah, who phoned from Kaneshie in Accra, said he was outraged by the sentence: "It would have been better if he had been set free, so that we know that he had chopped [stolen] our money for nothing" (*The Evening News,* Dec 12, 2001). "A 20-year-old girl suffering from chronic renal failure died at the Korle-Bu Teaching Hospital in Accra because she could not get ¢25 million to cover the cost of treatment," Mr. Sowah stated.

External loans contracted privately on the behalf of the people of Ghana were subject to much abuse and fraud, according to Mary Stella Ankomah, MP for Wassa-Mpohor in the Fourth Republic:

A member of parliament for the Wassa-Mpohor constituency has disclosed that the government pays agency fees on loans it contracts. Miss Ankomah also said that the government pays what it terms "exposure fees" before loans are granted to the country.

The MP explained that the government claims it pays middlemen, who . . . negotiate loans on its behalf, a certain percentage that these agents demand.

She said when the minority MPs smelt some fishy deals in the whole exercise, they invited the Deputy Minister of Finance, Mr. Victor Selormey, to explain the term "agent and exposure fees" to the House.

According to Miss Ankomah, the Minister said there are some benevolent Ghanaians in the United States who negotiate loans for the country under the condition that they are paid a certain percentage. Under one of such conditions, the MP said the government paid out 27 percent of an $8 million loan recently given to the country by an European country.

The MP wondered how a country with a Minister of Finance and an economic team which oversees the economic performance of the country should contact an agent in contractual bids. She described the Minister's explanation as a big farce. (*The Independent*, Aug 28 - Sept 4, 1996; p.1)

In 2000, the Rawlings regime entered into a secret contract with a shady company, New York Bay International, to buy government debt, mostly owed to contractors, at 5 percent discount. Under the first arrangement, New York Bay International (NYBI) was to buy a debt of 90 billion *cedis* ($12.8 million) from the government. But the only debt that was supposed to have been restructured was 52 billion *cedis,* which would have allowed the government to pay 8.9 billion *cedis* over a six-month period to NYBI. Investigations showed that even though NYBI did not completely absorb the debt, the government continued to transfer money into the accounts of the firm through a local commercial bank, far in excess of the value of debts the company had agreed to purchase. NYBI was neither registered to do business with government, nor passed through the Ghana Investment Promotions Center. With billions of *cedis* placed in its account in Ghana, NYBI, in turn, bought foreign currencies, notably dollars at any rate from both banks and foreign exchange bureaux and transferred the monies. "This was a major contributory factor which led to the free fall of the cedi against international currencies. Information available at the Ministry of Finance indicated that one of the directors based in the United Kingdom was an ex-convict" (*Daily Graphic,* August 22, 2001; p. 3).

In Kenya, Nairobi's deputy mayor, Abdi Ogle, demanded the resignation of the World Bank's country director for Kenya, Harold Wackman (a Canadian), accusing him of turning a blind eye to the embezzlement of an emergency loan of $77.5 million in July 1998 to repair infrastructure damaged by heavy rains. "Not a cent of this money has come to the City Council because it has disappeared into private pockets within the Ministry of Local Government," fumed Ogle, who also demanded the resignation of the minister, Sam Ongere (*Daily Graphic*, Jan 9, 1999; p.5).

The World Bank mission sent to Uganda in 1998 reported "widespread accusations of non-transparency, insider dealings and corruption" (World Bank, 1998; p.1). "The impression of the World Bank anti-corruption mission is that the prevalence of corruption in Uganda is highest in the areas of procurement, particularly military procurement, and reform, and privatization of public enterprises" (p.2). The report also noted that there is widespread institutionalization of bribery throughout the country, especially in dealings with the police and with the judiciary—areas in which President Yoweri Museveni's security apparatus was directly involved.

According to the bank's report, most of the funds raised through privatization had been embezzled. President Museveni's own brother and defense advisor, Major General Salim Saleh, had been forced to resign after it was revealed that he had improperly and secretly tried to buy a majority stake in the Uganda Commercial Bank (UCB). The World Bank itself shared a confidential report detailing many cases of corruption involving government officials with the Ugandan government prior to the Consultative Group meeting, a report later released to the public at the request of the Ugandan government (World Bank, Nov 1998; p.4).

The World Bank uncovered corruption in twelve contracts, with one researcher estimating that 20 percent of privatization had serious corruption problems. The most common allegations were of undervaluing, lack of open and transparent bidding process, and non-payment by the buyer. In June 1998, for instance, purchasers of privatized companies still owed the government $14 million. It has also been claimed that funds from privatization were used for the president's political party's election campaign.

Cases of large-scale embezzlement documented in the World Bank report included the stealing of donor funds disbursed to the ministries of health and education and to the Ugandan Electoral Commission, as well as funds disbursed to projects aimed at helping alleviate poverty, but which were embezzled and never benefited the intended poor. The World Bank report specifically targeted Vice President Wandira Kazibwe, whose office is being investigated for the loss of 3.4 billion Ugandan shillings in a valley dam scheme, which was paid for but never constructed.

In June 1999, the EU announced that it had suspended aid to Ivory Coast after discovering that about $30 million donated for health programs had apparently been misused. The Ivory Coast authorities arrested four senior government officials for questioning in connection with the alleged embezzlement (*BBC World Service*, July 18, 1999). And at the XIth International Conference on AIDS and Sexually Transmitted Diseases in Africa in Lusaka in September 1999, former Nigerian health minister Olikoye Ransome-Kuti accused some African governments of stealing the bulk of funds meant for the purchase of medical drugs. Kuti said many of the HIV/AIDS patients could be saved and the epidemic effectively controlled in the region if governments valued the lives of their people and looked critically at the ways funds were being spent. He added that it would not be helpful to appeal for international aid toward the procurement of drugs when the money was being stolen by the governments. "Donors no longer listen to our whines. I am also sure they will respond promptly when our governments demonstrate a determination to care for the people" (*PanAfrican News Agency*, Sept 13, 1999).

Mauritania, a poor arid West African country, also receives aid from wealthy Western countries. About 70 percent of it goes back as interest payments, and the rest is embezzled. "The chief opposition party, Union des Forces Democratiques, claims that since 1985, the government of President Maaouya Ould Sid Ahmed Taya has siphoned away $1.8 billion of aid money for itself and its supporters. When the party raised questions about the missing money, its leaders were promptly thrown in jail. Mohammed Ould Lafdahl, the chief opposition spokesman, says debt relief will go the same way as the original loans" (*The Economist,* Sept 23, 2000; p.52).

Evidently, the record of official development assistance in Africa under all phases has generally been dismal—a fact recognized by the donors and which underscores their unwillingness to provide more aid, a result called "donor fatigue." OECD aid to Africa fell by 22 percent between 1990 and 1996, decreasing by 18 percent to Sub-Saharan countries between 1994 and 1996 alone (DeYoung, 2000a; p.A1). Even humanitarian aid to Africa has been shrinking. Contributors to UN aid and development programs have provided slightly more than half of the $800 million requested in 1999 for African countries suffering from "complex emergencies"—the term applied when war and failed institutions, often combined with a natural disaster, leave vast numbers of people homeless and starving. Specific programs for some particularly problematic areas, such as the Great Lakes region of Central Africa, including the two Congos, Rwanda, and Burundi, have fared even less well (DeYoung, 2000b; p.A1).

In September 1999, the UN's World Food Programme announced it would curtail its feeding program for nearly 2 million refugees in Sierra Leone, Liberia, and Guinea after receiving less than 20 percent of requested funding. An emergency appeal during the summer to feed and shelter at least 600,000 Angolans who had been displaced in that country's long-standing civil war brought minimal initial response and predictions of mass starvation. In Africa's Great Lakes region of Congo, Burundi, and Rwanda, where wars have produced nearly 4 million refugees, the United Nations estimated it would need $278 million to take care of the refugees. By October 1999, only 45 percent of that amount had been donated.

Private organizations are also having difficulty raising funds for African relief operations. According to Mario Ochoa, executive vice president of the Maryland-based Adventist Development and Relief Agency (ADRA), which operates relief projects out of its own donations and under contract with donor governments, "If I were to go now and make an emergency appeal for, say, Rwanda, for $500,000 for food, I'd probably get about seventy or eighty thousand in contributions" (*The Washington Post,* Nov 26, 1999; p.A1).

The reasons for the decline are not hard to find. Critics have long said that foreign assistance was wasted by bloated aid agencies pouring money into the pockets of corrupt African governments. When the Soviet Union collapsed, Western powers no longer felt the need to purchase the cold war loyalty of such governments. With a less threatening world beyond their borders, donor nations came under pressure to attend to problems at home (DeYoung 2000a; p.A1).

A bucket full of holes can only hold a certain amount of water for a certain amount of time. Pouring in more water makes little sense as it will all drain away. To the extent that there are internal leaks in Africa—corruption, senseless civil wars, wasteful military expenditures, capital flight, and government waste—pouring in more foreign aid makes little sense. As a first order of priority, the leaks should be plugged to ensure that the little aid that does come in stays in. As President Reagan once stated: "Unless a nation puts its own financial and economic house in order, no amount of of aid will produce progress" (quoted by Bovard, 1986; p.2). To believe otherwise is a myth. But African dictators, impervious to reason, continue to believe that only more foreign aid would save Africa.

Perhaps the decline in foreign aid is just what Africa needs. As Maritu Wagaw wrote: "Let Africa look inside Africa for the solution of its economic problems. Solutions to our predicament should come from within not from outside" (*New African,* March 1992; p. 19). Additionally, there will be less aid money for Africa's finance ministers to steal.

Ghana's former finance minister Victor Selormey is in jail. Another, the former finance minister of Zambia, Katele Kalumba, was grabbed and charged with theft of $33 million while he was in office. "The police found him hiding in a tree near his rural home" (*The New York Times,* Jan 16, 2003; p.A8). Where else can a coconut-head hide?

Chapter 6

The First Generation Problems

Three decades after independence, uncertainty and fear still rule the African continent. The freedom and justice that many people sacrificed their lives for have been replaced by tyranny and oppression. And the promise of a decent living has been betrayed by misgovernance and corruption.

Most Africans fought so hard to liberate themselves from colonial rule only to be used and abused and their nations ruined by their own leaders. Today Africa has very little to show for its independence because of inhumane and incompetent leadership.

—Steve Mallory, publisher,
The African Observer, May 2–15, 1995; p.3.

I heard we have a new government. It makes no difference to me. Here we have no light (electricity), we have no water. There is no road. We have no school. The government does nothing for us.

—Simon Agbo, a farmer in Ogbadibo, south of Makurdi,
Benue state capital in Nigeria, in *The Washington Times,*
Oct 21, 1999; p.A19.

Thousands of Angolans are dying of hunger because the country is mismanaged and the holders of power have turned into a band of thugs who pretend to be managing a bank. Our bank. Our petrol. Our diamonds. Our riches. But above all, our children, parents, brothers and cousins, who they use as fodder for their diabolical cannons.

—From a pamphlet of *Parti d'appui démocratique
et du progrès d'Angola* (PADPA) circulated in Angola,
The Economist, Feb 3, 2001; p.47.

THE PREDATORY STATE

As discussed in chapter 3, most postcolonial African nationalist leaders and elites made some serious initial mistakes. They adopted the wrong ideology, socialism, which is alien to Africa, under which they spurned the private sector or the market economy, and placed primary reliance on the state to direct economic development (*dirigisme* or statism). Statism and socialism were bedfellows in many African countries. State participation in the economy was expanded to ensure "state ownership" of the economy under a regime of state controls on prices, interest rates, exchange rate, and rent. Even in the few countries, such as Ivory Coast, Kenya, and Nigeria, that did not opt for socialism, a large role was envisaged for the state in the economy. In the process, a state monster evolved that came to control almost every conceivable aspect of the economy. The all-powerful, omniscient, and omnipresent state held sway, knowing no bounds and holding no restraint against itself.

Africa was in a hurry to industrialize. The industrialization drive required the massive transfer of resources to the state. With its legislative powers, exercised by fiat, edicts, and diktats, the state extracted such resources from the peasantry, or the rural sector. Additional resources were secured by the state through foreign borrowing. When such foreign aid was not forthcoming, African governments simply printed money to finance their development programs.

In Africa's industrialization drive, state enterprises were acquired or built with breakneck speed. Factories and whole industries were acquired haphazardly—often more on considerations of prestige and emotionalism than economy or rationality. Africa had to "prove something"—that it too was "capable." Factories were established with little planning or study. In many cases, pre-feasibility studies were seldom done. Inordinate political interference ensured that state enterprises became employment mills, providing "jobs for the boys"—loyal supporters of the ruling regime. Overstaffing and swollen bureaucracy became the characteristic features of state enterprises in Africa. Packed with party hacks, they were handed over to cronies, whose management experience did not extend beyond bludgeoning opposition rivals and spitting venomous anticolonialism verbiage. Managed by pot-bellied incompetents, chosen for their fealty to the head of state, Africa's state enterprises became towering edifices of inefficiency, waste, nepotism, venality, and graft.

Personal and political factors influenced much of Africa's infrastructural development. African heads of state are notorious for placing modern airports and multilane highways that lead nowhere in their home towns: The late president Mobutu Sese Seko of Zaire attempted to transform his home-town, Gbadolite, into the "Versailles of the jungle." Some African politi-cians, eager to "bring development" to their home towns, just placed factories in their districts. Three of Nigeria's oil refineries were placed in the north for no reason other than tribal politics, as the northern Hausa/Fulani ethnic group has dominated the string of military regimes that ruled Nige-ria for much of the postcolonial period.

Africa's state-owned enterprises failed to deliver the goods—import sub-stitutes, which were supposed to conserve foreign exchange. Even when de-livered, the products were shoddy and of such poor quality that Africans preferred the imported variety. Nigeria's state-owned oil refineries could not produce refined fuel due to frequent equipment breakdown and lack of re-pairs. Inadequate refinery supplies, coupled with price controls, created acute fuel shortages in an oil-producing country! Only in Africa can such grotesque paradoxes occur. Eventually, refined petroleum products had to be imported anyway. This example is representative of many of Africa's state en-terprises, which were to produce such items as cement, steel, shoes, rubber, and food items. Thus, in the case of Nigeria, the investment in oil refineries did not pay off. Then foreign exchange had to be expended to import re-fined fuel. Why not sell off the inefficient state oil refineries and cut losses, then? Because that would be politically unacceptable. Thus, state employees are kept on the payroll when nothing is produced. Losses are covered by gov-ernment subventions, draining budgets.

State Overreach

A sensible person recognizes his weaknesses, his strengths, and the limits of his capabilities. Similarly, a government must also recognize its own limita-tions and strengths and concentrate on those tasks it can do best. The gov-ernment is best at providing what economists call public goods (defense, roads, bridges, parks, education, health care, law and order enforcement, etc.). The area where government is weakest is in production. Fishing, lum-bering, agriculture, manufacturing, mining, and commercial banking often require making quick decisions—not the hallmark of government. By its very nature, the government is excruciatingly slow in making decisions and should not get itself involved in directly productive activities. Here the profit motive clashes with politics, and the result is inefficiency, losses, and waste. This, however, does not mean the state or the government has no role what-soever to play in the development process.

Government action can be helpful in two areas. The first is the "devel-opment environment" the government creates, and the second is the way in which the government manages or conducts its own affairs. A government can play a positive role in development by making it easier for people to be more productive; for example, by providing a reliable telecommunication system. The proper role of an African government is to encourage, facilitate, and channel this creative human activity, not to suppress it, since innovation and creativity lie at the root of social progress. The government does not develop an economy; it is the people who do so. Therefore, it makes absolutely no economic sense for the government to seek to replace the activities of millions of people. If two heads are better than one, then certainly 14 million heads are better than the government's.

People are encouraged to be creative and productive through praise, reward, or incentives. In the marketplace, incentives are provided by prices, which act as signals to both producers and consumers. A rise in the price of a commodity sends a signal to producers—to produce more of the affected commodity. The rise in price serves as an incentive for increased production. By the same token, the rise in price sends a signal to consumers to curtail consumption. But by fixing prices, interest rates, wages, foreign exchange, and rent, the government blocks this signaling process and effectively destroys the system of incentives. Because a price control prevents the price of an item from rising, producers are not given the incentive to make more available—nor are consumers given the incentive to reduce consumption.

The second area where the government can play a useful role is by establishing an "enabling environment." The six requirements for such an environment are: security of persons and property, the rule of law, a system of incentives, a basic functioning infrastructure, some measure of freedom (intellectual, economic, and political) and stability (political, economic, and social). People must feel safe in order to go about their economic activities, and their property rights must be respected, too. Equally important is the state of the physical infrastructure: roads, bridges, telephones, ports, utilities, and educational facilities. Raw materials must be purchased for the production process, finished goods must be shipped to market. Reliable supplies of water and electricity, as well as a good network of roads and a stable communication system, are all vital for economic activity. But as we noted, postcolonial African governments did not establish an enabling environment for productive economic activity. Because they took on so many tasks, they performed none of them well. They had their fingers in every conceivable pot, as Africans would say. Obviously, it is far better for the government to take on few tasks and do them well rather than assume an enormous amount of tasks and do none well. What tasks can the government efficiently handle?

According to the World Bank (1989):

The state has an indispensable role in creating a favorable economic environment. This should, in fact, be its primary concern. It is of utmost importance for the state to establish a predictable and honest administration of the regulatory framework, to assure law and order, and to foster a stable, objective, and transparent judicial system. In addition, it should provide reliable and efficient infrastructure and social and information services—all preconditions for the efficiency of productive enterprises, whether private or state-owned. (p.55)

Providing an enabling environment alone is not enough. The second aspect of the role of government in development concerns how the government conducts its own affairs. As the World Bank (1989) put it:

Africa needs not just less government but better—government that concentrates its efforts less on direct interventions and more on enabling others to be productive. Every level of government should take measures to improve the performance of public administrations and parastatal enterprises. Institution-building is a long-term endeavor that requires a clear vision and a specific agenda. Special attention needs to be given to strengthening the policy analysis and economic management capabilities of governments.

Ultimately, better governance requires political renewal. This means a concerted attack on corruption from the highest to the lowest levels. This can be done by setting a good example, by strengthening accountability, by encouraging public debate, and by nurturing a free press. It also means empowering women and the poor by fostering grassroots and non-governmental organizations (NGOs), such as farmers' associations, cooperatives, and women's groups. (p.6)

Radical Africanists, who object to these suggestions as "strictures from an imperialist institution" (the World Bank), should look at the role of the government in their own indigenous economy. The main functions of traditional African governments were:

1. Defense against external aggression,
2. Maintenance of law and order,
3. The promotion of justice and social harmony within the kingdom, and
4. The promotion of trade and commerce.[1]

The role of the indigenous government in the economy was very limited for pragmatic, not ideological, reasons. In fact, "The chief function of the Ashanti administration was to ensure harmony in the society rather than to provide services requiring expenditure" (Busia, 1967; p.78). Within the context of these objectives, trade assumed primacy in peacetime.

One of the traditional roles of the African chief was to create a peaceful atmosphere for his people to engage in trade—the creation of an enabling environment. Even in agriculture, it was not the role of the indigenous government to interfere or dictate what crops the peasants should raise. What a peasant farmer cultivated was his own individual decision to make. The role of the chief in agriculture was to ensure that access to land was not denied to anybody, even strangers. Supervision or regulation of access did not constitute control over production.

In most cases across Africa, "there was no direct interference with production" (Wickins 1981; p.230). Such an interference would have been in direct and obvious antipathy to African philosophy. This philosophy held that the individual was part of a community whose interests were antecedent. Within the community, the individual was completely free to pursue any vocation he so wished. The tenet of African law which maintained that any harmful action against another individual was a threat to the whole society was applicable to the realm of economics. A restriction on the economic activity of an individual could place severe restraints on the economic welfare of the whole village or community. If the individual prospered, so too did his extended family and the community. The individual could prosper so long as his prosperity did not conflict with or harm the interests of the community. In such a clash, the community's interests were paramount. To the extent that such conflicts did not arise, the chief had no traditional authority or business interfering with an individual's pursuit of prosperity. Ultimately, the individual was answerable to his family and ancestors, not the chief, who merely acted as the intermediary between the living and the departed. The individual cannot blame the chief for his poverty or misery. This was a well-nigh universal African belief.

With trade, the historical evidence does not suggest obtrusive government interference, either. It hardly made sense for the chiefs to prevent their own subjects from engaging in trade. Traders were free enterprisers, taking the risks themselves. In fact, chiefs encouraged their people to engage in trade. Tribal government enterprises, the equivalent of state-owned enterprises, were not common in indigenous Africa.

Rather than act as the initiator or entrepreneur, the state should be a facilitator and *empower others* to initiate development. It is difficult to prescribe how much economic and political power the state should have, since there is no one single political-cum-economic system that assures stability, freedom, and security. The fact that the American system works well for Americans does not mean every African country must copy it. In every constitution, there is a cultural imprint and historical experience. The American democratic system has evolved through the centuries and reflects American cultural attributes and idiosyncrasies. But democracy, as an institution, can take different forms: American-style (or representative) democracy, European-style (parliamentary) democracy, and African-style (participatory or consensual) democracy. Similarly, capitalism, as an economic institution, can take different forms. As such, Africa must evolve or devise its own constitution and system, based upon its cultural heritage, experience, and aspirations. What this system should ultimately be is for the African people themselves to determine; it is not for this author or any African head of state to impose upon them.

The Regime of State Controls

As noted earlier, African governments took on more than they could chew. Statism or state intervention in the economy was pursued with a whole battery of controls on prices, exchange rates, interest rates, and other economic variables. These controls, together with other edicts and legislation, were intended to transfer huge resources to the state, which would, in theory, allocate them for development to benefit the whole country. By the early 1970s, practically much of Africa was under rigid state controls. Unfortunately, they had serious unintended but predictable consequences.

Officially, price controls were supposed to make commodities affordable to the masses. But the immediate effect of the imposition of a price control is the creation of a shortage. If the government fixes the price of a commodity, say bread, at $1 a loaf below its prevailing market price of say, $3, the commodity is rendered artificially cheaper, increasing the demand. But producers (bakers), forced to accept a lower price, would reduce the supply because the government-dictated price is insufficient to cover their costs. The result is a shortage—a first-generation problem. The shortage, in turn, may create a black market (a second-generation problem, a secondary unintended consequence) where hoarding, bribery, profiteering, and shady deals may flourish as the commodity is illegally traded above the official price. Measures designed to curb profiteering or hoarding attack the *second-generation problems.* In other words, such measures attack the symptoms, rather than the root cause of the disease—the price control itself. It is important to remember that the first-, second-, and even third-generation problems can be found in other government measures.

If the official price (price control) of bread is $1, but the cost is three times as much ($3) on the black market, this creates an incentive for anyone to seek to buy bread at the official price and resell on the black market to reap a huge profit—a practice that was known in Ghana as *kalabule.* As such, everyone would want to seek access to or acquire bread at the official price. Political connections or knowing somebody in the government can be an asset. Where such connections do not exist, every effort will be expended to establish one since connections can be profitable. From society's point of view, the distortionary effects of price controls wreak enormous economic damage. To illustrate this, imagine the price control was absent and the price of bread is the free market price of $3. In this case, if people found the price too expensive, they would either refuse to buy the commodity, buy a substitute, or produce it themselves. However, in creating shortages and allowing the commodity to be obtained cheaply from government sources, price controls induce people to "chase the commodity" or invest a substantial amount of effort and time in establishing the political connections needed to obtain the commodity at government-subsidized prices. Such efforts, which could better be spent elsewhere, are a waste of time from society's standpoint.

Contrary to popular misconception, price controls do not make commodities "affordable." Rather, they make them more expensive because of the hidden costs involved in searching for the scarce goods ("search costs") and the time wasted in standing in line. It is these hidden opportunity costs that render the commodity much more expensive. The hidden costs can be eliminated by simply removing the price controls. But most postcolonial African countries followed in almost lockstep fashion the rigid price-control script.

In Nigeria, price control—fixing the price of petrol (gasoline) at 26 *naira* per liter ($0.18 cents per liter, or 0.83 cents per gallon)—caused enormous shortages in tandem with inadequate supplies. Nigerians believe that, since their country is an oil-producing country, they are entitled to cheap gasoline prices. But its state-owned fuel-refining firm, NNPC, cannot produce enough gasoline to meet demand because most of its state refineries are out of commission. Funds allocated for repairs during the Abacha era were embezzled. "So it imports petrol (gasoline) at market rates, which it is then obliged to sell at a loss" (*The Economist*, April 26, 2003; p.42). To maintain that price control, Nigeria's governments spend about $2 billion a year subsidizing fuel. Since coming to office in 1999, President Olusegun Obasanjo tried on two occasions to remove subsidies on petroleum products. The economic reasons were cogent. First, cheap petrol encouraged waste of a declining asset. Second, the subsidies were costing the government money that could more usefully be spent on education, health care, or telecommunications. Third, since subsidized petrol cost only a third of the price of neighboring countries, much Nigerian petrol is smuggled across the border, leading to chronic fuel shortages in many parts of Nigeria. The entire situation is one of economic insanity: The government imports gasoline at market rates to sell at subsidized prices in Nigeria, but because prices are higher in neighboring countries, the same fuel is smuggled out, forcing the government to re-purchase and re-import presumably the same fuel into Nigeria, which will be smuggled out again in a never-ending cycle. But each time the government attempts to raise the price of fuel, deadly and violent strikes and protests ensue.

In June 2000, President Obasanjo tried to raise fuel prices by 50 percent. That move led to a general strike organized by the Nigerian Labor Congress (NLC) and riots that left dozens of people dead. President Obasanjo was forced to rescind the price hike. He tried again in January 2002, but this time went for only an 18 percent increase. The NLC promptly called for a general strike and the country ground to a halt. Shops and banks were closed. However, President Obasanjo fought back, declared the strike illegal, and arrested NLC leaders. Two days later, the strikers returned to work.

On June 20, 2003, Obasanjo's government tried again, announcing a 54 percent increase in the price of fuel. Nigeria's trade unions embarked on an eight-day general strike to protest the fuel price. "Labor leaders argue the steep price increases for petrol, diesel and kerosene would only aggravate poverty among Nigeria's 120 million people, 70 percent of whom live on less than one dollar a day" (*Allafrica.com,* July 7, 2003). At least 14 people were killed in violence during the 8 days of the strike. According to union leaders, 10 were shot dead by the police in Lagos during riots on the last day of the strike. Eventually, a compromise was reached between the NLC and the government on the price of 34 *naira* a liter ($0.24 a liter or $1.09 a gallon), which, by international standards, was very cheap. Of course, this would not solve the problem of gasoline/petrol shortages.

When President George W. Bush visited Nigeria on July 12, 2003, Franklin Okoye, a civil servant, pointed out that President Bush never saw real Nigeria. If Okoye were chaperoning Bush around Nigeria, he would have canceled all talks with Nigeria's politicians and scrapped the ceremonial functions as well. Instead, he would have fed President Bush a bowl full of *isi ewu,* a peppery Nigerian delicacy made of goat head that would have left Bush's taste buds numb. Then he would have taken President Bush to a gas station, where he would have spent all day sitting in his limousine, inching ever so slowly toward the pump, now and then sticking his head out into the choking smog to swear at line jumpers and curse the fact that an oil-rich country such as Nigeria does not have enough gasoline to go around.

"This is the real Nigeria," fumed Okoye during President Bush's visit; Okoye had to spend six frustrating hours baking in his Honda Prelude in order to fill his tank after the stations opened after an eight-day strike (*The New York Times,* July 13, 2003; p.A3). There was pandemonium as drivers tried to force their way, or buy their way, into the front of the unruly queue. Frustrated by the slow pace of things, a driver called Dele "reached into his wallet and pulled out a 200 naira bill—the equivalent of about $1.50 and a day's wage for many Nigerians—and handed it to a man with a handful of bills who then allowed Dele into a faster-moving gas line" (*The New York Time,* July 13, 2003; p.A3).

It is important to analyze the cases of Okoye and Dele because they illustrate an important concept economists call "opportunity cost." The six frustrating hours Okoye spent in the gas line could have been spent more productively elsewhere. Because he was a civil servant he did not bear this "opportunity cost"—he was absent from his job for six hours and did not lose any pay. Taxpayers or the government bore the cost of paying him for no work done. If he endures this ordeal twice a month, it would translate into 12 hours a month (or 144 hours a year) of lost productivity. Obviously, Okoye is not the only civil servant who wastes six hours in a gas line. If a million other civil servants do, the cost to the Nigerian government would be enormous, running in the billions of *naira.*

There is an additional cost as well. When civil servants spend part of their time chasing scarce commodities and gasoline, the rate of absenteeism skyrockets. This, in turn, means that getting normal government functions—such as obtaining a passport—takes much longer. And to speed up that process, bribes may have to be offered there, too!

Suppose, however, that Okoye was a taxi driver, earning 400 *naira* an hour. Assume that his Honda Prelude takes 10 gallons to fill the tank and one gallon is equivalent to 4.546 liters. At 34 *naira* per liter, it would cost him 1,545.64 *naira* to fill his tank, which, at the exchange rate of $1 = 144 *naira,* would amount to $10.73. But he wasted six hours in queue, costing 2,400 *naira* or $16.67. Therefore, the total cost of waiting for six hours to fill his 10-gallon tank was $27.40, which translates to $2.74 a gallon, which is even more expensive than in California! Of course, this analysis assumed that he was able to purchase gasoline after the six-hour wait—the length of wait assures no guarantees—and further that the taxi driver did not have to bribe to jump the line. If any of these cases apply, then the taxi driver would have paid more than $2.74 per gallon, which puts the price per gallon among the highest in the world.

The point of this discussion is to drive home the fact that price controls do not make commodities affordable. Okoye would be far better off if there were no price controls on gasoline and the price in Nigeria was the same as in Benin. If the price were $2.00 a gallon or 63 *naira* per liter, Okoye would have all the gasoline that he wanted and would not have to waste precious time waiting in a smog-choked queue.

Unfortunately, initial mistakes made were compounded, creating a crisis situation, which spawned second and third-generation problems—bribery to jump gas lines, the smuggling of cheap Nigerian gasoline to neighboring countries, absenteeism in the civil service, and hoarding of gasoline, among others. For decades, the energies of African governments were absorbed in managing crises and their attendant problems. Rather benightedly, many of these governments believed that more of the same bad medicine would cure the patient. Accordingly, more stringent government control measures were taken, which naturally aggravated the crises. Then the authorities called for more powers and yet more severe measures to deal with the new crises— gasoline shortages, hoarding, and smuggling, for example. In 1982, Ghana closed its borders to prevent the smuggling of cocoa to neighboring countries, where it fetched a higher price. In the late 1980s, Zambia also closed it borders to stanch the smuggling of cheap consumer goods to Tanzania and Zaire. Then, on August 9, 2003, Nigeria closed its border with Benin "over concerns about increased cross-border crime such as smuggling and people trafficking" (*The Washington Times* Aug 10, 2003; p.A11). Did Nigerian government officials need to be told that their policy of ridiculously cheap gasoline was what was fueling smuggling across the border to Benin, where gasoline was more expensive?

Of course, Benin would protest the border closure, claiming it violated the protocol of the Economic Community of West African States (ECOWAS), which permits free movement of goods and people. The border would be opened after a summit between the presidents of the two countries. Smuggling activity would resume, depriving Nigeria of much-needed gasoline. Threats would be issued: "Gasoline smugglers would be shot on sight!" But then, customs officials can always be bribed to look the other way. For much of the postcolonial period, most African governments have been engaged in such "crisis-management."

Rent-Seeking, Culture of Fraud, Bribery, and Corruption

The Byzantine maze of state controls and regulations provided the vampire elites with golden opportunities for self-enrichment. In Egypt, for example, securing an ordinary permit to put up a house required obtaining permits from no less than 30 government agencies with overlapping jurisdiction. In Ghana, securing a license to import a commodity required submitting an application in triplicate and getting approval from three levels of authority: the Ministry of Trade, the Ministry of Finance, and the Bank of Ghana, which resulted in an interminable waiting period during the 1970s. To set up a business in Nigeria, an entrepreneur had to comply with the 1963 Immigration Act, 1964 Indigenization Guidelines, 1968 Companies Decree, 1972 Nigerian Enterprises Promotion Decree (amended in 1973, 1974, and 1977), as well as other stifling regulations pertaining to what could be imported, who could be hired, and how much could be repatriated abroad. In 1977, dividend payments were restricted to 40 percent. According to Martin Plaut, a BBC Africa analyst,

> "The World Bank says that four-fifths of the most difficult countries in the world to do business are in Africa . . .
> Mozambique: 153 days to start a firm
> Congo: 155 days
> Nigeria: 21 procedures to register a business but just 3 in Finland
> Chad: 19 procedures
> Angola: Three years to enforce a contract."
> (BBC News, Sept 8, 2004. Web posted at http://news.bbc.co.uk/2/hi/africa/3638018.stm)

Compliance with the multiplicity of regulations was often frustrating and time consuming. Tempers flared when applicants and potential investors were endlessly shuttled back and forth to obtain permits from senior government officials who, more often than not, were absent for extended lunches with their young mistresses. Hucksters saw an opportunity to "expedite" the process and charge a "fee." Civil servants could also exploit the situation. They would suddenly run out of application forms for passports creating a contrived shortage. A bribe of say, $5 would promptly produce such an application form. In this case, a "shortage" of application forms is manufactured to enable the civil servant to extort a "premium," a "commission," or a "rent" for its "scarcity," as others do in a real black market. Economists call these kind of activities "rent-seeking." Rent-seeking activities retard economic growth—merely redistributing wealth and not producing it. Rent seekers become rich extracting "commissions" on contrived shortages.

Many demand bribes outright, exploit their positions in government, and manipulate the state's regulatory powers to supplement their meager salaries. "Because every permit has its price, Nigerian officials invent endless new rules. A guard outside a ministry demands a special permit for you to enter; a customs inspector invents an environmental regulation to let in your imports; an airline official charges passengers for their boarding cards" (*The Economist*, August, 21, 1993; Survey, p.5). Indeed, said Tony Nze Njoku, "Every official transaction provides an avenue to amass wealth, which leads to poor service and failed government programs" (*Finance and Development*, June 1998; p.56).

Almost every government regulation and nuance of policy can be exploited. Revenue collection, passport control, and even government stationery can all be diverted, manipulated, or used for illicit gain. In Cameroon, the Ministry of Finance and Economy is supposed to be open to the public at 11:00 A.M. "but for 500 Cameroonian francs the guards will let you in as much as three hours early" (*West Africa,* March 13–19, 2000 p.16).

The phenomenon of "chasing files" breeds a culture of fraud, bribery, and corruption. "In Cameroonian government administrative services, if you do not give money your file will not be processed. Documents will even be removed from them in order to render a file incomplete. If you do not 'talk well' your file will be sat upon, your child will not go to school, the magistrate will send you to prison" (*West Africa,* March 13–19, 2000 p.16).

Quite often, however, the ruling vampire elites take advantage of the same shortage situation they publicly lament and profit from their own mismanagement of the economy. They purchase commodities at government-controlled prices that they later resell on the black market to reap a huge profit. As journalist Ben Ephson explained,

Kalabule dates back to the late Acheampong's era when inflation was rising uncontrollably. It was at that time that chits were being issued, mainly to women to collect goods which were being sold on the open market. Non-bakers had huge allocations of flour and young girls just out of school were collecting weekly allocations of 100 bags of cement, ten cartons each of milk, milo, etc. [When Limann's civilian government was elected in 1979], party leaders felt those who helped the party come to power had to be rewarded. This reward came in the form of chits to collect flour, milk, sugar, beverages, wax prints etc., which were in turn sold to *Makola* [market] women. The party man gave the price to his contact man at $650, the contact man too had to chop, so—in turn gave it to the market woman at $750 and before it got to the actual baker, the price ranged between $850–950. The control price of a bag of flour was $114.00. (*West Africa,* Oct 4, 1982 p.2571)

In Rwanda, the late President Juvenal Habyarimana ran lucrative rackets in everything from development aid to marijuana smuggling. "Habyarimana and his in-laws operated the country's sole illegal foreign exchange bureau in tandem with the central bank. One dollar was worth 100 Rwandan francs in the bank or 150 on the black market. The president and his brother-in-law took dollars from the central bank and exchanged them in the exchange bureau." (*The Washington Post,* April 18, 1995; p.A17).

In Nigeria, "Abacha, the late head of state of Nigeria, increasingly monopolized the oil trade for himself,' said John Bearman, a London-based oil industry analyst. 'There's no deal that does not go through the presidential villa'" (*The Washington Post,* June 9, 1998; p.A19). In 1996 and 1997, more than $2 billion was diverted from the Nigeria's four state-owned oil refineries by corrupt finance and oil ministers, leading to the collapse of the refineries for lack of repairs. When price controls created gasoline shortages forcing Nigerian to import refined fuels, the vampire elites immediately saw a profitable opportunity and grabbed that trade too, skimming off a percentage. "The government subsidizes the sale price of gasoline and other fuels, but Abacha loyalists among the officer corps and civil service divert much of the available supply to sell on the black market or to neighboring countries" (*The Washington Post,* June 9, 1998; p.A19). In this way, they profit from the very problem they themselves created.

But then such smuggling aggravated the shortage situation—an all too familiar situation. At domestic service stations, long queues of vehicles would snake out around blocks. Scuffles and fights would often break out as some drivers or vehicle owners attempted to jump the queue. This then would create an opportunity for racketeering. Frustrated drivers would be willing to pay to jump the line and con artists, acting as though they were "station managers" or station workers with authority, would collect money from potential line jumpers. The public would clamor for a resolution to these problems. The obvious solution is to remove the price controls and reform the dysfunctional system. But such reform is anathema to the ruling elite and their cronies, who benefit from the rotten status quo. Their business empires will collapse if economic reform strips them of state controls. Economic liberalization may also undermine their ability to maintain their political support base and, thus, prove suicidal. So the government pretends it is solving the problem by taking more stern measures to combat smuggling—a second-generation problem. If a military junta is in power, it may threaten to close the borders or execute by firing squad anyone caught smuggling gasoline. A civilian government may place more personnel at the border to check smuggling. Increasingly, government manpower is absorbed with administering control measures—manpower that is not used productively. Again, note the distinction between first- and second-generation problems.

Import Controls

The richest opportunity, however, was provided by import controls, which were intended to curtail the volume of imports and thereby conserve the scarce foreign exchange needed to import machinery and other equipment essential for development. Import controls and licensing were the tools often employed to reduce the huge demand and match it to the available supply of foreign exchange. But import controls and licenses became the most fraud-ridden systems.

To import an item, a permit or a license was required from the Ministry of Trade. The licenses quickly became scarce. Ministers quickly discovered that they could use the labyrinth of controls to enrich themselves. Ministers and government officials at the trade ministry demanded bribes—10 percent of the value of the import license—before issuing them. The withholding of licenses was then used to punish political rivals and businesses associated with the opposition. In the late 1980s, import licenses were denied to the publications *Free Press* and *Ashanti Pioneer* in Ghana and *Footprints* in Liberia for their criticism of government policies. In Ghana, the administration of import licenses was most notorious for its gross malpractices, which were exposed by various commissions of enquiry: See Akainyah (1964); Abrahams (1965); and Gaisie (1973). These commissions revealed that, with the payment of a bribe—usually 10 percent of the value—importers could import anything, sending the volume of imports out of control. Imports were often over-invoiced to enable importers to keep some foreign exchange balances abroad. For example, suppose a product cost $100 to import from Britain. Through a secret agreement between the Ghanaian importer and the British suppliers, the item would be invoiced for $250 and the invoice presented to the Ministry of Trade or the Bank of Ghana for payment, as all foreign exchange transactions were managed by the government. Upon payment of the invoice, the difference ($150) would be split between the Ghanaian importer and the British supplier. Similarly, exports were also under-invoiced. These schemes drained the country of much-needed foreign exchange. Since foreign exchange was scarce, civilians would connive with certain bank officials to defraud the Bank of Ghana of hard-earned foreign exchange. Then more commissions of enquiry were set. And on and on; nothing learned.

The Patronage System and Governance

Finally, state controls conferred upon the head of state—unintentionally perhaps—an enormous amount of economic and social power. Monopolization of political power had already been attained under the decrepit one-party state systems. The head of state soon discovered that the power to direct economic activity and to channel resources to the state could be used capriciously in a variety of ways:

• To channel development to certain areas of the country, such as his hometown,
• To undertake "social engineering" or indoctrination

- To maintain his political support base and buy new supporters, and
- To punish rivals or the opposition.

Although African strongmen and officials administering state controls initially did make the effort to "spread development" to areas long neglected by the colonial administrators, they soon started to use the control regime for more selfish, political, social, and sinister purposes. Resources siphoned by the state could be used to buy political support (clientelism). Before long, state controls were being used by African leaders to advance their own selfish economic interests as well as those of their kinsmen and supporters, to silence their critics, and to punish political opponents. State controls also allowed African leaders to extract resources which were then used to build huge personal fortunes and to generate a "spoils system" (patronage) to reward political supporters. According to Taylor (2004), "The problem for African development is that whilst individuals within such patronage networks may benefit handsomely, the system fundamentally fails to promote economic growth and development and in actual fact rapidly sabotaged the high aspirations of independence" (p.5).

Africa's autocrats also need political support. The spoils system enabled them to dispense patronage to loyal supporters, cronies, and tribesmen as well as buy new political support. In Malawi, the late Life-President Banda used the instruments of the state to pay his political supporters by transforming them into commercial agricultural estate owners whose prosperity and economic security depended upon their personal loyalty to the president. According to Libby (1987):

> At the center of political power in Zaire is the president and his personal allies who have control over vast powers of patronage that originate from the president. For example, the Bank of Zaire, SOZACOM (the now defunct state-owned mining marketing organization), and the Gecamines (the state mining company) were under the president's personal control and were administered on his behalf by his family and close political allies. Thus Mobutu and his political allies use their control of the state apparatus not only to enrich themselves but more importantly to bind the ruling class together in support of the regime. (p.273)

In Malawi, Banda was able to rip off economic surplus from peasant producers and transfer it to the estate sector through two commercial banks: his holding company—Press Holdings—and the parastatal Agricultural Development and Marketing Corporation (ADMARC). "Between 1972 and 1981, Press Holdings was the single largest recipient of ADMARC's loans. About 27.9 million *kwacha* (about $65 million) was transferred to the president this way" (Libby 1987 p.191). These were huge sums of money the president could use to buy political support.

Strongmen can channel low-interest loans and contracts from public agencies to their friends and allies. According to Kwame Ashaai, a columnist, "In Rawlings Ghana, procurement or public works contracts are awarded to contractors, not on basis of ability to do the jobs well, and at the lowest costs, but on basis of affiliation and connections with the ruling NDC party or its top brass, or on basis of agreement to pay for the contracts" (*Free Press* Oct 30–Nov 5 1996; p.5). In Ivory Coast, companies with links to President Konan Bedie's family allegedly grew fat in financial services and commodity trading, while others gobbled up the most profitable privatized state companies (*The Economist,* Dec 12, 1998; p.46). In Nigeria, for example, the late head of state, General Sani Abacha, used state controls to grant a business set up by his oldest son, Ibrahim, extensive privileges. The business, Delta Prospectors Ltd, mines barite, a mineral that is a source of barium and an essential material for oil production. "In the spring of 1998, shortly after Delta had announced that its operation had reached full production, the Abacha government declared a ban on imports of barite, making the Abacha-owned company the monopoly provider for the huge Nigerian oil industry" (*The Washington Post* June 9 1998; p.A19).

State workers may be provided with subsidized housing and transportation or given "essential commodities" (sardines, corned beef, tinned milk) at government-controlled prices. In Senegal, people were rewarded for their vote with bags of rice; workers in pro-government trade unions got the best pay and conditions; student party members were first in line for scholarships (*The Economist,* Apr 18, 1998; p.44). Some patrons may supply their clients with opportunities for illegal gain from public office. Corruption is another such opportunity—accepting or extorting bribes for decisions or actions taken in a public capacity. Other opportunities include theft of public property, the illegal appropriation of public revenues (fraud), and nepotism.

Strongmen may also "reward their clients by granting preferential access to resources which are subject to government regulation, permits. For example, favorable allocation of import or other licenses. All these allocations of non-governmental benefits can become counters in the game of factional maneuver. Corruption and misuse of public office has reached exceptional levels also in Nigeria" (Sandbrook 1993, p.94). "One of General Abacha's main sources of patronage is the system that enables a lucky few to buy foreign exchange at 22 *naira* to the dollar, while others pay 80" (*The Economist* Nov 9 1996; p.46). And "In Rawlings' Ghana, import permits, bank loans, etc. are awarded on orders of ministers, and only to friends, relatives, NDC members, or those who pay huge bribes. Businessmen and women who have

NDC connections often enjoy tax exemption, penalty waivers, or get their tax obligations reduced. They may even be left to go free when caught evading taxation, or to have made false declarations regarding tax liabilities" (*Free Press,* Oct 30–Nov 5, 1996; p.5).

Soldiers can be bought with pay increases, subsidized housing, commodities, and faster promotions. In 1993 General Ibrahim Babangida "rewarded nearly 3,000 of his most loyal military chiefs by giving them new Peugeot sedans, which cost the equivalent of $21,000 each in Lagos. A senior university professor, for example, earns about $4,000 a year, while a nurse or mechanic is lucky to bring home more than $1,000" (*The New York Times,* Dec. 2, 1993; p.A3).

The success of the patronage system in buying political support, however, depends on the ability of the strongman or center to generate the resources required to appease or purchase the support of the major social groups. Such resources may be capriciously seized through exorbitant taxes, steep hikes in excise duties on imports, gasoline prices, and through various legislative edicts and structures, such as price controls, value-added tax (VAT), marketing boards, and other state controls. Alternatively, the strongman may attempt to generate such resources artificially—on paper, by printing money. The net result is declining production, tax evasion, escalating government expenditures, recourse to the central bank for financing, and, ultimately, inflation.

Regardless, the dispensing of patronage to buy political support has resulted in soaring government expenditures and bloated, inefficient African bureaucracies that waste scarce resources. "Jobs for the boys" in the civil service, government boards, and public corporations become unproductive charges to the state: "In 1984, 20 percent of Ghana's public sector workforce was declared redundant by the Secretary of Finance" (*West Africa,* Jan. 27, 1986; p.178). "This country had 50,000 civil servants who were consuming 51 percent of the nation's wealth," complained Guinea's reformist prime minister, Sidya Toure (*The Washington Times,* Oct. 17, 1996; p.A19). In Kenya, "the civil service has grown by 10 percent to 500,000 in ten years, whose salaries take up half the budget; another third currently goes in repayment of internal and external debts" (*The Economist,* April 19, 1998; p.42). But trimming these bureaucracies, as demanded by the imperatives of economic reform (or structural adjustment), has been anathema to the ruling elites since it cripples their ability to maintain their political support base. In Ghana, the total number of cabinet and deputy portfolios reached an astonishing 88 in 1995. Similarly, in 1996,

President Robert Mugabe of Zimbabwe has upped his cabinet by two to 28. That takes the number of officials with ministerial status to 54. Economist

Eric Bloch attributes Mugabe's move to an entrenched system of patronage: "It is regrettable. People continue to be rewarded for loyal past services even if we can't afford that reward. It's incomprehensible that Zimbabwe should require a cabinet of a greater number than the U.K., France or South Africa when we have a population that is a fraction of those countries." (*The African Observer,* May 23–June 5, 1996; p.23)

South Africa has a 25-member cabinet and 17 deputy portfolios.

To facilitate the dispensing of patronage and reduce any threat to their power, the ruling elites usurp control over all key state institutions: the army, police, civil service, state media, parliament, judiciary, central bank, and educational system. These institutions are packed with trusted lieutenants, cronies, supporters, and tribesmen. Professionalism in these institutions is destroyed and replaced with sycophancy. State institutions become paralyzed and begin to decay. Laxity, ineptitude, indiscipline, and inefficiency thus flourish in the public sector. Rule of law is for the oppressed people; official bandits are exempt. The functions of state institutions become debauched. The police are themselves highway robbers and judges are crooks. The worst institution is the military—the most trenchantly perverted institution in Africa. In any normal, civilized society, the function of the military is to defend the territorial integrity of the nation and the people against external aggression. In Africa, the military is instead locked in constant combat with the very people it is supposed to defend.

It is important to recognize that economic progress in Africa will be elusive unless the key institutions enumerated above are wrestled out of the control of the ruling vampire elites. This requires the establishment of *independent institutions:* An independent central bank, an independent media, an independent judiciary, an efficient civil service, and neutral and professional armed forces. As I indicated in chapter 2, the provision of Western aid should be conditioned upon the establishment of these independent institutions and not on the promises or rhetoric of Africa's coconut leaders.

FAILED INDUSTRIALIZATION BID

Almost everywhere, the industrialization drive, launched with state enterprises and development planning, failed miserably to engineer development. In its wake, economic atrophy, repression, and dictatorship followed with morbid staccato. As Mabogunje (1988) asserted, "It is generally agreed that the false start in all African countries has been due largely to the high level of governmental and bureaucratic domination of the economy with its consequences of inefficiency, profligacy and inappropriate control" (p.25).

Though a few African state enterprises operated with efficiency, "the overall image of the majority of these public enterprises is a depressing picture of inefficiency, losses, budgetary burdens and poor products and services" (Etukudo, 2000; p.23).

In fact, in the early days of their establishment, some public enterprises were modestly profitable. For example, in Nigeria, the former Electricity Corporation of Nigeria, the government railway, the commodity boards, as well as the regional marketing boards all generated surpluses that were reinvested in development projects. The then Eastern Nigeria Marketing Board provided £5 million for the establishment of the University of Nigeria at Nsukka (Udoji, 1970; p.220). In Uganda, the Uganda Development Corporation had in 1967 a gross turnover of over £22 million and an investment of over £5 million in seven projects. In Kenya, especially in the 1970s, state-owned banks spurred growth and were important in the establishment of non-bank financial institutions as well as extensive rural banking (Etukudo, 2000; p.23).

For the most part, however, public enterprises were unprofitable and chronically inefficient. In 1976, when Somalia installed a plant to box bananas, it discovered that "the quantity needed to make the plant break even exceeded the entire national output of bananas" (*Journal of Economic Growth*, 2: 3, 1987; p.4). According to *the Wall Street Journal* (July 15, 1985),

> Togo built an oil refinery big enough to serve half a dozen West African countries. But Togo doesn't produce any oil. Hundreds of millions of dollars went to build five-star hotels and international airports in the remote jungle villages of Ivory Coast President Houphouet-Boigny and Zairian President Mobutu Sese Seko. Shortly after independence, Madagascar bought a jet plane and proudly named it "The Revolution." Now, Chase Manhattan is trying to repossess "The Revolution." (p.18)

A tin can manufacturing plant in Kenya had such high production costs that cans full of vegetables could be imported from Asian competitors for cheaper than the cost of the Kenyan company's cans alone. The Kenyan government estimated that over $1.4 billion had been invested in state enterprises by the early 1980s. Yet, their annual average return had been 0.2 percent (Goldman, 1992; p.10).

Civil war reduced Sudan to a vast open-air latrine and rubbish dump. Telephone service is non-existent since lines have been cut for years. Electricity and water supplies are sporadic. State-run schools are often closed, and doctors are more often than not on strike. Army and rebel forces have indiscriminately mined all roads and fields surrounding major towns. Out of this chaos flew the state-owned Sudan Air with nationalistic pride. As the *Wall Street Journal* (June 23, 1990) described it:

The airline's timetable is meaningless; flights routinely skip scheduled stops, make unplanned layovers of several days, leave without passengers—or most commonly, don't leave at all. In late March, 1989, Sudan Air pilots went on strike. It was an empty gesture; the airline's entire fleet was already grounded due to maintenance problems and lack of jet fuel.

In 1983, a Sudan Air 707 landed at night in the White Nile. Though accounts differ, pilots say the navigator mistook the river for the runway. In 1988, officials in London declared a Sudan Air plane unfit and sent it home empty. Passengers joke that the airline's international code, SD, stands for "sudden death." (p.1)

Nigerian Airways' airbuses were routinely seized for nonpayment of maintenance and landing fees overseas. For two weeks in July 1989, over 1,000 Nigerians were stranded at Heathrow Airport waiting for Lagos-bound flights by Nigerian Airways (*West Africa* August 3—13, 1989; p.1305). At least it has a better safety record, according to an anonymous reader who posted this on an Internet discussion forum:

Nigerian Airwaste
"Good morning, Ladies and Gentlemen. This is your captain welcoming you on board of Nigeria Airwaste.

We apologize for the four-day delay in taking off, it was due to bad weather and some overtime I had to put in at the work.

This is flight 126 to Lagos.

Landing in Lagos is not guaranteed, but we will end up somewhere in the South. If luck is in our favor, we may even be landing on your village!

Nigeria Airwaste has an excellent safety-record. In fact our safety standards are so high that even terrorists are afraid to fly with us!

It is with pleasure, I announce that starting this year over 50% of our passengers have reached their destination. If our engines are too noisy for you, on passenger request, we can arrange to turn them off!

To make your free fall to earth pleasant and memorable, we serve complimentary Bongo tea and Okin biscuits!

For our not-so-religious passengers, we are the only airline who can help you find out if there really is a God!

We regret to inform you, that today's in-flight movie will not be shown as we forgot to record it from the television.

But for our movie buffs, we will be flying right next to Air Barka, where their movie will be visible from the right side of the cabin window.

There is no smoking allowed in this airplane. Any smoke you see in the cabin is only the early warning system on the engines telling us to slow down!

In order to catch important landmarks, we try to fly as close as possible for the best view. If, however, we go a little too close, do let us know. Our enthusiastic co-pilot sometimes flies right through the landmark!

Kindly be seated, keep your seat in an upright position for take-off and fasten your seat-belt.

For those of you who can't find a seat-belt, kindly fasten your own belt to the arm of your seat. And for those of you who can't find a seat do not hesitate to get in touch with a stewardess who will explain how to fasten yourself to your suitcase."

Enjoy Nigeria Airwaste!

(Circulated on Nigerian Internet discussion forums Nigeriaworld and Naija-Politics in January 2003)

Some attempts were made by African governments to privatize loss-making state enterprises but there was often fierce resistance from state workers. In Tunisia, for example, the government ran the airline, the steel mill, the phosphate mines, and 150 factories, employing a third of Tunisian workers. Before 1990, 35 companies were sold off, but fewer than 20 have sold since.

Private businessman Afif Kilani bought one such company called Comfort, a featherbed for 1,200 workers who built 15,000 refrigerators a year. Mr. Kilani paid $3.3 million for the place in 1990. Five years later, he had whittled the workforce down to 600 workers who made 200,000 refrigerators a year. "Like all state companies, its point had been to support the maximum number of jobs," he said. "It was social work. A sort of welfare" (*The Wall Street Journal* June 22, 1995; p.A11).

It is estimated that up until the 1970s, "at least 50 per cent of the corporations in Nigeria and Ghana had had public inquiries conducted into their operations" and that between 1960 and 1966 the Nigerian Railways alone had 13 inquiries into its activities (Udoji, 1970; p.219). Following a special committee set up in 1961 by the federal government of Nigeria, a public policy statement was issued to the effect that public corporations should enjoy an appropriate measure of independence and should not be subjected to direct government interference in their day-to-day activities. But political interference in the affairs of the corporations continued unabated. "Chairmen usurped the powers of chief executives, ministers usurped the powers and functions of both chairmen and chief executives. The management of some of the corporations was chaotic as it became a hotbed of power struggles" (Etukudo, 2000; p.27). In such a chaotic situation, the finances and general management of these enterprises were in such a parlous state that, in 1986, the Nigerian federal government issued instructions to the effect that "the volume of non-statutory transfers to all economic and quasi-economic parastatals will constitute no more than 50 per cent of their present levels. Public enterprises were required to provide the balance from price increases, charges, tariffs and rates." A similar injunction was issued in Zambia by former President Kenneth Kaunda to the Zambia Industrial and Mining Corporation Limited (ZIMCO) and its subsidiaries to the effect that they "were business enterprises first and state-owned companies thereafter." They were therefore to operate "no less efficiently than any other business undertaking" (Etukudo, 2000; p.29).

In 1958, when Guinea gained its independence from France, it was considered to have the richest potential of Francophone Africa. It had one-quarter of the world's bauxite as well as copious reserves of gold and diamonds. Prior to independence, Guinea was exporting food to neighboring French colonies, thanks largely to its fertile land. In addition, thousands of tons of bananas, pineapples, and coffee were shipped to Europe.

Proclaiming a doctrine of "Marxism in African clothes," the first president, Ahmed Sekou Toure, set the country on a rigid course of state planning and controls. Unauthorized trading became a crime. Police roadblocks were set up around the country to control internal trade. Foreign trade was monopolized by the state and smuggling was made punishable by death. Currency trafficking attracted stiff penalties, ranging from 15 to 20 years in prison. Farms were collectivized and food prices fixed at below-market levels. Private farmers were forced to deliver annual harvest quotas to "Local Revolutionary Powers." Thousands of Guineans, who protested Toure's dictatorial rule, were imprisoned or executed. By 1984, at the time of Toure's death after 26 years of tyrannical rule, Guinea, once a food exporter, was spending a third of its foreign exchange earnings from bauxite on food. Further, saying "nyet!" to Toure's crass revolution, as many as two million Guineans had fled to neighboring countries and Europe to live as voluntary exiles. The same Marxist/socialist experiment was attempted in Ghana.

I will now look at the privatization problems in depth in several African countries.

Ghana

At independence in 1957, Ghana started on the development road with the same per capita income of $200 as South Korea, which made Ghana one of the richest countries in the developing world. Its civil service, rooted in British tradition, was fairly efficient. Foreign exchange reserves stood at $400 million and the country was the world's leading producer of cocoa. Its first president, Dr. Kwame Nkrumah, launched an ambitious industrialization program that hope to achieve in a decade what it took others a century. Foreign companies were nationalized and state monopolies established. A bewildering array of legislative controls pertaining to prices, interest, and exchange transactions were imposed. By 1965, agricultural production had plummeted and food shortages had appeared in the country, which once used to export food.

A master plan—the Seven-Year Development Plan—was drawn up to launch Ghana into the industrial age. Factories were built and whole industries set up at incredible speed. Technical institutes cropped up, and even an atomic energy commission was established at Kwabenya. But it became apparent that the drive toward industrialization was governed more by considerations of prestige than rationality. Not surprisingly, Ghana's Seven-Year Development Plan achieved little if anything by way of development. The indictment by Tony Killick (1978) was more scathing:

> The 7-Year Plan, then, was a piece of paper, with an operational impact close to zero. Why? It could be argued that this was due to defects in the plan itself, to shortages of staff to monitor and implement it, and to the intervention of factors beyond Ghana's control, especially the falling world cocoa prices of the early and mid-sixties. [But] in retrospect, we see an almost total gap between the theoretical advantages of planning and the record of the 7-Year Plan. Far from providing a superior set of signals, it was seriously flawed as a technical document and, in any case, subsequent actions of government bore little relation to it. Far from counteracting the alleged myopia of private decision-takers, government decisions tended to be dominated by short-term expediency and were rarely based upon careful appraisals of their economic consequences. The plan was subverted, as most plans are, by insufficient political determination to make it work. (p.143)

The state enterprises established by Nkrumah were intended to produce consumer goods that were previously imported in the hope that foreign exchange would be saved and employment created. The businesses were hastily and haphazardly established. In many cases, feasibility studies were not done to determine the economic viability of the enterprises. About 74 percent of the total inputs into the manufacturing sector were imported (Killick, 1978; p.201). Thus, there were delays in the importation of inputs—either due to the insufficient allocation of import licenses, managerial incompetence, or scarce foreign exchange. The delays idled production. Since workers in state enterprises were seldom terminated or furloughed, they were paid even when they produced nothing. The enterprises were saddled with chronic inefficiency and underproduction. Nkrumah's state enterprises could not deliver the goods and when they did, the final products were more expensive than the imported substitute.

The government of Ghana estimated that at the end of the 1966, actual manufacturing output was only one-fifth of the single-shift capacity of installed plant. Even the 1965 Annual Plan, prepared by the government itself, showed that actual production in the state industrial enterprises was only 29 percent of their capacity. Of the 20 state manufacturing enterprises that were in operation in 1964, only 10 were working to half or more than half of their optimum capacity. In three cases, the actual production was even less than 10 percent of the full capacity. In one case (the paper bag division of the Paper Conversion Corporation at Takoradi), the rate of utilization was as low as 3.5 percent. On average, the 20 state manufacturing enterprises were using only 42 percent of their total productive capacity (Ahmad 1970; p.116).

Underutilization was extensive during the 1960s. In March 1966, as many as 13 of the State Fishing Corporation's 17 fishing vessels had been tied up at home and abroad for want of repairs or attention. Six of them were at Japanese ports incurring daily mooring charges of $50 (*Daily Graphic,* Nov 17, 1978; p.6).

Worse, the state enterprises turned out to be inefficient at saving foreign exchange. Steel (1972) concluded from his study that:

> Existing structure and utilization of manufacturing capacity represents a very costly and inefficient method of gaining foreign exchange and raising national income. Even worse, 24 percent of output was produced at a net loss in foreign exchange, taking into account all foreign exchange costs of capital and domestically-produced inputs. (p.226)

In other terms, an item that could be imported for $10 was being produced and sold by Ghana's state enterprises for $15. That many state enterprises were net users of foreign exchange is further supported by a study by Killick (1978). He showed that between 1966 and 1970, when the quantity of imports of industrial raw materials went up by nearly one-half, gross output per manufacturing establishment actually declined in real terms by 9 percent and that constant-price value-added per establishment went down by a remarkable 2 percent over the same period (p.197). In other words, the contribution of state enterprises to the national output was negative.

It is ludicrous to even ask how profitable the state enterprises were. At the time of the coup in Ghana in 1966, only 3 or 4 of the 64 state enterprises were paying their way (Garlick, 1971; p.141). Killick's calculations on some selected state enterprises showed that in 1964–65, 23 of them made losses totaling 14,116,000 *cedis.*

More disturbing was the co-existence of certain loss-making public enterprises with private firms that can be assumed to have been profitable by virtue of their continued existence. Cases in point were State Fishing, State Construction, State Transport, State Footwear, and State Housing (Killick, 1978; p.218). In fishing, for example, the private company, Mankoadze

Fisheries Ltd., had been remarkably successful while its government counterpart was plagued with excess capacity. In 1967, three of the State Fishing
Corporation's vessels were sold to Mankoadze and in January 22, 1979,
Colonel S. M. Akwagyiram, Commissioner for Agriculture, "praised the
spectacular results of Mankoadze for defying the numerous odds it encountered in the past 20 years to build the biggest African-owned fishing company on the African continent" (*Daily Graphic* Jan 22, 1979; p.3).

On another test of efficiency, Killick (1978) showed, using available frag-
mentary evidence, that the state enterprises, which tended to be more capital-intensive, had lower labor productivities than their private counterparts.
The productivity achieved by workers in the state enterprises barely ap-
proached 50 percent of the level achieved by workers in the private sector
(Killick, 1978; p.223, Table 9.2).

Evidently, these state enterprises, more often than not, were riddled with
gross inefficiency, waste, and bureaucratic corruption. The following snip-
pets of information provide some limited insight into the sordid performance of Ghana's state enterprises:

- Ghana's State Meat Factory at Bolgatanga, which produces the VOLTA
  corned beef, was closed for 9 months. Yet, employees received full pay
  (*West Africa*, Nov 30, 1981; p.2884).
- "The Boatyard Division of GIHOC at Mumford Village in the Apam
  District (Central Region) has launched only 6 vessels with a workforce
  of 40 employees since its establishment 9 years ago" (*Daily Graphic* Aug
  14, 1981; p.8).
- A Yugoslav company built a mango-processing plant in Ghana with a
  capacity exceeding the entire world's trade in canned mangoes. When
  the factory was commissioned in 1964, it was discovered that the supply of mangoes came from a few trees scattered in the bush (Killick,
  1978; p.229).
- The Ghana government owns nearly 90 percent of the companies
  doing business in the country. There are nearly 340 plus state-owned
  enterprises. Out of this number, only 17 have posted improved figures
  to date (*Ghana Drum* Oct 1992; p.17).
- In 1972, the government took over the African Timber and Plywood
  Company. Before the takeover, "production was 75 percent of installed
  capacity but this has fallen to a woeful 13 percent" (West *Africa* Oct
  12, 1981; p.2422).
- In 1976, the government of Ghana took over R. T. Briscoe, a foreign
  company. "Before the take-over, the company was producing 241 buses
  in 1974. After the take-over, production was 12 buses in 1977 and only
  6 buses in 1978" (*Daily Graphic*, Jan 18, 1979; p.1).

- In 1980, the government of Ghana voted 80 million *cedis* for the Ghana National Reconstruction Corps, a reconstituted State Farm Organization. At the end of the farming season, only 864, 0000 *cedis* was recovered (*Daily Graphic,* July 21, 1981; p.5).
- For 14 months, from November 1978 to January 1980, the State Jute Bag Factory was closed due to a shortage of raw materials. Yet, the 1,000 workers received full pay for the entire period of closure (*Punch* Aug 14–20, 1981; p.4).
- The pre-fab factory started by the Russians in 1962 has not produced a single home. Yet, 500 Ghanaian workers and 13 Soviet experts were drawing salaries for a period of 6 years (*Daily Graphic* Dec 6, 1978; p.5).

Clearly, Nkrumah's industrialization strategy was an unequivocal failure. The massive investments in state enterprises turned out to be black elephants. Killick (1978) summed up the situation quite tersely:

> State enterprises were unprofitable—absolutely by comparison with public enterprises in other developing countries and by comparison with private enterprise in Ghana—and they were unprofitable despite considerable monopoly powers (and excessive effective rates of protection). State enterprises, then, failed to fill the entrepreneurial gap, to propel the economy forward and to generate the surpluses which Nkrumah demanded of them. (p.227)

But getting rid of these unprofitable and inefficient state enterprises has been a chronic headache. For example, the water supply situation in Ghana's cities and regional capitals has suffered from inefficiencies over the years. They worsened over the past two decades due to poor urban development, population growth, and Ghana Water's own decrepit facilities and corrupt management practices. The state-owned corporation "employs 14 people per 1,000 customers—but according to one international expert, that should be down to about five. And half of Ghana Water's daily production of 120 million gallons is unaccounted for, lost through leaks and unpaid bills" (*BBC World Service* Aug 13, 2003, www.bbc. co.uk).

Attempts to rectify the situation, including a $140 million project to improve the system in 1989, failed to get water flowing through the taps. Most homeowners in urban cities had to purchase water tanks at the considerable expense of 3 million *cedis* (or $400) because the taps ran only for a few hours for two or three days a week. In some parts of the capital city (Accra), such as Teshie-Nungua, Madina, and Adenta, residents paid between 500 *cedis* and 1,000 *cedis* (5–12 cents) per bucket of 4 gallons from private suppliers. The official Ghana Water rate was 64 *cedis*.

The World Bank sought to "bribe" the Ghana government to privatize the water supply system with an interest-free loan of $150 million to reequip the state-run Ghana Water Company and hire new management. Immediately, opposition was registered from the country's National Coalition against the Privatization of Water (CAPW). The anti-privatization lobby argued that access to water is a human right. "You can't privatize something as close to air as water, and allow market forces and profit motives to determine who can and who cannot have some to drink," said Ameng Etego, spokesman for the CAPW (*BBC World Service* Aug 13, 2003; www.bbc.co.uk). "We agree that there's need to improve efficiency and root out corruption at Ghana Water. But for the World Bank to insist that we privatize before it gives us a loan is plain blackmail. We should use the money to address the management problems internally," he added. But the *real* issue was not whether private suppliers earn a profit or not. Rather, it was having access to water at 500 *cedis* or not having water at 64 *cedis*.

Tanzania

In Tanzania, Nyerere's industrialization and social transformation were also a stunning fiasco. In 1967, Tanzania's ruling party adopted the Arusha Declaration establishing a socialist state where the workers and peasants controlled and owned the means of production. Banks, insurance companies, and foreign trading companies were nationalized. Nyerere stated as one of his principles of socialism that: "It is the responsibility of the state to intervene actively in the economic life of the nation so as to ensure the well-being of the all citizens." After 1967, the Tanzanian state became predominant in all spheres. The state took over all commercial banks, insurance companies, grain mills, and the main import-export firms, and acquired a controlling interest in the major multinational corporation subsidiaries and the sisal industry. A "villagization" program ("*Ujamaa*") was adopted to encourage the communal production, marketing and distribution of farm crops.

In 1973, Nyerere undertook massive resettlement programs under "Operation Dodoma," "Operation Sogeza," "Operation Kigoma," and many others to create "communal villages" or *ujamaa*. Peasants were loaded into trucks, often forcibly, and moved to new locations. Many lost their lives and property in the process. To prevent them from returning to their old habitats, the government bulldozed the abandoned buildings. By 1976, some 13 million peasants had been forced into 8,000 cooperative villages, and by the end of the 1970s, about 91 percent of the entire rural population had been moved into government villages (Zinsmeister, 1987; p.13). All crops were to be bought and distributed by the government. It was illegal for the peasants to sell their own produce. This was in clear violation of traditional African practices.

Between 1967 and 1973, the number of rural villagers who were officially designated as residing in *Ujamaa* villages increased from one-half million to two million (or an estimated 15 percent of the rural population). However, according to Japheth M. M. Ndaro, director of the Institute of Development Planning at Dodoma, during the period 1961–70, the inhabitants of Dodoma devised and adopted strategies that did not conform with the political slogan of nation building that was dominant in the early 1960s. In some parts of the district, the concept of *Ujamaa* actually stifled local initiative. "All in all, the Arusha Declaration of 1967 and the *Ujamaa* Policy of 1968, which marked an important milestone in the development of the country as a whole, did not inspire the people of Dodoma to engage in development initiatives that were alien to their socio-cultural environment" (in Taylor and Mackenzie 1992; p.178).

Even worse, forced settlement later proved to be an ecological disaster. UN agencies estimated that about one-third of Tanzania is threatened by desertification due to deforestation, overgrazing, overcultivation, and population increase because of the government's policy of villagization. "Critics say this caused lower farm yields and increased land degradation since families were settled regardless of land fertility or livestock numbers" (*New African* Nov 1991; p.35).

The agricultural economy was left devastated by state controls. Production of most crops showed a steady decline after 1974. Overall output of food crops rose only 2.1 percent between 1970 and 1982, well below the population growth of 3.5 percent. By 1981, a food crisis had gripped the nation, turning it into a net importer of basic foodstuffs. The country had to import one million tons of grain to avert population starvation. The towns and cities had to be supplied with imports of grain costing as estimated 2,000 million shillings (Libby 1987; p.254). In 1971–72, grain imports were 135,000 tons, including 90,000 tons of maize. In 1972–73, grain imports dropped to 90,000 tons, of which 80,000 tons were maize. However, during the next year from August 1973 to July 1974, Tanzania was forced to import over 500,000 tons of maize alone (*African Business* 1979; p.21). For eight years (1974–1982), Tanzania's income per capita had remained stagnant at $210 (World Bank 2000a; p.35). Exports of agricultural produce were similarly affected, impairing the country's capacity to earn foreign exchange:

> Exports of cotton have fallen to pre-independent volumes and sisal output is less than a third of its 1961 total. In the last ten years, the annual cashew exports fell from 140,000 to 30,000 tons. The total tonnage of all export crops

was 20 percent less in 1984 than it had been in 1970. Production of basic food crops, such as maize, rice and wheat, have also declined to half their 1972 levels. And, as could be expected, food imports have doubled. (Zinsmeister, 1987; p.33)

After the Arusha Declaration of 1967, the Tanzanian state became predominant in all spheres. The state took over all commercial banks, insurance companies, grain mills, and the main import-export firms, and acquired a controlling interest in the major multinational corporation subsidiaries, coffee estates, and the sisal industry. No role was envisaged for private investors. Within a decade, however, more than half of the 330 state-run enterprises set up by Nyerere became scandalously inefficient and broke. Tanzania's state enterprises could barely produce. They were characterized by overstaffing and high overheads that perpetuated a costly elitist rule by bureaucrats. The government-run factories operated at 10 to 30 percent of capacity. For example, the state-owned Morongo Shoe Company (MSC) was financed by the World Bank. Based on abundant supplies of hides and skins, the project was supposed to be a low-technology, economies-of-scale activity that would expand the country's exports. About 80 percent of the shoes were to be shipped to Europe. But when the plant became operational in the 1980s, "MSC achieved just over 5 percent capacity utilization. By 1986, the figure was below 3 percent. Most of the machines were never used, quality and design were abysmal, and unit costs were very high and the factory was eventually abandoned" (Luke 1995; p.154). Another example is the state brewery that produced the local Safari beer. Production was hideously inefficient and quality-control nonexistent. A stray cockroach could now and then be spotted in the bottled brew. In 1993, the government sold part of its stake to a South African company.

The entire industrial sector contributed only 8 percent to GNP in 1998. The government sector was hideously overmanned, employing some 75 percent of the formal labor force. The Nyerere socialist failure would have been even more devastating had it not been for the generous external assistance it received.

Between 1978 and 1981, over $3 billion in foreign aid poured into Tanzania. By the early 1980s, foreign charity was paying for over 16 percent of the nations' GNP, including 60 percent of the development budget and more than half of all imports. Still, the economy floundered. The *New York Times* (Oct 24, 1990) reported that, "at first, many Western aid donors, particularly in Scandinavia, gave enthusiastic backing to this socialist experiment, pouring an estimated $10 billion into Tanzania over 20 years. But when Nyerere left the stage, the country's largely agricultural economy was in ruins, with its

26 million people eking out their living on a per capita income of slightly more than $200 a year, one of the lowest in the world" (p.A8).

The 1990 World Development Report by the World Bank noted that Tanzania's economy contracted an average of 0.5 percent a year between 1965 and 1988. Average personal consumption declined dramatically by 43 percent between 1973 and 1988. Infrastructure crumbled under Nyerere's rule. *The Economist* observed that for all the aid poured into the country, Tanzania only had "pot-holed roads, decaying buildings, cracked pavements, demoralized clinics and universities, and a 1988 income per capita of $160 (lower than at independence in 1961)" to show for it (June 2, 1990; p.48). A dilapidated telecommunications system was also a feature of Tanzanian society. The Tan-Zam railway completed by the Chinese operated under low capacity due to lack of railway engines. The Tanzanian Railways Corporation, with support from Canada, operates a rail service on other tracks. But since the tracks are of a different gauge, the engines cannot be used on the Tan-Zam line.

Delivery of social services collapsed under Nyerere's tenure. The Muhimbili Medical Center, where the Dar-es-Salaam University of Medicine, is based and which serves as the only referral hospital for all Tanzanians, often had no drugs and was in a state of complete collapse for much of the 1990s. Educational institutions similarly crumbled to such an extent that government officials sought medical care overseas—as was the case with Nyerere himself—and sent their children to foreign schools.

In 1996, Denmark and even Canada suspended aid to Tanzania, citing rampant corruption. Senior government officials and major politicians were brazenly exempting themselves from paying taxes. In 1993, there were over 2,000 such exemptions, costing the treasury $113 million. When corruption first reared its head in the early 1970s, Nyerere set up a Corruption Bureau. But very quickly, bureau officials themselves became corrupt and one of its top officials was himself seen bribing an airline official to secure a ticket for Tanzanian Airways.

Similarly, Zambia under Kaunda, according to *The Washington Post* (Sept 12, 1995), fit the classic mold of the command economy: "Through companies it controlled, the state ran virtually everything, from the cultivation of maize to the baking of bread to the mining of copper. Payrolls were heavily padded, with employees receiving housing, cars and free airfare on the national airline. Even food was subsidized" (p.A12).

In Mozambique, FRELIMO sought to replicate Tanzania's model by establishing an embryonic socialist state replete with collectivized agriculture, crop-growing schemes, village political committees, and health programs. The party took over about 1,000 "fortified villages" that the Portuguese regime had created to isolate FRELIMO. The socialist government converted them into communal villages involving a million people, later establishing other villages after the Limpopo and Zambezi Valley floods in 1977 and 1978, and still more following the resurgence of MNR guerilla war in Manica and Sofala.

According to Libby (1987):

> The centerpiece of Frelimo's rural social program for Mozambique was the collectivization of agriculture into communal villages and cooperative farms. Agricultural cooperatives were intended to provide an integrated production base for the communal villages. Hence, villagization was designed to increase food and cash crop production and to make available common facilities for farming as well as provide social services such as education and health comparable with *ujamaa* villages in Tanzania. (p.216)

Uganda

In Uganda, in contrast to Ghana, there was no ideological basis to statism, nor strident rhetoric about colonialism and imperialist enemies. But there was an enemy nonetheless. As in Nigeria, the enemies were the foreign companies and expatriates. Until 1971, the Ugandan economy enjoyed a fairly robust growth. Gross domestic product grew at 4.8 percent per annum between 1963 and 1970, giving a respectable increase in per capita terms of at least 2 percent. The country also maintained a reasonable saving rate, averaging 13 percent, which permitted the implementation of an ambitious investment program without adverse effects on domestic prices or the balance of payments. Though exports grew slowly, earnings were more than adequate to cover import requirements, leaving a healthy current account surplus on the trade balance in most of the years. Even the government was running a sizable budget surplus during the latter part of the 1960s, which helped finance a significant proportion of development outlays. The turning point came after 1970, when Idi Amin seized power.

I have railed persistently about the scourge of the military in Africa as the bane of Africa's development. Africans should note what happens to an economy when the apparatus of the state falls in the hands of reckless military brutes. As the World Bank Mission to Uganda in 1982 observed:

> From the early 1970s, and especially following the change of government in 1971, the situation deteriorated abruptly. The adverse impact of developments under the military regime on the country's economy is of continuing concern. In particular,

a. Many of the country's best administrators, managers, entrepreneurs, book-keepers, teachers, and traders left the country (including most of the Asian population during the so-called "economic war" of 1972);

b. The parastatal sector, which had already been expanded during the early 1970s, became bloated with the addition of numerous abandoned or confiscated industries (others were given to inexperienced private owners). This whole process was undertaken in a haphazard and chaotic manner, with little concern for proper transfer of ownership, compensation and financial control and little regard for managerial constraints in the parastatal sector; and

c. The administrative system, in both government and the parastatal sector, was increasingly geared to fear and favoritism. Many civil service and parastatals positions were filled by political appointees, and there was little reward for technical competence or scope for open discussion of economic strategy or policies. Fiscal responsibility was virtually non-existent, leading to widespread misuse of funds and corruption. (p.4)

The process actually began with the "Nakivubo Pronouncements" of 1970, in which the state sought 60 percent participation in a number of private industrial, commercial, and financial undertakings. The military regime initially toned down this policy, reducing the participation rate to 49 percent and the number of nationalized companies to 17, including banks, one of the oil companies, and some manufacturing and mining companies. But the nationalization drive was revived during the "economic war" of 1972, spearheaded by Idi Amin.

The results of these asinine policies under Amin were stagnation of GDP from 1970 to 1978, a fall in the saving rate to 8 percent, deteriorating infrastructure, and the destruction of productive assets. Many agricultural processing units were closed down and equipment frequently broke down and was not fixed.

A war broke out in late 1978 between Uganda and Tanzania that eventually led to the downfall of Idi Amin. Extensive damage was caused by artillery bombardment around Mbarara and Masaka in the southern part of Uganda. Though the war was brief, military rule took a devastating toll on the Ugandan economy. When the Commonwealth team of experts arrived in Uganda in mid-1979, the evidence of destruction and disintegration was everywhere. They found:

• Crops were damaged and livestock killed, either due to the direct impact of military activities or to provide food for the soldiers and marauders;
• Many houses, factories, and public buildings were gutted or partially destroyed, especially around Mbarara and Masaka;

- School supplies, textbooks, and writing materials were looted;
- Food, clothes, and furniture were taken from shops and houses;
- Office records were lost or destroyed;
- Tools and equipment were taken from workshops; and
- Thousands of cars and trucks were stolen (World Bank Report on Uganda, 1982; p.8)

The war in Uganda imposed severe hardships and difficulties. These problems were not by themselves insurmountable and could be overcome with a stronger administration and resource base. But the World Bank mission was not optimistic. As it reported:

> The years of military regime had left the economy short of skilled manpower and foreign exchange, and the administrative system virtually collapsed. With such deep-rooted and pervasive problems, it would have been difficult for any government, with the best of intentions and support, to implement an effective rehabilitation program. In Uganda, where the government has changed four times during the last three years and where the security situation has remained unsettled, it is not surprising that initial progress was slow. (p.8)

Following the ouster of Idi Amin, international agencies held the first aid donors' meeting in Paris in November 1979 to help successive Ugandan governments rebuild their economy. In June 1981, the IMF agreed to a $197 million standby facility and after the first debt rescheduling in November 1981 at the Paris Club, Uganda came under IMF tutelage. The government of Milton Obote announced an economic recovery program for 1982–1984, which concentrated on the main export sectors and pressing social needs. A further program was announced for 1983–1985, which covered more than 100 projects and gave more emphasis to industry. Unfortunately, Obote began an Idi Aminesque pogrom, sparking a rebel insurgency that led to his ouster by Yoweri Museveni in 1986.

In June 1987, the Museveni regime reached an agreement with the IMF, securing a 3-year Special Drawing Rights (SDR) 63.25 million structural adjustment facility.[2] The country began a comprehensive policy and institutional reform program to deregulate the economy, eliminate direct state involvement in most of the public services, institute a major privatization program, reform the civil service, and embark on a public expenditure reform and a decentralization process.

Macroeconomic stability was achieved and maintained in the 1990s. Annual inflation rates dropped from 66 percent in 1986 to 15 percent in 1993 and below 5 percent per year for most of the second half of the 1990s. Interest rates fell from 240 percent in 1986 to 15 percent in 1993. Average income per capita rose from $200 in 1990 to $330 in 2000, a 65 percent increase. There was a significant reduction in the incidence of poverty from 56 percent of the total population in the 1992 to 35 percent in 2000. Between 1994 and 1997 Uganda posted a real GDP growth rate of 8 percent, the highest in Africa. In response to its reforms and performance, foreign aid poured in, amounting in 2000 to some 53 percent of the total government budget, or 13 percent of GDP. Uganda's macroeconomic performance showed an average real growth rate close to 7 percent per year, leading the bank to declare Uganda an economic success story in 1998.

Uganda is one of the few African countries that has been willing to embrace the stringent structural adjustment programs that the World Bank deems vital to restore fiscal discipline and monetary stability, and has been an important advocate for the World Bank's programs in Africa. Since 1987, the World Bank has provided an estimated $790 million in adjustment support, in addition to an estimated $1 billion in project support in the agriculture, infrastructure, and social sectors.

By African standards, Uganda has performed well and President Yoweri Museveni has made credible, serious, and committed efforts at reform. Unfortunately, dangers lurk behind the corner. First, Uganda's economic recovery is not sustainable as it is "aid-induced." Dependent on the international community for 55 percent of its budget, it is doubtful if the recovery can be sustained if the aid spigot is turned off. Second, massive coffee exports have been the prime engine of the country's economic growth. A fall in coffee prices could pose a serious threat to Uganda's recovery. Indeed, in 2000, coffee prices began to fall in international commodity markets. By May 2001, coffee prices had plummeted to a 20-year low and in 2004 remained at a 30-year low. The slump in prices reduced export income. In 1996, Uganda's export earnings from goods and non-factor services stood at $786 million. However, they fell to $596 million in 2000 (Bank of Uganda, 2001). Thus, Uganda's economic performance remains highly vulnerable to commodity price fluctuations.

Third, recent information indicates that fiscal discipline is slipping with government expenditures spiraling out of control—fed by huge expenditures for military adventures in the Congo. Contrary to efforts to implement measures for improving the efficiency and transparency of the privatization process, progress in this area was significantly slow, including measures for reforming the ministries and the civil service. Revenue receipts have been inadequate to meet rising expenditures. Indeed, tax collection has been characterized by highly corrupt and inefficient tax administration. The banking system also came under severe pressure due to weak prudential regulations and supervision. Those insolvent ones were ultimately closed. In an uncertain economic environment reflecting poverty, scant gains in human and social development, Uganda is now ravaged by the HIV/AIDS epidemic. Although President Museveni has earned high marks in the battle against HIV/AIDS, this disease has led to a reduction in life expectancy that has adversely affected the working population, and created a large number of orphans, as well as great pressure on the government's health budget.

Fourth, the decrepit political system could unravel the economic recovery. Uganda is a de facto "one-party state" with the political arena dominated by President Museveni's National Resistance Movement. Constitutionally, Ugandans can form any political party they wish but they cannot campaign nor hold rallies since it is illegal to assemble more than 6 persons for a political function. President Museveni, who declared in 1986 when he became president that no African leader should be in power for more than 10 years, was a different president in 2004. Rather strangely, he has tried to block or override a constitutional clause that limits his tenure to two terms. It is the same African disease encountered in Angola, Chad, Guinea, and Namibia, where incumbents seek to gut the two-term rule they themselves agreed to. But as Africans would say, "Power sweet them. Once they taste it they don't want to let go."

Fifth, progress on economic reform is in danger of being throttled by corruption, which has become a serious problem in Uganda and has penetrated all levels of society. A recent review by the opposition group, Uganda Debt Network (UDN), claimed that Uganda has been ranked among the most corrupt countries of the world and that 80 percent of business in Uganda pays a bribe before accessing a service. UDN further estimates that more than 1 trillion Ugandan shillings (equivalent to more than $700 million at current exchange rates) have been lost through corruption in government departments from 1984–1999 (*UDC Newsletter,* Jan 2003; pp.1–4). Indeed, studies by the Inspector General's office have revealed that the police, judiciary, and health departments are the most corrupt in the country. Public disgust and intolerance of corruption have been growing, fed by press reporting and parliamentary investigations. Although Uganda has taken steps to create anticorruption agencies, there has been a lack of political will to provide adequate resources for these agencies to function effectively. As a result, corruption, especially in relation to privatization, continues almost completely unabated. In the year 2000, Transparency International ranked Uganda as the third most corrupt country in the world—a slippage since the country was ranked 12th in 1996.

President Yoweri Museveni has pledged to root out corruption but few believe him and to date only limited progress has been made. International donors expressed their strong collective concern about corruption in Uganda at the November 1997 Consultative Group meeting on Uganda held at World Bank offices in Paris. Almost all the delegates cited corruption as a serious impediment to Uganda's economic progress.

Hardest hit has been the privatization program—an important component of structural adjustment programs and often a precondition for loans from the World Bank and the IMF. In 1992, in accordance with loan conditionalities, the government of Uganda began a privatization effort to sell off 142 of its state-owned enterprises. However, in 1998, the process was halted twice by Uganda's own parliament because, according to the chair of a parliamentary select committee, Tom Omongole, it had been "derailed by corruption," implicating three senior ministers who had "political responsibility" (*The East African,* June 14, 1999). The sale of these 142 enterprises was initially projected to generate 900 billion Ugandan shillings or $500 million. However, by the autumn of 1999 the revenue balance was only 3.7 billion Ugandan shillings. This discrepancy occurred due to the government's mismanagement of the privatization process covering three parastatals: The Ugandan Commercial Bank (UCB), illegally bought by Museveni's brother; the Uganda Airlines Corporation; and Trans-Ocean.

Ugandan Commercial Bank was the largest bank in the country, controlling over 80 percent of the commercial banking market. It was sent into bankruptcy by brazen looting of the ruling clique. Senior members of the ruling National Resistance Movement (NRM) took huge loans worth over 62 billion shillings ($164.5 million), which were later declared as "bad debts." *The Monitor* (Oct 26–28, 1994) reported that "the names behind UCB's bad debts include some of the most famous and prominent politicians, soldiers, bankers and businessmen." The paper went on to reveal military officers collectively owed the bank at least 281.25 million shillings.

As noted in chapter 5, the World Bank mission sent to Uganda in 1998 reported "widespread accusations of non-transparency, insider dealings and corruption," involving President Museveni's own brother, Major General Salim Saleh (World Bank, 1998). Cases of large-scale embezzlement documented in the World Bank report included the stealing of donor funds disbursed to the ministries of health and education and to the Ugandan Electoral Commission, as well as funds disbursed to projects aimed at helping alleviate poverty, but which were embezzled and never benefited the intended poor. The World Bank report specifically targeted Vice President Wandira Kazibwe, whose office is being investigated for the loss of 3.4 billion Ugandan shillings in a valley dam scheme which was paid for, but never constructed.

President Museveni himself, together with the presidents of Rwanda and Burundi, were directly accused by a United Nations panel of taking advantage of the civil war in the Democratic Republic of Congo and engaging in systematic plunder of the country's mineral resources. The United Nations Panel of Experts on the Illegal Exploitation of Natural Resources and Other Forms of Wealth of Congo was set up in June 2000 and headed by Madam Safiatou Ba-N'Daw (from Ivory Coast).

Its report, released in mid-April 2001, found "mass-scale looting" of stockpiled minerals, coffee, timber, livestock, and money by the armies of Rwanda, Uganda, and Burundi. Military and government officials then exported the diamonds, gold, and a composite mineral called coltan to line their own pockets and enrich a network of shell companies owned by well-connected associates. The Panel said between September 1998 and August 1999, the occupied zones of Congo were drained of existing stockpiles of minerals, agricultural and forest products, including livestock. "Regardless of the looter, the pattern was the same. Burundian, Rwandan, Ugandan and/or Rally for Congolese Democracy (RCD) soldiers, commanded by an officer, visited farms, storage facilities, factories, banks, and demanded that the managers open the coffers and doors. The soldiers were then ordered to remove the relevant products and load them into vehicles" (*New African*, June 2001; p.4). When resource stockpiles were looted and exhausted by occupying forces and their allies, the exploitation evolved to an active extraction phase. The looting was facilitated by the administrative structures established by Uganda and Rwanda.

According to the panel, "The Central Bank of Uganda has reportedly acknowledged to IMF officials that the volume of Ugandan gold exports does not reflect [the] country's production levels but rather that some exports might be 'leaking over the borders' from Congo. The Central Bank reported that, by September 1997, Uganda had exported gold valued at $105m, compared with $60m in 1996 and $23m in 1995" (*New African*, June 2001; p.4). But the panel found Uganda's exports "suspicious" for many reasons: "(a) Uganda has no known diamond production; (b) Diamond exports from Uganda [began] only in the last few years, totaling $3 million, coinciding surprisingly with the occupation of eastern Congo; and (c) the need [for Uganda] to control the rich diamond zone near Kisangani and Banalia." Uganda has also become an exporter of niobium, another mineral similar to coltan, but the panel says Uganda had "no production [of niobium] prior to 1997," coinciding with its presence in Congo.

The panel contended that Rwandan authorities themselves admitted that the country "has no production of diamond, cobalt, zinc, manganese and uranium. Yet Rwanda has been exporting diamonds." Rwanda's production figures, according to the report, displayed some irregular patterns for gold and coltan starting from 1997. Rwanda took in at least $250 million in 18 months by exporting Congolese coltan (*The Washington Post*, May 2, 2001; p.A18).

"Key individual actors including top army commanders and businessmen on the one hand, and government structures on the other, have been the engines of this systematic and systemic exploitation," said the report. President Yoweri Museveni of Uganda and Paul Kagame of Rwanda are, at the very least, politically involved, according to the panel of experts, which spent close to seven months in the region. The report, written by five experts, goes so far as to say the two leaders "are on the verge of becoming godfathers of the illegal exploitation of natural resources and the continuation of the conflict." (*The Washington Times*, April 17, 2001; p.A13)

Zaire

Zaire's economic crisis emerged in 1974 and for four straight years its gross national product contracted by 16.8 percent. The worst year of the crisis was in 1978, when output was 17 percent below the level of 1974; the manufacturing sector was operating at about 40 percent of capacity; the inflation rate (December 1977 to December 1978) averaged 100 percent; real wages and salaries were at one-fourth of the 1970 levels; and malnutrition was on the rise.

While external factors, such as the depressed level of copper prices and the closing of the Benguela Railway in November 1975, played a role, the principal causes of the crisis were internal: The heavy external borrowing, hastily conceived and poorly implemented experiments of *zairianization* and "radicalization" deficiencies in management of the economy, misallocation of the country's resources, and the pervasiveness of corruption.

By far, however, the most significant factor in the causation of the Zairean crisis was the *zairianization* or nationalization measures of 1973–74. It needs to be borne in mind that, around this time, Nigeria and Ghana were also pursuing the same "indigenization" programs (see for example Nigeria's Indigenization Decree of 1972 and Busia's Ghanaianization Law of 1970).

In Zaire, the state took over a wide variety of businesses, including the small trading and transport firms, which constituted the lifeline of the rural areas. In manufacturing, however, the impact of zairianization was somewhat mitigated by the fact that the state did not take over the large firms but restricted their retail outlets. As the World Bank Mission to Zaire reported in 1979:

Zairianization led in many instances to the destruction or dispersion of the capital stock, as many plantations were abandoned by the new owners after selling their newly acquired assets (trucks and other movable equipment); it disrupted marketing by causing an exodus of small expatriate intermediaries who traditionally played a vital role in the distribution of inputs and consumer goods as well as in the collection and commercialization of farm output. To take one example, the decline in palm oil production of about 30 percent between 1974 and 1978 is attributable in part to the negative effects that *zairianization* had on the output of small plantations, which had been significant as a group. (Report on Zaire; p.15, paragraph 26)

The brunt of the nationalization measures were borne by the manufacturing sector, including agro-industry. Sixty-two firms in 11 of 12 manufacturing sector branches—which accounted for about two-thirds of total sector sales—were nationalized. A large number of firms in the commercial and construction sectors were also affected. Although nationalization had a widely varying impact on individual enterprises, it produced a generalized effect on the working environment by causing a progressive attrition of expatriate managerial and technical staff, abrupt changes in commercial (supplier-client) relationships, and severed or significantly altered relations with former foreign parent companies.

The World Bank (1979) concluded that:

> The most adverse effects of the *zairianization*/nationalization measures, however, were perhaps the neglect of maintenance and repair, the discouragement of private investment by either foreigners or nationals, and pervasive financial mismanagement. This has been widely recognized by the Zairian authorities; nationalization was a reaction to the failure of *zairianization;* and retrocession a reaction to the failure of nationalization. (Report on Zaire; p.15)

Living standards deteriorated. Income per capita dropped from $210 at the time of independence to $160 in 1988 (World Development Report, 1988). A 1980 official Trade Union Enquiry revealed that 1,061 *zaires* (about $235) a month were needed for a diet that would barely keep the body and soul together for a typical urban family. The average wage in June 1981 was 23 *zaires* per month, which was worthless in the face of inflation raging at 85 percent. Even the professional class was suffering. Medical doctors, for example, were getting between 500 and 800 *zaires* a month in 1982.

Social conditions were deteriorating alarmingly. At Mama Yemo General Hospital (named for Mobutu's mother) unattended patients were dying because there were no bandages, no sterilization equipment, no oxygen, and no film for x-ray machines. The dead often remained in the intensive care unit for hours before being removed because there was no room for extra bodies in the morgue (Lamb, 1985). One-third of infants died before the age of five.

Health clinics at the university campuses in Kinshasa and Lumumbashi had to shut down because the medicines intended for use there had been diverted to the black markets. Agricultural produce destined for market often rotted on the ground because the transportation system had broken down. The government news agency closed down for lack of paper, and two of Air Zaire's planes (a Boeing 747 and a Douglas DC-10) were repossessed. What happened?

Part of the suffering of Zairians emanated from the collapse of the copper market in the late 1970s and early 1980s. Copper, which accounts for some 60 percent of Zaire's foreign exchange earnings, experienced overcapacity and increasing competition from optical fibers (which can replace copper in some applications, such as underground telephone cables). Another part of Zaire's woes stemmed from the civil war that raged through the Shaba province in 1977 and 1978. But the predominant cause was the egregious system of government instituted in Zaire: kleptocracy—government by armed looters.

Presiding over an empire of graft and venality, President Mobutu himself boasted on the TV program CBS *60 Minutes* in 1984 that he was the second-richest man in the whole world. Together with his close family and friends, Mobutu owned more than 26 expensive properties including a 32-room mansion in Switzerland, a 16th-century castle in Spain, a huge vineyard in Portugal, and an estate in the Ivory Coast. At home, he had 11 palaces, including one on the northern border in his ancestral village of Gbadolite, known as the "Versailles in the Jungle," where liveried waiters served pickled quail tongues and chilled French wines.

The top group that ruled Zaire, the Gang of Five, were Mobutu; Litho Moboti, his uncle; Seti Yale, his security adviser; General Bolozi Gbudu, head of military intelligence (and married to two of Mobutu's relations); and Moleka Liboko, his nephew and a businessman. They all came from two clans originating from Mobutu's father's village, Gbandolite (the Gbande tribe) on the northern Ubangi River in Equateur province.

Zaire in the late 1970s was receiving nearly half of all the aid money the Jimmy Carter administration allocated for black Africa. But that aid failed to improve conditions. "Of every dollar coming into Zaire, whether in the form of foreign aid or a business contract, Zairian officials reportedly took twenty cents off for their personal cut. In 1977, Zaire's coffee crop was valued at $400 million. Only $120 million made it to Zaire's treasury" (Lamb, 1985). Meanwhile, Mobutu strutted about the world stage while his African people starved. Slowly but steadily, Zaireans watched helplessly as their hopes and future were squandered by the Gang of Five.

In 1997, Zaire imploded. President-for-life Mobutu Sese Seko was driven out of office by a rebel insurgency, led by Laurent Kabila. Mobutu died in exile in Morocco. But as Africans would say: "We remove one coconut and the next coconut comes to do the same thing!" A year and a half later, Kabila faced a rebel insurgency himself—just like Charles Taylor of Liberia, who himself led an insurgency to remove General Samuel Doe from office. The insurgency against Kabila drew in the armies of Angola, Namibia, Chad, and Zimbabwe, supporting the Kabila government, and the armies of Uganda and Rwanda, supporting the rebels. This plunged Zaire (now renamed the Democratic Republic of the Congo) into yet another orgy of violence and war that claimed more than 3.5 million lives.

Zimbabwe

Upon independence in 1980, President Robert Mugabe openly stated his determination to make Zimbabwe a one-party nation and his Zimbabwe African National Union (ZANU) party "a truly Marxist-Leninist party to ensure the charting of an irreversible social course and create a socialist ideology." Indeed, in December 1982, all 57 ministers and deputy ministers in Mugabe's cabinet arrived at the Harare airport to greet visiting Ethiopian leader Mengistu Haile Mariam—black Africa's archapostle of Marxism-Leninism. Inheriting an economy that was hobbled by racial inequalities under the former white-minority regime, there was a strong need for statism, to correct injustices committed by white colonialists.

At independence, Zimbabwe had the most broad-based economy in Africa. It had an iron and steel industry and a diversified industrial infrastructure, which was meticulously built by the racist Ian Smith regime to ensure self-sufficiency after the imposition of sanctions following the Unilateral Declaration of Independence (UDI) from Britain in 1965. Its mining, chemical, and construction industries were relatively advanced technologically. But ownership and control of industries and the economy lay in the hands of white settlers.

After independence, Mugabe did not embark upon any program of wholesale expropriation and nationalization. In December 1982, the Mugabe government introduced a Transitional National Development Plan 1982–83 to 1984–85. The strategy was for growth, equity, and transformation. The private sector, dominated by white settlers, was to continue to function but with increased state control and participation. For example, shortly after independence in 1980, the Zimbabwe Mass Media Trust was set up to buy out the country's five main newspapers. Mugabe argued that the newspapers were owned by the South African Argus newspaper group and that the news was racially biased. Nathan Shamuyarira, the minister of information, declared that the purchase was motivated with a "view to getting the right news through to the consumer." Who could challenge that objective? But as in Nkrumah's Ghana, each repressive measure in Zimbabwe was dressed in either anticolonialist or antiracist garb. In 1981 the editor of the *Umtali Post* was dismissed on Mugabe's order after she raised questions about the presence of North Korean military instructors in the country. Nor could journalists or even members of parliament investigate allegations of corruption in high echelons of the government.

As elsewhere in Africa, the socialism introduced by Mugabe was of the "Swiss bank" variety that allowed him and a brigade of kleptocrats to rape and plunder the treasury for deposit in overseas bank accounts. It became evident that Mugabe and his lieutenants were a determined bunch of bandits who had wrapped themselves in socialist garb. Less than two years after independence, a wave of corruption scandals began to sweep the country. For example, at the Ministry of Education phantom teachers were added to the government payroll, and their salaries were collected by teachers already on the payroll. *New African* (Dec 1987) reported the extent of the corruption:

> Civil servants at all levels, workers in parastatals and private organizations and bank tellers have been appearing in court with monotonous regularity for dipping their hands in the kitty. Government critics point fingers at the leadership of the country for the malaise saying that a lot of Ministers are the ones, who, through their "get rich quick" tendencies started the "each one for himself and God for us all" survival syndrome. The critics point to the massive wealth which many Ministers have amassed in the seven short years of independence. It is a common secret that several leaders have thrown the country's avowed policy of socialism to the winds and have used their positions to acquire wealth in the form of hotels, houses for rent, ranches, farms, buses and stores. (Dec 1987; p.58)

As early as 1982, Edgar Tekere, a maverick and also a nationalist who fought alongside Mugabe for Zimbabwe's independence, decided to fight against this incipient "Swiss bank" socialism. He declared: "We all came from Mozambique with nothing; not even a teaspoon. But today, in less than two years, you hear that so-and-so owns so many farms, a chain of hotels and his father owns a fleet of buses. Where did all that money come from in such a short period? Isn't it from the very public funds they are entrusted to administer?" (*New African,* March 1989; p.21) University students also protested, saying that Zimbabwe's revolutionary heroes had been betrayed by corrupt and ideologically bankrupt leaders (*New African,* Dec 1988; p.23).

According to *The Zimbabwe Independent* (April 27, 1999):

> The 1999 Zimbabwe Human Development Report (funded by the UN Development Program) is eloquent on the straits to which the Mugabe regime

has reduced Zimbabwe, hitherto one of Africa's richest and most developed countries. Per capita income has fallen back to what it was a generation or more ago and the grotesque appropriation of wealth by the governing elite—every minister is rich and most are at least US dollar millionaires—has produced one of the most unequal societies in the world. Poverty is increasing rapidly: 61 percent of the population is now below the poverty line. Zimbabweans are now suffering rapid declines in health and life expectancy. (p.22)

The myriad of state controls and regulations imposed by the Mugabe regime created a gold mine of opportunities for illicit enrichment by government bureaucrats and cronies. As noted in the previous sections, state controls create artificial shortages and rent-seeking activities. In the early 1980s, such an activity erupted into a scandal that drew much attention.

At that time, Zimbabwe had only one car assembly plant, Willowvalle Motor Industries in Harare. Owing to a shortage of foreign exchange created by a combination of import, export, and exchange controls as well as the refusal of Mugabe to deal with apartheid South Africa, a chronic shortage of vehicles developed. Ration coupons or chits were issued by the government to allocate scarce vehicles. But some government officials used their positions to gain access to an inordinate number of chits. They then used their excessive allocation of chits to purchase automobiles and later resold them on the black market at three times their purchase price—*kalabule* in Ghana.

Mugabe's statist, Marxist-Leninist policies failed to improve the lot of the people, whose economic welfare progressively deteriorated. By 1989, people were already fed up with Mugabe. On Africa Day, "only about 8,000 people went to listen to President Mugabe deliver a speech at Rufaro Stadium in Harare. Within hours after the stadium was cleared, 40,000 people paid to watch soccer at the same stadium. People have reasons to be apathetic. They complain of high taxation, unemployment, corruption among government and party officials and price hikes" (*New African* Dec 1989; p.20).

The economy declined progressively. Corn production dropped sharply from 2 million tons in 1981 to 620,000 in 1983. Zimbabwe, once a food exporter, was rapidly becoming a food importer. Shortages of commodities and foreign exchange were becoming rampant. "The cost of living has risen astronomically since independence in 1980. Inflation is running around 20 percent per annum and most people are having to dig deeper into their pockets to survive" (*New African* Dec 1987; p.58). The unemployment rate was 50 percent in the urban job market in 1989 and corruption was getting worse. By 1999, things had gotten progressively worse.

According to the *Zimbabwe Independent* (April 27, 1999):

There is no *mealie* meal—the staple diet—in the shops, apparently because of foul-ups by the government marketing board. Every day the government promises that mealie meal will soon be in the shops. Meanwhile bread, rice, potatoes and other substitutes are also sold out. Inflation is running at 47 percent and shopkeepers, unsure what will happen to the currency next or that today's takings will buy tomorrow's supplies, often opt for pre-emptive price increases. With interest rates at 55 percent car sales have halved (causing job losses in the country's Mazda assembly plant) and the property market has frozen solid. (p.25)

By 1999, the Zimbabwean state had effectively ceased to function. Desperate for revenue, the government not only imposed stiff hospital fees that many could not afford but also sacked all the nurses. Of the country's 16 district hospitals, 5 were still lying idle in 1999, two years after being built, due to lack of medical staff. The parastatal oil company, NOCZIM, looted by its managers, ran up a debt of Z$4 billion. In 1999, the department of social welfare announced that it lacked transport to ship grain to 54,000 starving families in the Guruve district. "No-bid government contracts, such as the one to renovate Harare's international airport, were awarded to Mugabe's nephew and other relatives" (*The Washington Post*, May 5, 2000; p.A23).

In 1990, subsidies to Zimbabwe's parastatals amounted to 6.9 percent of total recurrent expenditure or 34.5 percent of the budget deficit. This was aggravated by a phenomenal expansion of the civil service (bureaucracy) after independence in 1980. There were 62,035 total civil servants in 1980; in 1989 the total came to 181,402 (Five-Year Development Plan, 1990–1995).

The state-owned Air Zimbabwe was long plagued by Mugabe's habit of commandeering its planes and kicking off passengers whenever he wanted to go on one of his frequent trips with his wife, Grace. Her enormous mansion in Borrowdale was built on land bought from the state for less than a seventh of its commercial value (*The Zimbabwe Independent*, April 27, 1999; p.25).

Zimbabwe Mining Development Corporation (ZMDC) was set up through an act of Parliament of 1982 to develop mines owned by the state. It was hoped that the parastatal would grow its portfolio, generate foreign exchange, and create jobs. Given that the mining sector accounted for about 5 percent of the gross domestic product (GDP), it was assumed that state participation in the industry was only logical and strategic. But ZMDC never lived up to expectations. According to the state-owned *The Herald* (January 22, 2003),

Its holdings shrank from over 10 mines to the three in 2003: Elvington Mine, Sabi Gold Mine and Jena Mines, which were bought from Trillion Resources of Canada. Two of ZMDC's flagships, Kamativi Tin Mine and Mhangura

Copper Mines (MCM) closed in 1994 and 2001 respectively. ZMDC has also disposed of Bar 20 to Forbes and Thompson mines and is no longer operating Merits Limited, Peneast Mining Company and KY Refractories.

The situation at the remaining mines became precarious. Sabi ceased operations and teetered on the verge of collapse. It owed Trust Bank $618 million and required at least $Z1.2 billion to pay off the debt and exploit the mineral resources at the mine.

Workers at ZMDC alleged that management had been left to run down the parastatal. They cited favoritism and profligacy as contributory factors to the poor performance of ZMDC. But ZMDC chief executive Isaiah Ruzengwe denied the allegations: "None of ZMDC mines were closed because of mismanagement. In fact, a government institution can never be closed because of mismanagement because Government will act to remove that management and replace it and examples are galore in Zimbabwe" (*The Herald* Jan 22, 2003). The chief executive perhaps needed brain surgery.

According to *The Zimbabwe Independent*, (April 27, 1999):

> Given the government's spendthrift ways, its steady refusal to slim down the bloated patronage state administration and the elite's determination to steal everything that is not nailed down and quite a bit that is, the result has been to deliver Zimbabwe into the hands of the IMF/World Bank. Ministers bilk on whatever bills they can, the infrastructure falls to bits before one's eyes and the state searches ever more desperately for revenue. School fees have been pushed up to the point where many parents are having to take their children out of school and illiteracy is increasing for the first time in a century. (p.25)

Mugabe angrily rejected the criticism of those who blamed the government for Zimbabwe's economic crisis. It was, he said, the fault of greedy Western powers, the IMF, the Asian financial crisis, and the drought (*Zimbabwe Independent* April 27, 1999; p.26). Naturally.

Egypt

The tale of gross inefficiency, profligacy, and mismanagement can be recounted in one state enterprise after another in the postcolonial period. The experience of Egypt was even more dramatic. Back in 1993, foreign investors took one good look at Egypt and drew a loud yawn. Its economy was suffocating under a leviathan bureaucracy. Inefficiencies at state enterprises were titanic, illustrated by the case of Pyramid Beverage Co., which produced the country's flagship beer, Stella. Its reputation quickly became legendary. Beer drinkers in Cairo soon learned to inspect each bottle before they purchased the product because many arrive on store shelves flat or half full. An occasional bean has been seen floating in an unopened bottle of Stella. Pyramid Beverage was founded in 1897 by Heineken Co., the giant Dutch brewery, but was nationalized under Gamal Abdel Nasser's version of "Arab socialism" in 1961.

In 1993, the Egyptian government hosted a delegation from Heineken to see if it was interested in buying back Pyramid Beverage. After inspecting the factory, the delegation said: Thanks but no thanks. And to add insult to injury, they informed the government that they would rather invest their money in Latin America and South Africa, according to Adeeb Mena, who then headed the commercial section of Pyramid Beverage.

"It was very humiliating," said Hamad Fahmy, chairman of the government holding company that owned the brewery (The Washington Post, May 8, 1996; p.A27).

The factory was in a sordid state: antiquated equipment, factory grounds filthy with heaped trash, and with paint flaking from the ceilings. The work force was bloated. The company employed 3,000 workers, about 10 times the number Heineken estimated was needed to produce the same quantity.

The Egyptian government cleverly changed the name of the brewery to Al-Ahram Beverages Co. Still, there were no takers. An attempt to sell 10 percent of the shares in 1996 flopped badly.

Another foreign company, Owens Corning, which sent a group of executives to Egypt in 1993, reached a similar conclusion: Egypt was not yet ready. Company executives could not even get a firm date for a meeting with the Egyptian government commission that was supposed to approve their investment.

Though Egypt had agreed with the World Bank and IMF on an ambitious economic restructuring program to privatize moribund state-owned enterprises and curb inflation and budget deficits, reform was proceeding at a glacial pace. From 1992 to 1995, only 3 of its 314 public-sector companies were sold to private investors. Analysts pointed to the huge resistance to privatization from public-sector managers and workers that had to be contended with. Even within the government circles, there were many who believed privatization amounted to selling off the nation's assets too cheaply to foreign interests. At one point the IMF became so frustrated at the pace of reform that it suspended its loan program to Egypt.

In 1997, Al-Ahram Beverages was sold to Luxor Group and has gone through further restructuring that has resulted in better quality products and wider distribution. Sales were up 13 percent to 168 million Egyptian pounds ($49.3 million) in the year ending June 1998, while net income rose 25 percent to 67.6 million pounds (Wall Street Journal, Jan 12, 1999; p.A19).

Shaking off decades of "socialist hang-over" has been tough. Overstaffing in Egyptian companies still remains a problem. State enterprises were often employment mills for party faithfuls and there was the tendency to pad pay rolls. Though pay scales were meagre, state workers often enjoyed free medical care and subsidized housing and transportation. "The public sector is better than the private sector," said Abdel Ghani Azouz, 43, a fermentation worker at Pyramid Beverages Co. in 1994 (*The Washington Post* May 8, 1996; p.A29).

Nigeria

Nigeria differed from other African states in three respects: a large population, a federal constitution, a major gold strike in the form of oil, and economic liberalism. It eschewed doctrinaire socialism and adopted federalism at independence in 1960. But, as Fieldhouse (1986) noted, "Lagos, exactly like Accra, aimed to concentrate the largest possible share of the national product in its own hands, to expand the public sector and to develop import-substitution industry by means of tariffs, import licensing and other stimuli" (p.151).

Soon after independence, federalism ran into problems, which originated from two key pieces of legislation. The first was the 1951 Macpherson Constitution. This replaced the 1947 Richards Constitution, which created three houses of assembly for the three different regions: the North, the East, and the West. The new Macpherson Constitution set up a House of Representatives and a Council of Ministers at the center. The ostensible reason was to secure a more unified government. But it came at a crushing political cost, concentrating enormous powers in the hands of the federal government. The military, dominated by the northern Hausa, captured and monopolized the state for 29 out of the 39 years of Nigeria's independence, until civilian rule was ushered in 1999.

The second was a 1970 law that in effect gave all mineral rights in Nigeria to the federal government. Revenues were then, in theory, distributed throughout the country. With the discovery of oil in the early 1970s, much oil revenue flowed into government coffers, accounting for more than 80 percent of government revenue. The states could not raise their own revenues, but had to rely upon handouts from the central pot, the amount of which corresponded to the population in the states. Because of this setup, there has always been a dispute over population censuses. Fierce competition inevitably developed among politicians, organizations, state governments, and the various ethnic groups to capture the central pot or at least gain access to it. Politics has often been seen as a way of gaining access to fantastic wealth. Much time is wasted over how to share the spoils of office. This often stirred ethnic chauvinism. The group that dominated the administration handed out the best jobs and contracts to its friends and kinsmen. The ethnic minnows left out clamored for their own states and even threatened secession (the Biafran War of 1967). New states were created for some: 7 in 1976, 2 more in 1987, and 9 in 1993. By 2003, the number of states had reached 36. The Ogoni in the Niger Delta are the latest clamoring for their own state. Their grievances are real. They sit on top of billions of dollars of oil reserves. But "we get no benefit from it, absolutely none," complained Chief Edward Kobani, a senior elder of the Ogoni. Nor was revenue from Nigeria's immense mineral wealth used to lift the people out of poverty.

With the huge influx of oil money, Nigeria's governments embarked upon extravagant public projects. This created other strong constituencies to lobby aggressively for budgetary allocations. The state expanded public expenditure programs enormously to provide social services and utilities. Primary education was made free and mandatory, which created a huge market for the construction of school buildings and provision of textbooks through the state, thus creating the conditions under which influence-peddling, bribery, and corruption flourished.

Though Nigeria's industrialization policy began in the mid-1950s, the major state-support system began after 1960, and gained further impetus with the discovery of oil. The industrialization policy, based upon import-substitution, was largely driven by emotional, nationalistic goals. From the colonial period to the early 1960s, most of the industrial investment was by foreign firms, so that, in 1963, 68 percent of the ownership of large-scale industry was foreign (Fieldhouse 1986; p.152). Accordingly, in the 1970s, Nigeria increasingly adopted a policy of "indigenization" as did many other African countries, such as Ghana, Zaire, and Zimbabwe. Certain sections of the Nigerian economy were reserved exclusively for Nigerians.

The state apparatus was utilized ostensibly to protect Nigerians from foreign exploitation. The First Development Plan (1962–68) called for economic independence and stated that indigenous businessmen should control an increasing portion of the Nigerian economy. The 1963 Immigration Act and the government's 1964 statement on industrial policy, when taken together, were designed to encourage personnel, equity, and local-content indigenization (Biersteker 1987; p.71). In 1966, an Expatriate Allocation Board was created in part because of a large influx of Lebanese and Indian merchants engaged in both wholesale and retail sales of textiles goods in the Lagos trading area.

In April 1971, the state acquired 40 percent of the largest commercial banks and the Nigerian National Oil Company (NNOC) was established with the government keeping majority participation. In 1975, the government acquired 55 percent of the petroleum industry and 40 percent of National Insurance Company of Nigeria (NICON). The following year, the acquisition was extended to other insurance companies when the government took 49 percent of their shares. Heavy industry and manufacturing, such as gas liquefaction, iron and steel-making, petrochemicals, and fertilizers, were to be held by the state. The Nigerian Enterprise Promotion Decree of 1972 ordered foreign businesses in a number of specified fields to transfer part or all of their equity to private Nigerian investors or businessmen. Twenty-two activities were scheduled to become the preserve of Nigerian nationals, and another 33 foreign enterprises were to be excluded from foreign participation unless above a specified size and with at least 40 percent Nigerian ownership of the equity (Fieldhouse, 1986; p.153).

The restrictions were extended in 1977 to cover both the range of manufacturing and proportion of equity. Nigerians were to hold 40 percent equity in all unlisted enterprises. To achieve this goal, oil money was funneled through state credit agencies to state holding companies and favored individuals. Schemes were started to provide credit and facilities to small-scale Nigerian entrepreneurs. The Approved Manufacturers Scheme, begun in 1955, was expanded to provide industrial estates to would-be manufacturers with little capital.

Although manufacturing output and the number employed in manufacturing did increase, it came at great economic and social cost. Graft, corruption, and political patronage ensured that much of the oil money was frittered away on prestigious projects—motorways, Ajaokuta steel mills, inefficient state enterprises, and luxury imports—from aircraft engines to Mercedes Benzes. One business tycoon impatient for the delivery of his Rolls Royce had it air-freighted!

Most of Nigeria's state enterprises are triumphs of towering inefficiency, producing well below their installed capacity. For example, if a factory could produce 100,000 electric bulbs a month (its capacity) and produced only 10,000 bulbs, it was utilizing only 10 percent of its capacity. Now, consider the rate of capacity utilization of a random selection from the Central Bank's 1992 annual report: Nigerian machine tools, 8 percent; Nigerian paper mill, Jebba, 12.1 percent; Nigerian Newsprint Manufacturing Company, 13.3 percent; Jukura Marble Plant, 1 percent; the Nigerian Sugar Company, an impressive 72 percent. The Nigerian National Paper Manufacturing Company did not make anything at all: "construction work which started in 1977 was yet to be completed due to lack of funds" (*The Economist,* Aug 21, 1993; survey p.9). Two of Nigeria's Airbuses were impounded in 1988 by the French company Sorgema for non-payment of debt. In March, Aer Lingus of Ireland impounded spare parts, worth about $20 million, which were stored in Dublin, "because of the airline's (Nigeria Airways') failure to pay for the maintenance of its fleet of Boeing 707 aircraft" (*West Africa,* March 20–26, 1989; p.454).

Rather strangely, Nigeria chose highly capital-intensive techniques for its state enterprises. Initial estimates placed the capital costs of the Aluminum Smelter at Ikot Abasi in Nigeria at $1.2 billion, making this project 60 percent more costly than comparable projects elsewhere in the world. The government had already expended $450 million by early 1991 (World Bank, 1994; p.251). Then the Nigerian government built a six-vehicle assembly plant that was largely dependent on imported materials. The range of models produced was so wide that production runs were extremely short; the multiplication of plants also ensured that all operated at very low levels in capacity. As a result, some recorded a negative value-added in manufacturing: Just the costs of assembly in Nigeria were in excess of the cost of importing a fully built vehicle from overseas (Chazan et al., 1992; p.255).

The rest of the oil money was squandered by corrupt politicians and military bandits in hideous displays of wealth amid appalling poverty and squalor. A recent World Bank study reckoned that capital flight during the 1980s reached $50 billion. "Over 3,000 Nigerians have Swiss bank accounts," lamented the Christian Association of Nigeria. Army chiefs parked Maseratis and even Lamborghinis outside plush government villas while their children attended expensive schools in Britain.

Riding high on an oil boom, the government of Shehu Shagari decided to build a new capital at Abuja, about 30 miles northeast of Lagos, at an estimated cost of $16 billion. Never mind that millions of Nigerians in the slums of Lagos lacked running water, medical care, and educational facilities. Eventually, the cost of the capital soared to $25 billion—officially. Unofficially, most critics believe it was more than double that. But such frivolous extravagance was not unique to Nigeria alone. President El Hadj Omar Bongo of Gabon, an oil-producing country with a foreign debt of $1 billion, built a $27 million conference center with a façade of imported Italian marble just in time for the 1977 summit meeting of the Organization of African Unity in the capital of Libreville (*Time,* Jan 16, 1984; p.28).

Thus, in Nigeria, as in Ghana, "the record of public policy as an instrument of economic development was very poor. Industry was extremely inefficient. Agriculture experienced virtually no growth" (Fieldhouse, 1986; p.159). The increase in national income, occasioned by the higher oil prices and larger volumes of oil exports, was partly absorbed by a state apparatus that was increasingly politicized and linked to private interests and partly squandered on import-substitution industrialization, involving huge investments with little return. In July 1999, the new Nigerian president Olusegun

Obasanjo announced a new privatization program. He lambasted Nigeria's large public sector, where some of the more than 1,000 state-owned enterprises have been losing millions of dollars annually. "State enterprises," he declared, "suffer from fundamental problems of defective capital structure, excessive bureaucratic control or intervention, inappropriate technology, gross incompetence and mismanagement, blatant corruption and crippling complacency" (*UN Recovery*, April 2000; p.8).

The supreme irony of Nigeria's economic development is that, despite the flow of substantial oil wealth, the country entered the new millennium with real income per capita about the same as it was at independence in 1960 and heavily burdened by debt. The drop was more dramatic in the 1980s. In 1980, income per capita stood at $1,029—the fifth highest in Sub-Saharan Africa. By 1990, it had dropped to a woeful $266. This sharp decline in economic performance was not due to external economic adversities. In fact, between 1970 and the early 1980s, when oil prices collapsed, $100 billion in oil money flowed into Nigerian government coffers. On top of this, Nigeria accumulated a $35 billion foreign debt.

Senegal

The posture of Francophone African states after independence was somewhat bizarre and paradoxical. Having won political independence, they yearned for economic sovereignty; yet French commercial influence was dominant and pervasive. In Senegal, Leopold Senghor, who assumed the presidency upon independence in 1960, was socialist-oriented. President Senghor maintained in most essentials an open economy and trade. At the political level, however, his ruling party, *Union Progressiste Senegalaise (UPS)*, "monopolized power, with Senghor, as president, the sole focus of decision-making. The party took control of all organs of government, politicizing the bureaucracy at all levels. The bureaucracy, already large, grew substantially" (Fieldhouse, 1986; p.213). A substantial portion of state revenue went to feed a political and administrative elite that had grown accustomed to a French standard of living.

Though Senghor's ideological orientation was socialism and "Negritude," there was hardly any direct state involvement in economic life. The state's main economic function consisted in controlling credit and banking. *Banque Nationale de Developpement* and *Union Senegalaise de Banque* were established in the 1960s and the state invested in some new industrial ventures, such as the industrial free zone, the naval repair base, a petrochemical complex, and tourist facilities. The bulk of the industrial enterprises were left to the French.

Senghor supported French international policies in exchange for economic aid, military support, and a favored position for Senegalese products on the French market. Senegal's export economy has always been monoculture: the cultivation of groundnuts. By supporting the price of this commodity above world prices until 1967, France reinforced this overdependence on a single crop and did not help to diversify agriculture. It was in this sector that the state was most directly involved.

Direct state involvement in groundnut production stemmed from the need to free the peasant producer from domination by the largely French trading companies, which previously marketed more than 50 percent of the groundnut crop, distributed over 75 percent of imported food and manufactures, sold to peasants, and provided much of the credit, along with Lebanese and African middlemen, for the production system. Although Senegal had no marketing boards, as in Anglophone Africa, a stabilization fund was set up in 1958 to even out fluctuations in market prices, and *Societes de Prevoyance,* an alternative cooperative means of marketing produce, was established with the aim of creating a system of rural cooperatives. *Societes de Prevoyance* would not only control the buying of the groundnut crop but also dispense credit and disseminate technical knowledge. But to carry out this scheme, a very complex bureaucratic machinery was set up—of course—upon the advice of the ever-indispensable French advisors in Dakar. Thus,

> Control of all sales of groundnuts was vested in an *Office de Commercialisation Agricole (OCA),* which had a monopoly of buying from the co-operatives and at first the remaining private buyers. OCA would then sell either to the processing companies in Senegal or to importers of groundnuts in France. To promote agricultural improvement, *Centres Regionaux de l'Assistance au Developpement (CRADs)* were established, provided with finance for credit by the new *Banque Senegalaise de Developpement (BSD),* later by *Banque Nationale de Developpement Senegalaise (BNDS).* The co-operatives were supervised by the *Service de la Cooperation (SC),* part of the Ministry of Rural Economy. (Fieldhouse, 1986; p.215)

Clearly, the structure was highly bureaucratic and centralized. Bureaucratic incompetence resulted in widespread cases of embezzlement, financial chaos, shortages of agricultural inputs, food, and trade goods, with wide variations in prices. These reinforced rural economic inequalities and enabled the local cooperative officials to enrich themselves (Samoun, 2000; p.28). In fact, "The state apparatus became one of direct exploitation of the peasantry. The co-operatives organized the rural world and the state appropriated the surplus" (Cruise O'Brien, 1981; p.287). Senegalese farmers revolted, threatening the political stability as well as the interests of the civil servants and the French capitalists. To quell the growing revolt, Senegal asked the European Union for a grant to cover the peasantry's debt—a request that was supported by France (Cruise O'Brien, 1981; p.287). Groundnut producers did not benefit either from the end of private marketing or the creation of a state monopoly with related development services.

When the Senegalese state opted for industrialization through import substitution, its special relationship with France created a problem. The share of private Senegalese capital in the domestic ownership of industry was a tiny 3 percent (Fieldhouse, 1986; p.224). The preponderance of French- and Lebanese-owned industry made it difficult even for the most enterprising Senegalese to find a niche in industry, except in the "informal sector." Thus, while some modest industrialization and expansion was achieved, it furthered the interests of French companies. Private and public French capital was favored over local private or public investment in the creation of infant industries that were supposed to lead the development of the local economy. A contradiction soon became apparent—attempting to achieve economic independence while allowing unrestricted penetration of French capital.

Ivory Coast

Similarly in Ivory Coast, French economic interests shaped the country's industrialization program. Upon independence in 1960, President Felix Houphouet-Boigny chose to maintain the existing close relationship with France. Known as Le Vieux, Houphouet-Boigny ruled single-handedly for 30 years, until November 1990 when he was forced by popular demand to appoint a prime minister. Under his leadership Ivory Coast was a one-party state led by the *Partie Democratique de Cote d'Ivoire (PDCI)*, the sole legal party, which ruled for 39 years from 1960 to 1999.

Houphouet-Boigny proscribed opposition parties with the constant refrain "that his life was under threat from opposition figures working in collusion with juju-men and their gris-gris" (*West Africa*, July 13–19, 1992; p.1171). He took responsibility for all policy decisions. The press was tightly controlled by the government and faithfully reflected the party line. All civil servants were party members.

For 40 years after independence, Ivory Coast was characterized by a continuous "coup d'etat"—by a small minority who managed to control the political and the economic power, who became a rentier class and whose interests were protected by the French state (Leymarie, 2000, http://www.monde-diplomatique.fr). The development of the economy was aimed toward serving the needs of the entrepreneurial farmers allied to French big business. Accordingly, European presence expanded tremendously in the postcolonial period. Gradually, however, the new African government began to expand its power over the economy. It took an increasingly active role in the allocation of resources and the redistribution of wealth. In 1970, the government implemented a five-year national plan that affirmed the government's desire to become more actively involved in the allocation of resources.

The central government began to invest in prestigious but inefficient projects, such as the creation of a new capital city and large hydroelectric plants. These projects were financed largely by annual World Bank loans, which did not require that the projects make a financial return. Rather, investment in these projects assured the central government of a steady flow of capital and the employment of a loyal cadre of followers. It was widely known that much of the loans were being squandered, yet the foreign bank loans poured in. Ivory Coast's public long-term debt was $4.7 billion in 1980, or 40 percent of its GDP. Debt grew to $6.8 billion in 1984, more than 85 percent of its GDP that year (Berthlemy and Bourguignon, 1996; p.70).

While not overtly socialist in ideology at independence, the Ivorian state increasingly became actively interventionist. It took an active role in planning, in the provision of infrastructure, in the extraction of surplus from the peasantry, and in investment. It also took minority shareholder positions in private productive enterprises. In 1966, the *Caisse de Stablisation et de soutien des Prix des Productions Agricoles* (or Caisse) was established to fix producer prices for cocoa and coffee, operate a reserve stabilization fund, and extract profits for the state—much in the same way that marketing boards operated in Anglophone Africa, with slight variation.

According to Berthlemy and Bourguignon (1996; p.30), "Initially, the Caisse was to be only a price stabilization device and an instrument for controlling export crop markets." However, with the increase in coffee and cocoa world prices in the mid-1970s, it became an additional source of revenue for the government and virtually abandoned its original stabilizing function. Between 1960 and 1990, Caisse made significant profits every year except for 1972, 1989, and 1990. This profit was achieved by fixing the prices to the producers at a much lower level than the prices on the international market. In 1984 and 1985, coffee and cocoa producers received on average only 37 percent of the international prices paid to Caisse.

Increased state activity led to greater direct public control and stimulation of cash-crop production. By 1979, 33 state enterprises had been established. Among them were SODESUCRE, to stimulate cane-sugar production to produce refined sugar, which was exported; SODERIZ, to increase rice production and eliminate imports; and SODEPALM, to increase palm-oil and coconut-oil production.

Industrialization was very limited and adapted to the needs of cash-crop farmers. The industrialization program consisted of two elements. The first—"manufacturing"—consisted of processing local raw materials for export, the second, "import based industries," produced consumer goods for the local market with imported inputs. Extreme care was taken so that Ivorian industries would not compete with French ones. In fact, most of the industrial plants were subsidiaries of French companies, and the list of industries set up in Ivory Coast excluded the possibility of economic takeoff (Destanne de Bernis, 1981, p.112). The state retained ownership of the plants, but their operation and technology, especially in textile and construction sectors, were controlled by French capital. Managerial and technical staffs were drawn from the expatriate community. The plants relied on imported inputs, often overpriced. Consequently, profits were quite low, leaving little room for taxation (Leymarie 2000, http://www.monde-diplomatique.fr).

Houphouet-Boigny once described this economic philosophy as "state capitalism" but it transmogrified into "crony capitalism." Many of his associates enriched themselves fabulously under his watchful patronage. The agribusiness parastatals became "private fiefs of the managing elite" (Fieldhouse, 1986; p.193). In the 1970s, Henri Bedie, the minister for the economy and finance, was dismissed for embezzlement and fled the country, later to become the chargé d'affaires of the Ivorian Embassy in Washington, D.C. "Rehabilitated," he returned to become the chairman of the Ivorian national assembly. His name resurfaced in a number of financial scandals, regarding his ill-fated plans to expand the country's sugar industry that rocked the country in the 1980s.

Another Houphouet-Boigny associate, Emmanuel Dioulo, the former mayor of Abidjan, fled to Europe in March 1985 to avoid criminal charges of embezzlement and fraud. His company, COGEXIM, "had failed to repay loans worth $58 million to the *Banque Nationale de Development*" (*West Africa,* May 1–7, 1989; p.677). He received a presidential pardon and indemnity from prosecution upon his return to the country on March 3, 1986. In April 1989, Dr. Theodore Kouba, another executive member of the ruling PDCI, was charged with extorting CFA 6.8 billion ($21.8 million) from executives working for the Abidjan-based Continental Bank, the African Development Bank, the World Bank, and from some 800 Ivorian teachers under the pretext of building estate houses for them.

In 1983, Houphouet-Boigny himself stunned the nation by declaring on television that: "Yes, I do have assets abroad. But they are not assets belonging to Cote d'Ivoire. What sensible man does not keep his assets in Switzerland, the whole world's bank? I would be crazy to sacrifice my children's future in this crazy country without thinking of their future" (*La Croix* [Paris], March 13, 1990). In the *Guardian Weekly* (London), Paul Webster claimed that Houphouet-Boigny "was siphoning off French aid funds to amass a personal fortune as high as 6 billion pounds sterling" (June 17, 1990; p.9).

Ivory Coast's economic development strategy, supported with massive infusion of World Bank loans and French aid, was based on the extraction of large surpluses from small holders (peasant farmers)—for example, through 40 percent or higher taxes on cocoa—for investment by the state. In his 1988 New Year's address to the nation, Houphouet-Boigny admitted that the country's farmers had over the years sacrificed 80 percent of the value of what they produced to enable the government to finance economic development. But the sums were channeled into inefficient and unprofitable state corporations, and over 80 percent of the development that took place was concentrated in Abidjan and other urban areas, bypassing the rural peasants. The president's proteges used the rest of the peasants' money for self-enrichment and deposited it overseas. In 1990, "the central bank calculated that some CFA 130 billion ($456 million) are spirited out of the country illegally each year" (*Africa Report* May-June, 1990; p.14).

To be sure, in the 1960s and 1970s the Ivory Coast did enjoy robust economic growth, averaging 6 percent annually—one of the highest growth rates in Africa—and earning praise from the World Bank and other international donors. However, the windfall earnings from cocoa and coffee in 1976 and 1977 were splurged on imports, and the country borrowed recklessly to finance a consumption binge. Its foreign debt soared from $1.66 billion in 1975 to $8.45 billion in 1987 and $14 billion in 1988 for a country of 16 million people. An economic crisis emerged in 1979, debts were rescheduled, and a structural adjustment agreement was signed with the IMF and the World Bank in 1981. An initial success, with GDP growth registering 5 percent in 1985, led the World Bank and the IMF to throw all caution to the wind. A hasty 1985 IMF report, ignoring all signs of social discontent, huge disparities in income, and the lack of institutional infrastructure, was effusive in its praise, declaring Ivory Coast "a success story"— a model of free market success.

Falling commodity prices and scandalous mismanagement brought the crisis back in 1988. GDP growth turned negative (−6.4 percent) with an income per capita of $830, down 36 percent from $1,290 in 1978. Blaming the declining market on Western commodity speculators, President Houphouet-Boigny asked all public sector employees, students, and teachers for a "solidarity tax"—cuts in wages and allowances, 40 percent for civil servants. The official price paid to cocoa and coffee producers was reduced by 50 percent for the 1989 to 1990 growing season. These measures provoked unrest and riots amid calls for political reform.

Viewing the vast basilica Houphouet-Boigny was building for himself at Yamassoukrou at the cost of $360 million and taking a cue from the dramatic developments in Eastern Europe, the workers opposed the tax. They took to the streets in February and March 1990 to vent their anger at the government. They dismissed his argument that Western commodity speculators were responsible for the collapse of the markets and demanded his resignation, pointing to the basilica as a paramount example of his failed leadership. Irate workers demanded the prosecution of the *grotos*—the corrupt ruling elite—accusing "Houphouet-Boigny and some of his powerful government ministers of having hidden away in Europe sums said to exceed the foreign aid that Western donors have poured into Ivory Coast" *(The Washington Post* March 26, 1990; p.A17). When Houphouet-Boigny insisted that there were no billionaires in the Ivory Coast, a tract revealed that Minister of Primary Education Odette Kouame, appointed in 1985, owned a castle on Boulevard Latrille in Cocody and another in her own village.

Houphouet-Boigny steadfastly rejected the protesters' demands for multiparty democracy, claiming "tribalism was still the main obstacle to the achievement of national unity—the prerequisite for a change in the status quo" *(Africa Report* May-June 1990; p.16) and unleashing his security forces on the protestors with tear gas, stun grenades, and truncheons. Schools were closed and 120 teachers were arrested *(West Africa,* April 2–8, 1990; p.558).

By May 1990, the Ivorian "miracle" had gone bust. The country's 13 bishops issued a pastoral letter, deriding the situation as the "Ivorian malaise" *(West Africa,* Aug 6–12, 1990; p.2251). Mounting pressure—through strikes and demonstrations—forced Houphouet-Boigny to legalize other political parties and to hold multiparty elections in November 1990. But Houphouet-Boigny handily won a seventh term in a presidential election generally regarded to have been rigged.

Social discontent against the corrupt ruling oligarchs bubbled to the surface again in 1992 when angry citizens took to the streets to protest hopeless life in perpetual poverty. University students boycotted end-of-year examinations to protest the government's new education policy, which required them to pay higher bus fares. Unemployed youth also went on the rampage, blocking midday rush hour traffic. Producers of the country's cash crops joined in. Years of neglect by the government had left them bitter. Apart from good access roads, every other social service was in short supply. At an October 1992 meeting at Anyama, on the outskirts of Abidjan, the farmers demanded better prices for their produce. (Again in 2003, the farmers renewed their demands, refused to sell their cocoa, and burned several tons of produce to protest low prices.)

In 1993, Houphouet-Boigny passed away, and power-hungry stalwarts within the ruling PDCI party could not even wait for his burial before jostling ferociously to succeed him. Said a desperate Philippe Yace, a challenger: "I would be happy to become president, even if just for two weeks" (*New African,* May 1994; p.41). Ordinarily, the prime minister, Alassane Ouattara, should have taken over, but he was outmaneuvered by Henri Konan Bedie, the speaker of the parliament. Bedie, who hails from the same ethnic group as Houphouet-Boigny (Bauole), assumed full control but departed from Houphouet's style of governance: dialogue and consensus with opposition forces.

In 1994, Bedie launched a highly xenophobic and ethnically divisive campaign of "Ivoirité"—Ivorian-ness—ostensibly to check the influx of foreigners. But opposition leaders said the campaign was to promote his Baoule ethnic group and prevent Ouattara, a Muslim for the north, from ever becoming president. "After 1994, after Ouattara left, all (Muslim) northerners lost important jobs," said sociologist Abdou Toure. "I was fired from UNESCO, Ali Coulibaly was fired as main television broadcaster, General Abdoulaye Coulibaly was fired as air force commander. We were replaced by Baoules," Toure said (*The Washington Times,* Oct 10, 1996; p.A17). Many African immigrants, notably from neighboring Burkina Faso and Ghana, were harassed and forced to leave.

For the presidential elections in 1995, Bedie rammed through parliament an electoral code designed to ensure his victory and changed the president's term of office from five to seven years. Protests led to violent clashes with security personnel on October 16, 1995, and five lives were lost. "Only a politician like Bedie could have made such a mess of things," said an irate World Bank official. "Only he could have turned an economic success story into a political nightmare that this is turning out to be" (*The Washington Times,* October 19, 1995; p.A14).

Crony capitalism continued unabated. In May 1998, the *French Weekly* published the fortunes of African heads of state, placing President Houphouet-Boigny's fortune at 35 billion FF ($6 billion) and clocking President Henri Bedie's at 2 billion FF—$300 million (reprinted in the Nigerian newspaper *The News,* Aug 17, 1998). Companies with links to President Konan Bedie's family grew fat in financial services and commodity trading, while others gobbled up the most profitable privatized state companies. In June 1999, the EU suspended aid to Ivory Coast after discovering that about $30 million donated for health programs had apparently been embezzled through dubious accounting, overbilling, and failure to deliver goods. One example was baby weighing scales; a single scale would normally cost about $40 but was billed by the health ministry at $2,445. Subsequently in July,

Communications Minister Daniele Boni Claverie revealed that four senior government officials of the Health Ministry were being held for questioning.

In August 1999 Ouattara was proclaimed leader and presidential candidate of the Assembly of Republicans (RDR), a breakaway group from the ruling party. Bedie grew nervous and panicky. On November 12, 1999, 11 leading members of RDR, including 4 members of parliament, were jailed for two years for allowing others to cause public disorder. Nine more were charged with public order offenses. On November 26, the police sealed whole areas of Abidjan and arrested 8 more leaders of the RDR in a northern town. The crackdown further widened ethnic and religious divisions, leading to events that culminated in a military coup. The rebellion not only was against appalling socioeconomic conditions and the tyrannical excesses of the Bedie regime but was also a sharp rebuke of French and World Bank policies in the Ivory Coast. On December 24, 1999, Bedie was overthrown by General Robert Guie.

Disavowing any interest in politics, General Guie vowed to create the necessary conditions for a real democracy with a view to holding fair and transparent elections within a year. He would not stand for election, he said; he had only come to "sweep the house clean" and return to the barracks. But after tasting power for a few months, he found that "power sweet," as Africans would say. He decided to run for the presidency in the elections he had scheduled for October 2000. Since he needed a political party, he asked the very political party he overthrew on charges of corruption to choose him as their presidential candidate! O coconut-head. When none of the parties would have him, he decided to run anyway as the "people's candidate" in the October 27 elections. When early returns showed that General Guie was losing, he ordered his soldiers to raid the Electoral Commission and sack the commissioners. The vote was then counted in secret and General Guei declared the winner. But angry Ivorians poured into the streets of Abidjan, demanding that General Guie step down from power. He fled Ivory Coast in a helicopter on October 29 and Laurent Gbagbo became the new president. But that did not end Ivorian troubles. Gbagbo resurrected *Ivoirité* to debar Ouattara from seeking the presidency. A mutiny by soldiers in September 2002 degenerated into civil war and state implosion. By January 2003, the Ivorian miracle has morphed into a ghastly nightmare.

SUMMARY

The experience with industrialization through state ownership and development planning proved to be an unmitigated disaster in postcolonial Africa. Industrial output across Africa declined, with some regions experiencing deindustrialization. The state enterprises established under Africa's various development plans failed to deliver:

> There are countless examples of badly chosen and poorly designed public investments, including some in which the World Bank has participated. A 1987 evaluation revealed that half of the completed rural development projects financed by the World Bank in Africa had failed. A cement plant serving Cote d'Ivoire, Ghana and Togo was closed in 1984 after only four years of operation. A state-run shoe factory in Tanzania has been operating at no more than 25 percent capacity and has remained open only thanks to a large government subsidy. (World Bank, 1989; p.27)

By 1980, Africa had more than 3,200 state enterprises (SEs), most of which were financed by the World Bank, the African Development Bank, and foreign loans. By the beginning of the 1990s, there were 4,000 state enterprises. These state enterprises, set up with foreign loans, turned out to be hideously inefficient, underutilized, unprofitable, and overstaffed. "Rather than conserving foreign exchange, as proponents had argued, import substitution industries (in Africa) had frequently proved to be import-intensive, as capital goods and many of the components used in manufacturing had to be imported" (Chazan et al., 1992; p.254). As we have seen, the number of these "black elephants" in Africa is large.

Africa's state enterprises consumed about one-fifth of its GDP while contributing only one-tenth of its GDP (World Bank, 1993). In Niger, the cumulative deficit of 23 loss-making SEs exceeded 4 percent of Niger's (GDP) in 1982. In 1990, subsidies to Zimbabwe's parastatals amounted to 6.9 percent of total recurrent expenditure or 34.5 percent of the budget deficit (Five Year Development Plan, 1990–1995). In Tanzania, between 1976 and 1979, one-third of all state enterprises were losing money. In Benin, more than 60 percent of all SEs suffer losses. In Togo, the losses of just eight state enterprises reached 4 percent of GDP in 1980, while in Ghana, 65 percent of all state enterprises still had losses in that year. In 1984 there were 235 state enterprises in Ghana. Kenya's government estimated that over $1.4 billion had been invested in SEs by the early 1980s. Yet, their annual average return had been just 0.2 percent of invested capital (Goldman 1992; p.10). E. A. Sai, member-secretary of Ghana's Committee of Secretaries, echoed these sentiments:

> Apart from a few success stories in the management of public enterprises in Africa, such as in the Kenya Tea Development Authority, Botswana's Meat Commission, Tanzania's Electricity Company, The Guma Valley Water Company of Sierra Leone and Ghana's Volta River Authority, the record of state enterprises had been poor. (*West Africa* May 16, 1988; p.897)

Indeed, in a speech at the International Conference on Privatization on February 17, 1987, in Washington, D.C., the former president of the African Development Bank, Babacar N'Diaye, himself admitted that:

It is now generally accepted that over time the majority of public sector enterprises or entities have not performed efficiently. Instead of accumulating surpluses or supplying services efficiently, a good number of these enterprises have become a drain on the national treasuries. Due to this poor performance, coupled with the growing recognition of the costs of ineffective public enterprises in terms of foregone economic development and the scarcity of domestic and external resources for public sector expenditure, reappraisal of the strategy of heavy reliance on the public sector has become imperative. From this reappraisal, a view has emerged—the need for enhancement of the role of the private sector in development. We in Africa are facing a great challenge. We believe that the creation of a conducive environment for the growth of the private sector, an important agent of economic growth, is essential.

Thus, statism, hegemonic state participation in and direction of the economy, was a complete failure in Africa. Nowhere on the continent did it succeed in allowing African countries to achieve their economic potential. Between 1965 and 1985, Africa's economy grew by a miserable 1.1 percent rate. The rate of growth for all of black Africa was a negative 14.6 percent for the same period (World Bank, World Development Report, 1988). The record was no less impressive in the "capitalist" African countries: Cameroon, Ivory Coast, Malawi, and Senegal. Ivory Coast and Senegal were often described as "success stories" for achieving what may be called "spectacular" growth. But they were the biggest aid receivers on the continent. Ivory Coast, as we saw, imploded in September 2002. Senegal received more than $500 million a year from the IMF, World Bank, and France—almost $100 per person in the 1980s. "Without that aid Senegal would be considered one of the region's basket cases," said *The Wall Street Journal* (July 29, 1985; p.18). Moreover, according to *West Africa* (Feb 10, 1986; p.282): "In 1973–1983, Senegal's GNP rose by an average of 2.6 percent from only 1.6 percent in 1965–70. But in 1984, it dropped by 4 percent in real terms to some $2,400 million. From 1965 to 1983, GNP per capita dropped by an annual average of about 0.4 percent."

CONCLUSION

After independence, African nationalists settled down to develop Africa—in its own image. They were in a hurry. Africa was to be developed not by capitalist or imperialist principles but by a socialist ideology under which the state not only participated in but captured the "commanding heights of the economy." Even those African countries, such as Ivory Coast, Kenya, and Nigeria, that were not so enamored with the socialist ideology envisaged and actively promoted state participation in the economy for nationalistic reasons—to promote "indigenization" (indigenous ownership of the economy) and to protect national assets against foreign exploitation.

State participation in the economy was, almost everywhere in Africa, to be achieved through a myriad of state controls, state ownership, and establishment of state enterprises and government regulations. Development was to be spearheaded by the state, which acted as the entrepreneur, the planner, and the investor. Industry was emphasized over agriculture, since all developed countries are "industrialized." Besides, agriculture was held in contempt as an inferior form of occupation. Worse, it reminded African nationalist leaders and elites of their colonial past.

The strategy for industrialization was import-substitution. The idea was that the production of commodities previously imported would save foreign exchange. The same foreign exchange could be used to import machinery and equipment needed to accelerate the pace of development.

Massive resources were needed for Africa's industrialization drive. Only the state, under the banner of socialism, it was argued, possessed the necessary powers to mobilize the requisite resources. These resources could be secured by running down the country's foreign exchange reserves. Where such reserves had been depleted, the peasants could be milked—à la Soviet example—through compulsory saving schemes and development levies under such slogans as "national sacrifice" and "belt-tightening." The remainder was to be sought through money creation and, as a last resort, borrowing from abroad. And foreign aid poured into Africa.

With such resources invested, African leaders surmised that they could transform Africa into a bountiful and prosperous continent. Kwame Nkrumah of Ghana, for example, dreamed of transforming Ghana into a "veritable paradise" and undertook to "achieve in a decade what it took others a century" (Nkrumah, 1973; p.401). Unfortunately, all did not go as planned.

The Byzantine maze of state controls and regulations created an artificial "scarcity economy" and rich opportunities for illicit enrichment. State controls on prices, imports, and foreign exchange, for example, created artificial shortages, which spawned a mountain of economically unproductive rent-seeking activities. Price controls created shortages and, in turn, black markets, where commodities were illegally sold above their government-controlled price. Much time and resources were expended chasing scarce goods. Bribes were offered to secure such goods. Government officials in charge of the distribution of scarce goods saw an opportunity to secure them at the cheap official price and resell them on the black market to reap huge profits. An official culture of bribery and corruption was spawned.

Africa's state enterprises established with foreign loans were egregiously inefficient and riddled with excess capacity, waste, and corruption. Obviously, these enterprises could not generate the return needed to repay the loans that were taken to establish them. Foreign loans taken for "general budget support" or to cover a budget deficit posed a problem when they disappeared into general government accounts. In that case, they could be used to pay civil servant salaries or even purchase weapons for the military. Under such circumstances, the loans were being "consumed" and not invested productively to generate a return. Investment in infrastructure is necessary for economic development, and foreign loans from the World Bank to build such infrastructure can be defended on economic grounds. Roads, bridges, schools, health clinics, telecommunications, safe drinking water, and a reliable supply of electricity are all vital to spur economic growth. But when the infrastructure is allowed to deteriorate and decay because of negligence its contribution to economic growth becomes negative or dubious. In other cases, portions of foreign loans simply disappeared into the pockets of corrupt government officials. Thus, foreign loans taken by African governments were not used productively. A debt crisis erupted when the time came to repay the loans. Debts were rolled over and more was borrowed to service existing debt, which really did not solve the problem.

Commodity scarcities, *kalabule,* hoarding, smuggling, bribery, inefficient state enterprises, budget deficits, and the accumulation of foreign debt were the first-generational problems, which fed upon themselves to create the second-generational problems—the subject of the next chapter. The "veritable paradise" promised Africans turned out to be famine, unproductive state enterprises, and a bazooka to the head.

CHAPTER 7

The Second Generation Problems

Africa can feed herself. Even without using any modern farming techniques such as pesticides and with only the most casual approach to maintaining the soil, the 51 countries of Africa presently have the potential to feed a population three times as large as that now living in the continent, even allowing for the fact that 47 percent of the land surface is useless for crops.

> —A Food and Agricultural Organization study cited in
> a *West Africa* editorial Dec 14, 1981; p.2959.

Africa today suffers from a "deadly triad" of interrelated burdens—food insecurity, HIV/AIDS and a reduced capacity to govern and provide basic services.

> —UN Secretary-General Kofi Annan
> *Africa Recovery* 17:1 (May 2003); p.37.

One of the remarkable facts in the terrible history of famine is that no substantial famine has ever occurred in a country with a democratic form of government and relatively free press. They have occurred in ancient kingdoms and in contemporary authoritarian societies and in modern technocratic dictatorships, in colonial economies governed by imperialists from the north and in newly independent countries of the south run by despotic national leaders or by intolerant single parties. But famines never afflicted any country that is independent, that goes to elections regularly, that has opposition parties to voice criticisms, that permits newspapers to report freely and to question the wisdom of government policies without extensive censorship.

> —Amartya Sen, recipient of the Nobel Prize in economics (1998)
> in the *Washington Times,* Oct 20, 1998; p.A12.

INTRODUCTION

The previous chapter examined the *first-generation effects* of statism: state direction of economic activity and planning with a plethora of state controls (price controls) and establishment of state enterprises to forge Africa's industrialization drive. To recap, state controls created commodity shortages while inefficient and unprofitable state enterprises—established with foreign loans—failed to deliver the goods. These initial problems may be considered "innocent," but they fed on each other, creating additional problems or secondary unintended consequences. In this chapter, we examine these *second generation* problems. For example, a food or agricultural crisis was produced when African agriculture—the livelihood of the majority of Africans—started its decline. The decline was not the result of a deliberate and malicious government policy to destroy agriculture. In fact, most African governments acknowledged the importance of agriculture. Rather, agriculture atrophied in many African countries because of the neglect occasioned by government obsession with industrialization, the imposition of price controls, civil war, and crumbling infrastructure.

Inadequate supply situations (commodity shortages), coupled with soaring government expenditures financed by printing money, resulted in inflation in many African countries. That, in itself, had undesirable consequences—for example, it discouraged savings and, thereby, depleted the funds for investment. Recall that the key to economic growth in Africa is investment, both domestic and foreign. Therefore, anything that discourages savings has a negative impact on investment.

To compensate for low domestic savings, African governments borrowed feverishly from abroad to establish state enterprises and initiate various development projects. But much of the loans were "consumed." In addition, the investment in state enterprises was generally unproductive. Investment projects failed and loans were squandered, producing a foreign debt crisis—the inability to service foreign loans on time.

Thus, one finds in many African countries the ludicrous spectacle of a government manned by a small cadre of incompetent and inexperienced bureaucrats attempting to manage a food crisis, a fuel crisis, a foreign exchange crisis, inflation, a banking crisis, a foreign debt crisis, and a development crisis all at the same time. At the end of the day, not a single one of them is resolved. The next day begins with the same crisis-management routine. Trapped in a perpetual crisis-management mode, government officials have little time to move the country in a new direction. Meanwhile, the problems multiply. Crises galore.

There is no scientific study that proves that Africans, as a people, are culturally more prone to bribery and corruption than any other people. However, when one lives in an economy beset by shortages and one must spend hours waiting in a gas queue, there is always the temptation to "jump the queue" or pay "something under the table" to avoid the ordeal. To expect Africans to resist this temptation is to expect them to be superhuman. And Africans do succumb to this temptation.

Distributors of "controlled commodities" in shortage find that they can exploit the situation by extracting rent and pocketing bribes. Ministers of trade discover that they can demand 10 percent of the value of an import license and enrich themselves. Refuse to pay the "10 percent commission" and one goes without the license. Report the minister to the police and it is *you* they will arrest and throw into jail! Hitch a defective political system—such as a military dictatorship or a one-party state system—to the state-controlled and crisis-laden economy and a train wreck (state collapse or implosion) is inevitable.

This is because the goat at the helm uses the state control system to enrich himself, to dispense patronage, allocate resources to his cronies and tribesmen, and exclude everybody else (the politics of exclusion). The rest of the population can eat grass. He acts with impunity because he has taken control over all the key institutions in the country: the military, the judiciary, the police, the media, the electoral commission, and even the central bank! Forget about parliament; it is a rubber stamp only. There is no opposition party because the country is a one-party state, political parties are banned. They can exist, but only on paper. Such is life in a coconut republic, where common sense has been murdered and lunacy is on meretricious display. Eventually, the republic implodes.

Resentment steadily builds in those excluded from the spoils of power. Fed up with the vampire state, people may simply pack up and vote with their feet, becoming economic refugees. Coup attempts are made to dislodge the gangsters from power, creating political instability. If the military is rigidly controlled or defanged with the creation of additional layers upon layers of security—special division forces, elite commando units, presidential guards, special presidential guards all checking each other—then a rebel insurgency or movement starts within an excluded group. Bridges are blown up, infrastructure mutilated—even by government forces to repel rebel advances. Paranoid, government forces vow to root out "rebel sympathizers" or "moles" within their midst—even in state apparatuses, like the National Assembly, leaving a trail of destruction. Said Mark K. Hollie, deputy chief clerk of Liberia's House of Representatives, after going through lawmakers' chambers that had been reduced to rubble: "This is the sacred property of the republic—damaged. These are government forces that did this. The government destroying the government" (*The New York Times,* Aug 20, 2003; p.A3).

Political instability engenders economic instability and insecurity. Capital flees the country and foreign investors stay away. Unable to generate sufficient revenue domestically, the African government becomes more and more *dependent* on foreign charity, Western donors, and multilateral institutions such as the World Bank and the IMF. In 2002, some 40 percent of Ghana's budget was externally funded; it was 55 percent in the case of Uganda. National sovereignty is surrendered when government budgets must be approved by Washington, London, or Paris. If external funding is insufficient, new money is printed, injecting excess liquidity into the system and fueling inflation. The cost of living soars. Unable to make ends meet, civil servants and workers agitate for higher wages or find ways of "chopping by their work small," as Africans would say. "Chopping by their work small" means inventing ways, fair or foul, of supplementing their meager wages. They may involve, for example, theft of office equipment and extortionary demands, such as tips and extra fees before providing application forms. The policeman, the customs official, and the judge who extort bribes before dismissing a traffic violation, allowing an item to pass through, or fixing a case all "chop by their work small." Bribery and corruption become more brazen as the cost of living rises and economic hardships become more severe.

Being the main and largest employer, the government initially resists demands for higher salaries because its expenditures would soar and add to the budget deficit. But the vampire elites feel the inflation pinch, too. So they award themselves hefty salary increases and a piddling squat for the proletariat. In 1995 Mugabe's government in Zimbabwe stipulated a 10 percent ceiling for annual salary increases for state workers. Less than a month later, top government officials awarded themselves increases exceeding 50 percent. In 1999, President Mugabe further tripled and quadrupled their salaries (*The Washington Post,* Dec 2, 1999; p.A37). In 2003, Mugabe increased his own salary by more than 1,000 percent and his top officials by more than 800 percent to compensate for inflation that was raging at more than 400 percent per annum.

Resentment continues to build as workers are squeezed by the rising cost of living. Unable to subsidize the price of food or gasoline, the government attempts to increase their prices. Food and gasoline riots break out, as occurred in Zambia and Zimbabwe over *"mealie"* (a national staple), and in Senegal and Nigeria over gasoline. There were waves of strikes by workers, nurses, and teachers to protest rising food and fuel prices. While the urban poor were rioting about food prices in Zimbabwe, President Mugabe ordered a fleet of brand new Mercedes cars for his cabinet ministers (*The Economist,* Aug 15, 1998; p.34). People become outraged. Sensing an opportunity, a military adventurer may step in and seize power, accusing the ousted regime of economic mismanagement and corruption.

The ouster of the regime adds to greater political instability. More capital flees the country. Foreign investors shun the country. The military junta finds the treasury empty or looted by elite *bazongas* (raiders of the public treasury). Desperate for funds, the junta appeals to Western donors and the international community for aid on promises of quick return to democratic rule. Coconut elections are held to return the military despot to power. Disgusted, foreign donors suspend aid to protest the lack of transparency in the elections. Investment falls on account of economic uncertainty and insecurity. Prices keep rising along with the cost of living. Civil servants demand higher wages.

Quite often, opposition groups compound these problems. Hopelessly fragmented, they are incapable of mounting any effective challenge. In Kenya's 1996 presidential elections, for example, 26 political parties emerged and fielded 13 candidates to challenge the incumbent, President Daniel arap Moi. Imagine. Further, opposition groups lack clear effective strategies. For example, the civil service is a military junta's most potent Achilles heel. Shut down the civil service and *any* military regime will collapse.

In Ghana, mass demonstrations and civil disobedience—the preferred choice of opposition groups—were ineffective and costly against Rawlings's military dictatorship. The success of these types of action would require the very type of mechanisms that are nonexistent: the right to public assembly and freedom of expression, often banned or denied by the tyrannical regime. Furthermore, they present the military junta with a concentrated blob of people, which the military, with their modern weapons, can annihilate in short order. This was the case in Ghana in 1995 when paramilitary forces fired into a mass demonstration protesting the imposition of the "vampire tax." More than four protesters were killed.

A more intelligent strategy is to exploit the weakness of the military junta: its numerical inferiority. The military has the weapons advantage but not the numbers advantage, which explains why virtually all of Africa's civil wars start from the countryside, where the military is stretched thin geographically and does not have the numbers to put down a rebel insurgency.

In March 1978, civil servants in Ghana went on strike to press their demands for better working conditions. The strike led to a chain of events that culminated in the ouster of the military regime of General I. K. Acheampong in July 1978. His successor, General Akuffo, did not address the grievances of the civil servants either. Another strike was called in November

1978. That too set in motion events that led to the overthrow of the Akuffo regime by Jerry Rawlings in June 1979. A report by the commission of enquiry, set up by the military regime itself, ironically concluded:

> Finally, the fact should not be overlooked that the Civil Service is, in the final analysis, *the* machinery of Central Government. Without it, the policies and plans of the Government will fail, and Government itself will collapse. (*Report of the Committee of Inquiry into the Civil Service Strike of November 1978;* p.67)

In 1989, civil servants in Benin went on strike to demand payment of their salary arrears. That strike, too, paralyzed the government and the country, setting in motion events that led to the ouster of Mathieu Kerekou in January 1990. Military regimes have proliferated in Africa, largely because of the lack of imagination on the part of opposition leaders, many of whom are too susceptible to "co-optation."

In Benin, Kerekou was replaced by Nicephore Soglo, a former executive director of the World Bank. He fared no better. Less than two years after he took power in 1991 as leader of an opposition alliance, a rift developed between the executive and the legislature. The National Assembly accused President Soglo of "solitary exercise of power" (*New African Yearbook,* 1999–2000; p.38). The president's wife delved into politics and attempted to transform the opposition alliance into a political party with her husband as the leader. Rebuffed, she formed the Renaissance of Benin party. The country lurched from one political crisis to another. In the end, Soglo was ousted in 1996 by Matthieu Kerekou, the former dictator!

And so on to the *nth generation problems.*

AFRICA'S AGRICULTURAL CRISES

In the new century, hunger remains a persistent problem in Africa. At the beginning of 2003, an estimated 25 million Africans required emergency food aid. Although famine is often closely linked to drought and, in some countries, war, UN Food and Agriculture Organization (FAO) Director-General Jacques Diouf noted that even when there is no drought or other acute crisis, about 200 million Africans suffer from chronic hunger (*Africa Recovery* 17: 1 [May 2003], p.1). Alarm was raised in 2001 by the International Food Policy Research Institute, a Washington think tank, in its 2020 Global Food Outlook, warning of rising hunger on the continent. The report noted that "without massive investment in irrigation, roads to take the harvest to market and crop research, Africa might have 49 million malnourished children by 2020, a rise of 50 percent" (*The Washington Post,* Sept 4, 2001; p.A12).

African agriculture provides livelihoods for "about 60 percent of the continent's active labor force, contributes 17 percent of Africa's total gross domestic product, and accounts for 40 percent of its foreign currency earnings" (*Africa Recovery,* Jan 2004; p.13). Yet, agriculture has performed abysmally. Farmers' yields have essentially stagnated for decades. Although total output has been growing, this growth has barely kept pace with Africa's increasing population. Food production in particular has lagged, so that the number of chronically undernourished people increased from 173 million in 1990–92 to 200 million in 1997–99. Of that total, 194 million were in Sub-Saharan Africa. In 1997, Africa's total food imports amounted to $14.69 billion, slightly more than what Africa received in foreign aid from all sources (World Bank, 2000b; p.107). By 2000, food imports had grown to $18.7 billion in 2000 alone (*Africa Recovery,* Jan 2004; p.14).

Since 1970 agricultural output has been growing at less than 1.5 percent— less than the rate of population growth. Consequently, food production per capita declined by 7 percent in the 1960s, by 15 percent in the 1970s, and by 8 percent in the 1980s. From 1961 to 1995, "per capita food production in Africa dropped by 12 percent, whereas it advanced by leaps and bounds in developing countries in Asia" (*The Economist,* Sept 7 1996; p.45). The decline continued. Using 1989–91 as the base year, food production per capita index for Africa was 105 in 1980 but 92 for 1997 (World Bank, 2000b; p.225).

The Democratic Republic of the Congo exported food when it was the Belgian Congo. Today, it cannot feed itself, and neither can postcolonial Zambia, Sierra Leone, Tanzania, or even Zimbabwe. These countries, once self-sufficient in food production, now face sharp escalations in food import bills. As much as 20 percent of the continent's export income in the 1980s was spent on food imports (Chazan, et al. 1992; p.259). In 1990, it had reached 40 percent.

At the micro level, the performance of Africa's economic sectors, except for mining and other extractive industries, has been weak. The most serious sectoral deterioration has occurred in agriculture. This is the life-blood of the African economy and accounts for "a much higher share of GDP than in other regions of the world" (ECA [UN], 1999; p.8). Three out of four Africans are engaged in agriculture, with women making the most significant contribution. They perform "some 90 percent of the work of food processing, 80 percent of food storage tasks, 90 percent of hoeing and weeding, and 60 percent of harvesting and marketing, besides load carrying and transport services."[1] But finding enough to eat has become a formidable challenge for many. "We cannot afford even a meal a day," said Andre Miku, a retired mechanic in Kinshasa, Congo. "We try to keep at least the children fed" (*The Washington Post,* Sept 14, 1998; p.A16).

No Sub-Saharan African country has been able to achieve food self-sufficiency. The paucity of agricultural "success stories" suggests an abundance of individual horror stories. In 1982, food output per capita in Angola, for example, was estimated to be half the level reached in 1972. Its coffee output was one-tenth of the 240,000 metric tons produced annually before independence. Some years back, Sierra Leone was not only self-sufficient in rice, but was also able to export large quantities to other African states. It is now importing rice. Nigeria used to export palm oil, which it now imports. "Nigeria spends $3 billion a year importing food—including rice, sugar, chickens, and milk—which it could grow for itself" (*The Washington Times*, July 18, 2004; p.A6).

The Causes of Africa's Food Crisis

Africa's agricultural crisis has been attributed to a host of factors, both external and internal. Among them are: protectionist policies of the rich countries, drought, poor soils, the use of "backward and primitive" technology, and increased competition from cash crops. These explanations, however, are unsatisfactory. It is true that the rich countries operate a battery of tariff and non-tariff barriers (duties, quotas, subsidies to domestic producers) against agricultural products from the Third World. The United States, for example, protects its sugar, tobacco, and peanut producers. The European Union will not permit free trade in agricultural products that compete with those of its member states, notably citrus fruits, wine, tobacco, vegetable oils, and tomatoes (*The Economist*, Sept 7, 1996; p.43). But why don't African governments retaliate by slapping tariffs on imports from Western countries? More important, if these restrictive trade practices were hurting African agriculture, the situation in Africa should be one of excess supplies or food surpluses looking for an overseas market. But this flies in the face of reality. The situation rather is one of *declining* per capita production, not excess supplies.

Droughts have often been blamed for Africa's agricultural decline. This indeed appears to be the case for the Sahelian African countries. Senegal's agriculture has been ravaged by drought in 15 of the 37 years since independence. In Burkina Faso and Mali, drought is a perennial problem. But for many African countries, droughts only exacerbate an already existing precarious situation. Food production per person had been declining in many African countries well before the 1983–85 droughts that wreaked havoc across the African continent. Furthermore, the agricultural economies of Angola, Chad, Ethiopia, Mozambique, Sudan, Uganda, and Zaire were shattered more by warfare and internecine strife than by drought.

Furthermore, the lack of access to modern farming equipment did not hinder African food production, just as access to modern technology does not guarantee high farm productivity. In the United States and Canada, for example, Amish communities prosper using nineteenth-century farming methods. The basic resource is the farmer himself. In Africa, it was the ordinary Ghanaian farmer who invented and perfected the superior heap fermentation method of cocoa production while agricultural scientists were developing the box fermentation method. Competition from cash crops did not hinder the production of foodstuffs. Two salient facts confute this conclusion.

First, in the 1950s, cash crops posed no threat to food production. In fact, Africa was exporting both cash and non-cash crops. Second, if it were true that cash crops were replacing foodstuff production, then one should expect to see increasing exports of cash crops as food production declines. Instead, the record shows that non-oil export production has been stagnant since 1970, a period during which the export volumes of all developing countries more than trebled. Export production has, in fact, declined in tandem with the decline in the production of food crops.

Nor do hostile world market conditions offer any credible explanatory power. Black Africa has not faced more adverse global conditions than other developing regions. According to a study by Charles Humphreys and William Jaeger, "Since 1975, Africa's non-oil commodity terms of trade have declined only half as much as those for all exports of primary commodities."[2] This is not to minimize the impact of negative external factors, which can be severe. The point is that other developing countries faced worse situations but have been better able to adjust than the countries of Sub-Saharan Africa.

There has been a general tendency on the part of African leaders to overplay the external factors, perhaps to provide justification for more food aid or to shift responsibility away from their own failed policies. If the agricultural sector were on a strong basis to begin with, it would have recovered quickly from an externally induced shock. What, then, caused Africa's agricultural crisis? A combination of vicious internal factors: civil wars, state interventionism, and wrong-headed policies.

Agricultural performance cannot be analyzed in a vacuum but must be studied within the context of its sociopolitical setting. For sociopolitical reasons, African leaders, until recently, generally neglected agriculture. When its importance was belatedly recognized, again sociopolitical factors conditioned or influenced the type of agricultural policy choices that African leaders made. Often, outsiders compounded the problem by failing to recognize the importance of these sociopolitical factors and tended to view the agricultural problem merely in terms of technological transfer and of increasing such inputs as tractors, fertilizers, etc. Even when the sociopolitical factors were recognized by outsiders, the tendency was to minimize their importance. Many foreign agencies and consultancies arrogantly assumed that traditional African ways of farming were useless and Western methods were invariably superior. As *The Economist* (Sept 7, 1996) observed:

> In the Sahel, the FAO bullied farmers into growing potatoes. They produced a bumper crop, which then rotted unsold in city markets where potatoes looked as exotic as bush rats or *kinkilaba* would in a western supermarket. The foreign foresters who persuaded West Africans to clear their acacias and plant non-indigenous trees also ended up apologizing. Within a few years it had become obvious that the native acacias were vastly more suitable than the imported substitutes. They needed less water and less attention and, crucially, sprouted leaves for goats and sheep to browse on during the dry season. (p.443)

Then there was the fisheries project, which Norwegian experts developed for the Turkana tribesmen at Lake Rudolf (now Lake Turkana). After the project was completed it was discovered that the Turkana people do not fish but raise goats and cows. As a further embarrassment, the cost of freezing the fish far exceeded the price they fetched in the markets (Whitaker, 1988; p.194).

When starvation became a threat and the importance of agricultural development was finally recognized, palpable confusion reigned, not only among African leaders but also among the international lending and food aid agencies, about the kind of strategies to adopt to combat the hunger. While the World Bank and the International Development Agency (IDA) were lending millions to African governments for the purchase of tractors, fertilizers, pesticides, etc., a 1981 report by the UN Food and Agriculture Organization (FAO) about the crop-bearing potential of African soils maintained that Africa could feed itself without the use of these aids.

An interminable argument over who was to blame is futile. The primary responsibility for choosing between "bad" and "good" projects rested with African leaders and elites. But their own predisposition made them vulnerable to foreign misjudgment. Recall that the elites were imbued with a peculiar mentality ("religion of development") that held the peasantry in contempt and frowned upon the traditional ways of doing things, including farming. Agriculture was an inferior form of occupation. Industrialization was all the rage. Agriculture also reminded their elites of the colonial status as suppliers of agricultural raw materials. Furthermore, in the African countries themselves, there was great confusion and inefficiency in attempts to solve the food crisis. While some countries were pursuing collective agriculture, others were adopting integrated rural development (IRD) strategies. Again sociopolitical factors influenced the choice of the strategy. The results, however, have nowhere been impressive in black Africa.

After independence, many African leaders adopted socialism as their guiding ideology and applied the same ideology to agriculture. But the socialization of agriculture—just like the other socialist experiments in industry and trade—failed miserably. We shall now look more closely at Ghana's agricultural crisis.

Ghana's Agricultural Crisis

When Nkrumah launched Ghana on the road to African socialism in the 1960s, he, like many African leaders, paid only lip service to peasant agriculture. The peasants, the chiefs, and the indigenous sector generally did not fit into the religion of development nor into the grandiose plans Nkrumah drew up to industrialize Ghana. His Seven-Year Development Plan (1963–69), for example, devoted only two paragraphs to the agricultural sector, and the 1965 foreign exchange budget allocated a mere $2 million to agriculture, compared to $114 million for manufacturing and $312 million for imports.

When Nkrumah eventually recognized the immense contribution that agriculture could make to the country's economic development, he took his socialist program of state participation to that sector as well. Collective agriculture was envisaged. But the indigenous agricultural sector was skirted in a somewhat dysfunctional comprehension of the logistics of local food production. Nkrumah believed that he could not rely on peasant farmers for a rapid agricultural revolution because they were "too slow to adapt or change their practices to modern mechanized scientific methods" (Uphoff, 1970; p.602). Nkrumah saw mechanization and socialization as the quickest way to achieve an agricultural transformation.

Accordingly, for Ghana's agricultural development, Nkrumah set up state farms, and mechanization was to be the guiding principle. The state farms were to use "modern" and "scientific" techniques and serve as models to the "illiterate" and "primitive" peasant farmers who produce the bulk of Africa's food. The State Farms Corporation and its ancillary organizations—Workers' Brigade and Young Farmers' League—were assigned the major task of creating "a complete revolution in agriculture on our continent (and) a total break with primitive methods and organization and with the colonial past" (Nkrumah 1963; p.27). The State Farms Corporation was to be a model of collective agriculture; the Workers' Brigade was to run settlement farms; Young Farmers were to be taught mechanized and scientific agriculture; and a Food Marketing Board was created to fix maximum prices for all foodstuffs and to improve the efficiency of the distributive system. After its establishment in 1962, the State Farms Corporation expanded its operations rapidly. But in less than five years, the State Farm experiment of collectivized agriculture had turn into a hopeless disaster.

Despite having the expertise of many of the Ministry of Agriculture's professional officers, ready access to capital and technical know-how, favorable allocation of import licenses, and above all government support, the State Farms achieved lower yields and smaller output per man than their "illiterate" peasant counterparts.

In 1964, the State Farm Corporation was cultivating only 3.3 acres per worker, compared to 5.1 acres per person in small-scale peasant farming. The acreage per worker was 1.5 in the case of the Workers' Brigade and only 0.9 for the cooperative farms managed by the United Ghana Farmers' Cooperative Council. In 1963–65 the State Farms absorbed 19.8 million *cedis* ($7.92 million) in subventions (Killick 1978; p.193). By the end of 1965, the State Farm Corporation had accumulated a net deficit of 17.25 million *cedis* after only three years of operation (Levine 1975; p.34).

Four years after Nkrumah's socialist fiasco, the situation had not changed much. The 1970 Agricultural Census showed that, although cultivated acreage per person had fallen on both state and peasant farms, that of the state farms (2.7 per worker) still lagged behind the peasant acreage of 3.6 per worker (Killick, 1978; p.193). The failure of the state farms was even recognized in official circles. The Abrahams Report (1965) noted that "the State Farms Corporation has not produced food-stuffs in sufficient quantities to justify their capital and current investment" (p.23, para. 63). The conclusion of the World Bank mission, which stayed in Ghana toward the end of 1965, was that neither the state farms nor the Worker's Brigade,

> had had success in achieving either its aim of significantly improving agricultural production or of attaining financial self-sufficiency. Indications are that workers of both agencies produce little more, if as much, as they and their families consume and that if engaged in traditional agriculture they would produce significantly greater quantities of farm produce at a much lower cost. (Cited in Killick, 1978; p.194)

By 1971, only a quarter of the total state farm acreage was under cultivation and the corporation in the field of food farming seemed to have had a negative impact on peasant food production. There is evidence to suggest that the peasant farmers "looked upon the State Farms with anxiety" because the corporation "was unceasingly backed by tax-payers money"; "feeling that their days are numbered," the traditional farmers had begun to "cut down on the scale of their farming" (Abrahams Report, 1965; p.23, para. 66).

The tragedy of Ghana's agricultural development was that successive governments after Nkrumah continued the scandalous state farms and price control system. In 1970, for example, when peasant farmers with primitive tools were producing 0.49 tons of rice per acre, the state farms were producing only 0.13 tons per acre (Killick 1978; p.229). In 1981, the Limann government reorganized the state farms into the Ghana National Reconstruction Corps (GNRC), but the results were the same. In 1983, peasant farmers were still producing 0.49 tons of rice per acre while the state farms managed to produce a mere 0.13 tons per acre. Out of the $71 million voted for those state farms in 1981, only $751,000 was recovered (*Graphic*, July 21, 1981; p.5). In one specific case, $720,000 was spent to house workers at a Ghanaian-German settlement project, but the farm earned only $95,216 from the sale of crops in the 1972–73 season (*Daily Graphic*, Aug 21, 1973; p.11).

Notice that the $720,000 was spent on housing alone. Add to this the wages of the workers; managers; cost of equipment and land preparation, etc. and the loss becomes greater. By December 1982, the total number of state farms established was 79, and only 37 were either actively or partially operating. Their collective debt stood at over $158 million (*Daily Graphic*, December 22, 1982; p.8).

The story of the Okumaning oil plantation, a state farm, is pathetic. The Okumaning State Farm was established in 1975 with a capital of $24 million and a 2,000-acre palm nut plantation. Out of that acreage, only 23 acres were maintained by February 1982; the rest of the palm trees were overgrown with weeds and secondary forest. The staff at the Okumaning farm was over 500. Total gross revenue generated by the farm over an entire four-year period was $34,000! Ripe fruit on the oil palm trees were left to rot at a time when Ghana had to import 57 percent of its national palm oil requirement from Benin (*Daily Graphic*, Feb 15, 1982, p.5; Nov 12, 1982; p.1; and Nov 20, 1982; p.2).

It may be recalled that the state farms in the Nkrumah era accumulated a deficit of about $18 million after three years of operation. But the GNRC accumulated a deficit of about $81 million in just one year! Despite this, parliament, on August 20, 1981, approved another whopping sum of $54.4 million for the same GNRC after rejecting an amendment calling for a reduction in the corps expenditure by $40 million (*Daily Graphic*, Aug 21, 1981; p.8). It was clear, even by 1982, that the entire agricultural revolution in Ghana was an unmitigated disaster, as shown in table 7.1.

It can be seen from table 7.1 that, in 1982, the production of local food crops was, in many cases, less than half of what it had been in 1970. For

Table 7.1   Production of Important Crops (Thousand Tons)

Item	1970	1982
1. Cereal (Total)	857.5	543.0
Maize	481.6	346.0
Rice	48.8	36.0
Millet	141.2	76.0
Guinea Corn	185.9	85.0
2. Starchy Staples (Totals)	6,077.2	4,431.0
Cassava	2,387.8	2,470.0
Cocoyam	1,136.0	628.0
Yam	909.4	588.0
Plantain	1,644.0	745.0

Sources: Ministry of Agriculture, Government of Ghana: Accra—*Quarterly Digest of Statistics,*
Sept 1982; p.74.

example, production of plantain, a Ghanaian staple, was 745,000 tons, a
substantial decline from the 1,644,000 tons produced in 1970.

In 1981, the Ghanaian vice president, Dr. V. W. W. de-Graft Johnson,
announced with much fanfare that the short-term crash agricultural program launched by the government was being embraced enthusiastically: "A
great many people responded positively to the call to go back to the land and
have already started to think food" (*Daily Graphic,* Oct 17, 1981; p.1). But
even the state-owned newspaper, *the Daily Graphic,* saw the "success" of the
cash program differently. In a cynical editorial, "Thinking Food Indeed," the
paper wrote:

> We must admit that the government deserves commendation for the zeal with
> which it attempted to tackle the problem and the subsequent importation of
> agricultural inputs and equipment, notably fertilizers, tractors, harvesters and
> cutlasses. We cannot however admit, or agree that there has been "a judicious
> use of these scarce resources." To start with all the cutlasses that were imported
> were the wrong type and had to be altered by local blacksmiths before they
> could be used. The scarce foreign exchange could have been used in import-
> ing raw materials for the local market factories, which would have produced
> the right types from the beginning. Apart from its resource and time saving,
> it would also have created employment for idle labor and machinery. Fertiliz-
> ers were imported in good quantity and on schedule but we are all aware of
> the ordeal that it went through at the port. And even the "Fertilizer Evacua-
> tion Committee" that the President set up, could not, in conjunction with the
> ministry of agriculture, supply the input on time. Tractors were imported al-

right, probably the greatest number in any financial year. But when these are found carting produce and human beings in the cities we certainly cannot be made to agree that this is a "judicious use." The situation is still grave indeed as food shortage persists and food prices keep rising at incredible rates. (*Daily Graphic,* Oct 19, 1981; p.2)

For much of the 1980s, Ghana therefore had to import maize from Mozambique—a war-torn country! "Ghana spends at least 72 million cedis annually on the importation of maize, the Ashanti Regional Secretary, Mr. Kwame Kessie said" (*West Africa,* Aug 23, 1982; p.2188). For much of the 1980s, Ghana's total imports of food stood at 200 million *cedis* ($85 million) annually (*West Africa,* Feb 7, 1983; p.370). In the 1990s, the food supply situation deteriorated further, with Ghana importing $100 million of one commodity (rice) in 1999 alone.

Other African Countries

Elsewhere in Africa, only lip service was paid to agriculture. Even though agriculture accounts for the livelihood of more than 70 percent of the population in Zambia and Zimbabwe and for 13 to 18 percent of the GDP, it only receives 6 to 9 percent of the budget in the respective countries. Agricultural research in Africa has generally dwindled due to underfunding. Research into peasant agriculture has generally been nonexistent since the focus has been placed on technologies suitable for adoption by large and medium-scale farmers. Nigeria allocated only 6.5 percent of federal spending to agriculture, and in Benin's Ten-Year Development Plan (1980–90) only 5.8 percent of total planned expenditures was earmarked for agriculture, contrasting with the 10 percent allocated to agriculture in the Third World.

In Mozambique, "the FRELIMO party neglected the countryside in favor of the industrial urban areas and large-scale state farms and plantations. However, this failed to consolidate Frelimo's control of the country and to reconstruct the economy" (Libby, 1987; p.224). Predictably, the output of cashew nuts declined from 216,000 tons in 1973 (pre-independence year) to 76,000 tons in 1977 (post-independence year); sugar declined from 383,000 tons in 1973 to an estimated 166,000 tons in 1978; and tea production fell from 18,700 tons in 1973 to 14,000 tons in 1978. Mozambique's only other major cash crop for export—cotton—also underwent significant decline in production. For example, cotton (lint) fell from 46,000 metric tons in 1974 to 20,000 tons in 1981 (Libby, 1987; p.220).

Food production in Mozambique, as in Ghana, also declined seriously. Cereals fell from 801,000 metric tons in 1974 to 478 tons in 1980; rice from 120,000 metric tons to 70 tons; and maize from 450,000 tons to 250 tons for the same period. There was a serious food shortage in Mozambique, as these figures attest. It is tempting to attribute the decline in food production to the on-going civil war. But the war merely exacerbated the effects of disastrous policies of statism. Ghana had no civil war but its state farms could not feed its people.

In Tanzania, collectivized agriculture was another resounding failure. Despite the government's commitment to agricultural self-reliance, the share of agriculture in development expenditure declined from over 20 percent in the mid-1960s to 10 percent in 1978–79. Many African governments reportedly devote as little as 3 to 5 percent of their budgets to agriculture (Chazan et al. 1992; p.264). On November 6, 1973, President Julius Nyerere of Tanzania declared, "to live in villages is an order." Accordingly, massive operations were launched that moved millions of peasants to new but scarcely suitable village sites with extensive destruction of property and with some use of force. Toward the end of the operation, there were 7,373 registered villages with a total population of 13,506,044 people.

The basis of the "villagization" (or *Ujamaa*) concept was to concentrate the peasantry in administratively and politically accessible units in order to implement a number of programs and measures aimed at raising the productivity of labor in household agriculture. The prototype of such programs was the National Maize Project (NMP), which was launched in 1975. It eventually covered a thousand selected villages, providing them with packages of improved seeds and fertilizers, management and supervision, and expanded storage facilities. Four years later, the NMP was absorbed into a new National Food Credit Program administered by the Tanzania Rural Development Bank. As *New African Yearbook*, 1993–94, explained:

> Though the theory of villagization sounded right on paper and was widely praised by development economists, it turned out to be an unmitigated disaster in practice. Despite the huge cultivable land area, the large labor force and the wide variety of crops that could be grown, production of most crops showed a steady decline from 1978 when the first effects of villagization should have been making themselves felt. Output of food crops rose by only 2.1 per cent between 1970 and 1982, well below the population growth of 3.5 percent. (p.373)

Unfortunately, the other African countries that did not follow a socialist path fared no better. Nigeria, for example, chose to rely much less on the state. Before it gained its independence in 1960, Nigeria was self-sufficient in food and a net exporter of palm oil. It made no serious effort at increasing food production, however, devoting only 6 percent of federal spending to agriculture until 1973, when the National Accelerated Food Production Project (NAFPP) was launched.

Almost all land in Nigeria is owned by the state. Farmers must lease it, and thus cannot use it as collateral for bank loans; all transactions involving land requires the approval of the state governor. When President Shagari came into office in 1979, he declared the "Green Revolution," the main priority of his administration, and ultimately directed the program himself. About 15 percent of the Fourth National Development Plan was allocated to agriculture. The basic thrust of Nigeria's agricultural strategy, under both NAFPP and the Fourth Plan, was to turn to its small-scale farmers to increase food production. Although the strategy made sense, Nigeria was not immune to policy mistakes and blunders.

The program envisaged providing small-scale farmers with high-yielding varieties of seeds, tractors, fertilizers, insecticides, and other equipment at subsidized prices. Under the NAFPP, for example, farmers were to pay half the cost of machinery over a three-year period. The Fourth National Plan expanded this basic service program. Despite the huge investment, the agricultural revolution failed. Food production per capita fell an average of 2.5 percent a year from 1960 to 1982.

During the 1970s oil boom, agriculture fell into dismal neglect. Many farmers rushed to the urban areas to cash in on the new jobs and opportunities. Increasingly, Nigeria turned to imports to feed its population. By 1980, food production had tumbled by nearly 10 percent and food imports represented 15 percent of all imports. Even cocoa production was affected, plummeting from 330,000 tons annually to 165,000 tons in 1980.

The Babangida administration reshaped agricultural strategy by placing more emphasis on rural development. The Directorate for Food, Roads, and Rural Infrastructure was created in 1986 for the purpose of boosting food production. But it failed because "many projects were conceived, designed and executed without consulting the local communities that [they] are supposed to benefit" (*West Africa*, July 20, 1987; p.1384). Policy blunders aggravated the crisis as well. *The Economist* (Aug 21, 1993) provided one such example:

> The story of wheat is a victory of political folly over common sense. General Babangida slapped a ban on wheat imports in 1987. This was supposed to be a breeze to encourage domestic farmers and bakers. There was only one snag: Nigeria has the wrong climate. The only wheat it can grow does not bake into decent bread. The result: bread prices soared; smuggling from French bakeries in Benin flourished; Nigerian millers and bakeries went bust; and states exaggerated the size of their modest wheat crops to get bigger fertilizer subsidies.

In Dec 1992, the government finally recognized the folly, lifted the ban, and bread prices dropped. (survey; p.10)[3]

For much of the 1990s, Nigeria's agricultural sector continued to be plagued by high labor costs, credit scarcity, corruption, and deteriorating infrastructure. Fertilizer, the main agricultural input, is often in chronic shortage due to diversion of the stock to unknown destinations by management and distributors of the National Fertilizer Company (NAFCON). So serious was feed shortage that "About 20 percent of poultry farmers packed up in 1994 and a further 40 percent of those who survived did so the following year" (*African Business,* Nov 1996; p.24).

Unable to feed itself, Nigeria gave up and turned to imports. By 2004, the country was spending $3 billion a year on food imports—including rice, chickens, and dairy products (*The Washington Times,* July 18, 2004; p.A6). To help feed the nation, in July 2004, President Olusegun Obasanjo invited about 200 white farmers from Zimbabwe, whose farmlands have been violently seized by the Mugabe regime, to resettle in Kwara state.

Senegal also followed this strategy of turning to the peasant farmers, rather than to the state, to produce food. But as in Nigeria, the system failed because the state still maintained control over every facet of input supply. "Peasants said ONCAD (the state monopoly peanut buying agency) distributed poor seeds, unless bribed, underweighed crops and generally 'creamed' farmers' profits" (*West Africa,* Mar 3, 1986; p.486).

Until 1974, Zaire (now the Democratic Republic of Congo) was in fairly good economic shape. But after that year, more and more of the country's investible resources were allocated by the state to the modern sector (mining

Table 7.2   Volume Indices of Agricultural Output (1970 = 100)

	1972	*1974*	*1975*	*1976*	*1977*
Coffee	118.5	116.0	88.0	162.1	95.8
Cotton Fibers	106.2	96.5	95.3	66.7	58.5
Palm Oil	97.3	85.4	85.0	75.4	61.5
Manioc	83.6	111.9	119.4	122.2	124.5
Maize	150.0	177.7	138.9	142.2	144.4
Rice	111.1	166.7	150.0	152.2	153.3
Sugar Cane	109.6	140.0	148.9	113.6	134.3

Source: Kinshasa, Zaire: Bank of Zaire, Ministry of Planning and World Bank Mission (1979) estimates.

and manufacturing and services), benefiting mostly the urban centers. By 1974, Zaire's population had doubled since independence in 1960, and the urban population had quadrupled. But agricultural production persistently stagnated and remained below the output in 1974, as table 7.2 indicates.

The agricultural sector has been shrinking in real terms and in relation to the economy as a whole. "Hence, while the country was once self-sufficient in food production and indeed was a major exporter of agricultural produce, it has become a major importer of foodstuffs. Hunger and malnutrition have now become widespread" (Libby, 1987; p.276).

Reasons for the Failure of Africa's Agriculture

Many factors account for the failure of the agricultural revolution in Africa. According to the Comprehensive Africa Agriculture Development Program (CAADP), embedded in New Economic Partnership for African Development (NEPAD), the reasons for Africa's agricultural stagnation are: "continuing dependence on uncertain rainfall, nutritional deficiencies in Africa's soils, small and dispersed domestic markets, the instability and decline of world prices for African agricultural exports, the small size of most farms, farmers' frequent lack of organization, the lack of rural roads, neglect of the particular needs of women farmers (who produce most of the continent's food), and the spread of HIV/AIDS" (*Africa Recovery*, Jan 2004; p.13).

We shall focus on three broad reasons, ignoring for the moment other factors like administrative ineptitude, corruption, financial problems, and HIV/AIDS. The first was the emphasis on mechanization, the second was the socialist ideology itself, and the third was the neglect, and often the downright denigration and exploitation of, peasant farmers. Little was done to assist the peasant farmers by providing them with improved infrastructure: feeder roads, tap-borne water, rural electricity, extension services, health clinics, etc. Instead, they were portrayed as "enemies" and persecuted under a myriad of government dictats, controls, and regulations.

The emphasis on "modern," "scientific" techniques and mechanization was particularly misguided and was yet more evidence of the preoccupation with the signs of modernity (religion of development). Mechanized agriculture was seen as a sign of progress, and African leaders who pursued mechanization did so with total disregard for experience and rationality. Considerable evidence had already accumulated that mechanization in Africa was generally unsuccessful (Dumont 1966, pp.56–59).

The obtrusive obsession with modern machinery by Ghanaian authorities was baffling. It makes no economic sense to import a tractor stripped down (no attachments) at a cost of $25,000 to work on a five-acre farm in

a country with surplus or redundant labor. To be effectively utilized, a tractor requires a farm size of at least 100 acres per worker. Nowhere in black
Africa does the average farm size, including the state farms, even approach
50 acres per worker. (The state farms in Ghana were cultivating only 3.3
acres per worker as against an acreage of 5.1 acres per person in small-scale
peasant farming.) Black Africa is not yet ready for large-scale mechanization
of agriculture. A child learns how to crawl first before he walks and runs.
One cannot jump from simple agricultural implements like hoes and cutlasses to tractors and combine harvesters. Neither can one jump from a
dugout canoe to a fishing trawler. But black Africa is a place where people
are trying to fly when they haven't even learned how to walk.

Indeed, functionally illiterate Ghanaian officials advocated mechanization with total disregard of past experience. An attempt at mechanized
farming in northern Ghana in the 1950s proved an expensive failure and
caused one official to conclude that "the fundamental lesson is, without
doubt, that new ways cannot at present compete with traditional methods
of agriculture as practiced in that region" (Agricultural Development Corporation Report, 1957; p.9). Also, in the 1930s, the United Africa Company (UAC) found that their attempts to grow cocoa on a plantation basis
could not compete with the traditional farming of this crop (Killick, 1978;
p.210n). Elsewhere in Africa considerable evidence was accumulating that
mechanization was generally unsuccessful; the failure of the famous
"groundnut scheme" in Tanzania may be recalled. Nevertheless, mechanization was the policy; by 1966 the total number of tractors in the country was nearly 4,000 but the rate of utilization was only 20 percent (Killick,
1978; p.172). Yet, the mentality persisted. Emblazoned on the front page
of the state-owned paper was the caption: "183 Tractors Arrive"—"The
Ministry of Agriculture has taken delivery of 183 tractors and 30 combine
harvesters. There are other farming inputs waiting to be cleared from the
port" (*The Daily Graphic,* Sept 19, 1980; p.1). Strange how a poor country
made increased production of food dependent upon the very inputs—tractors—that it did not produce. Most of the tractors imported into Ghana in
the 1980s worked for a few months, broke down, and were abandoned to
rust in the countryside.

The second general reason for the failure of collective agriculture was the
socialist ideology itself. As we saw in chapter 4, many African leaders, especially Kwame Nkrumah of Ghana and Julius Nyerere of Tanzania, mistook
the communalism of African tribal life—strong kinship ties and participation in local affairs in village meetings—as evidence that Africa was ready for
socialism. They were dead wrong. One can be socialistic or communalistic
without necessarily being a socialist or a communist—an important distinc-

tion African leaders failed to make. If socialism is an alien economic ideology then socialized agriculture cannot succeed in Africa.

The third, and perhaps the most important, reason for the failure of collective agriculture was the neglect and downright denigration of peasant traditional farmers. These farmers would have responded to the call to increase output had they been given the right incentives. As *Time* (June 6, 1986) put it:

> By and large, African peasants are capable farmers. The problem is that . . . African states provide little incentive to grow more food. The state-set prices are kept low to please city residents, but in many areas they are not high enough to pay farmers for the cost of production. Unable to make a living on the land, farmers join the exodus to the cities, compounding the hunger problem. (p.37)

Wharton (1966) also offered this view:

> Peasant and subsistence farmers are indeed "economic men" who respond positively and negatively as quickly as the most commercialized farmers in the modern world. The evidence is quite clear that the subsistence man is fully responsive to the opportunity for a larger income (higher gain beyond costs and efforts spent) as the next man. Such responsiveness takes a variety of forms ranging from the introduction of new crops to the adoption of new practices, even those at odds with existing cultural methods. (p.264)

And even the World Bank acknowledged as far back as 1982 in its World Development Report that: "Small farmers can be highly productive, typically producing more from each acre than large farmers do, despite the often considerable disadvantages of their limited access to services, markets and production inputs such as fertilizer" (*West Africa*, Aug 23, 1982; p.2147).

The bulk of Ghana's local foodstuffs is produced by peasant farmers, who account for about 95 percent of the total farming production. The rest of the operations in the agricultural sector is in the hands of medium and large-scale private individuals, commercial firms, public corporations, and cooperatives. These, however, are not significant; in 1974, for example, the commercial firms and public corporations accounted for less than 10 percent of the total food production. Yet, Ghanaian governments have generally viewed peasant agriculture as too "backward" and the techniques of production as too "primitive" to care about. Industrialization was more prestigious. But there were political and ideological reasons to shun peasant farmers as well.

Nkrumah, for example, felt that assistance to peasant farmers would create a bourgeois class that would undermine his political power (Fitch and Oppenheimer, 1966; p.67). Again, Nkrumah was quite explicit about this: "We would be hampering our advance of socialism if we were to encourage the growth of Ghanaian private capitalism in our midst" (Killick, 1978; p.63).

Too many agricultural projects crafted by the elites failed in Africa because they did not fit into Africa's unique sociocultural environment; and they did not embrace Africa's peasant farmers. Back in 1981, the European Economic Community (EEC), was forthright: "Many development projects failed in Africa because they were on too large a scale and were not adapted to the population and the environment they were supposed to benefit. The projects of most lasting value are generally those which are simplest and directly benefit the local community concerned" (*West Africa*, June 21, 1981; p.131).

Some attempts were made to reshape agricultural strategies to embrace the peasant farmers, but these state-mandated programs did not live up to expectations. Examples are the integrated rural development (IRD) programs that provided seeds, fertilizer, and other inputs directly to small-scale farmers and sought to improve the marketing and distribution of agricultural produce by providing infrastructural facilities (feeder roads, storage bins, wells, market centers, clinics, etc). Such programs were undertaken in Nigeria, Ghana, Sierra Leone, Burkina Faso, and Benin, to mention only a few countries.

In Nigeria, for example, maize, cassava, guinea corn, and rice farmers were assisted through cooperatives to receive production inputs such as tractors, seeds, fertilizers, rice threshers, irrigation pumps, and processing equipment, all of which they paid for at half price over three years.

In Burkina Faso and Benin, a novel IRD program, funded by the World Food Programme (WFP), was tried. Villagers built schools, clinics, dikes, sinking wells, and boreholes in a community development effort. They were paid no wages but received free daily food rations from the WFP. The scheme, introduced in Burkina Faso in October 1981, involved the distribution over five years of nearly 35,000 tons of food in 83 million rations costing over $33 million. In Benin, the scheme was introduced earlier (in 1975), and since then WFP has distributed nearly $8 million worth of food.

Unfortunately, the results of the IRD and WFP's food-for-work programs were rather disappointing. In Ghana, the fertilizer distributed to farmers ended up being sold "in bowls for between 415 *cedis* ($5.45) and 430 *cedis* ($10.9) a bowl in the Salaga district in the Northern Region" (*Daily Graphic*, Sept 10, 1981; p.8). The ordinary African peasant farmer does not understand tractors or fertilizers. Providing these inputs, even free of charge, is more likely to confuse him. He understands donkeys, compost, manure, and cutlasses (machetes). Furthermore, the IRD authorities who dispensed these inputs were too far removed from the villages to understand the needs of the local farmers. Because the programs were often target oriented, the authorities were more often concerned with quantities—how many farmers were reached, how many acres were developed, etc.

Although the WFP food-for-work program was laudable in its aim, the strategy was misguided, with the potential of undermining its own stated aim of increasing agricultural production. Consider a situation where community work programs, such as the construction of small irrigation dams or wells, increased rice production but rice farmers found it difficult to market their rice because of the free food rations. The second difficulty with WFP related to the fundamental fact that aid tends to induce dependency. A recent study of Burkina Faso's experience with food aid was quite revealing:

> So extensively has the food aid mentality permeated the way of life in Burkina Faso that rather than act as an incentive to community improvement, food aid has the opposite effect; it is an assurance that in spite of bad land-use practices that lead to eroded and exhausted soil and marginal harvests, there will be food to eat, there will be food aid.
>
> The use of food aid as an incentive to farmers to participate in community development has distorted their conception of value, long- and short-term, of the work and has concomitantly undermined the interest that a farmer usually has in the future of his community. Often, among the farmers who have received food aid in the past for participation in community development projects, the overriding concern is with food aid (when and just how much of it will be distributed) rather than with the development work or its effects on their village or their families. (*West Africa*, Mar 1, 1982; p.575)

Indeed, the study cited above noted that in two villages in Burkina Faso, work aimed at reclaiming a degraded piece of land was abandoned when it was learned that there would be no more free food. Some of the problems with agricultural development were elementary and should have been obvious to government officials in Africa.

Increasing agricultural production in Africa should not be rocket science. First, senseless civil wars destroy Africa's agricultural production capacity. Peasants cannot be producing food when they are fleeing from savage carnage and destruction. Second, the authorities need to recognize that peasant farmers produce the bulk (over 90 percent) of Africa's foodstuffs and about 80 percent of these peasant farmers are women. The environment in which the peasants find themselves to a large extent conditions or determines their economic behavior as well as the size, or the lack thereof, of the surpluses they generate. The environment the peasants face in Africa is composed of two parts: a traditional environment that delineates their indigenous value systems, attitudes, and motivations, and a national environment created by the government in power. In relative terms, the traditional environment is of greater importance since illiterate people tend to go more by custom and age-old practices than by convoluted national policies that they may not understand.

One pertinent feature of the peasants' traditional system is the large measure of economic and political freedoms they enjoyed under their traditional chiefs. These chiefs are closer to the peasants than central governments seated miles away in capital cities. The chiefs often understand the needs of peasant farmers, as well as those of their villages, much better than central governments. They also communicate much better with the farmers and command more respect from them than the government does. The British colonialists recognized this fact and used the African chiefs as intermediaries.

In traditional Africa, corrupt and autocratic chiefs are rare. Chiefly decisions are usually taken after consultation with an inner circle of elders. In fact, it is this inner circle of elders that makes decisions for the chief. A chief's role, by custom, is not autocratic but part of a consultative system of government—a fact that many foreigners, understandably, failed to see. An autocratic chief in Africa would be quickly removed or abandoned by the people. And unlike Fidel Castro of Cuba, the chief cannot stop anyone from leaving the village.

Under these circumstances, it makes more sense to have the traditional chiefs, rather than African governments, play the pivotal role in agricultural development, particularly since the chiefs are also the custodians of land. In many African countries, it is one of the traditional roles of a chief to play an active role in the village community's development. In Ghana, for example, villagers, under the leadership of their chiefs, provide free "communal labor" to build schools, clinics, markets, and other village infrastructure. An African peasant would work for free on a chief's farm rather than on a government farm. Furthermore, a peasant would handle agricultural tools, machinery, or property belonging to the chief with better care than he would government property. Property belonging to the chief is generally regarded as sacred since it forms part of ancestral wealth. This should not be confused with "socialized" or collectivized agriculture since the element of coercion would be missing. A peasant cannot be forced to work on a chief's farm.

Ghana's Experience with Price Controls

Perhaps nothing wrought more damage to Ghana's agriculture than price controls. They were introduced by Nkrumah in 1964 ostensibly to make food "affordable" and check rising food prices because of inadequate production. We saw the disastrous consequences of state controls on the price of gasoline in chapter 6 with gas lines in Nigeria. It is often easy and politically expedient to issue such an edict because it purports to demonstrate to party supporters that the government or politicians are "doing something about the high price." But price controls create more problems than they solve. They strangulate the economy, cause serious dislocations and distortions, and wreak incalculable damage, not to mention the huge amount of resources they cost both the government and the people. Although the strictures on price controls apply to both countries—Nigeria and Ghana—a separate discussion about Ghana's experiment is warranted because of the nature of the commodity—food. Whereas oil in Nigeria is produced and refined by a few firms and purchased by millions of motorists, food, on the other hand, is produced by millions of peasant farmers and consumed by almost everybody. Furthermore, food production is the backbone of peasant economic activity. Therefore price controls on food have the potential of wreaking far more economic and social damage.

Human beings everywhere operate by incentives. If a government pays farmers more than what they can get on the market, farmers will overproduce the commodity. This has been the case in the United States, Canada, and the EC countries, resulting in the persistent surpluses of wheat, maize, rice, cheese, and other dairy products that they have difficulty disposing of and ship off as food aid to the Third World. In the United States, the minimum prices guaranteed by the government—called "agricultural support prices"—are set above prices farmers can get on the market, creating a chronic excess supply situation. From an economic standpoint, this is a waste.

African farmers are no different from American farmers. Much of the smuggling of produce that occurs in Africa is simply movements of goods to places where they fetch higher prices. In the early 1960s, the producer price of cocoa in Ghana was higher than in Ivory Coast. Consequently, cocoa was smuggled into Ghana, culminating in Ghana's record 1965 crop of 494,000 tons. But this was reversed in the 1980s when the price in Ivory Coast was higher, resulting in Ghana's output of only 150,000 tons.

On the other hand, if a government pays farmers less than what they can get on the market, farmers will under-produce and the immediate effect will be a shortage. This was evidenced in the former Eastern-bloc countries such as Poland, Russia, China, and in many African countries, where there were chronic shortages of food. This economic fact has little to do with ideology; it is plain common sense.

In Ghana, price controls and various legislative instruments quickly became tools for the systematic exploitation of the peasant farmers. One undeclared intention was to milk the agricultural sector and transfer resources to the state. Another was to fix the prices of agricultural produce and render food cheap for the urban elites—the basis of political support for African governments. The prices peasants received for their produce were dictated by governments, not determined by market forces in accordance with African traditions. African chiefs do not fix prices. Bargaining over prices has always been the rule in all village markets.

Elsewhere in Africa, government policies to make food available at reasonable prices to the elites flouted not only economic laws but also common sense. Agricultural marketing boards were established, to which farmers were required to sell their produce at artificially low prices set by the government. No farmer in this world will sell a bag of maize at $100 a bag to the government when he knows he can get $200 on the free market unless he is forced. And if he is, the normal human reaction would be to cut back on production and grow something else other than maize.

When farmers switch production from a commodity whose price is controlled to one that is not, the result is shortages of the controlled commodity due to reduced supply. Generally, when a commodity is in short supply relative to demand, its price rises. One observes this even in Africa's own indigenous village markets. When fish is out of season, its price rises, and when there is a bumper catch of fish, the price falls. But ever-prescient African governments often refused to accept this economic fact. When the price of a commodity rose, their immediate reaction was to look for a conspiracy and impose price controls, which exacerbates the shortage situation.

In Ghana, the Marxist Rawlings regime denounced indigenous markets, which had been in existence for centuries, as dens of economic profiteers and saboteurs. It slapped stringent price controls on hundreds of goods during the 1981–1983 period. Not content with the commodity shortages occasioned by the price controls, the regime employed price inspectors and established Price Control Tribunals to hand down stiff penalties to violators:

- In June 1980, a magistrate, Mr. Kwadwo Asumadu-Amoah, jailed a 43-year-old petty trader, Madam Abena Amponsah, for three years at hard labor for making an illegal profit of $1.50 on 6 cakes of "Guardian" soap. The same magistrate handed down a three-year term at hard labor to an 18-year-old boy who made an illegal profit of fifty cents on a packet of matches. (*Graphic,* June 5, 1980; p.5)
- The Brong-Ahafo Tribunal imposed a 12,000 *cedis* fine on Grace Lamiere, a popular baker in Sunyani, for buying a bag of flour above the controlled price at Gonnorkrom. The Tribunal had earlier jailed Dora Mensah, also a baker, for 6 months and fined her 5,000 *cedis* for exchanging *cedis* on the black market. (*Ghanaian Times,* June 22,1982; p.8)

- An Accra trader, Umaro Shaibu, was jailed 4 years by the Price Control Tribunal in Accra for selling a bottle of "Sprite" for 7 *cedis* instead of 1.50 *cedis* (*West Africa,* Feb 28 1983; p.576).
- On March 11, 1983, at the Kumasi Central Market, a pregnant woman, Yaa Amponsah, had her 18-month baby flung to the ground and she herself slapped and kicked by a policeman who insisted on paying $1 instead of $5 for two tubers of yam. At the same market, another pregnant woman was dragged on the ground by soldiers for allegedly selling above the controlled price, causing her to miscarry the next day. (*West Africa,* March 20, 1983; p.487)

For all their faults, the British colonialists seldom perpetrated such heinous atrocities against Ghanaian peasants. Nor do even "backward" tribal chiefs use such force against their peasants. How did traders respond to these inanities?

> The brisk trading activities around Accra Central Market and the Orion Cinema Palace areas have slowed down considerably, following the coming into effect yesterday of the government's price control exercise in the Accra-Tema metropolitan areas. Most stores in this area did not open for normal business and only a handful of the large number of people, who previously sold various items on the pavements and sidewalks, could be seen.
>
> The few stores which opened for business had almost empty shelves unlike the situation last week and some stores had mounted notice boards reading "stock-taking." (*Daily Graphic,* Jan 18, 1982; p.1)
>
> *The Daily Graphic* (state-owned) reported that a section of market women and traders in Cape Coast would not "heed appeals." It said a market survey there had shown that traders would rather withdraw their goods than bring prices down (*West Africa,* Jan 25, 1982; p.272).
>
> Overland trade along Ghana's south-eastern frontier has declined about 70 per cent resulting in sharp fall in (customs) revenue. Observers attributed the fall in trade to the withdrawal of women traders in response to the strict enforcement of prices by the present PNDC government. (*Daily Graphic,* Feb 5, 1982; p.1)

The authorities, in turn, responded by wreaking destruction "as a warning to traders who had decided to withdraw their wares instead of reducing prices" (*West Africa,* Feb 1, 1982, p.286). "In January 1982, Air Force personnel destroyed over 400 tables and chairs belonging to traders at Apampam Store in Takoradi Central Market in a bid to enforce price controls" (*West Africa,* Feb1, 1982; p.286). Furthermore, "In February 1982, the PNDC Secretary for the Upper Region, Dr. Awdu Tinorgah, ordered a detachment of the Police Striking Force to enforce price controls, following the refusal of traders at the Bolgatanga Market to sell their items at controlled prices" (*West Africa*, April 26, 1982; p.1170).

Markets were burned down and destroyed at Accra, Kumasi, Koforidua, and other cities when traders refused to sell at government-dictated prices. In February 1982, "the Tamale Central Market was set ablaze, causing the destruction of large quantities of foodstuffs, drugs, and imported spare parts. Then John Ndeburge, the Northern Regional Secretary, set up a five-member committee of inquiry to investigate the circumstances leading to the incineration of the market" (*West Africa*, March 8, 1982; p.684). Imagine deploying air force personnel and a police striking force to destroy tables and enforce price controls. Economic lunacy was on the rampage.

Worse, the little food that there was in Ghana was being destroyed! When that failed to intimidate the market traders, the military government launched house-to-house searches for goods (*West Africa*, Feb 15, 1982; p.481). "The Rawlings government also declared that it would conduct unannounced searches of traders and stated that if any were found with hoarded goods they would be taken away to be shot by firing squad'" (Herbst 1993; p.26). This defied common sense. And the results of all these inanities?

Between January 1982 and April 1983, prices of locally produced goods rose by more than 600 per cent. The price of a bag of maize, for example, went from 500 *cedis* in January 1982 to 4,000 *cedis* in April 1983; and for nine months, bread disappeared completely from the markets (*West Africa*, July 11, 1983; p.1597).

Having jailed the traders and destroyed their markets, the government of Ghana discovered it had to feed them. But there was no food to feed the food traders it had jailed for allegedly selling or buying above government-fixed prices. Thirty prisoners died in Sunyani prison for lack of food; 39 inmates died at another (*West Africa*, July 15, 1983; p.1634). Imagine. For the economy as a whole, "GNP per capita declined from $483 in 1979 to $447 in 1981 while by 1983 living standards had fallen steadily to some 16 percent of 1972 levels. The Urban Consumer Price Index (1977 = 100) averaged 363 in 1980, 800 in 1981, 976 in 1982 and by May 1983 was at 2,222.6" (*West Africa*, March 19, 1984; p.618).

Instead of looking at inadequate food supplies, the Rawlings regime organized massive demonstrations to denounce "imperialists," "neocolonialists," and other imaginary enemies. *The Daily Graphic* carried cartoons portraying the United States and Britain as imperialist nations choking Ghana to death. Yet, in the same newspaper was a report that Ghana had received "500 metric tons of food and comprising sorghum grits and wheat soy blend from the American Government" (*Daily Graphic*, Feb 17, 1982;

p.4). There is no excuse for such economic lunacy. Wouldn't Ghana have been better off if all that time and energy wasted on demonstrations to denounce imperialism had been spent producing more yams or corn to reduce the dependence on food from "imperialist" nations?

Between 1982 and 1983, the government of Ghana had in its employment more than 300 price inspectors and more than 20 price control tribunals. It cost the government a substantial amount of resources to employ all these people to enforce price controls—an activity that did *not* result in even one extra tuber of yam being produced. The controls exacerbated the shortage situation. Wouldn't it have been wise and better for the economy if all those people had instead been placed on a farm to produce maize? As we saw earlier in this chapter, production of local staples like maize, rice, cassava, and yam in 1982 was half the level in 1974. Ghana therefore had to import maize from Mozambique.

I have come down hard on military regimes for their economically destructive and lunatic policies. The rigid enforcement of stringent price controls by a military regime in Ghana effectively destroyed the country's capacity to feed itself. For much of the 1980s, Ghana's total imports of food continued to soar, reaching 200 million *cedis* in 1982 (*West Africa,* Feb 7, 1983; p.370). The shortages created by price controls cost the country in other ways as well: lost output, reduced productivity, and absenteeism in the civil service. In the 1982–83 period, most civil servants were away from their desks, chasing after scarce commodities. Government business remained undone or took forever. A simple application procedure, for a passport, for example, took months instead of days.

Worse, price controls ended up making commodities more expensive to consumers if opportunity and search costs are factored in, as was done for gasoline shortages in Nigeria in chapter 6. More perniciously, price controls worsen the shortage situation over time and breed corruption. Commodity shortages induce people to hoard, which exacerbates the shortages. Government officials, charged with selling the commodity to the public at the control price, soon "exploit" the situation by diverting part of the goods to the black market to sell and pocket the price difference. Ordinary people may use their political connections to acquire the scarce commodity at the controlled price and sell it on the black market to make a killing—a practice that was known as *kalabule* in Ghana. All these activities exacted an enormous toll on the economy. The simple solution to all this waste of resources is to *remove the price controls.* In fact, no African government should ever, ever fix prices. Such practice was never part of indigenous Africa's village market culture. If the price of a commodity is too high, people should simply shun the product and buy a substitute. If African governments want more food produced, they should lift price controls. For example, in 1981, when Malawi, Somalia, and Zambia lifted price controls and raised prices paid to farmers, food production increased. The production of maize doubled in Malawi and by 1983, Malawi was producing enough maize for export. In Somalia, production of sorghum increased by almost 50 percent, largely due to increased prices to farmers. In 1985, when Ghana finally had the economic wisdom, at the instigation of the World Bank, to remove price controls, foodstuffs began appearing in the markets. But more still needs to be done to increase food production since the food situation in Ghana remains precarious. As the World Bank noted, "Little was done over the 1983–1994 decade to improve the productivity of the main food crops or to generate dynamic innovation in the small farmer sector" (World Bank, 1995). Improvements in infrastructure—feeder roads, building markets, electricity, clean water, etc. in the rural areas—were desperately needed in the 1990s:

> Accessibility to the farm gates is still a problem in spite of the much trumpeted rural development programs. Fifty percent of food prices in the urban areas are made up of transportation costs. Because of the unwillingness of transport-owners to ply the most impassable roads, the few that are ready to ply the roads charge exorbitantly, a cost which is transferred to the consumers in the urban areas. This in turn has created a situation where the ordinary Ghanaian spends 60 per cent of his income on food. (*African Observer,* May 29-June 4, 1997; p.14)

It was necessary to discuss Ghana's experience with price controls in detail because country after country that tried this insane experiment experienced exactly the same results. Let's look at Zimbabwe, for example.

Zimbabwe

Between 2000 and 2003, Zimbabwe faced a serious food shortage crisis and more than 11 million—over 80 percent of its population—faced hunger and starvation. Like its erstwhile Marxist counterpart, Comrade Mengistu Haile Mariam in the 1985 Ethiopian famine crisis, "the government, for months, denied that any serious food shortage was on the horizon, even as evidence mounted. Finally, the finance minister, Simba Makoni, publicly acknowledged the looming crisis and began laying the groundwork for an appeal for aid" (*The Washington Times,* Oct 16, 2001, p.A13).

The food shortages stemmed from an unlikely convergence of natural and political factors. Many parts of the country had suffered from drought, while others had been buffeted by severe flooding. In addition, violent land seizure, orchestrated by a government plan to redistribute much of the land owned by the country's small white minority, disrupted food production and discouraged investment in agriculture. The shortages sent the prices of staples soaring.

In October 2001, President Robert Mugabe announced that Zimbabwe was abandoning market-based economic policies and returning to socialist/statist policies. He imposed price controls on basic foods, warning that they would be strictly enforced, and that the government would seize firms that shut down, withheld their goods, or engaged in illegal profiteering. Mugabe railed: "Let no one on this front expect mercy. The state will take over any businesses that are closed. We will reorganize them with workers and, at last, that socialism we wanted can start again. Those tired of doing business here can pack up and go" (*The Washington Times,* Oct 16, 2001; p.A13). The rhetoric was eerily reminiscent of Ghana's lunatic experimentation with price controls in the Rawlings era.

Mugabe's government ordered price cuts of 5 percent to 20 percent on corn meal, bread, meat, cooking oil, milk, salt, and soap. Three days later, "Bread, cooking oil and margarine were unobtainable across the country; bread shortages were also experienced in Harare. A main bakery chain in Harare said the set prices did not take into account transportation, power and other costs; the chain had put 200 of its workers on shorter working hours as production was cut" (*The Washington Times,* Oct 16, 2001; p.A13).

The Mugabe government never learned, believing that *more* of the *wrong* economic medicine would solve the food shortage crisis. To halt the surging costs of staples like bread, government imposed more stringent price controls. The result? "The main effect has been a decline in supply from producers unwilling to settle for below-market prices" (*The New York Times,* Nov 10, 2001; p.A7). "Already, some farmers have been switching to more lucrative crops like soybeans and the pepper plant, from which paprika is derived. If the price of corn is held down too much, many more will abandon it, setting up much bigger shortages next year, the officials say" (*The New York Times,* July 18, 2001; p.A4).

Instead of looking at their own disastrous agricultural policies, African governments' instinctive reaction to a looming food shortage crisis is to look for a conspiracy. In Zimbabwe, President Robert Mugabe's government "repeatedly accused white farmers of withholding the staple grain to create false shortages in retaliation for its drive to seize white-owned farms for redistribution to landless blacks. *The Herald* (state-owned) quoted Agriculture Minister Joseph Made as saying some farmers involved were foreign nationals whose land had been taken off a list of farms targeted for compulsory seizure under agreements with their home countries" (*Reuters,* Jan 22, 2002).

Accusing them of hoarding, Zimbabwe's state grain board (Grain Marketing Board) impounded more than 36,000 tons of maize from white commercial farmers. This was almost an exact replay of Ghana's insane experimentation with price controls.

Obviously, Zimbabwean farmers would refuse to sell their grain to the GMB and sell it on the black market or to brokers outside the country. Indeed, this was precisely what happened. Zimbabwean farmers sold their grain across the border to brokers in South Africa, who in turn sold it to humanitarian relief organizations such as the World Food Programme, which in turn shipped the Zimbabwean grain *back* into Zimbabwe as food relief aid! According to the state-owned Zimbabwean paper, *Sunday Mail* (March 21, 2004):

> The grain shortages that hit Zimbabwe in the past two years were artificial as grain was exported and later re-imported into Zimbabwe as drought relief. Investigations show that some of the maize brought into the country as drought relief had actually originated in the country. Sources told *The Sunday Mail* last week that what has appeared in court following the arrest of farmer and businessmen Cecil Muderede, who is facing charges of externalizing grain and foreign currency, is only a tip of the iceberg. Muderede is facing charges of defrauding the GMB on 21 occasions of wheat valued at over $63 million and undisclosed amounts of maize. He also faces charges of defrauding Bak Storage of $13 million and of externalizing foreign currency to the tune of US$1.3 million. Sources have confirmed that there was massive externalization of maize and other products. The result was the food deficit which hit the country and threatened its security. There are also reports that some of the maize brought into Zimbabwe by the World Food Program as drought relief was actually Zimbabwean maize that had been externalized and bought by WFP on the open market in South Africa. (www.guardianandmail.com)

Rather than remove the price controls that had created the artificial shortages, the government opted to create more bureaucratic controls:

> Greater attention would now be paid to the marketing of agricultural produce and products. A full position of director of marketing had now been established in the Ministry of Agriculture and approved by the Public Service Commission. The director would operate just like other directors such as the directors of Veterinary Services, Engineering, Livestock Production and Development and Arex. Dr Made said his ministry would soon be announcing the producer prices. Farmers would soon be told the pre-planting price of wheat and of other crops. (*Sunday Mail,* March 21, 2004; (www.guardianandmail.com)

Zimbabwe's economic situation was deteriorating rapidly. According to Colin Powell, the U.S. Secretary of State, "reckless government mismanagement and unchecked corruption have produced annual inflation rates near 300 percent, unemployment of more than 70 percent and widespread short-ages of food, fuel, and other basic necessities" (*The New York Times,* June 24, 2003; p.A31). To finance its soaring expenditures, Mugabe's government re-sorted to printing money. But so severe were commodity shortages that even the "government ran out of the ink and the special paper needed to print enough notes to keep pace with inflation, currently 365 percent and rising" (*The Economist,* Aug 2, 2003; p.45).

It was déjà vu all over again—the annoying repetition of the agricultural policy blunders in Ghana. The wise learn from the mistakes of others while fools repeat them.

The Deadly Mix of AIDS and Famine

Africa's famine crisis has been aggravated by the HIV/AIDS pandemic, which has hit African agriculture especially hard. The lethal mix of famine and AIDS was particularly noticeable in Southern Africa during 2001–2003. Most of the countries in this region are fairly fertile, well wa-tered, and have traditionally been self-sufficient in food. However, it has faced a famine crisis largely because the region also has the world's highest HIV infection levels. The UN Joint Program on HIV/AIDS (UNAIDS) es-timated that infection rates in 2002 ranged from 15 percent of adults in Malawi up to more than 30 per cent in Swaziland and Lesotho and a stag-gering 39 percent in Botswana (*Africa Recovery,* May 2003; p.11). The World Food Programme (WFP) estimated that, in March 2003, the num-ber of people requiring food assistance in Zimbabwe stood at 7.2 million, or 52 percent of the population, and nearly 8 million more also needed food aid in Malawi, Zambia, Lesotho, Mozambique, and Swaziland (*Africa Re-covery,* May 2003; p.11).

The AIDS epidemic has taken a heavy toll on Africa's agricultural pro-duction. A study in a communal area in Zimbabwe has demonstrated that an adult death from the disease can immediately reduce a household's abil-ity to produce different foods. The declines average 61 percent for maize, 49 percent for vegetables, 47 percent for cotton, and 37 percent for ground-nuts. In Malawi, death rates among employees of the Ministry of Agricul-ture and Irrigation have doubled, almost all because of HIV/AIDS. In Namibia, studies indicate that agricultural extension workers spend one-tenth of their work time attending the funerals of people who died of AIDS (*Africa Recovery* 17; 1 [May 2003]; p.11).

Malawi, Lesotho, Zimbabwe, and Zambia are the three African countries that have been most devastated by the deadly mix of AIDS and famine.

Malawi's lush green countryside is crisis-crossed by several rivers, and Africa's third-largest lake can be found along its eastern border. Yet, Malawi is finding it increasingly difficult to find people to work its fertile land. The AIDS epidemic has caused an acute labor shortage. Malawi has an annual rate of 70,000 deaths from AIDS-related illnesses (including tuberculosis, malaria, and cholera), and life expectancy has fallen from 46 years to 36 years, according to the UN Development Program (*Africa Recovery*, May 2003; p.11). Partly as a result, Malawi has sought emergency food assistance, including donations of even maize—the key staple of East and Southern Africa.

With nearly one-third of working-age adults infected with the virus—the world's fourth highest HIV infection rate—Lesotho was unable to deal with crop failures, largely due to inclement weather over the period 2001–2003. In Zimbabwe, some 2.2 million people are infected with the virus, of whom 600,000 have developed full-blown AIDS. According to the Ministry of Health, 70 percent of hospital admissions are HIV-related, and the government expected the country's 2002/2003 agricultural production to fall far short of national needs. Since Zimbabwe used to be the breadbasket of the region, the food deficit would have ramifications on the neighboring countries.

In Zambia, the HIV/AIDS pandemic has not only devastated agricultural production and depleted the work force, but also affected every other aspect of life and society. By the end of 2000, between 40,000 and 90,000 people had died of AIDS, most of them men between the ages of 20 and 45 (*Africa Recovery*, May 2003; p.12).

INFLATION

Inflation is simply defined as a period of rising prices. It is generally due to two causes or a combination of them. The first is the demand factor. If people have lots of money in their pockets, they would want to buy more goods and their prices would rise, other things being equal. In this case, prices are "pulled up" by excess demand. The second is the supply factor. If demand remains "constant" and the supply of, say, foodstuffs falls due to poor rainfall, for example, the price of food would rise. Here, food prices are pushed by inadequate supply. The popular saying "too much money (or demand) chasing too few goods" reflects a combination of the two factors.

In Africa, inflation is of both the "supply push" and "demand pull" variety. Food prices, for example, are being pushed and pulled up because of declining production on a per capita basis and increasing demand. However, the more important cause of inflation in Africa has been a phenomenal rise in demand, occasioned by the injection of huge amounts of money into the economy.

Table 7.3 Per Capita Food Production and Money Supply—Inflation for Ghana, 1986–1994

	1986	1987	1988	1989	1990	1991	1992	1993	1994
Food Production/Capita	101	100	105	108	86	98	99	99	—
Money supply increase	44	53	45	53	11	14	53	28	50
Deflator	71.7	100	134	172	239	288	324	406	514
Rate of Inflation (%)	—	39	34	28	39	21	13	25	27

Source: *African Economic and Financial Data, UNDP/World Bank, 1996.* Washington, D.C.: World Bank Publication.

The first row of table 7.3 indicates per capita food production that was largely stagnant, while the second row indicates the annual percentage growth rate of the money supply. In 1987, for example, the increase in the money supply was an irresponsible 53 percent. The deflator indicates that what cost 1 *cedi* in 1987 cost 514 *cedis* in 1994.[4] The impact of excessive increases in the money supply on prices has been much greater as there were no extra goods—even food—to sponge off the excess liquidity.

The result was a worthless *cedi*. The black market rate for the *cedi* stood at 40 *cedis* to the U.S. dollar in 1981 (the official rate was 2.75 *cedis* to the dollar). Even after a "successful" economic recovery program and greater availability of goods, the black market rate for the *cedi* in 1997 was 2,250 to the dollar (the official rate was discontinued after the adoption of a weekly foreign exchange auctioning system in 1987). The basic source of excess liquidity has been mounting budget deficits and printing more money to finance them, as we saw in chapter 5.

Dealing with Inflation: Ghana and Nigeria

One would think that after having conducted their own meticulous research and arriving at the brilliant, earth-shattering discovery that too much money in circulation has been the cause of inflation and that the source of excess money has been their own runaway budget deficits, Ghanaian governments would take the initiative to eliminate the deficit by reining in their own expenditures. But that would be wishful thinking. They deal with inflation by blaming others (the imperialists), imposing price controls, hastily adopting ad hoc measures, or changing the currency.

Back in 1963–64, when food shortages appeared and prices of local foodstuffs began to soar, the Nkrumah government reacted by blaming food traders and their "neocolonial collaborators" and searched in vain for an imperialist conspiracy. The government imposed price controls on the traders instead of looking at production and the government's own inflationary policies. Successive governments continued this economic blunder, as we saw in the previous section.

Monetary Management, Currency Changes, and Banking Crises

> Career bankers are scrambling out of banks and finance houses and are looking for jobs elsewhere. Customers too are scrambling to withdraw their deposits. The bubble has at last burst for Nigerian banks.
> —Pini Jason, a Nigerian columnist in *African Business* May 1994; p.33.

Too often in Africa, government officials, betraying a singular lack of under-standing of conventional economic problems, hastily adopt wrong solutions with little forethought to deal with the wrong economic problems, thus com-pounding existing mistakes. Nigerian authorities provide a stunning tale of reckless financial mismanagement following the oil boom in the 1980s.

The discovery and exploration of oil fields in the early 1970s led to a booming economy. Oil quickly became the dominant sector of the econ-omy, accounting for more than 90 percent of exports and providing the fed-eral government with 80 percent of its revenue. The government went on a spending spree. It frittered away the oil bonanza on extravagant investment projects, a new capital at Abuja with a price tag of $25 billion, and highly ambitious Third Development Plans, upon the false projections of oil out-put and revenue. Agriculture was neglected and food imports rose rapidly. Elite *bazongas* (raiders of the public treasury) helped themselves to the rest of the oil money.

In 1981, oil prices fell precipitously. Export receipts plummeted from $22 billion in 1980 to $10 billion in 1983 and then to $6 billion in 1986. To maintain income and the consumption binge, Nigeria borrowed heavily and recklessly. Its foreign debts quadrupled from $9 billion in 1980 to $36 billion in 1990. Federal and state budgets sank into deficits. These were fi-nanced with the accumulation of more debt and the depletion of interna-tional reserves. External imbalance caused difficulties with debt servicing and forced the country to go into arrears.

To help improve balance, the Economic Stabilization Act of 1982 was passed. Stringent trade controls, the rationing of foreign exchange, a restric-tion on import licenses, an increase in duties, and the initiation of an im-port deposit program were adopted. These measures, however, failed miserably and an economic crisis emerged in 1983. Growth rates turned sharply negative. The GDP growth rate in 1983 was –6.7 percent; non-oil sector growth fell to –9.3 percent, and petroleum sector growth to –2.5 per-cent. By 1985, the distortions in the economy had reached alarming pro-portions. The exchange rate was grossly overvalued and the budget deficit out of control.

The government resorted to heavy domestic borrowing from the banking system to finance its profligacy. As the following table shows, in 1974, the Central Bank of Nigeria (CBN) loans to the government constituted less than 1 percent of the bank's asset portfolio. By 1986, they had reached 63 percent. Heavy government borrowing from the commercial banks also in-jected substantial liquidity into the economy.

To deal with the worsening economic situation, the government of Gen. Ibrahim Babangida adopted the IMF's structural adjustment program (SAP)

Table 7.4   Deficit Finance ($ millions)

	1975	1977
Central Bank		
Foreign Assets	3,454	3,635
Claims on Government	10	14,472
Claims of Private Sector	190	1,301
Claims on Commercial Banks	10	3,250
Claims on Other Financial Institutions	5	326
Total	3,669	22,984
Commercial Banks		
Reserves	331	1,506
Foreign Assets	64	1,740
Claims on Government	778	8,259
Claims on Private Sector	931	15,390
Claims on Other Financial Institutions	8	566
Total	2,112	27,461

Source: *International Financial Statistics,* 1987 (IMF). Washington, D.C.: IMF Publication.

in July 1986. Among other moves, trade was liberalized, price controls removed, and the banking system deregulated. The deregulation saw an explosion in the number of new banks. In 1973, there were 16 commercial and only 3 merchant banks. By 1984, there were 27 commercial and 11 merchant banks. In 1987, the total had shot up to 47 banks (32 commercial and 15 merchant banks) and in 1994 to 121.

The proliferation of banks sparked fierce competition for deposits, pushing interest rates to abnormally high levels. Newly established banks had difficulty attracting deposits and increasingly came to rely on the interbank market for funds. Seventy percent of these funds were controlled by about five older commercial banks that secured deposits at very low interests from their wide network of branches at about 18 percent. These funds were lent to the merchant banks and other borrowers at about 25 percent at the interbank market. The merchant banks, in turn, lent to their customers at about 33 percent. But at such rates, hardly any business could borrow for investment and make a profit.

The banks gambled, sinking their funds into highly speculative and risky ventures that promised fantastic rates of return. The foreign exchange market was one prime area of such speculation. Unfortunately, the gambles did not always pay off. In November 1992, the Central Bank of Nigeria declared

46 banks "insolvent." Alhaji Abdulkadir Ahmed, the CBN governor, "pin-pointed huge debts that are doubtful or bad, fraud and forgeries, boardroom quarrels and inept management" (*West Africa,* Feb 1–7, 1993; p.148). The governor explained further that:

> Most Nigerian banks, especially the state-owned ones, have poor loan portfolios—for state government-owned commercial banks, the proportion of classified loans (bad and doubtful) was 66.3 percent in 1991; while the proportion of privately-owned banks was 32 percent, and for merchant banks (all privately owned) the classified loan portfolio was only 27 percent. (*West Africa,* Feb 1–7, 1993; p.148)

Fraud soon started to threaten the integrity and stability of the banking system. Between 1988 and 1990, fraud cases rose 800 percent. In 1991, for example, a total of N360.2 million was lost. Of this, the loss to privately owned commercial banks was N25.5 million and N28.3 million for merchant banks. The bulk was incurred by state-owned banks. In May 1993, the CBN took over the management of five state-owned banks: African Continental Bank, Cooperative & Commerce Bank, Mercantile Bank of Nigeria, New Nigeria Bank, and Pan-African Bank. In January 1994, the CBN revoked the operational licenses of two banks (Financial Merchant Bank and Kapital Merchant Bank) for "total erosion of their capital bases and dissipation of the depositors' funds" (*African Business,* May 1994; p.31). Three weeks later, the Republican Bank Limited and Broad Bank of Nigeria Limited were suspended. But few of the fraudsters were prosecuted, as most had fled the country.

By January 1988, Nigeria's structural adjustment program had stalled. The banking system was in total disarray. Financial controls were either non-existent or hopelessly ineffective. The money supply registered a staggering 43.9 percent growth, against a ceiling of 15 percent. The rate of inflation accelerated to 45 percent in March 1989, compared to 25 percent in 1988.

To bring sanity into the banking system, both the government and the CBN resorted to desperate ad hoc measures to mop up excess liquidity. On April 5, 1989, the CBN issued a directive that the commercial and merchant banks should, within 21 days, recall all loans and advances with offshore guarantees and collaterals, since such loans were guaranteed with foreign exchange that should have been repatriated. About N1.03 billion (or $144 million) was involved. The directive sent panic in the banking system. Nineteen banks could not comply with the 21-day ultimatum.[5]

In May 1989, the government followed CBN action by ordering all government agencies to withdraw their funds from commercial and merchant banks and other nonbank financial institutions. This order "spread fears that some banks were about to collapse" (*African Business*, Oct 1989; p.25). Panic set in, triggering a run on the banks. Though the Nigerian Deposit Insurance Corporation was established in 1988 to protect depositors against bank failures, only it only covered N5,000, exposing large depositors to bank failures. "One notable multimillionaire caused panic when he gave his bank the mandatory seven days' notice to withdraw his N200 million" (*African Business*, Oct 1989; p.25).

On May 11, 1989, CBN bellowed out another directive: a 36-hour ultimatum, ordering all banks to render returns of all their foreign exchange transactions. Borrowers who had obtained credit on the guarantee that they had funds offshore suddenly found themselves having to sell off their foreign currency on the parallel market. This swelled the vaults of the banks with about N2 billion. CBN then raised the cash-reserve ratio. But the banks found a loophole by trading through nonbank financial institutions.

Consequently, 13 days later, on May 24, CBN issued yet another directive that prohibited all nonbank financial institutions from granting loans backed by foreign currency or foreign guarantees. This was followed by yet another directive on May 28: that all government ministries, agencies and corporations should withdraw their accounts—worth an estimated N6.5 billion—from the commercial and merchant banks and deposit them with the CBN. But soon after the directives—four in a single month—the federal government released N250 million to pay increased salaries and fringe benefits, raising the budget deficit from N5.6 billion to N12 billion in 1989. Unable to keep within the guidelines of the program, Nigeria abandoned structural adjustment altogether in 1990.

The Causes of Nigeria's Banking Crisis

Three factors underpinned Nigeria's banking crisis. The first culprit was a reckless and runaway government that was accountable to no one. The second was the autocratic style of monetary policy management by the CBN, which added more confusion and panic than calm during the turbulent times. The third factor was the complete breakdown of the rule of law, or the judiciary system, which helped spawn a culture of corruption that tolerated and even condoned egregious scams.

Excess liquidity in the banking system was a constant problem. But according to Ralph Osayameh, president of the Chartered Institute of Bankers of Nigeria, "The cause of that is government expenditure" (*West Africa*, Feb 1–7, 1993; p.153). Riven with graft and corruption, Nigeria's military governments have been unable to control soaring budgetary expenditures, necessitating accommodation by a servile central bank. Lacking basic economic literacy, Nigeria's military dictators issued decrees without even the pretense of thinking through their ramifications. Policy initiatives were taken erratically and haphazardly with stubborn refusal to learn from past mistakes.

Improved revenue collection would have helped narrow deficits, but weak administrative capacity and susceptibility to graft and venality limited its prospects. Fraud pervaded customs and other revenue collection agencies. For example, in 1992, the Ministry of Petroleum could not account for some N4 billion ($1.5 billion) in crude oil sales between 1980 and 1986. The probes, "war on corruption," and the vaunted rhetoric of "accountability" by Nigeria's military rulers were all crude oil jokes. "For all the promises of probity, the military elite [has been] as corrupt as any regime that preceded it, taking kickbacks on contracts and diverting government funds" (*Financial Times*, May 22, 1992; p.6).

The Babangida regime did not account for the $10 billion in oil windfall occasioned by the Gulf War in January 1991. When the Lagos correspondent of the *Financial Times*, William Keeling, charged a misuse of this bonanza in August 1991, he was promptly deported from Nigeria with less than 24 hours notice.

According to *The Washington Post* (July 21, 1992), "corruption robs Nigeria's economy of an estimated $2 billion to $3 billion each year" (p.A16). This allegation was confirmed by a report presented by Pius Okigbo, chairman of the panel on the Reform and Reorganization of the Central Bank of Nigeria. The report, presented to Gen. Sani Abacha on September 27, 1994, noted:

> Nigeria's military rulers squandered more than $12 billion of oil revenue without proper accounting between 1988 and June 1994. The money had been placed in special accounts set up in 1988 for special projects and to receive a windfall of oil revenue from the Gulf War. But Pius Okigbo called the handling of the accounts "a gross abuse of public trust." He said $21.2 billion— more than a third of the country's total foreign debt—was spent in less than 6 years on "what could neither be adjudged genuine high priority nor truly regenerative investment. Neither the president nor the governor of the Central Bank of Nigeria account to anyone for these massive extra-budgetary expenditures." (*African News Weekly*, Oct 14, 1994; p.3)

On the expenditure side, chaos reigned. Laid-down budgetary procedures were flagrantly skirted by top government officials. Virtually every agency in the public sector was riddled with corruption. *West Africa* reported, "The Nigerian Ports Authority has failed to account for the sum of N4.6 million provided by the federal government in 1987 to pay the salary arrears of dock-workers" (July 31-Aug 6, 1989; p.1266). Chief Olu Falae, secretary to the federal military government, announced after a debt verification exercise that "over N30 billion ($4.5 billion) of Nigeria's external debt was discovered to be 'fraudulent and spurious'" (*West Africa,* Sept 25-Oct 1, 1990; p.1614).

Those at the top were themselves ignoring budgetary guidelines. For example, in 1986, Gen. Babangida signed a SAP agreement with the IMF to rein in extra-budgetary spending and escalating defense expenditures. But even before the ink on that accord had dried, he had started the formation of his own private army (called the National Guards). He ignored the agreement and showered the officers of the Armed Forces with gifts of cars worth half a billion *naira*. The military also exempted itself from belt-tightening. In July 1992, his military regime took delivery of 12 Czechoslovakian jet trainers (Aero L-39 Albatros) in a secret deal believed to be part of a larger order made in 1991 and worth more than $90 million. Earlier in 1992, Nigeria had taken delivery of 80 British Vickers Mark 3 tanks, worth more than $225 million.

Their military posture notwithstanding, Nigeria's governments bowed to political pressure to increase public spending. In 1988, for example, a reflationary budget was introduced after demonstrations and riots in opposition to austerity. That budget raised the minimum wage, unfroze wages in the civil service, and removed the ban on civil service recruitment. In addition, it included such new expenditures as transit subsidies, meal subsidies, and training for civil servants, increasing total spending by more than 30 percent. Outside the public sector, rent-seeking interest groups agitated to undermine reform. For example, the Manufacturers Association of Nigeria demanded greater protection against imports, and large agricultural interests sought an increase in the number of items under import ban.

Heavy outlays were made on grandiose investment projects with little economic viability. Among them is the Ajaokuta Steel Plant, which was commissioned in 1979 and has cost more than $3 billion so far but is not yet fully operational. Another is the Aluminium Smelter Project at Ikot Abasi at a cost of $1.2 billion—60 percent more costly than a comparable project elsewhere in the world.

On the external front, the government's inability to sterilize oil revenue swings caused wide fluctuations in the money base. Uncertainty about its own faith in market reform led the government to establish a two-tier foreign exchange system in 1986. The official rate for the *naira* was fixed at the foreign exchange market (FEM), while the autonomous market was allowed to operate freely. The autonomous market was established to encourage those holding overseas accounts and non-oil export proceeds to repatriate their hard currency. But the two-tier system created its own problems.

As the overseas funds started to flow back, banks saw an opportunity for profit by charging foreign currency applicants higher autonomous rates, rather than the FEM rate. Also, the two-tier system created a lucrative opportunity for "round-tripping" or arbitrage: purchasing foreign exchange at the lower FEM rate and selling it at the higher autonomous rate. Even government agencies participated in this. In September 1988, the government reacted by banning "About 223 firms suspected of speculative bidding and other malpractices on the FEM and ordering all government establishments out of the autonomous market altogether" (*African Business*, March 1989; p.19). In December 1988, 132 more firms were banned from FEM participation, but most of them were the same government establishments that had been ordered out of the autonomous market.

According to Dr. Kalu Idika Kalu, a former finance minister,

> The mistake of 1986 when Babangida chose the Second-tier Foreign Exchange Market (SFEM), was that he chose a method of exchange-rate adjustment meant for the advanced countries whose entire economic system moves, whereas in developing countries, there are supply constraints which cannot adjust to instantaneous adjustment. And having chosen the wrong policy, Nigeria compounded her problem by saying that we didn't need the IMF loan. By so doing, we rejected the funding we needed to cushion the pressure of the chosen policy. This led to a total disregard for the law of supply and demand and invariably also created an incentive for massive corruption in the system and arbitrage in the banks. (*African Business*, January 1994; p.14)

One expects a government to learn from the blunders of its predecessors as well as the mistakes of other countries. But the remarkable characteristic of Nigeria's military rulers was their unyielding propensity to repeat not only their own blunders, but those of others as well.

Currency Changes

A new currency may be introduced by a government to facilitate exchange and the handling of everyday transactions. For example, if thousands or millions of the "old currency" are required to purchase an everyday item, such as bread, a "new currency," a unit of which exchanges for, say, 1,000 of the old units, would drastically reduce the amount of bills needed to be carried for daily transactions. And if this is the sole purpose of the change, then the old currency should never be demonetized and should continue to circulate until it is all withdrawn from circulation. But this was not the purpose for which the changeovers in Ghana and Nigeria were intended.

In February 1982, the military government of Ghana (the Provisional National Defense Council—PNDC) demonetized the 50-*cedi* note. (Ghana has meddled with its currency more than four times since independence in 1957). The public was asked to deposit these notes in their banks in return for chits that were supposed to be redeemed later but that never were. Ghana shut its borders for two years. The official reasons were: to mop up excess liquidity in the system, to crack down on tax evasion, to punish corrupt politicians, and to render useless large amounts of the currency circulating outside the country. Additionally, the exercise was intended to crush currency smuggling and thereby shore up the external value of the currency. The government insisted that "the withdrawal of the 50 cedi note was not against the poor or the genuine rich but rather it was meant to withdraw excess liquidity in the hands of a few greedy and corrupt businessmen" (*Daily Graphic,* Feb 24, 1982; p.1).

The other official reason for the currency change was to reduce excess liquidity in the banking system and ease inflationary pressures. But this was criminally dishonest. Borrowing from the central bank to finance soaring budget deficits has been the primary source of excess liquidity. Even Ghana's own 1978–79 budget statement admitted that "over the past 5 years, more than 70 percent of every budget has been financed by the Bank of Ghana, resulting in the injection of substantial amounts of money into the economy" (p.2; paragraph 6).

On February 13, 1982, exactly one day after the deadline for the deposit of the demonetized 50-*cedi* notes in Ghanaian banks, the PNDC announced that those whose bank balances exceeded 50,000 *cedis* would be subject to investigative probes to determine their compliance with tax obligations. In one stroke, this inane policy shattered confidence in the currency and dealt a devastating blow to the banking system, from which it is yet to recover.

Exactly the same phenomena were observed with Nigeria's currency change in 1984. The official reason was that "there was too much money in circulation" (*West Africa,* May 28, 1984; p.1106). Nigeria's Central Bank director of domestic operations at the time, Chief Nwagu, argued that the change was necessary to demonetize the N2 billion illegally acquired by corrupt politicians and held outside the country (*West Africa,* May 28, 1984; p.1107). But the fact of the matter is, when corrupt politicians rape and plunder their country, they take the booty out in foreign exchange, not in *naira.*[6]

When Nigerians deposited their old currency to exchange for the new one, "persons who had deposited up to N5,000 were informed they would have to produce their tax clearance certificates, showing that they paid their taxes over the last 3 years, before they could be allowed to withdraw any money" (*West Africa,* May 28, 1984; p.1108).

Nigeria's military government of Maj-Gen. Muhammadu Buhari changed the currency and sealed the country's borders, ostensibly to "catch big-time hoarders who had tucked money away overseas" (*West Africa,* May 28, 1984; p.1108). Nigeria reopened its borders in March 1986 after two years of closure.

Few economists would impugn the seriousness of the excess liquidity, tax evasion, corruption, and currency smuggling problems in Africa. But to attempt a resolution of these problems through currency changes was totally misguided. But then again, this was typical of military regimes, which resort to the "bazooka approach" in solving problems they do not understand.

Currency changes inflict an incalculable damage on the economy and suffer from three fundamental defects. First, they undermine confidence in the currency, both domestically and internationally, and wreak havoc with the banking system, thereby impairing the economy's capacity to develop. Second, currency change is the wrong solution to the problems of excess cash liquidity, tax evasion, corruption, etc. Third, currency changes are fraudulent; they often rob the innocent and illiterate masses of cash balances they have worked hard to accumulate legitimately.

The entire monetary system operates largely by confidence. The public keep their savings at banks upon the assumption that the safety and confidentiality of their deposit is assured. The whole banking and monetary structure would collapse if this assurance cannot be guaranteed and confidence in the currency is destroyed. Confidence in a currency enables money to serve its primary functions of medium of exchange and store of value. We use money because we are confident it will be accepted as a means of payment. We also keep our savings in money form because we are confident money will hold its value (store of value) for future use. The use of money is indispensable to a growing economy. Money facilitates exchange, trade, specialization, and promotes economic growth. Commenting on Mexico's peso crisis, Paul Gigot wrote: "A currency is a contract between the government and its people. When government betrays that contract, trust goes to zero. Especially if a government compounds the problem by printing more money or imposing wage and price controls" (*The Wall Street Journal,* Jan 13, 1995; p.A14).

If people have no faith in the currency, they would either rid themselves of the "unwanted" currency by spending it on physical assets (land, houses, durable commodities, etc.), thereby adding to inflationary pressures, or exchange it for foreign currencies, which would lead to a depreciation of its value. To understand this, imagine a situation where confidence in the *cedi* or the *naira* is so weak that Ghanaians and Nigerians keep their savings in the form of cars, cows, and goats. Such savings cannot be put to a productive economic use. In other words, they cannot be lent to business for investment to generate economic growth.

Suppose, on the other hand, that we keep our savings in money balances and deposit them at the banks. The banks keep a small fraction (say 20 percent) of our deposits in actual cash reserves in their vaults and lend the rest to business to finance industrial projects, create jobs, and accelerate economic development. Thus, the banks play a fundamental role in the economic development process. Technically called "financial intermediation," the process whereby banks collect small savings and lend them to business and government for investment purposes is crucial to rapid economic development.

This whole financial intermediation process operates by confidence. We, the public, keep our savings in the banks because of the confidence we have about their safety. If for some reason this confidence is destroyed or safety is threatened and we were to rush to the banks all at once to withdraw our money, the banks will not have sufficient cash to satisfy the massive withdrawals. Such a run on the banks will invariably spell bank failures, business failures, and general economic disaster. The Great Depression of 1933 in the United States was triggered by bank failure.

Banks cannot lend to business to invest if they do not have deposits from the public, and the public will not keep bank deposits if they are uncertain about their safety. If people have little confidence about the safety of their bank deposits, they will put their savings in socks, under mattresses, or in some other concealed place. If people have little confidence in the currency itself, they will rid themselves of it and keep their savings in physical assets such as houses, durable commodities that have high resale value, and foreign currencies. These are irrefutable elementary facts of monetary economics. They were observed in Germany after World War I, producing the notorious German hyperinflation. They were also observed in Brazil and Argentina in the mid-1990s.

Public Reaction

Currency changes invariably lead to some destabilizing speculations. Illiterates, despite their lack of formal education, are no simpletons. In Ghana, when "the news of the exercise (50 *cedi* note demonetization) leaked out, many people in Accra and other parts of the country went on shopping sprees, before the Feb 12, 1982 deadline to get rid of their notes" (*West Africa,* Feb 22, 1982; p.536). The demonetization of the 50 *cedi* notes also prompted speculation that the 20 *cedi* note would be next and some traders even refused to accept the 20 *cedi* notes (*Graphic,* Feb 12, 1982; p.4).

Such speculation and loss of confidence in the currency drove people to hold physical assets and foreign currencies. In Ghana, there was an added impetus because of the odious tax probes of individuals whose bank balances exceed 50,000 *cedis.* Who on earth would deposit more than these amounts in a bank and invite a tax audit? The public reacted by shunning the banking system and conducting business strictly on a cash basis. *The Mirror* reported "a sharp drop in the amount of money paid by the public into the various banks" (Jan 22, 1982; p.1). In response, the government ordered that "businesses are to be transacted in checks, not cash" (*Graphic,* May 27, 1982; p.1). Loss of confidence in the *cedi* and the subsequent flight from the currency drove Ghanaians to hold, among other things, foreign currencies, which they could only obtain at the black market. The results were soaring black market rates, which meant declining external value of the *cedi*—a result clearly opposite to what the demonetization exercise was intended to achieve, namely, shoring up the external value of the *cedi.* Within one year, the black market rate jumped from 40 *cedis* to 100 *cedis* to the dollar.

Each time an African holds a dollar or a pound, he/she renders an economic service to the American or the British economy. People all over the world hold dollars or pounds because of the confidence they have in the notes. One can take a 1910 U.S. dollar to the Federal Reserve and will be given exactly one modern dollar. Even some 1925 U.S. dollars, redeemable in gold, are still circulating in the United States, though the United States is no longer on the gold standard. To take this to the extreme, one can bury dollars or pounds, dig them up 50 years later, and still be able to use them. Could one use 1960 *cedi* or *naira* in their respective countries today? Even Lenin, a communist, displayed a remarkable understanding of this confidence factor when he remarked that the best way to wreck a capitalist system is to debauch its currency.

The second major criticism of currency changes is that they are the wrong solutions to the problems of excess cash liquidity, tax evasion, and corruption. Too much currency in circulation is the result of overissue in the past. Only the Bank of Ghana and the Bank of Nigeria, under orders from their respective governments, issue currency. Responsibility should be placed squarely where it belongs.

Under the gold standard, a central bank could only issue more currency after acquiring more gold. Similarly, when both Ghana and Nigeria were part of the British West African currency system in the 1950s, the two countries could issue more currency only after obtaining more pounds sterling or other foreign currencies. Today, with all African countries off the gold standard and out of the British West Africa Currency Board system, reserve assets used to back currencies are gold special drawing rights (SDRs), foreign exchange, and government securities.

In Ghana, government securities provide a whopping 85 percent backing of the *cedi*, while gold, SDRs, and foreign exchange provide only a tiny 6.7 percent. These securities were issued by the government of Ghana as a means of borrowing from the Bank of Ghana to finance gargantuan budget deficits. Here is how the system works:

Suppose the government of Ghana runs a deficit of 100 billion *cedis*. To borrow to finance this deficit, it issues government bonds for 100 billion *cedis,* which it sells to the central bank (Bank of Ghana). To pay for the these bonds, the bank literally goes to its basement and prints 100 billion crisp new *cedi* notes, which enter into circulation as soon as they are spent by the government.

Borrowing from the central bank to finance budget deficits has been the source of excess liquidity in Africa. The central banks, really extensions of their various respective African governments, have always stood ready to print the extra currency needed to finance huge budget deficits—a fact that Ghanaian governments themselves admitted. So how does a currency change solve that fundamental deficit problem?

A currency change is really an attempt to fool the public: to shift responsibility away from the government and blame corrupt politicians and greedy businessmen for too much money in circulation when it was the central bank itself that overissued the currency in the first place. If there is too much money in circulation the obvious solutions are to reduce those budget deficits and redeem part of the government securities held by the central bank; that is, repay a part of the government debt to the central bank.

More outrageous, especially in the Nigerian case, was the presumption that the large sums of *naira* abroad were illegally taken there by corrupt politicians and avaricious businessmen. The fact of the matter is, when corrupt politicians, or the elites generally, rape and plunder their countries, they take their booty out in foreign exchange, not in *cedis* or *nairas.* Those who take *cedis* or *nairas* out of the country are generally illiterate traders and migrant workers. These market traders have no access to foreign exchange at the central bank and therefore use whatever currency that is acceptable, *cedis, nairas* or *francs,* to trade along the West African coast. Migrant workers also repatriate some of their savings in *cedi* or *naira* form to their respective home countries. Now, what have these traders and workers got to do with corruption in government or excess cash liquidity so that a currency change is necessary to dispossess them of the *cedis* or *nairas* they have toiled to accumulate? It amounts to robbery.

Currency trafficking cannot be halted by currency changes. The only way to stop currency trafficking is seal off the borders completely, because whenever individuals cross borders, they do so with money and goods. Sealing off the borders not only contravenes stipulations of the Economic Community of West African States (ECOWAS) for free movement of people and goods but also flies in the face of African traditions. Before the continent was colonized, there were free trade routes criss-crossing Africa. These trade routes were indispensable in making a variety of goods available to Africans.

Ghana learned a painful lesson when she closed her borders in September 1982. Market traders, who were rather naively castigated as profiteers and hoarders, performed a vital service to the economy by buying *naira* on the black market, and traveling to Nigeria to buy scarce commodities to bring back to Ghana. It was an invaluable service because the government of Ghana could not provide the goods. When the borders were closed, this trading activity ceased and the markets became empty, accentuating an already precarious shortage situation.

It should also be remembered that currency regulations permit citizens to take an amount of their local currencies out of the country. In Ghana, this used to be 4,200 *cedis*. Why should anyone who legally took this amount out be dispossessed by a currency change?

The absurdity of this all lies in the fact that the amount of a nation's currency circulating outside its borders is directly correlated with the degree of confidence foreigners have in that currency. The important point is, currency outside the country is not available to raise purchasing power domestically. The economic advantage enjoyed by the United States or Britain, for example, is that they can increase their currency issue, but part of this increase will flow out of the country into the hands of foreigners; not all that increase in the money supply remains in their countries to wreak inflationary damage.

Until the *naira* was changed, Nigeria enjoyed this enviable position because the *naira* was almost an "international currency" in West Africa. This status provided an outlet for excess *naira* to safely leave the country. By changing the *naira* and effectively shattering foreign confidence in it, this outlet became closed. Thus, any further overissue of the *naira* to support budget deficits will remain in Nigeria and unleash its fullest inflationary havoc. In both countries, loss of confidence and flight from the currency also drove people to hold foreign currencies, which they could only obtain on the black market.

Finally, a currency change imposes unnecessary, unfair, and exorbitant costs on both the illiterate masses and the country at large. Many illiterate rural folks had toiled all their lives to legitimately accumulate life savings, which they stashed away under mats, in jars, closets, etc. Where they keep their savings is their own prerogative. The government cannot force them to keep their savings in banks; neither can the government force anyone to hold a currency he/she does not want. Civilians are persuaded to do things, not forced or ordered—a fact that is not understood by African military governments. Many of these rural folks have to search for their savings and trek miles to the nearest bank in highly inaccessible regions of the country to exchange their money. Missing the deadline meant a whole life savings gone down the river. Indeed, this was exactly the case in certain parts of Ghana: "Large bundles of ¢50 notes were found thrown into the River Aboabo in Kumasi. According to a Ghana Broadcasting Corporation correspondent, several others were also thrown away near the Kumasi railway station" (*West Africa*, March 1, 1982; p.618).

The country also paid dearly because of poor timing and ineptitude. Before the currency was changed, Ghana had paid Thomas de La Rue of London £1,266,210 to print 119 million additional *cedi* notes of the "old" currency. "The currency change therefore meant that the ¢119 million newly-printed notes were worthless and were destroyed on orders of the SMC II" (*Ghanaian Times*, Nov 12, 1981; p.3).

Ghana's banking system has yet to recover from the 1982 economic inanity. After this misguided currency change, Ghanaians continued to shun the banking system, leading to large amounts of cash being held outside the system. What fool was going to put his money in a bank and invite a tax audit? *West Africa* magazine stressed exactly the same point in its May 8–14, 1995 issue:

> "No sense putting money in the bank," says Hilal El-Jamal. "Dig a hole and bury it, or better, build something with it."
>
> Some economists estimate that 50 percent of Ghana's currency is lying idle, tucked away somewhere or sunk into partially completed building. For the individual, it is a good investment. For the country it is disastrous . . .
>
> "That is what makes the economy worse," says home appliance dealer Hussein Bakri. "Everybody is hiding their money or using it to build houses. Ghana imports rice, can you believe it? And refined sugar, too." (p.718)

Consequently, when cocoa farmers presented their government-issued "Akuafo Checks" (Farmers' Checks) to the banks for payment, the banks had no money. In an irate editorial, the state-owned *Ghanaian Times* (Jan 5, 1995) berated:

An aged farmer of a village near Offinso, Ashanti, collapsed while in a queue at a bank to cash her "Akuafo Check." She was rushed to a hospital. According to the Ghana News Agency report, the farmer had been in the queue every successive day at the bank for two weeks up to the day of her collapse without succeeding in cashing her check. She accused the bank staff of serving only favorites, who are those ready to offer bribes. Farmers in other cocoa growing areas complained bitterly of similar experiences. Some of them journey every day for up to three weeks before succeeding to cash even 200,000 *cedis* (or $200). The period of waiting is short for those who can pay bribes. One eye witness account said that a farmer had to haul a big sheep to the house of the bank manager to get his check cashed the next day. The bank branches that indulge in this disrespectful and insulting treatment of cocoa farmers are said to give the excuse that moneys for the Akuafo Checks are dispatched to them in insufficient quantities and late. (p.2)

Cocoa farmers, cheated or frustrated in their attempts to cash their government checks, reacted by abandoning the production of cocoa, the export of which provides the country with 50 percent of its foreign exchange. Such a decline in cocoa exports can be traced to an insane monetary exercise undertaken in 1982 when the government pried into the bank accounts of private individuals. In fact, in the same issue of *The Ghanaian Times* (Jan 5, 1995), Jacob Frimpong hit the nail on the head: "The practice in the past where private accounts were forcibly revealed to the public should be discouraged" (p.5). I say not discouraged but outlawed. Only then would the public have sufficient trust in the confidentiality of bank accounts for them to deposit moneys in the banking system, which in turn would provide the banks with the cash needed to pay cocoa farmers.

Like their Ghanaian counterparts, the Nigerian public reacted by shunning the banking system. Rather than deposit their savings at banks, "Several people went on spending sprees, buying among other things, cars, airline tickets, anything that could later be sold" (*West Africa,* May 24, 1984; p.1106). Why should Nigerians keep their savings in commercial banks? To survive, the banks had to offer fantastic rates to attract depositors and invest in highly speculative ventures. Many did not make it. In November 1992, the Central Bank of Nigeria declared 46 banks as "insolvent." By September 1, 1993, literally all the commercial banks in Nigeria were unable to meet their obligations to customers. "Depositors were in most cases not allowed to withdraw amounts in excess of N1,000 (in some cases, even less), irrespective of their credit balances" (*African Business,* Oct 1993; p.17). The banking system nearly collapsed.

Nigerians chose to keep their money balances outside the country, although crooks and corrupt politicians engaged in flight of capital. The Morgan Guaranty Trust Company estimated that Nigeria's foreign debt of $32 billion would have been only $7 billion had there been no capital flight (*Business Week,* April 21, 1986; p.14). Capital flight accelerated in the 1980s as policy zigzags further undermined confidence in the banking system. By 1990, as the Lagos National Concord (Aug 16, 1990) reported, the staggering sum of $32 billion owned by Nigerians in foreign bank accounts was equivalent to Nigeria's huge foreign debt. A year earlier (in April 1989) the Christian Association of Nigeria had revealed that more than 3,000 Nigerians held Swiss bank accounts and that Nigerians were near the top of the list of Third World patrons of Swiss banks (*West Africa,* April 10–16, 1989; p.570). As a result, commercial banks in Nigeria still have difficulty attracting deposits and have to offer fantastic rates for short-term deposits—six months or less.

In both countries, the changeover produced a loss of confidence and flight from the currency. The black market rates of exchange soared. If Nigeria's military thugs did not learn from Ghana's blunder did they learn from their own mistakes? Emphatically no! In August 1987, Gen. Babangida limited debt-service ratio at 30 percent of export revenue, sending foreign investors scampering for cover. On March 5, 1992, the foreign exchange market was deregulated but in December, trading was suspended for about a week to probe irregularities. Foreign exchange controls were reimposed in October 1993 when Gen. Sani Abacha seized power. Believing in the power of the gun rather than the market, he fixed the value of the naira at N22 to the dollar. Interest rates were also pegged, stifling bank profitability and sending several banks to the brink of financial collapse. In January 1995, Gen. Abacha reintroduced the second-tier system, leaving the official rate fixed at N22 to the dollar while the rate on the parallel (autonomous) market was N80. Nothing, it seemed, had been learned.

Admittedly, policy acrobatics by the federal government did not create an environment conducive to sound monetary management. Further, the CBN did not have much room for independent action when there was a gun trained on its head. However, the CBN exacerbated the banking crisis with its own autocratic style of management, by issuing last-minute directives with little consultation with bankers and demanding compliance within unreasonable time-frames. This cavalier style of management did little to calm the banking public and in fact aggravated panic situations. For example, in April 1993, CBN yanked a whopping N33 billion ($1.31 billion) from the vaults of the banks. Before banks could recover from the cash squeeze, CBN introduced Open Market Operations, selling N250 million in treasury bills. But in late August, CBN reversed itself and "released N1.5 billion in the form of loans to bail out 14 banks which were adversely affected by the withdrawal of government funds from the banks" (*African Business*, Oct 1989; p.26). But "By Sept 1, 1993, literally all the banks were unable to meet their obligations to customers. Depositors were in most cases not allowed to withdraw amounts in excess of N1,000 (in some cases, even less), irrespective of their credit balances" (*African Business*, Oct 1993; p.17).

Above all, however, discipline must be restored in the public sector and the rule of law enforced. Almost every public official in Nigeria is on the take. Says Anthony Ebeh in *African News Weekly* (May 27, 1994):

> A major cause of our problems in Nigeria is that our leaders have a primitive concept of public office. Public office in civilized societies, including some non-Western nations, is seen as a way to provide selfless service to one's nation. It is a way to give back to one's country. Public office is cherished and respected. Public office holders are generally accountable to the people they serve. However, in the Nigerian context, public office is seen as a huge opportunity to enrich self and kindred. This explains why Nigeria is now one of the poorest nations in the world. In Nigeria, public office is seen as a means to acquire wealth and personal aggrandizement. By all standards, this concept of public office is primitive. (p.7)

In Francophone Africa, there has been relative price stability because the central bank is independent of the central government although, it should be noted, the central bank is tied to the French monetary system. Consequently, this region has performed better economically than the rest of Africa. Perhaps not only should the independence of central banks be enshrined in all African constitutions but also the governors of central banks should be rotated within various regions in Africa. For example, governors of the ECOWAS countries (West Africa) may be rotated with, say, the Ghanaian governor serving a five-year term at the central bank of Nigeria and the Nigerian governor serving the same term in Sierra Leone or vice versa. Such rotation would remove the governors from coming under undue political pressure to print money to accommodate profligate government spending.

AFRICA'S FOREIGN DEBT CRISIS

Total African foreign debt rose 24-fold since 1970 to a staggering $350 billion in 2002, which was equal to its yearly GNP, making the region the most heavily indebted in the world. (Latin America's debt amounted to approximately 60 percent of its GNP.) Currently debt service obligations absorb about 40 percent of export revenue, leaving scant foreign exchange for the importation of capital goods, essential spare parts, and medical supplies.

Only about half of the outstanding debts are actually being paid, while on the other half arrears are continually being rescheduled.

A large chunk of Africa's foreign debt—about 80 percent—is owed to Western governments and multilateral financial and development institutions such as the World Bank, the IMF, and the UNDP. The loans were extended to African governments under various foreign aid programs at concessional rates (below market interest rates with a grace period and a longer term to maturity) to finance development projects and to fund structural adjustment (economic restructuring) and democratization programs in Africa. The general consensus among African development analysts is that foreign aid to Africa has not been effective. All that aid failed to spur economic growth, arrest Africa's economic atrophy, or promote democracy. The continent is littered with a multitude of "black elephants" (basilicas, grandiose monuments, grand conference halls, and show airports) amid institutional decay, crumbling infrastructure, and environmental degradation. Further, structural adjustment loans from the World Bank and the IMF made little impact on poverty reduction in Africa. The World Bank's own 1994 Report, *Adjustment Lending in Africa,* confirmed this. The bank evaluated the performance of 29 African countries for which it had provided more than $20 billion in funding to sponsor structural adjustment programs over a ten-year period, 1981–1991, and concluded that only six African countries had performed well: The Gambia, Burkina Faso, Ghana, Nigeria, Tanzania, and Zimbabwe, giving a failure rate in excess of 80 percent. The bank's "phantom list" of economic success stories, however, kept shrinking or evaporating. As noted in chapter 1, by 2001, the old success stories had expired and the World Bank was trotting out new ones: Benin, Botswana, Madagascar, Mali, Mauritius, Mozambique, and Uganda.

Mistakes on Both Sides

Regarding foreign borrowing by African governments, it is generally agreed that mistakes were made on both the donor and recipient sides, as we saw in chapter 5. First, on the donor side, the allocation of foreign aid was often determined more by ideological considerations: To support cold war allies such as Mobutu Sese Seko of Zaire, General Samuel Doe of Liberia, and General Siad Barre of Somalia; and to woo various Marxist leaders from the Soviet bloc—for example, Flt./Lte. Jerry Rawlings of Ghana, Joaquim Chissano of Mozambique, and Jose Eduardo dos Santos of Angola. Second, much Western aid to Africa was tied—that is, requiring a certain percentage to be spent in the donor country. For example, 80 percent of U.S. aid is spent on American contractors, subcontractors, goods, and services. Chinese aid is nearly 100 percent tied. This common practice of tying aid, however, reduces its effectiveness as it unnecessarily restricts the ability of the recipient to purchase goods from sources that may be cheaper than the donor's. Third, Western governments and development agencies failed to exercise prudence in the grant of aid and loans to African governments. Much Western aid to Africa was used to finance grandiose projects of little economic value and to underwrite economically ruinous policies. Fourth, foreign aid allocations were often cocooned in bureaucratic red tape and shrouded in secrecy. The programs lacked transparency and the people being helped were seldom consulted. More maddening, the West *knew* that billions of dollars were being transferred to Swiss and foreign banks by greedy African leaders and elites. Yet, the West continued to pump in more aid and credits, knowing full well that much of it would be stolen and end up in overseas bank accounts, while the rest would be used to buttress the repressive capacity of the tyrant in power or extend a lifeline to his incompetent regime. It would be naive to pretend that foreign credit institutions knew nothing about the rampant corruption in recipient countries. As *The Wall Street Journal* (July 14, 1998) reported in the case of Indonesia:

> World Bank officials knew corruption in bank-funded projects was common but never commissioned any broad reports tracking how much was lost to it—in part, some bank officials say, because they feared having to confront the Suharto government.
>
> Not only did the World Bank lend money and credibility to Gen. Suharto, but critics say, it tolerated and in some ways may have inadvertently stoked the corruption and economically corrosive practices that increasingly characterized the Suharto regime until its collapse. (p.A1)

Fifth and finally, SAPs or adjustment lending failed because of design flaws, sequencing, pedagogical inanities, and other factors. The commitment to reform has demonstrably been weak in Africa. Even when reform—both economic and political—is accepted, it is poorly implemented. While implementation problems cannot be blamed on the World Bank or the donors, the programs sponsored by the donors were themselves fraught with design flaws. In many cases, SAPs amounted to reorganizing a bankrupt company and placing it, together with a massive infusion of new loans or capital, in the hands of the same incompetent managers who ruined it in the first place. Additionally, SAPs assumed development occurred in a vacuum—as if civil wars, environmental degradation, infrastructural deterioration, and a general state of terror and violence in Africa have no effect on economic development. Accordingly, the World Bank lent billions to various African countries to restructure economies that were being ravaged by civil war: Algeria, Angola, Burundi, Ethiopia, Mozambique, and others. Of course, there were blunders on the recipient side as well, as noted in chapter 5.

How An African Country Falls into Debt

An African country contracts foreign debt on two fronts: balance of payments and government budgetary finance. The balance of payment account shows accounts receivable from and payable to the rest of the world. If the country must pay the rest of the world $5 billion *more than* the rest of the world owes the country, it is said to have a $5 billion balance of payments deficit. The balance of trade, on the other hand, is simply the difference between merchandise imports and exports. If *"invisibles"*—principally services such as tourism, transportation costs (airline charges) and insurance—are added, then the trade balance becomes the current account balance.[7] Adding the *capital account* makes it the balance of payment. Thus,

Merchandise or Visible Trade Balance = Exports − Imports
Current Account = Visible Trade + Invisibles
Balance of Payments = Current Account + Capital Account

Now consider the balance of payments accounts for Africa in 1998.

Table 7.5   Africa's Balance of Payments, 1998

Accounts Receivables	
Foreign Aid from all sources	$17.0 billion
Total Exports (Merchandise and Services)	$157.7 billion
Net Foreign Investment	$6.3 billion
Private Transfers	$9.1 billion
Total	$190.1 billion
Accounts Payable	
Total Imports (Merchandise and Services)	$184.6 billion
Total External Debt Service payments	$23.4 billion
Total	$208.0 billion
Balance of Payment Deficit	$17.9 billion

Source: *African Development Indicators*, 2000, Washington, D.C.: World Bank, 2000.

The difference between the two creates a balance of payment deficit of $17.9 billion, which means Africa owes the rest of the world $17.9 billion more than the rest of the world owes Africa.If Africa has no foreign exchange reserves, which is often the case, then it must borrow $17.9 billion to cover the shortfall; that is, incur a $17.9 billion debt. To correct this, Africa must earn more abroad (increase export revenue, attract more foreign investment and remittances from African expatriates) or reduce its imports.

African governments claim they cannot earn more from exports because of declining terms of trade, Western agricultural subsidies, and trade barriers. As we shall show in the next chapter, this argument has little validity. The *physical volume* of exports has been declining and therefore it is not a question of Africa not being able to earn enough because of low prices. Burundi's coffee exports, Ivory Coast's cocoa exports, and Sierra Leone's diamond exports have been devastated not because of low world market prices but by senseless civil wars.

Greater opportunities exist in reducing imports, and if one looks closely at the composition of imports, one finds such a range of items as Mercedes Benzes, weapons, and food imports. In 1998, for example, Africa spent $15 billion on food imports and another $15 billion on the import of arms and the maintenance of the military. Obviously, if Africa could feed itself, it wouldn't need to import food and the balance of payment deficit would be only $2.9 billion. And would Africa's military dictators cut back on arms imports and the military?

The second area where foreign debt is incurred is in budgetary finance. It should be noted that the two areas may overlap. For example, imports of weapons and arms are often part of government budgetary expenditures. But it is best to keep the two areas separate in our analysis of them here.

Again, if African governments have no reserves, they beseech Western donors for aid to cover the deficit. About 40 percent of Ghana's budget is financed by foreign aid and 55 percent of Uganda's. If African governments do not receive what they asked for, they simply print money to finance the budget deficit, which brings in its wake inflationary consequences as discussed earlier in this chapter.

The fact of the matter is, no government or nation can forever spend beyond its means. Nor can it borrow forever to cover a budget shortfall. If it badgers foreign creditors every year for a loan, eventually the creditors will lay down conditions before they grant further loans because they want to ensure that past loans are repaid. The so-called conditionalities are designed to ensure that the government lives within its means, which means balancing its budget by trimming its expenditures or raising more revenue. It is precisely here that all the polemics about structural adjustment, foreign aid conditionalities, and debt relief arise, because conditionalities are demanded by the World Bank, IMF, Western governments, and creditors.

The World Bank, IMF, and Western governments are demonized for making outrageous demands on poor African countries. Charges of "neocolonial interference" are hurled by African leaders. According to *New African* (Dec 2001), "Rawlings openly said that the IMF and the World Bank compounded his problems in office and were responsible for some of the economic and other difficulties facing the country" (p.14). For his part, President Sam Nujoma of Namibia dismissed the IMF and the World Bank as "the imperialists' well-organized machinery to get Africa's cheap labor and raw materials for their economic development" (*The Economist*, Jan 17, 2004; Survey, p.16).

This highly charged emotional rhetoric is rather puerile and diverts attention from the real issue: The elimination of massive budget deficits. *Any* student of economics would acknowledge that a government cannot forever produce deficits and finance them by printing money. Budget deficits can be eliminated by curtailing government spending, raising taxes, or doing both.[8] Colonial exploitation, neocolonial machinations, or solar eclipses have nothing to do with African governments living beyond their means. But the moment the World Bank enters the discussion and suggests cutbacks in government spending, common sense flies out of the window and the whole issue becomes politicized. If African governments abhor World Bank conditionalities then they should go elsewhere for loans. After all, the World Bank is not the only place where they can borrow money.

This is not to defend the World Bank, which has its own problems and blunders. But a further look at the composition of government expenditures reveals a bloated, inefficient, and wasteful public sector; corruption; huge subsidies to unprofitable state enterprises; and soaring expenditures on the military and security forces—all of which add little or nothing to GDP. The World Bank or Western donors have little to do with these wastes. If African governments detest being told what to do then they should act responsibly. Wasteful government expenditures should be trimmed by selling off unprofitable state enterprises, reducing the size of the bloated government bureaucracy, placing more emphasis on the private sector, and moving toward a market economy. As we saw in chapter 6, oil-producing Nigeria, for example, cannot produce enough gasoline to meet demand because its state-owned refineries have broken down. It imports gasoline at market prices and sells it at subsidized prices to the public. The subsidies cost the Nigerian government about $2 billion annually. But gasoline imports do not alleviate the shortage because of smuggling. Gasoline in Nigeria costs only a third of the prevailing price in neighboring countries, so it is smuggled out of the country, forcing the government to import more at market rates and costing more in subsidies. This is economic lunacy.

But African governments do not wish to live within their means.[9] They refuse to cut budget expenditures. They need the swollen state bureaucracy and all the patronage it affords to buy political support. Civil servants do not want their jobs and salaries cut. If military pay is cut, the soldiers might stage a coup and overthrow the government. If Nigeria is told by outside regulators to remove price controls on gasoline and stop paying subsidies, the government might respond by saying that doing so would be too "politically sensitive" and that riots might ensure. Furthermore, they say it is hypocritical for the West to demand the removal of subsidies when the West itself pays agricultural subsidies to its farmers. Unfortunately, that is mixing apples and oranges. Western agricultural subsidies, which should be removed, must not be used by African governments to justify payment of subsidies to inefficient state-owned enterprises. Unwilling to trim government expenditures, they perform crass acrobatics on reform. If there are any cuts at all, they are made on those items that are not politically sensitive, such as road construction, health care, education, etc. because they do not have an easily organized constituency. For example, cuts in health care or education affect the poor, who have no political say and are not well-organized. But these are precisely the infrastructures needed to help Africa grow. A frustrated World Bank official then tells an African government: "If you are not willing to reduce expenditures, then raise sufficient taxes to balance your budget in order to avoid printing money to finance the deficit."

The African government agrees and proceeds to tax anything that moves. But Africans are already overtaxed. Even villagers are openly defying tax officers. Recall from chapter 2 that, in Senegal, the Loulouni district chief was thrown out of the village when he tried to collect taxes on February 2, 1995. When the chief returned with a battalion of police and paramilitary gendarmes, enraged villagers met them with clubs and hunting rifles and beat them (*African News Weekly,* March 3, 1995; p.5). In Ghana, the Rawlings regime imposed "vampire taxes" and even "latrine fees." Overtaxed, the people rebelled, staging *"Kume Preko"* ("Kill me now") demonstrations, forcing the government to rescind its decision, although a vampire tax was subsequently reintroduced.

There are several problems with raising more government revenue through taxation. First, the tax base is small. Only a small proportion of the population (the elites) work in formal sector employment and are more likely to complain if their taxes are raised or evade them. Second, and as a result, the bulk of government revenue, as table 7.6 shows, is derived from

"indirect taxes." These are taxes on commodities such as gasoline, beer, cig-
arettes, and imported commodities. The problem here is that they can be
evaded through smuggling. Goods cheaper in neighboring countries can be
brought in through porous borders. Furthermore, indirect taxes also have inflationary potential. Desperate for revenue, the Ghana government raised
gasoline prices by 100 percent in 2003. Such a huge increase would affect
transportation costs and, thus, food prices, since the cost of transporting
food from the farms to market had increased. Even after slapping on vampire taxes, latrine fees, and huge increases in the price of gasoline, they still
cannot balance the budget.

For 10 years, from 1988 to 1998, the Rawlings regime in Ghana presented to the World Bank a balanced budget. But year after year, a huge
deficit emerged at the end of the fiscal year, which required the government
to borrow more and print more money to finance it. As it turned out, the
budget figures were "cooked" to present a more favorable situation and projected revenues did not materialize because of rampant corruption—
especially in the Customs and Excise department.

Table 7.6　Africa's Budgetary Expenditures and Revenues, 1998

Budgetary Expenditures	
Current Expenditures	
Wages and Salaries	$46.0 billion
Other Goods and Services	$35.8 billion
Interest Payments	$26.2 billion
Subsidies and Transfers	$4.9 billion
Other Expenditures	$17.0 billion
Capital Expenditures	
Military Weapons and Hardware	
Development Projects	$27.7 billion
Total	$157.6 billion
Budgetary Revenues	
Taxes on Income and Profits	$41.4 billion
Taxes on International Trade and Transactions	$18.6 billion
Indirect Taxes	$54.9 billion
Non-Tax Revenue	$19.0 billion
Total	$133.9 billion
Budget Deficit	$23.7 billion

Source: *African Development Indicators*, 2000, Washington, D.C.: World Bank, 2000.

For much of the 1980s and 1990s, these sort of acrobatics and chicanery on budgetary reform took place in Africa under the very eyes of the donors. At the end of the day, no real reform occurred. The public sector remained bloated. Chronic budget deficits persisted. Structural adjustment programs failed miserably. A phantom list of economic success stories was trotted out. Ghana, for example, declared a "success story" by the World Bank in 1994, was in the highly indebted poor country (HIPC) intensive care unit six years later. The World Bank became part of this economic charade and fraud because it never caught on to the chicanery and duplicity of African leaders. It, like the Clinton administration, invested so much capital in the euphonious verbiage of African despots and allowed itself to be duped.

An African government may seek foreign aid (or economic development assistance) for three main reasons. One is for general macroeconomic stability, to reduce inflationary pressures. Another is for budgetary support, to finance a budget deficit, as we have discussed above. The third is project specific—to finance specific development projects.

Suppose, for example, Nigeria borrows $50 million from a foreign commercial bank for a project. This debt must be serviced by making an annual payment of $4 million in foreign exchange a year for 20 years, after which the principal and interest will be paid. Whatever Nigeria uses the loan for, that activity must either generate or save Nigeria at least $4 million a year in foreign exchange for the next 20 years. Otherwise, Nigeria would have to secure the foreign exchange elsewhere to service the loan.

Some projects may not earn or save the foreign exchange directly but rather enhance the country's capacity to do so. Loans taken to finance road construction, education, and medical care fall into this category. But they depend on too many factors to be productive. A road may deteriorate because of neglect. Universities may be closed because of riots. The educated may flee ("brain drain") rather than stay in the country and help it earn foreign exchange. We shall exclude these indirectly productive activities for the sake of simplicity.

Other projects may earn foreign exchange directly but may be plagued with problems. The project may cost more upon completion (cost overruns). Or it may cost less but bring in only $2 million a year. Or it may last for only six years. Or the project may not produce any revenue for five years (long gestation period). Or the loan may be misappropriated to import Mercedes Benzes. Or part of the loan proceeds may be squandered. Any of these cases could create a problem. In this case, Nigeria would have to service the debt by taking foreign currency from its current foreign exchange earnings, which will leave the country with less foreign exchange for other things. Thus, if an African government takes a foreign loan for an activity that does not earn or save foreign exchange in amounts at least equal to the cost of servicing, there will be problems with servicing the debt in the future.

A "debt crisis" simply means an inability to meet service obligations on an existing debt; that is, paying interest and principal on time. But in case after case in Africa, foreign loans were squandered, leaving countries unable to make timely payments. Some of the external loans were used to finance reckless government spending to establish grandiose loss-making state enterprises and other "black elephants"; or to purchase weapons to slaughter the African people while the rest was simply squandered.

Africa's debt crisis or "problem loans" originate from three basic missteps, as we saw in chapter 5. First, many of the loans were simply "consumed" and therefore did not generate the returns needed to repay the loan. Second, in many other cases, the loans were indeed "invested" in projects, but the projects turned out to be hopelessly unproductive. Third, some of the foreign loans that were contracted from shady operators were of a questionable nature.

No Unconditional Relief for Legitimate Debt

At their June 19, 2000, summit in Cologne, Germany, leaders of the G-8 nations agreed to forgive up to $70 billion of the debts of desperately poor countries in Asia, Latin America, and Africa. Of the 41 countries eligible for the program, 32 are in Africa. The Cologne Debt Initiative was designed to provide deeper, broader, and faster debt relief than a similar program launched by the World Bank and the IMF in 1996 for highly indebted poor countries (the HIPC Initiative). The HIPC Initiative provided debt relief to those poor countries that undertook the necessary micro- and macroeconomic adjustments over a period of six years. Although most of the targeted countries were in Africa, only eight countries, including five in Africa, had qualified for debt relief, totaling $6.5 billion, by September 1998. The Cologne Debt Initiative retained the World Bank and IMF's requirements for economic restructuring under HIPC but laid greater focus on social investment, hoping that debt relief would release resources for investment in health, education, and social needs. Further, it reduced the time needed to qualify from six to three years.

Invoking the biblical exhortation of 'forgiveness,' an odd coalition of religious groups, the Vatican, charity groups, and Hollywood actors, operating under the banner Jubilee 2000, called for outright debt cancellation without conditions to provide the poor countries a fresh start at the dawn of the new millennium. For example, ActionAid, a London-based charity, argued that writing off Sub-Saharan African debt would provide resources to save the lives of 21 million children by the year 2000 and provide basic education to 90 million girls and women.

Over the past two decades, OECD countries have cancelled more than $3.2 billion of Africa's debt, lowering debt service by more than $125 million per year. But African governments are demanding outright cancellation. At a May 6–8, 2000 conference held in the Ethiopian capital, Addis Ababa, African policymakers lambasted the World Banks HIPC Initiative as "half-hearted and far from adequate," offering only the "choice between the devil and the deep blue sea." Invective was liberally dished out: To use the debt overhang or debt initiative as a whip to enforce unquestioning acceptance of the economic orthodoxy—the so-called Washington consensus that is being promoted by some international financial institutions—is tantamount to blackmail and therefore unviable and immoral (*New African*, Aug 2000; p.4). They charged that Africa's crushing foreign debt cannot be repaid. It has crippled its economic performance and seriously impeded its ability to carry out reform.

Forgiveness is a magnanimous and noble act of compassion, but unconditional and outright debt forgiveness will only compound Africa's economic crisis. It amounts to canceling a credit card debt and granting the consumer access to the same credit cards. This only rewards past mismanagement, indiscretion, and reckless spending. Like a tax amnesty, it penalizes those countries that did not borrow irresponsibly to the hilt. And what incentives do African countries have to meet their debt obligations when another round of debt relief may be expected to be provided in the future? Even more troubling, the biblical canon invoked to drive this debt cancellation campaign was selectively interpreted: "Repent and thy sins shall be forgiven." No such repentance has been forthcoming on either the lender or the borrower side. Bad debts do not occur in a vacuum; it takes two to create them.

To be sure, the highly indebted countries are desperately poor but poverty is no excuse for loan default. Muhammad Yunus, founder and facilitator of the micro-credit movement, loans money to the "poorest of the poor" in 60 countries. Supported by his Grameen Bank, he provides $2.7 billion to poor people, 98 percent of whom swiftly repay the loans. Nor is there any iron-clad guarantee that resources released by debt relief would actually be spent on education, health care, and other social needs, and not used to build palaces, purchase arms, or to fund capital flight. For example, Uganda, the World Bank's supernova, has had $650 million of its debt canceled. Yet, it has spent an equal amount prosecuting a war in neighboring Congo and crushing rebel insurgencies within its own territory. In fact, the first item President Yoweri Museveni of Uganda purchased after obtaining debt relief was a new presidential jet!

Given that mistakes were made by both donors and recipients, it is clear that corrective action must be taken by both sides. The loans cannot be repaid, and some debt relied is needed. However, two types of debt must be distinguished. The first is debt contracted *legitimately*—that is, with the consent and authorization of the people on whose behalf the debt was contracted. Illegitimate debt is contracted without the consent of the people.

On legitimate debt, steps must be taken to ensure that an African country does not fall into the debt trap again. On the donor side, greater transparency and more input by the African people—not only their governments—are required. Clearly, those on whose behalf loans are being contracted must have a say on the terms of the loans and the uses to which these loans are put. On the recipient side, unconditional debt relief without a concomitant fundamental change in errant debt-producing behavior would be meaningless. Outright debt relief without conditionalities would do Africa more harm than good. Therefore, Africans would like to see the following conditionalitities attached for debt relief:[10]

1. There must be full public accounting of external loans. The loans were contracted on behalf of the people and they must know who took what loan and for what purpose. A Nigerian journalist, Tony Nze Njoku, complained bitterly:

> The genesis of Africa's external debt burden is wide and multifaceted. But most of these debts and loans were never accounted for or of any real value to the people of the countries involved. Rather, the loans provided a gold mine for government officials. The selection of the few projects financed with these loans was not based on sound economic parameters but on the whims of power brokers in the government. It is unlikely that international financial aid will be properly accounted for in a setting viewed as corrupt. Aid is seen by African government officials as a source of self-enrichment since hard currencies are involved. Officials in donor countries cooperate with their counterparts in recipient countries to divert aid into their own pockets so that aid exists only on paper. (*Finance and Development,* June 1998; p.56)

In Ghana, General Emmanuel Erskine, the 1992 presidential candidate of the People's Heritage Party, demanded that the former National Democratic Council government of Jerry Rawlings be made to account for every *pesewa* of loan they collected from the donor community and all proceeds from the divestiture of state companies: "We have taken many loans for projects as a nation and once a new government is in place, the past government should not hide anything from the people. They must tell us how the loans were used and also be prepared to give clarification when the need arises" he declared (*Ghanaian Chronicle,* Jan 19–22, 2001; p.5).

2. There must be repatriation of the loot stashed abroad by corrupt Africa leaders. At the fifth African African-American Summit held in Accra, Ghana, on May 25 1999, Mr. Clifford Abubacar Weaver, Vice-President of Boston-based African-American Seafoods, stunned African leaders present by laying down conditions for a bail-out of Africa: Return stolen loot or no aid.

Weaver claimed that during the last 10 to 20 years over $450 billion had been given to Africa by the IMF/World Bank, European banks, and the Arab countries. But, he said, only 22 percent had been reinvested in Africa. "Where is the rest of the money?" he plaintively asked. African school children don't have pens and pencils, hospitals, or decent roads because, according to Weaver, African politicians have ripped off their countries. "These politicians have ripped off the British, the Europeans, the Asians and the Arabs and now they want to rip off the last group of people on earth which is the African-American. These people need to empty their bank accounts. It is useless to keep pouring water in the well. Let there be a summit to deal with what has happened to the $16 billion that they have hidden in American, British, European and Japanese banks. Why is it there in the first place?" (*The Ghanaian Chronicle,* May 26, 1999; p.1).

3. Debt relief should be restricted to only the 16 African countries (out of 54) that are democratic: Benin, Botswana, Cape Verde Islands, Ghana, Kenya, Madagascar, Malawi, Mali, Mauritius, Namibia, Nigeria, Sao Tome and Principe, Senegal, Seychelles, South Africa, and Zambia. Or, debt relief should be given to only those African countries that have a free media. According to Freedom House's 2003 survey, only 8 out of 54 African countries have freedom of the press and of expression: Benin, Botswana, Cape Verde Islands, Ghana, Mali, Mauritius, Sao Tome and Principe, and South Africa.

4. Debt relief can be tied to the promotion of economic growth with the creation of "debt-free zones." In this scenario, a debtor African nation meets a consortium of creditor governments (for example, the Paris Club) and designates an area of its country—say 100 square miles—as a free industrial zone, in which companies from the creditor nation can operate freely for the next 20 years. Companies operating in this zone would enjoy certain benefits, such as zero profit tax, and waivers on imports and custom duties. The management of this zone would be in the hands of the creditor government, with observer status granted the debtor government to ensure compliance with domestic industrial regulations for, say, the protection of the environment and child labor. The zone may choose to establish its own judicial, security, electrical, or water supply systems, if domestic supplies are felt to be unreliable. It also may choose to set its own wages, provided these are not below the domestic level. Disputes with the domestic government shall be subject to international mediation. The zone shall not engage in political activity. The exact terms, of course, would be negotiated between

the debtor nation and the creditors. Participation in such a zone would be open to the nationals of creditor governments and exiles of the African country. Once a final agreement has been reached, the African country's entire foreign debt would be canceled.

At their Toronto meeting in 1999, the G-7 countries decided to write off half of the debts of the "poorest" African nations. Since then, Ghana and Zambia have been rewarded with partial debt cancellation for progress on economic and political reform. However, a better way to take care of the debt problem is by creating debt-free zones. Such an arrangement confers enormous benefits on both parties. For the creditor nation, say the United States or Britain, it opens up markets and investment opportunities. Foreign companies are guaranteed repatriation of profits and minimal government interference. The debtor nation, through this arrangement, may gain not only the cancellation of its debt but also more foreign investment, technology transfer, and employment opportunities for its citizens. Furthermore, the more efficient management of the debt-free zone would serve as a demonstration model for the government and the rest of the economy.

The debt-free zone also could serve as a "magnet" and attract entrepreneurs, skilled labor, and resources, thereby forcing an intransigent African government to match the incentives provided by the zone or face an exodus of domestic firms to it. Even more important, it could encourage the return of African exiles abroad. Most would like to return to their home countries and run their own private businesses but are wary of government assurances that their businesses would be safe. However, they may feel safer and assured not only in debt-free zones but also in private industrial zones.

The World Bank, USAID, and other donor agencies should encourage the establishment not only of debt-free zones but also of private industrial zones (PIZs). PIZs are free economic zones that are not controlled by the government and can be considered for those African countries that are not in immediate need of debt relief.

Cancellation, Moratorium, or
Repudiation of Odious Illegitimate Debts

There is something maddening about Africa's foreign debt and the time has come for Africans to send a strong message to the international lending communities: Loans to illegitimate governments are not redeemable under international law. If entities wish to continue loans to illegitimate African governments, they should do so at their own risk. The African people shall not be held liable to repay foreign loans contracted on their behalf without their authorization. What is being applied here is an international legal instrument known as "the principle of odious debts." According to Adams (1991):

> Odious Debts is about a tax revolt. The Third World's debts were accumulated without public knowledge and consent, with most people benefiting not one whit. Having paid once with their environment as the loans financed destructive development projects—among them hydro dams flooding rain forests and irrigation schemes destroying farmland—the Third World populace finds odious the proposition that it pays one more. (p. 3)

The idea was applied in 1923 when the Royal Bank of Canada sought to recover debt from a new government in Costa Rica. The new Costa Rican government successfully argued that the debt had been incurred by the former dictator and not by the country's people. "If a despotic power incurs a debt, not for the needs or interest of the state but to strengthen its despotic regime and to repress the population that fights against it . . . then this debt is odious to the population of the state," said the government. "The creditors have committed a hostile act with regard to the people, they can't therefore expect that a nation freed from a despotic power assume the odious debts, which are the personal debts of that power," it added (Adams, 1991; p.23).

In South Africa, apartheid was defined by the United Nations as "a crime against humanity." By 1982, as the campaign for international sanctions grew, lawyers for U.S. banks publicly warned that a majority government might not repay apartheid debts: "If the debt of the predecessor is deemed to be 'odious' and the debt proceeds are used against the interests of the local populace, then the debt may not be chargeable to the successor" (*New Internationalist,* May 1999; p.24). Archbishop Njongonkulu Ndungale, who took over the Truth and Reconciliation Commission (TRC) after Bishop Desmond Tutu, argued that: "South Africa's foreign debts were largely incurred under the apartheid regime to suppress the majority population. Thus, they should be declared odious and written off" (*Financial Post,* May 10, 1999; p.6). Indeed, South Africa itself set an example when its first black government took office. It cancelled Namibia's debt to South Africa. "We did not ask whether the debt was payable or unpayable. Nor did we impose any condition on our neighbor. We merely declared those debts as immoral, odious debts incurred while Namibia was occupied by the apartheid regime," said Archbishop Ndungale (*Financial Post,* May 10, 1999).

Earlier in 1999, the Latin American and Caribbean Jubilee 2000 Coalition described the foreign debt of member nations as "illegitimate because in large measure, it was contracted by dictatorships, governments not elected by the people, as well as by governments which were formally democratic but corrupt. Most of the money was not used to benefit the people who are now being required to pay it back" (*Financial Post*, May 10, 1999). Activists want legitimate debts to be repaid, illegitimate debts ones repudiated.

Should this "doctrine of odious debts" be applied to the debt of African countries? There is absolutely nothing wrong with Africans calling for a review of their foreign debt obligations. Westerners do that all the time. However, a note of caution should be sounded here. However odious a debt may be, it should not be unilaterally repudiated by Africans, as the late General I. K. Acheampong, the former head of state of Ghana, did. That action resulted in the cancellation of all foreign credit to Ghana. Instead, the case should be taken to the world court at The Hague, European Court of Justice, or the Court for International Settlement in Geneva. After negotiations, perhaps Ghanaians, Congolese, and South Africans may end up paying a fraction of their foreign debts. This was the approach taken by Russia, after the collapse of the Soviet Union, in its February 1999 negotiations with the London Club, which represents 600 Western commercial banks. Essentially, the negotiations were about restructuring some $23 billion of Soviet-era debt. Russia also sought "to restructure an additional $40 billion of Soviet-era debt owed to the Paris Club of government creditors" (*Wall Street Journal*, Jan 21, 1999; p.A10).

Nobel laureate, former chief economist of the World Bank, and former chairman of the Council of Economic Advisers Joseph Stiglitz made a persuasive case for the repudiation of much of Iraq's odious debt, exceeding $60 billion. He wrote:

> Iraq needs a fresh start, and the only real way to give it one would be to free the country from what some call its "odious debts"—debts incurred by a regime without political legitimacy, from creditors who should have known better, with the monies often spent to oppress the very people who are then asked to repay the debts. Most of Iraq's current debt was incurred by a ruthless and corrupt government long recognized as such.
>
> Of course, Iraq isn't the only country that would like to see its debts forgiven. Why should the Congolese be forced to repay Cold War loans made by Western countries to buy Mobutu's favor—especially since the leaders knew full well that the money was going not to the people but to Mobutu's Swiss bank accounts? Why should Ethiopians have to repay the loans made to the Mengistu "Red Terror" regime—loans that made it possible to buy the arms used to kill the very people whose friends and relatives must now repay the

loans? Chileans today are still paying off debts incurred during the Pinochet years, and South Africans are still paying off those incurred under apartheid. (*Atlantic Monthly,* Nov 2003; p.39–46)

Stiglitz suggested the creation of an "international bankruptcy" court, under the auspices of the United Nations, to deal with debt restructuring and relief and to ensure a fair sharing of the burdens. "Governments and banks that lend money to oppressive regimes would be put on notice that they risk not getting repaid, and the contracts and debts of countries with outlaw regimes would be re-examined once those regimes are no longer in power" (*Atlantic Monthly,* Nov 2003; p.39–46).

Conclusion

From the previous four chapters, it is apparent that Africa's developmobile is kaput, driven into a swamp of corruption, grotesque inefficiency, and arrant mismanagement. Instead of discarding it, the ruling vampire elites cling to their pet toy—their pride and glory, furiously mumbling about neocolonial conspiracies, colonial legacies, and the slave trade but never at their own incompetence. The development model they adopted after independence had many defects:

1. It envisaged statism or state-directed economic development
2. It emphasized industry to the neglect of agriculture, the main occupation of the Atingas
3. It was based upon aping alien ideologies or systems and, therefore, could not engender "organic development" (chapter 4)
4. It required massive investible resources, which Africa lacked, thereby necessitating heavy foreign borrowings (chapter 5)

Economic problems quickly emerged. The state proved itself no more prescient in balancing demand and supply than millions of ordinary people operating through the market system. State enterprises, established with huge foreign loans, failed to deliver the goods. The industrialization drive discombobulated. Price controls and other state controls on foreign exchange, imports, and rent created chronic shortages, exploited by the same government officials and private citizens with political connections. A culture of smuggling, rent-seeking activities, *kalabule,* bribery, and corruption was spawned (chapter 6). The neglect of peasant agriculture, among other things, led to declining food production per capita. Desperate for cash to sustain profligate spending, African governments resorted to printing money. With inadequate agricultural and industrial production to mop up excess liquidity, a serious inflation problem emerged. As their economies stagnated or contracted, African governments found it increasingly difficult to service the foreign loans they took to finance unproductive investment projects or "black elephants" called state enterprises (chapter 7). Could Africa have avoided these pitfalls? Is there a better way to develop Africa?

We look at these questions in the next chapter.

CHAPTER 8

How to Develop Africa

When, if ever, black people actually organize as a race in their various population centers, they will find that the basic and guiding ideology they now seek and so much need is embedded in their own traditional philosophy and constitutional system, simply waiting to be extracted and set forth.

—Chancellor Williams (1987; p.161).

We have had to go back to our roots. We have to go back to our traditional ways of solving our problems, traditional ways of working together. Otherwise, Boosaaso, a port in war-torn Somalia, would not have peace.

—Gen. Mohamed Abshir, Boosaaso's de facto administrator in *The Washington Post,* March 3, 1996; p.A239.

Unfortunately, the leadership that took over from the departing colonial authorities did not go back to our past to revive and revitalize our democratic roots. They took the line of least resistance and convenience and continued with despotism, autocracy, and authoritarianism. But the basic democratic culture is still there.

—Dr. Adebayo Adedeji, former executive secretary of UN Economic Commission for Africa and director of the African Center for Development and Strategic Studies in Nigeria, in *Africa Report,* Nov/Dec 1993; p.58.

WHY THE STATIST/SOCIALIST MODEL FAILED IN AFRICA

Africa's disastrous postcolonial economic record provides overwhelming evidence that the state-controlled socialist economic model can never be used to develop Africa successfully. First, the inherent superiority of the statist model has not been proven convincingly in any part of the Third World. Second, even if such a model can be adjudged superior, Africa lacks the necessary supporting inputs to make the model work: an efficient administrative machinery, honest and dedicated civil servants, as well as an effective communications network. Africa lacks all these. Third, the statist/socialist model benefited only the ruling vampire elites. Only they rode about in Mercedes Benzes. Only they purchased commodities at government-controlled prices. Only they had access to government-subsidized housing. Even their funerals were paid for by the government. But there were also more practical reasons why statism failed miserably in Africa.

Multiplicity of Economic Objectives

Development under the direction of the state *(dirigisme)* led to the establishment of many state enterprises under hastily drawn industrialization programs, which were intended to achieve a multiplicity of objectives, some of which were noneconomic and contradictory. To compound the problem, many of the goals were nebulous. Nkrumah's Seven-Year Development Plan, for example, had more than 13 objectives, ranging from attaining economic independence, social justice, and African unity to "breaking the stranglehold of neocolonialism." Some state enterprises were expected to turn a profit and at the same time generate employment. But since many stood as shining pieces of "modern development," they were subjected to all kinds of political interference. Many were overstaffed with political functionaries and cronies. In some African countries, state controls and public enterprises were expected to check the activities of foreigners and multinational corporations. Some state enterprises were supposed to earn or save the country foreign exchange.

In many places in Africa, foreigners and foreign companies were quite productive. This was especially the case of Lebanese in West Africa; Asians in Uganda, Kenya, and other East African countries; and Belgians in Zaire. When Idi Amin expelled the Asian merchants in the mid-1970s, and Zaire expelled foreign nationals and seized their companies, as well as their property, the GNP in both countries suffered severely. In 1972, Idi Amin nationalized British investments worth more than £250 million and expelled all 50,000 Asians, confiscating assets worth more than £500 million, which he distributed to his cronies. The economy collapsed. Exports of sugar, coffee, and tea slumped, as peasant farmers resorted to smuggling to escape confiscatory taxes from Amin's rapacious gang. By the time Amin was kicked out by Tanzanian soldiers in 1979, average incomes in Uganda were 40 percent lower than in 1971, when he seized power. President Yoweri Museveni invited the Asians back and offered to return about 40 percent of their assets confiscated by Amin. The result? According to *The Economist* (Aug 23, 2003), "Uganda is one of only a handful of African states to have seen a substantial reversal of the flight of capital and skills. Asians, 15,000 of whom now live in Uganda, have invested an estimated $1 billion in the last decade or so" (p. 37).

There have been cases upon cases where an African government has nationalized a foreign-owned company, only to mismanage it. Consider, for example, two documented cases from Ghana. In 1976, the government of Ghana took over R. T. Briscoe, a foreign company. "Before the takeover, the company was producing 241 buses in 1974. After the takeover, production was 12 buses in 1977 and only 6 buses in 1978" (*Daily Graphic*, Jan 18, 1979; p.5). Four years earlier, in 1972, the government of Ghana had also taken over the African Timber and Plywood Company, a private company. The results were the same. Before the takeover, "production was 75 percent of installed capacity but this has fallen to a woeful 13 percent" (*West Africa*, Oct 12, 1981; p.2422).

Economic progress suffers whenever an activity is transferred by the state from productive into unproductive and inefficient hands. Even the so-called backward and illiterate chiefs recognized this:

> Nana Kwadwo Bosea Gyinantwi IV, Omanhene of Drobo Traditional Area, called on the government to allow foreign firms like UAC (Ghana Ltd), G. B. Ollivant and Cadbury and Fry with long standing experience in the cocoa industry to purchase and evacuate cocoa produce because the [state-owned] CMB and its agencies have proved incapable of handling the industry alone.
>
> He said since many expatriate companies in the country had in the past dealt with the cocoa industry with precision, there was no point in saddling the CMB with a load it could not carry. (*Daily Graphic*, Sept 21, 1981; p.5)

It is true that Africa was "exploited," however that term is defined in the past by the colonialists. But the persecution of expatriates in Africa often borders on xenophobic hysteria. Foreigners have always been welcome in Africa—a view shared by Diop (1987):

> In addition to the two previously mentioned cities, Timbuktu and Djenne, known as far as Asia and Europe, there were Biru, Soo, Ndob, Pekes, and so on. In all these centers foreign nationals had their own quarters in which they could live in utmost security with their goods, while pursuing their business. For the most part these were Arabs from North Africa, Egypt, and Yemen, and Europeans, especially Spaniards. Some of them were even students in Timbuktu. Black Africa was hospitable to foreigners. We already know that

the king of Djenne wished for there to be more foreigners than natives in his capital. (p. 133)

Even in some native political systems, foreign nationals played a role. It may be recalled that the king of the Asante Empire in the nineteenth century had Muslim record keepers as well as a Dutch advisor. King Alfonso of Angola also had Portuguese representatives at his court in the eighteenth century.

In this era of globalization, efficiency ought to be of prime consideration, regardless of tribal affiliation, race, or religion. If a foreigner, a Muslim, or a Martian performs satisfactorily, he/she should be kept on the job. If not, then sack him or her. In fact, in certain economic spheres or areas of governance, foreign expatriates have decisive advantages because they are insulated from the local web of social and cultural obligations. For example, when an expatriate says "there are no more import licenses," Nigerians would accept that as final. But when a Nigerian minister of trade says the same thing, it is interpreted as "come to my house at 7.00 p.m. with a bottle of whisky, an envelope stuffed with cash, and l will give you one."

In Ghana, the government itself recognized the attributes of the expatriate. In 1970, for example, Ghana Airways signed an agreement with Aer Lingus of Ireland to manage Ghana's airline for a fee of 3 million *cedis* ($1 million). Even the Bank of Ghana "employed the services of an expatriate, one Mr. Anderson, to streamline affairs in the Bank" (*Punch*, Oct 16–22, 1981; p.3). Also in 1981, the Limann administration placed the management of the country's shipping line (the Black Star Line) in the hands of Philippine nationals. And a government-appointed committee for increased gold output stated that: "The State Gold Mining Corporation (SGMC) must embark on a crash program to recruit not less than 100 'experienced expatriates' within 18 months to help increase gold production" (*Daily Graphic,* June 22, 1981; p.1).

In July, 2004, President Olusegun Obasanjo invited about 200 white farmers, whose farmlands have been violently seized by the Mugabe regime in Zimbabwe, to resettle in Kwara state. Bukola Saraki, the governor of the state, said: "When we found oil [in the Niger delta], we didn't ask people in southern Nigeria to look for shovels to dig for it. We brought in foreigners with expertise. Our land is an asset that is not being utilized. The only way to do that is to bring in people with the necessary skills" (*The Washington Times,* July 18, 2004; p.A6). In this case, while white Zimbabwean farmers should be welcome in Nigeria, unfortunately—as we shall argue in chapter 10—the governor erred by abandoning his state's peasant farmers. Foreign expertise should augment, not replace the local expertise.

Pragmatism ought to rule. The issue is not whether Africans are "inferior" or "unqualified" or the expatriate "superior" and more "qualified." Rather, it is a question of getting the job done in an establishment. If an African cannot do it, he should be fired, just as the expatriate should. At the same time, however, it would be unwise to insert expatriates in certain areas; for example, peasant agriculture. The hysteria about the employment of expatriates obfuscates the issue and plays into the hands of incompetent African officials.

The disbarment of foreign nationals provided many African governments with the rationale to create employment for their nationals and party supporters. Africa's state sector became hopelessly overstaffed. More than 20 percent of Ghana's civil service was declared redundant in 1984 by the secretary of finance (*West Africa*, Jan 27, 1986; p.1607). In fact, Ghana's state-owned shipping line, the Black Star Line, had so many redundant employees that 254 were paid for three years (1981–84) to simply stay home! (*West Africa*, Aug 6, 1984; p.1607). Back in 1966, a bamboo processing factory was found to have spent just 219 *cedis* ($72) on raw materials whereas wages and salaries amounted to 16,184 *cedis,* and the State Fishing Corporation "as of October 1, 1968, had on its payroll 435 sea-going personnel, despite the fact that for months it had no vessel fishing" (Killick 1978; p.237). In fact, in 1966, the minister of finance listed "overstaffing" and "indiscipline" as one of the major factors militating against efficiency of public enterprises (Killick 1978; p.237). Nigerian Railways has six times the staff per traffic unit of European railways. In February 1987, some 30 percent of all ministries in Sierra Leone were considered superfluous (*West Africa*, June, 1988; p.1762).

In Ghana, blatant cases of overmanning were often for political reasons and had a whole history dating back to the 1970s. One excellent example was Ghana's State Gold Mining Corporation, which was investigated by the Amamoo Commission (1971). Its report noted that:

> The basic cause of the present weakness of the corporation is political in nature. Since it was formed in 1961 no Government has provided the Corporation with the conditions necessary for its success. One reason for this is that Governments have tried to pursue contradictory objectives. Governments have tended to speak with two voices about the duties of the Corporation. With one voice they justify the necessity for the Corporation on social, noncommercial grounds, i.e., on the need to prevent unemployment. With the other voice, however, they talk of the Corporation in commercial terms, stressing the need to obtain profits and criticizing the management for having to depend on budgetary subsidies. (p. 8)

Another example of political interference and lack of accountability is supplied by the case of Ghana's Industrial Development Corporation (IDC), set up to promote industrial investment. A 1958 report by W. Arthur Lewis, the famous economist from the West Indies, noted that:

> The IDC has suffered greatly from outside interference in the shape of Members of Parliament and other influential persons expecting staff appointments to be made irrespective of merit, redundant staff to be kept on pay-roll, disciplinary measures to be relaxed in favor of constituents, business to be purchased at inflated prices, loans to made irrespective of security etc. (qtd. in Killick, 1978; p.245).

When the opposition charged that the IDC served more to the whims of politicians, the minister of works, N. A. Welbeck, retorted: "But that is proper; and the Honorable Member too would do it if he were there!" (Killick 1978; p.245).

Misaligned priorities were not unique only to Ghana. In Zambia, a country with critical shortages (of tires and auto spares, for instance), China was busy building a giant new headquarters for the country's only political party (*The Wall Street Journal,* July 29, 1985; p.18).

In addition, there has been a rather consistent tendency on the part of African leaders to select development projects that emphasize grandeur rather than economy. In Ghana, there was notable predisposition on the part of the government to opt "for modern capital-intensive techniques and projects." Uphoff (1970) cited a pharmaceutical factory, where a relatively modest design was turned down in favor of another that eventually cost nearly ten times as much and that included "eleven bungalows for managers, a handsomely fitted administration block, a large cafeteria with one of the biggest and most modern kitchens in Ghana, and housing for experimental animals better than those in which most Ghanaians lived" (p. 562).

Administrative Ineptitude

Some of the reasons for the poor performance of the state enterprises and other development projects generally have been poor project planning, lack of feasibility studies, improper siting of industries and projects, poor coordination, and implementation that emanated from defective administrative machineries.

The civil service is characterized by low morale, lack of discipline and accountability, predisposition toward graft, nepotism, and low productivity. African governments have always been aware of the defects in the civil service machinery but instead of tackling the problems they have blamed their predecessors, the "colonialists." Nkrumah was well aware of these defects:

It has long been apparent that the administrative machinery we inherited was not designed for a country working within the framework of an overall development plan, and in which the activities of individual agencies of the nation are directed to clearly defined goals of development. An effective reform of the governmental machinery is therefore needed if the 7-Year Plan is not to falter on the inadequacies of administration. (Nkrumah 1973; p.199)

Reform of the government machinery never materialized. To rectify the defects in the "colonially" inherited machinery, he created more ministries and public institutions. When no improvement was forthcoming he lamented that:

It amazes me that up to the present many civil servants do not realize that we are living in a revolutionary era. This Ghana, which has lost so much time serving colonial masters, cannot afford to be tied down to archaic snail-pace methods of work which obstruct expeditious progress. We have lost so much time that we need to do in ten years what has taken others a hundred years to accomplish. (Nkrumah 1973; p.157)

Twelve years after Nkrumah's overthrow the civil service standard of efficiency had not changed much, as the Okoh Commission (1978) noted: "The standard of discipline is generally low both in terms of compliance with civil service code and in the enforcement of disciplinary action. There is widespread feeling that some superior officers lack self-disciplining themselves. They are thus unable to set the right examples for the sub-ordinates to follow" (p. 2).

Defects in the civil service machinery not only resulted in poor project planning but also in administrative blunders and financial mismanagement. There is extensive evidence for these, but suffice it here to give a few dramatic examples.

In Ghana, two tomato canneries were built in different parts of the country. The capacity of either one of them would have met the total domestic demand (Killick 1978; p.229). It took six years to complete Ghana's state footwear corporation factory and by the time it was ready to go into production much of its equipment was obsolete (Killick 1978; p.231). The Ghana government-owned sugar factory at Komenda, after completion, stood idle for more than a year because it lacked a water supply system (Killick 1978; p.231).

In Uganda and Angola, some high-rises lack glass panes and running water. In Mali, a Soviet-built cement factory at Diamou was designed for a capacity of 50,000 tons a year. Beset by regular breakdowns, it produced only 5 tons in 1983 (*Time,* Jan 16, 1984; p.27). Furthermore, according to *The Wall Street Journal* (July 29, 1985):

The U.S. built 50 crop storage depots in Senegal and placed them in locations the peasants never visited. In Uganda, a railroad expert discovered to his amazement that a repair shop built with foreign aid was seven times as large as the one he ran in Germany. A fifth of Ivory Coast's foreign borrowing went to build two sugar mills that started production just four years ago and now are closed. In Sudan, the Soviets built a milk bottling plant at Babanusa. Babanusa's Baggara tribesmen drink their milk straight from the cow and there aren't any facilities to ship milk out of Babanusa. The 20-year old plant hasn't produced a single bottle of milk. (p. 18)

Delays in project completion—with consequent cost overruns, poor co-ordination, and in some cases the absence thereof—all took their toll on the efficiency of the state enterprises. In 1975, Nigeria purchased a Russian-made steel-making furnace. But it was built on a site so remote from iron and coal mines as to render it useless. Subsequently, Russian, German and French technicians spent billions of *naira* to make it operational. The most outrageous blunder, however, was what was dubbed Africa's largest paper mill, the Nigerian National Paper Manufacturing Company. It was conceived under the Third National Development Plan (1975–80) to produce 100,000 tons of paper yearly, to earn about 150 million *naira* from exports and save the nation 250 million *naira* in imports. It was initially estimated to cost only 85 million *naira* in 1976.

By 1979, the cost has been revised to 350 million *naira* from where it jumped to 450 million *naira* three years later. By 1986, it was estimated that an additional 275 million *naira* was needed for completion. When the government could not provide the funds, a Canadian company proposed a loan of $135 million (which then was the equivalent of 275 million *naira*) to complete the required project in return for lifting of crude oil of an equivalent amount, but this offer was rejected. By 1989, only 55 percent of the project had been completed, according to Professor Ganiyu Jawando, chairman of the Nigerian company. According to *New African* (Aug 1989):

> The project was then almost forgotten until last November, (1988) when President Ibrahim Babangida paid a visit. He was shocked by what he saw: "The Iwopin Paper Mill is becoming a classical example of how not to plan and execute a major strategic operation," he said. "It is a sad reflection of bad planning, bad implementation and bad use of public funds which have characterized our life since independence." (p. 24)

Many of Africa's state enterprises were set up with either no prior feasibility studies or improperly done studies. Where these studies were done at all, they mostly were done by the very companies or individuals who were peddling their equipment for factories under supplier credit arrangements—a clear conflict of interest. For example, in Ghana, a Yugoslav company recommended and built two tomato canning factories on an assumed price of 1 *pesewa* per pound of tomatoes when farmers were receiving from the ordinary market traders 5 1/2 to 9 *pesewas* in one center and up to 15 *pesewas* in others (Killick, 1978; p.230). In a similar fashion, the British consultants and engineers who built and managed Ghana's steelworks at Tema based their analysis on an assumed price for electric power that was only 30 percent of the going rate for other industrial consumers (Killick, 1978; p.230). That officials were aware of these shortcomings and conflicts of interest is borne out by a remark by the minister of finance that the foreign suppliers who undertook the feasibility studies "were more interested in selling than in anything else" (Killick, 1978; p.230). Lest one be inclined to ascribe these failures to a lack of administrative skills, note should be taken of an observation made by the World Bank in reference to Ghana's State Farm Corporation: "The most simple calculations of costs and returns would have indicated the lack of viability inherent in many of the Corporation's projects prior to their implementation" (Killick, 1978; p.230).

Venal Tendencies

African governments are characterized by overspending, wasteful practices, willful extravagance with public funds, and financial irregularities and profligacy. Many projects have failed in Africa because they were riddled with graft and corruption. According to the World Bank's 1983 World Development Report:

> Corruption seriously undermines the effectiveness of government. Over time, corruption tends to corrode popular confidence in public institutions. Rent-seeking can become an obsessive pre-occupation. Public officials will do nothing without bribes and many people are unproductively employed in securing their favors or buying their silence. Corruption tends to favor those with economic or institutional power. Some corruption is on such a scale that it has major economic consequences; it may stimulate the illegal export of capital or result in large projects being awarded to contractors (often multinational companies) according to the size of their bribes rather than the quality of their performance. (p. 117)

Much of the failure of government policies in Africa can be explained by corruption because it goes hand in hand with administrative inefficiency. Administrators may expedite the approval of a project without checking its viability either because they have a personal interest in it or are promised a cut. In some instances a viable project is shelved indefinitely because the appropriate minister was not adequately "settled," as Nigerians would say. Not only does corruption undermine administrative efficiency but it also impairs the government's ability to formulate and implement development policies.

As we saw in chapter 6, in most African countries, the import control program required licenses or official permission before goods could be imported. But in Nigeria, an importer could obtain the license with payment of a 10 percent bribe. It was the same story in Ghana, where even government-appointed commissions of enquiry revealed this malpractice. In Senegal, when the state-run company to distribute fertilizer and seed was closed, "auditors discovered that most of the company's $250 million in bad debts were owed by about half a dozen politically well-connected businessmen" (*The Wall Street Journal*, July 29, 1985; p.18).

Failed Grand Initiatives in the Past

In the postcolonial era, African governments have not proven themselves to be more competent at managing resources more efficiently than the private sector. Since independence, African leaders have announced all sorts of grandiose initiatives and mega-plans at various summits. Nothing is subsequently heard of them after the summits: The Lagos Plan of Action (1980); the African Priority Program for Economic Recovery (1985); the African Alternative Framework to Structural Adjustment (1989), the United Nations Program of Action for African Recovery and Development (UNPAERD); the United Nations New Agenda for African Development (UNNADAF); the Abuja Treaty (1991); and others. In the late 1980s, there was much excitement about the creation of the African economic community. Nothing was heard of it since. At the thirty-fifth OAU Summit in Algiers (July 15, 1999), President Thabo Mbeki of South Africa shocked the delegates by reminding them that little has been done to implement the 1991 Treaty of Abuja, which established an African economic community (*The Washington Times*, July 15, 1999; p.A14).

There were other grand initiatives too: The Algerian and South African initiative, the Millennium Partnership for the African Recovery (MAP), and the Omega Plan, spearheaded by President Abdoulaye Wade of Senegal. They were finally integrated into a single plan called the Compact for African Recovery (COMPACT) by the Economic Commission for Africa (ECA). Subsequently, COMPACT metastasized into the New Partnership for Africa's Development (NEPAD). All these plans committed African leaders to democratic ideals; establishment of peace, law, and order; respect for human rights and basic freedoms; and a better management of their economies, among other things. They also entreat the international community, especially Western nations, to work in partnership with African leaders to help them to realize their goal.

NEPAD

The New Partnership for Africa's Development (NEPAD)—a synthesis of these plans and touted by Presidents Thabo Mbeki of South Africa, Olusegun Obasanjo of Nigeria, and Abdoulaye Wade of Senegal—was presented at the G–8 Summit in Genoa in 2001 for Western financial support. NEPAD seeks $64 billion in Western investments in Africa. The official NEPAD document undertakes "to respect the global standards of democracy, whose core components include political pluralism, allowing for the existence of several political parties and workers' unions, fair, open, free and democratic elections periodically organized to enable the populace to choose their leaders freely." It also includes a "peer review mechanism" by which African leaders who misrule their countries would be subject to criticism by fellow African leaders according to commonly agreed standards. NEPAD was trumpeted as "Africa's own initiative," "Africa's Plan," "African crafted," and therefore "African owned." While African leaders deserve credit for at least making the effort to craft an "African initiative," NEPAD is fatally flawed in many ways.

Badgering the West

First, its pitch and analysis are faulty. Playing the guilt trip card, NEPAD claims that the impoverishment of Africa has been "accentuated" by the "legacy of colonialism" and other historical "legacies" such as the cold war and the unjust "international economic system." Colonialism subverted Africa's "traditional structures, institutions and values," creating an economy "subservient to the economic and political needs of the imperial powers" (para 21). Africa has been integrated into the world economy as "supplier of cheap labor and raw materials, draining Africa's resources rather than industrializing Africa" (para 21). Colonialism, according to NEPAD, retarded the development of an entrepreneurial and middle class with managerial capability. At independence, Africa inherited a "weak capitalist class," which explains the "weak accumulation process, weak states and dysfunctional economies" (para 22)—the same old colonialism claptrap. Insufficient "rate of accumulation" in the postcolonial period led to "patronage and corruption" (para 25). The "vicious circle" of "economic decline and poor governance" has confirmed Africa's peripheral and diminishing role and "marginalization" (para 26). More recent reasons for Africa's dire condition include "its continued marginalization from the globalization process" (para 2).

Back in August 1999, representatives of African governments met in Accra and issued a declaration: "Africa is demanding $777 trillion from Western Europe and the Americas in reparation for enslaving Africans while colonizing the continent" (*Pan African News Agency,* August 18, 1999). It added that the money would be demanded from "all those nations of Western Europe and the Americas and institutions, who participated and benefited from the slave trade and colonialism." Dr. Hamet Maulana and Debra Kofie, co-chairpersons of the commission, urged that worldwide monitoring and networking systems be instituted to ensure that reparation and repatriation will be achieved by 2004. Problem is, U.S. GNP is only $10 trillion and the amount asked—$777 trillion—exceeds the combined sum of the GNPs of the entire Western world. According to the British government's Office of National Statistics, "The United Kingdom—that is England, Wales, Scotland and Northern Ireland—is officially valued at $8.8 trillion, a sum that includes all of its property and buildings, machinery, roads, bridges, planes, trains and automobiles. It also includes all the money deposited in its banks and other financial institutions. Plus everything on the shelves at Harrods" (*The New York Times,* Jan 1, 2004; p.A4). While slavery and colonialism did harm Africa, this card has excessively been overplayed by African leaders to conceal their own failures. The truth is, African leaders themselves have marginalized Africa.

To be sure, unfair trade practices—trade barriers and agricultural subsidies—are legitimate issues of concern for the Third World, but they are peripheral to the core issue of Africa's underdevelopment. Africa's exports consist mainly of cash crops (cocoa, cotton, coffee, bananas, sisal, etc.) and minerals (gold, diamonds, oil, titanium, cobalt, copper, etc.). Trade barriers and agricultural subsidies in the West affect only a few African exports, such as cotton (Burkina Faso, Mali, Sudan), peanuts or groundnuts (Gambia, Senegal, Sudan), sugar (Mauritius, Mozambique, South Africa), tobacco (Malawi, Zimbabwe), and beef (from Botswana, Namibia). Only a few African countries such as Ivory Coast, Mauritius, and South Africa export manufactured goods, which can encounter trade barriers in the West.

Consider the effects of Western subsidies on the cash crop cotton, for example. In Mali, cotton farmers hitch their one-bladed plows to oxen and take two weeks to till 10- to 20-acre plots, from which the cotton is eventually picked by hand. In contrast, the Mississippi Delta growers tend giant spreads of 10,000 acres or more in air-conditioned tractors using global positioning satellite systems to determine the proper amount of fertilizer to

apply to sprouting seedlings on each particular acre. In all, it costs 82 cents
to produce a pound of cotton in Mississippi versus only 23 cents a pound in
Mali (*The Washington Post,* June 8, 2003; p.B2). However, the higher-cost
American producers are in business because of government subsidies. In
2002, President Bush signed into law a piece of legislation that paid more
than $3.4 billion in subsidies to America's 25,000 cotton farmers. Thus,
U.S. government subsidies allow American farmers to produce more cotton,
which will depress world prices, making it difficult for Malian farmers to
compete.

In Burkina Faso, Benin, Chad, and Mali, cotton production accounts for
5 to 10 percent of the gross domestic product (GDP), 30 percent of trade
balance, and more than 60 percent of export receipts. But Mali, Burkina
Faso, and Benin have each lost $43, $33 and $28 million respectively in ex-
port receipts because of the effects of subsidies. African countries as a whole
lost about $300 million U.S. dollars in 2001–2002 because of depressed
world cotton prices, thanks to the U.S. subsidies, which have brought the
global cotton price down by 25 percent. Benin, Burkina Faso, Mali, and
Chad are demanding the gradual elimination of the subsidies over a three-
year period, from 2004 to 2006.

It is not Western agricultural subsidies, however, that have hurt African
food agriculture. As we saw in chapter 7, food production per capita has
been declining and Africa's food import amounts to some $18 billion annu-
ally. The recent civil war in Ivory Coast, for example, cut the country's cocoa
exports by half and disrupted agricultural exports of neighboring countries
that pass through Ivory Coast. In Burundi, coffee production has dropped
by more than 50 percent because of civil war/strife that has engulfed that
small country of 8 million people since 1993. In Malawi, crime has risen so
sharply that some farmers have refused to grow crops. And while the U.S.
maintains import quotas against Zimbabwe's tobacco exports, the industry
has virtually been destroyed by President Robert Mugabe's violent seizures of
white commercial farmland to remedy "colonial injustices."

This erosion of Africa's share of world trade was caused not so much by
trade barriers but rather a host of internal factors. Among them are the neglect of agriculture occasioned by the overemphasis on industrialization, raging civil wars, crumbling infrastructure, and misguided socialist policies that
exploited Africa's farmers through a system of marketing boards and price
controls. For example, trade barriers do not block exports of oil, diamonds,
gold, coltan, and other minerals from Africa. Yet, paradoxically, countries
that produce them—Angola, Congo, Equatorial Guinea, Gabon, Nigeria,
Sudan, among others—have been wracked by war, poverty and social destitution. In fact, Africa's diamonds have fueled such barbarous civil wars in

Angola, Congo, and Sierra Leone that human rights activists in the West have called for a boycott of Africa's "conflict diamonds."

A keynote speech by the new African Union (AU) secretary-general, Amara Essy, to mark the New Year on Jan 3, 2002, in Addis Ababa, Ethiopia, did not provide Africans with hope or assurance. He "accused the international community of failing the continent; their refusal to alleviate Africa's huge debt burden continues to compromise its development" (IRIN, Jan 3, 2002). It is the same old drivel about the international community failing Africa, as if it is the international community that is responsible for the flagrant violations of human rights on the continent.

NEPAD and African Self-Reliance

Second, NEPAD talks of "self-reliance" and argues forcefully that Africans must be "masters of their own destiny." It rails against "the credit and aid binomial" that has led to a "debt deadlock," and perpetual rescheduling (para 3). In fact, the plan is a cleverly designed vehicle to extract more foreign aid and credit. It says that Africa needs to secure more aid and more credit (para 145), and furthermore, that the "bulk" of Africa's capital needs up to the year 2015 "will have to come from outside Africa" (para 147). The apparent contradiction stems from an aid-dependency trap African leaders seem incapable of breaking out of.

NEPAD as a Western Model

Third, it turned out NEPAD was modeled after a *foreign plan:* the U.S. Marshall Aid Plan, which rebuilt Europe after World War II. Recall that the development that took place in postcolonial Africa was dismissed as "development-by-imitation." American farmers use tractors; so too must African farmers. Rome has a basilica; so, too, must Yamassoukrou, Ivory Coast. Now comes NEPAD. How could it be "African crafted" when it is a copy of the Marshall Aid Plan? How could Africa claim ownership over someone else's idea?

At a forum organized by Kenya's Mazingira Institute, the African Academy of Sciences, and the Regional Office (Horn and East Africa) of the Heinrich Boell Foundation, the keynote speaker was Prof. Adebayo Adedeji. As the UN undersecretary-general and executive secretary of the ECA, Adedeji was instrumental in creating five initiatives to jump-start Africa's economic growth. Aid, he said, had failed to solve Africa's problems for four decades and was not about to. "No Marshal Plan will work in Africa's underdeveloped markets. It worked in Germany because of Germans' hard work and intellectual resources . . . Africa requires building anew; not rehabilitation or reconstruction," said Adedeji (*East African,* [Nairobi], May 6, 2002).

NEPAD and Exclusion

Fourth and more serious was the blatant dishonesty and double-speak that infected NEPAD. Speaking at the four-day OAU Civil Society conference (June 10–14, 2002), President Obasanjo of Nigeria noted that the involvement of civil organizations is required in order to make the ongoing establishment of African Union and NEPAD successful. "I would like to reiterate that much of what Africa has today gained in the areas of political and social sphere have been derived from the direct influence of Civil Society Organizations (CSOs). This attitude should continue," he added (*Daily Monitor* [Addis Ababa], June 14, 2002). Prime Minister Meles Zenawi of Ethiopia on his part said that the role of civil society is essential in making sustainable development in Africa. Meles noted that the success of NEPAD lies in the collective efforts of all Africans at the grassroot levels (*Daily Monitor* [Addis Ababa], June 14, 2002). NEPAD also claims to be "people-oriented." Yet, NEPAD was "crafted" without consultation with Africa's NGOs and civic groups.

No civic group, church, political party, parliament, or democratic body took part in its formulation. Only a small coterie of African leaders deliberated on the document, excluding the political leadership of the rest of Africa. In fact, most governments and civil society organizations in Africa first learned about NEPAD from the Western media when President Thabo Mbeki presented it in Davos at the World Economic Forum in January 2001. It had resulted from a chaotic evolution: The Millennium Partnership for African Recovery (MAP), crafted by presidents Mbeki and Bouteflika, was merged with the Omega Plan, spearheaded by President Abdoulaye Wade of Senegal, to create the Compact for African Recovery by the Economic Commission for Africa (ECA), which subsequently metastasized into NEPAD. In fact, President Mbeki admitted to this lack of popular consultation in a letter to the African National Congress (ANC):

> Quite naturally, up to now, our governments have led the processes of African transformation represented by the AU and NEPAD. Nevertheless, the 2001 Lusaka Summit of the OAU directed the Member States to popularize both the AU and NEPAD among the African masses. In reality, however, much needs to be done to give effect to this decision. The establishment of the Pan African Parliament (PAP) further emphasizes the need for the empowerment of our people to play their role in changing their lives for the better. Our movement must respond to this challenge and ensure that we both supply the people with

the knowledge they need, as well as organize them actively to participate in what inevitably will be a protracted struggle for the victory of the African renaissance. (*ANC TODAY*, On Line Voice of the African National Congress, July 9–15, 2004. Web site: www.anc.org.za/ancdocs/anctoday/2004/at27.html)

A furor erupted in Africa when it became clear that NEPAD was crafted more to placate Western donors rather than to address issues of concern to the African people. On January 9, 2001, representatives of some 200 social movements, organizations, and institutions meeting in Bamako, Mali, issued "The Bamako Declaration," which strongly condemned the lack of consultation with civic society. Another joust came in March 2002, when the Southern African Catholic Bishops Conference (SACBC) slammed NEPAD, calling the plan "ambiguous" and some of its proposals "dubious." The bishops averred that "NEPAD may not achieve its purpose because of lack of consultation with those the plan would affect" (*Mail and Guardian* [Johannesburg], March 8, 2002). In fact, such has been the history of other grandiose initiatives and megaplans announced by African leaders at various summits to address Africa's woes. They cease to exist after the summits.

Problem is, the architects of NEPAD do not even take African Unity seriously. Instead of working collectively to advance NEPAD as an "African initiative," South Africa has spearheaded NEPAD with Nigeria, Algeria, and Senegal, in a group now known as "the powerful G–4" (group of four), leaving the other countries chafing with little role to play.

On June 5, 2002, African leaders met in Durban, South Africa to fine-tune the details of the ambitious recovery plan for Africa. But bitter acrimony engulfed the endeavor and tension emerged over the powerful G–4 steering NEPAD. Irate at being excluded from the core group because of allegations of corruption in his government, Kenyan President Daniel arap Moi left in a huff, barely 24 hours after the opening of the summit, without making any formal addresses. His team of government officials subsequently withdrew from panel discussions on NEPAD and headed home. Kenya also complained that South Africa was rushing ahead with NEPAD without explaining the program to the rest of Africa. Libya, whose leader Col. Ghaddafi has been one of the architects of the AU, was also incensed at being left out of the plan. "Libya has let it be known that it is not happy at being excluded when it was a major force behind the creation of the AU," an African ambassador said, adding that explanations by some ministers that Libya was still largely isolated internationally had gone down badly with Ghaddafi. Zambian Foreign Minister Katele Kalumba also admitted there were tensions as NEPAD got off the ground (*Sunday Standard On Line*, June 9, 2002).

Never mind the absurdity of dictators standing in judgment of other despots. Even before the plan was launched, there was backpedaling on the "peer review mechanism." President Mbeki of South Africa has been reticent on how to implement peer review. "He talks vaguely about market reaction to the reviews, and a system of credit ratings for participating countries. Zambia's Levy Mwanawasa, who was elected in dubious circumstances in Jan 2002, argues that 'peer review must not be about isolation.' And Mozambique's Joaquim Chissano says it is too early to talk of peer pressure, even on countries as badly governed as Zimbabwe" (*The Economist,* June 22, 2002; p.44).

When the peer review mechanism was formally launched at the March 2003 Abuja meeting, it was "intended as a voluntary 'self-monitoring' system by which participating African countries subject themselves to ongoing examination by other Africans in such priority areas as peace and security, democracy and political governance, and economic and corporate management" (*Africa Recovery,* May 2003; p.8). At the Abuja meeting, only 10 out of 54 African countries officially acceded to the African Peer Review Mechanism (APRM)—Algeria, the Republic of Congo, Ethiopia, Ghana, Kenya, Mozambique, Nigeria, Rwanda, South Africa, and Uganda, with Botswana and Senegal indicating their intention to accede. APRM's funding was to come from African institutions, businesses and individuals "in order to affirm African ownership of the mechanism" (*Africa Recovery,* May 2003; p.8). Obviously, such a mechanism would not work if only the "good guys" signed up and there are no costs to the "bad guys" for nonparticipation.

Nonetheless, on June 26, 2002, the presidents of Algeria, Nigeria, Senegal, and South Africa traveled to Kananaski, Alberta (Canada) to present NEPAD to the G–8 Summit for funding by the rich nations. Mercy Muigai, an unemployed Kenyan woman, was unimpressed:

"All these people [African leaders and elites] do is talk, talk, talk. Then if they do get any money from the *wazungu* [white men], they just steal it for themselves. And what about us? We have no food. We have no schools. We have no future. We are just left to die." (*The Washington Times,* June 28, 2002; p.A17)

Africa's Leaky Begging Bowl

The fact is, the resources Africa desperately needs to launch into self-sustaining growth and prosperity can be found in Africa itself. The problem is intellectually astigmatized leadership, which is programmed to look only one way—outside Africa, principally in the West—for such resources, which results in hopeless aid dependency. At a workshop organized for the Parliamentary Sub-Committee on Foreign Affairs at Ho, Ghana, Dr. Yaw Dzobe

Gebe, a fellow at the Legon Center for International Affairs at the University of Ghana, stressed the need for the AU to look within the continent for capital formation to build a viable continental union with less dependency on foreign aid. "With an accumulated foreign debt of nearly $350 billion and estimated capital requirement of more than $50 billion annually for capacity building, it is time Africa begins to look within for capital formation. Experience in the last 40 years or more of independence and association with Europe and America should alert African leaders of the fact that there are very limited benefits to be derived from benevolence of the development partners" (*Daily Graphic,* July 24, 2004; p.16).

Africa's investment process may be compared to a "leaky bucket." The level of the water therein—GNP per capita—is determined by inflows of foreign aid, investment, and export earnings relative to outflows or leakages of imports (food, luxury consumer items), corruption, and civil wars. Recall table 7.5, which depicted Africa's balance of payment situation in 1998. It showed a balance of payment deficit of $17.9 billion. This had to be financed by new borrowing, which would increase Africa's foreign debt, or by the use of reserves, which were nonexistent for most African countries. This number, however, does not tell the full story. Hidden from view is a much grimmer story—the other more serious leakages.

According to one UN estimate, "$200 billion or 90 percent of the sub-Saharan part of the continent's gross domestic product (much of it illicitly earned), was shipped to foreign banks in 1991 alone" (*The New York Times,* Feb 4, 1996; p.A4). Capital flight out of Africa is at least $20 billion annually. Part of the capital flight out of Africa represents wealth created legitimately by business owners who have little faith in keeping it in Africa. The rest represents loot stolen by corrupt African leaders and politicians. Recall the charge by Nigerian President Olusegun Obasanjo, that corrupt African leaders have stolen at least $140 billion from their people in the decades since independence (*London Independent,* June 14, 2002. Web posted at www. independent.co.uk).

Foreign aid has not been spared, either. Says *The Economist* (Jan 17, 2004): "For every dollar that foolish northerners lent Africa between 1970 and 1996, 80 cents flowed out as capital flight in the same year, typically into Swiss bank accounts or to buy mansions on the Cote d'Azur" (Survey; p.12). At the Commonwealth Summit in Abuja, Nigeria on December 3, 2003, former British secretary of state for international development, Rt. Hon Lynda Chalker, revealed that 40 percent of wealth created in Africa is invested outside the continent. Chalker said African economies would have fared better if the wealth created on the continent were retained within. "If you can get your kith and kin to bring the funds back and have it invested in infrastructure, the economies of African countries would be much better than what there are today," she said (*This Day* [Lagos], Dec 4, 2003). On October 13, 2003, Laolu Akande, a veteran Nigerian freelance journalist, wrote that:

> Nigeria's foreign debt profile is now in the region of $25-$30 billion, but the president of the Institute of Chartered Accountants of Nigeria, ICAN, Chief Jaiye K. Randle, himself an eminent accountant and social commentator has now revealed that individual Nigerians are currently lodging far more than Nigeria owes in foreign banks. With an estimate he put at $170 billion it becomes immediately clear why the quest for debt forgiveness would remain a far fetched dream. (www.nigeriaworld.com/columnist/laoluakande/articles.html)

In August 2004, an African Union report claimed that Africa loses an estimated $148 billion annually to corrupt practices, a figure which represents 25 percent of the continent's Gross Domestic Product (GDP). "Mr. Babatunde Olugboji, Chairman, Independent Advocacy Project, made this revelation in Lagos while addressing the press on the survey scheduled to be embarked upon by the body to determine the level of corruption in the country even though Transparency International has rated Nigeria as the second most corrupt nation in the world" (*Vanguard*, Lagos, Aug 6, 2004. Web posted at www.allafrica.com).

Back in the late 1980s, Sammy Kum Buo, director of the U.N. Center for Peace and Disarmament, lamented that "Africa spends about $12 billion a year on the purchase of arms and the maintenance of the armed forces, an amount which is equal to what Africa was requesting in financial aid over the next 5 years" (*West Africa*, May 11, 1987; p.912). Since then, this amount had increased for all of Africa: "Excluding South Africa, spending on arms in sub-Saharan Africa totaled nearly $11 billion in 1998, if military assistance and funding of opposition groups and mercenaries are taken into account. This was an annual increase of about 14 percent at a time when the regions economic growth rose by less than 1 percent in real terms" (*The Washington Times*, Nov 8, 1999; p.A16). Total expenditures on arms and militaries exceed $15 billion annually and are already included in total imports.

Civil wars continue to wreak devastation on African economies. They cost Africa at least $15 billion annually in lost output, wreckage of infrastructure, and refugee crises. The crisis in Zimbabwe, for example, has cost Africa dearly. Foreign investors have fled the region and the South African *rand* has lost 25 percent of its value since 2000. Recall that more than 2 million Zimbabwean refugees have fled to settle in South Africa, and the South African government is preparing a military base at Messina to house as many as 70,000 refugees. Since 2000 almost 60,000 physicians and other professionals have left Zimbabwe (*The Washington Post*, March 3, 2002; p.A20).

According to *The Observer* [London] (Sept 30, 2001), Zimbabwe's economic collapse had caused $37 billion worth of damage to South Africa and other neighboring countries. South Africa has been worst affected, while Botswana, Malawi, Mozambique, and Zambia have also suffered severely.

As we have seen, neglect of peasant agriculture, the uprooting of farmers by civil wars, devastated infrastructure, and misguided agricultural policies have made it difficult for Africa to feed itself. Therefore, Africa must resort to food imports, spending $15 billion in 1998 (World Bank 2000a; p.107). By 2000, food imports had reached $18.7 billion, slightly more than donor assistance of $18.6 billion to Africa in 2000 (*Africa Recovery*, Jan 2004; p.16).

Here is a breakdown of how Africa loses money:

Corruption	$148 billion
Capital Flight	$20 billion
Expenditures on Arms and Military	$15 billion
Civil War Damage	$15 billion
Food Imports	$18 billion
Total Other Leakages	$216 billion

Recall that NEPAD seeks $64 billion from the West in investments. However, from the table, if Africa could feed itself, if the senseless wars raging on the continent would cease, if the elites would invest their wealth—legitimate or ill-gotten—in Africa, and if expenditures on arms and the military are reduced, Africa could find itself with the resources it needs for investment. In fact, more resources can be found if corrupt leaders would disgorge the loot they have stashed abroad—a condition we previously established for debt relief. This constitutes the new way of looking at the investment issue: plugging the leakages and repatriating booty hoarded abroad. The leadership, of course, would prefer crawling before Western donors with a bowl in hand to beg for more foreign aid, mumbling about the slave trade, colonial injustices, and an unfair international economic system. Enough. A new approach or a new paradigm is imperative.

Africa's Development Model goes Kaput

The existing approach to development envisioned the process as embarking on a journey from a state of underdevelopment to a developed state. The road was strewn with innumerable obstacles. Earlier development literature in the 1960s and 1970s was replete with a host of these obstacles: low income, low investment, low savings, illiteracy, high population growth rates, and so on. It was believed that removing these "obstacles" with foreign aid from Western donors was all that was needed to spur development. Few paid any attention to the *condition* of the vehicle for the journey.

In virtually all African countries, the tools of development were state controlled or owned. By the early 1980s, however, the development model (or the developmobile) had broken down with a host of crises: agricultural crisis, foreign debt crisis, inflation, etc. In addition, fiendishly clutching control was a reckless and unskilled megalomaniac who proclaimed himself "leader-for-life" but who had no idea how the country worked and viewed it as his personal property. He blamed any failure on the colonialists. He surrounds himself with his cronies, tribesmen, mistresses, sycophants, and other patronage junkies, who, in turn, have brought along their relatives, tribesmen, and friends. With all of these rascals stealing from the people, the system soon collapses, leaving a trail of crises in its wake.

This development crisis situation confronts many African countries. It has three dimensions, relating to the leader, the condition of the state apparatus, and the environment. It is important to recognize that fixing one without the other would make little difference to the development process. For example, changing the leader through democratic elections alone would not mean much if the government had broken down. Witness Ivory Coast, Liberia, Nigeria, and Zambia. Therefore, questions of accelerating development (becoming a developed state) must be deferred until the system is fixed. We can argue forever whether this situation inherited from the colonialists was defective or not, but that would be pointless.

Every society that seeks to move from point A to point B on the development stage needs a working state system. And every system must operate in a stable, standard way which requires maintenance and care. The problem is, the word "maintenance" does not even exist in the official lexicon of African governments, who drive new systems into the ground and then abandon them. In other words, you can't neglect to put oil in the engine of a car and when the engine seizes up, claim that the vehicle colonialists bequeathed you was defective.

Systems and Institutions

Regardless of horsepower, shape, or color, a vehicle is an amalgamation of systems: ignition system, fuel system, electrical system, cooling system, transmission system, suspension system, brake system, as well as other systems. Each system is designed for a specific purpose and must be in good working condition for the vehicle to operate efficiently. When a system breaks down, it must be repaired promptly. Parts designed for one system cannot be used to repair another. Oil, a lubricant, cannot be used as a coolant in the radiator. Periodic maintenance and repair are imperative for optimal operating efficiency of each system.

Institutions are to a society what systems are to a vehicle. A society has such institutions and systems as the military, the police and law enforcement, the political system, the economic system, the educational system, the judiciary system, the banking system, the civil service, and the media. Each institution has a specific function to play and should not be cross-matched with different functions. For example, the role of the military is to defend the territorial integrity of the nation and protect its citizens, while that of the judiciary is to enforce the rule of law and assure justice. Soldiers cannot be placed in civil judicial or political roles, because they are not trained for such roles. These institutions can also provide institutional checks against each other; for example, the police against the judiciary and verse versa.

But in Africa, the institutions that are supposed to provide the checks and balances have been corrupted by the ruling vampire elites. They raid state-owned corporations and the national treasury with impunity. They go scot-free because of the enormous powers afforded them by two defective systems they themselves established: the economic system of statism and the political system of sultanism, through which enormous economic and political power have been concentrated in their hands. Where parliament exists, it is a rubber stamp and not likely to probe deeply into the collapse of a looted, state-owned corporation. And the crooks escape apprehension because they control the very key institutions (the media and the judiciary) needed to expose their nefarious activities and prosecute them.

Other systems in the state (or development vehicle) are also perverted. The civil service was packed with party hacks, cronies, and tribesmen. It eventually became bloated, inefficient, and riddled with corruption. The educational system produced functionally illiterate elites. The judiciary system failed to uphold the rule of law. The judges themselves are crooks, the police highway bandits. The banking system was subject to manipulation by the ruling elite to siphon billions of dollars into overseas accounts. The media in most African countries was taken over by the state and gagged or used as a propaganda mouthpiece for the ruling vagabonds. The remaining private newspapers were cowed into silence with criminal libel suits, assassinations, and onerous registration requirements. But the most discredited and perverted institution in Africa has been the military-cum-security forces, lacking even an elementary understanding of their basic function in society. Instead of protecting the people, security forces train their guns on them.

Thus debauched, the institutions and systems in Africa's states have become dysfunctional and the "developmobile" kaput. Internal systems malfunction. The warlords in Congo, Liberia, Sierra Leone, Somalia, and other

African countries do not care about the condition of the state or the people. Rather, they battle ferociously to determine who should be in control.

Meanwhile, multilateral financial institutions, such as the World Bank, the IMF, Western governments, and donor agencies trip over themselves to offer aid and conflicting advice. Initially, they preoccupied themselves with removing obstacles to development by building highways, bridges, dams, and schools to improve literacy rates, and sinking bore holes for drinking water, for example. This was pointless since the state had broken down. Subsequently, in the 1980s, they shifted their focus to fixing various parts of the state: structural adjustment (economic reform) and democratization. But the IMF and World Bank did not understand that the state needed a *complete overhaul*, not just piecemeal reform.

Not to be outdone, Africa's politicians and intellectuals argue furiously and endlessly over who would be a better leader: a Hausa, Yoruba, Tutsi, Hutu, Kikuyu, Muslim, or a professor. No one is talking about fixing the institutions or systems. If the "developmobile" is kaput, then what is the sense in arguing over who would be the "best" leader or whether a six-lane highway must be built?

In summary, Africa's developmobile is going nowhere because of institutional breakdown (dysfunctional systems) and the megalomaniac drivers, who have "gone bonkers." Their development priorities are oriented toward self-aggrandizement and self-perpetuation in power. It is an African tragedy because no nation can develop when it is ruled by a phalanx of rabid bandits who stay in office forever. As George Soros, the billionaire financier, observed succinctly: "The main cause of misery and poverty in the world is bad government" (*The Wall Street Journal,* March 14, 2002; p.B1).

Institutional Reform

Back in the 1980s and 1990s, nearly all the development models assumed that all other things were equal and all Africa needed to take off was a massive infusion of foreign aid or capital. This orthodoxy, which became known as "capital fundamentalism," assumed that the country had the "absorptive capacity" to utilize effectively the capital it received from abroad. In other words, it had the right institutions, the right environment, and the capability to utilize foreign aid or investment. For example, that the country was at peace (no civil wars), property rights were respected (government thugs did not arbitrarily seize private property with impunity), and that the rule of law prevailed (the head of state and his ministers did not loot the treasury).

Today, most of these assumptions can be seen as profoundly erroneous and misguided. An "enabling environment" has not prevailed over much of postcolonial Africa. In fact, Africa's investment climate has deteriorated progressively over the decades. What now prevails is antithetical to development. The infusion of vast amounts of foreign aid into Africa achieved little results. The Washington consensus has now shifted its focus to "governance," but its fatal flaw is its presumption that the mafia state or the coconut republic will or is capable of reforming itself. A *new approach* is needed.

Sustainable, long-term development for Africa—or the blueprint for Africa's prosperity—entails a four-step reform process. The first step involves "changing the driver"—replacing the corrupt, incompetent, sit-tight "life-presidents" with more capable leaders. This is why democracy is important. Democracy itself does not guarantee economic prosperity; it only ensures that bad economic policies are not repeated by offering a peaceful means of changing failed leaders through the ballot box. Violent military coups engender political instability and a rebel insurgency could degenerate into destructive civil war. But democracy cannot be imposed from the outside or stage-managed through a series of coconut elections by the incumbent. It must be nurtured internally, which requires freedom of speech, of expression, of the media, of assembly, and of association. Recall that only 8 out of the 54 African countries had a free media in 2003 (www.freedomhouse.org).

The second step requires repairing dysfunctional systems: rebuilding key state institutions such as the military, the police, the judiciary, the banking system, the civil service, and the electoral commission, among others, in order to ensure secure property rights, the rule of law, and accountability.

The third step entails "cleaning up the environment." Civil wars, armed banditry, corruption, capital flight, and military vandalism must end. Infrastructure must be repaired to ensure reliable supplies of social amenities such as clean running water, electricity, phone service, health care, and education. Meaningful development cannot occur in a country engulfed by civil war. No one would invest in such a country, except perhaps arms merchants. And it makes no sense to supply foreign aid to build roads, schools, hospitals, and bridges only to have them blown up by rebel insurgents. Nor does it make sense to invest in a country where lawlessness and open plunder of the treasury are the hallmarks of the ruling bandits. These factors are all internal and are all highly interdependent. These internal problems are symptoms of more fundamental diseases. Treating the symptoms without attacking the root causes is an exercise in futility. For example, the root cause of most of Africa's civil wars is power. Rebel soldiers want power. Peace talks only treat the symptoms. The establishment of a mechanism or system for peaceful transfer of political power addresses the root cause.

This suggests that an environmental cleanup would require attending to the systemic breakdown by fixing malfunctioning institutions (the judiciary, the political system, the economic system, etc.) as the first order of priority. The experience of several African countries in the 1990s is instructive at this juncture: Some leaders were merely changed without reforming their dilapidated systems/institutions: Zambia in 1991 (from Kenneth Kaunda to Frederick Chiluba); Liberia in 1996 (from Samuel Doe to Charles Taylor); Ivory Coast in 1999 (from Konan Bedie to Robert Guie in 1999 and from Guie to Laurent Gbagbo in 2000); and Nigeria in 1999 (from Abusallam Abubakar to Olusegun Obasanjo).

Once all the three steps have been taken, the fourth step requires laying down a *development strategy* to get from point A (state of underdevelopment) to point B (developed state) *faster*. Admittedly, each African country is "different" and one size or strategy may not fit all. However, there are enough commonalities to delineate what should *not* be done.

Regarding the sequence of steps, a furious debate ("leaders versus institutions") continues to rage over which problem to address first: bad leaders or bad institutions. A failed despotic leader would not allow the institutions to be reformed because that would strip him of power and expose his own crimes. If pressured, he would only undertake phony or cosmetic reforms to placate Western donors. Kenya is a case in point: The corrupt Moi regime set up a commission of enquiry in 2000 to satisfy IMF demands and then passed a law to declare that same commission unconstitutional. Progress on corruption began to be made when the Moi regime was tossed out but then the new Kibaki regime began stalling, prompting violent demonstrations on July 7, 2004. The chicanery of Africa's despots knows no bounds. To ensure their political survival, some African despots suddenly change their tune, don a reformist garb and become democracy converts. But their brutal past misdeeds strip them of any credibility to advance a reformist agenda and the populace become suspicious of their intentions.

Only new leaders can have the credibility and the clean hands to carry out necessary institutional reform. Also, civil society needs to be galvanized as the motivating force behind political reform. The prescription, therefore, is new leadership in tandem with reformed institutions, since the former alone will not suffice. Once these are in place, the next question should be: What is the appropriate *development strategy?* It should be obvious that it cannot be the failed "import-substitution" industrialization strategy of the 1960s. This new strategy must be agriculture-based for the simple logic that agriculture is the primary occupation of the vast majority of Africa's peasants.

However, in many African countries, fixing the broken state may well-nigh be impossible. Reform of political and economic systems, as well as the country's institutions, is anathema to the ruling vampire elites. They are simply not interested in relinquishing or sharing power. Period. The democratization process has stalled and economic reform, despite tutelage by and billions of dollars from the World Bank, has produced only a phantom list of economic success stories. Institutions such as the judiciary, the media, the military, and the central bank are yet to be reformed. In short, the Bongos, the Eyademas, the Ghaddafis, the Mugabes, the Nguemas, among others, are just not interested. African mafia states and coconut republics won't reform themselves. Therefore, two alternatives suggest themselves.

The first is to buy them out. In fact on July 1, 1998, that exact proposal was advanced in Nigeria, where kamikaze plunder by a string of military bandits had reduced a mineral-rich country to rags:

> The proposal [to lay-off officers above the rank of major] was one of many presented to General Abubakar as part of wide-ranging consultations to ease the military out of office without threatening the fragile stability of Nigeria or risking a coup by hard line officers. It urges the regime to spend more than £1 billion on generous early retirement packages for middle and top-ranking officers. "No one is saying who would be the person to do it [sack most of the officer corps], but there is a widespread feeling that an investment of $2 billion (£1.2 billion) or $3 billion on ensuring that the clear-out would be painless—in return for a democratic future (would be money well spent. Consider the enormous cost of the last five years of military rule, in terms of lost investment, money stolen by government members, human lives destroyed and deaths," one of General Abubakar's advisers said. (*Times Newspapers*, July 1, 1998; p.4)

In Guinea, "the government bought off angry soldiers threatening to mutiny by giving them $7.6 million after an emergency meeting among the ministers of finance and planning and the central bank governor" (*The Washington Times*, June 24, 1999; p.A16). Or consider Zimbabwe, where the tyrannical and erratic rule of President Robert Mugabe had not only wrecked the economy but also caused more than $37 billion worth of damage to neighboring countries. Would $500 million be too much to buy out Mugabe and his thugs and send them off to Jupiter?

Recall that there are three Africas: modern and traditional Africa, and an informal sector stuck between them. Modern Africa—the abode of the elites, dysfunctional government (mafia state) systems, and institutions—does not work. It is hopelessly lost. For decades, much effort and billions of dollars have been spent to cajole, bribe, and browbeat the ruling elites to reform modern Africa. Greater returns can be achieved elsewhere.

Traditional Africa—the home of the Atingas—however, does function, albeit at low levels of efficiency. The second strategy is give up or bypass the modern sector—which will eventually implode anyway if the ruling elites do not come to their senses to save themselves. If after more than 40 years of independence from oppressive colonial rule and if after decades of "education" the ruling elites still have no grasp of such elementary concepts as "freedom," "democracy," "the rule of law," "accountability," "decentralization," and "devolution of authority," they are beyond redemption.

In traditional Africa, kings were not above the law and were severely restrained in the exercise of their powers against their people. The king of the Asante (of Ghana) might appear absolute, but he "had to procure the consent of the chiefs, and the chiefs the consent of the elders, in order to bring about group action" (Carlston, 1968; p.127). "Akan kings (in Ghana) had no right to make peace or war, make laws, or be directly involved in important negotiations such as treaties without the consent of their elders and/or elected representatives" (Boamah-Wiafe, 1993; p.169). Even in the rigidly controlled kingdom of Dahomey (Benin), Boahen and Webster (1970) found that,

> Although the king's word was the law of the land yet he was not above the law. Dahomeans like to recount how king Glele was fined for breaking the law. When gangs of men were working co-operatively either on state roads or building a house for one of their members, it was a law that a passer-by must approach the leader and make an excuse as to why he could not break his journey to assist in the work. Permission was almost inevitably given, the law being largely designed to reinforce courtesy. King Glele's procession passed one such group without asking to be excused. He was stopped by the headman and fined many cases of rum and pieces of cloth for breaking the law. The fact that the kings of Dahomey [now Benin] were prepared to obey the laws they themselves created was the difference between arbitrary despotism and despotism which realized that its power and position rested ultimately, no matter how indirectly, upon the will of the people. (p. 108)

The Zulu king also had to obey the law of the land. At the South African Government Commission on Native Law and Custom in 1881, Zulu king Cetshwayo was asked why he did not use his vast authority to prevent girls from being given in marriage sometimes without their consent. The Zulu king replied thus, through an interpreter:

> The King says he cannot alter a law like that, because it has been the custom, in Zululand ever since the nation was created. Every king has agreed to the law and so must he. The nation would say that anyone who tries to change that law was a bad king. Yes, the king would change it if the chief of the land were willing to make a change in that way. If there is a certain law which the king wishes to be known in the country, he declares it at the feast of the first

fruits. The king has a discussion with the chiefs about it, and they give out the law, but he cannot make a law without their consent. He consults the chiefs and gives his reasons, and if they conclude to agree to it, it is the law, but he cannot make a law against the wishes of his chiefs. (Olivier, 1969; p.145)

Note the similarity in the Asante and Zulu kingdoms: Without the consent of chiefs or elders, the king could make no law. His authority was also delegated through the bureaucracy to the heads of smaller territorial units, the provinces or principalities. In central Africa, delegation of authority usually amounted to delegation of almost all authority save religious—and on a few occasions, even religious authority was delegated (Bohannan, 1964; p.192). "Most traditional constitutions require the king to delegate almost all of his authority to other leaders and officials. Custom and tradition set limits to the authority of the king, his cabinet, and advisors" (Boamah-Wiafe, 1993; p.168). In fact, delegation of authority was necessary for practical reasons. The king's authority "cannot be exercised by any other means over an area larger than a few square miles" (Curtin, et al., 1988; p.31).

The constitutional articles, principles, and economic institutions Africa needs to develop are already there—in traditional Africa. Africa does not need to copy from Jupiter. Enough development by imitation. The continent is already littered with putrid carcasses of failed imported systems. Said *The New York Times* (June 21, 1994):

> Everywhere the point is the same: Africans cannot just transplant foreign models, like the [Western] parliamentary system, and hope it will take root in native soil. "It's a mistake to copy Western democracies because it's artificial," observed Cyril Goungounga, an engineer and national assembly deputy in Burkina Faso. "Look at the U.S. You elect a President. He's in office for four years, eight years. Then he's out. That's what the Constitution says. We have a Constitution too," he said. "But it doesn't work. It's just a piece of paper. Because we have two civilizations here. The Western one on top, where everything is fine and differences are submerged in talk of national unity. And a parallel one underneath, an African one, where ethnic groups are a reality." (p. A8)

Take what is there—in Africa's own backyard—and build upon, improve upon, or modernize it. Return to Africa's own indigenous economic heritage of free village markets, free enterprise, and free trade. Only Botswana returned to its traditional roots and built upon its indigenous institutions. Not surprisingly, "Only one African country, Botswana, has consistently been well governed since independence. Not coincidentally, average incomes in Botswana have grown faster than anywhere else in the world in the past 35 years, from bare subsistence to over $3,000 a year" (*The Economist,* Jan 17, 2004; Survey; p.4).

Botswana ought to be the "African model" that should be replicated across the continent—from Zimbabwe to Nigeria. It is preposterous to seek to establish a "Marxist-Leninist" state in any African country. Marx and Lenin bear no relevance to indigenous African heritage.

CHAPTER 9

The Indigenous Economic System[1]

Before 1890 there was no cocoa production in the Gold Coast or Nigeria, only very small production of cotton and groundnuts (peanuts), and small exports of palm oil and palm kernels. By the 1950s all these had become staples of world trade. They were produced by Africans on African-owned properties.

—Peter Bauer, 2000; p.57.

INTRODUCTION

Of all of Africa's social organizations, the least understood is probably the indigenous economic system. The myth of "hunters and gatherers" persists, giving the impression that Africa had no economic institutions or culture before contact with the Europeans. Inexorably tied to the land, Africans supposedly eked out livings from primitive agriculture. Trade and exchange were supposedly unknown, since self-sufficiency and subsistence farming were the operative goals. Books on precolonial Africa dwelled excessively on the "backwardness" of African technology. But Africa did have economic institutions.

West Africa was particularly noted for its indigenous economic development. As Elliott Skinner (1964) observed:

The peoples of [precolonial West Africa] had economies which made agricultural produce available in amounts large enough to be sold in rural and urban markets; craft specialization often organized along the line of craft guilds, whose members manufactured goods to be sold in these markets; different kinds of currencies which were nearly always convertible one to another and, later, to European denominations of values; and elaborate trading systems, external as well

as internal. Goods produced in even the smallest West African societies were circulated in local market centers, and ultimately by porters, caravans, and boats,
to the large Sudanese emporiums from which they could be shipped to Mediter-
ranean areas in exchange for foreign products. (p.205)

Africans engaged in a wide variety of economic activities. Although
mostly primary—agricultural, pastoralism, hunting, fishing, and wood-
working—there were also crafts and other industries such as clothweaving,
pottery, brassworks, and the mining and smelting of iron, gold, silver, copper, and tin.

Agriculture was the primary occupation of Africans, and the basic unit
of production was the extended family. Each family constituted itself into
a working unit or labor force and acted as an operative economic entity that
produced goods and distributed the fruits of labor as its members saw fit,
allowing for individual discretion and reward. Within the family, there was
specialization of labor and sexual division of occupation. Different crops
were raised by different members and certain tasks were reserved for
women. For example, the cultivation of food crops (domestic staples) was
almost everywhere a female occupation. The majority of Africa's peasant
farmers today are women. In Ethiopia, however, women raised goats in addition to farming.

What a person grew on the land was his own free decision to make. The
produce was private property. Even among the Kalahari Bushmen, "all that
a woman gathered belonged to her alone" (Marshall, 1973; p.113). How
much a person shared with his kinsmen and how much he kept for himself
was an individual decision to make. There was rarely a mandated, propor-
tional distribution of produce among the extended family. As M. J. Field
(1940; p.62) observed of the Ga people of Ghana, "in farming every married man has his own farm though all help each in clearing, so problems of
division of produce do not arise."

In much of indigenous Africa, all the means of production were owned
by the natives, not by their rulers, the chiefs, or by tribal governments. Feu-
dalism was not commonplace in Africa, except in Abyssinia (Ethiopia). That
means, in popular language, that all the means of production were privately
owned. The hunting spears, fishing nets, cattle, pots, huts, farm produce,
fish, textile looms, gold jewelery shops, and various tools and products were
all privately owned. As Gray (1962) observed of the Sonjo of Kenya:

Generally speaking, property is privately owned among the Sonjo. The only important exception is the building plots upon which houses are built. These are
owned communally. The other forms of property are owned by individuals.

Thus, a piece of property such as a field, a beehive, or a goat, at any given time can be traced in ownership to an individual. According to Sonjo law, a man has ultimate ownership rights in his own property and in all property possessed by his patrilineal descendants for as long as he lives. When he dies, these rights are inherited by his heirs. (pp. 45–46)

Centuries ago when Africa was sparsely populated, unoccupied land belonged to no one. Anyone could use natural waters and pastures. But as soon as a man sunk a well or built a dam, he could exercise exclusive rights over the water it contained (Schapera, 1953). "The man who first came with his followers to settle in a previously unoccupied area was usually termed the 'owner of the land' and his heir would continue to receive respect for his primacy" (Colson, 1953). Among the Tonga, who occupy the plateau of southern Zambia, the owner was called *ulanyika* and the Dagaaba of northern Ghana used the word *tendaana*.

On the inherited land, family members exercised only usufructural rights. A son had the right of use but could not sell the land. Ownership and control remained within the lineage. Lineage control over the land was exercised by the elders, and in some small tribes, by the chief. Communal ownership is really a misleading description of this system for it implies open access by all in the village to any piece of land, which was certainly not the case. Clearly, if what obtained was communal tenure, then shifting cultivation would be possible only when the whole community moved to another location. As Bohannan and Bohannan (1968) contend, "Communal tenure is an illusion that results from viewing the systematic exploitation by kinship groups of their environment through the distorting lens of western market-oriented and contract-dominated institutions of property and ownership" (p.88). The more accurate description is family or lineage ownership. All those who trace their ancestry to a certain individual are entitled to use his original plot of land. The individual farmer makes his own determination about what to cultivate on that land.

Africans engaged in a variety of industrial activities in the precolonial era. In Benin, "the glass industry made extraordinary strides" (Diop, 1987; p.136). In Nigeria, "the cloth industry was an ancient craft" (Olaniyan, 1985; p.104). Kano attained historical prominence in the fourteenth century with its fine indigo-dyed cloth, which was traded for goods from North Africa. Even before the discovery of cotton, other materials had been used for cloth. The Igbo, for example, made cloth from the fibrous bark of trees. The Asante also were famous for their cotton and bark cloth (*kente* and *adwumfo*).

Economists define capital as anything that is not wanted for its own sake but aids in the production of further goods. Thus, Robinson Crusoe's fishing net is a capital good, as are tractors, industrial machines, and scythes. By popular usage, however, capital has come to mean funds or money needed to operate or start a business. In indigenous Africa, capital funds were generally scarce. There were banks in colonial Africa, but the natives lacked the collateral to obtain credit. To secure initial startup capital for fishing and commercial operations, they turned to two traditional sources of finance. One was the "family pot." Each extended family had a fund into which members made contributions according to their means. While members were not coerced to contribute, failure to do so effectively extinguished one's access to the pot.

The fund was used for both consumption and investment. For example, it was used to cover funeral expenses, weddings, the educational costs of the more gifted among them, extension of the family house, or as capital. Among the Ewe seine fishermen of Ghana, the family pot was called *agbadoho*. Members borrowed from this pot to purchase their fishing nets and paid back the loans.

The second source of finance was a revolving credit scheme that was widespread across Africa. It was called *susu* in Ghana, *esusu* in Yoruba, *tontines* or *chilembe* in Cameroon, and *stokfel* in South Africa.[2] A group of say ten people would contribute perhaps $100 into a fund. When the fund reached a certain amount, say $1,000, it was handed over to the members in turn, who would invest the cash into an endeavor. To be operational, such a scheme required a liberal dose of trust among members and somehow the natives managed to make it work. In fact, for many businesses in the indigenous and informal sector, the loan club was the primary source of capital.[3] One could also borrow money by pledging farms, a practice common in Ghana and Nigeria (Hill, 1986; p.12). If borrowing was not possible, one could form a partnership with a person with capital. "A common arrangement involved three partners who shared the returns from a venture equally. In trading ventures, one partner supplied the capital, one transported the goods and braved the hazards of the trail, and the other organized the partnership, which in some cases involved little more than getting the capitalist in touch with someone who had the stamina and courage to make the trip" (Miracle, 1971; note 2, p.401).

Profit was never an alien concept to Africa. Throughout its history, there have been numerous entrepreneurs. The aim of traders and numerous brokers or middlemen was profit and wealth. In the brokerage business, the middlemen kept a fixed proportion of the proceeds. For example, among the Egba and Ijebu brokers of palm oil in Nigeria in the 1850s, a quarter of the price went to the broker and three-quarters to African suppliers (Newbury, 1971). Profit calculations were always on the mind of African traders. For example, "The Nupe saw to it that the prices of goods corresponded closely to variations in supply and demand, and above all, to seasonal fluctuations. They also made sure that distance between the area of production and market, and the additional labor and loss of time involved in transport, entered into the calculation of price and profit" (Skinner, 1964; p.218).

Profit made was private property; it was for the traders to keep, not for the chiefs or rulers to expropriate. On the Gold Coast in the seventeenth century, there existed men of wealth, such as the Akrosang brothers and Edward Barter of Cape Coast, Aban and John Kabes of Komenda, John Kurankye of Annomabo, Asomani and Peter Passop of Akwamu and Accra, and John Konny of Ahanta (Daaku, 1971). Chiefs did not sequestrate their wealth for equal distribution to all tribesmen.

The natives chose what to do with their profit. The traditional practice was to share the profit. Under the *abusa* scheme devised by the cocoa farmers of Ghana at the beginning of the twentieth century, net proceeds were divided into three parts: A third went to the owner of the farm, another third went to hired laborers, and the remaining third was set aside for farm maintenance and expansion. Under the less common *abunu* system, profits were shared equally between the owner and the workers. Variants of this profit-sharing scheme were extended beyond agriculture to commerce and fishing.

PROPERTY RIGHTS

Looting and arbitrary seizures of property by undisciplined soldiers was not a feature of traditional African society. Even the chief could not dispossess someone of his property without a full council hearing. When disputes pertaining to property arose, a chief's court adjudicated the matter. On precolonial African law and custom, Frances Kendall and Leon Louw (1986) observed that: "There were no powers of arbitrary expropriation, and land and huts could be expropriated only under extreme conditions after a full public hearing" (p. 18). This view is corroborated by Koyana (1980):

> Only in cases of, for example, the commission of a grave offence against the community, abandonment of the land, or when the chief required the land for himself or for another chief, was this right exercised. There could therefore be "despotic acts" giving evidence of an unbridled exercise of power, but there was *always* the safeguard that the powers were not exercised recklessly. Public opinion would always be taken into account. There were also always the councilors whose advice was as a rule taken into account by the chief. *In practice, therefore, the rights of the individual were never nullified.* (p.69) (emphasis added)

FREE MARKET, FREE TRADE TRADITION

Some goods produced by the natives were traded or sold in markets. Market development was inevitable even if self-sufficiency was the preferred form of making a living, for it was physically impossible for one homestead to produce everything it needed on the farm. By necessity, a surplus had to be produced to exchange for what could not be produced. In earlier times, such exchanges were done by canvassing from hut to hut, a time-consuming process. A market was simply a place where exchanges could be made more easily. Where exchanges occurred regularly, a marketplace would naturally develop. The institution of a marketplace, then, evolved naturally. As noted in chapter 4, markets were everywhere in West Africa. There were the small village markets and the large markets that served as long-distance interregional trade centers.

Precolonial rural markets in West Africa provided for the needs of local producers, consumers, and traders. If the rural population and the volume of transaction were sufficiently large, the rural market operated daily. Otherwise, the rural market operated periodically. The periodic markets were organized on a cyclical basis of every three, four, five, and sixteen days to feed the daily markets. Each rural community had a market day. Where a cluster of villages existed, market days would be rotated among them. An important characteristic of rural markets was the segregation of vendors or merchants according to the products they sold. Tomato sellers, for example, were all seated in one section of the market. The economic object was to promote competition, but there appeared to be a social one as well. It made it easier to locate a merchant. For example, a child in search of his mother at the market could be readily reunited if he indicated the product she sold. Another distinctive characteristic of rural markets was the seating arrangement. Market traders seated themselves facing the homesteads or villages from which they came—should flight from the market be necessary. The seating arrangement also made it easier for a lost child to find his mother; for example, if the child knew what his mother sold and from which village she came from.

Market Regulations and Controls

Generally, economic activity in African markets was not controlled by political authorities. Existing rules and regulations were aimed more at the preservation of law and order, the collection of market tolls, the use of standard weights and measures, and the supervision of the slaughter of cattle. For example, to prevent fighting in the Igbo market, there was a strict rule against carrying machetes or large knives. Traders generally sat with others from their villages. There apparently were no price controls.

In the Mossi markets:

There are no official restrictions on the kinds of goods which may or may not be sold. In pre-European times slaves and eunuchs were the common stock-in-trade of the major markets and of some of the smaller ones as well. The only active supervision that existed and still exists concerns the butchering of meat. Every person who sells meat in the market must exhibit the skin of the butchered animal in a public place so that there will be no question as to the ownership of the animal. If the meat in question is the remains of a cow killed and half-eaten by a lion, then the village or district chief must be notified before the meat enters the market. (Skinner, 1962; p.219)

Kojo Yelpaala (1983) also found that, in Dagaaba markets, "There was the freedom to buy and sell any commodity within the market environment (*daa*). Free and voluntary interaction between buyers and sellers produced a market-determined price. When this condition was violated, the transactions were said to result in *fao* (robbery) in the sense that the buyer or seller might extort a price lower or higher price than the market-determined price, thereby reducing social welfare" (p. 370).

The Importance of Markets

The village market performed vital economic, social, and political functions that were well understood by the chiefs and the people. In fact, as Skinner (1962) observed of the Mossi of Ghana, "whenever and wherever there is a large gathering of Mossi there is a market. The rural market is the center of Mossi social life, and friends as well as enemies meet within its confines. What Mangin [a British explorer] wrote some 40 years ago is still true: 'Every self-respecting Mossi—man or woman, child or elder—must go to market at least once in a while were it only to look and to be looked at, if he can put on some handsome clothes.' Except for the Moslems who are now experimenting with a form of Purdah, there are few persons who do not go to market" (p.168). Among the Akan of Ghana, Daniel F. McCall (1962) noted that the marketplace was not only "the source of food and clothing for the family, it is the place where the wife and mother spends most of her waking day" (p.65).

The rural market served many purposes:

- It provided peasants with the opportunity to exchange goods or occasional agricultural surpluses and to purchase what they could not produce themselves.

- It provided an indispensable avenue for social intercourse: to meet people, to gossip, or to discuss and keep abreast of local affairs. Dancers, singers, musicians, and other artists often went to the markets to display their skills. Work parties and weddings often took place at the markets.
- It served as a center of interethnic contact and channels of communication (White, 1987; p.41). It was at the market that important information about foreign cultures, medicine, product improvements, and new technologies was exchanged. As such, the market acted as an integrative force, a place for cultural and normative exchange.
- It often served as the meeting place for important political events such as *durbars* and village assemblies convened by the traditional rulers.
- It served as an important area for communication and dissemination of information. Among the Mossi of Ghana, "the market is the main communication center of Mossi society and news of happenings in the region can be heard there. If a *new* person is in an area one can be sure that the people in the market will know about him, or that he will sooner or later visit the market" (Skinner, 1962).
- Most marketplaces were associated with religious activities. Markets were consecrated with shrines associated with them. The consecration emanated primarily out of the need for peace and calm at the market place. It was believed "such consecration would guarantee that supernatural sanctions would back up the political authorities in their maintenance of peace in the marketplace" (Bohannan, 1964; p.215).

In the 1850s, an American missionary, T. J. Bowen, provided a vivid description of the importance of Yoruba markets:

> The most attractive object next to the curious old town itself—and it is always old—is the market. This is not a building, but a large area, shaded with trees, and surrounded and sometimes sprinkled over with little open sheds, consisting of a very low thatched roof surmounted on rude posts. Here the women sit and chat all day, from early morning till 9 o'clock at night, to sell their various merchandise. The principal marketing hour, and the proper time to see all the wonders, is the evening. At half an hour before sunset, all sorts of people, men, women, girls, travelers lately arrived in the caravans, farmers from the fields, and artisans from their houses, are pouring in from all directions to buy and sell, and talk. At the distance of half a mile their united voices roar like the waves of the sea. (Bascom, 1984; p.25)

In East Africa, studies by Gulliver (1962) also showed that markets were extremely important to the Arusha because markets provided them their "main opportunity for personal contact with the Masai in the conscious efforts to learn and imitate all they could of Masai culture" (p.46).

Clearly, the marketplace was the heart of indigenous African society, the center not only of economic activity but also of political, social, judicial, and communication activities. Perhaps the easiest way to annihilate an ethnic group was to destroy its markets. For such a destruction would assail the *very* core of the society and the extended family itself. The importance of markets in traditional African society has not diminished even today. As *West Africa* magazine (April 3–9, 1989) reported:

> Sixty years ago Cotonou was a cluster of villages surrounded by lagoons. Today, it is the economic capital of Benin with a population of 170,000. Its nerve centre is the Dantokpa Market. Animated from early morning to late at night, scores of small retailers line its *voms,* or streets. Mobylette repair shops, dressmakers, millers preparing corn flour and cabinet-makers carving red wood ply their trades next to traditional healers patiently waiting for clients. Vendors of pimento, peppers, spices and vegetables with piquant odors stand behind their stalls, while itinerant peddlers are everywhere selling dried fish, potato-fritters and corn flour.
>
> Near the old port are the stands selling textiles, the domain of the "Mama Benz". These vigorous business women usually ride in shining Mercedes cars, hence their name. Impressive by their girth and the sumptuous cloth they wear, their spectacular success has been built on the sale of colorful textiles, most of which they import from the Netherlands. (p.514)

In indigenous Africa, the occupational system and the family structure were functionally related. Women have always dominated market activity in Africa. A benighted attempt to destroy or reduce the scale of operations of an indigenous African market and the consequent decline in female participation in market activity would send shock waves through the entire family system. The market was so important in indigenous Africa that Skinner (1962) asserted emphatically that: "No African chief can refuse to hear a case brought to his attention at market (though he may postpone it until a regular court hearing). These courts may be the same as—but are often different from—the arbitrating facilities for settling disputes which arise among sellers and customers within the marketplace itself" (p.63).

Market Prices

To effect trade, direct barter was the medium of exchange in the early stages of African market development. Goods were exchanged directly. In many communities, however, various commodities were used as currency, including cloth, cattle, salt, iron bars, cowrie shells, beads, firearms, mats, and gold dust.

Every African today will declare that prices in the village markets are generally not determined or fixed by the village chief or king. This is a fact that has been true for centuries and must be stated emphatically since many modern African governments are ignorant of it.

Prices on indigenous markets traditionally have been influenced by several factors: the forces of supply and demand, scarcity, time of day, status of the consumer, relation with the seller, quality of the product, its degree of necessity, bargaining skills and competition. In general, prices are determined by the normal forces of supply and demand, while the other factors merely shave off or add a few pennies so that two different consumers do not pay exactly the same price. Thus price discrimination exists in indigenous African markets.

Skinner (1964) observed that "Mossi merchants were very aware of the principles of supply and demand and held goods out of the market when prices fell, in order to obtain later higher prices" (p.222). Vansina (1962) also found that prices on Kuba markets in Zaire "behave in exactly the same way as prices do in European markets. The price is set by the relation of supply and demand. When shrimps first appear on the market, they fetch a high price. Later on, the price falls" (p.235). On the Konso markets of southern Ethiopia, Kluckhorn (1962) discovered that "supply and demand was the basic adjustment mechanism for prices" (p.86).

Marguerite Dupire (1962) observed that on Fulani markets, "The price of millet and of salt, essential elements in the life of the nomad, vary in proportion to their scarcity. That of millet is at a minimum after the harvest and at a maximum just before the next harvest—variations on the order of one to four—while salt is less expensive at the return of the caravans which bring it back from the salt mines of the Sahara" (p.36).

The status of the buyer also affected how much one paid for a commodity. Europeans would affirm that in indigenous markets they paid higher prices than the natives. That was one reason why many sent servants to make purchases for them. As well, the price of an item was often influenced by the time of day. Toward the end of the market day, most traders were in a hurry to get home or reluctant to carry home unsold goods. Africans knew that was the best time to obtain good bargains.

In most indigenous African markets, haggling was the process by which prices were determined. Because prices were not fixed by any village or government authority, people bargained. Tardits and Tardits (1962) provided a description of such a bargaining process on South Dahomean markets:

Bargaining is the rule. Prices asked by sellers as well as buyers are always higher or lower than those which are finally agreed upon. Long debates ensue in which praise and insults have their place. A customer looks at a fish tray; the merchant asks 425 francs for 40 fish; the customer offers 350 francs. After a short discussion, the merchant is ready to sell. The customer then withdraws the offer and proposes 300 francs; the discussion goes on till the seller has accepted; the buyer thinks it over a second time and says: '275 francs.' The merchant finally agrees but the customer drops the proposed price down to 200 francs. At this point, the merchant refuses to sell. Discussion starts again until at last the bargain is concluded for 225 francs. (pp.106–107)

Peasants and chiefs understood these price gyrations. If the price of an item was too high, the traditional response was to bargain down the price. If it did not come down enough, a substitute was purchased, especially in the area of farm produce. For example, cocoyam, cassava, or plantain could be substituted for yam. One was not "forced" to buy yams if they could not afford it. When the price of a commodity remained persistently high, the natives either produced it themselves, as often happened in the case of yams, or traveled to the source to obtain it more cheaply. Tales of traders trekking long distances to buy goods more cheaply at the source are legion. Similarly, various meat substitutes could be purchased if the price of, say, chicken was too high.[4] African chiefs did little to interfere with the day-to-day operations of the village market. Nor did they impose price controls on the market. It was never the traditional role of chiefs to police how prices were set. Even wages were not fixed by any village authority (Hill, 1986; p.110). To all intents and purposes, the African village market was an open and free market, however "primitive." Only rarely did a chief intervene in market transactions.

Role of Women in the Distribution of Goods

Upon close study of Africa's rural economy, one cannot fail to be impressed by the participatory role of women. Today the majority of Africa's peasant farmers—about 80 percent—are women. Women also dominate rural markets and trade. In Yoruba, "local farm produce—either cash crops or food crops—are marketed at the local market, almost invariably by women" (Hodder, 1962). This is not a recent phenomena. Female participation in market activities has always been a tradition. It was the result of the traditional division of labor on the basis of sex.

The object in trading, as everywhere, is to make a profit. The Yoruba women "trade for profit, bargaining with both the producer and the consumer in order to obtain as large a margin of profit as possible" (Bascom,

1984; p.26). And in almost all West African countries, women kept the profits made from trading. "A Ga woman also makes money by her trading. A man has no control over his wife's money, but any extra money she can extract from him for herself can never be reclaimed" (Field, 1940; p.54). "In South Dahomey, commercial gains are a woman's own property and she spends her money free of all control. Trade gives to women a partial economic independence and if their business is profitable they might even be able to lend some money—a few thousand francs—to their husbands against their future crops" (Tardits and Tardits, 1962; p.110).

Traders frequently reinvest part of their gains to expand their trading activities and spend part to cover domestic and personal expenses, since spouses have to keep the house in good condition, replace old cooking utensils, buy their own clothes, and educate their children. Historically, another important use of trade profits was the financing of political activity. According to M. I. Herskovits and M. Harwitz (1964), "support for the nationalist movements that were the instruments of political independence came in considerable measure from the donations of the market women" (p.377).

In fact, it can be asserted that there is no black African leader, past or present, whose mother or grandmother did not engage in trade, the traditional role of women in Africa. Clearly, any event, whether government policy, a civil war, or a calamitous occurrence, that disrupts agriculture or diminishes the scale of market activity would have a disproportionately adverse effect on African women. That in turn would have ramifications throughout the family structure and the entire society.

The Role of Government in the Indigenous Economy

Indigenous African economies were based on agriculture, pastoralism, markets, and trade. Both the rulers and the natives appreciated the importance of these activities. Indigenous governments created the necessary conditions for their subjects to conduct their activities. Even with agriculture, the tribal government did not interfere or dictate what crops the peasants should raise. The role of the chief or kings in agriculture was to ensure that access to land was not denied to anyone, even strangers.

In most cases across Africa, "there was no direct interference with production" (Wickins, 1981; p.230). The tenet of African law that maintained that any harmful action against another individual was a threat to the whole society was applicable to the realm of economics. A restriction on individual's economic activity placed severe constraints on the economic welfare of the whole society. If the individual prospered, so too did his extended family and the community. An individual could prosper so long as his pursuit of prosperity did not harm or conflict with the interests of the community. The society's interests were paramount. Unless an individual's pursuit of prosperity conflicted with society's interests, the chief or king had no authority to interfere with it. This was a well-nigh universal African belief.

With this in mind, it would hardly make sense for the chiefs to prevent their own subjects from engaging in trade. Traders were free enterprisers, taking the risks upon themselves and reaping the benefits. As Kwame Y. Daaku (1971) observed:

> Those who so desired and ventured into distant places in pursuit of trade could rise to higher positions in the traditional setup. Along the coastal towns, successful traders began to display their affluence by surrounding themselves with a host of servants. Some were raised to the status of headmen or elders. They built themselves magnificent houses on which some of them even mounted a few cannon. The rise of these people was not only a coastal phenomenon. In practically all the forest states there came into prominence men like Kwame Anteban of Nyameso in Denkyira, whose wealth became proverbial. (p.179)

Occasionally, the kings and chiefs had farms and other economic enterprises operated for them. For example, the Asante kings had royal gold mines, and the chiefs in East and southern Africa had others take care of some of their goats and cattle. But these animals were mainly for consumption by royalty and guests—the leaders' farms and animals were not supposed to support the people as a whole. This point is crucial. The people performed these services out of the reverence they hold for their traditional chief. He is an embodiment of his people, their hopes and aspirations. Further, the chief has no property. Any gift to the chief becomes "stool property"—the property of the office. If the chief is removed, he cannot take such gifts or "stool property" with him. Nowhere in the history of Africa is there evidence of chiefs and kings operating tribal government farms to feed the people. The natives fed themselves, built their own huts, and provided for themselves.

Nor did the kings and chiefs operate tribal government enterprises. The craft industries were owned by individuals or families, not by the chief or the state. The ruler might choose to have an enterprise, but, again, it was mostly used for his own benefit, not that of the natives. It was the same with trade. As Daaku (1971) noted in the case of the Akan of the Gold Coast, "Apart from the occasional trading organized for and on behalf of the chiefs, trading, like all other vocations, was primarily an affair of individuals. Much of it was conducted by a man and his family, that is, his wives and children and/or with his sister's sons. It was never an affair of the state" (Daaku, 1971; p.174).

Only in very, very few instances was trade monopolized and controlled by the state. The exceptions include the kingdoms of Dahomey, Asante, and Mossi. The Dahomey kingdom was centrally planned, and Dahomeans were the most heavily taxed West Africans in the nineteenth century. Inevitably, the kingdom collapsed under the weight of its bureaucracy and maze of regulations. In fact, fewer than twenty out of thousands of commodities were reserved strictly for chiefs. According to Robert Bates (1983), the most frequently mentioned objects of chiefs' monopoly were ivory, kola, slaves, cattle, skins, and parts of game killed (p.55). Everything else was a free commodity.

In conclusion, state intervention in the economy was the exception rather than the rule in precolonial Africa. As Bates (1983) observed, "In precolonial Africa, the states underpinned specialization and trade; they terminated feuds; they provided peace and stability and the conditions for private investment; they formed public works; and they generated wealth, if only in the form of plunder. In these ways, the states secured prosperity for their citizens" (p.40).

THE INDIGENOUS SYSTEM: A SUMMARY AND ASSESSMENT

Foreign observers who came upon African natives' profit-sharing schemes hastily denigrated them as "primitive communism." Many African leaders also considered the same schemes as proof that the indigenous system was "socialist." Both groups were wrong. Many tribal societies had no state planning or direction of economic activity. Nor were there state enterprises or widespread state ownership.

The means of production were privately owned. Huts, spears, and agricultural implements were all private property. The profit motive was present in most market transactions. Free enterprise and free trade were the rule in indigenous Africa. The natives went about their economic activities on their own initiative and free will. They did not line up at the entrance of the chief's hut to apply for permits before engaging in trade or production. What and how much they produced were their own decisions to make. The African woman who produced *kenkey, garri,* or *semolina* herself decided to produce those items. No one forced her to do so. Nor did anyone tell fishermen, artisans, craftsmen, or even hunters what to produce.

In modern parlance, those who go about their economic activities on their own free will are called "free enterprisers." By this definition, the *kente* weavers of Ghana; the Yoruba sculptors; the gold, silver and blacksmiths; as well as the various indigenous craftsmen, traders, and farmers were free enterprisers. The natives have been so for centuries. The Masai, Somali, Fulani, and other pastoralists who herded cattle over long distances in search of water and pasture also were free enterprisers. So were the African traders who traveled great distances to buy and sell commodities—a risk-taking economic venture.

The extended family system offered them the security they needed to take the risks associated with entrepreneurial activity. Many development experts overlooked these positive economic aspects of the much-maligned extended family system. Although this system entailed some "sharing" (which was not forced or proportionate), it also provided the springboard for Africans to launch themselves into highly risky ventures. If they failed, the extended family system was available to support them. By the same token, if they were successful, they had some obligation to the system that supported them. The Fanti have this proverb: *"Obra nyi woara abo"* ("Life is as you make it within the community").

Even in commerce, African states lacked state controls and ownership. In Gold Coast, for example, gold-mining was open to all subjects of the states of Adanse, Assin, Denkyira, and Mampong. Chiefs did benefit from mining: Some chiefs taxed mining operations at the rate of one-fifth of the annual output and in some states, all gold mined on certain days was ceded to the throne. But the mines were in general not owned and operated by the chiefs. Any villager could mine or pan for gold on any unoccupied land. Foreign entities needed mining concessions from the chiefs.

Much of the indigenous economic system still exists today, where African governments have not destroyed it through misguided policies and civil wars. Female traders still can be found at the markets. They still trade their wares for profit. And in virtually all African markets today, one still bargains over prices.

INDIGENOUS AFRICA UNDER COLONIAL RULE

When Africa was colonized, the colonialists sought to control indigenous economic activities to their advantage. Africa's colonial history is replete with successes and failures of these policies. For example, on the Gold Coast (now Ghana), European mining companies sought legislative curtailment of indigenous mining operations without success. The two operated side by side throughout the colonial era.

Notably absent during that era were state or colonial government enterprises. A few large European firms and companies dominated the field, but *no indigenous economic activity* was reserved exclusively for the colonial government or European companies. Nor would the colonial administrations have been successful had they attempted such repression, which would have entailed an extraordinary expenditure of resources. Africa then had not developed the communications and transportation networks needed for effective control of the natives and their economic activities and cost was one reason the British adopted the policy of "indirect rule"—administration through the chiefs.

For the most part, the natives were free to go about their economic activities. In West Africa, European settlement was confined to the urban enclaves and the rural areas were left almost intact. In central and southern Africa, the story was a little different. The plunder and barbarous atrocities against the native in King Leopold's Congo need no belaboring. In southern Africa, where the climate was more congenial to European settlement, there were widespread land seizures, massive dislocation of the natives, and restrictions on their movements and places of residence. Apartheid South Africa's pass laws and land seizures in Angola, Namibia, Mozambique, and Zimbabwe can be recalled. Nonetheless, despite the formidable odds, the natives could open shops and compete with the European firms. Many did and were successful. There were rich African shopkeepers as well as timber merchants, transport owners, and farmers during the colonial period. African natives have always welcomed foreigners and foreign firms provided they were willing to play fair. And given the opportunities and access to capital, African natives showed themselves capable of competing with the foreigners.

THE GOLDEN AGE OF PEASANT PROSPERITY

The period 1880–1950 may be characterized as the golden age of peasant prosperity in Africa. Though colonialism was invidious, one of its little-known and acknowledged "benefits" was the peace it brought Africa. The slave trade and competition over resources had fueled many of the tribal wars in precolonial Africa—just as competition over mineral resources, in particular diamonds, fueled wars in Angola, Congo, Liberia, and Sierra Leone in the twenty-first century. The slave trade generates intense emotional reaction among blacks. Unfortunately, however, there is much confusion and mythology about African participation in that abominable trade, which I have tried to clarify in an addendum at the end of this chapter.

The abolition of the slave trade in the 1840s eliminated a causus belli and made apparent the need to provide an alternative to the trade in human cargo. Toward this end, cash crops were introduced into Africa. About this time, the industrial revolution was gathering momentum in Europe. Factories needed raw materials and markets for manufactured products. Colonies could provide both: raw materials and markets. Tribal wars and rivalries virtually came to halt, although they flared up occasionally. Their amelioration gave Africa a much-needed atmosphere of peace for productive economic activity. In addition, skeletal forms of infrastructure (roads, railways, bridges, schools, post office, etc.) were laid down during this period, which greatly facilitated the movement of goods and people. This infrastructural development really gave production and economic expansion a tremendous boost. The secret to economic prosperity in Africa is not hard to find. A mere three terms unveil this secret: *peace, infrastructure,* and *economic freedom.*

It is instructive to note that the economic system used by the natives of Africa to engineer their economic prosperity in the 1880–1950 period was their own indigenous system. Except for a few places in Africa, notably in the Portuguese colonies, plantation agriculture was unknown. Cash crops were grown by peasant farmers on their own individual plots, using traditional farming methods and practices. In other words, the natives prospered using their own existing indigenous system with only minor modifications and improvements. For example, the cultivation of cocoa was not mechanized; it was a highly labor-intensive undertaking. Transportation of cocoa in the early twentieth century was by human porterage, which gave rise to the pricing of cocoa by the "head load." The building of roads and the introduction of motor vehicles tremendously improved the transportation of cocoa and boosted exports, and there were other improvements as well: insecticides, spraying machines, and so on. But the basic system of land tenure and the peasants' discretion over what crops to grow etc. were unchanged. African peasants were generally not forced to cultivate any cash crops. Forced labor in the French, Belgian, and Portuguese colonies was mainly for construction purposes.

The fundamental point is that African natives had the *economic freedom* to decide for themselves what crops they could cultivate—cash crops or food crops—and what to do with the proceeds. This economic freedom was a notable feature of their indigenous economic system. Indeed, Kendall and Louw (1986)—two white South Africans—noted: "The freedom that characterized tribal society in part explains why black South Africans responded so positively to the challenges of a free market that, by the 1870s, they were out-competing whites, especially as farmers" (p.4).

Though this freedom was circumscribed under colonialism in central and southern Africa, the peasants prospered during the colonial era. Why, then, were they unable to continue prospering after independence? The answer is obvious: Their economic freedom was somehow snatched from them. According to the Heritage Foundation and *The Wall Street Journal* Index of Economic Freedom (2004) only 9 African countries could be classified as "mostly free" in 2004: Botswana, Uganda, South Africa, Cape Verde Islands, Morocco, Mauritania, Tunisia, Namibia, and Mauritius. No African country received a "free" rating.

The move away from economic freedom came first in South Africa, where according to Kendall and Louw (1986):

> Black success had tragic consequences. White colonists feared black competition and this fear, combined with the whites' desire for cheap labor, resulted in a series of laws that systematically denied blacks access to the marketplace and stripped them of any meaningful form of land ownership (p.4).
>
> The truth is that white farmers felt threatened by blacks. Not only were blacks better farmers but they were also competing with white farmers for land. Moreover, they were self-sufficient and hence not available to work on white farms or in industry, particularly in the Transvaal gold mines where their labor was badly needed. As a result a series of laws was passed that robbed blacks of almost all economic freedom. The purpose of these laws was to prevent blacks from competing with whites and to drive them into the work force. (p.12)

In 1869, 1876, and 1884 the Cape Assembly passed a series of Location Acts (the first set of apartheid laws) that sought to protect white farmers from black competition and to force blacks to become wage laborers by working for white farmers. Then came the Native Land Act of 1913; the rest is history. Even during the apartheid era, South African officials grudgingly acknowledged the industriousness of black farmers. For example, in 1985, the Development Bank, a quasigovernment agency, began financing small agricultural credit programs, which involved dispensing a package of aid (seed, fertilizer, a few implements, and basic advice) to black subsistence farmers at a cost of $150 per farmer. According to the bank's general manager, Johan Kruger, these programs were "quite remarkably successful." The farmers significantly upgraded the production of about 25,000 of these smallholdings and greatly improved their ability to feed their families. "The perception that blacks can't farm and that people can't make a living on small pieces of land in South Africa is a fallacy," Kruger said. "Provided they have the necessary support services and infrastructure, black farmers have shown that they can farm as well as whites" (*The Washington Post,* Dec 29, 1990; p.A14).

In the rest of Africa, the turn toward statism and the attendant restrictions on economic freedom came after independence. Support services and infrastructure were not provided by new elites. Traditional Africa was castigated by the elites as "backward and primitive." Peasant agriculture was neglected in favor of industry. Chiefs and Africa's traditional rulers were stripped of their power and authority. Foreign ideologies were imposed on the Atingas, and their economic freedom was wrenched from them by "Swiss-bank socialists," while their economic prosperity was taxed and squandered by vampire elites through a series of edicts, state controls, and decrees, as we saw in chapter 6.

After independence, many African governments not only nationalized European companies, ostensibly to prevent "foreign exploitation," but also debarred the natives from many economic fields. For example, after Ghana gained its independence, mining operations were monopolized by the state, and indigenous gold-mining was declared illegal. In fact, "Anyone caught indulging in illegal gold prospecting, popularly known as 'galamsey' (gather them and sell), will be shot, a PNDC representative announced to a workers' rally in the Western Region" (West Africa, March 1, 1982; p.618).

In many other African countries, the natives were squeezed out of industry, trade, and commerce, and the state emerged as the domineering, if not the only, player. Indigenous operators were not tolerated. Indeed, there was a time when the director of the Club du Sahel, Anne de Lattre, would begin her meetings with the frightening remark, "Well, there is one thing we all agree on: that private traders should be shot" (West Africa, Jan 26, 1987; p.154). Under Sekou Toure of Guinea's nonsensical program of "Marxism in African Clothes," unauthorized trading became a crime. The prices the Atingas received for their produce were dictated by governments, not determined by market forces in accordance with African traditions.

Resources extracted from the Atingas were spent to develop the urban areas for the elites. Botswana was the only black African country in the postcolonial period that did not persecute its Atingas but rather went back and built upon their indigenous roots. It paid off handsomely. In elegant brevity, Newsweek (July 23, 1990) put the issue poignantly: "Botswana built a working democracy on an aboriginal tradition of local gatherings called kgotlas that resemble New England town meetings; it has a record $2.7 billion in foreign exchange reserves" (p.28).

BOTSWANA: THE SHINING BLACK ECONOMIC STAR

Ensconced in the Kgalagadi (Kalahari) basin, Botswana possessed all the ingredients for another postcolonial black African economic disaster. Doomsayers gave the country less than five years to self-destruct and evaporate.

When it gained its independence from Britain in September 1966, Botswana (formerly Bechuanaland) was one of the twenty poorest countries in the world with per capita income of only $40. Mines, commercial and farming enterprises were mostly owned by South Africa. There were only five kilometers of tarred road. Its society was composed of nine ethnic groups.

In addition, about 75 percent of the country's 592,000 sq. km. was desert, bordered by largely infertile areas. The bulk of its largely illiterate population (about 80 percent) lived on only 20 percent of the land area. There was a late-blooming diamond industry and a poor cattle industry, but the country lacked the technical know-how to develop other natural resources. Constantly threatened by drought, which in 1985 caused a serious loss of 1,500 jobs, and dependent on neighboring countries, which kept it held hostage to extraterritorial occurrences, Botswana additionally had to deal with foreign wars and the subsequent refugees.

After the ignominious 1976 Sharpeville massacre, thousands of students fled South Africa to seek refuge in Botswana. Soon afterward, a new wave of refugees from Rhodesia swelled the numbers encamped in Botswana from 3,000 to 21,000 by mid-1979, placing severe strains on budgetary resources and social facilities. Furthermore, Botswana was violently attacked throughout the eighties by both Zimbabwe and South Africa, who accused it of harboring guerillas among the refugees.

At independence, Botswana's prospects of surviving as a viable politico-economic entity were just about equal to those of Mali or Burkina Faso (former Upper Volta). Cameroon, Nigeria, and Zaire were far more blessed with richer mineral wealth endowment, luxuriant vegetation, modestly developed infrastructure, and an economically active population. Even Ghana was in a better "take-off" position. Yet, in spite of all its handicaps, Botswana has managed to register an impressive rate of economic advance, astonishing by *any* standard.

In a little less than two decades (1966 to 1986), Botswana's rate of economic growth averaged an astounding 8 percent per annum while the South African economy was limping along at a miserable 1.5 percent per annum between 1965 and 1985. In 1988, for example, Botswana's minister of finance and development planning, Vice-President Peter Mmusi, indicated that average real growth rate was running at 14 percent annually and that per capita GDP was 2,800 *pulas* ($1,450)—ten times greater than it was in 1978 (*African Business,* Sept 1988; p.35). Back in 1983, real GPD growth rate was a dizzying 26.3 percent and GDP per capita exploded from 755 *pulas* in 1982 to 2,145 *pulas* in 1986. By 1991, GDP per capita had reached 5,950 *pulas* ($2,439). Its GNP per capita of $2,530 in 1991 was the third highest in Africa, after oil-rich, sparsely-populated Gabon ($3,780) and South Africa ($2,560) (*African Business,* Sept 1993; p.14). Botswana's foreign debt was $543 million in 1992 and its reserves stood at $3.4 billion, which, on a per capita basis, were the highest in the world. Its debt service ratio in 1992 was an insignificant 3.4 percent, compared with the 53 percent of most African countries.

The first diamond mine to open was Orapa in 1971. By 1988, diamond production had reached 15.2 million carats, earning about 85 percent of Botswana's export earnings of 2,205 million *pulas* ($1,095 million). The beef industry, too, underwent phenomenal expansion, despite the denigration of African cattle and the devastating droughts of 1965–66 and 1982–84 that killed off a third of the national herd. Botswana began to export meat to the European Economic Community (EEC), which pays almost four times the world price for this meat because of its quality. The Bostwana Meat Commission's meat processing plant at Lobatse is the second largest in the world. There are other slaughterhouses in Maun and Francistown to help Botswana meet its 19,000 metric ton EEC quota.

Botswana's economic performance has not been matched anywhere on the African continent in the postcolonial period. Apart from Botswana, exceptions to the general economic atrophy has been pitifully few. Recall the difficulty the World Bank and Western governments have had in finding "economic success stories" in Africa as durable as Botswana's. Across black Africa, Botswana remains a shining star.

THE KEYS TO BOTSWANA'S SUCCESS

Although various analysts have attributed Botswana's success to its mineral wealth in diamonds, a combination of factors have contributed immensely to create the environment vital for economic prosperity. Foremost has been the *absence of civil and political strife.* Botswana society is multiracial, composed of ethnic Batswana, Europeans, and Asians. These various groups *live peacefully together.* Blatant acts of discrimination or ethnic chauvinism are not common in Botswana. By contrast, violent ethnic clashes, senseless and endless civil wars, and civil strife rage in at least fifteen other African countries (Angola, Burundi, Chad, Congo, Eritrea, Ethiopia, Ivory Coast, Liberia, Nigeria, Rwanda, Sierra Leone, Somalia, Sudan, Uganda, and Zimbabwe).

Second, Botswana enjoys *political stability.* This stability was not engineered by a military dictator or by declaring the country to be a one-party state. Botswana is a parliamentary democracy based upon a multiparty system. The main political parties are the ruling Botswana Democratic Party, the Botswana National Front, and the Botswana People's Party. Multiparty democracy, contrary to the claims by Presidents Moi of Kenya, Kaunda of Zambia, and other African dictators, did not degenerate into "tribal politics" in Botswana.

Third, the Botswana government has pursued strikingly *prudent economic policies,* allowing pragmatism, rather than emotional rhetoric, to prevail. The Botswana government's commitment to mixed economy has not been directed toward nationalization—no such takeovers have occurred—but rather toward the provision of good infrastructural support. Revenues from minerals, customs union payments, and donor funds were devoted largely to investment in infrastructure and to providing greater public access to basic needs: water, health care, and primary education. In Botswana, parastatals were only established to plug the gaps or overcome the deficiencies in the private sector, rather than to compete with or seek to replace the private sector, as was the case in many African countries, especially Tanzania, which took a "socialist" bent.

Fortunate enough to have an ex-minister of finance as president (Masire), the government pursued judicious macroeconomic policies of saving windfalls and avoiding excessive government spending during export boom years. These savings provided the cushion to ride out the lean years. By contrast, when sharply rising oil prices boosted exports from $4 billion in 1975 to $26 billion in 1980, Nigeria went on an import binge. It splurged on prestigious projects, including a $25 billion new capital at Abuja, while vampire politicians transferred as much as $15 million a day illegally out of the country. Nigeria even neglected agriculture, preferring to import food using cheap oil dollars. Rising public expenditures fueled by oil revenues shifted production from agriculture to services. When the price of oil collapsed, so did Nigeria's export receipts. By 1986, they were down to $6 billion, while external debt rose from $5 billion in 1980 to $25 billion in 1986. The booms in coffee, cocoa, and copper prices in the 1970s elicited similar extravagant spending by governments in Ghana, Ivory Coast, Kenya, Uganda, and Zaire. Other Third World countries such Mexico, Brazil, and Colombia acted similarly, squandering windfall profits from export booms only to find themselves in a debt crisis when markets collapsed.

Fourth, largely due to Botswana's openness and a vibrant press, there is a refreshing absence of corruption—the bane of many African regimes. Botswana has a lively *free press* and *freedom of expression.* Apart from the government newspaper, *The Daily News,* and the government monthly magazine, *Kutlwano,* the country has three weekly private newspapers and four locally produced monthly magazines. The local publications are *not* subject to censorship. In addition, foreign papers and magazines are widely available.

Commenting on the political process in Botswana, Professor Patrick Mulotsi, a lecturer in sociology at the University of Botswana, was quite pithy: "If you look at the prerequisites of liberal democracy, the rule of law has been highly respected. A lot of people can say a lot of things with relatively little fear. There has been a lot of response by the ruling party to debates with the opposition" (*The New York Times*, May 16, 1990; p.A6).

Botswana can find solutions to its economic problems because *it permits free debate and freedom of expression*. By contrast, the rest of black Africa is mired in an economic quagmire, for want of ideas and solutions to extricate itself. Intellectual repression prevents those with ideas from coming forward. Besides Botswana, only seven other African counties (Benin, Cape Verde Islands, Ghana, Mali, Mauritius, Sao Tome & Principe, and South Africa) of the remaining 54 countries tolerate freedom of expression and criticism of foolish government policies. And many of these same countries have ratified the Organization of African Unity's Charter of Human and Peoples' Rights, Article 9 of which guarantees freedom of expression.

Fifth, Botswana did not ignore its *indigenous roots*. It built upon its native system of *kgotlas*, whereby chiefs and councilors meet "under a tree" to reach a *consensus* on important matters. In fact, cabinet ministers are required to attend weekly *kgotla* meetings. As Fred Dira, an African journalist, explained:

When they were initiated, *kgotla* meetings were meant to be totally apolitical. They were to be meetings at which government ministers and members of parliament would brief local communities about official policies and programs, or about issues discussed or to be discussed in parliament. It was also part of the tradition of *kgotla* meetings that if they were convened by the president or any of his ministers, the respective members of parliament would not only be present, but would also be given some role to play at the meeting. This was in recognition of the fact that at such meetings, MPs shared the role of host with the chiefs. (*Mmegi/The Reporter*, May 12–18, 1995; p.7)

Such was the case in 1991, when the government tried to explain a $25 million Okavango River irrigation project to the villagers at a *kgotlas* in the northern town of Maun. Irate villagers let loose their opposition: "'You will dry the delta! We will have no more fish to eat! No more reeds to build our houses!' a village elder screamed" (*The Washington Post*, Mar 21, 1991; p.A3). For six hours, they excoriated government officials for conceiving of such a dastardly project. Buckling under the wrath of the people, the government canceled the project. Only in Botswana could this happen, giving true meaning to such terms as "participatory development," "bottom-up development approach," "grassroots development," and "popular participation in development."

Furthermore, in Botswana, "Chiefs still exercise considerable local authority and influence which can act as a check on too precipitate action by the government and can even swing local elections" (Colclough and McCarthy, 1980; p.38). In the rest of black Africa, chiefs saw their powers and authority reduced: The indigenous system of participatory democracy and the tradition of reaching a consensus were spurned, and, in their place, African elites and intellectuals erected one-man dictatorships and de facto apartheid regimes.

Of course, Botswana has had problems with income distribution and AIDS. But its economic success demonstrates that Africa does not have to renounce its indigenous culture to advance economically. The Japanese did not. "Japan's postwar success has demonstrated that modernization does not mean Westernization. Japan has modernized spectacularly, yet remains utterly different from the West. Economic success in Japan has nothing to do with individualism. It is the fruit of sheer discipline—the ability to work in groups and to conform" (Editorial in the *Bangkok Post,* quoted in *The Washington Times,* Nov 9, 1996; p.A8).

ADDENDUM: MYTHS ABOUT
AFRICAN PARTICIPATION IN THE SLAVE TRADE

The slave trade continues to evoke strong emotional reaction among blacks. While it was an ignoble practice that saw millions blacks shackled and deprived of basic human dignity, certain myths continue to persist. For example, as we saw in chapter 4, the slave trade did not take place on Africa's west coast alone. While the Europeans organized the Atlantic slave trade, the Arabs ran the East African slave trade. But one hears little or nothing about the latter, much less reparations from Arab countries. There are other more pertinent myths that often cause a rift between black Africans and black Americans, who tend to associate the entire traditional African system with slavery. Three such misconceptions may be identified:

1. Africans were selling themselves off into slavery before the Europeans arrived on the continent.
2. African chiefs just went to the market place and grabbed some of their people to sell off as slaves.
3. Slaves in Africa had no rights and were mistreated.

Slaves in precolonial Africa were mostly war captives from intertribal warfare. Suppose there was a war between two neighboring tribes—the Ashanti and the Fante—over access to land or the sea and 5,000 Fantes were taken prisoner. The Ashanti king had the following options:

a. To keep the 5,000 Fantes in prison, which meant feeding, clothing, and sheltering them—an economically expensive proposition.
b. To execute them—a very inhumane prospect.
c. To sell them off as slaves and use the proceeds to purchase weapons to defend his Ashanti people.
d. To absorb and integrate them into Ashanti society—a long, arduous, and dangerous process since the loyalty of former combatants to their new society could not be guaranteed.

African traditional rulers often chose sale (the third option) because it was the most humane and economically expedient. In addition, the Ashanti king also exercised the fourth option by absorbing former war captives or slaves into Ashanti society. To make their integration into Ashanti society as smooth as possible, the king was forbidden to disclose the slave origins of any of his subjects.

The claim that "Africans were selling their own kind into slavery" is often made by those who fail to make distinctions between the traditional ruler (chief or king), his people, and his subjects. The Ashanti king's subjects include not only his Ashanti people, but also people of other ethnicities. The duty of the traditional ruler is the survival of his people or tribe—not other tribes. It would make absolutely no sense for the Ashanti king to sell off his own people into slavery. For one thing, he would be committing an ethnic suicide by depopulating his own tribe, making it easier for his tribe to be routed by a more powerful neighboring tribe. For another, there were traditional injunctions in many tribal societies against selling off one's kin into slavery and the king can be removed from office for such an infraction. Instead, his role was to protect or minimize any external threat to his people. And if this meant depopulating or selling off the entire Fante tribe into slavery, the better off his Ashanti people would be. It would mean less competition for resources. It must also be said that Africa's traditional rulers did not know of the fate that awaited African slaves in the Americas or Arabia.

Now, it is true the Ashanti king did sell Fante prisoners of war as slaves and therefore participated in the slave trade, but the Ashanti king did *not* sell his own people. The Fantes were *not* his people. Many Europeans and black Americans did not make that distinction. To them, it was a black African king selling black Africans, and therefore, blacks were selling off their own kind. Preposterous.

It is strange that such distinctions are made elsewhere but not in regards to the slave trade in Africa. It may be recalled that medieval Europe also fought tribal wars—between the Flemish, French, and the Germans—and they were also enslaving one another. But one doesn't hear the expression,

"The Europeans were enslaving their own kind" because a distinction is made between Germans taking French slaves and vice versa. The same distinctions should be made regarding the slave trade in Africa; for example, the Ashanti king taking Fante slaves.

Second, slavery was not peculiar to Africa alone. Before the twentieth century, many societies in the world practiced some form of slavery. Prisoners of war, political opponents, and religious dissidents were often enslaved in Old England. For example, in 1530 in England, under the reign of Henry VIII, a vagrant picked up for the second time was whipped and had half an ear cut off; taken for a third time, he was "to be executed as a hardened criminal and enemy of the common weal" (Marx, 1915; p.806). Seventy-two thousand vagrants were thus executed during that reign. In the time of Edward VI (1547), "if anyone refused to work, he shall be condemned as a slave to the person who denounced him as an idler" (Marx, 1915; p.806). The owner of such a slave might whip him, chain him, and brand him on the cheek and forehead with a letter "S" (for slave), if he disappeared for two weeks. If he ran away a third time he was executed. An idler vagabond caught on the highway was branded on the chest with a "V" (for vagrant). The same laws were in effect during the reigns of Elizabeth (1570s) and of Louis XVI in France. The supporters of Monmouth's rebellion in England were sold by the Queen. Cromwell's Irish and Scottish prisoners were sold to the West Indies and non-Muslims who opposed the Sokoto jihad were sold to North Africa.

Criminals in Europe and Africa could be executed, transported or sold. Europeans favored execution; Africans favored sale.

In the eighteenth century there were 300 different offences in Britain for which one could be executed. In Dahomey, there were only two, for the king preferred to sell rather than execute his troublemakers. Those who could not pay their debts were sold for life or until the debt was paid. Among the Yoruba, debt slaves (pawns) were called *Iwofa,* among the Asante, *Awowa,* and among the Europeans indentured servants. About a quarter of a million white debt slaves entered America before the nineteenth century (Boahen and Webster, 1970; p.69).

Third, slavery in Africa was not of the inhumane chattel variety. Slaves in Africa enjoyed certain rights and privileges. Generally, there were no slave markets in black Africa because of the value black Africans place on humanity. According to historians, the slave markets that were in Africa could be found in North Africa (or Arab North Africa)—in such places as Fez and Tripoli. Slaves in Africa enjoyed many rights. In precolonial Africa, social conditions were such that,

All the white minorities living in Africa might own Black slaves, but slaves and white masters alike were all subjects of a Black Emperor: they were all under the same African political power. No historian worth his salt can permit the obscuring of this politico social context, so that only the one fact of Black slavery emerges from it. (Diop, 1987; p.92)

There was, however, an important distinction between the slave/master relationship in Africa and that in Europe between serf/lord, which is often overlooked. In Africa, slavery was more of a social distinction without economic consequence. The African slave, "instead of being deprived of the fruits of his labor, as was the case with the artisan or the serf of the Middle Ages, could, on the contrary, add to it wealth given him by the 'lord'" (Diop, 1987: p.2). Slaves of the kings of Mali and the Askias of Gao "enjoyed complete liberty of movement. Thus, an ordinary slave of Askia Daud, a native of Kanta, was able to carry out a pilgrimage to Mecca without his master's knowledge" (Diop, 1987; p.153). Boahen and Webster (1970) reaffirmed this view:

> Slaves had many privileges in African kingdoms. In Asante, Oyo and Bornu, they held important offices in the bureaucracy, serving as the Alafin's Ilari in the subject towns of Oyo, as controller of the treasury in Asante, and as Waziri and army commanders in Bornu. Al Hajj Umar made a slave emir of Nioro, one of the most important of the emirates of the Tokolor empire, and in the Niger Delta states slaves rose to become heads of Houses, positions next in rank to the king. Jaja, who had once been the lowest kind of slave, became the most respected king in the delta, and was no exception; one of the Alaketus of Ketu, and Rabeh of Bornu, rose from slave to king. (p.69)

The privileges accorded them, however, varied from tribe to tribe. In Nigeria, the treatment of slaves was by no means harsh; nor was their lot deplorable. The majority were integrated into the society and the respective families of their owners in order to retain their loyalty, prevent rebellion, and get the best out of them (Falola, 1985; p.99). The slaves were free to some extent; they could intermarry among themselves, own property, and redeem themselves if they had the means.

Among the Lobi of Gabon, slaves were considered as "new children." The Massangou of the Chaillou Hills in Gabon incorporated slaves (war captives) into the entire community to replace those lost in war. In Dahomey, the children of slaves were free people incorporated into the master's family with all the rights except the right to inherit political leadership (Simiyu, 1988; p.59). But in Senegal, slaves (*djem*) were closely associated to power.

They were represented in royal courts and many became de facto ministers (Diop, 1987; p.2).

To avoid the ugly connotations associated with commercial slaving, Vaughan (1986) suggested the use of the term, *limbry:* "Existing data, albeit tenuous, suggest that about 80 percent of African societies had *limbry*" (p.174). In contrast to commercial slavery, African "limbries" "were not on the whole mistreated, dehumanized or exploited" (Vaughan, 1986; p.174).

CHAPTER 10

The Atinga Development Model

Small-scale farmers in Kenya argue over the best corn varieties to plant, just as Iowa farmers. I have seen resourceful Africans in Kenya, South Africa and Zimbabwe create and run inexpensive, well-regulated minivan transportation networks into far-flung corners of their countries. Africans in all walks of life value sound business and pragmatic rule of law.

—William J. Gutowski, Jr., a professor of geological
and atmospheric sciences at Iowa State University, Des Moines,
Iowa, who has lived in South Africa, Zimbabwe, and Kenya;
The Des Moines Register, July 8, 2003; p.11A.

INTRODUCTION

The object of economic development is to raise the living standard of the "average African." He is not an elite. He is a peasant—an illiterate, poor and rural person, whose primary occupation is agriculture. Throughout, we have called him Atinga. The elites were more obsessed with industrialization, missile technology, and nuclear power than with the Atinga's peasant agriculture. Arrogantly, they then later marched off to "educate" the Atingas about "modern and scientific" farming techniques while feeding them empty revolutionary slogans. That approach got Africa nowhere.

The new approach turns that old paradigm completely upside-down. It places Atinga full-square at the center and starts from the bottom-up, rather than the old top-down. It seeks to liberate the Atingas from the chains of tyranny, exploitation, oppression, poverty, and disease that vampire elites have shackled them with. Instead of marching off to the villages to "teach" Atinga, it allows *him* to teach the dysfunctional elites a thing or two about agriculture and governance. After all, the Atingas have been farming for centuries. And the elite better listen: First, there is a treasure trove of valuable knowledge embedded in Atinga's traditional system that the elite can discover, extract, and still use. This is especially true of traditional medicine. Second, as we saw in chapter 1, the Atingas are rebelling against exploitation by the mafia state by reducing the production of export cash crops and smuggling their produce to where they fetch higher prices. To bring economies back up, changes must be made.

Africa's salvation does not lie in blindly copying foreign systems but in returning to its own roots and heritage and building upon them. As Williams (1987) advised: "When, if ever, black people actually organize as a race in their various population centers, they will find that the basic and guiding ideology they now seek and so much need is embedded in their own traditional philosophy and constitutional system, simply waiting to be extracted and set forth" (p.161). Says Robert Guest, editor of the Africa region for *The Economist* magazine,

> When Japan's rulers decided in the nineteenth-century, that they had to modernize to avoid being colonized they sent their brightest officials to Germany, Britain and America to find out how industrial societies worked. They then copied the ideas that seemed most useful, rejected the Western habits that seemed unhelpful or distasteful, and within a few decades Japan advanced enough to win a war with Russia—the first non-white nation to defeat a European power in modern times.
>
> Japan's example should be important for Africa, because it shows that modernization need not mean Westernization. Developing countries need to learn from developed ones, but they do not have to abandon their culture and traditions in the process. Africans face the same challenge now that Japan faced in the nineteenth century: how to harness other people's ideas and technology to help them build the kind of society that *they*, the Africans, want" (Guest, 2004; p.23).

After a long series of experiments with or blind imitation of foreign models, it is beginning to dawn on Africa's elites that they do not have to reject their traditional heritage in order for Africa to develop. The Swahili word for this concept is *majimbo*. It stands for the idea of local initiative and trust in traditional wisdoms. The same idea is conveyed by the mantra, *African renaissance*.

THE NEW DEVELOPMENT STRATEGY

To combat hunger and poverty in Africa, the new development strategy must be agricultural and rural based. Even NEPAD recognized this by emphasizing that "agriculture will provide the engine for growth in Africa" (*Africa Recovery*, Jan 2004; p.13). It makes no sense—none whatsoever—for Africa to receive $18.6 billion in foreign aid and spend about the same on food imports. Furthermore, agriculture is the main preoccupation of African peasants. If one seeks to help them, agriculture in their rural or traditional setting is the place to go. Their techniques may be "primitive"—donkey transport rather than trucking; dug-out canoes rather than nuclear-powered fishing trawlers; cutlasses (machetes) rather than tractors; manure rather than chemical fertilizers; *susu, esusu, tontines* or rural revolving credit banks rather than banks with ATMs—but these have worked for generations.

Occam's Razor

Quite often, African elites defy logic by concocting convoluted solutions to simple problems—possibly out of the need to impress or to make themselves useful. But Occam's Razor states that for every complicated solution to a problem, there is a much simpler one.

In 1999, Heifer International donated a goat, named Mugisa, to Beatrice Biira's family in a Ugandan village. By selling Mugisa's milk and offspring, Miss Biira's family was able to send her, and later her seven brothers and sisters, to school. She showed such promise in primary school, breezing through first, second, and third grades in three months each. She went on to win a full scholarship for a postgraduate year at Northfield Mount Hermon School, a boarding school in Northfield, Mass. "Without the goat, Miss Biira would almost certainly never have gone to school or finished filling out applications to 11 American colleges and universities, from Manchester College in Indiana to Harvard" (*The New York Times*, January 25, 2004; p.Wk.11).

African elites would never consider giving a goat to Beatrice's family; they would prefer a more complicated solution involving a shiny fleet of air-conditioned tractors with global positioning systems (GPS), combine harvesters, and fishing trawlers. The fancy gadgetry the elites imported for Africa's development journey has all gone belly-up. Meanwhile, the *tro tros, mutatos* (mammy lorries), and dug-out canoes of the Atingas continue to ply the roads and the seas.

The "KISS" Principle

African peasant farmers do need better technology to increase their productivity, but the operative principle here should be "keep it simple, stupid" (KISS). Menker Wolde Kiross, the former head of rural technology at the Ministry of Agriculture in Ethiopia, developed a simple foot-driven water pump that cost about $1,000 to develop. The original idea was based on a design from Kenya which Menker modified. It draws water from a depth of 7 meters and pumps over 9 meters high, providing about one liter per second and can water around a hectare a day. It costs $130 to buy. "This is a very simple piece of equipment with almost no moving parts or nuts and bolts which means the farmers themselves can maintain it," says Menker, who, with four other people, owns Mamjad Engineering in the capital (http://www.scienceinafrica.co.za/index.htm).

Menker and his team—he employs around 30 people—also build a mobile sprinkler that works with the pump so farmers can walk and irrigate their land. His other developments in recent years include a modern-style beehive—that is now being used all over the country—and a mobile seed cleaner. He also developed a hand-driven maize sheller.

The important considerations here are practicality, functionality, economy, and results. But the functionally illiterate elite yam-head in Africa would insist that American farmers don't use such primitive technology and insist on a complicated modern technology because it would "prove" that Africa is not "backward" and is "catching up." In fact, as we have observed in chapter 6, the overarching obsession with the "modern" to "prove something" betrays the intellectual backwardness of Africa's elites who are left to explain why an oil-producing country such as Nigeria, plagued by constant gas shortages, must import refined petroleum products, after spending $6.7 million on a space program.

THE VILLAGE DEVELOPMENT MODEL

The village model starts at the village level with the assumption that there is *peace, order,* and *economic freedom*—that is, the country is not wracked by conflict and the Atingas are free to produce what they want, sell wherever they want, at whatever prices they choose to charge. It takes what is there and attempts to build upon it to improve its efficiency. In most cases, this would entail a mere reorganization of the existing ways of doing things. If Atinga produces 300 bushels of corn a year, the object is to raise his productivity to, say, 1,200 bushels a year, using whatever technology that is *locally available.* Applying the KISS principle, such technology must be simple and inexpensive.

The ingredients and strategies of this Village Development Model involve three basic steps:

1. Setting up a Village development committee or council (VDC) under a traditional ruler, say a chief, who still commands authority and re-

spect. The chiefs constitute Africa's most important human resource. They are closer to the people, understand their needs, and command their respect. It defies common sense to exclude them in any rural development strategy.

The functions of the village development council would be to provide some basic infrastructure and the following services on a 50–50 cost-sharing basis with either a district or a regional administration:

- Education by building simple schools for elementary education,
- Clean water through the provision of bore wells for common usage,
- Health care by building a simple clinic, encouraging the interaction between traditional and modern medicine,
- A civic center or hall,
- A market, a market, a market, and
- Feeder roads.

2. The second step is to mobilize capital for investment. Capital can be raised through participation in and modernization of existing revolving credit schemes (microfinance).
3. The third step is investment in cottage industries by the cheetah generation (young African graduates). The state or government should be left out of this.

Throughout this book, we have emphasized *peace*. Economic activity cannot take place in an atmosphere of conflict, violence, and chaos. But a peaceful environment has eluded Africa and must be established as a first order of priority.

Why Peace Has Been Elusive

Since 1970, more than forty wars have been fought on the continent. Year after year, one African country after another has imploded with deafening staccato, scattering refugees in all directions: Sudan (1972), Angola (1975), Mozambique (1975), Ethiopia (1985), Liberia (1992), Somalia (1993), Rwanda (1994), Zaire (1996), Sierra Leone (1997), Congo DRC (1998), Ethiopia/Eritrea (1998), Guinea (1999), and Ivory Coast (2001).

Some wars never end (Algeria, Burundi, Somalia, Sudan, Western Sahara) while others restart after brief lulls. At least fourteen African nations are currently wracked by conflict and civil strife. Populations have been decimated, infrastructure destroyed, and homes of the Atingas razed. The economic toll has been horrendous: devastated agriculture, deepening poverty, declining investment, increasing social misery, and a massive refugee population of mostly women and children. Children are abducted into child soldiery and women fall prey to marauding soldiers, turning refugee camps into breeding grounds for the spread of AIDS. Since women constitute the majority of Africa's peasant farmers, Africa's agriculture has been hardest hit. Leaders of the warring factions don't care one hoot about the wanton destruction they wreak, and the pain and suffering they inflict on the Atingas.

The vast majority of Africa's conflicts are intra-state in origin. They are not about driving away colonial infidels, or redrawing colonial boundaries. They are about political power, pure and simple: power to plunder resources; power to allocate resources to oneself, cronies, and kinsmen; power to perpetuate oneself in office; and power to crush one's enemies. The wars invariably pit an autocratic "government" on one side against a rebel group, representing a politically excluded group, on the other.

A bitter lesson in the postcolonial era is that no African government has successfully put down a rebel insurgency, which is different from a secessionist bid. The former seek to overthrow or replace an existing government while the latter is an attempt to break up and set up a separate, independent state—for example, Biafra, Cabinda, etc. A tyrannical regime may succeed temporarily in suppressing a rebel insurgency—as in the Cameroon in the 1960s and Zimbabwe in the 1980s—but it does not crush it, only to erupt again.

Nearly all the rebel insurgencies start from the countryside, where government troops are thinly spread and virtually nonexistent. Fighting is sporadic and can drag on for years, leaving much destruction and death in its wake. Demoralized government troops (loyalists in the case of the Ivory Coast) abandon posts or join the rebels (Ethiopia, Somalia, Sierra Leone, Zaire). Unemployed and restless youth join the rebels, in hopes of gaining positions or improving the economic livelihood. They use their guns to pillage and plunder (such has been the life of child soldiers).

Various attempts are made to reach a peace accord without success. Peace accords are essentially a blueprint for joint plunder of the state. A "government of national unity" (GNU) is often proposed to "bring the rebels into the government." A certain number of ministerial or government positions are reserved for rebel leaders, but nobody is satisfied with what they get at the peace talks. Inevitably, resentment lingers and squabbles erupt over who gets what posts, leading to the resumption of conflict again (Angola in 1992, Congo in 1999, Sierra Leone in 2000, and Ivory Coast in January 2003). In the case of Ivory Coast, there were "disagreements over the distribution of cabinet posts and the January peace accord was greeted by a week of anti-French and anti-rebel demonstrations in parts of the country" (*Africa Recovery*, May 2003; p.3).

More than 30 such peace accords have been brokered in Africa since the 1970s with an abysmal success record. Only Mozambique's 1991 peace accord has endured, while shaky pacts hold in Angola, Chad, Liberia, and Niger. Elsewhere, peace accords were shredded like confetti even before the ink on them was dry, amid mutual recriminations of cease-fire violations. The most spectacular failures were: Angola (1991 Bicesse Accord, 1994 Lusaka Accord), Burundi (1993 Arusha Accord), Democratic Republic of the Congo (July 1999 Lusaka Accord), Rwanda (1993 Arusha Accord), Sierra Leone (1999 Lome Accord), Ivory Coast (2003 Accra Accord). All collapsed because they adopted the Western approach to conflict resolution.

The cornerstone of this approach, often foisted on Africa by well-intentioned Western donors, is direct face-to-face negotiation between warring factions. It works if factional leaders want peace or must pay a price for the mayhem they wreak—assumptions that grotesquely confute reality. The fact is, war is "profitable" to warlords as a conflict situation provides them with the opportunity to rape women, pillage villages, and plunder natural resources, such as gold and diamonds. For rebel soldiers, their weapons are often their livelihoods, and many government soldiers live by looting too because they have not been paid by their commanders. Several officers have grown rich by seizing control of diamond fields. The war also gives the government an excuse ("national security") to suspend development projects and provision of social services and keep its defense budget secret, thereby shielding padded contracts to cronies from scrutiny.

None of the war combatants pay any price for the destruction they wreak. Rather, they are "rewarded," gaining respectability. Back in 1993, the late Somali warlord, Mohammed Farar Aideed, was transported in U.S. military aircraft to Addis Ababa to take part in peace negotiations. (Aideed forces were subsequently responsible for the deaths of 18 U.S. Rangers in Mogadishu.) The most outrageous appeasement, however, was that of Foday Sankoh, the barbarous warlord of Sierra Leone, whose band of savages (the Revolutionary United Front) chopped off the limbs of people, including women and children who stood in their way. The 1999 Lome Accord rewarded RUF with four cabinet positions and Sankoh himself with the ministry of mines.

Africa's own indigenous conflict resolution mechanism provides a better approach. It requires four parties: An arbiter, the two combating parties, *and* civil society or those directly and indirectly affected by the conflict (the victims). For example, in traditional Africa, when two disputants cannot resolve their differences by themselves, the case is taken to a chief's court for adjudication. The court is open and anyone affected by the dispute can participate. The complainant makes his case, then the defendant. Next, anybody else who has something to say may do so. After all the arguments have been heard, the chief renders a decision. The guilty party may be fined, say, three goats. In default, his family is held liable.

The injured party receives one goat, the chief another goat for his services, and the remainder are slaughtered for a village feast for all to enjoy. The latter social event is derived from the African belief that it takes a village not only to raise a child, but also to heal frayed social relations. Thus, traditional African jurisprudence lays more emphasis on healing and restoring social harmony and peace than punishing the guilty. Further, the interests of the community supersede those of the disputants. If they adopt intransigent positions, they can be sidelined by the will of the community and fined, say, two goats each for disturbing social peace. In extreme cases, they can be expelled from the village. Thus, there is a price to be paid for intransigence and for wreaking social mayhem—a price exacted by the victims.

We now look at two cases where the traditional structures can be useful in restoring peace.

Benin City (Nigeria)—A Haven of Tranquility

When American journalist Glenn McKenzie, working for the Associated Press, visited Benin City in Nigeria, he was stunned to find an "island of calm in a modern Nigeria exploding with tangled regional, ethnic and religious hostilities." While traditional Nigerian cleavages (northerner vs. southerner, Muslim vs. Christian, Hausa vs. Yoruba) all existed in microcosm in that southern city of 500,000, they had not caused the conflagrations that periodically engulf the country. Even with the inception of civilian rule in May 1999, after decades of brutal military rule, more than 10,000 people had died in deadly ethnic and religious clashes by 2003. But the violence had not touched Benin City. "It is safer here than the Bank of England," said Idris Sanni, a prominent Muslim and ethnic Hausa community leader (*The Washington Times,* June 8, 2000; p.A16)

Many observers credit the city's Bini ethnic majority, which once ruled over an empire stretching hundreds of miles to the east and west, with maintaining tribal and religious peace and stability. The empire, which was dismantled by the British colonialists in the late nineteenth century, bears no relation to Nigeria's western neighbor, the modern country of Benin. The Bini are a distinct and majority ethnic group inside Benin City but minor ethnic group outside it, where the Yoruba, Igbo (or Ibo), and Hausa peoples dominate.

The Bini king, N'Edo Erediauwa, has a reputation as a peacemaker. According to McKenzie, the King frequently goes on state radio to make long addresses about the need for peace and [...] community leaders to prevent quarrels from escalating int[...]

When a Hausa man murdered the [...] of the Bini high priest several years ago, the royal family call[...] d urged Bini subjects not to seek revenge.

> "Under no circumstance do we want violence to destroy us like other Nigerian cities," said the priest, Nasakhare Isekhure.
>
> The word of the king, or *"oba,"* is law for most people here. He lives in a sprawling mud and log palace that is Benin City's biggest building and he is revered by followers as a demigod.
>
> Local Muslim and Christian leaders regularly pay homage to the *oba* for his influential advisory role in Edo state government and in recognition that many Christians and Muslims also believe in Bini mysticism and the *oba's* spiritual powers. (Glenn McKenzie, Associated Press, in *The Washington Times,* June 8, 2000; p.A16).

This is just one example of how traditional rulers can be useful in restoring peace; they can also be useful in conflict resolution. After its long civil war, "Mozambicans settled 500,000 property claims with only verbal agreement mediated by village chiefs. Mozambique has no psychiatric care, but local healers cleared up numerous cases of severe post-traumatic stress disorders" (*The News and Observer,* Jan 4, 1998; p.A18). In Rwanda after the 1994 genocide which saw the slaughter of more than 800,000 Tutsis, the government found that the formal court system would never be able to try more than a third of the over 100,000 suspects. To restore peace, reconciliation, and justice, the government turned to the traditional courts—*gacaca.* According to *The Economist* (May 17, 2003), "They got off to a flying start: in Oct 2001, Rwandans elected 258,208 *gacaca* judges, including 19 for each of the country's 9,170 cells (tiny administrative united sometimes as small as 200 people). The people in each cell are supposed to assemble before these judges on a patch of grass (*gacaca).* By hearing testimony from everyone who was there during the genocide, the judges are supposed to identify the culprits, and then pass judgment on them" (p.42).[1]

If Africa's traditional courts can be useful in conflict resolution, then Africa's traditional chiefs can be useful in the economic development of the Atingas.

Rural Development Under a Traditional Chief

It is indisputable that chiefs play a crucial role in the development of any given country. Being the closest to their subjects, traditional rulers are expected to spearhead and successfully execute developmental projects in their areas; like building schools and clinics, sinking boreholes and other ventures to uplift the living standards of their people. And the Zambian Government knows that very well. That is why it has, from time immemorial, sought a closer working relationship with traditional rulers. Without their involvement, nothing tangible would be achieved.

Our traditional leaders are people who command a hearing and therefore, whatever they say, the general public heeds their advice and counsel.
—Editorial, *The Times of Zambia* (Ndola), Feb 4, 2004.

Under the direction of a chief or a traditional ruler, schools, clinics, civic centers, and markets can be built with "communal labor." The chief, with the concurrence of the council of elders, may set a day or two aside and summon able-bodied men to contribute free labor for the construction of schools and markets. Consider these cases taken from Ghana:

Inhabitants of the 62 towns and villages in the Mamprong area in the central region have contributed $250,000 for the establishment of a rural bank.

Disclosing this to the "*Graphic*" at Mamprong, Nana Abedu said he had already offered his own building to house the bank. He said his people were prepared to offer communal labor (free) and are collecting a levy of $50 per head as their contribution towards the government's efforts to provide them with electricity and good drinking water. (*Daily Graphic,* Sept 15, 1982; p.8)

At the swearing-in ceremony presided over by the Ashantehene, Nana Bosu Brako, the newly installed chief of Achiase assured the Asanthene that he would lead his people to establish a large community farm, proceeds from which would be used for development projects in the area. (*Daily Graphic,* Oct 14, 1982; p.4)

A 5-year Development Plan estimated at $4 million has been drawn up by the Akrodie Traditional Council to improve the area.

Projects envisaged under the plan include the construction of a secondary school, renovation of elementary school buildings, tarring of streets and extension to the local health care.

Launching the plan at Akrodie, the Omhahene, Nana Dankwa fanin Ababie, said all the projects would be undertaken through communal labor.

Voluntary contributions of $300 per elder, $200 by young men and $100 per woman have been levied. Nana Ababio said proceeds from the sale of foodstuffs from 27-hectare farm near Akrodie would be used to meet part of the projects cost. (*Daily Graphic,* Jan 6, 1983; p.8).

The people of Bibiani District are sponsoring the facelift project of the Bibiani's Government Hospital at a cost of more than $200,000 through voluntary contributions. (*Daily Graphic,* Dec 3, 1982; p.8)

The rural locality of Tonka, in northern Mali, is an example of the endeavors that villagers in Africa are already making, despite extremely adverse conditions. By digging simple irrigation canals from a local river and lake, Tonka's 4,500 producers, organized in village cooperatives, have been able to increase their output of rice, millet, sorghum, potatoes, cassava, beans, and other foods. Tonka's marketplaces now attract buyers from other regions in Mali, and even from across the border in neighboring Mauritania. Thanks to the additional incomes they have earned, Tonka's residents have been able, during the past four years, to help finance the construction of nine primary schools, four health clinics, several wells, two livestock markets, a warehouse and several sanitation facilities. (*Africa Recovery,* Jan 2004; p.13)

Of especial importance is the building of a market and the providing of roads or access to the market:

In Sikorola, a village in western Burkina Faso, farmers generally benefit from adequate rains and more fertile soils. But their efforts to expand output are hampered by the area's very poor physical infrastructure. "We are ready to produce more maize and potatoes," says one member of the Siguizani family, "but there is no road to transport the crop."

Sikorola is not unusual. Across Africa, paved rural roads scarcely exist. Much produce is taken to market by cart or bicycle over unpaved roads or by foot along narrow paths cut through the brush. Africa has the lowest density of paved roads of any world region. Out of 1.8 mn kilometers of roads in sub-Saharan Africa, only 16 per cent are paved.

Moreover, many of Africa's paved roads have deteriorated badly from overuse and inadequate maintenance. Because of poor road quality, lorry drivers in rural Cameroon may charge an extra CFA1,000-CFA2,000 ($1.70-$3.40) for just a short trip of 6 kilometers. Higher transport costs raise the prices farmers must charge, reducing their competitiveness in both domestic and international markets. (*Africa Recovery,* Jan 2004; p.14)

In fact, this Atinga development model already exists in KwaDumisa, Natal (South Africa). The following section summarizes the findings of an important study by Themba Mbhele, "What Does A Rural Destination Area Look Like? Institutions and Livelihoods in KwaDumisa," in *Development Southern Africa,* 15, no 4, (Summer 1998).

KwaDumisa: A Successful Village Development Model

From time immemorial, African poor have used migration as a common strategy to change their livelihood options. They have "voted with their feet" to seek better economic opportunities elsewhere. Mbhele (1998) noted that one particular rural area on South Africa's eastern seaboard, KwaDumisa, although itself poor and beset with economic hardships, was attracting in-migration. Curious, he set out to investigate why KwaDumisa was serving as a magnet—seen as an area of opportunity and, in particular, what factors were attracting poor people to the area.

KwaDumisa is a rural quasi-urban settlement in KwaZulu-Natal, 80 km south of Durban, South Africa. A sandy coastal plain, it is sparsely populated with 13,000 people. The governance of this tribal area, subdivided into four districts, falls under the jurisdiction of a young, educated chief with links to the ruling African National Council. The land is hilly with poor soil fertility but adequate rainfall. The area is surrounded by large commercial sugar farms and Sappi forests, suggesting an economic potential that is yet to be tapped. But KwaDumisa residents lack access to basic social services: clean water, electricity, telecommunications, feeder roads, and public transportation. However, KwaDumisa has a fairly reliable taxi service that serves agricultural interests by transporting produce to selling points. It also has a relatively well-developed housing infrastructure.

Mbhele (1998) found that what were attracting migrants to the KwaDumisa were "good leadership and a resultant sound institutional system, provision of infrastructure and the possibility of pursuing multiple livelihood strategies in an economic climate of high unemployment" (p.668). The most important, he claimed, was the *institutional system*. The area is run along traditional lines with the usual interface with local statutory authority, the Ugu regional council, but leadership roles in KwaDumisa have been developed by women, who play a strong role in civil society.

Good leadership has provided the foundation for a good institutional system in which transparency rules; fairness and justice are upheld; and decision-making decentralized. As a result, the institutional system is relatively *free of corruption*. The decentralized approach to leadership has not only prevented political violence but has also reduced crime. This factor has led to relative *peace*, which in itself is a powerful attraction.

Another important aspect of KwaDumisa's institutional decentralization is the respect for civil liberties and economic freedom. Interest groups and economic actors can pursue their own agendas without interference or *diktats* by the tribal authority. Where the involvement of the tribal authority is mandatory, a more consultative approach is adopted. For example, agricultural development is handled by the *troika:* the Village development council, the agriculture lobby, and the tribal authority.

Mbhele (1998) gave four reasons why this institutional system has served as the major attractor. The first and most important factor is the role played by the traditional chief, who practices political and religious tolerance. As we have often observed, the traditional African chief's role is not to prescribe which political ideology or religion his people should subscribe to. Chiefs do not declare their villages to be one-party states. In KwaDumisa, people of any political affiliation may come to the area and may hold meetings, although political rallies are not allowed. This has brought about *peace* to an area where violence was endemic. The chief's practice of tolerance permeates his administration system, where land and other resource are not allocated along party lines. As a result, commercial agriculture has flourished.

The criminal justice system, though similar to that in most communities in KwaZulu-Natal, works effectively in KwaDumisa. The tribal authority has no jurisdiction over criminal cases, which are referred to the South African police service, but does preside over civil cases, such as stock and crop theft. These are handled by headmen, or *indunas,* through negotiations with the culprits. If they break down and the culprits refuse to make restitution, their property may be seized or they and their families may be expelled from the area. Again, note that in traditional Africa, a family is held *collectively* liable. If a boy steals a goat, his family is responsible for returning the goat or making restitution. Among the Somali, this same traditional law extends to murder, in which case a blood price (*mag*) is exacted. "If the perpetrator and the victim are of different clans and the murder was intentional, the *family* of the victim may ask for the death of the murderer. If the murderer escaped, the family of the victim is entitled to put to death two people of the murderer's family or tribe, preferably people of equal status as the victim" (van Notten, 2003, p.45). In KwaDumisa, the tribal court system has helped create an environment of fairness and justice, in which the rule of law prevails. According to Mbhele (1998), "this is appreciated by the community and has become a major magnet to the area" (p.670).

Besides the traditional setup, the second attraction to the area relates to development matters. The development committee (or village development council) is made up of community members and headmen. The committee has a very strong and dedicated female chairperson, who is influential with both the chief and the regional council chair. Thus, the village development council knows and can respond to the developmental needs of the people.

The third reason for the institutional system being such an attraction is its support for agriculture. The local extension officer's innovativeness and dedication to the community have earned her strong community support. Again, note that the local extension officer is a woman—a choice based on the fact that more than 70 percent of Africa's peasant farmers are women.

Mbhele (1998) continued that, apart from the institutional organization, the community has organized itself into clubs that empower their members both economically and socially. These clubs include *stokvels* (credit-lending clubs, like *susu,* and *esusu*), agricultural projects, and burial societies. Umbrella bodies for the clubs have developed and are financed by club subscriptions. These bodies interact with the development committee, offer new ideas, and promote capacity building. The *stokvels* appear to be most successful at improving community life. According to Mbhele (1998), "These informal credit-lending clubs have provided funds for investments in housing, education and cultivation" (p.673).

Access to agricultural land, coupled with a sound institutional system where tenure is fairly secure, has also been a major attraction. Again, note that in traditional Africa, "strangers" may gain access to land to farm after the payment of a token gift to the chief and strangers exercise usufructural rights only.

The fourth magnet has been the provision of infrastructure. "Although many of the basic services are not available, feeder roads have made the development of agricultural potential possible, as well as weekly commuting to major economic centers. The large number of traditional healers practice in the area" (pp.669–76).

Building Markets

As we have shown, the market is the nerve center of traditional Africa, where important commercial, religious, and even political activities take place. Destroy a market and one would wrench the life and soul out of a traditional African community. The market has three decisive advantages. First, it would provide *incentives* to the Atingas to *increase* production. Whereas before he produced just enough to feed his family (subsistence agriculture), the establishment of a market would encourage him to produce more so that he could sell the surplus to purchase things he may want. Second, the market affords other profitable opportunities; for example, he may find it more profitable to grow beans than corn. Third, market tolls would provide the village development council with revenue.

Indigenous markets still do exist in Africa but are not well organized. In the urban areas, they are chaotic, crowded, and open-air affairs that are at the mercy of the elements. An *improvement* to the market system would be *any* undertaking that increases the volume of trade and enhances the *freedom,* convenience, as well as the safety of transacting business at the market. The necessary *support services and infrastructure* would entail providing the following:

1. Roads and transportation networks to facilitate the shipment of goods and people to and from the market; improved buildings that provide better protection from the weather (rain and sun).

2. Electricity or lighting to enable the market to extend opening hours, toilet facilities, and security or secure areas where traders can leave their wares.
3. A general atmosphere of peace, security, order, and *freedom* for traders to conduct their business.

Recall that the period 1880 to 1950 was one of unparalleled peasant economic prosperity in Africa. The colonialists did not undertake much by way of development. But at least there was peace and a fair degree of *economic freedom* for Africans to produce, and sell what they wanted, and at what prices they wanted. In addition, the colonialists, in some cases, built a few markets for African natives. After independence, African nationalists and elites could not initiate *real* development because they were hostile to markets, erroneously thinking they were Western capitalist institutions.

In a fascinating story, *Washington Post* reporter Emily Wax recounted a story that drove home the importance of markets in famine-stricken Ethiopia.[2] She found two villages, Dilfaqaar and Dere Kiltu. Both suffer from the same lack of rainfall, yet the situation in one was of famine and the other of relative plenty. The reason? One had a market, the other did not.

Dere Kiltu's inhabitants are subsistence farmers. When they could not grow food, they were unable to feed themselves. Dilfaqaar, on the other hand, is a market town where trading flourishes. When local food supplies were cut off from nearby farms, Dilfaqaar's traders purchased food from farmers and suppliers who come in from Addis Ababa and other far-away cities. Likewise, meat, which is plentiful in some parts of Ethiopia, was brought to Dilfaqaar by traders. Wax found slabs of butchered meat hanging from the inside of kiosks waiting to be spiced, cooked, and served in Dilfaqaar. The stalls of the market were stocked with fat watermelons and bundles of the gray grain used to make *injera,* Ethiopia's spongy bread.

Donkey Transportation

Anybody who has been to rural Africa would affirm that the poor—mostly women—are overworked. Not only do they raise children but they are also peasant farmers, cultivating food. They go to their farms every day, trekking miles and carrying heavy loads on their heads. At harvest time, they carry out their produce from their farms on their heads! Some of these farmers are pregnant women with babies on their backs, too! There is a physical limit to the weight any human being can carry. Whatever cannot be carried is left on the farms to rot. Indeed, in Ghana, there have been instances upon instances of food rotting on the farms for lack of labor to take it out.

Back in the early 1980s, when food scarcities hit Ghana, people resorted to the consumption of all sorts of creatures to survive. Ghanaian columnist Ebow Goodwin was shocked. He wrote: "Oh God! What is this nasty world coming to? I have heard of people compelled by want, famine, and deprivation take to the ending of very strange insects, reptiles, carnivores. I have heard of people consuming frogs, lizards, earthworms, and dogs" (*The Punch*, Aug 28–Sept 3, 1981; p.2).

At exactly the same time that people were consuming lizards and frogs to survive, food was rotting on the farms. Consider these stories:

> About 3,000 large-scale food crop and cocoa farmers in four villages in the lower Afram plains district have appealed to the government to come to their aid now with transportation facilities to end the persistent, perishing of tons of farm produce in the area.
>
> They claimed that because of lack of hired labor in the area to help cart foodstuffs and cocoa they could only carry just a few *head loads* over a distance of about 19 kilometers to the nearest market at Nketepa.
>
> Sometimes volunteers offer to charge $100 for a bag of maize from Dentenkrom to Ohemaa, a distance of about five kilometers. (*Daily Graphic*, Dec 18, 1981; p.8)

> Reports from Krombakese in the Brong-Ahafo Region say that 6 million tubers of yam and more than 330,000 bags of rice, maize, millet, groundnut and pepper are locked up on farms in the area for lack of labor to take out the produce.
>
> Nana Opoku Ababio, chief of Dromankese, told *The Ghanaian Times* Accra, that, "thousands of perishable items such as tomatoes and cassava often got rotten and had to be thrown away every season." (*West Africa*, Jan 4, 1982; p.61)

Donkeys or horses with simple wooden carts can be helpful to the Atingas in getting harvest produce to the markets. A horse-drawn cart doesn't need a tarred road surface; it can travel over bush paths. Carts do not require foreign exchange to import oil; nor do they need much maintenance. In rural Ethiopia, donkeys are Atingas' best friends. "My donkey helps me carry water five miles back and forth, four times a day," said Lakech Mulugeta. "We travel many miles together. We never leave each other" (*The Washington Post*, Feb 18, 2003; p.A18). The animals bear the loads of firewood, water, and food that otherwise are borne on the backs of rural women whose physical labor shapes the Ethiopian landscape. Donkeys are extremely important to poor people because they work full time, seven days a week, and need little water or food. The donkeys are overloaded and overworked. Providing the poor with more donkeys would help. (Recall the story of Beatrice, a young Ugandan girl, whose family was given a goat.) Hitching a cart to the donkey would also ease the burden somewhat, and providing small credit to purchase donkeys would help many peasants. A donkey can cost the equivalent of about $25, which is a large sum in rural Ethiopia.

THE INFORMAL SECTOR: FREE ENTERPRISE RULES

A cursory look at Africa's roadsides reveal petty traders hawking all kinds of goods—ranging from *kenkey*, fish, toilet rolls, and dog chains to bread and even puppies. Then there are tailors, artists, sculptors, and artisans, who make various items such as carvings, iron gates, furniture, sweeping brushes, and clothes in their homes and then take them to the roadside to set up shop. These people are very hardworking and entrepreneurial, and must be admired because they are not wards of the government. Theirs is a daily struggle for survival. Such people—working for cash, mostly untaxed and unregulated and often with no permanent workplace—make up what economists call the "informal economy." In major Nigerian cities, "something like 53 percent of the economically-active population is in the informal sector," according to Akin Mabogunje, an economist at the Development Policy Center, a think tank in the southern city of Ibadan (*The Washington Post*, July 7, 1998; p.A5). "In smaller towns, it is 80 percent." These people are free enterprisers, but the roadside is not where they should be doing business. In fact, their activities there can be—and often are—hazardous. Vehicular traffic and trading do not mix. People get run over. Further, roadside activity can spill completely onto the road and block traffic.

Pompously stuffy African government officials think that slowing down traffic makes the road "people friendly" because the risk of knocking down pedestrians is reduced. The fad now is to place "high jumps" (speed bumps) on the road to slow down traffic, but the high jumps provide opportunities to armed robbers. At night, they hide behind the bushes near these high jumps. When a motorist slows down to scale the bumps, they pounce from their hideouts, fling open the passenger door, grab whatever is visible, and escape into the bush.

Further, slowing down traffic to a crawl creates two additional problems: First, it increases gasoline consumption. Automobiles are designed to run efficiently at certain speeds: 30–40 mph. At slower speeds and in lower gears, gasoline consumption is increased, which makes little sense for a country that must import oil. Second, slower traffic creates an immense pollution problem. A vehicle that is not operating efficiently does not burn fuel cleanly, which pollutes the air—the more so with diesel-powered trucks and buses.

The African government periodically bans roadside trading, sending an armada of policemen to drive away those selling dog chains at the traffic lights. A day or two later, the traders are back doing their businesses. No one in government ever thinks of providing an alternative place for these traders.

A problem crying out for a solution is really a business opportunity—an opportunity to make a profit. Virtually all the goods and services purchased in a normal economy were designed to solve some human problem—clothing, housing, or transportation problems, for example. Thus, problems at the roadside are really investment opportunities. For example, a market may be set up some distance away from the roadside. Some bright lights and stalls may be put in place and then the stalls may be rented out to generate revenue to recoup the initial investment. Or some abandoned warehouse can be found, painted, and refurbished into a showroom in which roadside furniture makers can display their wares. Better yet, the warehouse can be turned into a "factory" with the roadside furniture makers being employed as "workers." Another idea is to build a simple food mart with stalls for locally prepared food. A food market set some distance away from the road provides a safer and more convenient and hygienic place and environment to purchase food.[3] The roadside businesspeople are industrious and enterprising but are not well organized and lack capital. By reorganizing them and providing them with a little capital, the entrepreneur can make not only money for himself but also help solve a social problem.

In addition, there are all sorts of industries in traditional Africa: metal ware, pottery, glass, iron-working, gold, silver-mining, basketry, leatherworks, woodwork, clothing, and others. Craftsmen, artisans, goldsmiths, and blacksmiths produce all types of goods. In many traditional communities, the craftsmen organize themselves into guilds. There are guilds of carpenters, masons, woodworkers, potters, weavers, glass-makers, iron-ore miners, blacksmiths, and silversmiths. With a little reorganization, these craftsmen can become important exporters of *nonconventional* goods.

Most Western tourists leave Africa laden with an expansive collection of cultural artifacts: wooden drums, carvings, musical instruments, *kente* strips, basketry, bark cloth, etc. The poor in Africa have skills in producing these items. With a little capital and reorganization, these items can be produced more efficiently for export and provide the poor with a steady source of income.

Rural women in Uganda are skilled in producing beautiful mats, but they lack capital. At a conference organized by the Inter-Regional Economic Network (IREN) in Mombasa in November 2003, I met a black American, Cyril Boynes, who impressed me greatly. He had invested $1,200 of his own money, and organized about 20 Ugandan women into a cooperative to turn their mats into handbags. He brought samples to the conference and I bought one for $20.

If only Africa's elites would follow Cyril Boynes' example.

Raising Capital/Micro Credit

In the rural and informal sector, capital funds are generally scarce. There are banks, but the banks are hardly an option for the poor since the banks demand residential or postal addresses which the poor do not have, as well as collateral. Before opening accounts, banks also demand a minimum deposit of 50,000 *cedis* in Ghana, as well as evidence of regular income, impossible to provide for most petty traders, who keep records in their heads. To secure their intial startup capital for their fishing and commerical operations, the poor turn to two traditional sources of finance: the "family pot" and a revolving credit scheme, such as susu in Ghana, esusu in Yoruba, tontines or chilembe in Cameroon, and stokval in South Africa.[4] The second option is most popular with peasants as discussed in chapter 9.

In Ghana, the majority of susu clients are women, who form between 70 and 90 percent of susu clients. They are mostly petty traders and have difficulties satisfying the banks' conditions for accepting customers. "Women prefer the susu scheme because other forms of banking services are closed to them," says Sarah Ocran, a gender and development officer with the Third World Africa Secretariat, an advocacy nongovernmental organization in Accra. (*Public Agenda* [Accra], May 29, 2001)

Ghanaian journalist George Koomson provided a riveting account of another variation of the *susu* scheme that has been transformed into a saving scheme among petty traders in Ghana. Doing *susu* or making *susu* means giving money regularly to a collector for safekeeping with the aim of accumulating a targeted amount of money, often for a specific purpose: to purchase a capital or consumer good or to pay for some needs. *Susu* collectors make daily rounds among the petty traders, who may give according to their means. The daily savings handed to a collector may range from a modest 1,000 *cedis* to a high 50,000 *cedis* ($5). If a client chooses 1,000 *cedis*, she must give the collector the same amount for at least 31 days. At the end of 31 days, clients are entitled to take their entire savings, minus a day's contribution, which is retained by the collectors as their commission. *Susu* clients do not earn interest on amounts saved.

Susu serves important functions. First, it protects daily earnings from competing claims and ensures that there is working capital to restock supplies at the end of the month. Second, *susu* rewards the hard-working. One can only borrow or "collect" if one pays in, and one can only pay in if one works hard. "One woman, Esi Amissah, 45, who operates an eating place for example, operates four different types of susu accounts. She reportedly uses one to pay for utility bills, the second, for her four children's school fees, the third for supporting her business and the fourth for unexpected expenses" (*Public Agenda*, Accra, May 29, 2001).

Money collected by *susu* collectors is disbursed as advances or payment to those whose payments are due. Money that is not disbursed is checked, and kept locked up in the *susu* collector's house or store, usually in box or a compartment, until he is able to take it to the bank, usually the next day.

If the same *susu* scheme were brought to the West and modernized, it would be called a credit union! By definition, a credit union is a financial institution that lends only to its members. In Bangladesh, the astonishing success of the Grameen Bank, which modernized a similar microcredit, is world acclaimed. Muhammad Yunus, founder and facilitator of the "microcredit movement," provides more than $2 billion in loans money to the "poorest of the poor" in 60 countries. He has shown that even in the highly indebted countries, poverty is no excuse for loan default. His repayment rates often hover around 98 percent—a recovery rate that formal commercial banks can only dream of.

In South Africa, the Grameen Bank operations have been replicated by the Small Enterprise Foundation (SEF), which began operations in 1992 in rural areas where some 64 percent of the population live below the poverty line and some 30 percent below half the poverty line. Its *modus operandi* is group-based microcredit. In group-based lending, personal guarantees among a small, five-person group replace the conventional lending requirement for collateral. Since inception, SEF has disbursed in excess of 57,000 loans while maintaining an excellent recovery performance of less than 0.1 percent bad debts over this period. Currently SEF serves 12,500 poor clients.

For the urban jobless, however, community ties are weak and peer pressure may not be sufficient to ensure repayment. Accordingly, a slight variation of the Grameen model was development by Start-Up Capital, a charity based in Cape Town, South Africa. Would-be borrowers must pass through a five-day basic business course known as "township MBA," and put up 100 *rand* (or $10) of their own money as a surety. After that, they can borrow 300 *rand* and, if they repay this on time, they can raise ever-larger loans. The borrowers' business plans are not scrutinized, as that would require too much administrative manpower. Thus, Start-Up Fund's overheads are low: Two staff with computers deal with 15,000 customers. Combined with fairly high interest rates (3.25 per cent per month), the surety fund covers what few bad debts there are, and pays for the township MBAs as well. Most borrowers are women, and four-fifths of those who pass through the scheme are soon either employed or self-employed. "Now that the organization makes a profit, its director, Tony Davenport, has started to raise capital from investors instead of donors" (*The Economist,* Oct 31, 1998; p.42).

Genuine economic development must come from small-scale projects, and with microcredit, the Atingas can lift themselves out of poverty and prosper. On June 24, 2002, the BBC posted on its website the successful tales of three African entrepreneurs.[5] The following is a short account of their stories.

Bamako, Mali.   In the space of five years, Mariam Jaras Dirassouba rose from being a housewife to a bank manager. She had been unemployed with no access to credit and few opportunities to generate cash to support her family. Her story began when she and a group of Malian women started borrowing small sums of money of up to $50 from an Oxfam-backed local organization. With their loans, the women started money-making projects, including selling spices or kindling in the local markets. Their success led the women to demand training to set up a cooperative bank to help their friends and neighbors. When the number of women grew to 260, the bank was in a position to issue big loans of $1,000 or more to finance much more ambitious business plans, including a mango juice factory and a cloth-dying business. Mme. Jaras Dirassouba became the manager. Thus, the women gained the skills to access the formal banking system while giving other women the chance to borrow money to start out in business.

Kebemer, Senegal.   Collecting rubbish gave a new financial freedom to a group of women in the small town of Kebemer. The women borrowed money to buy a horse and cart, employed rubbish collectors, and earn a salary by cleaning up the streets on a daily basis. Since the local authorities lacked funds, garbage piled up, causing illnesses among the children playing outside. When people saw the benefits of the daily service, they were willing to pay for it. The project has not only reduced health problems, but it has also created income and employment for 20 people. The idea of a new force of dustbin women was first conceived in 1998 and got off the ground after Christian Aid provided the loan for the first horse and cart. The women then earned enough money to buy more than 300 dustbins, and 10 horses and carts, and employ administrators to organize the project, spanning 500 homes. There were profits left over to invest in new money-making projects, including traveling to Mauritania and Gambia to buy shoes for resale in their local towns.

Dekaya, Ethiopia.   Bee-keeping is a traditional activity in Dekaya in southern Ethiopia, using hives made out of hollow logs. Farmers introduced more innovatively designed hives from Germany while still making the hive out of local wood. The improvements raised productivity, with each hive producing about 26 kg of honey, compared to the 3 kg produced with the old-fashioned method. About 150 farmers benefited from the new technology, after Action for Development provided technical training and the loans for the first hives to be used. The farmers then set themselves up as a cooperative, with the aim of securing their own loans from banks to buy new hives in the future. With such success, the children could go to school, have access to better accommodation, and one man has been able to build a new house with the money raised from selling honey.

INVESTMENT STRATEGY

Complete Overhaul of Elite Mentality

Africa is still mired in poverty because horse-drawn carts, donkeys, garbage collection, and chiefs do not fit into the functionally illiterate elite's scheme of things. To them, development is synonymous with industrialization, modern and scientific methods. The developed countries are industrialized, *ergo* development means industrialization. As we noted in chapter 4, instead of utilizing the chiefs for rural development, they were stripped of much of their traditional authority after independence. In some African countries such as Ghana, Mozambique, Nigeria, and Zimbabwe, chieftaincy became politicized and the chiefs lost their reverence and respect.

  Few of the informal activities described here would interest Africa's dysfunctional elites because they see the tasks as too "dirty." For example, compost or animal waste can be used for farming, eliminating the government's dependency on imported chemical fertilizers. Ghana had a comprehensive plant that could supply half of all the country's fertilizer needs! The article "World's Richest Compost Produced In Accra" in *Ghana News* (July 1981), a publication of the Ghana Embassy, noted that:

> The compost produced by the Accra City Council's $22 million composting plant at Teshie is one of the richest in the world. But the plants' 120 tonnes

of compost a day is not being put to proper use as a rich organic fertilizer for Ghana's agricultural needs.

Mr. Martin Meyer, a Swiss agricultural expert, established that the Accra compost contains all the vital nutrients needed by plants.

The use of compost, he further emphasized, could double and sometimes triple the cereal and vegetable harvests of Ghanaian farmers.

Compost from the plant at Teshie could cut by half Ghana's reliance on chemical fertilizers. (p.14)

Did the same government make use of the compost? Of course not! On September 7, 1981 the Cabinet instead decided to allocate £6.5 million to import supplies so that work on a fertilizer project at Cape Coast, which was stopped, could go ahead (*Daily Graphic,* Sept 7,1981; p.1). And then in December 1981, came this report: "The ministry of agriculture is to import 19,050 metric tones of fertilizer for the 1982 farming season. The contract, which is worth about $8,996,607.50 has been awarded to UKF of Holland" (*Daily Graphic;* Dec 14, 1981; p.5).

There are lots of fish in the sea but the elites can't catch them. Rather, foreign vessels come and poach in Africa's waters, take the fish to their countries, turn them into *Tinapa* (canned mackerel), and ship them to Africa for the elites to queue in the hot sun. A little bit of history would help here.

The Ghana Navy has arrested two out of 15 foreign tuna vessels which were found fishing in Ghana's territorial waters. This was disclosed by Commander Kofi Aryeetey, officer-in-charge of the Eastern Naval command.

According to him, tuna poaching has become so lucrative that about 20 foreign vessels, mainly of Spanish origin, are attracted *daily* to Ghana's shores. Commander Aryeetey stated that about $25 million dollars worth of tuna were illegally taken out of the country last week. (*Daily Graphic,* Dec 17, 1981; p.1)

Ghana government elites never gave the native fishing industry any assistance or sought to reorganize it. It was too "backward." Instead, the government established the State Fishing Corporation. And how did it perform? That corporation became an economic disgrace, as we saw in chapter 6. The catalogue of mismanagement, corruption, and inefficiency is too long to fully recount, but a few examples will suffice. In 1977, two senior officials of this corporation were indicted for their involvement in the "Sekondi Fish Deal" in which more than $3 million was allegedly lost to the state (*West Africa,* Aug 8, 1977; p.1647). Then "Three ratings of the State Fishing Corporation (SFC) have been placed in custody at the Sekondi Naval Base in connection with the looting of more than 400 cartons of fish aboard the corporations vessel

'Drabon'" (*Daily Graphic*, July 18, 1981; p.8). Ship captains were involved: "When the captain of 'MV Ayensu' Mr. Akporyo stole 88 cartons of fish on board, only half was recovered" (*Daily Graphic*, Nov 24, 1982; p.1). So lucrative was the looting on board the SFC vessels that a senior refrigeration assistant who tried to report it, Mr. Fred Otoo, "was 'electrocuted' on board 'MV Asubone' under mysterious circumstances" (*Daily Graphic*, Nov 24, 1982; p.1). That scandalous state corporation was sold off in the late 1990s.

And what about the previous discussion of donkeys and carts to ease the problem of food evacuation from the farms? "The Minister of Agriculture, Mr. N.Y.A. Agbesi said the Government is making efforts to solve the problems of labor on the farms with the introduction of *mechanization at all levels*" (*The Ghanaian Times*, Oct 10, 1981; p.8). Mechanization at all levels?

The "tractor mentality" still prevails among Nigerian government officials. In July, 2004, President Olusegun Obasanjo invited about 200 white farmers, whose farmlands have been violently seized by the Mugabe regime in Zimbabwe, to resettle in Kwara state. Bukola Saraki, the governor of the state, said: "in Kwara, we don't have oil, but we have 2.3 million hectares [5.7 million acres] available for agriculture" (*The Washington Times*, July 18, 2004; p.A6). Much of that land along the Niger River is fertile and is seldom farmed and the governor has been spearheading a national drive to wean Nigeria off its oil-based revenue and make it self-sufficient in food. (The country spends $3 billion a year on food imports.) But the governor's "Back to the Farm" campaign launched in 2003 flopped miserably. The governor discovered that "Kwara's peasant farmers, most in their 60s and 70s, were unfamiliar with modern technology and had no capital to buy tractors" (*The Washington Times*, July 18, 2004; p.A6).

The governor's approach to peasant agriculture defied common sense. Illiterate peasant farmers cannot be expected to be familiar with modern technology and have the capital to buy tractors! An agricultural program involving peasant farmers based upon such ridiculous premises cannot be expected to succeed. The governor's solution to the agricultural debacle was to invite white commercial farmers from Zimbabwe, saying: "When we found oil [in the Niger delta], we didn't ask people in southern Nigeria to look for shovels to dig for it. We brought in foreigners with expertise. Our land is an asset that is not being utilized. The only way to do that is to bring in people with the necessary skills" (*The Washington Times*, July 18, 2004; p.A6).

There is nothing wrong with bringing in foreigners with the necessary skills to help Africa develop its resources. But that doesn't mean governor should abandon the peasant farmers in his state. He should have asked why the land was not being utilized. Did he think of giving incentives to his peasant farmers? Mohamed Alasan, a local farmer, was unimpressed by the governor's rationalization: "We want the whites to come and run the sugar estate because they won't mismanage it" (*The Washington Times*, July 18, 2004; p.A6).

Asked to explain the perennial food crisis in Ethiopia, President Meles Zenawi responded: "The problem is, we have too many people for the level of agricultural technology we are using. We have used these methods for centuries, but it's urgent that we update them" (*The Washington Post*, Feb 6, 2003; p.A32). Aid agencies disagreed. "The crisis would be less acute, according to aid agencies, if villages such as Dere Kiltu had the kind of water projects that would make it possible to grow food without large amounts of rainfall. Collecting water for cooking, bathing, drinking and washing clothes is an all-day chore in Dere Kiltu, performed by women walking with large yellow jugs. When water is scarce, there is not enough to irrigate crops" (*The Washington Post*, Feb 6, 2003; p.A32).

The tragedy is, war and politics, not water projects and markets, preoccupy the minds of the ruling elites. Between 1998 and 2001, Ethiopia and neighboring Eritrea fought a devastating, expensive war. Both countries reportedly spent $1 million dollars a day on the fighting, at a time when foreign donors were pulling out of development projects. And during the 1984 famine, Mengistu's military government, known as the Dergue, systematically moved farmers whom they believed to be disloyal and resettled them into camps where they died of famine.

The Hippo Generation

Donkeys, horses, carts, and small-scale projects are essential for the Atingas to raise their productivity. To make this happen, it is important to distinguish between two types of elite: the hippo and cheetah generations. The hippo generation are of the 1950s and 1960s—stodgy, pudgy, and wedded to the old colonialism/imperialism paradigm with an abiding faith in the potency of the state. They sit tight in their air-conditioned government offices, comfortable in their belief that the state can solve all problems. All the state needs is more power. And they ferociously defend their territory since that is what provides them with their wealth. The whole country may collapse around them, but they are content as long as their pond is secure. There are three key areas where the mentality of the hippo generation needs to be revamped.

First, the "government" does not solve all problems. Quite the contrary: Government creates problems. As such, the primary responsibility for taking steps to solve a problem must originate from the local level. Therefore, local institutions and government must be strengthened, which in turn requires greater decentralization of power.

The advantage in decentralization resides in the fact that the "development" or capital expenditures can be reduced considerably, with greater efficiency of results. For example, suppose the Akwadidi town needs a new school. The local "village development council" may be asked to draw up its plans and put up half of the cost. It may levy head taxes, poll taxes, market tolls, etc. to raise the money. The national or regional government may put up the remaining half. Thus, not only would the national development budget be cut but also corruption and malpractices in contracts would be minimized, as accountability at the local level would be better enforced.

Second, the content of education needs to be overhauled. The hippo generation overemphasized the literary type of education: the acquisition of university degrees and instruction in such subjects as history and the arts. The emphasis should rather be placed on vocational education to teach students such skills as cart-making, horse/donkey breeding, welding, brick-making, sewing, basketry, auto mechanics, etc. Instead of building more universities, African governments should be building more vocational schools. The advantage is that a graduate from a vocational school, with little capital, can immediately employ himself or herself. The university graduate, on the other hand, must often wait for the government to employ him.

Third, government does not create wealth, only redistribute it. Wealth is created in the private sector, not in the government sector. Therefore, those African elites who want to get wealthy—and there is nothing wrong with wanting to be rich—should seek their own place in the private sector, even if they have to produce and sell donkey carts. And there is nothing wrong with becoming rich by producing donkey carts or services the poor want.

The richest person in the United States—Bill Gates, with a personal fortune of more than $60 billion—made his money in the private sector, by producing Microsoft computer software, which has raised the productivity of both poor and rich workers. He has provided a valuable service to society and has something to show for his wealth. By contrast, the richest persons in Africa are heads of state and ministers, who use the government machinery to extract wealth from the backs of the suffering masses. Politics, therefore, has become the gateway to fabulous wealth in Africa. So every educated fool wants to be the president—not to produce anything in the private sector. As a result, there is always ferocious competition for the presidency and ministerial positions—competition that often degenerates into civil strife and war. Congo, Liberia, Sierra Leone, Somalia, and other African countries have been thoroughly destroyed. Yet, educated clods and barbarous warlords fight ferociously to death over who should be the next president.

If the hippo generation were to seek their wealth in the private sector, both Africa and the hippos would reap immense benefits. For one thing,

Africa would start producing again. For another, it would save the hippos' their own hides because, come a change of government, no one would haul them before commissions of enquiry and prosecute them over ill-gotten wealth if they had made that wealth in the private sector. Unfortunately, the sit-tight hippos are beyond redemption.

The Cheetah Generation

Africa's hope lies with the cheetah generation—the new and angry generation of Africans discussed in the prologue. They tend to be young African graduates, who are dynamic, intellectually agile, and pragmatic.

Angry at deteriorating economic conditions in Ghana, thousands of cheetahs marched through the streets of the capital city, Accra, to denounce the ruling regime of President Rawlings. "If Jerry Rawlings says the current economic crisis is due to external forces and therefore, beyond his control, then he should step aside and allow a competent person who can manage the crisis to take over," Atta Frimpong demanded (*The Ghanaian Chronicle,* Nov 29, 1999; p.1). Appiah Dankwah, another protestor, blamed the NDC government for mismanaging the resources of the nation.

The cheetah generation has no qualms about getting their hands "dirty" and, as such, it is this generation that can initiate small-scale projects in the informal and rural sectors to help the Atingas and make money in the bargain. Money can be made by helping the poor, and there is nothing immoral about that.

My proposal, then, is that the cheetah generation invest in cottage industries to produce wooden carts. Donkeys and horses can be bred. Horse- or donkey-drawn carts can be sold to the Atingas for $50 or so. There are many other cottage industries that can be started by the cheetah generation.

Cottage Industries

Just like the illiterate folks, the cheetah generation can organize investment clubs to set up cottage industries or projects.[6] Here are some examples recounted by *Washington Post* columnist David Ignatius.[7]

India. Joe Madiath for the past 24 years ran a rural development program called Gram Vikas in the Indian state of Orissa on the Bay of Bengal, the poorest areas in the country, with more than 40 percent of its people living below the poverty line. Madiath believes in solving the sanitation needs of the people to improve their health. This requires improving their water supply, their waste disposal, and providing toilets. So Madiath built toilets for about 12,000 families in 120 villages, asking villagers to share the cost by contributing $20 per family. He seeks to expand to 100,000 families and 1,000 villages, which will generate gross income of at least $2 million.

Brazil. Ismael Ferreira runs the Small Farmers Association in his home region of Bahia in northeastern Brazil. The area is so dry that the only crop that grows easily there is a cactus-like plant called sisal, whose fibers can make rope or thread. Ferreira, whose father was a sisal farmer, decided to make do with what they had. He started a carpet factory to weave sisal thread into products that could be sold in global markets. The operation now has annual revenues of about $7 million and employs about 650 families.

East Africa. Martin Fisher, co-founder of a group in East Africa called ApproTEC, is a Stanford-trained Ph.D. in engineering. He went to Africa in the 1980s and decided that the best way to fight rural poverty was to build simple, cheap machines—"appropriate technology"—that could help people earn some cash. His group designed and built sturdy, hand-powered machines: a $38 pump that can irrigate a small, one-acre plot, allowing a farmer to plant several cash crops and make an annual profit of $1,200; a $490 block press that can make building blocks from soil and a bit of cement and earn someone about $10 a day; a $510 hay baler that will allow farmers to feed livestock through the dry season and can earn them a profit of up to $50 a day.

Cameroon. Gisele Yitamben started her Association for the Support of Women Entrepreneurs in Cameroon in 1989 after she concluded that women in Africa had no access to credit. In the years since, she has worked with more than 5,000 women, opened a four-story resource center in the city of Douala, and is about to start a radio station that will provide information about health and education.

Similar projects can be started. Mention must be made of a young Nigerian engineer and industrialist, Emeka Okafor, residing in New York, who publishes a host of practical ideas at the website: www.timbuktuchronicles. blogspot.com. However, cottage industries should be selected according as to how they satisfy one or more of the following criteria. A project must be:

1. Geared toward improving the life of the ordinary African, the illiterate and semi-literate folks.
2. The target group should be found mostly in the informal and traditional sectors—precisely the sectors most neglected by nearly all African governments in their postcolonial development efforts.

3. Capital requirements should be modest, not exceeding, say, $20,000 for one project, so that risks can be spread.
4. Technological requirements should be labor intensive and should represent a modest improvement upon existing technology. High tech may be fashionable but dogmatic insistence on using solar energy to make *garri* (cassava meal) makes little economic sense. If larger charcoal-fired kilns can be used to produce *garri* more cheaply, they should be used. After all, it is the plentiful supply of *garri* that is desired—not that it is produced with solar energy, charcoal, or natural gas to impress some foreigners. Whatever fuel and technology are economical ought to be used.

Projects can be envisaged in the following areas:

Food Process and Distribution

Peasant agriculture, especially the production, processing, and distribution of local foodstuffs, remains the backbone of the economies of many African countries. It employs the vast majority of ordinary Africans and contributes a hefty chunk to the GDP. Yet, it is the area that has been most shunned by postcolonial African governments and is in need of serious investment. Due to poor organization and inadequate transportation facilities (lack of feeder roads, etc.), at least 30 percent of the locally produced foodstuffs is lost through spoilage. Thus, anything that preserves, processes, and facilitates the shipment of foodstuffs to the market (or the consumer) would be a worthwhile investment. Accordingly, the following projects fall in this category:

1. *Garri*/Starch-Making Enterprise (Cottage Industry). This author visited one such enterprise in Cape Coast, Ghana, where the owner explained his operations: How the cassava is ground, the starch extracted, and *garri* made and bagged. He needed a little capital—less than $5,000—to expand his operations. An investment of this nature can be recouped in less than a year because there is always a demand for *garri*. In addition, industrial starch has now become an export commodity, being championed under a new export initiative.
2. Grain Silos. The author also visited a village in Elmina, which has been experiencing periodic shortages and surpluses of maize. As there were no storage facilities, the villagers could not store grain surpluses to tide them over during the lean season. Simple silos can be built, where farmers can store their produce for a fee, which could be paid in grain. A simple silo can be constructed for less than $200.

3. Grain Milling Machines and Oil Presses. Milling centers can be established at strategic points where farmers can take maize, peppers, or millet to be milled into flour and bagged. A milling machine, for example, costs about $3,000 to install. The author was told that operators charge 20,000 *cedis* ($2) to mill one bag of maize in 10 minutes. If the machine mills only 10 bags a day, that would generate $20 a day. That translates into $100 for a five-day week or $400 for a month. Evidently, the $3,000 investment can be recouped in less than a year. Such centers may also have oil presses that would press groundnuts (peanuts) into vegetable oil and palm nuts into palm oil.

4. Markets/Food Distribution Depots. At various "junctions" on trunk roads in Africa, one finds people selling a few items on rickety and ramshackle tables: bread, cassava, bunches of plantain, bottles of palm oil. Doing business this way is not only inefficient but also dangerous as well, as noted in chapter 9. Mixing people and vehicular traffic is never a good idea.

Land may be sought from the chief of the town and a simple market constructed, say 40 yards from the road. Put in market stalls, starting with, say, 10 of them and providing them with locks and keys so that traders can secure their wares at the market without having to carry them back to their homesteads. Provide a night watchman, lighting, and driveways from the main road to the market. The stalls may be rented out at, say, 25,000 *cedis* (or $2.50) a month. Ten of them would yield 250,000 *cedis* a month or 3 million *cedis* a year. Twenty of them give 6 million *cedis* in annual revenue. In a few months, the market will become crowded and bustling with activity because it will act both as an attraction and inducement. Knowing that a market exists, farmers would be encouraged to produce more, increase their surpluses, and take them to the market. Such a market can be constructed for less than $50,000, or 500 million *cedis*. Conservative figures have been used here but stall rents can be raised when business picks up in order to recoup the investment in two or three years for another market to be built elsewhere or the existing one expanded.

5. Food Brokers. Instead of a market, a food depot can be constructed where produce can be purchased in bulk from farmers and then taken to corresponding depots in the urban centers to be sold to market women or even work establishments (canteens), hospitals, and educational institutions. This, however, would involve a more substantial investment than building a simple market.

6. Yam/Cassava Contest. Semi-annual or annual agricultural fairs can be organized, contests held, and prizes awarded to the Atinga who pro-

duces the largest tuber of yam or cassava. The contest can be organized in such a way that it generates revenue and boosts yam or cassava production at the same time. The benefits of increased yam/cassava production for the country are obvious. Less obvious are ways to use the contest to generate revenue. Here is how:

Award the farmer who produces the biggest tuber yam a bicycle, with the second prize being a donkey-drawn cart, and the third prize a transistor radio. Assume the total cost of the prizes to be $500. Rules of the competition would be such that any farmer can enter the contest by paying for as many entries as he or she likes, but the entries are not returnable or refundable. This is the key. Those who purchase lottery tickets do not have their money refunded if they do not win. After the contest and award of prizes, the yams can be sold to recoup the outlay.

If an entry sells for $1 and 1,000 peasant farmers enter the contest, $1,000 would be generated. Further, most peasant farmers, to improve their chances of winning, would submit three, four or even five entries. And as word spreads, more farmers from far away villages—2,000, 3,000 or more—may enter the contest, generating $5,000 or more for a contest that spent only $500 on prizes. A contest such as this also has social benefits. And every effort must be made to ensure that the winner is actually a peasant farmer.

7. Commercial farms or plantations. These are self-explanatory.
8. Fishing. This is another area with high profit potential, as there is always a high demand for fish. An investment club can start at the production (catching) end. It could purchase a dugout canoe for $5,000 (50 million *cedis*), give it to a fishing crew and work out a "work-and-pay" arrangement whereby the crew pays the club 3 million *cedis* a month for 3 years, after which time the canoe becomes their property. This is a no-hassle type of investment. Every month, the investment club simply collects 3 million cedis. After 3 years, the club would collect a total of 108 million *cedis* for a 40 million *cedi* investment, giving at least a 56 percent annual rate of return. There is no reason why the club should start with only one canoe; it can start with two. After a year, it will have 72 million *cedis* from the two canoes, which it can use to purchase a third or a fourth canoe and so on.

The uniqueness of this type of investment resides in the fact that there are already skilled fishermen in Africa. But due to their poverty, raising a small amount of $5,000 to buy a dugout canoe is beyond their means. Borrowing from a bank is out of the question because they are illiterate, not well organized, and have no collateral. All that the investment club does is to organize them into a fishing crew, purchase a canoe for them, and let them use their own skills to bring in the fish. No training, equipment, or housing is required. This type of operation can easily be upgraded with boats that are *wider* than the dugout canoes so that bigger catches of fish can be landed—a change Ghana government officials should have encouraged but bypassed in favor of modern pleasure boats.

Transportation

Because of the collapse of municipal bus service and public transportation, this area is one of the most profitable in the informal sector. But it is not yet efficiently put to use.

1. Taxi/Tro-Tro/Bus service. With a modest investment of $10,000, an investment club can purchase two minibuses and recoup the investment in less than two years.
2. Auto Repair Shops. There are highly skilled auto mechanics or "fitters." All that is needed is a little organization and capital. An investment club can build a repair shop, consisting of several bays, which can be rented out to recoup the initial investment.
3. Auto Rest Stops. Such stops seldom exist on Africa's trunk roads—a factor which contributes to the high rate of fatal road accidents. Night driving in Africa is extremely hazardous; the more so when drivers are tired with no place to rest.

   An investment project of this nature can take several variations. It can take the shape of a simple rest stop that provides toilet facilities and refreshments (snacks and drinks). Such a rest stop must be set at a little distance from the main road. It may take six months to a year to put up such an establishment, and the cost may exceed $50,000. This cost may rise rapidly if a restaurant is added or a motel/hotel for overnight stay.

Social Services

There is a whole range of social services that can be provided *profitably.* Note the emphasis on "profitably." An investment club is not a government outfit that obtains its revenue from taxes. It must raise its funds privately and make a return on them. And providing a service to the poor and making a profit at the same time is not necessarily unethical. The market women who sell bread and *garri* do not do so for altruistic reasons but hope to make a profit. The key is providing a quality product or service at prices the poor can afford to pay. The following services may be considered:

1. Public Toilets and Baths. Fees can be charged for these services.
2. Health Care. Simple clinics and/or dispensaries can be established and interfaced with traditional medicine. About 80 percent of Africa's population still rely on native medicine. This native sector is not well organized and quackery is prevalent. However, it should not be dismissed outright and strategic investment here and there could yield huge dividends.
3. Vocational Training Schools. The possibilities here are endless. An investment club can rent premises to instruct and train people to enter a variety of vocations: auto mechanics, carpentry, sculpting, masonry, welding, donkey breeding, cart construction, etc. This is the most neglected aspect of Africa's educational program. Fees can be levied so that the investment can be recouped.
4. Adobe Housing. Somehow, African elites have gotten this idea that only cement should be used in house construction. But cement houses are simply beyond the reach of many poor Africans. Cheaper materials, such as lumber and adobe, can be used. Adobe literally means "hardened mud" or sun-dried earth, and there is nothing wrong with adobe houses. Adobe construction has been used for centuries around the world. Approximately half of the people in Africa, Asia, and Latin America live in houses built using sun-dried earth. Famous buildings that still stand today have used variations of this method of building and bear witness to the strength and durability of this alternative method: the National Museum of Mali, Bamako, Mali, completed in 1982; a mosque in Tamale, Ghana; Pan African Institute Development (Ouagadougou, Burkina Faso); and many residential buildings in New Mexico, California, and Germany. This author found them in Albuquerque, New Mexico. When well constructed, adobe houses can last, but traditional mud houses in Africa do not; they are allergic to rain because of the way the mud is used. The cost of an adobe block is approximately 30 percent less than the cost of a comparatively sized cement block. In addition, adobe has several other advantages. The thick walls can provide good insulation against sound, heat, and cold. It is also termiteproof and fireproof.[8] An adobe brick-making machine can be purchased for less than $10,000.

Other Projects

There are many other projects that can be considered that do not fit the categories above. One is tailoring or dressmaking. There are lots of skilled tailors in Africa. Five good ones may be assembled at some premises. Two or three industrial sewing machines may be purchased for them at a cost of about 8 million *cedis* (or $800). Standard yarn or material worth 3 million *cedis* may be purchased for them to start with. Assume the total investment comes to 20 million *cedis* because they will need other things as well, such as a buttonhole-making machine. They would be required to produce and sell, say, shirts. All they have to do is to bring the investment club 2 million *cedis* a month. In less than a year, the investment more than recoups itself.

SUMMARY

The tragedy of Africa is that it is a continent with so much economic potential mired in abject poverty. More ironic is the fact that the resources and the blueprint Africa desperately needs to launch itself into the economic stratosphere already exists in Africa itself. The real problem has been leadership and a hippo generation who look to the wrong places for Africa's salvation. All the grand initiatives and plans crafted to resuscitate Africa's economic development came to ignominious grief. NEPAD, from all indications, will suffer the same fate.

The blueprint for Africa's economic recovery can be found in Africa's own backyard: In its own indigenous economic institutions, which have been castigated as "backward and primitive." These institutions comprise free enterprise, free village markets, and free trade. All that is required is to take what is there, build or improve upon the existing institutions, and unleash the creative and entrepreneurial energies of the African people. Given peace and economic freedom, they responded remarkably to economic stimuli and prospered during colonial rule. This does not suggest colonial rule was preferable. But in spite of all its abhorrent limitations, colonial rule did establish some peace and some rudimentary infrastructure—roads, railways, ports, and some schools. Botswana provided the same environment and incentives, transforming itself into a shining black African economic star.

The strategy entails three steps. The first requires establishing a village development council under the direction of an African chief or traditional ruler. The African chief is an important human resource and ought to be used. In many rural parts of Africa, chiefs command far more respect and reverence than modern African governments, and the most effective way of reaching African peasants is through their chiefs or traditional rulers. A village development council or committee can be set up under the chiefs, as we saw with KwaDumisa village in South Africa. Such a development council can provide basic social amenities such as clinics, schools, other infrastructure on a cost-sharing basis with provincial or regional administration and ensure that peace prevails in the community.

The second step is to mobilize capital by improving upon or modernizing existing microcredit schemes. Once mobilized, the funds should be invested in cottage industries by the cheetah generation.

The World Bank, the IMF, and foreign development agencies cannot be expected to craft such a strategy for the obvious reason that they are not very knowledgeable about the cultural norms of the Atingas. Such a strategy must be home-grown. But then again, the hippo generation are more interested in doing the "Babangida boogie" on state-owned "Nigeria Airwaste"!

CHAPTER 11

Epilogue and Conclusions

Africa will have to rely upon Africa. African Governments will have to formulate and carry out policies of maximum national and collective self-reliance. If they do Africa will develop; if they don't Africa will be doomed.

—Julius Nyerere, ex-president of Tanzania, in an October 9, 1997, speech at the University of Edinburgh, Scotland.

It is really difficult to ask foreign investors to come and invest on our continent when our own people are not investing here. There is no better factor to convince foreign investors than for them to see that our own people, both those based at home and those in the Diaspora, invest in Africa.

—Alhaji Bamanga Tukur, President of the African Business Round Table on business partnership with New Partnership for African Development (NEPAD) at the Commonwealth Business Forum on December 3, 2003 in Abuja, Nigeria; *This Day*, Lagos, Dec 4, 2003.

The average African is poorer (now) than during the age of colonialism. Whereas colonialists had developed the continent, planted crops, built roads and cities, the era of *uhuru* had been characterized by capital flight as the elite pocketed money and took it outside their countries. Among them were the late Nigerian dictator Sani Abacha. The money Abacha had plundered had been discovered in Switzerland . . . In the 1960s African elites/rulers, instead of focusing on development, took surplus for their own enormous entourages of civil servants without plowing anything back into the country. The continent's cash crops, like cocoa and tobacco, were heavily exploited by the state-run marketing boards with farmers getting little in return.

—Moeletsi Mbeki, Chairperson of the South African Institute of International Affairs, and brother of President Thabo Mbeki (*The Mercury*, Sept 22, 2004.)

MONUMENTAL LEADERSHIP FAILURE

This book owes no one any apology. Africa is a mess—economically, politically, and socially. Despite Africa's vast natural resources, its people remain mired in the deadly grip of poverty, squalor, and destitution while buffeted by environmental degradation and brutal tyranny. Most Africans are worse off today than they were at independence in the 1960s. African leaders have failed Africa. African politicians have failed. African intellectuals have failed Africa, too. The failure is monumental and the international community is fed up with incessant African begging.

Within a mere four decades after independence from colonial rule, Africa has been reduced to a broken, dysfunctional continent by wretched institutions and execrable leadership. Again, distinctions must always be made between *leaders* and the *people,* as well as *modern* and *traditional* leaders.

It is true African nationalist leaders waged an arduous liberation struggle against the colonialists to win independence for their respective peoples. The annals of postcolonial Africa are full of their sacrifices and gallantry. Historical accounts include such indefatigable efforts as those of Dr. Kwame Nkrumah of Ghana, Patrice Lumumba of Congo, Dr. Apollo Milton Obote of Uganda, Robert Mugabe of Zimbabwe, Samora Machel of Mozambique, to name a few. These leaders were purpose-driven individuals, selfless in their determination to liberate their people and improve their lot. Upon the attainment of independence, they were hailed as heroes. In the beginning, they all meant well for their people but good intentions were not enough. Lacking experience in government, these leaders were bound to make mistakes. Indeed, they did—aplenty. But they never learned from them or put in place mechanisms to correct them. The vast majority set the *wrong priorities* for their countries and took the *wrong approach* to their countries' development. And when problems emerged, they performed the *wrong diagnosis* and sought *wrong solutions* from the *wrong places.* Simple and honest errors that were initially made were compounded by stubborn refusal to admit mistakes. As heroes and semi-gods, they were infallible. They continued to bask in the glory of the liberation era and lost touch with their people. As Kenyan columnist Henry Ochieng pointed out:

> After the attainment of independence, many of these "heroes" grew into quarrelsome old men. They could not understand why their rabble-rousing speeches no longer elicited the same awe, or never had the selfsame electrifying effect on the masses. They also refused to understand why the people could not identify with their desire to die in power (and many actually did realize that desire). They were caught in a time warp. Most of these old politi-

cians failed to move with the people. The people, after independence quickly wanted to get to the next stage from liberation that the independence struggle was all about, while the leaders continued to bask in the euphoria of kicking out the colonial master. For them, it was a continuous party that could only end with their death. So, when talk of popular revolt against them begun to waft through the air, their only response was to become repressive—hoping they could suppress the clamor for change. They failed. (*The Monitor* [Kampala], Jan 22, 2003; p.4)

In an unusual editorial, *The Independent* newspaper in Ghana wrote: "Africa today is politically independent and can be said to have come of age but apart from Thabo Mbeki and Yoweri Museveni, we are sorry to openly admit that most of our leaders have nothing to offer except to be effective managers for the IMF and serve as footnotes to neocolonialism. Most of the leaders in Africa are power-loving politicians, who in or out of uniform, represent no good for the welfare of our people. These are harsh words to use for men and women who may mean well but lack the necessary vision and direction to uplift the status of their people" (*The Independent*, Ghana, July 20, 2000; p.2).

In the summer of 2004, humanitarian crises were brewing in the Congo, Sudan, and southern Africa. In Sudan, Arab militiamen called *janjaweed,* backed by an Arab government, were exterminating people with black skin, creating a massive humanitarian crisis in the Darfur region. The militias' systematic destruction of wells, agriculture, and villages had left more than 2 million people in need of food aid. When U.S. Secretary of State Colin Powell called upon the Sudanese government to stop the genocide, Sudan's foreign minister, Mustafa Osman Ismail, accused the U.S. of "meddling in Sudanese affairs" (*The New York Times,* July 23, 2004; p.A3). The AU delegates, partying at Addis Ababa in late June, decided to send monitors to Sudan, and, then later, troops to protect the monitors, not the people being slaughtered.

Southern Africa faces what UN Special envoy James T. Morris described as "the most serious humanitarian crisis in the world today" (*The Washington Post,* June 23, 2004; p.A17). Nearly five million Zimbabweans were starving but President Mugabe told Britain's Sky News that the nation no longer needed food aid. "We are not hungry. It should go to hungrier people, hungrier countries than ourselves," he said. "Why foist this food upon us? We don't want to be choked. We have enough" (*The Washington Post,* June 23, 2004; p.A17).

Charles Taylor, for six years the warlord president of Liberia, stole nearly $100 million of his country's wealth, leaving it the poorest nation on earth, according to a close review of government records, an investigation by United Nations experts, and interviews with senior Liberian officials (*The New York Times,* Sept 18, 2003; p.A3). Taylor stole government money to buy houses, cars, and sexual partners, senior members of his government said.

These leaders never care about their people. They starve them, butcher them, loot their wealth, and destroy their countries. These leaders have become a big embarrassment to UN Secretary-General Kofi Annan, himself an African. He ripped into them at the Organization of African Unity Summit in Lome, Togo, in July 2000. According to Ghana's state-owned newspaper, *The Daily Graphic* (July 12, 2000),

> U.N. Secretary-General Kofi Annan told African leaders that they are to blame for most of the continent's problems. Mr. Annan said Africans were suffering because the leaders are not doing enough to invest in policies that promote development and preserve peace. He told the OAU Summit that Africa was the only region where the number of conflicts was increasing and pointed out that 33 of the world's 48 least developed countries were African.
>
> Mr. Annan said African leaders bear much of the responsibility for the deterioration of the continent's security and the withdrawal of foreign aid. "This is not something others have done to us. It is something we have done to ourselves. If Africa is being bypassed, it is because not enough of us are investing in policies, which would promote development and preserve peace. We have mismanaged our affairs for decades and we are suffering the accumulated effects." (p. 5)

There was a reason why Kofi Annan lashed out at African leaders. During a brief stop-over in Accra after the summit, he disclosed in a Joy FM radio station interview that "Africa is the region giving him the biggest headache as the UN Security Council spends 60 to 70 percent its time on Africa. He admitted sadly that the conflicts on the continent embarrass and pain him as an African" (*The Guide,* July 18–24, 2000; p.8). The UN boss said that as an African Secretary General, he gets a lot of support from the region. However, the conflicts in the region impede the full development of the continent. "When you mention Africa today to investors outside, they think of a continent in crisis, and no one wants to invest in a bad neighborhood" he noted (*The Guide,* July 18–24, 2000; p.8). Earlier in the year at a press conference in London in April, 2000, Annan "lambasted African leaders who he says have subverted democracy and lined their pockets with public funds, although he stopped short of naming names" (*The African-American Observer,* April 25–May 1, 2000; p.10).

The leadership in Africa is a despicable disgrace to black people. I won't back down from these "harsh words" because I am angry—very angry—and

I am not alone in feeling this way. Truth be told, said Nigerian student Akira Suni, "Almost without exception, they (African leaders) are a big disgrace to humankind. Apart from indulging in their usual foolish rhetoric, what have they done to satisfy even the most basic needs of our people" (*BBC News Talking Point*, April 16, 2001, www.bbc.uk.co). Said Guinea's opposition leader Mamadou Ba of his country's head of state General Lansana Conte rather laconically: "He wouldn't hurt a fly, but he has nothing upstairs" (*The News & Observer*, 4 January 1998, p.18A).

Few of the modern African leaders took responsibility for the mess they have plunged Africa into. They blamed everybody except themselves. But even Africa's children can see through their fraudulent antics. Chernoh Bah, President of Children's Forum, contended that Africa's socio economic problems are a direct repercussion of incompetent and corrupt political leaders who usurped political office via the gun. "Some blame colonialism for Africa' plight while others blame the continent's harsh climatic conditions. I think the reason is the kind of political systems we have had over the past decades," he said. (*Standard Times* [Freetown], April 2, 2003; standardtimes@hotmail.com). Other African children are voicing their outrage at the contumacious failure of African leaders to bring development to the continent. At the United Nations Children's Summit held in May 2002 in New York, youngsters from Africa ripped into their leaders for failing to improve their education and health. "You get loans that will be paid in 20 to 30 years and we have nothing to pay them with, because when you get the money, you embezzle it, you eat it," said 12-year-old Joseph Tamale from Uganda (*BBC News*, May 10, 2002).

Those who disagree with this strong indictment should name 10—just 10—good African leaders out of the 198 Africa has had between 1960 and 2004. Or, name just 10 crises African leaders have been able to resolve *without begging the international community for aid*. Even if 20 "good" leaders can be named, 20 out of 198 reflect a preponderance of leadership failures.[1] From 1960 to 2003, only 19 African heads of state retired and the same number lost an election. Only one African head of state lost an election between 1960 and 1989—the prime minister of Mauritius. By contrast, 12 leaders lost elections between 1990 and 1999. Since then, 11 have been voted out of office but often, their replacements were no better. According to *The Economist* (Jan 17, 2004):

Of the 107 African leaders overthrown between 1960 and 2003, two-thirds were killed, jailed or driven into exile. This combination of risks and rewards gave African leaders a compelling reason to cling to power. They gagged the press, banned dissent, and turned the security services into private militias. (Survey, p.5).

Since 1990, one African country after another has imploded with deafening staccato:

- In 1990, Liberia was destroyed by the regime of *General* Samuel Doe;
- In 1991, Mali by the regime of *General* Moussa Traore;
- In 1993, the Central African Republic was destroyed by the military regime of *General* Andre Kolingba;
- In 1993, Somalia was ruined by the regime of *General* Siad Barre;
- In 1994, Rwanda by the regime of *General* Juvenal Habyarimana;
- In 1995, Burundi by the regime of *General* Pierre Buyoya;
- In 1996, Zaire by regime of *General* Mobutu Sese Seko;
- In 1997, Sierra Leone by regime of *General* Joseph Momoh;
- In 1999, Niger by the regime of *General* Ibrahim Barre Mainassara;
- In 2000, Ivory Coast by the regime of *General* Robert Guie.

Note the frequency of the title "*General.*" The paucity of good leadership has left a garish stain on the continent. More distressing, the caliber of leadership has deteriorated over the decades to execrable depths. The likes of Charles Taylor of Liberia and Sani Abacha of Nigeria even make Mobutu Sese Seko of Zaire look like a saint. The slate of postcolonial African leaders has been a hideous assortment of military coconut-heads, quack revolutionaries, crocodile liberators, "Swiss bank" socialists, briefcase bandits, semi-illiterate brutes, and vampire elites. Faithful only to their private bank accounts, kamikaze kleptocrats raid and plunder the treasury with little thought of the ramifications on national development. Billions of dollars in personal fortunes have shamelessly been amassed by African leaders while their people wallow in abject poverty. At an African civic groups meeting in Addis Ababa, Ethiopia, in June 2002, Nigeria's President, Olusegun Obasanjo, claimed that "corrupt African leaders have stolen at least $140 billion (£95 billion) from their people in the decades since independence" (*The London Independent,* June 14, 2002; http://www.independent.co.uk).

The fortunes of African heads of state were published by *French Weekly* (May, 1997) and reprinted in the Nigerian newspaper, *The News* (Aug 17, 1998):

1. General Sani Abacha of Nigeria 120 billion FF (or $20 billion)
2. President H. Boigny of Ivory Coast 35 billion FF (or $6 billion)
3. Gen. Ibrahim Babangida of Nigeria 30 billion FF (or $5 billion)
4. President Mobutu of Zaire 22 billion FF (or $4 billion)
5. President Mousa Traore of Mali 10.8 billion FF (or $2 billion)
6. President Henri Bedie of Ivory Coast 2 billion FF (or $300 million)
7. President Denis N'guesso of Congo 1.2 billion FF (or $200 million)

8. President Omar Bongo of Gabon 0.5 billion FF (or $80 million)
9. President Paul Biya of Cameroon 450 million FF (or $70 million)
10. President Mengistu Haile Mariam of Ethiopia 200 million FF (or $30 million)
11. President Hissene Habre of Chad 20 million FF (or $3 million)

Name one *traditional* African leader who looted his tribal treasury for deposit in Swiss banks. Said Kwame Toure (Stokely Carmichael), former founder of the Black Panther Party in the United States, "[Modern] African leaders are so corrupt that we are certain if we put dogs in uniforms and put guns on their shoulders, we'd be hard put to distinguish between them" (*The Washington Post*, April 8, 1998; p.D12).

The crisis in modern leadership has many manifestations. It is characterized, among others, by the following dispositions and failings: The "Big Man" syndrome, obsession with power rather than use of power for good, puffed-up posturing, intolerance to dissent, indifference to the welfare of their citizens, subordination of national interests to personal aggrandizement, super-inflated egos, misplaced priorities, poor judgment, reluctance to take responsibility for personal failures, and total lack of vision and understanding of even such basic and elementary concepts as "democracy," "fairness," "rule of law," "accountability," and "freedom." Some African leaders are given to vituperative utterances, outright buffoonery, stubborn refusal to learn from past mistakes, and complete absence of cognitive pragmatism.

The prosperity or poverty of an African country often depends on the existence of good or bad government; it is the political leadership that creates the environment within which development proceeds. This environment may be conducive to development by unleashing the creative and productive energies of the majority—the Atingas—or it may be so repressive that it stifles local initiative and renders self-sustaining growth difficult to achieve. As Krauss (1983) remarked: "The fundamental issue facing the LDCs in the 1980s will be that of the proper 'policy environment' to further their economic development" (p. 3). This observation is ruthlessly true for Africa.

Political Leadership Crisis

There is a serious political leadership crisis or a leadership deficit in Africa. African leaders exhibit certain idiosyncrasies that inhibit economic development. Perhaps an inferiority complex or intense nationalistic pride drove many African leaders to become obsessed with prestigious projects. The grander the project, the better it made them look. Never mind the costs or profitability. Africa's airlines are excellent examples. Each country wants to have its own—a fleet of one or two planes. Do not ask about flight schedules in Africa. The airlines do not leave when they are supposed to—sometimes they are delayed for days—and arrive when they are not expected. Recall the "Nigeria Airwaste" parody in chapter 3. The president can commandeer an airplane for a personal trip.[2] In January 2004, President Mugabe commandeered an Air Zimbabwe jet for a vacation to Indonesia. When the *Independent* newspaper reported it, government officials did not dispute the facts but objected strongly, saying the use of the word "commandeered" in the article amounted to "a criminal defamation of the president" (*The Washington Post*, July 23, 2004; p.A24). Mugabe had every reason to vacation in Indonesia. The London *Financial Times* reported in February 2003 that Mugabe had stashed a personal fortune worth $100 million in Malaysia (cited in *The Washington Times*, Jan 15, 2003; p.A13).

Afflicted with religion of development, each African leader seeks to collect as many symbols of modernism and prestige as possible. Nkrumah best exemplified this proclivity among African leadership. In exile after 1966 and responding to charges of economic mismanagement and wasted expenditure on projects of grandeur, he asked:

> How can the obvious evidence of modernization and industrialization of Ghana, such as new roads, factories, schools and hospitals, the harbor and town of Tema, the Volta and Tefle bridges and Volta Dam be reconciled with the charge of wasted expenditure? You only have to look around you to see what we achieved. . . . We built more roads, bridges and other forms of national communication than any other independent African state. We built more schools, clinics and hospitals. We provided more clean piped water. We trained more teachers, doctors and nurses. We established more industries. (Nkrumah 1973; pp. 394–417)

Tragically, only the quantity and the status of modernism mattered. It is this disposition of African leaders and their obsession with signs of modernism that make them susceptible to exploitation of all kinds. At this very moment, if some unscrupulous foreign equipment peddler went to Africa with a laser-powered tractor and promised to provide finance, he would find a ready market among some eager African leaders. But does Africa need laser-powered tractors at this stage in its development?

Few African leaders understand how an economy works. Most operate under the delusion that they can make food, general commodities, and foreign exchange cheap and copiously available simply by fiat; for example, by imposing state controls on prices. Military despots are the worst, thinking that they can just order merchants to sell their goods at such and such prices.

The fact is, no government in this world, not even the U.S. government with all the supercomputers at its disposal, can fix and control the price of, say, maize (corn). Those African leaders who arrogantly set out to impose food price controls not only fail to make food cheap but also betray their own economic illiteracy and ignorance of their own African heritage. Traditional Africa was not characterized by chiefs imposing state controls on prices and trade.

Again, it is important to distinguish between *modern* and *traditional* African leaders. I have persistently railed against the *modern* leaders because they are such a disgrace and their leadership is a far cry from *traditional* African leadership. Modern African leaders treat their countries as their own personal property and the treasury as their private bank account. Traditional African leaders don't. The modern leaders insist on being praised and worshiped. Every word they utter must be heralded with praise—even when their tail is on fire. They crave adulation and name everything after themselves. After he succeeded Kenyatta in 1978, Moi shaped the nation of 31 million with his image and name, dominating every facet of society for the 22 years he was in office:

> Moi's face is etched on the country's currency. The state-run evening news begins every night by saying, "His Excellency President Daniel arap Moi announced today . . ." There is a national holiday called Moi Day. Dozens of schools, hospitals, bridges and roads are named after Moi. There is Moi University, Moi Girls' School, Moi International Airport. Every business is required by law to hang his framed photograph. (*The Washington Post*, Nov 19, 2002; p.A15)

But Kenyans derided Moi's name as standing for "My Own Interest." Indeed, African leaders' notion of "the people" does not extend beyond the immediate confines of their extended families or tribesmen. "Government" is their private preserve, its key positions filled with their relatives, cronies, and kinsmen. As semi-gods, they cannot be criticized; such criticism is regarded as sacrilegious. This caliber of leadership is a scurrilous joke and an affront to the dignity of the African people. The supposedly "backward and illiterate" chiefs of Africa have a better sense of governance than the "educated" modern leadership. Said an irate Fred M'membe, editor of *The Post*, Lusaka, Zambia:

> Our leaders are incapable of being criticized without feeling rancor. When people say it is alien to our African culture to criticize leaders, they forget that in our traditional past even chiefs or kings were the subject of satirical orations and ribaldry. Even the ruthless Zulu dictator Chaka could be criticized openly.

Now try to make some of our leaders the subject of satirical orations and rib-
aldry and see what happens to you. In their mistaken belief, it is "Western" to
have freedom of the press and freedom of expression, which leaves us stuck in
a culture of zealous leader worship—a culture which would look primitive is
the eyes of our ancestors.

The acceptance of criticism implies the highest respect for human ideals,
and its denial suggests a conscious or unconscious lack of humanity on our
part. Intolerance must surely rank as one of the worst forms of immorality in
human affairs, yet our modern African societies have established a reputation
for intolerance that is difficult to match.

Until our leaders redress the imbalance between selfish pursuit of power
and concern for the human lives they are elected to protect, between arro-
gance and self-respect and humility, between intolerance and mutual tolerance, we will forever be marching backwards in very long strides. (Jan 5,
2004)

Africa needs a *new direction,* a *new approach* to its problems, and *new
leadership.* The current leadership is wedded to the old colonialism/imperi-
alism paradigm that is emotionally driven and lacks imagination. The rule
of law is not understood, priorities have been misplaced, and governance is
riddled with vapid corruption. Worse, the leadership has shown an appalling
inability to learn from its own mistakes.

The first generation of postcolonial leaders all meant well for their countries. They all wanted to develop their countries and close the gap between the
rich and the poor countries. But the means they chose to do so became seriously dysfunctional. The method was characterized by the following defects:

1. A political system based upon *sultanism* or "one-person rule" under
   one-party state systems;
2. An economic system based upon *statism* or state interventionism
   under the guise of socialism; and
3. A development strategy that can be characterized as "development-
   by-imitation" via import-substitution.

The leadership *ought* to have known that socialism, as an economic ideology, is alien to Africa. The one-party state system, copied from the Soviet
Union, could not be justified upon the basis of African tradition. More perfidious was the cultural betrayal. Chiefs were stripped of their traditional authority and shunned. Agriculture, the main occupation of the Atingas, was
neglected. Industrialization was all the rage. Huge foreign loans were contracted to establish Africa's industries. But Africa's industrialization drive
under state hegemony and controls sputtered.

By the late 1970s, the first-generation problems were emerging. Inefficient state enterprises failed to deliver the goods and racked up losses upon losses instead. Price controls created commodity shortages, foreign exchange scarcities, and rent-seeking activities. State controls also created lucrative opportunities for illicit enrichment. Administrators of import controls and licenses extorted "commissions." *Kalabule,* bribery, corruption and smuggling appeared. Further, state controls were employed to punish political rivals or the opposition and state enterprises became employment mills for a network of cronies. A huge patronage system emerged, which allowed the ruling party to maintain its lock on power.

These initial mistakes and problems were compounded, leading to the second-generation problems. Packed with party hacks, the civil service swelled and budget expenditures soared, producing chronic deficits. They were financed by borrowing recklessly abroad and by gunning the money supply. A huge foreign debt was contracted and inflation reared its head. Peasant agriculture, meanwhile, was neglected, castigated as an inferior form of occupation, and industry overemphasized. Misguided government policies of price controls and marketing boards accelerated the decline of agriculture. Agricultural production per capita fell steadily in the postcolonial period. However, price controls and misguided government policies alone are insufficient to explain the decline. In chapter 8 we emphasized that economic activity does not occur in a vacuum but in a development environment. We isolated some basic elements—including security of persons, property rights, rule of law, and stability—that must obtain in this environment. We argued that the development environment that prevails over much of Africa is inimical to productive effort. Elite bias against agriculture and Africa's interminable civil wars, for example, have done much to impede any agricultural revolution. Africa's civil wars are really *conflicts over power.* Virtually all erupted as a result of a dispute over some aspect of the *electoral process—or a struggle for power.* A mechanism must be established for peaceful transfer of political power *and* peaceful resolution of conflicts.

Internal problems, such as civil wars, corruption, and capital flight are really symptoms of two deadly diseases: *sultanism* and *statism.* While the state or government can play a role in the development process, the state, as it is conventionally understood, does not exist in Africa. What rather exists in many African countries is a mafia state—a government hijacked by gangsters, con artists, and scrofulous bandits, who use the machinery of the state to enrich themselves, their cronies, and tribesmen. All others are excluded (*the politics of exclusion*). This predatory state operates by extracting resources from the *productive* sections of the population (the peasant majority) and spending them in the urban areas and on the elites—a non-productive, parasitic class.

This state of affairs does not endure. Eventually it leads to destructive competition, instability, civil strife, institutional breakdown, and ultimately to the implosion of the state.

For the past few decades, the modern leadership has been absorbed with *defending* its failures and blaming them on someone else—often, external factors such as the legacies of colonialism, the lingering effects of the slave trade, Western imperialism, and a pernicious international economic system. The average intelligent person looks both ways before crossing a street or risks being hit by a truck. Africa is in bandages in the intensive care unit because its leaders looked only one way—at the external. The leadership scarcely looked at internal factors, such as its own incompetence, corruption, economic mismanagement, political tyranny, senseless civil wars, military vandalism, exploitation and oppression of the peasant majority, denial of civil liberties, and capital flight, among others. Now, the new gripe of African leaders is *globalization*—another external adversity.

Globalization: A New External Threat?

Globalization or the new global economy means an economy where the old rules no longer apply. Toward the end of the twentieth century, six new technologies—microelectronics, computers, telecommunications, new man-made materials, robotics, and biotechnology—interacted to create a new and very different economic world. Breakthrough technologies have allowed new industries (computers, semiconductors, lasers) to emerge. The same technologies provide opportunities to reinvent old industries and make labor more productive. The Internet has provided a new form of retailing and cellular phones, a new form for communication. As Thurow (1999) describes it:

> The old foundations of success are gone. For all of human history, the source of success has been the control of natural resources—land, gold, oil. Suddenly, the answer is "knowledge." The world's wealthiest man, Bill Gates, owns nothing tangible—no land, no gold or oil, no factories, no industrial processes, no armies. For the first time in human history, the world's wealthiest man owns only knowledge. (p. xiii)

Advances in microelectronics, robotics, and the Internet are creating what economists call the "third industrial revolution." In the first and second industrial revolutions, workers left agriculture (a low-wage sector) and entered manufacturing and mining (high-wage sectors). In the third industrial revolution, workers are leaving manufacturing and mining and entering the services sector, where they can apply their knowledge. The information technology and the spread of knowledge are, by themselves, creating ripple effects.

A global human rights standard is emerging, serving notice to tyrants that they can no longer butcher their people and hide it from the international community. The arrest of former Chilean dictator Augusto Pinochet in London in 1999; the establishment of a war crimes tribunal at the Hague; the indictment of Slobodan Milosevic, the former "Butcher of Belgrade"; and the indictment of former Chadian dictator Hissene Habre in Senegal in 2000 all serve as reminders of a global human rights standard. As well, environmental standards, as evidenced by the Kyoto Agreement of 1998, are also going global.

Far more important, however, are the changes in international trade. Advances in telecommunications and transportation have vastly expanded the boundaries of the marketplace. The wheat market is no longer localized in the Midwest; it is now global. Nor is the sale of Kenyan coffee confined to Europe alone; it can be sold worldwide. Economists define a market to be any setup that brings buyers and sellers into close contact. The Internet has led to an explosion of these contacts. A Kenyan coffee producer can be in touch via the Internet to a Japanese coffee maker in an instant. Economic decisions are increasingly being influenced by technology and other factors outside a country's territorial borders.

The World Trade Organization (WTO), various General Agreement on Tariffs and Trade (GATT) agreements, and the establishment of free trade zones—for example the North American Free Trade Agreement (NAFTA)—have further whittled down market barriers. Increasingly, we are witnessing a global market in goods, services, and capital, although immigration requirements still restrict the free movement of labor. These new developments should be welcomed. Anything that promotes or facilitates the free movement of goods, services, and capital should be encouraged since they will eventually increase world trade and prosperity.

Increased Opportunities and Greater Freedom

For Africa, the new global economy brings several benefits and challenges. The first is the phenomenal expansion in the market for goods from an African country. A Nigerian company would be able to tap into markets in Australia, the Far East, and even Africa. Access to new markets enhances the possibilities of growth, increased income, and employment. Second, the new global economy makes available to African consumers an immense variety of commodities, thus increasing the choice of goods available to consumers. The third is access to capital. Between 1990 and 1995 the net yearly flow of foreign direct investment into developing countries quadrupled, to over $90 billion. According to the World Bank, in 1995 a record $231 billion in foreign investment flowed into the Third World. Singapore by itself attracted $5.8 billion (*The Economist,* Nov 6, 1996; p.95). Africa can access this global capital.

The new global economy permits free flow of information via the Internet, faxes, and satellite dishes. The free flow of information is vital for an economy if investors are to make sound decisions. But the media is the first institution corrupt and despotic regimes—whether on the right or the left—go after. The pertinent characteristic of totalitarian or tyrannical political systems is the rigid control exercised over the *content and flow of information:* what can be said, printed, or disseminated by the people, editors, and publishers. They like to keep their people "in the dark" as they go about their evil and dastardly deeds. News is censored, the media monopolized by the state, journalists arrested and detained for writing critical reports. Very soon, these intellectually repressive tactics should be a thing of the past—thanks to the new global information super-highway. Jail a journalist and the news will be around the world in an instant.

This author places a very high premium on intellectual freedom and the media because they are a key part of the reform process. It is often easy to overlook the critical importance of "intellectual freedom"—a catch-all phrase embracing freedom of expression, press freedom, and free flow of information. Recall the crucial role played by *glasnost* in the collapse of the former Soviet Union and revolution in Eastern Europe. *Glasnost* means "openness," as in freedom of expression and thought. When people found that they could express their ideas and viewpoints freely, they began to demand change and a new system. The demands came from within. They were not dictated by so-called "American imperialists," the IMF, or the World Bank. With *blacknost,* Africans will make their own case for political reform, just as the Romanians did.

The Frustrations

Of course, there is a downside to the new global economy. Foreign capital can be quirky. Foreign investors are not imbued with any nationalistic ethos that would restrain them from leaving any Third World country. They can pull out at a moment's notice and, in fact, do so, triggering a run on foreign exchange reserves and a crisis: for example, Mexico in 1994 and the 1998 Asian crises.

Also, domestic industries may not be able to adjust quickly to the new economic order. Unemployment could occur in those businesses that are inefficient and therefore slow to compete. There are many such industries in

Africa, mostly state-owned. Third, government revenues could fall when import duties and tariffs are reduced or eliminated. However, the pain can be mitigated. Free trade also opens up new opportunities. Unemployed workers can be trained for jobs in the expanding industries and government revenue can rise with increased economic activity.

In the long run, however, the new global economy would expand the opportunities for Africa and enable its people lift themselves out of poverty. Unfortunately, there will be considerable resistance and numerous hurdles to overcome in order to enter the new economic order.

The Resistance to the New Global Economy

Resistance to globalization in Africa should not be confused with "antiglobalists" in the West. Westerners opposed to globalization tend to be farmers, union workers, or blue collar workers in steel, textiles, or manufacturing. They fear competition, loss of jobs, and diminution in their standard of living if corporations take jobs out of their countries to cheap-labor countries, or if cheaper imports are allowed into their countries to compete with their products. Sizable opposition also comes from Western farmers—especially sheltered and pampered French farmers—who fear increased competition from globalization and loss of government subsidies.

There is nothing wrong with antiglobalists in the West seeking to protect their own interests or agenda. But it is hypocritical and dishonest for them to cloak their agenda in the guise of helping the poor in Africa or the Third World. Their new gambit is to insist on *"environmental standards"*; that is, globalization or free trade agreements should only be entered into with Third World countries that follow the same environmental standards as the United States, for example, which smacks of *environmental imperialism*. At other times, antiglobalists in the West insist that globalization will lead to the exploitation of the people in the Third World. Why not let the poor in the Third World speak for themselves?

In Africa, the resistance to globalization generally comes from three sources: first, from government officials, who loathe to see economic control slip out of their hands. Export markets would no longer be guaranteed by special arrangements with former colonial masters. Cocoa from the Ivory Coast must compete on the same basis as cocoa from Brazil in France. A government that persists in maintaining exchange and interest rates that are out of line with market forces would lose capital. Room for independent fiscal and monetary policies will be severely restricted. To the extent that a country cannot pursue independent fiscal and monetary policies, it can be said that it suffers from some loss of sovereignty.

Second, vested business interests can also put up ferocious resistance to entry into the new global economy. There are some who benefit from the status quo—the sheltering of the domestic economy from foreign competition through tariffs and import controls. Competition from imports could force down prices and therefore profits. Powerful business interests with political connections could block the opening up of the economy. The resistance from this sector is often considerable in Africa, where the private sector is small or nonexistent and state or government-owned enterprises dominate the economic landscape.

Third, the intellectual class may also object to the opening up of the economy, arguing that it would set the stage for a new round of "neocolonial exploitation," in the light of the experiences of the Third World under colonialism and imperialism. They feel giant multinational corporations would be able to charge into a poor Third World country, exploit its resources, despoil its environment, rape its workers, and then leave.

Requisite Standards for the New Global Economy

Even if this resistance, formidable as it may be, can be overcome, there are additional obstacles to contend with. The new global economy demands certain standards: free flow of information, transparency, efficiency, and the rule of law. Assuring these standards requires political, economic, banking, and judicial reforms. Think of it this way: Consider the new global economy as a superhighway. To enter this highway, one's car must be in good shape. Else, it will sputter along, break down, or, worse, end up in a ditch. Metaphorically speaking, it is the unwillingness to "tune up their cars"—that is, reform their abominable political, economic, and banking systems—that precipitated the Mexican peso crisis in 1994 and the 1998 Asian crisis.

By all indications, Africa is not yet ready for the new global economy. In an address to the African Ministerial Forum on Integrated Transport in Africa (AMFIT), President Olusegun Obasanjo of Nigeria observed that:

> Poverty remains a major challenge, and most countries on the continent have not benefited fully from the opportunities of globalization. Africa's efforts to achieve economic growth have been hindered by conflicts, insufficient investment, limited trade, debilitating debt burden, and lately the impact of HIV/AIDS. Africa lacks basic infrastructure in many sectors, including transport, compared to the industrialized world. The gap in infrastructure constitutes a serious handicap to economic growth and poverty reduction on the continent of Africa. Improved infrastructure could—and would—transform the continent into investors' haven. (*This Day, Lagos*, March 11, 2003; www.allafrica.com)

President Bill Clinton signed the Africa Growth and Opportunity Act (AGOA) in March 2000 to open up U.S. markets for African goods, but four years later, few African countries had taken advantage of it. The continent is wracked by a never-ending cycle of civil wars, carnage, chaos, and instability. Economies have collapsed. Poverty, in both absolute and relative terms, has *increased*. Despite its immense wealth in mineral and natural resources, Africa is mired in grinding poverty. The statistics on Africa's postcolonial development record are abysmal. High taxes, rampant inflation, runaway government expenditures, unstable currencies, and high-level corruption have stunted Africa's economic growth potential. Infrastructure has decayed and crumbled in much of Africa. Roads, schools, and telecommunications systems are in shambles. In addition, censorship, persecution, detention, arbitrary seizures of property, corruption, capital flight, and tyranny continuously plague the continent. Investment—both domestic and foreign—is the way out of Africa's economic miasma and the key to economic growth and poverty reduction. But Africa repels, rather than attracts investment. "An estimated 40 percent of the continent's privately held wealth is stashed offshore" (*The Economist,* Jan 17, 2004; Survey, p.4).

To take advantage of the opportunities offered by globalization, African governments must clean up the prevailing business environment to attract investment; that is, they must reform their economic, political, and banking systems, as well as implement judicial reform. The rule of law must be instituted, infrastructure repaired, and some basic freedoms guaranteed. But as we saw in chapter 2, African leaders are just not interested in real reform. Period. The democratization process in Africa has stalled and only a handful of African countries can be termed "economic success stories." Much more needs to be done to establish an independent judiciary, an independent central bank, an independent media, and an independent electoral commission, not to mention a neutral and professional armed forces. The lack of commitment and seriousness on the part of African leaders is evidenced by the proliferation of gangster states, coconut republics, and collapsed states on the continent. If present trends continue, more states will implode.

AFRICAN RENAISSANCE

In recent times, various people, including this author, have propagated the idea that the impetus for reform and change in Africa must come from within. Back in 1993, the $3.5 billion international peace mission into Somalia failed miserably. As a result, this author coined the expression "African solutions for African problems." African solutions are less expensive, and, further, reform that is *internally generated* endures. Only Africans can save

Africa. An international conference on "Africa's Imperative Agenda," held in Nairobi in January 1995, emphasized this new philosophy. Conference participants expressed strong support for the following priority propositions:

1. Africa's human and natural resources are more than sufficient to revive progress if a concerted, determined effort is launched within each society, and coordinated regionally.
2. Such efforts will succeed only if Africans take full charge of them and formulate policies that are geared to meet national needs rather than win international approval.
3. Participatory political structures and "good governance" are essential preconditions for effective policymaking.
4. Only Africa can reverse its decline.
5. The criteria of success for economic policies must be the improved health and education of the population and increased employment and production. Therefore, the agricultural sector, which employs the vast majority of Africans, is central to economic revival.
6. The role of political leadership and government action has been downplayed and private sector efforts stressed in international debate. (*Africa Recovery*, June 1995; p.9)

It may be recalled that this plan of action does not differ substantially from the Atinga development model we laid out in chapter 10. It requires the establishment of peace, the provision of some basic infrastructure, the mobilization of capital through the revolving rural credit schemes, and the investment of funds in agriculture or agriculture-related cottage industries. Agriculture is the main occupation of Africa's peasant majority. Nothing complicated was envisioned—just modernizing the existing indigenous institutions to generate economic prosperity. It is an "African solution" that returns to Africa's roots and builds upon Africa's own indigenous institutions. This blueprint is already there in Africa and does not require billions of dollars in Western aid. Nor does our plan envision extensive involvement of the state. In a sense, this approach may be characterized as the "new African renaissance." Two African leaders—Presidents Thabo Mbeki of South Africa and Isaias Afwerki of Eritrea—have latched on to the African renaissance bandwagon. Let us briefly review their pronouncements.

In a speech entitled, "The African Renaissance: A Call to Rebellion," which was published in *The Nigerian* (Oct 1998; pp.28–29), President Thabo Mbeki of South Africa warned that Africa has no need for criminals who would acquire political power by slaughtering the innocents. "The time has come that we say enough and no more and by acting to banish the shame, remake ourselves as the mid-wives of the African Renaissance. The time has come that we call a halt to the seemingly socially approved deification of the acquisition of material wealth and the abuse of state power to impoverish the people and deny our continent the possibility to achieve sustainable economic development."

He claimed that Africa cannot renew itself where its upper echelons are mere parasites on the rest of society: their self-endowed political power ensures the African continent's place at the periphery of the world economy— poor, underdeveloped, and incapable of development. "The African Renaissance demands that we purge ourselves of the parasites and maintain a permanent vigilance against the danger of entrenchment in African society of this rapacious stratum with its social morality according to which everything in society must be organized materially to benefit the few."

President Mbeki then delved into a bit of history, an essential part of African renaissance, recalling with pride the African scholar and author of the Middle Ages, Sadi of Timbuktu, who had mastered such subjects as law, logic, dialectics, grammar, and rhetoric, and other African intellectuals who taught at the University of Timbuktu.

He asserted that the beginning of Africa's rebirth as a continent must start with the rediscovery of Africa's soul, captured and made permanently available in the great works of creativity represented by the pyramids and sphinxes of Egypt, the stone buildings of Axum, the ruins of Carthage and Zimbabwe, the rock paintings of the San, the Benin bronzes and the African masks, the carvings of the Makonde, and the stone sculptures of the Shona. He continued:

> The call for Africa is renewal, for an African Renaissance is a call to rebellion. We must rebel against the tyrants and the dictators, those who seek to corrupt our societies and steal the wealth that belongs to the people.
>
> To be a true African is to be a rebel in the cause of the African Renaissance, whose success in the new century and millennium is one of the great historic challenges of our time. (*The Nigerian,* October 1998; p.28–29)

Talk is fine, but it would be nice if President Mbeki would lead the rebellion against the Eyademas, the Ghaddafis, the Mugabes, the dos Santos, and others.

In a keynote address to the African Renaissance Conference held in Washington, D.C. on April 29, 1998, President Isaias Afwerki of Eritrea echoed similar sentiments. The conference was sponsored by the Southern Africa Grantmakers' Affinity Group of the Council on Foundations, the Congressional Black Caucus, and the John F. Kennedy Center for Performing Arts.

He raced through the catalogue of problems afflicting postcolonial Africa: perennial conflicts, grinding poverty, a widening gap with the developed world, and problems of political governance and economic management that have engendered a climate of apathy and despair to the peoples of the continent. This negative reality is at times writ large by the harrowing images of suffering women and children that appear on TV screens through real-time reporting, whenever the continent is struck by natural and manmade calamities.

He noted the historical patterns that governed the emergence of the postcolonial state, asserting that the propensity for imitating—in a wholesale manner—the political institutions and practices of the metropolis without rigorous scrutiny of their relevance and applicability to the local situation were major factors that derailed the process of nation-building from the onset. "Africa's lack of ownership of the shifting policies that were attempted at various junctures; and, the paternalism that often distorted its ties with its external partners were additional factors that stymied local innovation and dynamism to breed chronic dependency. The combined effect of these factors was to render the continent a basket case of retrogression and underdevelopment." [The keynote address was distributed by the Ethiopian Embassy in Washington, D.C.]

He then asked whether Africa would continue to be burdened by the mistakes and failures of the past to remain an impoverished and marginalized continent in the next millennium of increased globalization and world integration. He believed that the continent has the requisite factor endowments, and, more important, the political will and resolve to extricate itself from the abyss into which it has fallen. "This is underpinned by a solid faith in a new and dynamic Africa that will redeem itself to interact with, and integrate into, the global economy on an equal footing. It represents a belief in the inner strengths, capabilities and resilience of Africa."

According to President Afwerki, Africa's drive toward accelerated and sustainable development will remain elusive unless the continent recognizes, in a sober and thorough manner, its past failures and present weaknesses. "One of the key problems in the past has been Africa's wholesale imitation of the institutions and practices of the metropolitan Western countries. This has further been compounded by structural adjustment programs, and other lop-sided consultation mechanisms which serve, in reality, to impose external solutions to Africa's internal problems." He concluded:

Africa cannot continue to be spoon-fed, or survive for long, on an intensive care basis. Its policies and programs will have long-lasting impact, if and only if, they are home-grown; when, only when, all the stakeholders in the society participate in the formulation and implementation of the policies and programs that concern them. Africa will also not be able to articulate and periodically refine the vision, sense of purpose or ambition that are vital for success unless it first cultivates the culture of ownership of its policies and programs. [Speech distributed by Ethiopian Embassy in Washington, D.C.]

Unfortunately, African leaders who make such grandiose speeches do not realize that *they* are much of the problem. President Afwerki did not allow "all the stakeholders in the Eritrean society to participate in the formulation and implementation of the policies and programs that concern them." In May 2001, 15 senior members of the party, including government ministers and army generals, accused the president of working in an illegal and unconstitutional manner. The signatories said Afewerki had consistently refused to allow collective leadership, and failed to convene legislative bodies intended to regulate presidential powers (*BBC On Line,* May 31, 2001).

Where does the hope lie? Whom can the African people look up to to spark an economic rejuvenation?

The Feckless and Impotent West

To turn Africa around a whole slew of dysfunctional governments need to be thrown out of office (regime change). Coconut-heads need to be cracked open and common sense drilled into them. Stakes need to be hammered into the hearts of the vampire elites and Swiss-bank socialists fed to crocodiles. But Africans cannot—and should not—look up to the West for help in effecting this change, regardless of Western culpability for the mess in Africa.

First, the West does not understand Africa's problems; it thinks throwing money at them would solve them. Such money often ends up in the pockets of the same vampire elites who ruined Africa in the first place. It is an open secret that foreign aid to Africa has largely been ineffective; it doesn't reach the needy. Second, Western solutions don't work very well in solving certain uniquely African problems. We noted the 1993 Somali debacle above. Conflict resolution is another example as we saw in chapter 10. The Western approach requires direct face-to-face negotiations between combatants, whereas the traditional African approach includes an arbiter (a chief) and civil society. There are other areas as well, such as the institution of democracy. There are different *forms* of democracy: representative, parliamentary, and participatory democracy. Just because the West practices multiparty democracy does not mean Africa must choose *that particular form of democracy.*

Third, Africa's own history should caution Africans to be wary of foreigners who come to Africa bearing manna and solutions to Africa's problems. Foreigners come to Africa to pursue *their* interests. Americans, Arabs, French, Brits, and Russians all do the same. The Chinese don't go to Africa because they love black people; nor do Cubans. Therefore, if Africans give their problems to a foreigner to solve, he will do so to *his* advantage.

Fourth, even if the West or the international community is sincerely interested in helping Africa, it lacks the capacity to bring about change. The burden of colonial guilt, political correctness (racial oversensitivity), self-doubt, and diplomacy effectively prevents the West from criticizing corrupt, incompetent, and brutally repressive African governments and inane policies. Whites shy away from such criticisms for fear that they may be labeled "racist." Western governments prefer "diplomacy," "bribery," and forming "partnerships" with bandit African governments to cajole them into implementing reform. But crooked African governments are very adept at playing these games. In fact, diplomacy plays right into their hands. It is precisely here where the West, in my view, presents a more formidable obstacle to change in Africa—not by any malicious design but by default. The West has allowed itself to be suckered into playing diplomatic ping-pong with African despots that often ends in tragedy for the African people. Take Zimbabwe for example.

The West watches helplessly as a demonic maniac, Robert Mugabe, destroys the economy and the country. He has orchestrated violent seizures of white commercial farmland, claiming he is righting colonial injustices. Investors have fled, the economy is in tatters, and unemployment exceeds 70 percent. Millions face starvation and food aid given by the West is used as a political weapon—distributed to ruling party supporters. Independent newspapers critical of the government have been shut down.

Party officials control the information that Zimbabweans receive on the radio, television, and in most newspapers. The ruling party exerts outright control over all broadcasting and runs daily newspaper in the capital, Harare, and Mutare.

The government media tell Zimbabweans that Mugabe and his government are unfailingly benevolent and wise and that their main opponent, the Movement for Democratic Change, is a dangerous terrorist group that operates as a front for British efforts to re-establish Zimbabwe as a colony (*The Washington Post*, July 23, 2004; p.A24).

Mugabe blames Zimbabwe's woes not on his own stupid policies but on the IMF, imperialists, colonial injustices, and "snakes" (whites). Devilishly framed this way, the West is rendered impotent in dealing with Zimbabwe. Short of a military invasion to effect a regime change, there is little the West can do. Sanctions, such as travel bans against Mugabe and his lieutenants, are ridiculously futile. Appeals to Mugabe and his henchmen fall on deaf ears. Mugabe controls all the levers of power. The West can't help rectify the situation in Zimbabwe and it should say so. And if it can't, it should get out of the way. It would be cruelly immoral to raise the hopes of the oppressed people of Zimbabwe by pretending that it can.

Similarly, the West can't effect change in Sudan, Congo, Ivory Coast, and many other African countries. It shouldn't pretend it can by "exerting diplomatic pressure." It is this inclination on the part of the West to engage Africa's autocrats in implementing reform that allowed the West to be played for a dupe. Perhaps many Western governments and international financial institutions, such as the World Bank and the IMF, still haven't caught on to the chicanery and deviousness of Africa's despots. These autocrats loathe reform. They do the "Babangida boogie" and spin Western donors, the World Bank, and the IMF around. In this way, naïve Westerners become accomplices in this game of duplicity, which defrauds the African people.

I drove home this point by caricaturing a duplicitous African despot when I spoke at conference held on April 23, 2004, in Washington, D.C. The conference was organized by the Center for Strategic and International Studies (CSIS) to determine if President Bush's Millennium Challenge Account would help reverse Africa's economic slide. In attendance were Andrew Natsios, Chief Administrator for USAID, Daniel Kaufman from the World Bank, Clay Lowery of the Millennium Challenge Corporation, and other high government officials in the Bush administration. At my turn to speak, I thanked the moderator for his introduction and proceeded to give myself the "proper introduction." I said:

"I am Musugu Babazonga, the President-For-Life of the Coconut Republic of Tonga in the Gulf of Guinea. Don't mind Julius Nyerere of Tanzania; he called himself "Mwalimo" (Teacher), while Mobutu Sese Seko of Zaire changed his name to "Sese Seko Kuku Ngbendu Wa Za Banga," which, in the local Lingala language, meant, "The rooster who leaves no chicken untouched." And forget about Idi Amin who called himself "The Conqueror of the British Empire." My name trumps them all. My people call me the "Cutlass" (machete). Anyone who crosses my path is cut down—especially terrorists. I am fighting a war against terrorism.

I agree with all the speakers that rule of law, free and fair elections, transparency, accountability, stability, and foreign investment are all important in the process of economic development and rejuvenation. But we have all these in my country. It is an insidious form of racism and imperialism to claim that we don't.

I wrote the laws of the country myself and, since I am the ruler, we have the rule of law. I have been in power for 30 years, so we have stability. If U.S. Secretary of State Colin Powell calls my regime non-democratic and totalitarian, I will sue him for defaming and humiliating my people [Libya].

We have just concluded our first elections in 30 years and they were "free and fair." Those who opposed me are in jail, where they are free to say what they want [Togo]. Nobody bothers them there. I think that's fair. I won 99.92 percent of the vote. In fact, I would have won 110 percent if the opposition had bothered to get out of their graves to vote. Lazy bunch. So, you see, our elections were free and fair.

Yes, I take "development" very seriously. My pockets are well developed. We have "foreign investment" too. My wealth is safely invested in Riggs National Bank in Washington, D.C. and other foreign banks to protect against foreign exchange fluctuations [Obiang of Equatorial Guinea]. Yes, my country produces oil but the oil revenue is a state secret—to protect it from the prying eyes of imperialist enemies. My finance minister keeps the accounts at a secure place—in a tree [Zambia].

World Bank officials said we need less government spending so we are feverishly working on that. We have set up a Ministry of Less Government Spending [Mali]. The Bank also said we should privatize state-owned enterprises, so I sold them to my relatives and friends, who are in the private sector [Egypt, Kenya, Nigeria, Uganda, and Zimbabwe].

And I don't play with "accountability." My political opponents must account for every penny they spend and explain where they are at any moment of time. My security forces have been instructed to verify that information and must report to me every step my critics and political rivals take [Eritrea, Ethiopia, Togo, Zimbabwe]. I know who they are and where they live. So we have "accountability."

We have "Checks and balances" too. All government officials are required, by decree, to have bank accounts on which they can write checks and their bank accounts which must have positive balances. Bounced checks are not tolerated. So we have checks and balances.

President Bush says his Millennium Challenge Account (MCA) will give aid only to those governments that govern justly, promote economic freedom, and invest in the people. No problem there. In fact, my country should be the first to receive aid under that program.

I am the Constitution; I wrote it myself and set myself a two-term limit before our first elections. All the years I have held power before the Constitution came into effect didn't count [dos Santos of Angola and Rawlings of Ghana]. It is "just" because I have done a lot for my country. And if I don't like the two-term limit, I will change it [Deby of Chad, Conte of Guinea, Nujoma of Namibia, and Museveni of Uganda]. And when I retire, my son will take over [Mubarak of Egypt]. He will be freely chosen by me. So, you see, we have constitutional rule and I govern "justly." All the senior positions in my government are filled with my relatives, friends, and tribesmen [Burundi, Cameroon, Kenya, and Rwanda]. They love me, go ask them. We have two radio stations in the country and I own them. People can say what they want only on my radio stations because freedom of expression is an outmoded concept (Jonathan Moyo of Zimbabwe].

Movie theaters and television are forbidden to show pornographic material, which corrupts the minds of the young [Bashir of Sudan]. Violators are beheaded; they can appeal later. So, we are aggressively combating corruption of children. And we do actively promote economic freedom. My ministers can engage in whatever economic activity they like.

There is no famine in my country. The people are well-fed; they eat grass. Hey, cows eat grass too. Unfortunately, there are no cows left in the country because the people ate all the grass. If we are poor, it is because of Western colonial plunder and exploitation. So the West owes us—big time; in fact, $777 trillion!

We are waiting for the cash.

Can Africans expect help from the West to smash this coconut-head? Not very likely. First, the cold war has been replaced by the war on terrorism and the West now needs allies in this new war and all sorts of unsavory characters are offering help. Just as the West's preoccupation with allies in the cold war led it to overlook the excesses of the likes of Mobutu Sese Seko, Samuel Doe, and the like, the war against terror might well predispose the West to overlook the failings of President Babazonga. Remember, he claims he is fighting terrorists, too—just like Mugabe. Further, the West acts in its own interest, and if President Babazonga can be a useful idiot in the war against terror, the West might employ him. Second, the West may choose to handle President Babazonga "diplomatically" but, as we have noted, such "diplomacy" doesn't work. And if the West takes President Babazonga into custody, it might argue that he has "rights" and, therefore, he should be given access to a "fair trial"—as if he extended the same rights to his own people.

How about the African Union?

AU: A Hopeless Organization

Like the defunct organization that it succeeded, the African Union (AU) is hopeless and useless, which even the president of Tanzania, Julius Nyerere, recognized. In a speech at the University of Edinburgh on October 9, 1997, he said:

The Organization of African Unity (OAU) was set up by African states in 1963. Its name was as much an expression of hope as it was of serious intention; it was based on the principles of anti-colonialism, anti-apartheid, and non-interference in the internal affairs of member states. Being one of the hopeful, in a moment of extreme exasperation I later once described the OAU as a Trade Union of African Heads of State! We protected one another, whatever we did to our own peoples in our respective countries. To condemn a Mobutu, or Idi Amin or a Bokassa was taboo! It would be regarded as interference in the internal affairs of a fellow African State! (*PanAfrican News,* September 1998)

Former President Mandela skipped the 1998 OAU Summit in Burkina Faso and urged the younger generation of leaders to root out tyranny and put the continent on the information superhighway. "People are being slaughtered to protect tyranny," he said (*News wires,* June 10, 1998).

When the slaughter began again in the Congo in July 1998, the OAU quickly attempted to intervene. It issued a feeble call on the rebels "to lay down their arms." The call was ignored and fighting raged. Stung and intent on salvaging its reputation, the OAU summoned the Congolese defense ministers and government officials to broker a ceasefire. But guess what happened: The OAU seated only the government side to the conflict at the negotiating table. The rebels, the other side, had no seats. Inevitably, the attempt at ceasefire collapsed. Said an irate delegate: "We decided it would be a futile exercise. You cannot negotiate a cease-fire until you have identified all the belligerents and have invited them to talks" (*The Washington Times,* Sept 13, 1998; p.A11).

At the thirty-fifth OAU Summit in Algiers (July 15, 1999), President Thabo Mbeki of South Africa shocked delegates by stating that African leaders who took power by force would be banned from future OAU summits. And, rather than waste time bemoaning the effects of globalization, "African leaders should take steps to integrate the continent's economies," he told them. "Mere moral appeals from the have-nots to the haves are not likely to take us very far," he said, encouraging his OAU colleagues "to gain a profound understanding of economics, so that we can intervene in an informed manner." He expressed impatience with those leaders who simply complain that globalization is passing Africa by. He reminded them that little has been done to implement the 1991 Treaty of Abuja that established an African economic community (*The Washington Times,* July 15, 1999; p.A14).

Such straight talk must be applauded, but then again, President Mbeki seldom followed through by taking action. When asked about those leaders from Niger, Guinea-Bissau, and Comoros who had seized power in 1998, he replied: "Well, in the meantime, we will be working with them to return them to democratic society" (*The Washington Times,* July 15, 1999; p.A14). The following year, the OAU held its summit in Lome, Togo, which had been ruled for more than thirty-three years by General Gnassingbe Eyadema, who seized power in a coup.

The AU is preoccupied with providing a platform for African leaders to grandstand and announce grandiose plans to spark Africa's economic rejuvenation. The AU was nowhere to be found when Burundi's civil war flared up again in 2003. Nor has the AU taken a stance against the rape of democracy in Zimbabwe. Rather, it elected President Robert Mugabe of Zimbabwe as its new vice-chairman in July 2003.

As we argued in chapter 8, NEPAD, the new economic initiative for Africa, is a dud. It cannot even be called an "African plan" as it was modeled after the Marshall Aid plan—just as the AU is modeled after the European Union. There was no consultation with civic groups and other African parliaments when NEPAD was crafted. Worse, it seeks $64 billion in investments from the West. As we demonstrated in chapter 8, Africa's begging bowl leaks. Given that the leakages exceed the inflows, common sense dictates that, as a first order of priority, the leaks must be plugged. The resources Africa needs for investment can be found in Africa itself. Speaking at a Black Management Forum conference at Cape Town International Convention Centre on October 9, 2003, President Mbeki of South Africa observed that,

> NEPAD faced the grave danger of failure, posed by the lack of capacity in most countries. We are not going to achieve some of the programs we have set out to achieve because of the lack of capacity. Even if we do have the resources, the institutions do not have the capacity, and African renewal needs capacity. The embarrassing thing is that they (developed nations) have committed resources, but we do not have the capacity to implement. There are still too many of our people who are too poor and marginalized. This is what we must focus on as we enter the second decade of liberation. A combined effort of increased skills, economic growth, and economic transformation could go a long way in pushing back the frontiers of poverty. (*Cape Argus, Cape Town,* October 10, 2003)

To whom, then, should Africans look up to?

The Remaining Font of Hope

In Ayittey (1998), I stated that Africa's best hope lies with its intellectuals. They are a distinct and cohesive group among the elite class, which is made up of high government officials (heads of state, ministers, ambassadors, etc.), professionals (lawyers, doctors, accountants, teachers, etc.), politicians, and civil servants. The intellectuals are supposed to be *apolitical* and to understand such basic concepts as "democracy," "accountability," and "freedom." Yet, for much of the postcolonial period, this group has supplied the intellectual rationale to legitimize despotism and corruption. No military vandal would succeed in imposing his rule if judges did not swear in coup-makers, if the intellectuals did not serve under them, and if civil servants refused to carry out their orders. Unfortunately, the intellectuals have not risen up to the task.

Africa's intellectuals continue to prostitute themselves, selling off their principles and integrity to partake of the plunder, misrule, and repression of the African people. Said Ghanaian columnist Eric Bawah:

> Sometimes one cannot help but blame Africa's intellectuals for what is happening in some African countries. Many of these intellectuals happen to be educated by the tax payers' money but they turn out to collaborate with dictators and end up impoverishing their people while they grow rich and Epicurean. They disgracefully lick the boots of despots to the disadvantage of their people who look up to them for their wisdom. They throw dignity to the dogs and act as if they are hypnotized. How sad indeed. (*The Daily Guide*, Nov 20, 2001; p.6)

In fact, according to Col. Yohanna A. Madaki (rtd.), when General Gowon drew up plans to return Nigeria to civil rule in 1970, "academicians began to present well researched papers pointing to the fact that military rule was the better preferred since the civilians had not learned any lessons sufficient enough to be entrusted with the governance of the country" (*Post Express*, Nov 12, 1998; p.5). Nigerian senator Arthur Nzeribe once declared that General Babangida was good enough to rule Nigeria. When pressed, he confessed: "I was promised prime ministerial appointment. There is no living politician as hungry for power as I was who would not be seduced in the manner I was to invest in the ABN, with the possibility and promise of being Executive Prime Minister to a military president" (*The Guardian*, Nov 13, 1998; p.3).

Too many of Africa's intellectuals throw caution to the wind and grab every opportunity they get to serve the dictates of barbarous military regimes—even at great risks to themselves. There was the case of Phillips David Sesay, who had various academic degrees, including a doctorate in philosophy. As such, one would have expected him to know better. He was the head of Sierra Leone's chancery in Washington. For three years, he was not paid, yet he remained at the post—not out of an altruistic service to his country but a perfervid obsession with a government post. In 1996, he left his wife and son in Washington and returned to Sierra Leone in a hurry to accept promotion as acting chief protocol at the Ministry of Foreign Affairs.

That the former protocol at the ministry had worked with the barbarous junta for only four days and had fled the country did not bother Sesay, who took that post. Following a coup on May 23, 1997, Sesay himself fled the country. "When his plane landed in New York on 20 December 1997, Sesay's diplomatic passport with a multiple-entry permit to the U.S. was found to be insufficient. His visa was canceled at the behest of the State Department and he was placed in detention by the Immigration and Naturalization Service" (*The Washington Post*, Jan 2, 1998; p.A30). His case should serve as a lesson to African intellectuals who feverishly jostle for posts to serve under illegitimate military regimes.

Ghanaians would point to a swarm of intellectual prostitutes who sold out to join the military regime of Fte./Lte. Jerry Rawlings: Dr. Kwesi Botchwey, the former minister of finance; Totobi Kwakye, minister of communication, who as a student leader battled the former military head of state, Col. I. K. Acheampong; Dr. Tony Aidoo, a presidential adviser; Dr. Vincent Assisseh, a press secretary; and Kow Arkaah, the vice-president who was beaten up by President Rawlings in December 1995.

Vile opportunism and perfidious collaboration on the part of Africa's intellectuals allowed tyranny to become entrenched in Africa. Doe, Mengistu, Mobutu, and other military dictators legitimized and perpetuated their rule by buying off and coopting Africa's academics for a pittance. And when the academics fall out of favor, they are beaten up, tossed aside, or worse. And yet more offer themselves up. Such was the case of Paul Tembo, of Zambia.

Paul Tembo was Zambian president Frederick Chiluba's former campaign manager; he headed Chiluba's reelection campaign in 1996 and spearheaded the bid by Chiluba to seek an unconstitutional third five-year term in office. A divisive congress of the ruling Movement for Multi-party Democracy (MMD) ultimately voted to allow Chiluba to seek a third term but the decision was subsequently overturned. The congress also appointed an independent tribunal headed by Zambia's chief justice to probe accusations of corruption and abuse of office by Finance Minister Latele Kalumba, Home Affairs Minister Peter Machungwa, and Works and Supply Minister Godden Mandandi, who are among Chiluba's most trusted aides.

In May 2001, Mr. Tembo quit President Chiluba's MMD, saying the president had rigged internal polls to prevent him (Tembo) from becoming vice-president. In June 2001, Tembo joined the Forum for Democracy and Development (FDD) in a bid to unseat his former boss, and vowed to testify before the tribunal. On July 6, 2001, Tembo was shot dead execution-style at his home in front of his horrified wife and children. According to Tembo's attorney, "Three killers forced their way into the compound, roughed up Paul, led him to his bed, made him lie on it and then shot him in the back of his head. They made his wife watch" (*The Washington Times,* July 7, 2001; p.A5).

The government said in a statement: "The police are investigating this death and will spare no effort to ensure that the people involved are apprehended and brought before our courts of law" (*The Washington Times,* July 7, 2001; p.A5). The government even offered $13,000 to anyone with information leading to the arrest of the killers. But the opposition was not impressed. It immediately blamed the state, calling it a political assassination. The opposition FDD dismissed the government statement, noting that Tembo was due to give evidence at a tribunal investigating corruption and abuse of office by three Cabinet ministers: "This murder does not need much imagination for one to understand. He was killed because of the evidence he was supposed to give at the tribunal," said FDD chairman Simon Zukas. Another opposition leader, Anderson Mazoka of the United Party for National Development (UPND), slammed the state and dismissed its pledge to probe the death, saying it had failed to resolve similar cases in the past. One was the 1998 murder of former finance minister Ronald Penza, shortly after he was fired by President Chiluba.

The intellectuals and politicians prostitute themselves because of their belief that wealth can only be created in the government sector. But who can blame them when the chief bandit is the head of state himself? In March 2002, "the ex-wife of former Zambian president Frederick Chiluba claimed that her husband salted away some $2.5 billion from state coffers while he was in power. Vera Chiluba's revelations, published in the *Zambian Post,* shocked the country, which has a gross domestic product of little more than $3 billion" (*The Sunday Times,* March 31, 2002). Chiluba was placed under house arrest in 2003.

There have been so many African intellectuals who have ruined their careers, reputation, and lives by hopping into bed with corrupt and barbarous regimes. Intellectual prostitution, in the long run, does not pay.

Can the Mafia State Reform Itself?

Sadly, it does not appear likely that the African vampire state can be reformed. There are simply too many entrenched participants who benefit from the rotten status quo. Reform can mean committing collective suicide. It is a neopatrimonial state, where good governance principles advanced by the NEPAD would deprive such rulers of the means to maintain their patronage networks. It would be naïve to expect the ruling elites to implement broad accountability measures, and a functioning democracy would undermine their own positions. It would be nonsensical to expect Africa's autocrats to be the engines of reform and positive change on the continent. Billions in Western aid dollars were spent to bribe and cajole these African despots, but they adamantly refused to relinquish or share political power. Only 16 out of the 54 African countries are democratic. The World Bank and the IMF spent more than $25 billion in structural adjustment loans to help restructure 29 African economies to be market-based ones in the period 1981–1991. Fewer than six were adjudged to be "economic success stories." And without reform, more African countries and economies will collapse. Whoever thought Ivory Coast would blow?

The political and economic failings of African governments have prompted intensive debates and strident polemics, which have made it impossible for Africa to extricate itself from the current mess. Each time an African problem—such as economic mismanagement—is brought up for discussion, some benighted African government officials and intellectuals drag in extraneous historical factors that have no bearing on the issue. Africa is constantly being portrayed as a "victim"—as if the continent has no leaders. In fact, many of the hackneyed causes of Africa's woes bear little or no relevance to the current mess. The slave trade and colonialism have nothing to do with economic mismanagement.

True, the West supported some brutal African despots, such as Mobutu Sese Seko of Zaire and Samuel Doe of Liberia. But the West did not tell them to loot their national treasuries and slaughter their people. And, for balance, the East, as well the South, supported barbarous dictators in Africa, too.

African leaders refuse to take responsibility for their own failures, choosing instead to blame "external factors." The World Bank and the IMF, for example, have been demonized as "imperialist monsters" that are responsible for Africa's debt crisis, imposing "offensive conditionalities," and exacting their pound of flesh from poor, suffering African countries. If the World Bank and the IMF are really the "monsters" that African governments portray them to be, then why go to them? After all, the World Bank and the IMF are not the only places where African governments can borrow money.

If African governments do not wish for the World Bank and IMF to impose 'offensive conditionalities," why then don't these governments live within their means? As we observed in chapter 7, no government—not even the U.S. government—can spend beyond its means forever. This is not to defend the World Bank and the IMF, which have problems of their own. But constant demonization, demagoguery, and the polemics detract attention away from the real issue: budget expenditures that have careened out of control, producing chronic deficits that are financed by printing money. In 1992, Uganda's money supply went up by 68 percent; Kenya's increased by 47 percent. In 1993, Zimbabwe's money supply rose by a staggering 95 percent, and Togo by a whopping 105 percent in 1994 (World Bank, 2000a; p.62). The World Bank, the IMF, or Martians have got nothing to do with African governments irresponsibly gunning the money supply to finance election expenditures.

The African people are fed up with the claptrap their leaders serve up to avoid taking responsibility for their own reckless misgovernance and mis-management. One such African vented his frustration with the leadership. According to Obadina (1999),

> In 1990 a state governor in Imo state in southeastern Nigeria explained to a public meeting in the capital Owerri that his cash-strapped government was unable to solve the severe erosion problem devastating the region. After he had spoken an old man in the audience stood up and said "Since you and other black leaders have tried your best but have not been able to improve the lives of us ordinary people, why don't we ask the whites to come back. When the white man ruled us things were not this bad. Please ask them to come and save us". The statement, spoken with sincerity, met momentary silence in the audience followed by some laughter and applause. (p. 23)

The problem, however, is not so much rotten leadership with unchecked power as it is the lack of appropriate *institutions* or the existence of a huge *"institutional gap"* (Dollar and Pritchett, 1998). But then again, the leader-ship blocks the establishment of the institutions that will provide institu-tional checks against errant misrule and corruption. The mafia state takes over these institutions (the media, the military, the judiciary, etc.) and sub-verts them to serve the interests of the ruling bandits. Reform is anathema to the vampire elites. Ask them to open up the political system and they will hold coconut elections to return themselves to power. Ask them to reduce the size of the government by placing more emphasis on private enterprise and they will establish a ministry of private enterprise (Ghana).

For more than 30 years, the ruling elites have engaged in this kind of vile chicanery and acrobatics. Each time they are asked to reform their abom-inable systems, they throw up all sorts of objections and obstacles. It should be clear that the modern state sector is nonreformable. Billions of Western dollars have been expended to bribe and entice the ruling elites to reform the state sector but to no avail. It should be apparent that the *law of diminishing returns* dictates that investment elsewhere might yield positive results.

The alternative is to focus on the rural and informal sectors. After all, the vast majority of the African people can be found in these sectors. Common sense dictates that, if one is desirous of helping the real people of Africa, one goes to the sectors where one can find them, and they are not in the mod-ern, state sector. Helping peasants is not a complicated task and does not require massive amounts of Western aid. Their own indigenous economic institutions can be improved to engineer economic prosperity. The salvation of Africa rests on the backs of these peasants, not on the hippo generation of elites.

To lead the continent in a new direction, Africa's best hope lies with the cheetah generation. With small microcredit investment in cottage industries, this generation can turn Africa around. African leaders, politicians, and intellectuals have failed Africa badly. All these groups were looking for answers to Africa's problems in the wrong places when the blueprint for Africa's economic rejuvenation lies right at their feet. And worse, the issue of reforming the African state has become so polluted and politicized that the ruling elites do not see their own folly. Failed African leaders and the hippo generation should be left to their own devices. Eventually, their fate will catch up with them.

"President Frederick Chiluba of Zambia is a thief," said Zoran Zuze, 29. "He's a con man, and the MMD is like a mafia. We have told them to go, but they act like they cannot hear" (*The Washington Post*, January 2, 2002; p.A10).

Chiluba started out as a socialist, but in the opinion of many Zambians, he left the state house a wealthier man and Zambia a poorer nation. On August 5, 2003, Chiluba, the "Swiss-bank socialist," was arrested and "charged with stealing more than $40 million during his decade of rule" (*The Washington Times*, Aug 6, 2003; p.A13). And his finance minister, Katele Kalumba? Recall that police found him hiding in a tree near his rural home in January 2003. He was arrested and charged with stealing some $33 million when he was in office (*The New York Times*, Jan 16, 2003; p.A8). He could have saved himself all that grief if had made his millions in the private sector—by planting coconut trees for corrupt ministers to hide in!

From the Vampire State to the Coconut Republic

It may be recalled that the driving economic ideology in the postcolonial period has been statism. Originally, the regime of state controls was to enable African governments to spearhead economic development and capture the commanding heights of their economies. But state controls wreaked a treacherously pernicious havoc with Africa's political system as well. Africa's autocrats quickly discovered that not only could they use state controls and all their attendant powers to extract resources to enrich themselves, but also to punish political rivals and crush any opposition to their rule. Examples abound: from Ghana under Kwame Nkrumah, Guinea under Sekou Toure, Mali under Moussa Traore, Togo under Gnassingbe Eyadema, to Zimbawe under Robert Mugabe. Realizing that state controls can be used to their personal and political benefit, Africa's autocrats expanded their scope and tightened them. This provided the *modus operandi* for the evolution of many African states from neopatrimonial to vampire (mafia) states and eventually into coconut republics.

It is true, upon achieving independence, the newly emergent African political elites inherited a state system that lacked legitimacy, a stable government (with colonial administration gone), and the resources to administer the new state. "The initial tendency was to encourage an increased role for the state in most aspects of the economy. Industrialization and indigenization were the watch-words of the immediate postcolonial era and the state was to be the vehicle through which these twin goals could be achieved, primarily through nationalization" (Taylor, 2004). But the newly independent state evolved into a neopatrimonial order, where the "fathers" of the new nations (Nkrumah, Kenyatta, Nyerere, etc.) were to use resources extracted by a regime of state controls for general development of all. Over time, the ruling elites, as we noted, discovered that they could also use these resources to buy political support, crush their enemies, and illicitly enrich themselves.

In the 1970s, a rash of coups swept across Africa, overthrowing corrupt administrations. But rather than dismantle the statist interventionist behemoth and the venal patronage system and decentralize power, military juntas, which lacked the barest shred of legitimacy, concentrated more power in their own hands and proceeded to take their turn in plundering the state. Eventually, a mafia or vampire state emerged, where the government ceased to exist—hijacked by a platoon of uniformed bandits. The regimes of General Mobutu Sese Seko of Zaire and General Sani Abacha of Nigeria were classic examples.

With the progression of time, the vampire state hardened into a coconut republic. The ruling bandits wielded all power, committing heinous crimes, and plundering the national treasury with impunity. It is tempting to contrast a "banana republic" to a coconut republic. In a banana republic, one might slip on a banana peel but things *do* work—now and then—for the people, albeit inefficiently and unreliably. The water tap has a mind of its own: occasionally, it might spit some water and then change its mind. Buses operate according to their own internal clock, set according to Martian time—whatever that is. By the grace of God or Allah, they might arrive, belching thick black smoke. Food and gasoline are generally available but expensive, if one is willing to contend with occasional long lines and a few indignities from sellers. The police are helpful sometimes and protect the people, occasionally catching a real crook. There is petty corruption. Now and then, a million dollars here and a million there might be embezzled by government officials. Such a banana republic often slips into suspended animation or arrested development.

A coconut republic, on the other hand, is ruthlessly inefficient and lethal. It eventually implodes. Instead of a banana peel, one might step on a live grenade. Here, the entire notion of "governance" has been turned completely on its head by the ruling bandits. It is the people who must serve *them,* not the other way round. Their water taps run all the time; the people must collect rain water. There are inexhaustible supplies of food and gasoline for the thugs in power, but not for the people. And there are no buses for the people. Period. Those shiny buses that ply the road are for the vampire elites. The people can walk. The republic sits atop vast reserves of oil and exports oil. Yet, there is no gasoline for the people since the country's oil refineries have broken down. Funds earmarked for repairs had been looted, and refined petroleum products must be imported. The country may also be rich in mineral deposits—such as diamonds, gold, coltan. Yet, the mineral wealth has produced misery. When the Chad-Cameroon oil pipeline was completed in October 2003 and started exporting, there were high hopes that the oil boom would transform the lives of the Chadian people. But reality soon set in. "We thought with the petrol we could have everything—food, clothes, a better life," lamented Taraseem Pelagie, standing outside her mud hut. "There is nothing good coming from this oil. In five years, nothing will change" (*The Washington Post,* March 13, 2004; p.A16). And when the Chadian government received a bonus payment of $25 million from the oil deal, it spent $4 million to purchase weapons. Why? To suppress the people.

In Equatorial Guinea, President Teodoro Obiang Nguema came to power by overthrowing his uncle and shooting him in 1979. He survived in power by packing his government with relatives, torturing opponents, and rigging elections. "His would be a perfect banana republic, if it had bananas. Instead, it has oil—lots of it" (*The Independent,* March 16, 2004; www.independent.co.uk).

Obiang's fortunes turned to gold in the mid-1990s, when U. S. oil firms discovered vast offshore oil deposits. Overnight, the former Spanish colony shot from poverty-stricken obscurity to fabulous wealth, becoming known as the "Kuwait of Africa." Large oil companies, led by Exxon Mobil, invested $6 billion in operations that now pump 350,000 barrels of oil a day. It became Africa's third-largest oil producer, after Nigeria and Angola. But,

The vast majority of Guineans, however, have yet to taste that sweet bread. The majority of the vast state oil revenues—up to $700 million this year— has been salted into foreign bank accounts. Many are controlled by Mr. Obiang. Most of the country's 500,000 people scrape by on $2 a day, and human development indicators have barely budged since oil was struck. "There is no evidence that any of the oil wealth has gone to the people," said

Sarah Wykes of the lobby group Global Witness, which later this month will
release a report linking the Obiang regime to large-scale corruption and drug
trafficking. In Washington, the FBI has started investigating a $700m bank
account at the Riggs Bank, of which Mr. Obiang is apparently the main sig-
natory. One bank employee has already lost his job over the scandal. (*The Independent*, March 16, 2004; www.independent.co.uk)

In a coconut republic, the ruling elites have things backward. Basic common sense has been butchered and arrogant idiocy runs amok. It is here
where one finds oppressive tyrants chanting "People's Revolution" and vow-
ing to liberate their people when they are the ones standing on the necks of
their people. After September 11, 2001, several African leaders claimed to be
fighting terrorism when they themselves were the real state terrorists! The
regimes of Omar el Bashir of Sudan, Yoweri Museveni of Uganda, and
Robert Mugabe of Zimbabwe claimed to be fighting terrorists, and even former President Charles Taylor of Liberia established an anti-terrorist unit to
terrorize the people! In Taylor's coconut republic a gang of thugs welcomed
visitors at the airport:

"You," demanded a man with three identification cards swinging from his
neck, and a bottle of beer in his hand, accosting an arriving passenger.
"I am the visa officer and law requires you give me your passport".
Then he leaned in close and whispered: "I am suffering. No food. Help
me out".
"You don't have a real visa, you have to get one from me," commanded another man, who nodded and raised his eye-brows. "Whoever gave you this
visa is a liar".
"No, he's lying. Don't listen to him," cajoled yet another, who swooped in
with his own crew of nine friends and promised to retrieve precious luggage.
"We'll take care of you. That's the law, for true, true, true".
The truth is that there is no law in Liberia. In fact, there is no government,
only rough-hewn fiefdoms jostling to control a depleted nation. (*The Washington Post*, Sept 9, 2003; p.A1).

Under Charles Taylor, wheelbarrows served as ambulances for the people.
The public schools did not function; more than 70 percent of the population was illiterate. Yet, all government ministers had Ph.D.s, some even three
or four—all purchased, not earned. At the University of Liberia, Charles
Taylor offered 11,000 scholarships to his friends in 1997 but did not end up
paying their tuition bills. Nor did his government pay the salaries of university professors and public school teachers. Liberia had a judicial system, but
"Taylor named his friends who could not read or write to be judges and at-

torneys, and sentences were handed down on his orders" (*The Washington Post*, Sept 9, 2003; p.A18).

Liberia's capital, Monrovia, had a fire station painted bright red, but its only fire truck had no tires, headlamps, or even a hose. Wires dangled from the engine. With no running water in the city, firefighters "must jog or hitchhike to a creek three miles away to fetch water in buckets to put out a fire" (*The Washington Post*, Sept 9, 2003; p.A18).

A coconut republic can be run by cell phone. Charles Taylor was exiled for war crimes to Nigeria, yet he continued to run the country by remote control because the ministers left behind were too incompetent to make their own decisions. Moses Blah, a member of Taylor's army who became president when Taylor stepped down, was reportedly taking orders from Taylor about what to do with remaining government funds. "Charles?" asked Cecil Brandy, the minister of agriculture and a Taylor defender. "Oh, he's still in charge. I'm going to see him next week. What's wrong with that? We got business to contend with" (*The Washington Post*, Sept 17, 2003; p.A17). Said General Coocoo Dennis, a member of Taylor's inner circle, "He (Taylor) tells us to move the front lines, we are going to listen. He tells us to sit, we sit. There's no debate about that" (*The Washington Post*, Sept 17, 2003; p.A17).

In a coconut republic, national priorities are badly mangled. In Nigeria, where Taylor took refuge, the educational system is a shambles:

> "Education in Nigeria should be declared a disaster area in need of urgent attention," Registrar of the Joint Admissions and Matriculation Board (JAMB), Professor Bello Salim has said. Salim who made the declaration at an interactive session with media executives in Lagos yesterday said it was time to go beyond mere lip service to rescue the sector that is "producing illiterates".
>
> Painting a gory picture of the disaster that has befallen the sector, he said there are schools where two, three different classes are accommodated in one classroom. With each set of pupils facing different sides of the room, Salim wondered how they could learn.
>
> He also lamented today's university graduates, many of who are not as good as Standard Six graduates of old. He said although today's graduates can read and write, most do not understand what they are reading or writing."
> (*This Day*, [Lagos], January 28, 2004; p.4)

Yet, on January 29, 2004, Nigeria admitted it wanted to develop a ballistic missile capability and held talks with North Korea. Talks between Nigeria's vice-president, Atiku Abubakar, and his North Korean counterpart, Yang Hyong-sop, took place in Abuja (BBC News, Jan 29, 2004; www.bbc.co.uk).

If there is no food in the country, Zimbabwe's ruling bandits fly into South Africa and return, laden with huge bags of groceries. And the people? They can eat grass. Meanwhile, construction workers have feverishly put finishing touches to the retirement home of President Robert Mugabe in an exclusive area 18 miles north of Harare. The mansion has been estimated to cost about $5.25 million—a colossal sum in a country where factory workers barely earned £6 (about $13) a month. After adding landscaping, security, and interior decoration, the final cost is expected to exceed $8.4 million. The mansion is being put up at a time when vast numbers of Zimbabweans—some 5.5 million or about half of the population—face starvation and need hunger relief. Starving Zimbabweans not only foot the construction bill but also the cost of protecting the property by four uniformed police officers 24 hours a day! And there is nothing the people can do about that!

Whereas in a banana republic a million here and there might be stolen, in a coconut republic it is the entire treasury that is carted away. In pre-dawn raids, General Sani Abacha of Nigeria sent heavily armed trucks into the basement of the Central Bank of Nigeria and carted away billions of dollars, which were spirited out of the country by his henchmen in suitcases. "A Nigerian man and a banker accompanying him were arrested at the Lagos airport after trying to board a London-bound jet with $800 million in cash. Customs officials said the seizure was the biggest recorded in Nigeria. The banker accompanied the other man apparently so that customs officials would not ask questions. The money has since been deposited in the Central Bank of Nigeria" (*The Washington Times,* July 29, 1995; p.A7).

General Sani Abacha's family thought they were smart. They hired Usman Mohammed Bello—a Sudanese from Karsala—to look after their three children attending school in Amman, Jordan. Usman became a close confidante of Abacha, with access to several coded foreign accounts opened to him. The family trusted Usman and Abacha gave him diplomatic status in the Nigerian foreign office in Amman. He was also issued with both a diplomatic passport number, F317567, and a standard passport number, A104786. In 1998 Abacha was either poisoned or died from exhaustion after a Viagra-induced sex orgy—depending on upon which version one believes. A short transitional government led to the election of President Olusegun Obasanjo in March 1999, who vowed to recover Abacha's loot from abroad. On October 1, 1999, Usman Bello vanished. "Nigeria's State Security Service (SSS) established that the Sudanese might have salted away millions of dollars entrusted to him by the Abacha family and may also be privy to other financial transactions of the family overseas, especially in the Arab world" (*Weekly Insight,* July 19–25, 2000; p.1). A hysterical Abacha family appealed to Nigeria's police and government for help in catching him! Only in a coconut republic would thieves appeal to the police to apprehend a thief!

Even when the loot is recovered, it is quickly re-looted! About $709 million and another £144 million were recovered from the loot the Abachas had stashed abroad. But the Senate Public Accounts Committee found only $6.8 million and £2.8 million of the recovered booty in the Central Bank of Nigeria (*Post Express*, (July 10, 2000). The recovered loot itself had quickly been re-looted!

The following describe some of the unique characteristics of a coconut republic.

Presidential Eccentricities and Tomfoolery

In 1976, President Jean-Bedel Bokassa spent 25 percent of the GNP of the Central African Republic to crown himself "emperor"—just to prove that Africa too had come of age. If France once had an emperor, so too could Africa! Three years later, "Emperor" Bokassa was ousted in a popular uprising and fled the country. Years later, he returned to claim the throne and was thrown into jail. But his successors were no better.

On May 28, 2001, the country celebrated Mother's Day. The celebrations were marked by drinking, dancing, and women parading around town in their best outfits. Suddenly, unrelenting gunfire rattled through the night, in what appeared to be a coup attempt against President Ange-Felix Patasse.

Gunmen opened fire at about 1:00 A.M. on the president's residence, killing at least seven members of his presidential guard during several hours of fighting. Government spokesman Prosper Ndouba told Agence France-Presse there had been "many deaths among the attackers." But "the president is safe and sound," he told AFP. A government statement said loyal troops were in control and blamed the assault on "individuals who have yet to be identified" (*The Washington Times*, May 29, 2001; p.A11). Never mind that the government blamed the attack on individuals who were yet to be identified, but how "safe and sound" was the president?

According to the news report, "The president was reportedly warned about the impending night's violence but was so drunk from the celebrations that he did nothing to avert the threat. He was said to be sleeping off a hangover in a regional bank, the most robust-looking building in town" (*The Washington Times*, May 29, 2001; p.A11). Where else can he doze off except in a bank vault where he had stashed some loot? On March 15, 2003, a former army chief-of-staff and rebel leader, Francois Bozize, ousted President Ange-Felix Patasse from power.

In Ghana, after a spate of serial killings of more than 20 women in Accra, a protest demonstration was organized at the behest of the ex-first lady,

Nana Konadu Agyeman-Rawlings, to pressure the "authorities" into taking action. Those who followed Nana Konadu into the streets included the inspector-general of police, the deputy minister of the interior and some members of Parliament. In an editorial, *The Weekly Insight* (Nov 3, 1999) wrote: "One cannot help laughing at the recent demonstration. Clearly, these were the very 'authorities,' who needed to be pressured into taking action to resolve the murders but they were out in the streets demonstrating against themselves" (p. 2).

Fed up with 19 years of socialist misrule under President Abdon Diouf, Senegalese loudly demanded *sopi* (change) during the election campaign in 2000. Sensing an opportunity and ever so enterprising, President Diouf began using "change" as his campaign slogan! "He promises to modernize Senegal, prepare it for globalization, make government more effective and accessible, and toughen the laws on corruption. But the change most Senegalese want is a new government" (*The Economist,* Feb 26, 2000; p.56). The Senegalese kicked him out of office anyway.

A coconut republic is where a semi-literate General Samuel Doe of Liberia summoned his finance minister—"only to be reminded by aides that he had already executed him" (*The New York Times,* Sept 13, 2003; p.A4).

Farcical Rule of Law

The police protect *the ruling bandits!* In fact, if you report them to the police for stealing the people's money, it is *you* the police would arrest! On January 18, 1995, Ricardo de Melo, the editor of the Luanda-based *Impartial Fax,* was killed for writing stories about official corruption (*Index On Censorship,* 3/2000; p.86). On May 5, 2003, the weekly *Le Temps* in Gabon was suspended for three months after publishing an article about state mismanagement of funds (*Index on Censorship,* July 2003; p.146). In January 2000, Kenya's ruling party's (KANU) gang of thugs known as *Jeshi la Mzee* ("the old man's army") attacked a group of opposition leaders outside parliament who were protesting against the resumption of IMF assistance. "It was the protesters, not the thugs, who were arrested by the police" (*The Economist,* Feb 5, 2000; p.42). Said *The Economist* (March 16, 2002): "In Zimbabwe, the thieves are in charge and their victims face prosecution" (p. 18).

Indeed, the crooks are a law unto themselves. In October 1999, Henry Cassel, the deputy immigration director of Liberia and brother-in-law of President Charles Taylor, "pulled out a gun in broad daylight in a busy Monrovia street and shot dead a taxi-driver who had overtaken Mr Cassel's vehicle" (*The Independent* (Ghana), October 31, 1999; p.3).

In Kenya, the ever-competent, efficient, and highly professional police investigators routinely dismiss the mysterious deaths of prominent people as "suicides." During the Moi era, Nicholas Biwott, a member of Moi's Kalenjin tribe and considered to be President Moi's closest political confidant, was paid an official salary of Ksh 21,033 but was worth "hundreds of millions of dollars, chiefly in offshore holdings" (*The New York Times*, Oct 21, 1991; p.A9). Kenya's foreign minister Robert Ouko "clashed with Biwott during a trip to the U.S. over foreign accounts Biwott and other government ministers held in other countries" (*Financial Times*, Nov 27, 1991; p.4). Ouko was brutally murdered on his return to Kenya. Biwott was arrested by Moi and later released "for lack of evidence." According to Kenyan police investigators, "Foreign Minister Robert Ouko was presumed to have broken his own leg, shot himself in the head and set himself afire. Two years earlier, Kenyan officials suggested that a British tourist, Julie Ward, lopped off her own head and one of her legs before setting herself aflame" (*The Washington Post*, April 20, 2001; p.A19).

Vain Braggadocio and False Courage

Government thugs brutalize and intimidate people but all that façade of braggadocio, bravery, and invincibility evinced by the country's security forces are just that—hollow. They hide behind their uniforms and guns to terrorize the people. When it comes to beating up and shooting unarmed civilians, they can do so with efficient relish. But how really brave and courageous are Africa's policemen and soldiers?

On December 16, 1998, Corporal C. Darko and Constable K. A. Boateng at a police station in Accra, Ghana, were instructed to go and arrest Samuel Quartey, who was reported to police for being involved in a theft case. "When the suspect came out brandishing a cutlass (a machete), the police officers did what most people would have done—took to their heels with the speed of lightning that could have made an enviable record had they been timed" (*The Mirror*, Jan 2, 1999; p.1). As Ghanaians would say: "Some cutlass cut cutlass there, bor bor"—that is, there is some "greater power."

On July 23, 1998, Colonel Anthony Obi, Osun State's military administrator, strutted pompously to deliver a speech at a state function at Osogbo in the southwestern part of Lagos, Nigeria. As the *Daily Champion* (24 July 1998) reported:

Panic-stricken Nigerian officials ran for safety when first a rat and then a python, apparently drawn by the smell of the rat, made a sudden appearance.

The officials leapt up from their seats when the rat, described as having a "long snout and offensive smell," appeared from beneath the carpet by the high table. Colonel Anthony Obi, Osun State's military administrator, and his entourage nervously returned after security agents intervened and killed the beast. (p. 1)

Ambushed by a bunch of rag-tag cattle rustlers, Kenya's elite presidential guards quickly surrendered. Johann Wandetto, a reporter for the *People Daily,* a newspaper in Kitale, Rift Valley province, submitted a story in the March 6, 1999, edition with the title: "Militia men rout 8 crack unit officers: Shock as Moi's men surrender meekly." Wandetto was arrested and sentenced to 18 months in prison for what the court described as an "alarmist report" (*Index on Censorship,* 3/2000; p.99).

Much of the police force is composed of terrorists and bandits who scarcely know what their job is. On August 7, 1998, U.S. embassies in Nairobi and Dar es Salaam were hit by terrorist bombs, killing more than 250 people and injuring at least 5,000. In Nairobi, people rushed to the scene, dug into the debris with bare hands in frantic efforts to save the injured and the dying. Men ripped off their shirts to use as bandages; drivers threw out passengers to take the injured to hospitals. And Kenyan Police? They arrived at the scene "carrying truncheons and rifles, instead of spades and pickaxes" (*The Economist,* 22 August 1998, p.36).

Hoisted By Their Own Petard

The tyrants hold coconut elections to return themselves to power (Eyadema of Togo, Kagame of Rwanda, and Mugabe of Zimbabwe) but in the end they are hoisted by their own petard. Feeling increasingly insecure and paranoid, the gangster regime spends an inordinate sum on an elaborate security-cum-military structure to protect itself, suppress the people, and eliminate any threat to their rule. Since they came to power through illegitimate means (a military coup or rebel insurgency), they are ever so suspicious of everyone who might be harboring the same intentions. So the bulk of strategic positions in the police and military hierarchies are filled with personally loyal individuals: brothers and cousins, and tribesmen. Still, they can never trust their own militaries and therefore create other layers upon layers of security— Special Division Forces, Elite Presidential Guard, Secret Commando Squad—who are given better training and equipment, just in case one level fails. They then shower the security agents with perks and amenities. In Nigeria, former dictator Gen. Ibrahim Babangida rewarded "nearly 3,000 of his most loyal military chiefs by giving them new Peugeot sedans. Most Nigerians will never be able to afford anything like a new Peugeot 505, which costs the equivalent of $21,000 in Lagos. A senior university professor, for example, earns about $4,000 a year, while a nurse or mechanic is lucky to bring home more than $1,000" (*The New York Times,* Dec 2, 1993; p.A3).

Such expenditures on security for the ruling bandits have been a continuous drain on Africa's economies. As Africa's infrastructure and public services disintegrated, its dictators found the wherewithal to spend more and more on themselves and the military. But the irony is, their elaborate security system fails to protect them. Samuel Doe of Liberia, for example, spent huge sums to keep his soldiers happy. He also had crack presidential troops, secretly trained by the Israelis. But they could not protect him from Charles Taylor's 1,000 rag-tag rebels. Note that Charles Taylor was not even a soldier but an ex-civil servant. Similarly, Comrade Mengistu Haile Mariam also spent an enormous amount to build Africa's largest army, with 200,000 under arms. They, too, could not protect Mengistu from a band of determined Eritrean and Tigray rebels. In 1991, he fled to Zimbabwe. How safe was he there?

> Former Ethiopian dictator, Mengistu Haile Mariam panicked and ran yelling for help when a would-be assassin fired a single shot at one of his guards last fall, a Zimbabwe court was told. The Eritrean suspect, Solomon Haile Ghebre Michael, 36, pleaded not guilty Monday in the attack on the exiled Col. Mengistu, given asylum by President Robert Mugabe in 1991 after he fled Ethiopia. (*The Washington Times,* Thursday July 11, 1996; p.A10)

Quite often, it is the very same security apparatus that even overthrows them in the end—hoisted by their own petard. Such was the fate of the following coconut generals—all deceased—ousted by people from the very security apparatus they created.

On July 29, 1975, General Gowon of Nigeria was overthrown in a bloodless coup, planned and executed by some of his most trusted colleagues, including the commander of the Presidential Guard. Interestingly, General Joe Garba, who announced the overthrow, was Gowon's closest personal staff, in whom he confided in all matters of security. Ironically, reasons for the coup against Gowon were: inaccessibility, insensitivity, indecision, and lack of political direction. Strange that his own closest aide had no access to him. In 1998, General Sani Abacha of Nigeria was poisoned by members of his own inner security details.

In Rwanda, president Juvenal Habyarimana "fell victim to the monster he created" (*The Washington Post,* April 18, 1995; p.A17). His plane crash was plotted by his own allies in the military, who saw that he was edging closer to political reforms that would threaten their power.

But the next military buffoon doesn't learn. Being a product of that structure, with intricate knowledge of its inner workings, he repairs the weaknesses and strengthens the structure. Eventually he too is overthrown by the same security apparatus.

A year after taking office, Niger's president Maharanee Ousmane had tripled his personal fortune. As required by law, President Ousmane had declared a fortune of 51 million CFA ($89,000) and three houses when he took office in April 1993. A year later, "The poor West African country's Supreme Court said on April 28, 1994, that Maharanee had declared 160 million CFA ($280,000), with 57 million CFA held in cash and the rest in a local bank. Maharanee's list of property was 10 houses in Niger, livestock and poultry, three cars, two television sets, two video recorders and two gold watches" (*African News Weekly,* 20 May 1994, p.8).

He too placed his faith in a specially selected presidential guard. On January 27, 1996, came the coup. Did his presidential guard protect him? One looked at another and asked, "Me protect this thief? You lie bad." They threw down their weapons, scaled the presidential palace walls and dove into the Niger River to swim to safety. But the crocodiles got them.

General Ibrahim Mainassara, who overthrew Ousmane, vowed never to repeat that mistake. To calm international outcry at the rape of democracy in Niger, he held coconut elections on July 6, 1996 and used strong-arm tactics to return himself to power. He too didn't trust his own military. So he created Special Presidential guards and fortified his palace to make it impregnable. And just in case someone might entertain the idea of attacking from the air, he equipped the guards with powerful anti-helicopter machine guns. In May 1999, he left the country on an overseas trip. Upon return, his Special Presidential Guards were summoned to the airport to welcome him home—as was customary. When the president deplaned, they decided to try their new anti-helicopter machine guns. They opened fire, shredding the president's body beyond recognition. His wife, upon seeing the body pieces littering the tarmac, collapsed.

In Ivory Coast, ousted president Henri Bedie believed that the *gendarmerie* was strong enough to protect the state and his presidency against any potential threat. Accordingly, he gave hefty pay increases to the *gendarmerie* and the police and ignored the army. But when the coup came, "the *gendarmes*' commander refused to order his men to fight fellow Ivorians" (*The Economist,* Jan 8, 2000; p.42).

The military coconut-head General Robert Guie did not learn from Bedie's missteps. After seizing power in a December 1999 coup, General Guie claimed he had only come to "sweep the house clean" and return to the barracks. After tasting power for a few months, he decided that "power sweet, haba." So he decided to run for the presidency and asked the very political party he overthrew for corruption to choose him as their presidential candidate. Imagine. When none of the parties would have him, he decided to run anyway as the "people's candidate" in the October 27, 2000, elections.

When early returns showed that General Guie was losing, he ordered his soldiers to raid the Electoral Commission and sack the commissioners. The vote was then counted in secret and General Guei declared the winner. But,

> Crowds of Abidjan residents—angry at the general's attempt to steal Sunday's presidential elections—fought for a second day with troops loyal to Guie. The battle turned when key army units and the paramilitary gendarme force defected to the opposition, recognizing veteran opposition politician Laurent Gbagbo as the elected president. (*The Washington Post,* Oct 26, 2000; p.A33)

General Guie fled Ivory Coast in a helicopter on October 29, 2000. He returned to take part in Laurent Gbagbo's broad-based government but was killed in the September 2002 mutiny and abortive coup attempt that plunged Ivory Coast into civil war.

The futility of all these military expenditures and heavy armor was pointed out by Nobel laureate Archbishop Desmond Tutu back in 1990. Speaking at the Teachers Hall in Accra (Ghana) on November 25, 1990, he noted cogently: "Freedom is cheaper than repression. When you are a leader chosen by the people you don't need security. All the money spent on weapons doesn't buy one iota of security" (*Christian Messenger,* Jan 1991; p.1).

Indeed. Said Likulia Bolongo, the defense minister of President Mobutu Sese Seko during the 1996–1997 war: "I bought jet fighters. I bought MiG–23s. I bought armed helicopters. And I lost the war. When there's social unrest, it's difficult to win. It's the same feeling today" (*The Washington Post,* Nov 23, 1999; p.A24).

They never learn, do they? Like Africans would say, governance is like playing musical chairs with rats, cockroaches, hyenas, and bandits: "We struggle hard to remove one cockroach from power and the next rat comes to do the same thing." Liberians thought Charles Taylor would be better than Samuel Doe; Zambians thought Chiluba would be better than Kaunda; Malawians thought Muluzi would be better than Banda and the new president, Bingu wa Mutharika, elected in May 2004, would be better than Muluzi. But barely two months after President wa Mutharika was elected, he ordered parliament to move into a bombed-out sports complex so that he can use as his residence the new $100 million parliament building, which has 300 rooms, its own supermarket, and school. "The president needs enough room," his chief of staff said (*The New York Times,* July 22, 2004; p.A6).

The Coconut Cure

President Joaquim Chissano of Mozambique has a cure for what ails African leaders. He vouched for transcendental meditation. In a BBC World Service program *(Outlook)* on December 1, 2001, he remarked that he was introduced to that by former Zambian head of state Kenneth Kaunda in 1992 and had since made it his daily routine. He at one point ordered his military officers to practice it—an order he rescinded in 2000. "If there was collective meditation, perhaps there might be peace in Africa," President Chissano remarked. There is, however, a better *indigenous* African cure.

In Dar-es-Salaam, Tanzania, there is a place called "the magic corner," where all and sundry, including politicians, come to be relieved or cured of their problems. "Even those top leaders of the government come to that tree," said Shabuni Haruni, a private security guard. "Yes, during the election" (*The Washington Post,* Nov 12, 2001; p.A21).

Upon the payment of a small fee, a traditional healer would take a patient to a huge baobab tree, reputed to be the abode of ancestral spirits. Patients remove their shoes, kneel in front of the tree with their eyes closed. At one session described by *The Washington Post* correspondent, Karl Vick,

> Rykia Selengia, a traditional healer, passed a coconut around and around the head of her kneeling client. The coconut went around the man's left arm, then the right, then each leg. When she handed the coconut to the client, Mussa Norris, he hurled it onto a stone. It shattered, releasing his problems to the winds. (*The Washington Post,* Nov 12, 2001; p.A21)

At least the Atingas have their cure for mental dysfunction. And Africa's elites? Maybe this "coconut cure" should be prescribed for Africa's leaders and elites. Recall what Mercy Muigai, an unemployed Kenyan woman, said when the presidents of Algeria, Nigeria, Senegal, and South Africa traveled to Kananaski, Alberta (Canada) on June 26, 2002, to present NEPAD to the G–8 Summit for funding by the rich nations:

> All these people [African leaders and elites] do is talk, talk, talk. Then if they do get any money from the *wazungu* [white men], they just steal it for themselves. And what about us? We have no food. We have no schools. We have no future. We are just left to die. (*The Washington Times,* June 28, 2002; p.A17)

Now she wields the *real African cutlass,* unchained. Africans have no future because their leaders don't use their heads and the Western donors who give them money don't use theirs, either.

NOTES

CHAPTER 1

1. The Purchasing Power Parity (PPP) is used to facilitate international comparison of economic data since different countries use different currencies and exchange rates, and experience different levels of inflation. To compare economic statistics across countries, the data must first be converted into a common currency, say of $1 U.S. dollars, using an exchange rate. The next step is to take account of price differences (different levels of inflation) between countries. Thus, a PPP has the same purchasing power in Country A as it would have in the United States.
2. GDP measures domestic economic activity and includes such activity as oil production by foreign oil companies. But since foreigners producing oil in the Niger Delta are not Nigerians, their incomes are not included in Nigeria's national income accounts. Thus, GNP per capita figures are generally lower than GDP figures. They are also lower because Nigerians spend more abroad than foreigners spend in Nigeria.
3. Africa's population was estimated to be 770 million in 2001.
4. Recognizing that income per capita may be too restrictive, the United Nations employs a *Human Development Index*, which "combines measures of life expectancy, school enrolment, literacy and income to allow a broader view of a country's development than income alone, which is too often equated with well-being" (UNDP, *World Development Report, 2002;* p.34).
5. A family temporarily leaving the village may place their land in the custody of the chief to be reclaimed upon return. The chief may allocate such land to strangers or newcomers to the village upon the presentation of a token gift such as a bottle of schnapps (gin). Such newcomers or individuals can use the land as they see fit, provided it is not abused.
6. "UNICEF official warns African leaders to address AIDS" by Al Ebokem Fomenky, Panafrican News Agency, May 30, 2001.
7. For a comprehensive discussion of these institutions, see Ayittey (1991).
8. For a full report of the conference, see *www.para55.org/caretreat/ trad_med_mine.asp.*

CHAPTER 2

1. Each of the three broad category areas has sub-categories that must be satisfied for a country to be deemed eligible. For example, "Ruling Justly" specifies the following 6 benchmarks or indicators: civil liberties; political rights; voice and accountability; government effectiveness; rule of law; and control of corruption. "Encouraging Economic Freedom" also has 6 benchmarks and "Investing in People" has 4, bringing the overall total to 16 (www.mca.gov/Documents/methodology_report.pdf).

CHAPTER 3

1. In the words of the Babangida, one party was "a little to the left and the other a little to the right" (*West Africa*, June 21, 1992; p.232). But Nigerians promptly dismissed this "Babangida boogie" as "a little to the north and a little to the south." The two parties were dubbed the Northern Republican Convention and the Southern Democratic Party.

CHAPTER 4

1. This syllogistic error, as was earlier pointed out, risks being repeated in South Africa. There is an ocean of difference between apartheid and capitalism. In fact, the system of apartheid and its horrendous array of controls is not that much different from a Marxist or socialist system.
2. Survey results are published at the web site: www.freedomhouse.org.
3. It is important to distinguish between "modern" and "traditional" Africa. Traditional Africa is the home of the masses or peasants while the modern Africa has been the domain of the elites. Most of Africa's crises originate from the modern sector on account of elite misrule, mismanagement, and corruption.
4. For more on this discussion, see Ayittey (1991), chapters 7 and 8.
5. That statement, incidentally, applies with equal force not only to the Soviet economy but to all economic systems that use money.
6. The Japanese call their "parliament" *Diet* and the Israelis call theirs *Knesset*. What's the difference?
7. It should be pointed out, however, that a few "colonial chiefs," such as Felix Houphouet-Boigny, managed to serve well in that precarious position and earned the respect of both their people and the colonial administrators. At the age of five he became a chief himself. His uncle, Kourassi N'Go, was murdered by a fanatic named Allangba, who had never forgiven the Houphouet-Boigny family for having helped the French to extend their rule to this district in 1909. In 1932, Houphet-Boigny began his campaign to assist the Abengourou tribe, whose cocoa harvests were being bought at unjustly low price. In 1944, he founded the Syndicat Agricole Africain of the Ivory Coast. With this syndicate, the first of its kind in Africa, he prevented 20,000 small planters from being drafted for forced labor.
8. One example was the case of the Sengalese Blaise Diagne. In 1914, he was elected by the four communes of Senegal to represent them and defend their rights in the French Parliament. But he soon began an active campaign to recruit Africans throughout French West Africa for the French war effort. And worse, he vigorously defended the colonial policy of forced labor. Needless to say, he lost his people's support and in 1928 "won" the elections only with the help of brazen French rigging and falsification of election results.
9. Things however changed dramatically in the run-up to the June 1999 elections. Suddenly politicians of all stripes discovered the value of the traditional chiefs. In March 1999, the ANC, just in time before the election, decided the chiefs were entitled to hefty raises, pensions, and medical benefits. They would all be paid $1,000 a month, a very good salary by South African standards and twice as much as what they were getting before. To placate his traditional culture, President Nelson Mandela remarried Graca Machel in a traditional ceremony in his own Eastern Capte village, Qunu. Tony Leon, head of South Africa's liberal Democratic Party, took his campaign to Tzaneen, to pay his respects to Chief Muhlava. "South Africa," said Leon, "needed to carve a niche for traditional leaders where they could continue to be the voice of the people" (*The New York Times,* April 27, 1999; p.3).

CHAPTER 5

1. There was a political motive for paying peasant farmers low prices. Most African governments derived their political support from urban elites: workers, students, etc. African governments pursued a "cheap food" policy to ensure continued political support from this constituency. But this policy was economically stupid. As we have had the occasion to remark, price controls do not make food "cheap." Instead, they make food *more* expensive by creating shortages. This is true of *any* commodity whose price is controlled.
2. A more appropriate measure to use would be total production, but since most African economies are agricultural, I have used the per capita food production index.

3. Nigeria has been ruled by the military for 27 years out of its 35 years of sovereign existence.
4. Other questionable expenditure items included $2.92 million for a documentary film on Nigeria, $18.30 million for the purchase of TV/video equipment for the presidency, $23.98 million for Staff Welfare, Dodan Barracks, Aso Rock (the capital city), and a $500,000 gift to Ghana.
5. The currency over-issue itself was fraught with graft and venality. As an article in *West Africa* (Dec 14, 1981; p.3014) observed: "Top officials of the PNP Administration are alleged to have received £2.7 million commission on a 7 billion *cedi* currency printing contract awarded to British firms." In this environment inflation soared. By December 31, 1981, inflation was running at 116 percent (*Graphic*, Dec 10, 1982; p.1).
6. On July 10, 1954, President Dwight D. Eisenhower signed the Agricultural Trade Development Assistance Act, or Public Law 480, into law. The purpose of the legislation, the President said, was to "lay the basis for a permanent expansion of our exports of agricultural products with lasting benefits to ourselves and peoples of other lands." The U.S. has sent more than 106 million metric tons overseas over the past 50 years under Title II, the largest part of PL 480, and have kept billions of people from hunger, malnutrition, and starvation while creating thousands of jobs in the United States and abroad (Posted at: www.usaid.gov/our_work/humanitarian_assistance/ffp/50th/history/html).

CHAPTER 6

1. For a fuller discussion of these functions, see Ayittey 1991, chapter 8.
2. The Special Drawing Right (SDR) was created by the IMF in 1969 as an international reserve asset to supplement the existing reserves of member countries. Under the Bretton Woods fixed exchange rate system, the international supply of two key reserve assets—gold and the U.S. dollar—proved inadequate for supporting the expansion of world trade and financial development that was taking place. Therefore, the international community decided to create a new international reserve asset under the auspices of the IMF. However, only a few years later, the Bretton Woods system collapsed and the major currencies shifted to a floating exchange rate regime, lessening the need for SDRs.
   Today, the SDR has only limited use as a reserve asset, and its main function is to serve as the unit of account of the IMF and some other international organizations. The SDR is neither a currency, nor a claim on the IMF. Rather, it is a potential claim on the freely usable currencies of IMF members. The value of the SDR was initially defined as equivalent to 0.888671 grams of fine gold—which, at the time, was also equivalent to one U.S. dollar. After the collapse of the Bretton Woods system in 1973, however, the SDR was redefined as a basket of currencies, today consisting of the euro, Japanese yen, pound sterling, and U.S. dollar. It is calculated as the sum of specific amounts of the four currencies valued in U.S. dollars, on the basis of exchange rates quoted at noon each day in the London market. (Culled from the IMF website: www.imf.org/external/np/exr/facts/sdr.htm)

CHAPTER 7

1. FAO, *Women and Developing Agriculture*, Women in Agriculture Series, No.4 (1985), chapter 7.
2. *Finance and Development*, 26: 2 (June 1986), p.6. The terms of trade is the ratio of a country's export prices to import prices; it measures the purchasing power of its exports in terms of the imports they can buy.
3. Would the Nigerian government recognize the folly of controlling the price of gasoline and shelling out billions in subsidies?
4. The annual rate of inflation may be determined by finding the percentage changes in the indices. For example, in the case of Ghana, the rate of inflation in 1994 can be computed as (514 - 406) / 406 = 0.2660. Therefore, the rate of inflation in Ghana in 1994 was 26.6 percent.

5. Banks that could not recall all their offshore guaranteed loans were debited with the amount, totaling 1.3 billion *naira*, depriving the banks of funds.

6. Those who take the local currency out of the country are generally illiterate traders and migrant workers who have no access to foreign exchange at the central banks and therefore use whatever currency that is acceptable to trade along the West African coast. Why should these innocent traders be punished for the actions of corrupt politicians?

7. Merchandise trade is referred to as "visible" because one can actually see the goods entering or leaving the country. Insurance for imported goods and tourist expenditures by nationals in a foreign country are payments to foreign countries for services that are not visible. Suppose a Nigerian tourist spends $100 in Italy and a Nigerian consumer imports Italian products, say shoes, worth $100 into the country. In each case, the country would have to pay Italy $100. The import of shoes is merchandise trade (visible) whereas the tourist expenditure is "invisible."

8. "Supply side" economists, however, postulate that a government can cut taxes, spur economic growth, and raise incomes. Increased incomes would bring in additional tax revenues that will wipe out the budget deficit. This argument has great merit in Africa where the average African is overtaxed by the ruling vampire elites.

9. It may be noted that Argentina faced precisely the same problem. Its government refused to live within its means. Its provincial governments borrowed recklessly abroad to finance wasteful expenditures. The ruling elites wanted to protect their perks. In 2001, Argentina defaulted on its $121 billion foreign debt and the economy collapsed. Like African governments, Argentinean elites, too, blamed the IMF and the World Bank.

10. This author made these recommendations in a testimony before the U.S. Congressional House Sub-Committee on Africa on April 13, 1999.

CHAPTER 9

1. This chapter draws extensively from my earlier books (1991 and 1998), which may be consulted for more in-depth discussions.

2. The *skokfel* (or *stockvels*), however, was more than a rural credit scheme. It was an institution of mutual aid that provided support in case a member suffered a bereavement or went to jail. The support was invariably extended to the member's family (Iliffe, 1987, 136).

3. Three observations regarding the *tontines* may be instructive. First, they are not unique to Africa alone. Similar schemes exist in other parts of the Third World. These are called *hui* in China and Vietnam; *keh* in Korea; *tandas* in Mexico; *pasanaku* in Bolivia; *san* in the Dominican Republic; "syndicate" in Belize; *gamaiyah* in Egypt; *hagbad* in Somalia; *xitique* in Mozambique; *arisan* in Indonesia; *paluwagan* in the Philippines; *chit* fund in India and Sri Lanka; *pia huey* in Thailand and *ko* in Japan. Second, if the same *susu* scheme of the African natives were organized in the United States, it would be called a credit union. A credit union is simply an association of individuals who pool their savings together to lend only to themselves (the members). Third, these indigenous saving clubs still exist; "In Cameroon, a survey of 360 businesses showed that more than half started with help from the *tontines* or *chilembe*" (*South*, Feb 1989; p.25).

Also, "A sample of 398 village households in rural Niger in 1986 indicated that informal credit accounted for 84 percent of total loans and was equal to 17 percent of agricultural income. Informal *tontines* (rotating savings and credit associations) predominate. Out of a sample of 56 *tontines* in 22 villages, some had only 4 members, other more than 40. The average member contribution ranged from 100 CFA francs (25 cents) to CFA 25,000 ($70). The total size of all 56 *tontines*, as measured by member contributions per meeting, was the equivalent of $72,000. This suggests a promising base for deposit mobilization in rural Niger" (World Bank, World Development Report, 1989; p.113).

4. It may sound strange to the reader that an obvious point is being belabored here, but many postcolonial African governments did not understand this facet of indigenous economic culture. As we saw in chapter 6, they imposed price controls on peasant farmers and traders and arrested violators, charging them with "economic sabotage."

CHAPTER 10

1. Progress, however, has been slow due to sheer volume of the cases and low level of participation. Borland (2003) suggested that, "the Rwandan government may not have done enough to address the pervasive fear among Rwandan people of all ethnic groups, both inside and outside, of an outbreak of renewed violence" (p. 11). This fear, coupled with that of being victimized for testifying before the *gacacas,* has measurably reduced the level of participation.
2. "FamineReturns to Ethiopia, A Land of Relative Plenty in Drought-Stricken Areas, Subsistence Farmers Hit Hard," *The Washington Post,* Feb 6, 2003; p.A32.
3. The Free Africa Foundation, which this author heads, has acquired land from a local chief in Ghana to build one such food market.
4. They are discussed in depth in chapter 9.
5. Tales of Africa's entrepreneurs, Monday, June 24, 2002; http://news.bbc.co.uk/1/hi/business/2017335.stm#. More success stories can be found in Fick (2002).
6. This author helped establish and mentored such an investment club among Ghanaians in the diaspora, with the name Ghana Cyber Group (GCG). Their web site is: www.ghanacybergroup.com.
7. "Linking Poor Farmers to a Global Economy," *The Washington Post,* Sept 12, 2003; p.A31.
8. An adobe housing project was developed by Emma Tackie and is described at this website: www.earthbuilding.com.

CHAPTER 11

1. My next book, *Africa's Leadership Crisis,* will discuss the idiosyncrasies of modern African leaders, their deranged priorities, their brazen looting, and how they steal their people's money.
2. In 1993, I had to wait for six hours at Yaounde airport for an Air Cameroon flight to Nairobi. The reason? President Paul Biya had commandeered the plane for a trip to Douala.

BIBLIOGRAPHY

GOVERNMENT PUBLICATIONS

U.S. Government

U.S. Senate Committee on Foreign Relations Report (1996). *Economic Development and U.S. Development Aid Programs.* Washington, D.C.: U.S. Senate Committee on Foreign Relations, September 19.

USAID—Agency for International Development, Center for Development Information and Evaluation. Agency Performance Review (1998). Washington, D.C. PN-ACB–775.

Central Intelligence Agency (CIA) (2000). "Senegal," in *The World Fact Book.* Washington, D. C.: CIA publication. Also available at http://www.odci.gov/cia/publications/factbook/sg.html.

African Governments

"African Socialism and its Application to Planning in Kenya." Sessional Paper No. 10. Nairobi: Republic of Kenya, 1965.

Agricultural Development Corporation Report, 1957. Accra: Government of Ghana.

Budgetary Statement. Annually. Accra: Government of Ghana.

Economic Survey of Ghana. Annually. Accra: Government of Ghana.

External Trade Statistics. Periodically. Kampala: Bank of Uganda.

Five-Year Development Plan, 1990–1995. Harare, Zimbabwe. Government Printer.

Government Policies Toward the State Gold Mining Corporation. Inter-departmental Committee, Accra, Ghana: Government Printer, 1971 (Amamoo Report).

Report of the Commission of Enquiry into the Affairs of the Cocoa Purchasing Company Limited. Accra, Ghana: Government Printer, 1956 (Jibowu Report).

Report of the Commission of Enquiry into Alleged Irregularities and Malpractices in Connection with the Issue of Import Licenses. Accra, Ghana: Government Printer, 1964 (Akainyah Report).

Report of the Commission of Enquiry into Irregularities and Malpractices in The Grant of Import Licenses. Ministry of Information, Accra, Ghana: Government Printer, 1967 (Ollennu Report).

Report of the Commission of Enquiry Into the Structure and Procedures of the Ghana Civil Service. Ministry of Information, Accra, Ghana: Government Printer, 1978 (The Okoh Commission Report).

Report of the Commission of Enquiry into Trade Malpractices in Ghana. Accra, Ghana: Government Printer, 1965 (Abrahams Report).

Report of the Committee of Enquiry into Trade Malpractices (By the Ashkar Group of Companies). Accra, Ghana: Government Printer, 1973 (Gaisie Report).

Report of the Committee to Enquire into the Kwame Nkrumah Properties. Ministry of Information, Accra, Ghana: Government Printer, 1966 (Apaloo Report).

Report of the Committee of Inquiry into the Civil Service Strike of November 1978. Accra: Government Printer, April, 1979.

Revised Budget Statement, 1981–1988. The Provisional National Development Council. Accra: Government of Ghana.

Second National Development Plan 1970–74. Lagos: Government of Nigeria.

Serious Fraud Office Report, 1999. Accra: Government of Ghana.

Seven-Year Development Plan 1963–1970. Accra: Government of Ghana.

Tanzania's Second Five-Year Plan for Economic and Social Development. Dar-es-Salaam: Republic of Tanzania, 1967.

Books and Articles

Abdel-Fatau Musah et al. (2000). *Mercenaries: An African Security Dilemma.* London: Pluto Press.

Abraham, Kinfe (2002). *Somalia Calling: The Crisis of Statehood and Quest for Peace.* Addis Ababa: Ethiopian International Institute for Peace and Development.

Achebe, Chinua (1985). *The Trouble with Nigeria.* Enugu, Nigeria: Fourth Dimension Publishing.

Adams, Patricia (1991). *Odious Debts.* Toronto, Canada: Earthscan.

Adda, J., and M. C. Smouts (1989). *La France face au Sud: le miroir brisé.* Paris: Editions Karthala with the collaboration of the CNRS.

Adedeji, Adebayo, and Timothy Shaw (1985). *Economic Crisis in Africa.* Boulder: Lynne Rienner Publishers.

Ades, Alberto, and Rafael di Tella (1994). "Competition and Corruption." Working paper, Oxford, UK: Oxford University Institute of Economics and Statistics.

Adjaye, Joseph K. (1984). *Diplomacy and Diplomats in Nineteenth Century Asante.* Lanham: University Press of America.

Adkins, Lee, Ronald Moomaw, and Andreas Savvides (2002). "Institutions, Freedom, and Technical Efficiency." *Southern Economic Journal* 69: 92–108.

Africa Review 1988. Annual Series. Ed. Suzanne Cronje. Lincolnwood: National Textbook Company.

Aghevli, Bijan B., and Mohisin S. Khan (1978). "Government Deficits and the Inflationary Process of Developing Countries." *IMF Staff Papers:* September: 383.

Ahmad, Naseem (1970). *Deficit Financing, Inflation and Capital Formation: The Ghanaian Experience, 1960–65.* Munchen: Weltforum-Verlag GmbH.

Ainsworth, Leonard, and Mary D. Ainsworth (1962). "Acculturation in East Africa: Political Awareness and Attitude Towards Authority." *Journal of Social Psychology* 57.

Ake, Claude (1991a). "As Africa Democratises." *Africa Forum* 1, no. 2: 13–18.

———(1991b). "How Politics Underdevelops Africa." In *The Challenge of African Economic Recovery and Development,* ed. Adebayo Adedeji, Owodumi Teriba, and Patrick Bugembe. Portland, OR: Cass.

Allen, C., and G. Williams (1982). *Sociologies of "Developing Societies": Sub-Saharan Africa.* London: Macmillan Press.

Amin, S. (1971). "The Class Struggle in Africa." *Revolution* 1, no.9: 23–47.

———(1972). "Underdevelopment and Dependence in Black Africa—Origins and Contemporary Forms." *Journal of Modern African Studies* 10, no 4: 503–24.

———(1973). *Neocolonialism in West Africa.* London: Penguin.

Andreski, Stanislav (1969). *The African Predicament: A Study in the Pathology of Modernization.* New York: Atherton Press.

Ankomah, K. (1970). "Strengthening the public service for privatisation in Africa." Institute of Development Administration, *Journal of Sri Lanka* 7, no. 2, July-Dec., 132.

Apter, David (1965). *The Politics of Modernization.* Chicago: University of Chicago Press.

———(1972). *Ghana in Transition.* Princeton: Princeton University Press.

Arhin, Kwame (1985). *Traditional Rule in Ghana.* Accra, Ghana: Challenge Enterprises.

Aronson, Elliott, and David Mettee (1968). "Dishonest Behavior as a Function of Differential Levels of Induced Self-Esteem." *Journal of Personality and Social Psychology* 6, no. 4.

Austen, Ralph (1987). *African Economic History.* Portsmouth: Heinemann.

Ayittey, George B. N. (1981). "Effective Capacity to Save: An Alternative Approach to Development." Ph.D. diss. University of Manitoba, Canada.

———(1986a). "The Real Foreign Debt Problem." *The Wall Street Journal,* Apr 18.

———(1986b). "Kleptocrats Loot The Third World." *The Wall Street Journal,* Aug 15.

————(1986c). "Africa's Agricultural Disaster: Governments and Elites are to Blame." *Journal of Economic Growth*, 1, no. 3, third quarter.
————(1986d). "Famine in Africa: The Real Cause." *Journal of Economic Affairs*, 6, no. 2: 17.
————(1988). "African Peasants and the Market Economy." *Humane Studies Review* 5, no. 3 (Spring).
————(1991). *Indigenous African Institutions*. Dobbs Ferry, N.Y.: Transnational Publishers.
————(1992). *Africa Betrayed*. New York: St. Martin's Press.
————(1998) *Africa in Chaos*. New York: St. Martin's Press.
Balassa, B (1963). "The Problem of Growth in Less Developed Countries and Its Significance for OECD Policy." In *Special Report III: Trade Prospects for Developing Countries*. Paris: OECD.
Bandow, Doug (1986). "The First World's Misbegotten Economic Legacy to the Third World." *Journal of Economic Growth* 1, no. 4: 17.
Bandow, Doug and Ian Vasquez, eds. (1994). *Perpetuating Poverty: The World Bank, the IMF and the Developing World*. Washington, D.C.: Cato Institute.
Bankole, Timothy (1981). *Kwame Nkrumah: From Cradle to Grave*. London: Garvin Press.
Baran, P. A. (1952). "The Political Economy of Backwardness." *Manchester School of Economics* (January).
Barker, Jonathan S. (1971). "The Paradox of Development: Reflections on a Study of Local-Central Political Relations in Senegal." In *The State of the Nations; Constraints on Development in Independent Africa*, ed. M. F. Lofchie. Berkeley: University of California Press.
Barnes, Leonard (1971). *Africa in Eclipse*. New York: St. Martin's Press.
Bascom, William (1984). *The Yoruba Of Southwestern Nigeria*. Prospect Heights: Waveland Press, Inc.
Bates, Robert H. (1981). *Markets and States in Tropical Africa*. Berkeley: University of California Press.
————(1983). *Essays on the Political Economy of Rural Africa*. Berkeley: University of California Press.
Bator, F. M. (1958). "Anatomy of Market Failure." *Quarterly Journal of Economics* 4, no. 3: 159.
Bauer, Ludwig (1934). *Leopold the Unloved*. London: European Books, Ltd.
Bauer, Peter T. (1967). *West African Trade*. New York: Kelley.
————(1972). *Dissent on Development*. Cambridge, Mass.: Harvard University Press.
————(1984). *Reality and Rhetoric*. Cambridge, Mass.: Harvard University Press.
————(2000). *From Subsistence to Exchange*. Princeton: Princeton University Press.
Bayar, J-F. (1993). *The State in Africa: the Politics of the Belly*. London: Longman.
Bell, Morag (1987). *Contemporary Africa*. New York: John Wiley and Sons, Inc.
Bennell, Paul (1997a). "Foreign direct investment in Africa: Rhetoric and reality." *SAIS Review* (summer/fall): 127–139.
Berdal, Mats, and David M. Malone, eds. (2000). *Greed and Grievance: Economic Agendas in Civil Wars*. Boulder, Colo.: Lynne Rienner.
Berg, E. J. (1964). "Socialism and Economic Development in Africa." *Quarterly Journal of Economics* 4, no. 3: 549.
Bergner, Daniel (2003). *In the Land of Magic Soldiers: A Story of White and Black in West Africa*. New York: Farrar, Straus and Giroux.
Berman, B. (1984). "Structure and Process in the Bureaucratic States of Colonial Africa." *Development and Change* 15: 161–202.
Berthlemy, J. C., and F. Bourguignon (1996). *Growth and Crisis in Côte d'Ivoire*. Washington, D.C.: World Bank.
Bhagwati, Jagdish ed. (1974). *Illegal Transactions in International Trade*. New York: North-Holland.
Bhatia, R. J. (1973). "Import Programming in Ghana, 1966–69." *Finance and Development* (March).
Biddlecome, Peter (1994). *French Lessons In Africa: Travels With My Briefcase Through French Africa*. London: Abacus.
Biersteker, Thomas J. (1987). *Multinationals, the State, and Control of the Nigerian Economy*. Princeton: Princeton University Press.
Bing, Geoffrey (1968). *Reap the Whirlwind*. London: MacGibbon and Kee.

Birmingham, David (1981). *Central African to 1870*. London: Cambridge University Press.
Birmingham, Walter, I. Neustadt, and E. N. Omaboe (1966). *A Study of Contemporary Ghana*. Vol. 1. Evanston: Northwestern University Press.
Boahen, A. A. (1986). *Topics in West African History*. New York: Longman.
Boahen, A. A. and J. B. Webster (1970). *History of West Africa*. New York: Praeger.
Boamah-Wiafe, Daniel (1993). *Africa: The Land, People, and Cultural Institutions*. Omaha: Wisdom Publications.
Bohannan, Paul (1964). *Africa and Africans*. New York: The Natural History Press.
Bohannan, Paul and George Dalton, eds. (1962). *Markets in Africa*. Evanston: Northwestern University Press.
Bohannan, Paul and Laura Bohannan (1968). *Tiv Economy*. London: Longman.
Boone, Peter (1995). "Politics and the Effectiveness of Foreign Aid." NBER Working paper 5308. October.
Bouman, F. J. A. (1983). "Indigenous Savings and Credit Societies in Developing World." In Von Pische, J. D., Dale W. Adams, and Donald Gordon (1983). *Rural Financial Markets in Developing Countries*. Baltimore: John Hopkins University Press.
Bovard, James (1986). "The Continuing Failure of Foreign Aid." Cato Institute Policy Analysis, no. 65, January 31.
Brehm, J. and A. R. Cohen (1962). *Explorations in Cognitive Dissonance*. New York: Wiley.
Brown, W. A., and R. Opie (1953). *American Foreign Assistance*. Washington, D.C.: Brookings Institution.
Brunner, K., ed. (1969). *Targets and Indicators of Monetary Policy*. San Francisco: Chandler.
Brunner, K., and Alan Meltzer (1967). "The Meaning of Monetary Indicators." In *Monetary Process and Policy: A Symposium*, ed. George Horwich. Homewood, Ill.: Richard Irwin Inc.
Bruno, M. (1967). "The Optimal Selection of Export-Promoting and Import-Substitution Projects." In *Planning the External Sector: Techniques Problems and Policies*. New York: United Nations.
Bruton, Henry J. (1969). "The Two-Gap Approach to Aid and Development: A Comment." *American Economic Review* (June).
Bundy, Colin (1988). *The Rise and Fall of the South African Peasant*. Cape Town: David Philip.
Burawoy, M. (1976). "Consciousness and Contradictions: A Study of Student Protests in Zambia." *British Journal of Sociology* 78.
Burnside, Craig, and David Dollar (1997). "Aid, Policies and Growth." World Bank Working Papers, No. 1777.
Busia, Kofi Abrefa (1967). *Africa in Search of Democracy*. New York: Praeger.
Cadenat, P. (1983). *La France et le Tiers Monde: vingts ans de coopération bilaterale*. Paris: La Documentation Française.
Caincross, A. K. (1955). "The Place of Capital in Economic Progress." In *Economic Progress, Papers and Proceedings in a Round Table Conference*, ed. L. H. Dupriez. Louvain: International Economic Association.
Caldwell, Don (1989). *South Africa: The New Revolution*. Saxonwold: Free Market Foundation of Southern Africa.
Cardoso, F. H., and E. Faletto (1979). "Dependency and Development in Latin America." Available at www.rrojasdatabank.org.
Carew, G. M. (1993). "Development Theory and the Promise of Democracy: the Future of Postcolonial African States." In "Notes on the Centrality of the African State," by R. Rojas. Available at http://www.rrojasdatabank.org.
Carlston, Kenneth S. (1968). *Social Theory and African Tribal Organization*. Urbana: University of Illinois.
Casely Hayford, J. E. (1897). "Gold Coast Native Institutions." In *Ideologies of Liberation in Black Africa, 1856–1970*, edited by J. Ayo Langley (1979). London: Rex Collins.
Chabal, K. (1984). "People's War, State Formation and Revolution in Africa: A Comparative Analysis of Mozambique, Guinea-Bissau and Angola." In *State and Class in Africa*, ed. N. Kasfir. London: Frank Cass, pp.104–125.
Chaliand, G. (1969). *Armed Struggle in Africa*. New York: Monthly Review Press.

Chazan, Naomi, Robert Mortimer, John Ravenhill, and Donald Rothchild (1992). *Politics and Society in Contemporary Africa.* Boulder, Colo.: Lynne Riener Publishers.

Chenery, H. B. (1960). "Patterns of Industrial Growth." *American Economic Review* (September).

Chenery, H. B., and M. Bruno (1962). "Development Alternatives in an Open Economy." *Economic Journal* 4. no. 2.

Chenery, H. B., and A. M. Strout (1966). "Foreign Assistance and Economic Development." *American Economic 'Review* (September): 679–733.

Christensen, James Boyd (1958). "The Role of Proverbs in Fante Culture." *Africa* 28, no. 3 (July): 232–43.

Clapham, Christopher (1996). *Africa and the International System: The Politics of State Survival.* Cambridge, Mass.: Cambridge University Press.

———, ed. (1998). *African Guerrilla.* Oxford: James Currey.

Cleary, Sean (1999). "Angola—A Case Study of Private Military Involvement." In *Peace, Profit or Plunder? The Privatisation of Security in War-Torn African Societies,* ed. Jakkie Cilliers and Peggy Mason (1999). New York: Oxford University Press, pp. 141–74.

Cilliers, Jakkie, and Peggy Mason (1999). *Peace, Profit or Plunder? The Privatisation of Security in War-Torn African Societies.* New York: Oxford University Press.

Cilliers, Jakkie and Ian Douglas (1999). "The Military as Business—Military Professional Resources, Incorporated." In *Peace, Profit or Plunder? The Privatisation of Security in War-Torn African Societies,* ed. Jakkie Cillers and Peggy Mason. New York: Oxford University Press; pp.111–122.

Cohen, Ronald (1970). "The Kingship in Bornu." In Crowder and Ikime (1970). *West African Chiefs.* New York: Africana.

Collier, Paul (1999). "On the Economic Consequences of Civil War." In *Oxford Economic Papers* 51: 168–83.

———. (2000). "Doing Well Out of War: An Economic Perspective." In *Greed and Grievance: Economic Agendas in Civil Wars,* ed. Mats Berdal and David M. Malone (2000). Boulder, Colo.: Lynne Rienner, pp. 91–112.

Collier, Paul, and Anke Hoeffler (2000). "Greed and Grievance in Civil War." presented at conference on the economics of political violence, Princeton University, March 18–19, 2000, which was the updated version of their article "On the Economic Causes of Civil War" in *Oxford Economic Papers* 50 (1998): 563–73.

Colson, Elizabeth (1953). "Social Control and Vengeance in Plateau Tonga Society." *Africa* 23, no. 3: 199–211.

Colson, Elizabeth, and M. Gluckman, eds. (1951). *Seven Tribes of British Central Africa.* London: Oxford University Press.

Compagnon, Daniel (1998). "Somali Armed Movements." In *African Guerrillas,* ed. Christopher Clapham. Oxford: James Currey, pp. 73–90.

Coquery-Vidrovitch, C. (1977). "The Political Economy of the African Peasantry and Modes of Production." In *African Social Studies: A Radical Reader,* ed. Peter Gutkind and Peter Waterman (1977). New York: Monthly Review Press.

Crowder, Michael, and Ikime Obaro, eds. (1970). *West African Chiefs.* New York: Africana.

Cruise O'Brien, Connor (1981). "Factors of Dependence: Senegal and Kenya." In W. H. Morris-Jones and G. Fischer (1981). *Decolonisation and After: the British and French Experience.* London: Frank Cass.

Cumper, G. E. (1963). "Lewis' Two-Sector Model of Development and the Theory of Wages." *Social and Economic Studies* (March).

Curtin, Philip, Steven Feierman, Leonard Thompson, and Jan Vansina (1988). *African History.* New York: Longman.

Daaku, Kwame Y. (1971). "Trade and Trading Patterns of the Akan in 17th and 18th Centuries." In Meillassoux (1971). *The Development of Indigenous Trade and Markets in West Africa.* Oxford: Oxford University Press.

Damachi, V. G. (1976). *Leadership Ideology in Africa: Attitudes Towards Socio-Economic Development.* New York: Praeger.

Davidson, Basil (1969). *The African Genius: An Introduction to African Cultural and Social History.* Boston: Atlantic Monthly Press.

———. (1987). *The Lost Cities of Africa.* Boston: Little, Brown and Company.

———. (1981). *The People's Cause: A History of Guerrillas in Africa.* Harlow: Longman.

Decalo, Samuel (1976). *Coups and Army Rule in Africa. Studies in Military Style.* New Haven: Yale University Press.

DeGraft-Johnson, J. C. (1986). *African Glory.* Baltimore: Black Classic Press.

DeGraft-Johnson, K. E. (1964). "The Evolution of Elites in Ghana." In *The New Elites of Tropical Africa,* ed. P. C. Lloyd. London: Oxford University Press.

Destanne de Bernis, G. (1981). "Some Aspects of the Economic Relationship between France and Its Ex-colonies." In W. H. Morris and G. Fischer (1981). *Decolonization and After: the British and French Experience.* London: Frank Cass.

DeYoung, Karen (1999). "World Donors Ignore Signs of Promise in Sliver of Africa." *The Washington Post,* 26 November, 1999; p.A1.

Dickson, Kwamina B. (1969). *A Historical Geography of Ghana.* Cambridge: Cambridge University Press.

Diop, Cheikh Anta (1987). *Pre-colonial Black Africa.* Westport: Lawrence Hill and Company.

Djoleto, Amu (1988). *Hurricane of Dust.* London: Longman.

Dollar, David, and Lant Pritchett (1998). *Assessing Aid.* New York: Oxford University Press.

Doob, L. W. (1960). *On Becoming More Civilized.* New Haven: Yale University Press.

Dostert, Pierre (1987). *Africa, 1986.* Washington, D.C.: Stryker-Post Publications.

Douglas, Ian (1999). "Fighting for Diamonds—Private Military Companies in Sierra Leone." In *Peace, Profit or Plunder? The Privatisation of Security in War-Torn African Societies,* ed. Jakkie Cilliers and Peggy Mason (1999). New York: Oxford University Press; pp. 175–200.

Douglas, Mary (1962). "Lele Economy Compared with the Bushong: A Study in Economic Backwardness." In Bohannan and Dalton, eds. (1962). *Markets in Africa.* Evanston: Northwestern University Press.

Duffiled, Mark (2000). "Globalisation, Transborder Trade, and War Economies." In *Greed and Grievance: Economic Agendas in Civil Wars,* ed. Mats Berdal and David M. Malone (2000). Boulder, Colo.: Lynne Rienner, pp. 69–90.

Dumont, Rene (1966). *False Start in Africa.* London: Deutsch Limited.

Dupire, Marguerite (1962). "Trade and Markets in the Economy of the Nomadic Fulani of Niger (Bororo)." In Bohannan and Dalton, eds. (1962). *Markets in Africa.* Evanston: Northwestern University Press.

Dutton, Dean S. (1971). "A Model of Self-Generating Inflation: The Argentine Case." *Journal of Money Credit and Banking* 3 (May): 245–62.

Easton, Steven, and Michael Walker (1997). "Income, Growth and Economic Freedom." In *American Economic Review* 87, no. 2: 328–32.

Eberstadt, Nicholas (1988). *Foreign Aid and American Purpose.* Washington, D.C.: American Enterprise Institute.

———. (2000). "Pursuit of Prosperity South of the Sahara." *Washington Times,* August 27, 2000; p.B4.

Eckert, G. (1987). *Privatization of public enterprises: The case of Kenya.* Washington, D.C.: AAPAM publication.

Ellis, George W. (1914). *Negro Culture in West Africa.* New York: The Neale Publishing Company.

Ellis, Stephan (1998). "Liberia's Warlord Insurgency." In *African Guerrillas,* ed. Christopher Clapham. Oxford: James Currey, pp.155–171.

Etukudo, A. (2000). "Issues in Privatization and Restructuring in Sub-Saharan Africa." ILO Interdepartmental Action Program on Privatization, Restructuring and Economic Democracy Working Paper IPPRED-5. Available at http://www.ilo.org/public/english/employment/ent/papers/ippred5.htm.

Evans-Pritchard, E. E. (1963). "The Zande State." *The Journal of the Royal Anthropological Institute* 93, part 1: 134–54.

Fallers, L. (1963). *Equality, Modernity and Democracy in New States: The Quest for Modernity in Asia and Africa*. New York: Free Press of Glencoe.

———. (1967). *Bantu Bureaucracy: A Century of Political Evolution Among the Basoga of Uganda*. Chicago: Chicago University Press.

Falola, Toyin (1985). "Nigeria's Indigenous Economy." In *Nigerian History and Culture*, ed. Olaniyan. England: Longman Group Limited.

Fama, E., and J. MacBeth (1973). "Risk, Return and Equilibrium." *Journal of Political Economy* 81: 607–36.

Feierman, Steven (1974). *The Shaamba Kingdom*. Madison: University of Wisconsin Press.

Ferkiss, Victor C. (1966). *Africa's Search for Identity*. New York: George Braziller.

Fick, David S. (2002). *Entrepreneurship in Africa: A Study of Successes*. Westport, Conn.: Quorum Books.

Field, M. J. (1940). *Social Organization of the Ga People*. Accra, Ghana: Government of the Gold Coast Printing Press.

Field, Shannon (2000). "The Civil War in Sudan: The Role of the Oil Industry." Institute for Global Dialogue (IGD) Occasional Paper No.23. Braamfontein: IGD.

Fieldhouse, D. K. (1986). *Black Africa 1945–80*. London: Allen and Unwin.

Findlay, R. (1971). "The Foreign Exchange Gap and Growth in Developing Countries." In *Trade, Balance of Payments and Growth*, ed. J. Bhagwati et al. New York: North-Holland.

Fitch, Bob, and Mary Oppenheimer (1966). *Ghana: End of an Illusion*. New York: Monthly Review Press.

Forde, Daryll, and G. I. Jones (1950). *The Igbo and Ibibio-Speaking Peoples of South-Eastern Nigeria*. London: International African Institute.

Frank, A. G. (1969). *Capitalism and Under-Development in Latin America*. New York: Monthly Review Press.

Frenkel, Jacob A. (1977). "The Forward Exchange Rate, Expectations and the Demand for Money: The German Hyperinflation." *American Economic Review* 67: 653–70.

Friedman, Milton (1957). *A Theory of the Consumption Function*. Princeton: Princeton University Press.

Galli, Rosemary E., and Jocelyn Jones (1987). *Guinea-Bissau: Politics, Economics and Society*. London: Frances Pinter (Publishers) Limited.

Garley, John G. (1969). "The Radcliffe Report and Evidence." In *Monetary Theory and Policy*, ed. Richard Thorn. New York: Random House.

Garlick, Peter (1971). *African Traders and Economic Development*. Oxford: Clarendon.

Gibbs, James L., Jr., ed. (1965). *Peoples of Africa*. New York: Holt, Rinehart and Winston, Inc.

Gifford, P., and W. M. Roger Louis (1982). *The Transfer of Power in Africa: Decolonization 1940–1960*. New Haven and London: Yale University Press.

———. (1988). *Decolonization and African Independence*. New Haven and London: Yale University Press.

Glazier, Jack (1985). *Land and the Uses of Tradition among the Mbeere of Kenya*. Lanham: University Press of America.

Gluckman, Max (1959). *Custom and Conflict in Africa*. Oxford: Basil Blackwell.

———. (1965). *Politics, Law and Ritual in Tribal Society*. Oxford: Basil Blackwell.

Goldman, Maurice (1992). "End of Socialism?" *The Backgrounder*, a Heritage Foundation publication, no. 230.

Gourevitch, Philip (1998). *Stories from Rwanda*. New York: Farrar, Straus and Giroux.

Gray, Robert F. (1962). "Economic Exchange in a Sonjo Village." In Bohannan and Dalton, eds. (1962). *Markets in Africa*. Evanston: Northwestern University Press.

Grayson, Leslie E. (1973). "The Role of Suppliers' Credit in the Industrialization of Ghana." *Economic Development and Cultural Change* (April).

Grundy, K. (1971). *Guerrilla Struggle in Africa: An Analysis and Preview*. New York: Grossman.

Guest, Robert (2004). *The Shackled Continent*. London: MacMillan.

Gulliver, P. H. (1962). "The Evolution of Arusha Trade." In Bohannan and Dalton, eds. (1962). *Markets in Africa*. Evanston: Northwestern University Press.

Gutkind, Peter, and Peter Waterman (1977). *African Social Studies: A Radical Reader.* New York: Monthly Review Press.

Gutteridge, W. F. (1975). *Military Regimes in Africa.* London: Methuen and Co. Ltd.

Guy, Jeff. (1979). *The Destruction of the Zulu Kingdom.* London: Longman Group Limited.

Gwartney, James, Robert Lawson, and Randall Holcombe (1999). "Economic Freedom and the Environment for Economic Growth." *Journal of Institutional and Theoretical Economics* 155, no. 4: 1–21.

Haber, Stephen, Douglass North, and C. Weingast (2003). "If Economists Are So Smart, Why Is Africa Poor?" In *The Wall Street Journal,* July 30, 2003; p.A12.

Haessel, Walter, and A. G. Bloomqvist (1972). "The Price Elasticity of Demand for Ghana's Cocoa." *Economic Bulletin of Ghana* 2, no. 2.

Hagen, E. E. (1962). *On the Theory of Social Change.* Homewood, Ill.: Dorsey Press.

Hamer, John H. (1970). "Sidamo Generational Class Cycles: A Political Gerontocracy." *Africa* 40, no. 1 (January): 50–70.

Harbeson, John, Donald W. Rothchild, and Naomi Chazan (1994). *Civil Society and the State in Africa.* Boulder, Colo.: Lynne Rienner Publishers.

Harbison, F. H. (1962). "Human Resource Development, Planning in Modernizing Economies." *International Labor Review* (May).

Harden, Blaine (2000). "The U.S. Keeps Looking For a Few Good Men in Africa." *The New York Times,* August 27, 2000, section 4; p.1.

Harris, Joseph. E. (1987). *Africans and Their History.* New York: Penguin.

Hawkins, E. K. (1958). "The Growth of a Money Economy in Nigeria and Ghana." *Oxford Economic Papers* 10, no. 3: 354.

Heidenheimer, Arnold J., ed. (1970). *Political Corruption.* New York: Rinehart and Winston.

Helleiner, G. K. (1992). "The IMF, the World Bank and Africa's adjustment and external debt problems: An unofficial view." In *World Development* 20, no. 6 (1992): 787.

Herbst, Jeffrey (1993). *The Politics of Reform in Ghana.* Los Angeles, CA: University of California Press.

Herskovits, M. J., and M. Harwitz, eds. (1964). *Economic Transition in Africa.* Evanston: Northwestern University Press.

Higgins, Benjamin. (1959). *Economic Development.* London: Constable.

Hill, Polly (1958). "The Pledging of Cocoa Farms." Unpublished research paper, Achimota, Ghana.

———. (1970). *Rural Capitalism in West Africa.* Cambridge: Cambridge University Press.

———. (1972). *Rural Hausa: A Village and a Setting.* Cambridge: Cambridge University Press.

———. (1977). *Population Prosperity and Poverty: Rural Kano 1900–1970.* Cambridge: Cambridge University Press.

———. (1986). *Development Economics on Trial.* Cambridge: Cambridge University Press.

Hirschman, Albert O. (1958). *The Strategy of Development.* New Haven: Yale University Press.

———. (1965). "Obstacles to Development. A Classification and a Quasi-Vanishing Act." *Economic Development and Cultural Change* (July): 385.

Hitchens, Christopher (1994). "Africa Without Pity." *Vanity Fair* (November): 43–52.

Hodder, B. W. (1962). "The Yoruba Rural Market." In Bohannan and Dalton, eds. (1962). *Markets in Africa.* Evanston: Northwestern University Press.

Hoffman, P. G. (1960). *One Hundred Countries, One and One Quarter Billion People.* Washington, D.C.: Brookings Institution.

Holmes, Kim R., Bryan T. Johnson, and Melanie Kirkpatrick (1997). *Index of Economic Freedom.* Washington, D.C.: The Heritage Foundation and Dow Jones and Company.

Hopkins, A. G. (1988) *An Economic History of West Africa.* London: Longman.

Howe, Herbert M. (1998). "Private Security Forces and African Stability: The Case of Executive Outcomes." *Journal of Modern African Studies* 36, no. 2: 307–31.

Howell, T.A. (1972). *Ghana and Nkrumah.* New York: Facts on File, Inc.

Hull, Richard. W. (1976). African *Cities and Towns Before The European Conquest.* New York: W.W. Norton and Company.

Ibrahim, Abdullah, and Patrick Muana (1998). "The Revolutionary United Front of Sierra Leone: A Revolt of the Lumpenproletariat." In *Africa and the International System: The Politics of State Survival,* ed. Christopher Clapham. Cambridge, Mass.: Harvard University Press; pp. 172–194.

Iliffe, John (1987). *The African Poor.* New York: Cambridge University Press.

Indra de Soysa (2000). "The Resource Curse: Are Civil Wars Driven by Rapacity or Paucity?" In *Greed and Grievance: Economic Agendas in Civil Wars,* ed. Mats Berdal and David M. Malone (2000). Boulder, Colo.: Lynne Rienner; pp. 113–136.

Isichei, Elizabeth (1977). *History of West Africa Since 1800.* New York: Africana Publishing Company.

Italiaander, Rolf (1961). *The New Leaders of Africa.* Englewood Cliffs, N.J.: Prentice-Hall, Inc.

International Monetary Fund (IMF) (1986). *World Debt Tables.* Washington, D.C.: IMF.

Johnson, Paul (1993). "Colonialism's Back—and Not a Moment Too Soon." *New York Times Magazine,* April 18.

Keen, David (2000). "Incentives and Disincentives for Violence." In *Greed and Grievance: Economic Agendas in Civil Wars,* ed. Mats Berdal and David M. Malone (2000). Boulder, Colo.: Lynne Rienner.

Kelly, G. M. (1959). "The Ghanaian Intelligentsia." Ph.D. diss., University of Chicago.

Kendall, Frances and Leon Louw (1986). *After Apartheid: The Solution.* San Francisco: Institute of Contemporary Studies.

Kendall, Frances, Leon Low, and John Gurley (1985). "Radical Analyses of Imperialism, The Third World, and the Transition to Socialism." *Journal of Economic Literature* 23, no. 3: 87.

Kenyatta, Jomo (1938). *Facing Mount Kenya.* London: Secker and Warburg.

Khareen, Pech (1999). "Executive Outcomes—A Corporate Conquest." In *Peace, Profit or Plunder? The Privatisation of Security in War-Torn African Societies,* ed. Jakkie Cilliers and Peggy Mason (1999). New York: Oxford University Press, pp. 81–110.

Killick, Tony (1976). "Development Planning, Free Markets and the Role of the State." *Oxford Economic Papers* 41, no. 4 (October): 161–84.

———. (1978). *Development Economics in Action: A Study of Economic Policies in Ghana.* London: Heinemann.

King, Coretta S. (1984). *The Words of Martin Luther King, Jr.* New York: Newmarket Press.

Klein, Martin A. (1968). *Islam and Imperialism: Sine-Saloum, 1847–1914.* Stanford: Stanford University Press.

Kluckhorn, Richard (1962). "The Konso Economy of Southern Ethiopia." In Bohannan and Dalton, eds. *Markets in Africa.* Evanston: Northwestern University Press.

Klitgaard, Robert (1998). *Controlling Corruption.* Berkeley: University of California Press.

Knack, Stephen, and Philip Keefer (1995). "Institutions and Economic Performance: Cross-Country Tests Using Alternative Institutional Measures." *Economics and Politics* 7, no. 3: 207–27.

Koyana, Digby Sqhelo (1980). *Customary Law in a Changing Society.* Cape Town: Juta and Co. Ltd.

Kotecha, Ken C., and Robert W. Adams (1981). *The Corruption of Power: African Politics.* Washington, D.C.: University Press of America.

Krauss, Melvyn B. (1983). *Development without Aid.* Lanham, Maryland: University Press of America.

Lamb, David (1985). *The Africans.* New York: Vintage Books.

Lamb, Guy (2000). "A Literature Review on the Current Relationship between War and Economic Agendas in Africa." Center for Conflict Resolution Cape Town, South Africa. Available at http://ccrweb.ccr.uct.ac.za/staff_papers/lamb_relationships.html.

Lancaster, Carol, and John Williamson, ed. (1986). *African Debt and Financing.* Washington, D.C.: Institute for International Economics.

Langley, J. Ayo, ed. (1979). *Ideologies of Liberation in Black Africa, 1856–1970.* London: Rex Collins.

Lappe, Frances, and Joseph Collins (1979). *Food First: Beyond the Myth of Scarcity.* New York: Ballantine Books.

Lappe, Frances, and David Kinley (1980). *Aid As Obstacle: Twenty Questions about Our Foreign Aid and the Hungry.* San Francisco: Institute For Food and Development Policy.

Laurie, Nathan (1997a). "Trust Me I'm a Mercenary: The Lethal Danger of Mercenaries in Africa." Seminar on the Privatization of Peacekeeping, Institute for Security Studies, February 20, 1997.

———. (1997b). "Lethal Weapons: Why Africa Needs Alternatives to Hired Guns." *Track Two* 6, no. 2 (August): 10.

———. (2000). "The Four Horsemen of the Apocalypse: The Structural Causes of Crisis and Violence in Africa." *Peace and Change* 25, no. 2: 190–192.

Lee, H. K. (1957). *Climate and Economic Development in the Tropics.* New York: Harper and Row.

Leibenstein, Harvey (1957). *Economic Backwardness and Economic Growth.* New York: Harper and Row.

Leith, Clark J. (1974). *Foreign Trade Regimes and Economic Development: Ghana.* New York: Columbia University Press.

———. (1977). "The Role of Supplementary External Finance in Macro-Economic Stablization: Ghana." Mimeo, Department of Economics, University of Western Ontario.

Lessard, Donald, and John Williamson, eds. (1987). *Capital Flight and Third World Debt.* Washington, D.C.: Institute for International Economics.

LeVine, R. A. (1962). "Wealth and Power in Gusiiland." In *Markets in Africa,* eds. Bohannan and Dalton. Evanston: Northwestern University Press.

———. (1966). *Dreams and Deeds; Achievement Motivation in Nigeria.* Chicago: Chicago University Press.

LeVine, Victor (1975). *Political Corruption: The Ghana Case.* Stanford: Hoover Institution Press.

Lewis, I. M. (1962). "Lineage Continuity and Modern Commerce in Northern Somaliland." In *Markets in Africa,* ed. Bohannan and Dalton. Evanston, Ill.: Northwestern University Press.

Lewis, W. A. (1954). "Economic Development with Unlimited Supplies of Labor." *Manchester School of Economics* (May).

———. (1962) *Economic Problems of Development in Restless Nations: A Study of World Tensions and Development.* London: Allen and Unwin.

Leymarie, P. (2000). "Séisme dans le pré carré." In *Le Monde Diplomatique* (February). Also available at http://www.monde-diplomatique.fr..

Libby, Ronald T. (1987*). The Politics of Economic Power in Southern Africa.* Princeton: Princeton University Press.

Lloyd, P. C., ed. (1964). *The New Elites of Tropical Africa.* London: Oxford University Press.

Lofchie, M. F., ed. (1971). *The State of the Nations: Constraints on Development in Independent Africa.* Berkeley: University of California Press.

Louw, Leon, and Frances Kendall (1987). *After Apartheid: The Solution.* Los Angeles: Institute for Contemporary Studies.

Luke, David Fashole (1995). "Building Indigenous Entrepreneurial Capacity: Trends and Issues." In *Development Management in Africa: Toward Dynamism, Empowerment and Entrepreneurship,* ed., Sadig Rasheed and David Fashole Luke. Boulder, Colo.: Westview Press.

Mabogunje, A. (1988). "Africa after the False Start." Paper presented to the Twenty-Sixth Congress of the International Geographical Union, Sydney, Australia.

Mandela, Winnie (1985). *Part of My Soul Went with Him.* New York: W.W. Norton and Company.

Manning, Patrick (1988). *Francophone Sub-Saharan Africa 1880–1985.* New York: Cambridge University Press.

Maren, Michael (1997). *The Road to Hell: The Ravaging Effects of Foreign Aid and International Charity.* New York: The Free Press.

Marris, Peter (1968). "The Social Barriers to African Enterpreneurship." *Journal of Development Studies* (October).

Martin, G. (1986). "The Franc Zone, Underdevelopment and Dependency in Francophone Africa." In *Third World Quarterly* (January).

Martin, Phyllis M., and Partrick O'Meara, eds. (1986). *Africa.* Bloomington: Indiana University Press.

Marx, Karl (1867). *Das Kapital: A Critique of Political Economy.* Chicago: Kerr.

Matthews, Ronald (1966). *The African Powder-Keg.* London: Bodley Head.

Mauro, Paolo (1995). "Corruption and Growth." *Quarterly Journal of Economics* 2, no. 441: 681–712.

———. (1997). "The Effects of Corruption on Growth, Investment, and Government Expenditure: A Cross-Country Analysis." In *Corruption and the Global Economy,* ed. Kimberly A. Elliott. Washington, D.C.: Institute for International Economics.

Mazrui, Ali A. (2001). "Who Killed Democracy in Africa? Clues of the Past, Concerns of the Future." Paper presented at the "Conference on Democracy, Sustainable Development and Poverty: Are They Compatible?" Development Policy Management Forum, United Nations Conference Center, Addis Ababa, December 4–6, 2001.

M'baye, S. (2000). "Sénégal: Les Chantiers du Changement." Available at http://www.monde-diplomatique.fr.

Mbembe, A. (1999). "Les Frontières Mouvantes du Continent Africain." Available at http://www.monde-diplomatique.fr/1999/11/ MBEMBE/12706.

Mbhele, Themba (1998). "What Does A Rural Destination Area Look Like? Institutions and Livelihoods in KwaDumisa." In *Development Southern Africa* 15, no 4 (Summer).

Mbiti, John S. (1970). *African Religions and Philosophies.* New York: Doubleday and Co.

McCall, Daniel F. (1962). "The Koforidua Market." In *Markets in Africa,* ed. by Bohannan and Dalton. Evanston, Ill.: Northwestern University Press.

———, ed. (1969). *Western African History.* New York: Praeger Publishers.

McKinnon, Ronald (1964). "Foreign Exchange Constraint in Economic Development and Efficient Aid Allocation." *Economic Journal.*

———. (1973). *Money and Capital in Economic Development.* Washington, D.C.: Brookings Institution.

Meier, Gerald, ed. (1976). *Leading Issues in Economic Development.* New York: Oxford University Press.

Meillassoux, Claude (1962). "Social and Economic Factors Affecting Markets in Guro Land." In *Markets in Africa,* ed. Bohannan and Dalton. Evanston: Northwestern University Press.

———, ed. (1971). *The Development of Indigenous Trade and Markets in West Africa.* Oxford: Oxford University Press.

Melady, Thomas Patrick (1963). *Profiles of African Leaders.* New York: The MacMillan Company.

Menkiti, Ifeanyi (1984). "Person and Community in African Traditional Thought." In *African Philosophy: An Intro.,* ed. Richard Wright (1984). Lanham: University Press of America.

Mensah Sarbah, John (1897). "Fanti Customary Laws." In *Ideologies of Liberation in Black Africa, 1856 - 1970,* ed. J. Ayo Langley (1979). London: Rex Collins.

Merton, R. (1957). *Social Theory and Social Structure.* Glencoe, Ill.: Free Press.

Messing, Simon D. (1962). "The Konso Economy of Southern Ethiopia." In *Markets in Africa,* ed. Bohannan and Dalton. Evanston: Northwestern University Press.

Millikan, R., and W. W. Rostow (1956). *A Proposal: Key to an Effective Foreign Policy.* New York: Harper.

Miracle, Marvin P. (1962). "African Markets and Trade in the Copperbelt." In *Markets in Africa,* ed. Bohannan and Dalton. Evanston, Ill.: Northwestern University Press.

———. (1971). "Capitalism, Capital Markets, and Competition in West African Trade." In *The Development of Indigenous Trade and Markets in West Africa,* ed. Claude Meillassoux (1971). Oxford: Oxford University Press.

Monga, Celestin (1996). *The Anthropology of Anger: Civil Society and Democracy in Africa.* Boulder, Colo.: Lynne Rienner Publishers.

Morris-Jones, W. H., and G. Fischer (1981). *Decolonization and After: the British and French Experience.* London: Frank Cass.

Mukandala, R. S. (1992). "The State and Public Enterprise." In *Politics and Administration in East Africa,* ed. Walter O. Oyugi. Nairobi: Konrad Adenauer Foundation, Nairobi, ch. 5.

Murphy, Kevin M., Andrei Shleifer, and Robert W. Vishny (1993). "Why is Rent-Seeking So Costly to Growth?" *American Economic Review* 83, no. 2: 409–414.

Mussa-Nda, Mgumbu (1988). "A Greater Role for Local Development Strategies." *Regional Development Dialogue* 9, no. 2: 1–11.

Myrdal, G. (1971). *Asian Drama.* New York: Pantheon Books.

Nafziger, E. Wayne. (1993). *The Debt Crisis In Africa.* Baltimore: John Hopkins University Press.

Nellis, J. R. (1994). "Public Enterprises in Sub-Saharan Africa." In *State-Owned Enterprises in Africa,* ed. B. Grosh and R. S. Mukandala. Boulder, Colo.: Lynne Rienner.

Newbury, Colin W. (1971). "Prices and Profitability in Early Nineteenth-Century West African Trade." In *Development of Indigenous Trade and Markets in West Africa,* ed. Claude Meillassoux (1971). Oxford: Oxford University Press.

Newlyn, W. T., and D. C. Rowan (1954). *Money and Banking in British Colonial Africa.* Oxford: Claredon Press.

Nicol, Davidson, ed. (1969). *Black Nationalism in Africa, 1867.* London: Africana Publishing Corporation.

Nkrumah, Kwame (1957). *Ghana: An Autobiography.* London: Nelson.

———. (1962). *Towards Colonial Freedom.* London: Heinemann.

———. (1963). *Africa Must Unite.* New York: International Publishers.

———. (1968). *Handbook on Revolutionary Warfare.* London: Panaf Publishers.

———. (1969). *Dark Days in Ghana.* London: Panaf Publishers.

———. (1973). *Revolutionary Path.* New York: International Publishers.

Northrup, David (1978). *Trade without Rulers: Pre-Colonial Economic Development in South-Eastern Nigeria.* Oxford: The Clarendon Press.

Nurkse, R. (1953). *Problems of Capital Formation in Under-Developed Countries.* New York: Oxford University Press.

Nyang'oro, Julius E., and Timothy Shaw, eds. (1992*). Beyond Structural Adjustment in Africa: The Political Economic of Sustainable and Democratic Development.* New York: Praeger.

Nye, Joseph S. (1967). "Corruption and Political Development: A Cost-Benefit Analysis." *American Political Science Review* 61, no. 2 (June): 417–27.

Nyerere, Julius K. (1962). *Ujamaa: The Basis of African Socialism.* Dar-es-Salaam: Government Printer.

———. (1966). *Freedom and Unity: A Selection from Writings and Speeches, 1965–67.* Dar-es-Salaam: Oxford University Press.

Obadina, Tunde (1999). "Africa's Crisis of Governance." *African Business Review.*

Obichere, Boniface I. (1974). "Change and Innovation in the Administration of the Kingdom of Dahomey." *Journal of African Studies* l, no. 3: 325.

O'Connel, J. (1967). "The Inevitability of Instability." *Journal of Modern African Studies* 2, no. 2: 32.

Ogot, B. A. (1967). *History of the Southern Luo.* Nairobi: East African Publishing House.

Oguah, Benjamin Ewuku (1984). "African and Western Philosophy: A Study." In *African Philosophy: An Introduction,* ed. Richard Wright (1984). Lanham: University Press of America.

Olaniyan, Richard, ed. (1985). *Nigerian History and Culture.* London: Longman Group Limited.

Olivier, N. J. J. (1969). "The Governmental Institutions of the Bantu Peoples of Southern Africa." In *Recueils de la Societies Jean Bodin XII.* Bruxelles: Fondation Universitaire de Belgique.

Olson, Mancur (1996). "Big Bills Left on the Sidewalk: Why Some Nations are Rich, and Others Poor." In *Journal of Economic Perspectives* 10, no. 2: 3–24.

Onwuanibe, Richard C. (1984). "The Human Person and Immortality in Igbo Metaphysics." In *African Philosophy: An Introduction,* ed. Richard Wright (1984). Lanham: University Press of America.

Oyugi, Walter O., ed. (1988). *Democratic Theory and Practice in Africa.* Portsmouth, N.H.: Heinemann.

Person, Y. (1993). "French West Africa and Decolonization." In *Decolonization and African Independence,* ed. P. Gifford and W.M. Roger Louis (1988). New Haven: Yale University Press.

Pickett, James, and Hans Singer (1990). *Towards Economic Recovery in Sub-Saharan Africa.* New York: Routledge, Inc.

Pinchus, John (1970). "How Much Aid for the Under-Developed Countries." In *Economic Development, Readings in Theory and Practice,* ed. Theodore Morgan and George W. Betz. Belmont, Calif.: Wadsworth

Pinkney, Robert (1972). *Ghana Under Military Rule, 1966–69.* London: Methuen.

Polanyi, K. (1945) *Origins of Our Time: The Great Transformation.* London: Victor Gollancz.

Porteous, Samuel D. (2000). "Targeted Financial Sanctions." In *Greed and Grievance: Economic Agendas in Civil Wars,* ed. Mats Berdal and David M. Malone (2000). Boulder, Colo.: Lynne Rienner, pp. 173–188.

Prebisch, Raul (1950). *Economic Development of Latin America and Its Principal Problems.* New York: United Nations.

———. (1959). "Commercial Policies in the Under-Developed Countries." *American Economic Review, Papers and Proceedings* (May).

Rasheed, S. and E. Chole (2000). "Human Development: an African Perspective." Available at R. Rojas Databank .

Rauch, James (1995). "Bureaucracy, Infrastructure, and Economic Growth: Evidence from US Cities During the Progressive Era." *American Economic Review* 85, no. 4: 968–979.

Reno, William (2000). "Shadow States and the Political Economy of Civil Wars." In *Greed and Grievance: Economic Agendas in Civil Wars,* ed. Mats Berdal and David M. Malone (2000). Boulder, Colo.: Lynne Rienner, pp. 43–68.

Richards, Paul (1996). *Fighting for the Rain Forest: War, Youth and Resources in Sierra Leone.* Oxford: James Currey.

Ridker, R. (1967). "Discontent and Economic Growth." *Economic Development and Cultural Change* (October): 1–5.

Rimmer, D. (1966). "The Crisis in the Ghana Economy." *Modern African Studies* (May).

Roberts, Brian (1974). *The Zulu Kings.* New York: Charles Scribner and Sons.

Robinson, Ronald, ed. (1971). *Developing the Third World: The Experience of the 1960s.* Cambridge: Cambridge University Press.

Rose-Ackerman, Susan (1978). *Corruption: A Study in Political Economy.* New York: Academic Press.

———. (1996). *When Is Corruption Harmful?* Washington, D.C.: World Bank.

———. (1997). "The Political Economy of Corruption." In *Corruption and the Global Economy,* ed. Kimberly A. Elliott. Washington, D.C.: Institute for International Economics.

Rose-Ackerman, Susan, and Andrew Stone (1996). *The Costs of Corruption for Private Business: Evidence from World Bank Surveys.* Washington, D.C.: The World Bank.

Rosenstein-Rodan, Paul W. (1961). "International Aid for Under-Developed Countries." *The Review of Economics and Statistics* 5, no. 2: 131.

Rojas, R. (2000a). "Notes on the Notions of State and Development." R. Rojas Databank (www.rrojasdatabank.org).

———. (2000b). "The State, Civil Society and Development. A comparative Analysis." R. Rojas Databank (www.rrojasdatabank.org).

Rostow, W. W. (1960). *The Stages of Economic Growth.* Cambridge: Cambridge University Press.

Rothstein, Robert (1977). *The Weak in the World of the Strong.* New York: Columbia University Press.

Sachs, Jeffrey, and Sara Sievers (1998). "Foreign Direct Investment in Africa." In *World Economic Forum (WEF), The Africa Competitiveness Report 1998.* Cologne/Geneva: World Economic Forum, pp. 36–44.

Sandbrook, Richard (1993). *The Politics of Africa's Stagnation.* New York: Cambridge University Press.

Schapera, I. (1953). *The Tswana.* London: International African Institute.

———. (1955). *A Handbook of Tswana Law and Custom.* London: Oxford University Press.

———. (1957). "The Sources of Law In Tswana Tribal Courts: Legislation And Precedent." *Journal of African Law* 1, no. 3: 150–162.

Scott, James C. (1992). *Comparative Political Corruption.* Englewood Cliffs, New Jersey: Prentice-Hall.

Seers, Dudley (1983). *The Political Economy of Nationalism.* Oxford: Oxford University Press.

Saumon, Stephanie (2000). "External Domination via Domestic States: The Case of Francophone Africa." Available at http://www.rrojasdatabank.org/ssstate.

Shearer, David (1998a). "Outsourcing War." *Foreign Policy* 112 (Fall): 68–81.

————(1998b). *Private Armies and Military Intervention.* Adelphi Paper No.316. New York: Oxford University Press.

Simiyu, V. G. (1988). "The Democratic Myth In The African Traditional Societies." In *Democratic Theory and Practice in Africa,* ed. Walter O. Oyugi *et al.* Portsmouth, N.H.: Heinemann.

Sithole, Ndabaningi (1979). "Extracts from African Nationalism." In *Ideologies of Liberation in Black Africa, 1856–1970,* ed. J. Ayo Langley (1979). London: Rex Collins.

Skinner, Elliott P. (1961). "Intergenerational Conflict among The Mossi: Father And Son." *Journal of Conflict Resolution* 5, no. 1: 55–60.

————. (1962). "Trade and Markets among the Mossi People." In *Markets in Africa,* ed. Bohannan and Dalton. Evanston, Ill.: Northwestern University Press.

————. (1964). "West African Economic Systems." In *Economic Transition in Africa,* ed. M. J. Herskovits and M. Harwitz (1964). Evanston, Ill.: Northwestern University Press.

————. (1973). *Peoples and Cultures Of Africa.* New York: Doubleday/Natural History Press.

Smith, Michael G. (1962). "Exchange and Marketing among the Hausa." In *Markets in Africa,* ed. Bohannan and Dalton. Evanston, Ill.: Northwestern University Press.

Soyinka, Wole (1996). *The Open Sore of a Continent.* New York: Oxford University Press.

Stewart, Douglas B., and Yiannis P. Venieris (1985). "Socio-Political Instability and the Behavior of Savings in LDCs." *Review of Economics and Statistics* 17, no. 4: 67.

Tardits, Claudine, and Claude Tardits (1962). "Traditional Market Economy in South Dahomey." In *Markets in Africa,* ed. Bohannan and Dalton. Evanston, Ill.: Northwestern University Press.

Taylor, D. R. Fraser, and Fiona Mackenzie (1992). *Development from Within: Survival in Rural Africa.* New York: Routledge, Inc.

Taylor, Ian (2004). "Why NEPAD and African Politics Don't Mix." *Foreign Policy in Focus,* Feb 16, 2004, available at www.fpif.org.

Thomas, P. A., ed. (1969). *Issues in Privatization and Restructuring in Sub-Saharan Africa: Private Enterprise and the East African Company.* Dar-es-Salaam: Tanzania publishing house.

Thurow, Lester, C. (1999). *Building Wealth: The New Rules.* New York: Harper.

Tillett, Chris (1996). "Foreign investment: targeting and promotional strategies." Commonwealth Secretariat, London, Occasional Paper No. 2, mimeo.

Todaro, Michael P., ed. (1983). *The Struggle for Economic Development.* New York: Longman.

————. (1987). *Economic Development in the Third World.* New York: Longman.

Tollison, Robert D. (1982). "Rent-Seeking: A Survey." *Kyklos* 35: 4.

Udoji, J.O. (1970). "Reforming the Public Enterprises in Africa." In *Quarterly Journal of Administration* IV, no. 3 (April): 220.

United Nations Conference on Trade and Development (UNCTAD) (1995). Foreign Direct Investment in Africa. United Nations publication, Sales No. E.95.II.A.6. Geneva: United Nations.

————. (1997). "Foreign Direct Investment in LDCs: Prospects and Constraints." Report prepared by the UNCTAD secretariat for the pilot seminar on the mobilization of the private sector in order to encourage foreign investment flows towards least developed countries (LDCs). "Investment Opportunities in Pre-emerging Markets." Geneva, June 23–25, 1997, mimeo.

————. (1998a). *Trade and Development Report, 1998.* United Nations publication, Sales No. E.98.II.D.6. Geneva: United Nations.

————. (1998b). *World Investment Report 1998: Trends and Determinants.* United Nations publication, Sales No. E.98.II.D.5. Geneva: United Nations.

————. (1998c). *Trade and Development Report, 1998: Financial Instability and Growth in Africa.* United Nations Publication, Sales No. E.98.IL.D.10. New York: The United Nations.

————. (1999a). *"Investment Policy Review of Egypt."* Mimeo, Geneva: UNCTAD.

United Nations Development Program (1999). *Corruption and Integrity Improvement Initiatives in Developing Countries.* New York: UN Publications.

United Nations Development Program (UNDP) (2001). *Human Development Report* (Annually). New York: United Nations.

United Nations Economic Commission on Africa (ECA) (1999). *Human Capital Development and Endogenization of Geography as Framework for Africa's Competitiveness.* Addis Ababa, Ethiopia: United Nations.

United Nations Economic Commission for Latin America (1973). "Social Change in Latin America in the Early 1970s." New York: United Nations. Also available at http://www.rrojasdatabank.org..

United Nations Economic and Social Council (2000). "Summary of the Economic and Social Situation in Africa, 1999." (May).

United Nations Security Council (2000). *Report of the Panel of Experts on Violations of Security Council Sanctions Against UNITA,* p.26.

Uphoff, Norman T. (1970). *Ghana's Experience in Using External Aid for Development.* Berkeley: University of California Press.

Van De Walle, Nicolas (2001). *African Economies and the Politics of Permanent Crisis, 1979–1999.* New York: Cambridge University Press.

Van Notten, Michael (2003). *The Law of the Somalis.* Dobbs Ferry, N.Y.: Transnational Publishers.

Vansina, Jan (1962). "Trade and Markets Among the Kuba." In *Markets in Africa,* ed. Bohannan and Dalton. Evanston, Ill.: Northwestern University Press.

———. (1975). *Kingdoms of the Savannah.* Madison: University of Wisconsin Press.

———. (1978). *The Children of Woot: A History of the Kuba.* Madison: University of Wisconsin Press.

Vaughan, James H. (1986). "Population and Social Organization." In *Africa,* ed. Phyllis M. Martin and Patrick O'Meara (1986). Bloomington: Indiana University Press.

Venter A. J. (1996). "Mercenaries Fuel Next Round in Angolan Civil War." In "Current Conflicts." *Jane's International Defence Review* (June).

Von Pische, J. D., Dale W. Adams, and Donald Gordon (1983). *Rural Financial Markets in Developing Countries.* Baltimore: John Hopkins University Press.

Wanyande, Peter (1988). "Democracy and the One-Party State: The African Experience." In *Democratic Theory and Practice in Africa,* ed. Walter O. Oyugi et al. (1988). Portsmouth, N.H.: Heinemann.

Wedel, Janine R. (1998). *Collision and Collusion.* New York: St. Martin's Press.

Weisskopft, Thomas E. (1972). "The Impact of Foreign Capital Inflow on Domestic Savings in Underdeveloped Countries." *Journal of International Economics* (February): 25–28.

Werlin, Herbert (1973). "The Consequences of Corruption: The Ghanaian Experience." *Political Science Quarterly,* 88: 71–85.

Wharton, W. B. (1966). "Modernizing Subsistence Agriculture." In *Modernization: The Dynamics of Growth,* ed. M. Winer (1966). New York: Basic Books.

Whitaker, Jennifer S. (1988*). How Can Africa Survive?* New York: Harper and Row.

White, C. M. N. (1956). "The Role of Hunting and Fishing in Luvale Society." *African Studies* 15, no. 2: 75–86.

White, E. Frances (1987). *Sierra Leone's Settler Women Traders.* Ann Arbor: University of Michigan Press.

Wickins, Peter (1981). *An Economic History of Africa.* Oxford: Oxford University Press.

Wilks, Ivor (1975). *Asante in the Nineteenth Century: The Structure and Evolution of a Political Order.* Cambridge: Cambridge University Press.

Williams, Chancellor (1987). *The Destruction of Black Civilization.* Chicago: Third World Press.

Wilson, E. (1993). "French Support for Structural Adjustment Programs in Africa." *World Development* 21, no. 3: 331–347.

Wilson, Peter J. (1967). "Tsimihety Kinship and Descent." *Africa* 37, no. 2: 133–153.

World Bank (1979). *Report of Mission to Zaire.* Washington, D.C.: World Bank publication.

———. (1982). *Report of Mission to Uganda.* Washington, D.C.: World Bank publication.

———. (1984). *Toward Sustained Development in Sub-Saharan Africa.* Washington, D.C.: World Bank publication.

———. (1989). *Sub-Saharan Africa: From Crisis to Self-Sustainable Growth.* Washington, D.C.: World Bank publication.

————. (1993). *Regional Study on Public Enterprises Reform and Privatization in Africa.* Washington D.C.: World Bank publication.

————. (1994). *Adjustment in Africa: Reforms, Results and the Road Ahead.* New York: Oxford University Press.

————. (1995). *Ghana: Is Growth Sustainable?* Operations Evaluations Department. Report No. 99. Washington, D.C.: World Bank Publications.

————. (Annually). *World Development Report.* New York: Oxford University Press.

————. (1997a). *African Economic and Financial Data.* Washington, D.C.: World Bank/UNDP publication.

————. (1997b). *The State in a Changing World: World Development Report 1997.* Oxford: Oxford University Press.

————. (1998). *Uganda: Recommendations for Strengthening the Government of Uganda's Anti-Corruption Program.* Poverty Reduction and Social Development Section. Washington, D.C.: World Bank Publications.

————. (2000a). African Development Indicators 2000. Washington, D.C.: World Bank publication.

————. (2000b). *Can Africa Claim the 21st Century?* Washington, D.C.: World Bank publication.

————. (2001). *African Poverty at the Millennium.* Washington, D.C.: World Bank publication.

World Economic Forum (WEF) (1998). *Africa Competitiveness Report 1998.* Cologne/Geneva: World Economic Forum.

Wright, Richard A., ed. (1984). *African Philosophy: An Introduction.* Lanham: University Press of America.

Wrigley, Christopher (1960). "Speculations on The Economic Prehistory Of Africa." *Journal of African History* 1, no. 2: 189–203.

Yelpaala, Kojo (1983). "Circular Arguments and Self-Fulfilling Definitions: 'Statelessness' and the Dagaaba History." *Africa* 10: 349–385.

Young, Danielle M., and F. Michael Kunz (2000). "An Analysis of the United States Agency for International Development and Aid to India and Ghana." Available at http://www.usaid.gov/fani/Summary—Foreign Aid in the National Interest. pdf.

Zinsmeister, Karl (1987). "East African Experiment: Kenyan Prosperity and Tanzanian Decline." *Journal of Economic Growth* 2, no. 2: 28.

FOREIGN PERIODICALS

Daily Graphic, owned by the government of Ghana; a daily newspaper, Accra Ghana.

Ghanaian Times, owned by the government of Ghana; a daily newspaper, Accra, Ghana.

Punch, a privately owned weekly, Kumasi, Ghana.

West Africa, a privately owned weekly, London, U.K..

New African, a privately owned monthly, London, U.K..

INDEX